AFRICA YEARBOOK

AFRICA YEARBOOK

Volume 3

Politics, Economy and Society South of the Sahara in 2006

EDITED BY

ANDREAS MEHLER

HENNING MELBER

KLAAS VAN WALRAVEN

SUB-EDITOR

AMIN KAMETE

BRILL

LEIDEN • BOSTON
2007

This book is printed on acid-free paper.

A Cataloging-in-Publication record for this book is available from the Library of Congress.

ISBN 1871-2525
ISBN 978 90 04 16263 1

PRINTED IN THE NETHERLANDS

Contents

Preface

In May 2003, the Africa-Europe Group of Interdisciplinary Studies (AEGIS) encouraged some of its member institutions to publish an *Africa Yearbook* with a wider international appeal. As a joint undertaking, the African Studies Centre in Leiden (ASC), the Institute of African Affairs in Hamburg (IAA) and the Nordic Africa Institute in Uppsala (NAI) – all very active AEGIS centres sharing similar profiles – had accepted this challenge. The *Africa Yearbook* is herewith presented the third consecutive year to report on events during 2006. Since the last edition, the Dag Hammarskjöld Foundation in Uppsala (DHF) joined the original triumvirate as a fourth institutional partner. The basic format remains largely the same, but a few modifications are a visible consequence too. We have newly introduced an overview chapter dealing separately with the United Nations and Africa. While the three editors with overall responsibility remain the same, Amin Kamete from the NAI joined the team as a sub-editor with full responsibilities for the Eastern Africa section. We trust that the quality of the third volume is an indicator that we managed to maintain the high level of substantive and chronological information, which has resulted in positive appraisals since the *Yearbook* first appeared.

The country-specific articles continue to cover domestic politics, foreign affairs and socioeconomic developments in the states of sub-Saharan Africa during the calendar year under review. While we recognize the impossibility of finding fully objective indicators for the relative importance of each of the states, the length of the country specific articles aim to reflect the approximate weight of each country. The four sub-regions are each also introduced by means of an overview article. Further overviews summarise the general continental developments, the European-African relations and the United Nations and Africa.

The *Yearbook* is based on scholarly work, but oriented towards a wider target readership. It includes students, politicians, diplomats, administrators, journalists, teachers, practitioners in the sphere of development cooperation as well as business people or other travelers. Thanks to the support of the four partner institutions, the volume can be offered at a price attractive to this broad readership. Without pressing the individual contributions too much into a straight jacket, the volume is primarily concerned with providing factual (though not necessarily neutral) information. Each issue, in focusing almost exclusively on developments during the particular calendar year, will provide a completely fresh annual overview of events.

We wish to express our gratitude to all the contributors for their collaboration in this endeavour; to the partner institutions in AEGIS for encouraging us to embark on this ambitious project; to Amin Kamete for joining us as sub-editor; to Peter Colenbrander for his meticulous language editing; to Sylvia Steege for her unfailing coordinating assistance, to Rolf Hofmeier for continuous advice, to Brill Publishers for taking such professional care of publishing matters; and last but not least to our four institutions for providing the necessary support and opportunities to allow us to turn this idea into reality.

The Editors
(Hamburg, Leiden and Uppsala, June 2007)

List of Abbreviations

ABN	Autorité du Bassin du Niger (Niamey)
ACP	African, Caribbean, and Pacific Group of Countries (Lomé/Cotonou Agreement)
ADB	African Development Bank (Abidjan)
ADF	African Development Fund (Abidjan)
AFD	Agence Française de Développement (Paris)
AGOA	African Growth and Opportunity Act
AI	Amnesty International
APRM	African Peer Review Mechanism
AU	African Union (Addis Ababa)
BCEAO	Banque Centrale des Etats de l'Afrique de l'Ouest (Dakar)
BEAC	Banque des Etats de l'Afrique Centrale (Yaoundé)
CAR	Central African Republic
CBLT	Commission du Bassin du Lac Tchad (N'Djaména)
CEEAC	Communauté Economique des Etats de l'Afrique Centrale (Libreville) = ECCAS
CEMAC	Communauté Economique et Monétaire de l'Afrique Centrale
CEN-SAD	Community of Sahel-Saharan States (Tripoli)
CEPGL	Communauté Economique des Pays des Grands Lacs (Gisenyi/Rwanda)
CFAfr	Franc de la Communauté Financière Africaine (BCEAO; BEAC)
COMESA	Common Market for Eastern and Southern Africa (Lusaka)
CPLP	Comunidade dos Países de Língua Portuguesa
DAC	Development Assistance Committee (Paris)
DDR	Disarmament, Demobilisation and Reintegration
DRC	Democratic Republic of Congo
EAC	East African Community
ECA	Economic Commission for Africa (United Nations; Addis Ababa)
ECCAS	Economic Community of Central African States (Libreville)
ECOWAS	Economic Community of West African States (Abuja)
ECOMOG	ECOWAS Ceasefire Monitoring Group
EDF	European Development Fund (Brussels)
EIB	European Investment Bank (Luxemburg)

ESAF	Enhanced Structural Adjustment Facility (IMF)
EU	European Union (Brussels)
FAO	Food and Agricultural Organisation (Rome)
FTA	Free Trade Area
GDP	Gross Domestic Product
HIPC	Heavily Indebted Poor Countries
HRW	Human Rights Watch
ICG	International Crisis Group
IDA	International Development Association (Washington)
IDP	Internally Displaced Person
IFAD	International Fund for Agricultural Development (Rome)
IFC	International Finance Corporation (Washington)
IGAD	Intergovernmental Authority on Development (Djibouti)
ILO	International Labour Organisation (Geneva)
IMF	International Monetary Fund (Washington)
IOC	Indian Ocean Commission (Quatre Bornes)
IORARC	Indian Ocean Rim Association for Regional Cooperation (Port Louis)
MDGs	Millennium Development Goals
MRU	Mano River Union (Freetown)
NEPAD	New Partnership for Africa's Development
NGO	Non-Governmental Organisation
OECD	Organisation for Economic Cooperation and Development (Paris)
OIC	Organisation of the Islamic Conference (Jeddah)
OPEC	Organisation of Petroleum Exporting Countries (Vienna)
PALOP	Países Africanos de Lingua Oficial Portugesa
PRGF	Poverty Reduction and Growth Facility
PRSC	Poverty Reduction Support Credit
PRSP	Poverty Reduction Strategy Paper
PTA	Preferential Trade for Eastern and Southern African States (now COMESA)
SACU	Southern African Customs Union (Pretoria)
SADC	Southern African Development Community (Gaborone)
SAF	Structural Adjustment Facility (IMF)
SDR	Special Drawing Right (IMF)
TI	Transparency International
UAE	United Arab Emirates
UEMOA	Union Economique et Monétaire Ouest-Africaine (Ouagadougou)
UMA	Union du Maghreb Arabe
UN	United Nations (New York)
UNCTAD	United Nations Conference on Trade and Development (Geneva)
UNDP	United Nations Development Programme (New York)

UNEP	United Nations Environment Programme (Nairobi)
UNESCO	United Nations Educational, Scientific and Cultural Organisation (Paris)
UNHCR	United Nations High Commissioner for Refugees (Geneva)
UNICEF	United Nations Children's Fund (New York)
USAID	United States Agency for International Development (Washington)
WFP	World Food Programme (Rome)
WHO	World Health Organisation (Geneva)
WTO	World Trade Organisation (Geneva)

Factual Overview (as of 31 December 2006)

West Africa

Country	*Area (in sq km)*	*Population (in m)*	*Currency*	*HDI*	*Head of State*	*Prime Minister*
Benin	112,622	6.9	CFA Franc	0.428	Boni Yayi	
Burkina Faso	274,122	12.4	CFA Franc	0.342	Blaise Compaoré	Paramanga Ernest Yonli
Cape Verde	4,033	0.5	Cape Verdean Escudo	0.722	Pedro Pires	José Maria Pereira Neves
Côte d'Ivoire	322,462	17.1	CFA Franc	0.421	Laurent Gbagbo	Charles Konan Banny
Gambia	11,295	1.4	Dalasi	0.479	Yahya Jammeh	
Ghana	238,500	21.1	Cedi	0.532	John Agyekum Kufuor	
Guinea	245,857	8.1	Guinean Franc	0.445	Lansana Conté	
Guinea-Bissau	36,125	1.5	CFA Franc	0.349	Nino Vieira	Aristides Gomes
Liberia	111,370	3.4	Liberian Dollar	n.d.	Ellen Johnson-Sirleaf	
Mali	1,240,000	11.9	CFA Franc	0.338	Amadou Toumani Touré	Ousmane Issoufi Maïga
Mauritania	1,030,700	2.9	Ouguiya	0.486	Ely Ould Mohammed Vall	Sidi Mohamed Ould Boubacar
Niger	1,267,000	12.1	CFA Franc	0.311	Mamadou Tandja	Hama Amadou
Nigeria	923,768	139.8	Naira	0.448	Olusegun Obasanjo	
Senegal	196,192	10.5	CFA Franc	0.460	Abdoulaye Wade	Macky Sall
Sierra Leone	71,740	5.4	Leone	0.335	Ahmad Tejan Kabbah	
Togo	56,785	5.0	CFA Franc	0.495	Faure Gnassingbé	Yawovi Agboyibo

Central Africa

Country	*Area (in sq km)*	*Population (in m)*	*Currency*	*HDI*	*Head of State*	*Prime Minister*
Cameroon	475,442	16.4	CFA Franc	0.506	Paul Biya	Ephraim Inoni
Central African Republic	622,984	3.9	CFA Franc	0.353	François Bozizé	Elie Doté
Chad	1,284,000	8.8	CFA Franc	0.368	Idriss Déby	Pascal Yoadimnadji
Congo	342,000	3.9	CFA Franc	0.520	Denis Sassou-Nguesso	Isidore Mvouaba
DR Congo	2,344,855	54.8	Congolese Franc	0.391	Joseph Kabila	Antoine Gizenga
Equatorial Guinea	28,051	0.5	CFA Franc	0.653	Teodoro Obiang Nguema Mbasogo	Ricardo Mangue Obama Nfubea
Gabon	267,667	1.3	CFA Franc	0.633	El-Hadj Omar Bongo Ondimba	Jean Eyeghé Ndong
São Tomé and Príncipe	1,001	0.2	Dobra	0.607	Fradique de Menezes	Tomé Vera Cruz

Eastern Africa

Country	*Area (in sq km)*	*Population (in m)*	*Currency*	*HDI*	*Head of State*	*Prime Minister*
Burundi	27,834	7.3	Burundi Franc	0.384	Pierre Nkurunziza	
Comoros	2,166	0.6	Comoran Franc	0.556	Abdallah Sambi	
Djibouti	21,783	0.7	Djiboutian Franc	0.494	Ismail Omar Guelleh	Dileita Mohamed Dileita
Eritrea	125,000	4.5	Nakfa	0.454	Isaias Afewerki	
Ethiopia	1,121,900	70.0	Birr	0.371	Girma Wolde Giorgis	Meles Zenawi
Kenya	582,646	32.4	Kenyan Shilling	0.491	Mwai Kibaki	
Rwanda	26,338	8.4	Rwandan Franc	0.450	Paul Kagame	Bernard Makuza
Seychelles	444	0.1	Seychelles Rupee	0.842	James Michel	
Somalia	637,657	9.6	Somali Shilling	n.d.	Abdullahi Yusuf Ahmed (Somaliland: Dahir Riyale Kahin)	Ali Mohamed Gendi
Sudan	2,505,805	34.4	Sudanese Dinar	0.516	Omar Hassan Ahmad al-Bashir	
Tanzania	945,087	36.6	Tanzanian Shilling	0.430	Jakaya Kikwete	Edward Lowassa
Uganda	236,036	25.9	Ugandan Shilling	0.502	Yoweri Kaguta Museveni	Apolo Nsibambi

Southern Africa

Country	*Area (in sq km)*	*Population (in m)*	*Currency*	*HDI*	*Head of State*	*Prime Minister*
Angola	1,246,700	14.9	Kwanza	0.439	José Eduardo dos Santos	Fernando da Piedade Días dos Santos ("Nando")
Botswana	581,730	1.7	Pula	0.570	Festus Gontebanye Mogae	
Lesotho	30,355	1.8	Loti	0.494	King Letsie III	Bethuel Pakalitha Mosisili
Madagascar	587,041	17.3	Malagasy Franc	0.509	Marc Ravalo-manana	Jacques Sylla
Malawi	118,484	11.2	Kwacha	0.400	Bingu wa Mutharika	
Mauritius	1,865	1.2	Mauritius Rupee	0.800	Sir Anerood Jugnauth	Navinchandra Ramgoolan
Mozambique	801,590	19.1	Métical	0.390	Armando Guebuzo	Luisa Dias Diogo
Namibia	824,292	2.0	Namibian Dollar	0.626	Hifikepunye Lucas Pohamba	Nahas Angula
South Africa	1,121,038	45.6	Rand	0.653	Thabo Mvuyelwa Mbeki	
Swaziland	17,363	1.1	Lilangeni	0.500	King Mswati III	Absalom Themba Dlamini
Zambia	752,614	10.5	Kwacha	0.407	Levy Patrick Mwanawasa	
Zimbabwe	390,759	13.2	Zimbabwe Dollar	0.491	Robert Gabriel Mugabe	

I. Sub-Saharan Africa

The continent benefited economically from continued exceptionally high average growth rates. These reflected and were a partial result of the growing interest in its natural resources and in particular the energy sector as well as other strategic minerals. While the G8 summit in St. Petersburg showed little interest in honouring its declared commitment to Africa, the Chinese offensive culminated in a Sino-African summit attended by high calibre African representatives on a scale unprecedented outside the UN or the AU. The latter had to address political challenges in the form of Sudan's claim to the chairmanship but the organisation coped with the task. Notwithstanding this success, NEPAD and its APRM continued to lag behind expectations. While armed conflicts continued, progress was made in advancing the prospects for a non-violent future in a number of war-torn subregions. However, lasting peace remained a remote goal for many countries. The DR Congo, Mauritania and Uganda were among the most prominent cases of presidential and parliamentary elections held during the year. Notwithstanding the trend to seek relatively peaceful and legitimate transitions or continued political dominance, military attempts to change governments continued to rear their heads. AIDS and malaria remained among the scourges facing the people, and droughts and floods continued to threaten the bare minimum survival of millions of people.

Africa in the Global Economy

Overall, the continent witnessed another year of good economic growth. This, as well as the continued spectacular growth in trade with China and India compensated to a certain extent for the negative fall-out from the collapse of WTO trade liberalisation talks. The fifth annual report of the OECD and ADB in May predicted a growth rate for 2006 of 5.8% for Africa as a whole, while the IMF in November expected that sub-Saharan Africa would reach a figure of 4.8%. This represented a slowdown compared to 2005, due to a decline in oil production in some countries. However, the figure was driven up by high oil prices and upward movement of prices for metals such as gold, copper, zinc, nickel and cobalt, as well as uranium and bauxite. Many non-oil economies succeeded in withstanding the effects of high petrol prices by passing these on to consumers or benefiting from growth in non-fuel commodity production, higher foreign currency reserves, more investment and better agricultural production. Thus, oil importers were, as a whole, still expected to grow by approximately 4.5%. Oil-producing countries as a group were expected to reach an overall growth rate of 8% (May estimate). With inflation calculated to drop to an overall 6.9%, these IMF indicators, though usually higher than those used by the UN or World Bank, pointed to **robust economic growth**. Even non-mineral (agricultural) commodities shared to some extent in the boom, although some cash crops such as cotton and cocoa still experienced difficulties.

While expansion outweighed demographic growth, African economies would have to grow by at least 7% annually to cut poverty by 50% by 2015 as called for in the Millennium Development Goals. Only six countries, mostly north of the Sahara, were thought capable of this. Against this background, **illegal migration** to Europe continued in the face of tightening controls and soaring drownings in the Atlantic among young fortune-seekers. The Canary Islands saw an influx of more than 31,000 people. Spanish immigration authorities announced at year's end that some 6,000 men had died or gone missing, while thousands were repatriated to their countries of origin, especially in West Africa.

In order to speed up growth, the **World Bank** introduced the Africa Catalytic Growth Fund. More controversial was the bank's anti-corruption drive, spearheaded by its president, Paul Wolfowitz. European countries feared that this crusade could lead to a decrease in lending, in part because the concept of corruption could be unduly widened. Thus, Congo was deprived of funds as punishment for the spendthrift ways of its head of state and AU chairman, Sassou Nguesso, in the course of a mission to New York. Transparency International welcomed the new forcefulness but blamed Western governments for frustrating the recovery of money stolen from Africa and deposited in Western bank accounts, which reportedly totalled $ 140 bn. Britain as well as France pleaded at the annual World Bank-IMF meeting held in Singapore from 15 to 20 September for an extension of Africa's representation in the IMF. This led to a pledge that African representation would be improved in two years' time in line with a similar promise by Wolfowitz for the World Bank.

The global bank's soft loan institution, IDA, on 28 March announced that it would provide $ 37 bn in **additional debt relief** to Heavily Indebted Poor Countries to help them achieve the MDGs. This was part of the Multilateral Debt Relief Initiative (MDRI) proposed by the G8 summit at Gleneagles in 2005. Thirteen countries in Africa that had passed the completion point under the older HIPC initiative were now eligible for this. On 5 September, the ADB added its contribution by announcing a debt write-off for 33 African countries to the value of $ 8.5 bn.

The **G8 summit**, held in St Petersburg on 15–17 July, showed marginal interest in African issues. With the exception of the Gleneagles commitments on multilateral debt relief, most G8 pledges towards Africa were not kept. Instead of boosting global aid by $ 50 bn annually by 2010, this year Africa got less than $ 2 bn in additional aid, while the Gleneagles recommendations on financing improved health care faced a yearly shortfall of $ 10 bn.

On 24 July, negotiations within the framework of WTO's **Doha round** were suspended *sine die*. With especially the US, in an election year, not keen to concede more and preferring bilateral deals to the complex trade-offs inherent in global multilateral negotiations, trade arrangements were expected to become more regionalised and discriminatory. Africa would have little to offer in such bilateral settings. In the Doha round, most African economies would have received non-reciprocal concessions in terms of duty- and quota-free access to Western markets. By contrast, the US called off negotiations on a free trade agreement with Southern African countries in view of what was seen as insufficient trade concessions by those states. The US expressed its intention to seek new bilateral arrangements that would force African economies to open up key sectors to US companies. Rwanda and South Africa signed such bilateral deals. On 2 March, Benin, Burkina, Mali and Chad collectively filed a WTO proposal for the reduction of US domestic subsidies to its cotton farmers. By then, the US congress had finally agreed to stop subsidising the export of American cotton.

At the third **Sino-African summit** in Beijing on 3–5 November, Chinese President Hu Jintao boasted there were 'no strings attached' to Chinese assistance to Africa. Although much Chinese aid has been 'tied', i.e., involving compulsory purchase of Chinese goods, the president's statement referred to the refusal to attach political conditions to economic assistance other than the taboo on relations with Taiwan, thus contrasting with the conditionality of good governance in Western aid. The Beijing summit represented the culmination of a flurry of visits by Chinese dignitaries to 15 African countries. Amid worries about cheap Chinese imports damaging Africa's manufacturing industry (especially textiles in Southern Africa) and concerns over working conditions in Chinese companies and the influx of Chinese workers into Africa, Hu Jintao announced that China would double its aid to Africa by 2009, promising $ 2 bn in export credits, $ 3 bn in loans and a fund of $ 5 bn to encourage Chinese investments. Trade deals to a value of $ 2 bn were announced. The Chinese also declared their willingness to train more than 10,000 African professionals, improve Africa's agricultural production, education and health care, including the doubling of scholarships to African students, and construct dozens of hospitals. With competition between India and China heating up, the Indian Prime Minister Singh paid a visit to South Africa on 2 October.

African leaders responded with euphoria while Western powers, financial institutions and NGOs reacted with growing criticism. Amnesty International criticised China's aid to countries guilty of human rights violations. The US accused China of irresponsible lending that could lead to renewed indebtedness, and the president of the World Bank complained that the Chinese ignored environmental norms and human rights in their lending policies. Images of Africa as the arsenal of natural resources worth courting were developing alongside older ideas of Africa as the helpless recipient of aid. New figures testified to the significance of Asian-African interaction, most of which continued to be in the field of natural resource development. Chinese investment in African economies totalled nearly

$ 6 bn this year alone, with Beijing becoming Africa's third largest investor to the value of $ 29 bn in foreign direct investment. According to official Chinese sources, **Sino-African trade** was expected to reach a value of $ 50 bn at year's end. Africa now provided a quarter or more of Chinese oil needs, with Angola overtaking Saudi Arabia as China's biggest supplier. New trade agreements with Nigeria, while consolidating Chinese interests in Nigerian oil, covered a broad range of activities, from agriculture to health care and infrastructural development. Talks with South Africa involved nuclear power cooperation, among other issues, while Chinese companies were granted uranium exploration rights in Niger.

Concerns about **African-Asian asymmetries** persisted, however. Asia as a whole received 27% of Africa's exports, three times more than in 1990, but this did not even represent 2% of Asia's global imports. Asian exports to Africa were growing by 18% a year. In May, the Chinese agreed to a provisional deal limiting exports of textiles to South Africa, where 65,000 people had so far lost their jobs as a result of Chinese imports.

African Union

Controversy erupted when the AU Assembly held its sixth ordinary session, as originally planned, in the Sudanese capital Khartoum (23–24 January). Western governments and human rights NGOs criticised the venue and dreaded the prospect of the Sudanese regime, deeply involved in the bloodshed in Darfur, gaining the **annual Assembly chairmanship**. Although not an automatic prerogative, this position is usually awarded to the country hosting the summit. The outspoken president of the AU Commission, Konaré, lobbied heads of state to change the venue and avert Sudan's assumption of the Assembly chair. Khartoum's bid was supported by North and East African countries, but opposed by Central and West Africa, with Southern African nations divided. Consequently, the larger part of the Khartoum agenda was devoted to sorting out the presidency, ending in the decision to give it to Congo's President Sassou Nguesso on condition that Sudan gained the chairmanship in 2007, although the status of this proviso remained unclear. Some argued that this depended on an improvement in the conduct of Sudan's government, which disrupted summit fringe meetings of civil society groups that have customarily been held at (O)AU meetings since the 1990s.

The remainder of the summit agenda had to be rushed through or postponed. The question of the prosecution of former Chadian President Hissène Habré, accused of murdering and torturing thousands of people, was delegated to a committee of eminent jurists, on the advise that he be tried in Africa instead of extradited as demanded by a Belgian court. This was decided accordingly by the 7th Assembly summit in the Gambian capital Banjul on 1–2 July, which ordered **Habré's trial** by a court in Senegal.

Financial issues continued to plague the AU's functioning. The Pan-African Parliament (PAP) was provided with barely half of the promised $ 12 m. The parliament's total budget amounted to $ 24 m, of which the other half was to be furnished by individual member states, who failed to do so. The AU's general budget reached a total of $ 129.6 m, involving $ 69.4 m in operational costs and $ 60.2 m in programme expenses, the latter dependent on voluntary contributions despite objections from South Africa. While the number of member states sanctioned for non-payment of contributions dropped from 13 to nine, by July the organisation was said to face a deficit of $ 56 m. Discussion of the 2007 budget, targeted at $ 130 m, led to a stormy debate among ambassadors in Banjul on 25 June. Although it was approved, Konaré's criticism of member states' debts led to retaliatory action: the Commission was asked to moderate expenses while a scandal about an overcharged invoice of a Commission-subsidised conference of African intellectuals led to demands for an independent audit. Konaré, hated for his candour among some heads of state, especially Omar Bongo of Gabon and outgoing Assembly chairman Obasanjo of Nigeria, had called for a vast expansion of Commission powers. Apparently disappointed, the Commission president let it be known he would not seek re-election when his first term would be up for renewal.

Institutional evolution continued unabated with the establishment of the African Court on Human and Peoples' Rights, whose 11 judges were sworn in at the Banjul summit. In anticipation of its merger with the projected AU Court of Justice, the **human rights** court would only hear cases between citizens and their own governments. The new court's sister institution, the African Commission on Human and Peoples' Rights, suffered a setback when Zimbabwe persuaded member states to reject a critical report on human rights violations. The Commission also criticised the human rights records of Sudan, Ethiopia, DR Congo, Uganda and Eritrea. An African charter on democracy, elections and governance failed to win approval as it contained a ban on the extension of presidential terms through constitutional changes.

Political developments included the holding of the **first Africa-South America summit** in Abuja, Nigeria, on 26–30 November, at which the development of bilateral relations, regular summits and joined WTO postures were discussed.

The AU had little or no success in **managing conflicts**. This included the civil war in Côte d'Ivoire, which got some attention from President Sassou Nguesso. On Somalia, the AU continued to support the transitional government of President Abdullahi Yusuf Ahmed who at the Banjul summit managed to get support for lifting the UN's arms embargo. While it wanted this to defend itself against the Islamic courts union in place in Mogadishu, the AU called for dialogue between the opposing sides and continued its support for the idea of an IGAD peacekeeping force. This remained a non-starter, as Ethiopian intervention at year's end radically altered the strategic context. At the Khartoum summit earlier in the year, northern Somaliland applied for AU membership and, thus, international recognition as a separate state.

The biggest headache remained Darfur. The AU-mediated Darfur Peace Agreement (DPA), signed by Sudan's government and one of Darfur's rebel organisations in Abuja on

5 May, did not result in an end to bloodshed, as two other rebel groups representing, among others, Darfur's largest ethnic group, the Fur, refused to sign. With splits among rebel forces deepening and the Sudanese government realigning with one rebel force against the others, security worsened. Tensions between Sudan and Chad increased and later in the year Khartoum tried to assist in the overthrow of the governments of Chad and the Central African Republic. Despite a committed Commission president, who spent a night in an IDP camp and criticised African states for their inability to protect Darfurians, the **AU Mission in Sudan** (AMIS), was powerless to affect the situation. The peacekeepers, predominantly made up of Nigerian, Rwandan, Ghanaian and South African contingents, continued to struggle under a restrictive mandate that excluded enforcement action to stop ongoing massacres. Too thinly spread on the ground (7,000 men or one soldier for every 75 km^2), soldiers were forced to mount poorly equipped patrols and were faced with two to three months arrears in pay. Morale was low and commanders became increasingly frustrated as AMIS faced hostility from civilians, who accused it of failing to protect them and bias in favour of the DPA signatories, a charge AMIS denied. In July, South African troops were targeted and disarmed by rebel forces. The peacekeeping force also felt growing cash constraints. The US congress, in 2005 had declined to provide $ 50 m. This year the EU, which had funded 80% of AMIS financial requirements, spent $ 242 m, leaving little extra cash in hand. At the Khartoum summit, the Arab League pledged $ 170 m while Britain in February announced assistance worth $ 35 m. Before the Banjul summit, the AU's peace and security council threatened to withdraw AMIS, warning that money would run out unless the UN stepped in. The AU Assembly agreed but failed to win Sudan's approval for the deployment of a better funded UN force or for 'rehatting' AMIS with UN blue helmets. As Sudan and the AU's North African members opposed the decision of the UN Security Council on 31 August on a 24,000-strong UN peacekeeping force, the AU was forced on 21 September to extend the AMIS mandate till the end of the year.

NEPAD

Operating from its headquarters in Midrand, South Africa, which also hosts the PAP, the NEPAD secretariat this year again faced the difficulty of living up to the expectations created some five years ago. Considered as the official blueprint for the continent's socioeconomic development and an integral part of AU policy, NEPAD was mainly visible through its APRM. This was itself still a relatively new and innovative instrument in terms of African politics and had to date achieved limited results in strengthening so-called good governance. All NEPAD projects continued to depend to a large extent upon external funds, while African states were often reluctant to provide even the financial input for the APRM, which is a purely voluntary review process.

A stock-taking report on NEPAD was prepared by the UN secretariat, which through its different sub-organisations was the main supporter of NEPAD. The report was submitted to its economic and social council on 29 March at the 46th session later in the year. It concluded that the **implementation of NEPAD** showed constraints "concerning issues of coordination, collaboration and funding." One weakness identified was the lack of coordination at cluster level, resulting in a lack of predictable schedules for meetings and reduced opportunities for information exchange. Several UN agencies were, because of insufficient funding, limited in their ability to participate in cluster meetings. Technical assistance and other operational support to NEPAD programmes were as a result negatively affected.

G8 support for NEPAD, which has featured prominently since the initiative was created, was also confined within sobering dimensions. At its summit in St. Petersburg (15–17 July), only three African heads of state were invited as guests, Denis Sassou Nguesso (as chairperson of the AU), Alpha Oumar Konaré and Thabo Mbeki. This was the lowest such representation since the Okinawa meeting in 2000. The G8 was briefed by its 'sherpas' (the personal representatives on Africa to the heads of state created as a result of the summit in Genoa 2001) on the progress made with the Africa action plan adopted at the Canadian Kananaskis summit 2002 in direct response to and in support of NEPAD. It confirmed its commitments to support Africa's efforts to achieve the MDGs (which for most countries were still a remote prospect) and pledged particular support for the fight against disease.

The rosy picture presented did not match reality. Checking the earlier commitments against the measurable actions, it emerged once again that NEPAD had not received the degree of **material support** originally promised as a renewed commitment to Africa. The UN secretary-general's advisory panel on international support for NEPAD stated in its second report submitted to the UN General Assembly on 13 July that "aid should involve real fund flows." The secretary-general submitted his fourth consolidated report on progress in implementation and international support on the fifth anniversary of NEPAD's official establishment on 2 August. It stated that, "the momentum of international support ... is not yet strong enough to be irreversible" and that, "G-8 countries' official development assistance . . . needs to rise fast enough to deliver on their pledges."

This not unprecedented interplay between many words and **lack of action** was displayed by all the parties involved, i.e., mainly the African governments, the G8, other OECD countries, UN agencies and the NEPAD secretariat and resulted in the sobering conclusion presented by the chief executive officer of NEPAD, Firmino Mucavele, at the sixth session of the PAP. On 14 November, he concluded that, "programmes of NEPAD are not running at the speed we want to."

This is also true for the APRM, initiated in 2004 and completed by the end of the year in three countries (Ghana, Kenya and Rwanda) with differing experiences and results. Based on the insights to date, it may be concluded that it was largely the local (meaning national) framework for organising and implementing the APRM that set the decisive criteria, with the general and vague NEPAD standards playing a lesser role. Notwithstanding such reservations, the 6th **Africa Governance Forum** (AGF-VI) held on 9–11 May in Rwanda's capital Kigali and focusing exclusively on the APRM closed on an over-whelmingly positive tone. The AGF (whose first session had been held in 1997) considered itself a "UNDP flagship governance programme" and was undertaken jointly with the ECA. Its rather uncritical stance on the recent experiences again gave rise to the suspicion that, in the absence of any other pragmatic initiative, NEPAD and the APRM were, despite their shortcomings, considered to be the only viable option for advocating Africa's interests among mainly Western donor countries.

The **APRM** panel of eminent persons held its 15th meeting on 19–20 January in Khartoum to prepare for the 4th summit of the APR forum on 22 January. The two country review reports submitted by Ghana and Rwanda at the preceding summit six months earlier in Abuja were discussed. According to all evidence available, the APRM in the case of Ghana was considered best practice, while the review procedures in Kenya and Rwanda were more affected by controversies over the extent to which independent social actors had been given the opportunity to have their input into the findings and to what extent governments were prepared to accept the critical issues raised in the mission reports. Even President Kufuor of Ghana had earlier been rather reserved about accepting the recommendations, but by the time of the official debate of the report at the summit he indicated his government's willingness to respect the findings. He informed the august gathering, comprising several heads of state and/or government, that addressing the main issues raised in the programme of action would amount to some $ 5 bn. The summit commented in its communiqué "that the financing of the Programme of Action addressing the weaknesses is of a critical nature." Rwanda announced that it would implement the programme of action. At the end of April, Kufuor implemented one of the APRM report's recommendations through a major cabinet overhaul, in which the number of ministers was reduced from 88 to 70.

With São Tomé and Príncipe, Sudan and Zambia joining the **APRM process**, the number of countries prepared to undergo the voluntary assessment amounted to 25, almost half the total membership of the AU. Mozambique entered the queue as number 26 in August. Not all member countries, however, were willing to accede to the APRM. Among the reluctant countries were relatively 'shining examples' such as Botswana, but also Namibia. Namibia's foreign minister stated publicly during early March that his government fully backed NEPAD but had consigned the APRM "to the dustbin of history as a sham" and that Namibia would not sell its soul to reap financial benefits from developed countries. Meanwhile, APRMs were conducted during the year in South Africa and Uganda, among other countries, and an APRM support mission to Tanzania took place during 6 to 8 June.

Peace and War

A human security brief, updating the "Human Security Report" published for the first time in 2005, was issued by Simon Fraser University, Vancouver in December. It stressed that the number of state-based **conflicts** in Africa had declined from 13 to five in the period

2002–05 (the number of non-state conflicts from 24 to 14). Sub-Saharan Africa would no longer be the world's most conflict-affected region (that dubious distinction now belonged to Central and South Asia). The same report noted that in 2005 Somalia had experienced six conflicts, Nigeria three, while Ethiopia, Côte d'Ivoire and Sudan had two each. The logic of this form of counting becomes increasingly doubtful given the half-values assigned to peace agreements in some countries (Chad being the best case), which proved to be generally short. Above all, the validity of 'best estimates' of 'battle deaths' could be questioned, given the paucity of good data for virtually all spheres of life on the continent. Looking at the real horrors of ongoing conflict in the most affected part of Africa – the triangle involving Sudan, Chad and Central African Republic – the positive news produced by this initiative sounded utterly wrong.

However, some developments were clearly positive. The adoption of the comprehensive pact on security, stability and development in the Great Lakes region, signed by the heads of state of 11 countries on 15 December, was a major milestone towards peace right in the middle of the continent. It took six years of negotiations to come to this point. The leaders of Angola, Burundi, CAR, Congo, DR Congo, Kenya, Rwanda, Sudan, Tanzania, Uganda and Zambia agreed on far-reaching programmes in four fields of engagement: peace and security, democracy and good governance, economic development as well as humanitarian and social welfare. Given the complexity of those issues on the one hand and the limited capacities of most of the signatories on the other, a good helping of optimism was needed to believe in swift tangible results. In fact, responsibility for implementing the multifaceted programmes, such as the establishment of early warning and disaster prevention systems or cross-border development projects, would rest with the signing governments aided by a conference secretariat reporting to a sub-regional committee of cabinet ministers. This structure was in turn to advise the biennial heads of state meeting. A reconstruction and development fund financed by donors and Great Lakes governments is to be managed by the ADB. It is aimed at supporting reconstruction, development and subregional integration projects.

In **Burundi**, the far-reaching peace arrangements of 2005, which included elections, did not bear the expected fruits, as internal quarrels in all political camps continued and allegedly fabricated coup plots were denounced in a climate of growing paranoia. The last active rebel movement continued to attack several zones in the country. Peace negotiations began in Tanzania and a comprehensive ceasefire agreement was concluded on 7 September. It was, however, unclear whether it would bring lasting peace.

In **Uganda**, peace negotiations between the government and the rebel Lord's Resistance Army (LRA) began in earnest and led to a ceasefire agreement. By year's end, it was still not clear whether the positive momentum would hold. The presence of LRA in northeastern **DR Congo** was confirmed when the organisation attacked UN peacekeepers there. Over the year, Ituri province was very insecure, but further south the two Kivu provinces experienced a comparatively peaceful year, while the feared escalation in the southern Katanga provinces did not materialise. However, several serious incidents in the course of the elections and their aftermath, particularly in the capital Kinshasa, kept DR Congo on the list of countries to watch.

The Horn of Africa sub-region was the theatre for several serious civil wars. Rebel movements remained active in a number of regions of **Ethiopia** and clashed with security forces. Apart from this, a number of local violent conflicts and religious confrontations were recorded. More dangerous still was the involvement of the Ethiopian army in the **Somali civil war**, where it militarily supported the transitional federal government and intervened directly at year's end, while Eritrea backed the Union of Islamic Courts with ammunition and logistics, if not contingents of troops. This has to be seen against the background of the still volatile situation on the frontier between Ethiopia and Eritrea, where several incidents occurred during the year. The whole Somalia question could be interpreted as a proxy war between two neighbours conducted on Somali soil. Ethiopia had the backing of the US government for activities that were meant to foster sub-regional hegemony and were disguised as a contribution to the 'war against terrorism'. However, the situation clearly had some of the hallmarks of a major new sub-regional conflict in the making.

Further to the east, **Sudan** remained a conflict-ridden country. While the implementation of the comprehensive peace agreement between North and South, signed in early 2005, made only gradual progress, with at least one incident provoking fears of a late breakdown, the situation in the province of Darfur was more critical militarily. The government and a part of the leadership of the rebel Sudan Liberation Army (SLA) signed a peace agreement in Abuja, Nigeria, while a second wing of SLA and the Justice and Equality Movement (JEM) refused to sign. Fighting, therefore, continued or even intensified and resulted in heavy civilian casualties. Accusations of genocide were repeatedly voiced against the regime in Khartoum.

The spill-over of the conflict into neighbouring **Chad and CAR** was facilitated by the weakness of both regimes in the peripheries of both countries as a result of rebellions already taking place. Presidents Déby and Bozizé openly accused Khartoum of actively supporting those rebel movements. The N'Djaména regime narrowly survived a surprise attack on the capital and the already weak state in CAR saw two provincial capitals taken by rebel forces and vast stretches of territory lacking government control. France activated defence and cooperation agreements to support both governments with Mirage aircraft and military personnel. Civilians in both countries suffered enormously from rebel attacks and even more from retaliatory acts of government troops. A new wave of refugees from CAR to Chad was recorded.

One crisis meeting after another occurred in **Côte d'Ivoire**'s shaky peace process. On the ground, no major violent incident occurred, as both sides established their economic basis in their parts of the divided country. All international diplomatic efforts had at best limited success, but did not permit any thought of holding elections.

Nigeria's Niger delta saw another year of fierce battles between soldiers and militias, including army bombardments of villages. Officially, the army deplored 40 casualties within its ranks, giving an idea of the extent of the shoot-outs, described at times as 'local warfare'. The civilian casualties could only be estimated, with the figures ranging between several hundred up to about 1,000. Additionally, more than 150 foreign oil workers were taken hostage, not so much in protest against the state but to blackmail companies. However, army brutality alienated more and more local communities. Other states in the Nigerian federation were also affected by local armed conflicts.

Two **further hot-spots** in West Africa remained on the agenda: Guinea-Bissau intervened militarily against rebels of the Senegalese separatist movement in the Casamance region in March, testifying to the new alliance between Dakar and Bissau: about 10,000 people were displaced in the course of the fighting. Army barracks in northern Mali were attacked, raising fears of a new round of the Tuareg rebellion.

Elections

National-level presidential elections were held in 11 countries, legislative elections in seven, sometimes jointly as general elections (DR Congo, Uganda and Zambia). In two cases in a row, legislative elections preceded presidential ones (Cape Verde, São Tomé and Príncipe). Benin, Chad, Comoros, Gambia, Madagascar and Seychelles saw presidential elections only while Gabon had just legislative elections.

Arguably the two most important electoral developments took place in DR Congo and **Mauritania**. In the latter country a coup in 2005 had ended the rule of a rather authoritarian regime. A constitutional referendum was organised in June and permitted the holding of municipal and legislative elections in November–December. The overall trend was not completely clear as 25 political parties and 41 independent candidates won mandates, but there were new hopes for a more democratic and stable future for a country that had experienced its share of violent turnovers and societal tensions.

Much more international attention was given to the long-awaited national elections in **DR Congo** that had been preceded by a constitutional referendum in 2005. The relative success of this plebiscite provided the necessary dose of optimism to prepare for a poll in particularly difficult political and logistical conditions. With massive outside help (financial, technical and military), the operation was set in motion, not without serious hiccoughs. In the end, the incumbent Joseph Kabila was elected by a fairly clear margin (58%). However, the escalation of violence after an attack by the presidential guard on the residence of his best-placed rival, Jean-Pierre Bemba, which coincided with the announcement of the results of the first round of elections held on 30 July, plus serious new confrontations after the second round in November, underlined the need for the deployment of peacekeepers both from the UN and EU. In addition, the results showed the continuing divisions within the country with, roughly, the east voting for Kabila and the west for Bemba. Between the two rounds, Kabila concluded an alliance with the third-placed candidate, veteran politician Antoine Gizenga, promising to appoint him prime minister. This alliance secured the presidency for Kabila as well as a majority in parliament. Allegations of vote-rigging were voiced and the overall conduct of elections was certainly far from perfect. However, outside commentators generally expressed relief that the expected negative side-effects had been contained. This notwithstanding, a Herculean task lay ahead for those hoping to establish a political system even remotely resembling a stable and viable democracy.

Both other general elections, in Uganda and Zambia, confirmed the rule of the incumbents (Yoweri Museveni, Levy Mwanawasa) and their political parties. **Uganda** held its first multiparty elections since 1980. Party activities had been restricted for a long time and campaigning was also hampered now. However, the Ugandan opposition fared well, with presidential candidate Kizza Besigye officially receiving 37.4% of the votes. Even so, the electoral system facilitated victory for the ruling National Resistance Movement in 191 of the 284 seats in the National Assembly. In **Zambia**, Mwanawasa had more difficulty in being re-elected, winning only 43% of the votes, while his Movement for Multiparty Democracy (MMD) received just 73 of 150 seats. Only by adding the eight nominated MPs allowed under the constitution could MMD secure a majority. Supporters of second-placed populist Michael Sata staged demonstrations claiming that the vote had been rigged. Tensions remained high for a couple of days in both Lusaka and the Copperbelt, where Sata's opposition Patriotic Front was strong. By winning some crucial municipalities, the party had established itself firmly.

Presidential elections in **Chad** were run despite serious security concerns and calls by the opposition not to hold them in a year marked by more turmoil than ever; Idriss Déby stuck to his calendar and officially received close to 65% of the votes. The trustworthiness of those elections was as dubious as ever. Similarly, in **Gambia**, the nature of the elections reflected the authoritarian nature of the regime and led to an easy win for incumbent Yaya Jammeh in a climate of intimidation. Legislative elections in **Gabon** equally resulted in the confirmation of an overwhelming majority by the ruling party in parliament.

The island republics of Comoros, Seychelles, Cape Verde as well as São Tomé and Príncipe all held elections in quite divergent contexts. While the latter two republics were established democracies with elections considered routine and the Seychelles has enjoyed a solid 'partly free' rating for about 15 years without major hiccoughs, the **Comoros** are considered one of the most chaotic and coup-prone republics on the continent. The complex constitutional arrangements agreed upon in 2001 prescribed a rotation of the top position of federal president among the islands. After winning the primaries in Anjouan, Ahmed Abdallah Sambi, a businessman who considered himself a moderate Islamist, won the elections. Soon, tensions between the new Union government and the established island governments developed, but without fully escalating. In the **Seychelles**, James Michel, the candidate for the party that had ruled the country since 1977 was easily elected, winning 53.7% of the votes in elections considered largely free and fair.

Cape Verde's elections confirmed the incumbent President Pedro Pires in office, although by a very slight margin (51%). However, his 'Partido Africano da Independência de Cabo Verde' (PAICV) secured a wider margin in the legislative elections (41 of 72 seats). The opposition cried foul, but the complaints were rejected by the supreme court. Incumbent President Fradique de Menezes of **São Tomé and Príncipe** won by a comfortable majority in presidential elections, but his party had to form a coalition in parliament after earlier winning only a plurality of seats.

Madagascar and Benin, two Francophone countries that had experienced regime change after popular mobilisation in the early 1990s, held presidential elections, with one major difference: in **Benin**, most contenders from this period were excluded from the race by constitutional provisions. The hitherto unknown banker Yayi Boni therefore won those elections relatively easily. In **Madagascar**, the flamboyant entrepreneur Marc Ravalomanana stood for a second time and easily won the elections, gaining 54.8% of the votes and a wide margin over his closest rivals: the second, third and fourth placed candidates received between 9% and 11.6% of the votes. A bizarre coup attempt briefly interrupted campaigning two weeks before the elections, which experienced only minor irregularities.

Coup Attempts and the Struggle against Terrorism

Al-Qaida (AQ) was believed to operate from East Africa, particularly Somalia, but certainly with only a limited number of activists. This presence continued to be interpreted as a most serious threat to US and allied interests in the sub-region and it provided pretexts for intervention by both Ethiopia and the US in the notoriously unstable and divided country after the union of the Islamic courts had substantially extended its zone of influence between June and September. As a result (and as a self-fulfilling prophecy), ties between AQ and local Islamist organisations became more solid. No major terrorist attack was identified in Africa south of the Sahara, while AQ-affiliated groups were present and operated in northwest Africa and on the fringes of Sahelian states. These groups conducted small-scale attacks on government installations, raised funds, recruited personnel and conducted other support activities across the Sahara. The best-known group, the 'Groupe Salafiste pour la Prédication et le Combat' (GSPC) reportedly merged with al-Qaida in September and changed its name to Al-Qaida in the Islamic Maghreb (AQIM). AQIM/GSPC continued to operate in the Sahel region, crossing difficult-to-patrol borders between Mali, Mauritania, Niger, Algeria and Chad. It was speculated that the new alliance with AQ gave the group better access to resources and training. Only one major event in the framework of the US-sponsored trans-Saharan counterterrorism initiative, started in 2005, was recorded. In March, an exercise was held in Niger designed to enhance the training of US forces for operations in sub-Saharan Africa and to provide training to Niger's military ground forces.

One assassination attempt (in Chad) and two alleged but failed **coup attempts** in Gambia and Madagascar were reported, showing that democratic change was not the only avenue that political actors followed to change governments. Rumours of an imminent coup were voiced in Congo. Severe public unrest in Guinea ultimately aimed at regime change could hardly affect the security of President Conté, while the motives for mutiny-like unrest in certain of Burkina's security forces may have been less political in nature.

Epidemics and Disasters

In 2006, almost two-thirds (63%) of all persons infected with HIV worldwide were living in Africa south of the Sahara. According to the UNAIDS/WHO AIDS epidemic update issued in December, the estimated number was 24.7 m persons. Additionally, an estimated 2.8 m adults and children became infected with HIV, more than in all other regions of the world combined. With 2.1 m **AIDS** deaths, Africa south of the Sahara represented 72% of global AIDS mortality. All these figures contained an admittedly important margin of error (about 15%), but there was little doubt about the continuing drama. In 16 countries, at least 10% of the population was infected. According to WHO and UNAIDS, by December 2005 the number of people living in sub-Saharan Africa receiving antiretroviral therapy had increased more than eightfold to 810,000 (from 100,000) over a two-year period. This was cited as an example of the success of their campaign to improve access to antiretroviral medicines to treat HIV/AIDS. WHO's African regional office declared 2006 "the year of HIV prevention in the African region." The aim of the campaign was to again make a broad range of stakeholders more aware about the HIV/AIDS epidemic.

The WHO-inspired 'Africa Malaria Day' on 25 April was meant to highlight the need to provide universal access to artemisinin-based combination therapies and for these treatments to reach those who need them as quickly as possible. A total of 33 of the 42 **malaria**-endemic countries in Africa have adopted artemisinin combinations as first-line treatment, but only nine of these were implementing such treatment policies. About 80% of the more than 1 m malaria-related deaths globally occurred in African countries.

In May, the AU Commission in collaboration with UN agencies and other development partners held a special summit on HIV/AIDS, tuberculosis and malaria in Abuja, Nigeria, to take stock of progress to date and the way forward to achieve universal access to treatment for these diseases by 2010.

The potentially fatal H5N1 strain of the **avian flu** was detected in Africa when a commercial poultry farm in northern Nigeria raising chickens, geese and ostriches confirmed having detected the virus in samples taken in January. About 46,000 birds had to be slaughtered. Doubts were expressed about the ability of the authorities in the affected countries to manage a potential epidemic. Popular awareness was believed to be low, increasing the risk of a rapid spread of the dangerous disease.

An African regional health report was published by the WHO African regional office for the first time and launched at the opening of an international conference on community health in Addis Ababa on 20 November.

East Africa was hardest hit by new **drought**-related famine risks in the first half of the year. The January bulletin of the US-sponsored Famine Early Warning System (FEWS) warned of a pre-famine situation in Ethiopia, Djibouti, Kenya and Somalia affecting more than 5 m people. By September, the situation had worsened, particularly for northern Kenya. Heavy rains since October caused severe flooding in areas already suffering from high levels of food insecurity. Those rains were, however, expected to improve crop and livestock production in the medium term. The Sahelian countries experienced much better rainfalls and record gross grain production was expected for the 2006–07 growing season. FEWS also reported that, unlike previous years, food supplies remained adequate in most of Southern Africa as reflected by the stability of food prices across the region.

In December, Mozambique was affected by windstorms and heavy rains that caused inundations and destruction. Two Burundi provinces also suffered from heavy rains and substantial loss of homes and crops was recorded.

Andreas Mehler, Henning Melber and Klaas van Walraven

II. United Nations and Sub-Saharan Africa

The Economic Commission for Africa's 2007–09 business plan was officially launched on 16 November in Addis Ababa. At this ceremony, the declaration entitled 'Enhancing AU-UN Cooperation: Framework for the Ten-Year Capacity Building Programme for the African Union' was signed by the UN's secretary-general, Kofi Annan, and the chairperson of the AU Commission, Alpha Oumar Konaré. The ECA business plan was launched to illustrate how the ECA intends to scale up its support for the region's development efforts. Special emphasis was placed on regional integration and capacity building for the AU and its NEPAD programme. The total funding requirement for the three-year period 2007–09 amounts to $ 278.3 m.

Overall, the UN increasingly stressed the critical importance of a regional approach to conflict prevention, particularly with respect to cross-border issues such as disarmament, demobilisation and reintegration programmes, prevention of illegal exploitation of natural resources and trafficking in high-value commodities; and the illicit trade in small arms and light weapons.

The UN noted a steady increase in the insecurity levels facing its staff in Africa. On 22 January 2007, the UN press service announced that during 2006 a total of 11 UN personnel were killed in Africa. Many more were wounded.

UN peacekeeping in Africa continued to face challenges that taxed its capabilities. Crimes against humanity and ethnic cleansing in Darfur seemed to present the UN with the first test of its 'responsibility to protect' agenda adopted by the UN summit in 2005, amid loud proclamations that a disaster such as the inability to act over Rwanda would not happen again. Yet the UN response to Darfur showed that this agenda is in further need of support and consolidation. While Security Council resolution 1674 of 28 April praised the AU's civilian protection activities, the Security Council refused to turn to enforcement measures and instead insisted on the elusive consent of the Government of Sudan (GoS).

Peace and Security

On 12 October, Legwaila Joseph Legwaila, the secretary-general's special advisor on Africa, underlined the interrelationship between security, development and sustainable peace when he announced that all Africans must put in place the conditions for lasting peace or risk nullifying all the progress made in infrastructure, education, health and other areas under the region's common development strategy. In October, there were 18 different DPKO (UN Department of Peacekeeping Operations) missions. Only six of these were in Africa, yet they involved 58,238 out of 80,976 of the UN's serving military and police personnel, or approximately 72%.

During the year, the Security Council zealously debated African peace and security issues, pleaded, made condemnations and called upon African governments and armed groups to desist from any peace-obstructing and life-threatening activities. The UN clearly saw a continuing crucial role for **'African solutions'** (i.e., for ownership by African intergovernmental institutions and otherwise) to what have been mystifyingly dubbed 'African problems'. In this vein, the Security Council did not lose any opportunity to commend and thank actors such as the AU, sub-regional organisations (ECOWAS, SADC, IGAD), African states and individual mediators.

It was clear that the Security Council was working with sub-regional and other inter-governmental organisations to strengthen **partnerships** on peace and security, thus fulfilling the goals of the previous year's report of the 6th high-level meeting between the UN and regional and other international organisations (Security Council resolution 1631). These recommendations were also part of the 2005 World Summit outcome document. On 28 July, these priorities were given further weight in a report of the secretary-general entitled 'A regional-global security partnership: challenges and opportunities'. It argued for closer and more effective partnerships, based on a clearer division of labour that would reflect the comparative strengths of each organisation. For Secretary-General Kofi Annan, partnerships have been a priority especially with regard to Africa.

Burundi and Sudan were perhaps most emblematic of the growing UN and African cooperation with regard to policing internal wars and resolving conflict. The two peacekeeping missions, very different in nature and scale, provided ample examples of lessons needing to be learned on how the UN and African actors might work together. In relation to **Burundi**, the Security Council expressed its gratitude to AMIS (African Mission in Burundi), which had previously been deployed by the AU but had been integrated into ONUB ('Opération des Nations Unies au Burundi') in a unique co-deployment model. Continuing acts of hostility and human rights abuses committed by the 'Parti pour la libération de Hutu-Forces Nationales de Libération' (Palipehutu-FNL) and the Burundian army prompted the Security Council to call upon them to desist immediately. A comprehensive ceasefire agreement was signed on 7 September in Dar es Salaam by the government of Burundi and the Palipehutu-FNL. The mission was completed by the end of the year.

In stark contrast, the UN and the AU met with fierce opposition and all imaginable defiance on behalf of the GoS and the armed rebel groups. The two organisations held high-level meetings and sent a joint AU and UN technical assessment mission to **Sudan**. In the south, UNMIS (United Nations Mission in Sudan) retained a robust presence of more than 10,000 personnel, monitoring the ceasefire and the slow implementation of the comprehensive peace agreement signed by the GoS and the SPLM/A (Sudan People's Liberation

Movement/Army) in January 2005, and performing functions related to humanitarian assistance and the protection and promotion of human rights. On 31 August, the Security Council expanded the mandate of UNMIS to include its deployment to Darfur to support the early and effective implementation of the Darfur peace agreement of 5 May. Nevertheless, the widely expected re-badging of AMIS as a UN mission did not happen.

AMIS's military mandate in Darfur remained the only one GoS would consent to. GoS even denied entry to Jan Egeland, UN emergency relief coordinator, to Darfur and it declared that Jan Pronk, the secretary-general's special representative for the Sudan, must leave the country. Stymied by the lack of progress, the Security Council expressed full support for the inter-Sudanese peace talks and the signing in Abuja of the Darfur peace agreement between the GoS and the SPLM/A. It repeated its financial and military threats and referred those suspected of major war crimes to the International Criminal Court (ICC). AU and UN diplomacy ended in deadlock: at the end of the year GoS had allowed only the deployment of the UN light support package to AMIS (technical and logistical support). A UN/AU hybrid operation in Darfur seemed a very distant possibility.

At year's end, the threat to regional peace and security posed by the situation in Darfur with respect to **Chad** and the **Central African Republic** (CAR) demanded much attention from the world body. Fighting in **Somalia** also called for attention during the second part of the year. Fighting in Mogadishu prompted the Security Council to request the TFG (Transitional Federal Government) and the UIC (Union of Islamic Courts) to adhere to the ceasefire agreed on 22 June. The Security Council also stated its willingness to consider a request for a peace support mission if it judged that such mission would contribute to peace and security in Somalia. On 2 December, the UIC and the secretariat of IGAD reached an agreement, but the situation remained highly volatile.

A woeful standstill in **Western Sahara** prevailed throughout the year. Nonetheless, in October the mandate of the United Nations Mission for the Referendum in Western Sahara (MINURSO) was extended until 30 April 2007. In **Eritrea and Ethiopia**, UNMEE saw its mandate extended five times during the year. The troop numbers were reduced despite the fact that the military situation in the temporary security zone and adjacent areas remained volatile. On 24 February, the Security Council reiterated its demand that the parties permit UNMEE to perform its duties without restriction. Yet the government of Eritrea imposed restrictions on UNMEE's freedom of movement and detained several of its members and Ethiopia refused to abide by the decision relating to the border demarcation. On 29 September, the mandate of UNMEE was extended until the end of January 2007.

An equally difficult challenge existed in **West Africa**. On 9 August, the Security Council declared that transition from war to democratic rule was taking place in Sierra Leone, Guinea-Bissau and Liberia. Efforts were also under way to enable free and fair elections in Côte d'Ivoire. It was noted that the security situation in those countries remained generally stable, albeit fragile. The Security Council stressed the importance of cooperation between the UN office in West Africa, ECOWAS and the AU in peace consolidation initiatives, based on an integrated approach. In **Côte d'Ivoire**, security sector reform modalities and potential sanctions as well as the organising of elections plagued the slowly progressing agenda of the UNOCI mission (United Nations Operation in Côte d'Ivoire) and the French forces that supported it. In February, the Security Council decided on targeted sanctions for 12 months and travel bans against three alleged leaders of attacks on UN personnel and property. On 6 February, the secretary-general redeployed one infantry company from UNMIL (United Nations Mission in **Liberia**) to UNOCI for a limited time. The Security Council held numerous talks with Prime Minister Charles Konan Banny and encouraged him in his efforts to cooperate with President Laurent Gbagbo. On 2 June, UNOCI was strengthened by an additional 1,500 personnel. On 15 December, the mandate of UNOCI and the French forces was extended until 10 January 2007. The mandate of UNMIL continued. Security Council resolution 1712, adopted on 29 September, decided upon a phased, gradual consolidation, drawdown and withdrawal of UNMIL's troop contingent from April 2007, provided the security situation so permitted.

The main success during this difficult year in the life of the MONUC mission in the **DR Congo** was the holding of elections on 30 July. The electoral process was derailed by violent events such as the attack in January on a MONUC detachment resulting in the deaths of eight Guatemalan peacekeepers. MONUC received additional help: on 10 April ONUB temporarily redeployed one infantry battalion, a military hospital and approximately 50 military observers. In June, a temporary EU force was also mustered. Serious concerns were raised regarding the acts of violence perpetrated by armed groups: in May several Nepalese peacekeepers were kidnapped. Nevertheless, MONUC would stay until 15 February 2007.

In **Sierra Leone**, UNIOSIL's mandate was extended until the end of 2007 with a view to providing continued peacebuilding assistance to the government and preparing for the general elections scheduled for July 2007. The main task of this so-called integrated mission was assistance in peacebuilding and it was hoped that the elections would provide the exit strategy for the mission. On 16 June, the ICC expressed its willingness to allow the use of its premises for the trial of former President Charles Taylor.

At the end of the previous year, resolution 1645 fulfilled the decision of the September 2005 World Summit to establish a **peacebuilding commission**, and on 11 October a peacebuilding fund was launched. In Burundi, BINUB ('Bureau Intégré des Nations Unies au Burundi') was instituted in collaboration with the government for an initial period of 12 months, commencing in 2007. In Sierra Leone, the peacebuilding commission was also involved in ongoing work in support of peace-consolidation and risk-reduction efforts led by the government. In the CAR, the department of political affairs of the UN secretariat managed a peacebuilding support office (BONUCA) with a renewed mandate until end of 2007. In Guinea-Bissau the peacebuilding support office (UNOGBIS) worked in close cooperation with the Community of Portuguese-Speaking Countries, ECOWAS and the UN country team.

On 20 December, the Security Council backed the pact on security, stability and development successfully concluded by the countries of the Great Lakes region at the 2nd summit of the international conference on the Great Lakes region in Nairobi, Kenya, on 14–15 December.

Governance

The 61st session of the UN General Assembly witnessed the swearing in on 14 December of **Ban Ki-Moon**, former foreign minister of the Republic of Korea, as the new secretary-general in a General Assembly ceremony. Until the end of the year, he was the secretary-general designate, working alongside **Kofi Annan**, the outgoing secretary-general and second ever African to hold the post in the UN's history. Annan and Ki-Moon asked on 19 December that Jan Eliasson, former Assembly president during its 60th session in 2005–06 and Swedish foreign minister until October, serve as UN envoy for Darfur and under-secretary-general of the DPKO.

The Assembly adopted without vote several texts dealing with matters pertinent to the continent. These dealt with the 2001–10 decade to roll back malaria in developing countries, particularly in Africa; progress in implementing NEPAD and international support; and implementation of the recommendations in the secretary-general's report on the causes of conflict and promotion of durable peace and sustainable development in Africa. These texts were vague and declamatory in spirit and content, leaving a big gap between political rhetoric on the one hand and expected actions, timelines and results on the other.

The General Assembly convened its first-ever plenary session on **migration issues**, a UN high-level dialogue on international migration and development on 14–15 September. African speakers highlighted the growing number of migrants from the developing world heading to developing countries and, while agreeing that migrants'remittances to their home countries might contribute to poverty reduction, noted that migrancy underscored the problems of the nations the migrants left behind. Issues such as brain drain, the smuggling of migrants and the exploitation of immigrants working in poor conditions for little money were challenges that African speakers felt there was further need to address.

The 61st session took note of the report of the international criminal tribunal for the prosecution of persons responsible for **genocide** and other serious violations of international humanitarian law committed in the territory of Rwanda and Rwandan citizens responsible for genocide and other such violations committed in the territory of neighbouring states between 1 January and 31 December 1994. The completion-date had been postponed but the tribunal reported some significant progress and that it maintained good relations with the Rwandan government.

Kofi Annan highlighted in his last annual report to the General Assembly on 19 September how Africa was in great danger of being excluded from the benefits of globalisation and that it was the scene of some of the most protracted and brutal conflicts. With emotion, he declared that many of Africa's people felt they were unjustly condemned to be exploited and oppressed, generation after generation, since colonial rule had been replaced by an inequitable economic order on the global level, and sometimes by corrupt rulers and warlords at the local level.

The adoption on 13 December of the convention on the protection and promotion of the rights of persons with disabilities was the first major human rights treaty adopted in the 21st century. African states in many ways helped champion it by increasing the visibility of **disability-related issues** and making progress on these domestically as part of the ongoing African Decade of Persons with Disabilities, spanning the period of 1999–2009.

In the **DR Congo**, MONUC, in close cooperation with the UNDP, was involved in the largest electoral assistance project ever. The UN Democracy Fund in August unveiled its first beneficiaries, awarding $ 36 m in grants to 125 projects. At least one-third of grants were directed to projects focused on sub-Saharan Africa.

Human Rights

Countries such as the DR Congo, Chad and Sudan were in the limelight for UN human rights bodies and agencies. The issues of concern included gender-based violence and rape as a weapon of war in Sudan and Darfur, dumping of toxic waste in Côte d'Ivoire, the need to implement Uganda's national policy for IDPs, the continuing forced evictions in African states such as Angola and the risk of famine in the Horn of Africa.

The **Human Rights Council** was established in June, replacing the Geneva-based Commission on Human Rights, which had come under fire for excessive politicisation. It quickly became preoccupied with the gross human rights violations in Darfur and on 13 December decided to dispatch a high-level mission to assess the situation. Darfur was also at the centre of attention of the special advisor on the prevention of genocide, who was provided with additional support in the shape of an advisory committee on genocide prevention on 3 May 2006.

The OHCHR (Office of the United Nations High Commissioner for Human Rights) ran a **human rights programme for Africa**, which was to continue beyond year's end. Notably, the OHCHR has liaised with and helped enhance the operations of the African Commission on Human and People's Rights. The OHCHR also initiated and participated in consultations to establish an African human rights defenders' award.

Much to the anger of human rights and like-minded organisations, the General Assembly adopted a resolution on 20 December postponing action on a declaration on the rights of **indigenous peoples**. After an initiative by the Namibian representative, the text was amended to defer consideration of the draft declaration until some time before the end of the 61st session. The African group had expressed concerns about the declaration's potential effects on national sovereignty and on land rights. Some provisions ran counter to the national constitutions of a number of African countries and there was therefore thought to be a need for more consultations. Nonetheless, the African Commission on Human and People's Rights working group on indigenous people's rights expressed a wish for an agreeable resolution on rights for this vulnerable group in the African context.

Economic Performance and Development

The UN Economic and Social Council (**ECOSOC**) ad hoc advisory group in Guinea-Bissau provided an overview of current developments on 18 April. The advisory group on Burundi was terminated at the 2006 substantive session of ECOSOC, since it was foreseen that the peacebuilding commission would move in.

NEPAD continued to garner weighty support from UN agencies. On 13 July, the secretary-general's advisory panel on international support for **NEPAD** underlined the need for the UN to have an integrated framework for NEPAD support through the AU Commission. The panel therefore stressed the urgent need for the AU Commission and NEPAD secretariat to clarify the institutional relationship between them. UN support for NEPAD had previously been reviewed in a report considered on 29 March by the ECOSOC committee for programme and coordination. This report put pressure on African governments to address a range of institutional and partnership issues, including integrating NEPAD into AU structures and processes, providing greater support for the private sector and achieving more outreach to civil society. The UN supported a stronger role for the OSAA (Office of the Special Advisor on Africa) in periodically reviewing and monitoring the NEPAD programme and keeping the General Assembly and other organs up to date. A UN panel discussion on institutional challenges in implementing the NEPAD was organised on 12 October, OSAA's 4th panel discussion held on this theme. The progress in implementing the APRM involved among others the ECA, UNDP and the ADB in a meeting in May in Kigali.

On 21–23 February in Addis Ababa, the African regional preparatory meeting reviewed the implementation of the **Brussels programme of action** for the period 2001–05 for African LDCs. African stakeholders urged international partners to increase ODA flows and to expand HIPC debt relief to African LDCs. They urged the UN system, in particular the office of the high representative for LDCs, landlocked developing countries and small island developing states to remain involved and monitor activities. On 25 May, a report from the secretary-general on the implementation of the programme of action for LDCs (2001–10) showed that rapid population growth and urbanisation, environmental degradation and HIV/AIDS aggravate extreme poverty in LDCs, in particular those in Africa and the small islands.

On 26 April, ECOSOC debated a report on **recent economic trends** in Africa. The report found that economic conditions in the region have improved in the recent past but much remains to be done to reduce poverty and improve social conditions significantly. Oil-rich countries were expected to benefit from the continued strong performance of exports, thanks to high international oil prices. Delivery of promised aid and debt relief would allow African countries to boost expenditures in key sectors, including infrastructure and social services. Improvements in political stability were also thought to help. Interestingly, the report highlighted the need for policymakers in Africa to find ways to eliminate gender imbalances, because, while gender inequality harmed women primarily, it also imposed heavy costs on society as a whole.

The 5th ECA **African development forum** from 16–18 November in Addis Ababa centred on youth and leadership. The forum recognised that the political and economic marginalisation of youth is a structural source of conflict. A subsequent OSAA expert group meeting from 14–16 November aimed at identifying strategies for creating income-generating activities, integrating youth more fully into political life and enhancing community-based rehabilitation.

In June, an OSAA expert group meeting on **natural resources and conflict** was held in Cairo. It recommended that the international community support the AU-led process for developing minimum standards for natural resource governance; enhancing governmental and civil society capacity for natural resource management, including the strengthening of monitoring and enforcement mechanisms; involving the private sector as a partner in post-conflict reconstruction and development activities; and strengthening existing mechanisms, particularly the extractive industries transparency initiative.

ECA continued to prioritise the need for Africa to implement urgent and comprehensive national, regional and continental strategies to tackle the challenges of poverty eradication and job creation. Under the AU Commission's leadership, ECA, AU/NEPAD and ADB also tackled the crucial issue of a **land policy**. On 27–29 March, a consultative workshop was held in Addis Ababa as a first step in the joint process that was meant to usher in a land policy framework and guidelines, as well as the modalities for its implementation at country, sub-regional and continental levels.

The **UNDP 2006 human development report** contained some depressing figures. Disease and productivity losses linked to water and sanitation in developing countries amounted to 5% of GDP in sub-Saharan Africa, more than the region received in aid. Most of the 18 countries whose HDI score was lower than in 1990 were located in sub-Saharan Africa, as were 28 of the 31 low human development countries. Over 300 m people lack access to safe water and more than 500 m live without adequate sanitation. The UN Human Settlements Programme (UN-HABITAT) and the UN Department for Economic and Social Affairs (UNDESA) held a workshop in Nairobi in December for water utility managers across the continent. They called for increased financing and oversight, including innovative ways to raise funds.

Environment

At year's end, Secretary-General Kofi Annan unveiled the **Nairobi framework** that came out of the UN climate change conference in Nairobi. This outlined a plan by six UN agencies to help the poorest continent get a bigger slice of investment in clean technologies. The UN Africa **carbon plan** had yet to attract sufficient funds and to translate into a strategic framework of action.

Desertification was debated in the second committee of the General Assembly on 6 December and a draft resolution on the implementation of the UN Convention to Combat Desertification (UNCCD) in those countries experiencing serious drought and/or desertification, particularly in Africa, was approved.

On 27 June, UNEP released a study showing that Africa would not stay poor if the region's wealth of **natural resources** were effectively, fairly and sustainably harnessed. The study highlighted Africa's untapped potential for tourism based on nature and cultural sites. It also noted that the continent had suitable land to feed its people; abundant but little used water resources for irrigation, drinking and power generation; and produced nearly 80% of the world's platinum, more than 40% of the globe's diamonds and more than one-fifth of its gold and cobalt.

The Humanitarian Situation and Assistance

Among the many humanitarian crises in sub-Saharan Africa, UNOCHA (UN Office for the Coordination of Humanitarian Affairs) put special emphasis on the food security situation in Malawi; floods in Mozambique and, at the end of the year, in Somalia; the disaster-stricken parts of the Horn of Africa to which it had dedicated $ 1.7 m from a recently launched central emergency response fund in March; the difficult and deteriorating situation in CAR about which there was a need to raise awareness among donors; and in May, the DR Congo, which was pronounced to be the deadliest humanitarian catastrophe.

In July, the UN noted that six months after the launch of the **2006 humanitarian appeal** aimed at raising funds for relief efforts globally, the world body and its partners still required $ 3.1 bn to address the urgent needs of 30 m people affected by crisis in 31 countries. Jan Egeland, under-secretary-general for humanitarian affairs and emergency relief coordinator, was concerned about several under-funded appeals. The Horn of Africa regional appeal, which required some $ 119 m, had seen only $ 17.5 m committed. Less than one-quarter of the $ 1.6 bn required for humanitarian assistance to Sudan had been received. The Burundi appeal, for $ 123 m, had received just 25% of its requirements, while the action plan for the DR Congo had less than $ 184 m of the required $ 705 m – just 26%. Appeals for Liberia, Guinea and Côte d'Ivoire had also come up short of expected funds. On 20 April, the Security Council was told by Jan Egeland that the situation in northern Uganda was still bad, but that he saw hope in that the government was working with the international community on a concrete action plan to improve the humanitarian situation. Towards the end of the year, Jan Egeland announced that 4 m Darfurians were in need of humanitarian aid.

Refugees

In July, the General Assembly was told that UNHCR was working to protect, assist and find durable solutions for some 12.2 m people in Africa. A number of persistent challenges had to be faced in protecting and assisting these refugees. For example, eastern Chad, with around 120,000 IDPs, faced a crisis of internal displacement, while at the same time hosting more than 200,000 refugees from Darfur. The **UNHCR report for 2006** lamented the organisation's lack of sufficient core funding in recent years and noted that the tight earmarking of contributions had led to some refugee crises, mainly in Africa, receiving far less funding than crises in Afghanistan, the Balkans and Iraq.

At the beginning of the year, **major refugee populations** originated in Sudan (693,300 mainly seeking asylum in Chad, Uganda, Kenya, Ethiopia and CAR); Burundi (438,700 mainly seeking asylum in Tanzania, DR Congo, Rwanda, South Africa and Zambia); DR Congo (430,600 mainly seeking asylum in Tanzania, Zambia, Congo-Brazzaville, Rwanda and Uganda); Somalia (394,800 mainly seeking asylum in Kenya, Yemen, UK, US and Ethiopia); and Liberia (231,100 mainly seeking asylum in Sierra Leone, Guinea, Côte d'Ivoire, Ghana and the US). The UNHCR was involved with IDPs in Sudan (841,900), Somalia (400,000) and Liberia (237,800).

UNHCR continued work on improving conditions in areas of return in the DR Congo, on assisting with the repatriation of Burundian refugees and on its multi-year **HIV and refugee strategic plan**. Sub-regional AIDS initiatives, such as GLIA (Great Lakes Initiative on AIDS), were started. GLIA involves UN organisations, bilateral and multilateral donors, NGOs and the private sector working together with the six countries involved (Burundi, DR Congo, Kenya, Rwanda, Uganda and Tanzania). A consolidated version of the international guidelines on HIV and human rights was released during the year by the OHCHR and UNAIDS. UNHCR also released a note on HIV/AIDS and the protection of refugees, IDPs and other persons of concern, which provided detailed guidance on how refugee and human rights law applies when addressing the HIV-related needs of refugees.

Health and Diseases

The annual **UNAIDS report** confirmed that Africa remained the global epicentre of the AIDS pandemic. Among the notable new trends were the decline in national HIV prevalence in two sub-Saharan African countries (Kenya and Zimbabwe) and in the urban areas of Burkina Faso. HIV was spreading fastest in provinces linked by major transport routes to Malawi, South Africa and Zimbabwe. The report recommended that the needs of children who had lost one or more parents to AIDS – approximately 9% of children under the age of 15 in sub-Saharan Africa – be promptly and prominently included in national AIDS plans and strategies. It was shown that **feminisation** of the disease was occurring and that this had consequences for gender equity. In sub-Saharan Africa, infection rates have been growing far more rapidly for women than for men. Women accounted for 57% of HIV infections in the region, and young African women (aged 15–24) were three times more likely to become infected than men.

Female genital mutilation continued to take its toll on girls. According to the WHO, there are between 100 and 140 m girls in the world who have undergone such mutilation. In June, WHO published a study showing that women who have had genital mutilation are significantly more likely to experience difficulties during childbirth and that their babies are more likely to die as a result of the practice. Female genital mutilation is common in Burkina Faso, Ghana, Kenya, Nigeria, Senegal and Sudan.

Malaria caused more than 1 m deaths per year, of which 86% occurred in sub-Saharan Africa. The African group at the UN took a lead in putting together the resolution on efforts to roll back malaria.

An African **regional health report** came out in November focusing on public health. While drawing the world's attention to recent successes, the report sadly stated that HIV/AIDS, tuberculosis and malaria, and pregnancy-related conditions that kill mothers and babies remained colossal challenges. The African region has the highest neonatal death rate in the world. The UN Population Fund (UNFPA) reported that **women** may well experience more suffering than men because of the lack of access to reproductive health care systems. Liaison activities with African health ministers occurred as a result.

At an avian influenza donor conference in Bamako on 7 December, the UN Food and Agriculture Organisation (UNFAO) declared that Africa must be the centre of attention in the battle against the deadly H5N1 **avian flu** virus, since it suffered from a shortfall in funding.

Linnea Bergholm

III. African-European Relations

After many public discussions about European policy towards Africa in 2005, on the agenda in 2006 was the defining of activities and implementing promises, for instance at the meeting of European NGOs towards the end of the Austrian presidency of the EU in the first half of the year (22–23 June). It remained unclear, however, what impact the EU strategy – intended alike for the common programmes of the Commission towards Africa and for bilateral relations between EU member states and that continent – will have at the national level within Europe.

European institutions took **increasing official interest in the AU**. This interest included troika-level consultations, a visit by a European parliament delegation to the still embryonic Pan-African Parliament in Midrand, South Africa (8–9 May) and a meeting of both the European Commission (EC) and the AU Commission in Addis Ababa (8–9 October). One of the possible driving forces behind this increased interest is the increasing role of China in Africa in recent years, strongly symbolised in 2006 in the **China-Africa summit in Beijing** (4 November). The event was the third of it kind, but the first to involve heads of state and government. China's increased engagement spurred academic discussion in Europe of that country's role in Africa, discussion that was apparently partly motivated by a sense among some observers that Europe was losing political ground on its neighbouring continent.

European intervention in DR Congo had also to be interpreted in this light. Central Africa served as an arena for much of the discussion on the political and military capabilities of an autonomous European security policy, specifically the deployment of a European Force (**EUFOR**) **to the DR Congo**. The mission was largely unpopular among the European electorate and its mandate was criticised.

A broader debate between Europe and Africa was migration, even though not much immediate action resulted. The year 2006 saw **two major European-African conferences on migration**, the first being between the EU and African countries of origin or transit in Rabat (July). The conference was the result of the flow of migrants particularly via West Africa to southwestern Europe. Towards the end of the year, a ministerial conference on migration and development in Tripoli, Libya (22–23 November) again discussed the topic, this time with broader participation by the EU and African states. While both sides agreed on the need to manage migration between the two regions, the interests and policy emphases were different. While Europe aimed at curbing illegal migration and trafficking in human beings, the African participants focused rather on the link between migration and development, as well as legal obstacles to emigration to Europe and human rights issues.

Bilateral Relations between African and European States

The new **EU strategy for Africa** was a key document agreed during the UK's EU presidency in December 2005 and was debated and investigated by the British House of Lords in autumn 2006. The committee in charge focused its inquiry on the implementation of the strategy, including the extent of the EU's role in Africa, how the strategy would be financed, what the priorities for its implementation would be and how the EU could best work with the AU and sub-regional organisations to ensure its implementation.

Migration flows to southwestern Europe and particularly the Canary Islands off the West African Coast continued to be a much-debated topic in **Spain** and between that country and West African countries of origin and transit. The Spanish government emphasised the regional dimension of the issue and sought to discuss the topic in a broader European-African framework.

The **French** came to the **military assistance** of the regimes in **Chad** (starting in April) and in the **Central African Republic** (CAR) (intensifying in November). In Chad, French troops repelled rebel groups advancing on the capital N'Djaména and thereby seemed to have saved the regime of Idriss Déby (13 April). Throughout the year, Chadian authorities denounced Sudanese support for rebels attacking towns not far from the borders of both Sudan and the CAR (25–26 June; 21 October). In the CAR, French military jets and paratroopers intervened to recapture towns in the north near the Sudanese border that had fallen under rebel control. The intervention in the CAR was supported by CEMAC troops. Both military engagements were officially justified by defence agreements with the respective countries, and represented lingering French Africa policies that hearkened back to well-known patterns of the past. Through these interventions, France risked becoming engaged in the conflict in Sudan, whence rebel groups in both Chad and the CAR came and allegedly were supported. These strong-man interventions in Africa could not stem the increasing sense of *fin de règne* of President Jacques Chirac. The **French military presence** in Africa was reasserted, yet the lack of vision in French African policy was apparent, also in **Côte d'Ivoire**. France's political influence in the Ivorian quagmire decreased further: it remained mired in the conflict without being able to push either side to an agreement. Elections had originally been planned for October 2005. However, they could not be held on time because of delays in the preparations and were postponed to October 2006, a date that was also ultimately not met.

Institutional Development in the Regions – EU and AU

In 2006, several high-level meetings symbolised the **increased European interest in the AU**. The AU aimed at institutional transformation with a view to clarifying its internal governance. Clearer structures should emerge by strengthening the Commission (as the motor of the AU) and by promoting institutional rationalisation in Africa (e.g., between the AU and the regional economic communities). An updated 'implementation roadmap' for these reforms was elaborated at the AU summit in Banjul (1–2 July).

Despite the more favourable odds for Africa in international politics, one could hardly expect rapid change in EU policy-making towards Africa. **Implementation of the Africa strategy** and the European Consensus on Development was expected to be take time, not least because the goals were broad. The start was indeed slow, as the consultation process between the EU and the AU on a joint strategy has only just begun. Disagreements over Zimbabwe continued to loom large in the highest-level inter-regional meetings between Europe and Africa, even though meetings at working and sub-regional levels were taking place.

The regular meeting of foreign ministers in the **EU troika and Africa** took place in Vienna in the framework of the **EU-Africa dialogue** (8 May). In addition to the current EU presidency, represented by the Austrian foreign minister, Ursula Plassnik, the meeting was attended by her counterpart from Congo-Brazzaville, Rodolphe Adada, as chairperson of the AU. A second troika meeting between the EU and AU took place on 10 October in Brazzaville. The AU troika consists of the former, current and future (annual) chairmanship, i.e., in addition to the Congolese foreign minister, the foreign ministers of Nigeria and Sudan were present. The AU commissioners for economic affairs, Maxwell Mkwezalamba, and for peace and security, Said Djinnit, represented African continental institutions. On the European side, also present was the EU commissioner for development cooperation, Louis Michel and the foreign minister of Finland, as well as high-level representatives of the policy unit of the general secretariat of the Council of the EU. The main topic discussed at the meeting was the implementation of the EU strategy for Africa.

In October, the **commissions of both the EU and the AU met** for a third joint meeting in Addis Ababa, in which in addition to both commission presidents, ten commissioners each participated (2 October). At their meeting, the two regional organisations further discussed cooperation in their institutional development. Both regional bodies signed a support programme for **EU to AU assistance of € 55 m** and both institutions declared their willingness to exchange officials and to increase funding for the Erasmus Mundus postgraduate student exchange programme. They also agreed on an EU-Africa infrastructure partnership (see below). Recurring topics between the EU and AU were the political situation in African states, in particular in Darfur, the DR Congo, Chad and Uganda. Not mentioned in any of the public announcements was the situation in Zimbabwe.

A **meeting of the EC and African regional integration organisations** was held in autumn as a follow-up to the one held last year on the EU-Africa strategy consultation. The meeting had been postponed from May to autumn. Key issues on the European-African agenda were the planned economic partnership agreements and security questions, as well as a joint EU-Africa strategy.

Conflict and Security

In support to the emerging **African Peace and Security Architecture (APSA)**, the Council's general secretariat and the Commission in June 2006 presented a proposed 'European Union Concept for strengthening African capabilities for the prevention, management and resolution of conflicts', which was endorsed by the Council on13 November. The concept was elaborated in the wake the EU Africa strategy commitment to increase work with the AU, regional organisations and African countries on security issues. It elaborated the framework and objectives for EU support as well as the possible measures to be taken. It aimed particularly at combining EU and member state resources and instruments for future engagements. Already in April, the EU council of ministers had decided to extend the **Africa Peace Facility (APF)** from 2008 to 2010. Funding was increased to € 300 m for that period, to be provided from the 10th European Development Fund (EDF). The APF was meant to financially support African peacekeeping operations under an AU mandate, such as the smaller missions to the CAR (by CEMAC) in the past and the short-term AU-led mission in the Comoros during elections in spring 2006. The major APF-funded activity, however, was the **AU's mission to Darfur, Sudan (AMIS)**. The EU provided some police and military personnel and a total of € 242 m to AMIS, which, nevertheless, was considered a failure as it did not manage to stop the war. Political will in Europe to engage directly in Sudan was limited and the pre-eminence of AU activities was repeatedly emphasised. The AU mission to Sudan was supposed to end in December 2006, yet the regime in Khartoum did not agree to the deployment of a UN mission and played for time. There was no precedent for the suggested integrated AU-UN force that Khartoum suggested in place of a purely UN-led mission. Sudan was also covered in a wider strategy paper by the EC on the **Horn of Africa** (10 October). The interest in the region was best explained by its strategic value and the important activities by other powers such as the US and China. The EU, meanwhile, attempted to improve its interactions with IGAD. While the Commission's paper attempted to put the conflicts into a broader perspective and identify EU instruments to address various challenges in the region, the EU's presence and its policy impact in the area remained negligible.

The single key issue that stood out in European policy towards Africa in 2006 was the **elections in DR Congo**. Discussion about a **European military force** alongside the UN mission to Congo (MONUC) commenced in February when the EU expressed a general willingness to provide assistance. For the EU, the mission was politically important as it aimed at creating credibility for its unfolding common security policy as formulated in the **European security strategy** of 2003. This document called for the ability for autonomous European operations within a radius of 5,000 km, that is, most of sub-Saharan Africa. However, details of the mission proved tricky, as the Union faced continuing – and public – quarrels over the composition and the exact mandate of the EU force. Burden-sharing discussions within the EU pointed to a German lead of this peacekeeping mission, while the German government insisted on broad participation by other EU member states in the mission before it would be willing to accept the lead. The agreement was for 400–500 troops from other EU member states. On 27 April, two days after the UN mandate had been decided upon, the European Council agreed to the EUFOR mission to Congo, appointing Lt.Gen. Karlheinz Viereck (Germany) EU operational commander and Maj.Gen. Christian Damay (France) EU force commander. While EUFOR's mission was officially to assist the UN troops already deployed to Congo, it remained an autonomous, non-integrated mission. The elections in DR Congo were originally scheduled for June and were delayed several times because of political and technical difficulties, for example, with voter registration and the hesitation of President Joseph Kabila to officially invite the EU troops. Parliamentary elections and the first round of presidential elections finally took place on 30 July. When no candidate achieved the necessary absolute majority of votes, a second round of presidential elections was held in autumn (30 October). The EU mission was **deployed to Central Africa in the second half of the year**, with its official start on election day, 30 July. It was meant to function as a *force d'ordre* for four months during the elections. The force headquarters in Congo were in Kinshasa at the N'Dolo airfield. Most of the soldiers were stationed there, with a few EUFOR soldiers also stationed at the N'Djilli airfield. The largest part of the force was not stationed in DR Congo but in Libreville, Gabon, and were be deployed when they were needed. The mission itself and particularly its **mandate were highly contested**. The mission was declared to be mostly a deterrent to political forces that might want to contest the results of the election immediately after the counting of votes. Critics, including members of the European parliament, agreed that the EU had an interest in stability in Africa, but questioned the EU's capacity to work effectively in Africa and pointed to the risks of becoming caught up in a long conflict. Intervention should therefore be limited. This, on the one hand, meant a technically feasible, geographically restricted mission with a clear timeline until the end of 2006. On the other hand, these limitations potentially affected the value of the peace operation in DR Congo. One criticism was the restriction to the capital city of Kinshasa, in a vast country with particularly virulent conflicts in its eastern and southern provinces. Furthermore, it was argued, the strict deadline for the end of the mission was also known to potential political contestants, so the EU force deliberately created incentives to play for time and thereby reduced the deterrent impact. The **EUFOR mission ended on 30 November** after the final results of the election were announced. The last EU troops left Kinshasa before Christmas, after the Congolese opposition had accepted the incumbent as the newly elected president. However, the political situation in DR Congo remained tense and the peace was fragile.

The EU decided on a policy framework for support to **Security Sector Reform (SSR)** that aimed at greater coherence of EU activities across different funding modalities (from the EU budget and via the Common Foreign and Security Policy – CFSP – funding). The EC has supported SSR reforms in South Africa in areas of policing and justice reform and afterwards provided similar support in 25 other African countries. Activities under SSR included capacity building of law enforcement agencies and key ministries in the areas of justice reform, rule of law and civilian oversight. EU engagement with SSR in Africa also took place in the DR Congo in the area of defence and security policy, through its **EUPOL mission**, among others. EUPOL, an EU police mission in Kinshasa, had approximately 30 staff, and started in 2005. It was extended until 30 June 2007 (8 December).

Besides an observation mission alongside EUFOR in DR Congo, **EU election observation missions** were active in Uganda, Zambia and Madagascar in 2006.

Cotonou Partnership Agreement

In January, the **planning for the 10th EDF** started and a series of regional planning seminars at the highest political level were launched in the ACP regions. After discussions in the previous year, European states have committed € 22.7 bn to the EDF, covering the period from 2008–13. Discussions and planning were envisaged to continue until 2007.

In 2006, two programmes within the 10th EDF already took shape, one being the governance initiative, the second an EU-Africa partnership on infrastructure. In August, the Commission published the first outlines of the **governance initiative**, which arises from the renewed emphasis on governance in the European Consensus on Development. The initiative was approved by the council of ministers on 16–17 October. The governance initiative aimed at creating a **new incentive mechanism** that would give ACP partner countries access to funding, depending on their commitment to democratic governance reform programmes. Of the 10th EDF, € 2.7 bn was reserved for these incentive tranches, which were apparently meant to be more flexible funding alongside the funds planned to be provided by member states. A key instrument of this mechanism appeared to be a **'governance profile'** established by the Commission and EU member states for each ACP country. The draft profiles were collated at country level and contextualised in Brussels. These profiles, intended as an analytical tool, gave an overview of nine areas: political governance, the rule of law, control of corruption, government effectiveness, economic governance, internal and external security, social governance, the regional and international context and the 'quality of partnership'. The papers were intended to be – and in fact in some cases were – critical assessments of the governance situation. The assessment provided for an analysis of the current situation and trends, as well as the European perception of the respective ACP government's commitment to reform. The governance profiles were not published, as work on the profile continued throughout the year. The Commission announced that the profile's conclusions would be shared 'as appropriate' with the partner government during the programming of assistance. According to the EC, funding would be used to support "relevant, ambitious and credible reforms". Good performance and respect for the commitments made by the ACP countries, particularly in terms of good governance, the proper management of public funds and efficient administration would become key factors in the increase of the matching financial allocations to each country.

This initiative was also announced as part of European financial support to the **APRM**, an African self-assessment tool within the NEPAD programme. Twenty-six of 53 African countries have acceded to the APRM, some of them being North African non-ACP countries (Algeria and Egypt) or ACP members that are ineligible for EDF funding (South Africa).

To support the development of Africa's infrastructure – and presumably also to mark European engagement in an area where China is increasingly active – the Commission proposed an **EU-Africa partnership on infrastructure** (13 July). The partnership claimed to support the development goals of the AU and of NEPAD. Emphasis was laid on the establishment of transborder networks in transport, water, energy and communications. The funding needs for this area of cooperation were considerable. Funding for the EU-Africa partnership on infrastructure was to come from the EDF. In the 10th EDF, approximately € 5.6 bn was earmarked for infrastructure. Additionally, an **EU-Africa infrastructure trust fund** was set up. This new instrument aimed at allowing the EC and EU member states to co-finance projects with the European Investment Bank and with African and European financial and development institutions. Co-financing had been legally difficult within the EU in the past.

EU-South Africa relations were discussed as a **'strategic partnership'**, that is emphasis would be put on joint actions, beyond reactive political dialogue, that should also include regional and global issues. On 28 June, the EC published a proposal with this intent and this was taken up by the EU council of ministers on 17 October. Issues on the joint agenda included HIV/AIDS, the development of the UN, international terrorism, the Middle East and Zimbabwe. South Africa's 'quiet diplomacy' towards Zimbabwe was criticised in the EU paper for not having had the desired results.

Consultations under article 96 on the violation of essential elements of the Cotonou Agreement (i.e., democracy, human rights and the rule of law) were held with **Guinea, Mauritania, Togo and Zimbabwe**. While the EC claimed that progress could be observed in Guinea, Togo and Mauritania, relations with Zimbabwe continued to be 'problematic'. The EU renewed its sanctions against the regime of Robert Mugabe – including a travel ban for key figures in the regime – for a further year. The restrictive measures have been in place since 2002 without having achieved the isolation of Robert Mugabe within Africa.

EU Development Cooperation

In autumn, the EC staged the first **European Development Days** (13–17 November) in Brussels. In addition to a trade fair on European national development programmes, the event provided an opportunity for high-level thematic discussions, including a former African presidents' roundtable and an EU-Africa business forum. The Development Days were subsequently declared an annual event, to take place in the capital of the EU country holding Council presidency at that time.

Agreement on the EU's financial framework between 2007 and 2013 included **reforms to budget organisation**. This reorganisation was needed to achieve greater effectiveness and efficiency. With most past and prospective ODA increases being channelled through member state's bilateral programmes – because the financial framework placed an absolute cap on EU spending on external relations – it was already foreseeable that the need for efficient use of resources would become more urgent. While the EC accounted for 20% of European ODA, this share was expected to fall to 15% by 2010, if ODA commitments were met by member states, hence the approaches like the EU-Africa infrastructure trust fund noted above. Yet, the increases decided upon within the framework of the EU budget would result in a de facto doubling of aid through the EC until 2013. While regrouping activities may in the short run only amount to the relabelling and refiling of ongoing activities, these structural changes potentially implied wider political consequences.

Particularly contentious in the rearrangement of external affairs activities was the combination of **development cooperation and economic cooperation** in one so-called instrument. Much legal wrangling between parliament and the EC arose out of this grouping, mainly based on concerns that the development focus and assistance to poor countries could be diverted to key strategic partners. Parliament thus initially rejected this combination of tasks under one heading for fear of losing its powers of oversight.

Changes within the EC's programmes in development cooperation were pursued under the slogan of increasing efficiency and aid effectiveness. With regard to the second source of funding for European-African development cooperation, the general EU budget, the Commission decided on a **re-organisation of thematic programmes** under the budget. After years of incremental addition of new thematic lines and subsequent cleaning-up, the Commission suggested the filing of all expenditure on foreign assistance under seven thematic headings instead of the current 15. Thematic budget lines, as they are called, aim at policy objectives that were not covered by country or regional programmes such as the Cotonou Agreement with ACP states. Programmes were to include **human and social development** ('investing in people', thus bearing the same title as the criteria under the US Millennium Challenge Account), including, *inter alia*, health, gender equality and culture. Civil society activities were curiously grouped with sub-national state bodies in a programme labelled **non-state actors and local authorities**. Early planning for the 10th EDF was criticised for lack of civil society involvement. Discussions within the EU have also given consideration to the possibility of EU development assistance being used in the fight against terrorism. In future, these activities will be funded through the **stability instrument** within external relations.

Trade and Development

The EU continued to conduct **negotiations on Economic Partnership Agreements (EPAs)** with six ACP sub-regions. According to the Cotonou partnership agreement, EPAs are supposed to replace existing non-reciprocal trade preferences in 2008. In its progress report on the implementation of the EU Africa strategy (12 October), the EC admitted that the "atmosphere surrounding the EPA negotiations [was] not good and that major political difficulties [might] arise." This, the Commission claimed, was mostly due to a lack of financial support by EU member states. **Aid for trade** was particularly emphasised in this context: the EU has collectively pledged € 1 bn per year in aid for trade by 2010, of which a substantial part would be spent on Africa.

The EU-West Africa discussions were apparently slow. Negotiations with the **West Africa** grouping – consisting of ECOWAS plus Mauritania – proceeded only in autumn (6 October) to the **second stage of negotiations**, during which the actual text of the agreement would be drafted and discussed. In the first phase of the negotiations, from 2004 until October 2006, general questions on regional economic integration had been discussed, grouped in five thematic technical clusters, namely regional markets (free-trade area, common external tariff and trade facilitation), technical and sanitary and phyto-sanitary standards and measures (SPS), services and investment, other trade related issues and the analysis of productive sectors. The negotiations with the **Central Africa grouping** had reached a similar stage. This grouping consisted of CEMAC and São Tomé and Príncipe. Only in late autumn (24 November) could both sides agree to proceed to the next stage, which consisted of drafting the actual EPA text until December.

Negotiations with **Eastern and Southern Africa (ESA)** appeared to be more advanced. The group consisted of COMESA minus Egypt and Libya with overlap into Central Africa (DR Congo) and SADC (Swaziland). Representatives from the EU and the ESA region have come together at several meetings. A session in Mauritius (17 July) agreed that development should be anchored in the EPA, both with a dedicated chapter and across the sectoral chapters in the trade agreement. Shortly after this discussion round, a trade negotiating session was held, both at technical and senior levels (24–26 July). The Commission reported good progress on the issues already under discussion (market access, agriculture, fisheries) and talks began on trade-related issues and services. At the end of August 2006, a **first draft EPA text** was submitted by ESA, which was discussed at a meeting of ambassadors and senior officials of the EU and ESA in Mombasa (27–29 September).

Negotiations with **SADC** faced a bumpier ride. They **had been suspended** at technical level in late 2005 at the request of SADC, mainly due to questions about the regional composition of SADC. EU-SADC negotiations were subsequently continued **without DR Congo** (which joined the Central Africa grouping), but continued to be tricky because of the linkages between the EU-South Africa Trade and Development Cooperation Agreement (TDCA) and the future EPA: South Africa is closely linked to its neighbours in a customs union (SACU). In early 2006 (7 March), SADC presented its EPA framework, which was discussed on the same date by senior officials as well as during a senior officials meeting in Swaziland on 18 May. In autumn, the EC tried to adapt its EPA directives to allow for conditional inclusion of South Africa into the EPA with SADC (28 November). Since the senior officials meeting in May, negotiations had been suspended, as the EU needed to conduct internal consultations with its constituents before being able to reply officially to the SADC framework.

Sven Grimm

IV. West Africa

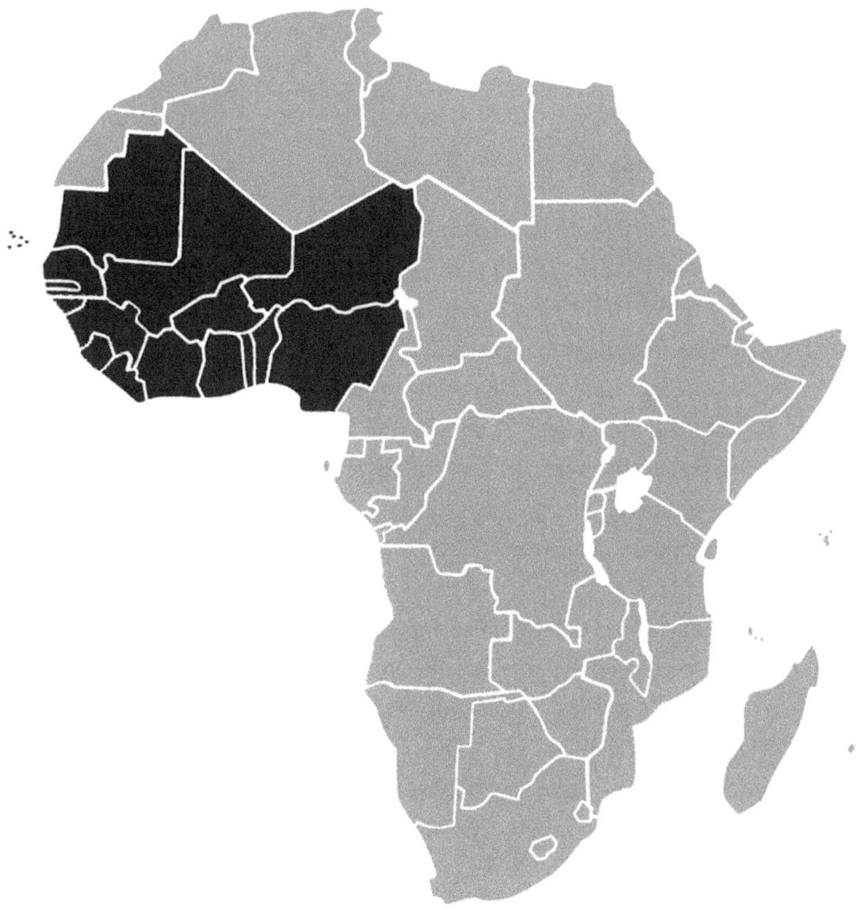

The comparative quiet that characterised 2005 by and large continued. Only a couple of countries faced elections, while the political scene in others was affected by the prospect of electoral confrontations in coming years. Yet other countries entered a downward phase in political instability. While the political impasse in Côte d'Ivoire continued with low levels of violence, life in Nigeria carried on under the mark of violent confrontations, which did not, however, threaten the federation with break-up. Mutinous exchanges involving soldiers and elite security police in Burkina Faso stood out as a more remarkable example of violence, together with an alleged but failed coup attempt in Gambia. Chronic insecurity in the remote desert areas of Mali and Niger persisted. The southwestern forest zone remained calm as the newly elected government of President Johnson-Sirleaf assumed power in Liberia, assisted by the removal of former warlord-president Charles Taylor to the

Netherlands. Social instability, however, continued to pose threats, notably in Guinea. Massive protest again tore at the political fabric in Niger. The sub-region's human rights situation remained mixed. The upturn in the economy continued with growth rates averaging from 3% to 6%. High petrol prices continued to have an uneven socioeconomic impact. Ongoing exploration for natural resources increased the involvement of Asian operators.

Politics and Elections

The most remarkable elections took place in **Benin**, where incumbent President Kérékou was constitutionally barred from standing for another term in view of his age, as was his main political adversary of the 1990s, Nicéphore Soglo. With Kérékou's refusal to amend the constitution to his advantage, the presidential elections, held on 5 and 19 March, led to a renewal of the political class. Yayi Boni, the president of BCEAO who had never been involved in Beninese politics, won by a comfortable margin in polls which, despite some minor problems, represented model elections. Signifying the electorate's desire for change, this peaceful renewal helped consolidate the pluralism of political life and, just as during the advent of multipartyism in the early 1990s, confirmed Benin's **exemplary role** in the sub-region.

Electoral developments in **Mauritania** also went some way towards improving the quality of political life after a coup d'état in 2005 had overthrown the government of President Ould Taya. A nationwide registration campaign was followed by a referendum for which 76% of the electorate turned out to give approval to a new constitution stipulating a limit of two five-year terms for the president and an age limit of 75. Municipal polls were organised on 19 November simultaneously with elections for parliament, of which the second round were held on 3 December. The polls, deemed relatively free and fair by international observers, were marked by a high turnout and the participation of numerous political parties, many of which had previously been banned. Presidential elections are set to follow at a later date.

Legislative and presidential elections in **Cape Verde** proceeded without too many problems, despite complaints of irregularities by the opposition candidate, who was defeated by a narrow margin. The supreme court rejected his allegations of irregularities in voter registration and voter cards as insignificant to the overall result, which confirmed incumbent President Pires and his prime minister, José Maria Neves, in office. All the same, a new voter registration initiative was commenced to update the register.

Politics in **Nigeria** were considerably affected by the prospect of presidential polls in 2007. Remarkably, the senate put an end to the aspirations of President Obasanjo for a third term by halting amendment of the constitutional provision restricting the number of terms for both governors and the head of state to a maximum of two. The subsequent updating of the electoral register, however, got bogged down in various difficulties, forcing an extension of the exercise into the new year.

Presidential elections did little to reduce **repression in Gambia**, primarily because of an alleged but foiled coup attempt by the military's top brass that shook President Jammeh's confidence to the core. A wave of arrests ensued, with disappearances and alleged killings and the torture of some of the plotters, followed by the announcement of snap elections to be held on 22 September. Despite a memorandum of understanding among political parties brokered by the Commonwealth in 2005 to enhance a peaceful vote, the polls were marked by various forms of intimidation by Jammeh's government, whose position was enhanced by the holding of the AU's 7th summit in Banjul. Jammeh won by a comfortable margin, though this was reduced in comparison with the two previous presidential elections. Similarly, well organised local elections in **Burkina Faso**, which led to an overwhelming victory by President Compaoré's party, could not prevent **spectacular clashes** between some lower ranks in the army and elite security police towards the end of the year.

Politics in other countries were dominated by the imminence of future polls. In **Mali**, some politicians began to jockey for position ahead of the 2007 presidential elections. Some political realignments took place, bringing to the fore two major electoral coalitions that would compete for presidential office. Criticism was levelled at the consensus model underlying the political order, which was said to restrict the healthy working of competitive and representative politics. A new electoral law was voted in that excluded a 30% quota for female representation on electoral lists. In **Senegal**, President Wade announced his wish to run for a second seven-year term in 2007 (28 July). This was backed by the ruling 'Parti Démocratique Sénégalais' in October. The unofficial election campaign opened with the release from prison on 7 February of former Prime Minister Idrissa Seck, who had been held on charges of threatening state security and misappropriation of funds. On 4 April, Seck declared that he would stand for president. Realignments took place among opposition parties resulting in several new electoral coalitions. President Kabbah of **Sierra Leone** in July announced that presidential and parliamentary elections would be held in 2007. Boundary delimitation of electoral districts commenced, followed by voter registration in September. The newly established Peoples Movement for Democratic Change of Charles Margai, popular among the young, brought the total number of political parties to 28, of which at least three were deemed serious contenders. In **Guinea**, draft laws were prepared to create an independent electoral commission, among other things. **Ghana**, finally, already began to see some preparations ahead of the general elections scheduled for 2008. Despite protests and a temporary boycott of parliament by the opposition National Democratic Congress, the government got approval for its plan to enfranchise Ghanaians in the diaspora on the grounds of their economic contribution to the country through remittances. Most Ghanaians abroad, however, were deemed to support the ruling New Patriotic Party, in which covert campaigning began for the succession of its leader, President Kufuor.

Human Rights

The human rights record continued to be mixed. Developments with a sub-regional dimension involved the extradition by Nigeria of former warlord and head of state of Liberia **Charles Taylor** to the special court for Sierra Leone, to stand trial for his involvement in that country's civil war. For security reasons, Taylor was flown to The Hague, where the court would hold the trial on the premises of the International Criminal Court. In a related case, on 7 June a Dutch businessman and former associate of Taylor was sentenced by a court in the Netherlands to eight years imprisonment for violation of the UN arms embargo on Liberia. By contrast, the AU at its Banjul summit decided that former President **Hissène Habré** of Chad, accused of having murdered and tortured thousands of people, be tried in Africa instead of being brought to Belgium, which had demanded his extradition. Senegal, where Habré had been living since 1990, was asked to prosecute him. Accordingly, the Senegalese government announced that it would revise its laws to permit the trial on its soil.

In the course of **anti-corruption campaigns**, Benin's former head of national police was jailed for embezzlement. More dramatically, in Côte d'Ivoire a pollution scandal involving the illegal dumping of toxic waste, resulting in several deaths, led to the resignation of the Ivorian government on 6 September. The head of the customs service and the governor of Abidjan district were suspended on charges of corruption and neglect, but this action became ensnared in the continuing rivalry between the prime minister and the president, who reinstated the officials. In addition, two French officials of the Dutch-registered company involved were arrested. In Ghana, a so-called Whistleblower Bill was passed enabling individuals to disclose malpractices in the public interest. The country's road transport minister resigned when he was investigated on corruption charges and was found guilty of conflict of interest, perjury and abuse of power. A similar investigation of the president was inconclusive, but the vendetta against the former government of Jerry Rawlings, under the guise of anti-corruption operations, continued. Likewise, in Nigeria anti-corruption campaigns, which had led to the recovery of billions of dollars, targeted among others several state governors, but in some cases involved dubious impeachment procedures amounting to political in-fighting. Its most dramatic victim was Vice-President Atiku Abubakar, who was accused of corruption and sacked in the run-up to the presidential elections of 2007, in which he was considered a rival to President Obasanjo's political ambitions. In Sierra Leone, the actions of the anti-corruption commission in previous years, involving high-profile people, did not lead to actual prosecutions. Instead, a report concluded that the death of the chief immigration officer, Gloria Newman-Stuart, in 2005 had been caused by stress as a result of false accusations of corruption. In sharp contrast to this, President Conté of Guinea interfered with judicial procedures on 16 December when he personally went to the country's central prison and ordered guards to release two of his friends, one of whom was the former vice-governor of the central bank, arrested for embezzlement of $ 21 m. In Cape

Verde, the minister of economic affairs resigned after being accused of passive corruption. More spectacularly, in Niger the ministers of health and education lost their jobs over their involvement in a massive corruption racket, which had led to the embezzlement of $ 7.8 m over a five-year period and violent protests by students in the capital. In Liberia, one of the first acts of President Johnson-Sirleaf was the sacking of more than 17,000 non-existent civil servants in a drive to clean up the bureaucracy. Senior officials of the former government, too, were arrested on corruption charges.

Arrests of journalists on defamation charges took place in Benin, Niger and Senegal, among others. In Senegal, a new law tightened control of audiovisual media, but the country also saw the appearance of new media publications. In Mali, a radio journalist was beaten up by unknown assailants, while harassment of journalists in Nigeria decreased somewhat. In Mauritania, a new media law was passed enabling newspapers to operate without permits. The regulation of audiovisual media was also liberalised.

New evidence emerged of the persistence of slavery in that country, although it had been abolished several times in the past. Several human rights NGOs that had operated illegally in Mauritania for years now received official recognition. Political prisoners were also released, although ill-treatment of detainees continued and several Islamist activists were arrested. Nigeria's human rights record was again marred by extra-judicial killings – which also took place in Burkina – as well as politically motivated murders, which served as an ugly prelude to the 2007 elections. Prison reforms, however, led to the release of thousands of inmates who had been vainly awaiting trial for up to a decade. The human rights record of Gambia was disfigured by the reprisals against members of the military accused of involvement in the coup attempt of 20 March. In Togo, fewer than half the refugees who had fled the electoral violence of 2005 returned home for fear of political reprisal. Several human rights reports on the 2005 turmoil were published. In Niger, hundreds of thousands of Chadian immigrants were threatened with deportation in the course of tensions in the far east, although the government backed down at the 11th hour.

Trials involving 70 soldiers accused of participation in the 2002 mutiny in Niger finally commenced, leading to several convictions. The long-running Zongo saga in Burkina led to the acquittal of one person because of lack of evidence, while another, who had been sentenced to ten years, was released on grounds of good behaviour. Both men were former members of the presidential guard, which made the case politically contentious. In Sierra Leone, the trials of various people accused of war crimes or crimes against humanity during the civil war continued, still without any convictions.

Legal reform developments occurred in various countries. In Mali, a debate took place on the abolition of the death penalty, which had not been carried out for over 25 years. Togo adopted a new abortion law liberalising the termination of pregnancies in cases of rape, incest or a handicapped foetus. A new rape law in Liberia, making it a non-bailable offence, was an attempt to tackle what amounted to one of the worst scourges still affecting the country. Benin strengthened its legislation against trafficking in children, who were reduced to conditions of slavery in foreign countries. UNICEF applauded the move. Attempts to legalise homosexuality in Ghana came to naught.

Conflict, Instability and Violence

The impasse in **Côte d'Ivoire** continued, but the violence appeared to maintain a downward trend. In January, there were attacks on the UN headquarters in Abidjan while some UN camps in Daloa and Guiglo in the west also came under fire. Renewed violence broke out near Bangolo in the west at the end of April, leading to a new deployment of UN troops. Towards the end of the year, on 5 December, opposition protests led to a few casualties in Abidjan and Agnibilékrou, in the northeast. For the most part, however, the conflict was marked by mediation attempts that failed on the issues of disarmament and the voter identification process in the run-up to forthcoming elections. As in 2005, presidential elections scheduled for October were again postponed, while the interim period plus President Gbagbo's mandate were extended for another year. Attempts to mediate a settlement by ECOWAS led to threats against citizens of ECOWAS member states on 4 October, prompting sharp condemnation by ECOWAS.

There were no such sub-regional repercussions of the violence marking **Nigeria**, which was much larger in scale and affected many levels of society and many of the federation's regions, notably Anambra state and the Niger Delta. Violence in the southeast involving struggles for power and revenue among militias, vigilantes and government forces erupted between May and August and led to a dusk-to-dawn curfew in Onitsha in June. Dozens of people were killed. Violence also marked the oil-producing Delta, and was characterised by murders, bombardments, kidnappings of more than 150 foreign oil workers, armed robberies and shoot-outs between soldiers and militia groups. Dozens of casualties were reported. In the run-up to the 2007 election year, several contenders for office were assassinated in contract killings. Armed robberies targeting long-distance buses, banks and bureaux de change remained a serious problem in cities across the country. Some of the robbers became the victims of extra-judicial killings by the police. The national census on 24–25 March, a prelude to the 2007 elections, was marred by violent incidents that cost several lives.

More important from a sub-regional perspective were the clashes between government troops in Guinea-Bissau and rebels from the separatist movement in the **Casamance** region in Senegal in March. Some 10,000 people were displaced in the fighting, which demonstrated the closer ties between the Senegalese and the government of President Vieira. The spectacular clash between members of the military and elite security police in the heart of **Burkina**'s capital, Ouagadougou, on 19–20 December also had sub-regional implications. While the number of casualties was limited, the summit meetings of UEMOA and ECOWAS scheduled for 22 and 23 December had to be painfully postponed. The clashes pointed to undercurrents of discontent in the armed forces and suggested President Compaoré's position was less secure than was thought.

The desperate social situation in **Guinea** led to massive strike action and protests on a number of occasions, without, however, threatening the security of President Conté's regime. The same was true of **Niger**, which saw another year of urban protests over the cost of living, but without jeopardising the government's stability as much as the previous year. Crime in **Liberia**'s capital of Monrovia had no explicit political repercussions, but nation-wide animosity towards the Mandingo section of the population in this regard continued to worry observers. **Togo** witnessed a remarkable downturn in instability as compared to the political turmoil of 2005, as the inter-Togolese dialogue, sponsored by the EU, resumed and led to an accord with the opposition on a transitional government and parliamentary elections for 2007. The accord did not bring to an end the harassment of returning refugees, however.

Potentially more serious for national stability were attacks by rebels/bandits in some **Sahelian countries**. Attacks on army barracks in Mali's Kidal region led to an accord with the government promising renewed investments in the north. Similar promises were made in Niger but could not prevent clashes between smugglers and government forces near Agadez and Arlit. A widely publicised kidnapping took place in the border region with Chad, when 23 Western tourists were abducted by men claiming to be members of a former movement of Toubou rebels, who issued various political demands. Two Italians were held hostage for two months until Libya secured their release on 12 October.

Socioeconomic Developments

Growth, averaging 4.8% for the entire sub-region (ADB-OECD figures), indicated that the upturn phase continued, although this said little about the distribution of income, prevalence of poverty and persistence of bottlenecks. The difference between oil-producers (or countries exporting mineral resources generally) and oil-importing countries masked an important distinction. For example, Senegal's performance disappointed at 3.3%, a substantial reduction compared with previous years, and partly the result of high oil prices. This was comparable to Niger's growth, forecast at between 3% and 4%. Nevertheless, GDP growth in Cape Verde, which had made such progress towards economic stability that no further IMF financial support was needed, was expected to reach 6%, i.e., still in the range of previous years. The IMF gave estimates of 4.5% for Benin, 4.2% for Guinea-Bissau and even 7.8% for Liberia, these figures representing in part donor-funded expenditure. GDP growth for Burkina was estimated at 6%, much higher than the previous year. Gambia's growth rate stood at a suspicious 7.1%, demonstrating the sometimes limited utility of such statistical indicators (the IMF gave an annual estimate of 5.7% for the previous years). Ghana's economy, however, continued to be robust, with its 6.2% estimate markedly above an average population growth of 3%. Guinea's growth rate of 5% (IMF estimate) clearly pointed to the significance of its mineral exports rather than a reduction in poverty, as did that of Sierra Leone (7%). The similar growth rate in Mali (around 5%) fed on higher gold prices but was dampened by demographic growth. At 14.1%, Mauritania held the sub-regional record, indicating the effects of oil production, which commenced this year. Nigeria benefited less, at 5.3% (ADB-OECD figures). The worst performers were Togo (an IMF estimate of 2%) and, predictably, Côte d'Ivoire, which grew by only 1.2% despite the start of oil production – an actual contraction in view of demographic growth at 2%.

Generally, these figures were insufficient to tackle the problem of **poverty** in any meaningful way. Poverty in Gambia was estimated to affect more than 70% of the population. In Liberia, this rose to more than 86% for the countryside and half the population of the capital – significantly higher than in a Sahelian country such as Mali, where urban poverty dropped to some 20% (from approx. 26% in 2001) but rural misery, too, remained stuck at well over 70%. For Sierra Leone, rural poverty stood at an overall 82%, measured against a yardstick of $ 2 a day. In neighbouring Guinea, only 19% had access to electricity. The cost of living, moreover, rose in several countries, partly as a result of high petrol prices. These were the backdrop to the numerous strikes that took place in Guinea, and fuelled protest marches in Burkina and, especially, Niger, where for the second year running urban life ground to a halt during the spring and early summer. Cereal harvests in Niger were generally good, however, as in neighbouring Mali. **Food security** in Guinea-Bissau suffered as a result of a 25% fall in rice production because of drought and breaches in sea dykes.

Against this background, illegal **migration to Europe** continued unabated, with the sub-region providing the major part of young fortune seekers trying to gain entry, especially via the Canary Islands. In Senegal, which accounted for over 30,000 migrants, the issue became an important topic in the run-up to the presidential elections of 2007. The government became involved in diplomatic clashes with France and Spain and tried to encourage youngsters to stay at home by initiating a donor-funded agricultural programme. Malians, however, were said to be the largest group of Africans trying to enter Europe illegally. The EU promised additional aid to manage migration flows. Cape Verde obtained EU aid to help patrol the archipelago's waters and in September announced its intention to suspend the ECOWAS agreement on the free movement of citizens by re-imposing the visa requirements that had earlier been scrapped.

West Africa's **hydrocarbon resources** continued to grow in importance. The sub-region's major producer, Nigeria, benefited considerably in terms of foreign currency reserves and falling debts, even though the volatility of the Niger Delta led to a cut in production by oil companies costing the country $ 4 bn in the 2006 fiscal year. Natural gas production was becoming more important. Despite this, domestic fuel shortages, indicating structural anomalies, continued to disrupt economic life. Mauritania joined the club of oil producing countries and, for the first time, oil exports overtook cocoa exports in Côte d'Ivoire. Guinea-Bissau had high hopes of offshore prospecting and similar exploration was planned off the coast of Guinea. Oil exploration also continued in Niger, which announced the discovery of major coal reserves in the Tahoua region that could help reduce dependence on firewood for energy needs.

High gold prices benefited the economies of Burkina, Mali, Ghana and, to a lesser extent, Niger. Gold was the most important export product in Mali – generating 70% of its export revenues – and the second largest for Burkina (after cotton) and Niger (which suffered drops in cattle exports). Ghana and Mali were the continent's largest gold producers, along with South Africa. **Mineral production** generally went up, accounting for 25% of public revenues in Guinea (which benefited from international rivalry for its large bauxite deposits), and Sierra Leone, which saw the (re)start of rutile and bauxite production as well as increased exports of diamonds and gold. Liberia, however, still struggled to get back on to its feet after the end of civil war, with part of its economy remaining under Security Council sanctions and international supervision. Uranium exports were expected to rise in Niger, where Canadian and Chinese companies were awarded concessions for the exploration of new deposits.

Increased **Asian interest** in mineral resources, however, continued right across West Africa, buttressed by the disbursement of development aid and commitments to help improve infrastructural facilities. An Indian investment firm, for example, obtained interests in Togo's mining sector including iron ore, chromite and manganese. The Chinese made grants and loans and took on major new commitments in a broad range of development projects, notably infrastructural facilities, in numerous countries in the sub-region. Gambia and Burkina Faso, in contrast, benefited from ties with Taiwan. Ghana was one of the few countries also to suffer from (mainland) Chinese activity, which created serious problems in its textile industry.

The **cotton producers** Benin, Burkina, northern Côte d'Ivoire, Mali and Togo faced new problems. As in neighbouring Togo, production of cotton in Benin – the country's major export – plummeted compared to the previous year, in part due to low world prices that led to renewed smuggling. With a quarter of Burkina's population dependent on cotton-generated incomes, many Burkinabè peasants switched to food production, while their president, Blaise Compaoré, openly derided the US for its subsidies to American cotton producers. Cotton exports from Mali, which suffered from managerial problems in addition to the depressed global market, more or less stagnated, while production in northern Côte d'Ivoire declined further, also as a result of shortages in inputs, marketing problems and infrastructural deterioration.

EU **development subsidies** were disbursed to a range of countries, including Benin, Mali, Niger, Nigeria, Cape Verde, Mauritania and Togo – both of which benefited from a resumption of aid in the wake of improved political stability – and Guinea, where the Chinese now rivalled European and US influence. American disbursement of development funds continued under the Millennium Challenge Account programme, for which Benin, Burkina Faso, Cape Verde, Ghana and Mali qualified.

West Africa saw a limited outbreak of **avian flu** of the dangerous H5N1 strain. Starting in Nigeria, it spread to northeastern Niger, necessitating culling operations in both countries. Benin closed its borders to Nigerian poultry but the disease also spread to Mauritania and Côte d'Ivoire, where an outbreak in Abidjan also led to culling. In this context, Mali opened its doors for the establishment of an African office of the World Organisation for Animal Health.

The **toxic waste** scandal in Côte d'Ivoire resulted in an alleged 14,000 people falling ill, while another 40,000 required medical help. A controversy about **uranium contamination** in Niger's mining town of Arlit led to protest marches by the city's population.

Nigeria was said to harbour 4 m people infected with **HIV/AIDS**, the largest number after South Africa and India. The country, nevertheless, made some strides in the combating **polio**, which affected nearly 1,000 people in the north. Torrential rains in Niger led to a limited outbreak of **cholera**, while Mali faced an outbreak of **yellow fever**. Both countries suffered an epidemic of **meningitis** – in Niger of a dangerous strain resistant to existing vaccines and affecting at least 1,500 children.

Sub-regional Organisations: Cooperation and Conflict

ECOWAS held its 29th ordinary summit in Niger's capital, Niamey, on 12 January. The summit re-elected President Tandja as chairman of the Authority of Heads of State and Government, a move that again thwarted the ambitions of Gambia's President Jammeh. The summit also re-elected Ghana's Ibn Chambas as executive secretary for another four-year term and approved the 2006 budget of $ 121 m. The 30th ordinary summit meeting was held in Abuja on 14 June, while the next conference scheduled to take place in Burkina's capital, Ouagadougou, on 22 December had to be postponed because of the clashes between army soldiers and elite security police.

The organisation took several decisions relevant to its **institutional framework**. It was agreed that the community's court of justice would be strengthened. Moreover, the organisation's secretariat would be restructured into a full-blown nine-member commission, with a president, vice-president and seven ordinary members from among the member states, each of whom would provide commissioners on a rotational basis. However, the commission must always include someone from Nigeria in recognition of that country's status in the sub-region, its hosting of the organisation's headquarters in Abuja and its 60% share of the ECOWAS budget. The reforms closely followed the example of the AU, which itself was inspired by the EU model, and were to be enacted as of January 2007. The commissioners, with a four-year mandate, are to have genuine power to initiate and have more focused roles in their respective areas of competence, ranging from politics and security to various forms of economic and technical cooperation. In addition, the ECOWAS parliament, made up of member-state parliamentarians, was provided with a new structure. The lifespan of the consultative body will be four years and it was agreed that member state delegations would reflect the political composition of their national bodies, while at least 30% of delegation members are to be women. After a transition of four years, the 115-seat ECOWAS parliament is to be elected by way of direct universal suffrage. On 14 November, the body elected Mahamane Ousmane, chairman of Niger's National Assembly, as parliamentary speaker during the transition period. He succeeded Nouhoum Ali Diallo of Mali.

As far as **economic and technical cooperation** was concerned, the organisation provided $ 450,000 budgetary support to the West African Power Pool (WAPP) to facilitate the initiation of a programme involving nine generation and transmission priorities over the next 17 years and aimed at integrating and harmonising national electricity grids to increase the sub-regional power supply. The object would be to provide energy to at least 50%–60% of West Africans in the next ten years, in line with the Millennium Development Goals. Generating capacity would have to be increased from 10,000 megawatts to 17,000 by 2023. The World Bank had already promised $ 450 m for the realisation of WAPP. In addition, the West African Gas Pipeline (WAGP) was discussed, with a view to providing excess electricity for industrial and commercial purposes by transporting natural gas from Nigeria to Benin, Togo and Ghana and later to other member states. The heads of state and government also approved an action plan for the implementation of the ECOWAS Regional Agricultural Policy (ECOWAP) to improve productivity and attain food self-sufficiency. The ECOWAS Common External Tariff (CET) was given a four-band structure ranging from 0% to 20% for different categories of goods imported from outside the sub-region to align it with the tariff structure of the Francophone member states united in UEMOA, which already operates a common tariff regime. A roadmap was envisaged by both organisations to produce a uniform tariff regime by January 2008. While this dimension of sub-regional cooperation had bedevilled ECOWAS since its inception, the free movement of persons also remained a problematic issue, within and outside the sub-region. The ECOWAS Authority expressed concern about illegal migration of West African youngsters to Europe and appealed for humane treatment of those forcibly repatriated. Together with Central African countries organised in CEEAC, ECOWAS discussed questions related to trafficking in persons with the UN Office on Drugs and Crime (UNODC) in Nigeria in July. With respect to sub-regional travel, an ECOWAS travel certificate was agreed that would be cheaper than national passports and would be issued by member states. At that point, only Benin, Guinea and Senegal had issued ordinary ECOWAS passports to the benefit of their citizens.

On their common frontier, **Benin and Burkina** confronted some of the problems associated with cross-border traffic. The two countries have had a longstanding dispute over a 68 kilometre area in the frontier region that led on 18–19 January to an incident and the closure of the common border by Benin. ECOWAS Executive Secretary Chambas appealed to the leaders of both countries to exercise restraint and avoid actions that would impinge on their bilateral ties. He also recalled the satisfactory manner in which Benin and Niger had resolved their border dispute, through adjudication by the International Court of Justice in The Hague. Chambas called for a peaceful solution and contacted the foreign ministers of the two member states. On 23 January, representatives of Benin and Burkina met to discuss the issue. An ECOWAS fact-finding mission was deployed to **Guinea-Bissau** on

1 May, comprising members of the ECOWAS council of elders, to assess that country's return to a degree of stability. The organisation endorsed the establishment of an International Contact Group for Guinea-Bissau (ICG-GB) to assist Guineans with political stabilisation and economic recovery. It was recommended that ICG-GB should at least include – besides Guinea-Bissau itself – Sierra Leone and **Liberia**. The ECOWAS mediation and security council, meeting on 13 June, appealed on Liberia's behalf for the lifting of UN sanctions and the travel ban imposed on certain of its nationals. The council also condemned the attacks on army barracks in **Mali**'s northern region.

ECOWAS's concern with **Gambia** proved more contentious. A fact-finding mission in August advised opposition parties against boycotting the presidential elections, appealed for equal access to the media and called on all political parties to refrain from using inflammatory language. It also recommended a large election observer mission, which endorsed the polls as transparent and credible, noting that no violence or intimidation had taken place and that the logistics for the elections had been in proper order. Although the fact-finding mission preceding it had met with Gambia's Independent Electoral Commission (IEC), the observer mission failed to pronounce on the dismissal and detention of the IEC chairman and one of its members and the chairman's replacement by someone else. The detention of a journalist in the run-up to polling day was also left unmentioned.

Côte d'Ivoire, however, remained ECOWAS's biggest headache. Expressing full support for Prime Minister Konan Banny and the 'Groupe de Travail International' (GTI) in which ECOWAS took part, the organisation noted with concern the attacks on the UN mission in Abidjan in January. Its outrage over the threats made against citizens of other ECOWAS member states only masked its powerlessness in relation to the Ivorian deadlock. On 6 October, the organisation simply recommended to the AU the extension of the transition period by another year, together with the mandates of President Gbagbo and his rival, Prime Minister Banny. The successful mediation of the national dialogue in **Togo** was the work of President Compaoré of Burkina and thus took place outside the ECOWAS framework.

Issues of **collective security** were tackled, among them the draft ECOWAS convention on small arms and light weapons. This convention, whose draft was approved by independent experts in March, will replace the moratorium enacted in 1999 and include a mechanism to monitor violations of its provisions and to impose sanctions where these occur. The convention was approved by the heads of state during their summit in Abuja on 14 June. Chiefs of defence staff of ECOWAS countries met in Niamey in March to discuss the roadmap for the ECOWAS Standby Force (ESF), to form part of the AU's overall African Standby Force (ASF). The ESF is expected to be functional in 2010. To this end, the defence chiefs called for the harmonisation of training programmes and joint military exercises. ECOWAS is coordinating the standard operating procedures for the ASF. A conference on counter-terrorism questions, which also involved Central African countries, was organised in Spain on 25–26 May.

UEMOA faced the challenge of finding a successor to Konan Banny, the chairman of the BCEAO who had been called to become prime minister of Côte d'Ivoire at the end of 2005. While Senegal and Niger argued that this post should not automatically go to another Ivorian, Côte d'Ivoire opposed this on the grounds that it is the principal supplier of the bank's capital. The tenth UEMOA summit, held in Niamey at the end of March, could not resolve the issue, nor that of the succession to the chairmanship of the 'Banque Ouest-Africaine de Développement' (**BOAD**) based in Togo, whose head, Yayi Boni, was suddenly called to the presidency of Benin. The chairmanship of both West African institutions was assured by interim measures. On 24 November, BOAD signed cooperation deals with Chinese banks to a value of CFAfr 46 bn on technical cooperation and credits. UEMOA held a pledging conference with donors on 3 November in which it received aid exceeding its requests for the purpose of its 'programme économique régional' for the period 2006–10 (CFAfr 2.44 bn). UEMOA's operating budget for 2007 was approved during a ministerial meeting in Ouagadougou on 16 December (CFAfr 84.1 bn).

Klaas van Walraven

Benin

The political year was dominated by the presidential election, the fourth since the beginning of the new democratic regime in 1990. The peaceful and free electoral process reinforced the pluralism of political life and the stability of the regime. The success of Yayi Boni, a newcomer who had never been involved in politics, symptomised a widespread desire for change. It also saw the renewal of political actors, a new will to fight against impunity for people suspected of embezzlement and a diplomatic activism involving presidential visits to several countries. Benin continued to face economic difficulties as well as increasingly pronounced social inequalities.

Domestic Politics

At the beginning of the year, there were major uncertainties concerning the **presidential election** scheduled for March. There were still questions concerning its organisation. Mathieu Kérékou, president since 1996 (he was re-elected in 2001) was barred from putting himself forward as a candidate, since the 1990 constitution imposed a 70-year age limit on prospective candidates and limits the number of successive terms to two. The age limit also applied to his principal political adversary over the past 15 years, Nicéphore Soglo (president from 1991 to 1996). The exclusion of these two prominent figures served to increase the uncertainty surrounding this election. In July 2005, President Kérékou had stated he would not amend the constitution in order to stand again.

In January, the question of the **electoral budget** that had begun in November 2005 remained unresolved. The government contended that it did not have the means necessary to finance the election. While the 'Commission Electorale Nationale Autonome' (CENA) had already reduced its budget by CFAfr 10 bn, civil society organisations mobilised to force the government to respect the electoral schedule and provide the requisite funds. Labour unions issued ultimatums and threatened to go on strike and organise demonstrations. After issuing a fresh ultimatum to government demanding that it provide funding by 17 January, six unions declared a 48-hour strike within the administration beginning on 24 January. Few went on strike within the ministries, but in Cotonou public schools were closed and only minimal service was available at the main hospital. 'FORS Présidentielle 2006' ('Front des Organisations de la Société Civile pour l'Organisation d'Élections Démocratiques, Libres, Pacifiques et Transparentes'), a coalition of very active NGOs opened a 'fonds d'appui citoyen' in order to receive direct funding from citizens. With foreign sponsors funding the election in part, the government finally gave in and provided CENA with a budget of CFAfr 6.6 bn.

Tensions developed at the governmental level. Pierre Osho, the state minister in charge of national defence and one of those closest to President Kérékou, **resigned** on 12 January, protesting the finance minister's handling of the electoral process. He was replaced by another friend of the president, retired Colonel Martin Dohou Azonhiho, a strongman during the pre-1990 revolutionary regime. On 15 February, the minister of foreign affairs, Rogatien Biaou, was dismissed and imprisoned for a couple of days for an illegal transaction concerning the Beninese embassy in the US.

Nonetheless, the electoral process proceeded as normal, particularly after 21 January, with the registration of voters, the distribution of voting cards and the submission of candidatures to CENA. More than 3.9 m voters were registered, approximately 30% more than in the previous election. The **increase in voters** heightened concerns about fraud. Thirty-three people submitted their candidatures. On 30 January, the constitutional court published the final list of 26 candidates authorised to stand as presidential candidates.

Presidential favourites were Adrien Houngbédji of the 'Parti du Renouveau Démocratique' (PRD), chairman of the National Assembly (1991–95) and former state minister, who had finished in third place in the first round of the last two presidential elections; Bruno Amoussou of the 'Parti Social-Démocrate' (PSD), also one-time chairman of the National Assembly (1995–99) and former state minister, who finished fourth after the first round in 1996 and 2001; and Léhady Soglo of the 'Renaissance du Bénin' (RB), son of former President Soglo and his deputy mayor in Cotonou. From the end of 2005, the little-known candidate Yayi Boni, an economist and president of the 'Banque Ouest Africaine de Développement' (BOAD), began to gain in popularity. He announced his decision to resign as the head of BOAD once the constitutional court had validated his candidature. Antoine

Idji Kolawolé, chairman of the National Assembly, and several former Kérékou ministers (Lazare Séhouéto, Luc Gnacadja, Daniel Tawéma) were also candidates, as were two women (Marie-Elise Gbédo and Célestine Zanou).

The **first round** was held on 5 March and involved more than 17,000 polling stations. Several problems were reported in the south. Many polling stations located in the suburbs of Cotonou opened late because of a lack of election materials (ballot boxes, bulletins). Observers speculated that these problems were caused by some of Kérékou's supporters and advisors. However, in a pronouncement on the day of the first round, it was President Kérékou who criticised what he saw as the lack of transparency and the evidence of fraud, although none of the other political leaders or non-partisan actors agreed with him. The following day, Kérékou told foreign diplomats in Cotonou that the election was not fair.

The results were pronounced by the constitutional court with Yayi Boni obtaining 35.6%. Houngbédji followed with 24.1%, Amoussou 16.5% and Soglo with 8.5%. A second round was necessary between Yayi Boni and Houngbédji. Soglo, Amoussou and A.I. Kolawolé, who had finished fifth, coordinated their support for a candidate, thereby creating a **political alliance** called 'wologuédé'. The alliance decided to support Yayi Boni after the first round. None of the other candidates appealed for a vote in favour of Houngbédji. The **second round** took place on 19 March, after the government refused to postpone polling day by three days because of the very late proclamation of the results of the first round by the constitutional court. Indeed, conditions were better than during the first round, and Yayi Boni was elected president with 74.5%. On 22 March, after the constitutional court published the results, Houngbédji conceded defeat and congratulated his adversary.

Yayi Boni's victory raised great hopes. He was presented as an exconomically capable man (as shown by his record as chair of BOAD) and as a new and independent political figure who had never been involved in politicking. He had never put himself forward for election, or been a minister or had political allegiances. Moreover, he could not be linked to a single ethnic group or geographical area, since his parents hailed from the centre and north and his wife from the south. He was emphatic about the importance of religion in his personal life, having been born into a Muslim family but become an evangelical Christian when he was young. His triumph meant that there was a deeper willingness to change in the country. His main campaign slogan was: "It may change, it must change, it will change."

On 6 April, Yayi Boni was inaugurated as the new president. Seven other African heads of state participated in the ceremony in Porto-Novo. The following day, he appointed his first **cabinet** consisting of 22 ministers, many of them new to Beninese politics. None had been minister before and some had a technocratic profile without any party affiliation, with the exception of four ministers belonging to political parties from the 'wologuédé' alliance. The president also appointed one of Houngbédji's advisers, Pascal Koukpaki, as one of his main ministers, for development, economy and finance. Former NGO leader Edgar Alia became minister in charge of security and local government and Issifou Koguidro was appointed minister of defence. There were five women in the new government, including Mariam Aladji Boni Diallo as minister of foreign affairs, the first woman to be appointed to this position.

Yayi Boni's success and the preparations for the parliamentary elections (see below) led to a **reconfiguration** of the **political landscape**. In May, partisans of the new president created a new political alliance made up of 27 parties and dubbed 'Alliance Kauri' – the cowry shell being the emblem of Yayi Boni's campaign. The 'wologuédé' alliance improved its position, while Houngbédji's PRD remained in opposition. While the new cabinet largely met with popular approval, in the course of the year three ministers were forced to step down after the president had criticised them for being inefficient or independent. On 27 July, Albert Tévoédjré, a well-known political leader and previous UN special representative in Côte d'Ivoire, was appointed 'mediator of the republic', a kind of ombudsman.

One of the first decisions of the new government was to **audit** ministries and public companies (about 60) in order to evaluate their financial situation and possible mismanagement. On 7 December, P. Koukpaki published the results of this audit, pointing out high levels of embezzlement and recommending the repayment of the sums involved to the ministry of finance. In the same vein, the government aimed to recover unpaid personal and company taxes to a value of CFAfr 40 bn. A list of the main debtors was published together with the sums due.

On 4 June, Séfou Fagbohoun, one of Benin's principal businessmen, was arrested and jailed in the course of investigations concerning the privatisation and management of SONACOP, the former national oil company sold to Fagbohoun. Fagbohoun was also politically active, being chairman of the political party for which Kolawolé had stood as president. On 22 February, the former general director of national police, Raymond Fadonougbo, was jailed in Cotonou for embezzlement. These events and initiatives demonstrated a new willingness to fight **corruption** and mismanagement in public life, while as a goodwill gesture to the electorate school taxes, compulsory for primary public school enrolment, were abolished in October.

After the presidential election, political life was largely dominated by preparations for the **parliamentary elections** scheduled for March 2007. A new controversy over budgetary matters arose, with a majority of MPs proposing that the legislative election be postponed and combined with the local elections scheduled for 2008 in order to reduce operating costs. This proposal would involve prolonging the current legislative term by one year. A broad majority of MPs, including Yayi Boni's supporters, approved this proposal, 71 of the 83 MPs voting in favour of it on 23 June. However, President Yayi Boni disagreed with the proposal, which also met with sharp hostility from civil society. The parliamentary bill was thrown out by the constitutional court, which argued that nothing could justify such a law. Hence, on 11 December the government decided that the parliamentary election would take place on 25 March 2007.

On 28 September and over the following days, a **national census** took place with the aim of improving the electoral process, especially voter registration. Documents such as birth certificates were handed out to people during public meetings in towns and villages in the hope that these would facilitate the distribution of voting cards and reduce electoral fraud.

On 30 January, Benin strengthened its legislation against the **trafficking of children**, that is the selling of children to dealers who took them to foreign countries, where they were reduced slavery. This new law, approved by UNICEF, aimed at stiffening the punishments for traffickers and employers.

In a different case, on 21 April Rachidi Gbadamassi, the mayor of Parakou – the third city of the country, in the north – and president of the 'Association Nationale des Communes du Bénin' (ANCB), was released from jail. He had been imprisoned in November 2005 after the **assassination** of magistrate Sévérin Coovi, the president of the court of appeal in Parakou. He remained under suspicion of involvement.

Whereas the Paris-based NGO 'Reporters sans Frontières' classified Benin among the better African countries as regards **press freedom** and the media had a positive impact on the electoral campaign, private newspapers remained rather unprofessional. Thus, on 15 and 17 September, four journalists were arrested and jailed for defamation of the head of state, having published articles about the president's family. They were quickly released, however. On 1 December, two others journalists were sentenced to six months imprisonment after they were found guilty of defamation in a private affair.

The year ended with the celebration of the centenary of the death of **Behanzin**, the last ruler of the kingdom of Danhomey before colonisation. The commemoration served as an opportunity for Yayi Boni to call for national unity.

Foreign Affairs

On 18–19 January an incident in the frontier region with **Burkina Faso** led to the rapid closure of the border by Beninese authorities. It was linked to a long-running border conflict over a 68 kilometre area between the two countries. On 23 January, representatives of Benin and Burkina Faso met to resolve the incident. The events in Sémé on the frontier with **Nigeria** on 30 and 31 January were more serious. Some Nigerians tried to free a man who, after crossing from Nigeria, was arrested by Benin police, leading to several hours of street fighting that left from four to ten people dead. This region, which includes the principal checkpoint between the two countries, is characterised by heavy traffic in goods and people.

After his investiture, Yayi Boni introduced a new style in **Beninese diplomacy** involving presidential visits to several countries, especially in Africa, Europe and Asia, the principal aim of which was to obtain financial support and increase foreign investment. In Africa, he principally visited countries with oil resources. On 7 April, Yayi Boni paid his first visit to Nigeria and from 17 to 30 April he went to Libya, Gabon and Congo. Yayi Boni subsequently visited Niger, Burkina Faso, Mali, Senegal and Côte d'Ivoire. He went to Togo on 16–17 June and Ghana on 20–21 June.

France was visited on 28–30 June. Bilateral cooperation deals were signed and French budgetary assistance was increased from € 1.5 m to € 4.5 m. Yayi Boni paid a visit to Belgium on 10–12 July, where he met the European Commission president, José Manuel Barroso. In October, he was back in Belgium and travelled to Luxemburg and Germany to improve bilateral cooperation with these countries. He also called attention to the problems related to cotton production and demanded an end to subsidies by developed countries.

Yayi Boni's numerous visits to **Asian countries** symbolised the change in Beninese diplomacy: much more emphasis was laid on meeting businessmen and discussing Benin's investment opportunities. After Japan (4–6 July) and Singapore (6–8 July), Yayi Boni paid a one-week visit to China from 27 August to 3 September, in the course of which several agreements were signed. He sought Chinese cooperation in the impending exploration and exploitation of offshore oilfields. On 4–5 November, he took part in the Sino-African summit in Bejing, followed by a visit to Seoul, where he met future UN Secretary-General Ban Ki-Moon and was one of the few African leaders to attend the Korea Africa summit. Yayi Boni's Asian tour ended with a visit to Vietnam and Laos.

In sharp contrast to his predecessor Kérékou, who paid his last official visit as president to the **US** in February, Yayi Boni only visited Washington from 11 to 15 December, meeting President Bush and the directors of the World Bank and IMF.

Aiming to reinforce its diplomatic influence, the government on 25 August adopted a training plan for its diplomats. It also introduced changes in several of its principal embassies, including Brussels, Geneva, New York and Addis Ababa, as well as countries with important economic potential.

Two Latin-American presidents visited Benin, Brazilian President Luiz Inácio 'Lula' da Silva (9–10 February) and the Venezuelan Hugo Chavez (2 August), who inaugurated the first embassy of his country in Benin. However, it was the visit of the French minister of the interior, Nicolas Sarkozy, the presidential hopeful, that had the profoundest echo in the country (18–19 May). Sarkozy's policy of selected immigration of foreign workers in France drew much African criticism. Student unions and civic associations organised demonstrations to protest the visit and MPs boycotted the reception at the French embassy. Sarkozy met President Yayi Boni and the minister of the interior, inaugurated a market in Cotonou and called for a new partnership between France and Africa.

Socioeconomic Developments

On 8 February, Benin banned the importation of poultry from Nigeria after the discovery there of the H5N1 **avian flu** virus. Two days later, a special plan was adopted to strengthen border and national controls. Although no cases of avian flu were discovered, the scare provoked a strong decrease in the sale of chickens in urban markets.

On 22 February, during his last visit to the US, President Kérékou signed the financial agreement related to subsidies under the **Millennium Challenge Account** framework. This financial support ($ 307 m over five years), approved by the US government, aimed at improving Benin's business and foreign investment climate. Benin was one of nine African countries selected for this support.

Nevertheless, **cotton**, the country's main export, remained the most important source of concern. Production for the 2005–06 season reached only 192,000 tonnes (as against 426,000 for the previous season and a forecast of 500,000). Many of the 400,000 cotton producers smuggled part of their harvest to neighbouring countries, because of the payment difficulties experienced in Benin. In trying to resolve the crisis, the new government declared in April that it would pay CFAfr 15 bn (€ 23 m) to producers. This sum corresponded with the state deficit associated with the subsidised purchase of cotton over the three past seasons. In May, the government revised the institutional framework for cotton producers' representatives, companies importing products necessary for cotton production and shelling companies. In November, it prohibited the import of edible oil for six months in order to protect local cotton seed oil factories. While the president stipulated an objective of 500,000 tonnes for 2006–07, production for the coming season was expected to stall at 250,000 tonnes because of the poor quality of imported production material and despite the changes introduced by government. Government also aimed to diversify agricultural production and announced the strengthening of the oil palm sector in partnership with a Malaysian company.

On 1 August, Yayi Boni announced a 20–30% decrease in the cost of communications by cellphone. At the same time, 'Benin Telecom's' deficit increased. In December, government concluded an agreement with foreign partners to invest CFAfr 12 bn to save the company.

The new government showed great interest in the **oil sector**, in which it also tried to interest various foreign oil companies. In March, the previous administration had decided to take control for 90 days of SONACOP, the oil company purchased by Séfou Fagbohoun as part of a murky transaction in 1999. This requisition included gas stations. In May and on 31 August, Yayi Boni's government decided to extend the requisition for another 90 days. In June, Fagbohoun, chairman of the SONACOP board, was prosecuted for financial mismanagement.

On 22 May, Yayi Boni presented his policy on **major projects**, including the construction of a highway between Cotonou and Bohicon (135 km to the north); urban road works, especially between Cotonou and Porto-Novo; and the construction of a new airport near Cotonou. The total value of these projects was estimated at CFAfr 1,350 bn over five years. The president also presented a social housing project involving 13,000 new dwellings and aimed to boost the tourist sector with the planning of a new resort, including luxury hotels, near Cotonou. The importance of this sector to the economy was estimated at CFAfr 23 bn a year.

In 2006, Benin benefited from two major EU **subsidies**, € 23 m for the rehabilitation of the road network between Banikoara and Kandi in the north and € 22 m to finance the national poverty reduction programme. Poverty reduction also benefited from funds from the ADB ($ 22 m). GDP growth was estimated at 4.5% as against 2.9% in 2005 – itself significantly below the original estimate of 5.3% (see *Africa Yearbook 2004*).

Cédric Mayrargue

Burkina Faso

Well-organised local elections and an impressive diplomatic profile in the sub-region combined with periods of strong civilian discontent and violent incidents involving sections of the military and the police. This situation pointed to social undercurrents in what, on the surface, appeared to be a neatly organised society. At the economic level, positive assessments of the country's economic performance both by the regime and multilateral organisations contrasted with social protests and the negative perceptions of ordinary people. President Compaoré's position could thus be weaker than the results of this year's municipal elections suggested.

Domestic Politics

In January, after Blaise Compaoré had been re-elected as president the previous year, Prime Minister Ernest Paramanga Yonli put together his **third cabinet**. Except for the appointment of the two leaders of the largest opposition party, 'Alliance pour la Démocratie et la Féderation – Rassemblement Démocratique Africain' (ADF-RDA), as minister of transport (Gilbert Ouedraogo) and acting minister of higher education (Hyppolite Ouedraogo), no major changes were made to the cabinet.

At the start of the year, the forthcoming municipal elections dominated political discussions. They had been scheduled for 2005, prior to the presidential elections, but the new law reducing the presidency from seven years to five years made it necessary to delay them until 12 February 2006. Additional postponements were needed because the expiration of the legal mandate of the 'Commission Électorale Nationale Indépendante' (CENI) following the presidential elections. Municipal polls were scheduled for 12 March but only took place on 23 April. The legal foundations for the municipal elections lay in the new laws on decentralisation, adopted in its final version on 21 December 2004. These distinguished two levels of territorial entity, regions (made up of various existing provinces) and municipal communities and resulted in a total of 13 regions and 49 urban and 302 rural **municipalities**. Elected deputies would choose a mayor as well as vice-mayor from their midst and set up committees for general, social and cultural affairs, economic and financial matters, as well as one for environmental and development issues. Several deputies would also be selected to serve on the regional council, a support structure for the regional governor. In the new decentralised system, budgets would only be allocated and administered at the level of the region and the municipality. Even though the 'haut commissaire' and the 'préfet' were to continue representing the state at the level of the province and 'département', they would not have budgetary autonomy in the future.

With its abundance of **financial resources**, Compaoré's party, the 'Congrès pour la Démocratie et le Progrès' (CDP) was able to put up candidates in every constituency, in contrast to the other 47 parties, which had only a limited number of local strongholds. Moreover, due to the strong association of the CDP with state institutions and facilities, it could make more promises to the electorate and engage the services of celebrities such as cabinet ministers in the three-week campaign in April. The 'Mouvement Burkinabè des Droits de l'Homme et des Peuples' (MBDHP) had vainly proposed that independent candidates should be allowed to stand in order to limit the dominance of political parties and to give local people greater opportunity to influence the political process within their communities.

The CDP's campaign showed that the party was determined to regain lost ground. In 2000, the municipal elections had been strongly influenced by the aftermath of the murder of prominent investigative journalist Norbert Zongo, on 13 December 1998. The suspicion voiced at the time was that Zongo had been murdered by members of the military at the instigation of Blaise Compaoré's younger brother François, and this had boosted the opportunities for opposition parties. The town of **Koudougou** in particular became one of the opposition's strongholds, first of the ADF-RDA and later – after an internal split in June 2003 – of the 'Union Nationale pour la Démocratie et le Développement' (UNDD) led by Hermann Yaméogo, son of former President Maurice Yaméogo, whose cousin Marcelin had become Koudougou's mayor. However, just before this year's municipal elections, journalists received anonymous letters stating that Hermann Yaméogo had obtained substantial sums of money from the Gbagbo regime in Côte d'Ivoire. This created negative fall-out so that even his own supporters reproached him for making choices that suited the Compaoré regime. In the end, CDP took two-thirds of the Koudougou vote.

Similar shifts occurred in Bobo-Dioulasso and Ouahigouya. In the former, the CDP ousted three ADF-RDA mayors and in Ouahigouya it prevented Gilbert Ouedraogo from obtaining the seats that would have allowed him to rebuild his image as a serious alternative to the CDP. In the campaign, it was especially Compaoré's right-hand Salif Diallo, minister of agriculture and the CDP's regional head, who challenged Ouedraogo's dominance in the north. The **CDP was successful** both in places where it had to regain ground and where it had been supported all along, notably in Ouagadougou and the rural municipalities. The CDP victory was overwhelming. Of the 3,807,424 registered voters, 1,870,017 Burkinabè turned out (49.1%). The top three parties took 85% of the votes. The CDP won 12,793 seats out of 17,786, leaving 1,572 for the ADF-RDA and 600 for the 'Union Pour la République' (UPR), hence nearly becoming the 'winner takes all' ('tuk giuli' in the major local language, Moore).

In June–July, developments in the **Zongo affair** once more dominated public debate, this time in relation to the trials of Ousseni Yaro and Marcel Kafando, former members of the presidential guard. While both had been found guilty of murdering David Ouedraogo in 2000, with Ousseni Yaro sentenced to 10 years, in June the judge ordered Yaro's release on grounds of good behaviour. On 31 May, a judge ordered a new cross-examination of Kafando and a prosecution witness, who retracted a statement on the basis of which Kafando had been charged with murder and arson in connection with Zongo's death (February 2001). In the light of these new developments, Kafando was acquitted on 19 July. Moreover, the judge ordered that the investigation of Kafando and any other person for the murder of Zongo be abandoned. Confirmation of this decision on appeal on 16 August meant that no further attempts would be made to find out who murdered Zongo. The court ruled that the case could be reopened only if sufficient new incriminating evidence was provided. An attempt by Robert Ménard, secretary-general of 'Reporters sans Frontières' (RSF), to have new material admitted was rejected on 23 October. These rulings, together with the fact that Kafando had never served time in prison, but had stayed at home sick; that Yaro had been regularly seen on the streets of Ouagadougou; and that the complicity of Compaoré's younger brother had never been seriously investigated, reinforced popular perceptions of the regime's impunity.

On 4 December, **Joseph Ki-Zerbo**, one of the country's leading academics and politicians, died. Well known internationally and the recipient of numerous prizes, Ki-Zerbo represented the 'Parti pour la Démocratie et le Progrès/Parti Socialiste' in parliament. Numerous obituaries for this pan-Africanist of the first hour celebrated Ki-Zerbo's intelligence and integrity.

At year's end, there were **deadly clashes** in the streets of Ouagadougou between the lower ranks of the military and members of the elite security police, 'Compagnie Républicaine de Sécurité' (CRS). This episode began when on 17 December CRS police prevented a group of soldiers from taking seats for which they had no proper tickets for a concert in the football stadium. In retaliation, the soldiers attacked the central police station in the heart of Ouagadougou on 19 December. Shots were fired, killing one soldier and wounding three. This unleashed more violence the following day, with police headquarters coming under heavy machine gun and rocket fire for the entire day. Soldiers stole ammunition, opened prison doors (releasing 600 inmates) and robbed petrol stations. In all, two police officers and three soldiers were killed and several civilians wounded. The government was forced to postpone the ECOWAS and UEMOA summits scheduled for 22 and 23 December in Ouagadougou.

Immediately after the violent incidents, Minister of Defence Yéro Boly and Djibrill Bassolé, minister of security, gave a press conference, deeply deploring the events and promising to improve the relationship between the different security forces, characterised by different hierarchical systems. Questions about the causes of the violence were also raised in the press. While army mutinies have been rare since Blaise Compaoré came to power, the rank and file have voiced **complaints** about worsening conditions of service, including health insurance and pension packages. Lower ranks have felt alienated from their superior officers, who over the years had secured additional tasks and privileges linked, among other things, to their participation in international peacekeeping missions. Rumour had it that most of the officers had left Ouagadougou during the fighting.

The gradual reduction of the army's lower ranks combined with the proliferation of **special security services**, such as the CRS, formed the background to this conflict. The elite but controversial CRS, whose deployments included fighting highway banditry, triggered considerable criticism from MPs and human rights associations when on 28 October they executed three businessmen/criminals in Bogande on suspicion of being bandits. The later incidents in Ouagadougou more generally pointed to powerful undercurrents in the armed forces suggesting that Compaoré's position was weaker than intimated by the outcome of the local elections.

Foreign Affairs

As a sign of improved bilateral relations, President Compaoré paid a visit to **Mauritania** on 16 and 17 March. In the past, Libya and Burkina had allegedly supported rebels against former President Maaouiya Ould Taya. The coup d'etat in Mauretania by Colonel Ely Ould Vall in August 2005 opened up the possibility of restoring relations with Burkina. At Nouakchott, the two presidents proclaimed their wish to collaborate in the fields of agriculture and cattle keeping. Burkina's state-run newspaper 'Sidwaya' asserted that Mauritania's new president could benefit from Compaoré's expertise in conflict resolution, as shown in Chad, DR Congo, Sudan, Liberia, Togo and with regard to Touareg rebels. This report was also an allusion to the progressive change in role of Compaoré in the sub-region, developing from meddler in conflicts into a potential and effective mediator.

This shift could be clearly observed with regard to relations with **Togo** and Côte d'Ivoire. After the death of President Eyadéma in February 2005, Compaoré chose to support his son Faure Gnassingbé in the hope of improving relations. Under Eyadéma, these had been marred by mutual accusations of subversion, notably in the border regions. However, with the onset of the crisis in Côte d'Ivoire, Lomé became the major port for Burkina's trade, including cement and cotton, making it worthwhile for Compaoré to try to improve ties and leading him to step in as mediator in the dispute over Togo's fraudulent presidential elections in 2005. This year, on 20 August, he successfully mediated the signing of an agreement to resolve the crisis by forming a government of national unity and organising parliamentary elections. The agreement was co-signed by Compaoré.

With the growing presence of mainland **China**, Compaoré chose to express his loyalty towards his Taiwanese allies, who had given extensive aid in the construction and health sectors since 1994. On 22 September, he once more supported Taiwan's request to become a full member of the UN. He stated that with its 23 m inhabitants, Taiwan should be allowed a mature status on the international scene. Compaoré visited Taipei from 19 to 23 November. He stressed that he wanted to strengthen bilateral relations with regard to both economic collaboration and issues of democratisation.

Burkina's head of state also strengthened his international profile within the **ECOWAS** framework, even though its summit in Ouagadougou had to be postponed because of the fighting in the capital. It was expected, however, that Compaoré would be elected ECOWAS chairman in 2007 to replace President Mamadou Tandja of Niger, who had held the position for a second consecutive year. This development would have relevance for Compaoré's position as mediator in the civil war in Côte d'Ivoire.

Socioeconomic Developments

Multilateral organisations such as the World Bank and IMF, together with Burkina's government, continued to praise Burkina's economic performance. **Growth** figures were up again this year, to 6%. These positive assessments continued to trigger forms of aid. On 17 and 18 May, a meeting took place with the regional coordinator of the Millennium Challenge Account (MCA), the US donor fund for which the country had qualified in November the previous year. Earlier in 2006, a national coordinators' team had been appointed and reported on the initial results of their tour of Burkina's 13 regions. They proposed several projects to be funded with the $ 4 bn to be made available in the near future.

Despite this international optimism, there were ample signs that the effects of growth were unevenly distributed. In June, a large movement principally made up of labour unions organised **protest marches** under the slogan 'La Vie est Chère'. Rising petrol prices increased the prices of imported goods, among other things. The government was blamed for the fact that petrol prices were higher than in neighbouring Mali.

More setbacks came from the cotton sector. With more than a quarter of the population dependent on cotton-generated incomes and the crop comprising 60% of the country's export revenues, farmers would receive only $ 0.30 a kilogram for their next harvest, i.e., 9% less than the previous year. Even the SOFITEX cotton-buying company was struggling to survive, its expenses of around $ 80.45 m outstripped its income over the last two years. Meanwhile, many Burkinabè farmers tried to switch from cotton to cereals such as corn, millet and soya beans, but cereal prices were even more volatile and the crops themselves more vulnerable to the periodic droughts. This year, a 100 kg bag of maize cost just $ 6.03 compared to $ 50.28 two years earlier. The US, which has heavily subsidised 25,000 of its **cotton** farmers, was blamed for the low price of cotton. In October, President Compaoré told US farmers and congressmen in a video conference organised by the World Bank that cotton was essential to alleviating poverty in his country as well as in Benin, Mali, Niger and Chad. "But our economies have been reformed so that there are no forms of subsidies for farmers", he said. "While alas, certain [Western] countries have chosen to flout the rules of the market."

Compaoré continued his role as a free market champion. On 30 December, a contract was signed with Maroc Telecom providing it control of 51% of the shares of Burkina's **telecommunications** company ONATEL. The state sold its majority share in ONATEL, together with its cellphone division Telmob, for $ 290 m. Maroc Telecom planned to integrate ONATEL's services into wider sub-regional communication networks. Both company and government officials expected that information and communication technologies would play a major role in furthering social and economic development.

Gold, the country's second largest export after cotton, was the most promising sector. Gold prices continued to climb, peaking in June at $ 680 per ounce and falling back a little to $ 600 per ounce in the second half of the year. The government received $ 2.5 m in annual taxes from mining companies, which were active at Taparko, situated between Kaya and Dori (High River Gold), at Essakan in the northeast (the largest deposit worked by the South African firm Gold Fields and the Canadian firm Orezone) and Youga, near the border with Ghana (the Canadian junior Etruscan). Gold production was expected to reach 8,700 kg in 2007 – a nearly sixfold increase over 2005. The country's potential was now compared to that of Ghana and Mali, West Africa's largest gold producers.

From 4 to 7 December, the PROMIN event took place ('Journées de promotion minière du Burkina') organised by the ministry of mining with the object of attracting additional capital. The event, the third of its kind, was attended by representatives of several mining companies. A large delegation visited the Taparko site, slated to open as an industrially exploited open pit mine in 2007.

On 17 August, a serious accident occurred at Poura mining site, Burkina's first industrial mine, dating back to colonial times. The mine was closed in 1999, but ever since illegal miners had continued to work the shafts, a haphazard activity, particularly during the rainy season. The accident, caused by a blast, cost the lives of three people and another five were injured. The incident rekindled discussions on how to promote safety in **artisanal mining**, also in view of the widespread use of mercury and other chemicals. In addition, environmental problems would have to be addressed.

In tackling problems of **infrastructure**, Burkina saw the completion of the tarred road between Kaya and Dori. This, and the road between Ouagadougou and Kongoussi expected to be ready the following year, are important for mining companies as well as for the export of vegetables. The latter are cultivated on irrigation sites that are the result of ongoing development initiatives by the ministry of agriculture in dry season agriculture involving the cultivation of vegetables, maize and rice on fields adjacent to lakes created by artificial dams. In March and June, the minister of 'l'Agriculture, de l'Hydraulique et des Ressources Halieutiques', Salif Diallo, inaugurated dam-building projects in Bagré and Andékanda. The 'Agence française de Développement' provided the $ 14.5 m needed for the first, while the second was financed ($ 6 m) by the 'Banque Islamique de Développement' (BID) together with the Burkina government. Oumarou Kanazoe, by far the largest builder in Burkina Faso and a close associate of the Compaoré regime, was given the responsibility for these public works. A first national conference on dams took place on 5 December. National and international experts and engineers discussed the role of dams in socioeconomic development, as well as solutions for the social and technical problems related to the construction of dams and the maintenance of irrigated areas. The World Bank announced that $ 50 m would be made available for new irrigation projects, both large- and small-scale.

In December, the president announced that his presidency of ECOWAS would serve to put economic growth high on the sub-regional agenda.

Sabine Luning

Cape Verde

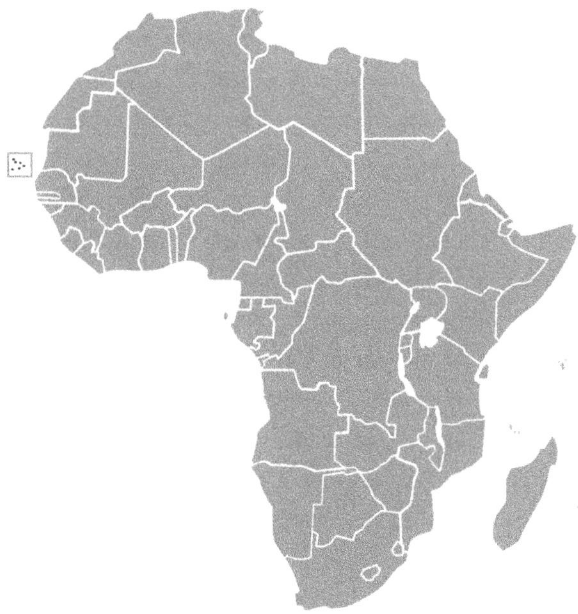

Prime Minister José Maria Neves was confirmed in office when the ruling 'Partido Africano de Independência de Cabo Verde' (PAICV) won an absolute majority in the legislative elections in January. In March, President Pedro Pires (PAICV) was re-elected for a second term. Economic growth, driven by private and public investments, continued and the country succeeded in attracting further inflows of both development aid and private foreign investment.

Domestic Politics

In the **legislative elections** of 22 January, the ruling PAICV and the government of Prime Minister José Maria Neves were confirmed in office. The PAICV won 52.3% of the votes and 41 seats in the National Assembly, while the major opposition party, 'Movimento para a Democracia' (MpD) gained 44% of the ballots and 29 seats. The 'União Cabo-Verdiana Independente e Democrática' (UCID) won 2.6% of the votes and two seats. Two other small parties participating in the elections secured no seats. PAICV and MpD contested the elections in all constituencies, whereas the three smaller parties only participated in areas where they expected considerable electoral support. The average voter turnout was 54.2%. After the elections, the leader of the MpD, Agostinho Lopes, accused the victorious PAICV of electoral fraud. In February, the MpD formally contested the validity of the election results in the supreme court, alleging irregularities during the electoral process. The court confirmed some deficiencies in the process but rejected the appeal on the grounds that they had not influenced the overall results.

Prime Minister Neves's **new cabinet**, inaugurated on 10 March, remained largely unchanged. The number of women in the executive was increased from three to six. The new female members were the minister of employment, Sara Lopes; the secretary of state for agriculture, Rosa Fortes; and the adjunct secretary of state to the minister of finance, Leonesa Fortes. The former justice minister, Cristina Fontes Lima, took over the state reform and defence portfolio and was replaced by José Manuel Andrade. The government included four new secretaries of state. The government's priorities for the five-year term were to increase annual economic growth to more than 10%, reduce unemployment to less than 10%, intensify the fight against drug-related crimes, establish a special partnership with the EU and strengthen bilateral relations with Angola, South Africa, China and the US.

In the **presidential elections** held on 12 February, incumbent Pedro Pires (PAICV) was re-elected with 51% of the votes. The rival candidate, Carlos Veiga (MpD), lost by a margin 3,342 out of a total of 169,824 valid votes. Veiga defeated Pedro Pires by a very narrow margin of 24 votes in Cape Verde, but obtained only 49% of the total ballots due to the fact that two-thirds of the votes cast by emigrant communities abroad went to the incumbent. Voter turnout was 53%. Veiga attributed his defeat to irregularities, such as voter registrations after the deadline and the use of false voter cards, and contested the results in the supreme court. However, on 12 March the court refused his appeal, arguing that the irregularities that had occurred had been insignificant to the overall electoral result. President Pires's inauguration ceremony on 22 March for his second term was attended by Presidents Cavaco Silva of Portugal, Abdoulaye Wade of Senegal and Nino Vieira of Guinea-Bissau. While President Pires called for unity and reconciliation in his speech, the day before in Praia about 3,000 supporters responded to Carlos Veiga's call to demonstrate against electoral fraud and for fair elections in the future.

In light of the alleged irregularities in **voter registration**, the government proposed to change the electoral law to enable the postponement by one year of the updating of the voter registration due in June. It argued that this measure would restore confidence in the electoral process and would save funds that would otherwise be spent on updating electoral registers known to be flawed. The MpD, however, rejected the amendment of the electoral law as unconstitutional and instead proposed a mixed-party commission to be elected by the National Assembly to discuss the revision of the electoral system. On 30 May, the government lost the parliamentary vote in favour of amending the electoral law to postpone the updating of voter registration. In the voting, the government fell short by five votes of the necessary two-thirds majority to approve the law. The government then agreed to conduct the new voter registration in June so as to update the register for the local elections in 2008.

On 23 May, the first NATO troops arrived in Cape Verde in preparation for the 'Steadfast Jaguar 2006' manoeuvres as part of the **NATO Response Force** (NRF), a rapid deployment force for peacekeeping, humanitarian and security operations, established in 2002. From 15–28 June, around 7,000 French, German and Spanish (and US) troops participated in NATO's first military exercise in Africa. The exercise, which brought together the land, sea and air components of the NRF to test its operational capacity, took place on the islands Santiago, Santo Antão, Fogo and Sal.

On 10 September, the MpD elected Jorge Santos, the former mayor of Ribeira Grande, Santiago island, as its **new leader** to replace Agostinho Lopes, who resigned after five years as leader following the party's second successive defeat in the legislative elections. For the first time, the MpD leader was elected directly by party members. However, less than 10,000 of the 30,000 members participated in the vote. Santos won almost 9,000 votes. He promised to modernise and rejuvenate the party by encouraging new members to join.

In September, João Serra, the finance minister, stepped down for health reasons after two years in office. Cristina Duarte, a former consultant with FAO, became his successor. She promised to continue the policy of sound fiscal and economic management to further improve the country's record of economic stability and growth.

In late November, a corruption scandal prompted the **resignation of the minister** for the economy, growth and competitiveness, João Pereira Silva. The leader of the MpD, Jorge Santos, accused the minister in the National Assembly of passive corruption arising from a technical and financial assistance contract that the state tourist development company, 'Sociedade de Desenvolvimento Turístico das Ilhas da Boa Vista e do Maio', had signed in January with the private 'Sociedade Lusa de Negócios-Cabo Verde'. Prime Minister Neves admitted the contract contained some irregularities and promised to renegotiate it. However, he rejected any evidence of corruption. Nevertheless, the National Assembly appointed two commissions to inquire into the dealings of the tourist development bodies.

On 1 December, the government suffered another defeat in the National Assembly when a bill aimed at increasing **politicians' salaries** by 20% failed to achieve the necessary two-thirds majority. The government justified the salary raise, which benefited MPs, the presidency and the heads of the municipalities, by reference to the cumulative inflation rate since the last salary increase. However, Jorge Santos, leader of the opposition MpD, rejected the proposal, arguing that the population would not accept it. Public-sector trade unions, which had accepted a 3.5% salary raise at the beginning of the year, also condemned the government's bill.

Foreign Affairs

In order to combat **illegal immigration** and trafficking in people, the minister of internal administration, Júlio Lopes Correia, asked in April for assistance from the EU. During a visit to Praia on 19 April, Portuguese Foreign Minister Freitas do Amaral promised to support Cape Verde in obtaining from the international community the means to patrol the archipelago's territorial waters. On 23 May, the European Commission announced measures to help Spain to combat illegal immigration to the Canaries, including the extension of its border-surveillance operations to Cape Verde, Mauritania and Senegal.

The Spanish foreign minister, Miguel Ángel Moratinos, paid a visit to the country in June to sign bilateral agreements on the struggle against illegal immigration and organised crime. On 11 August, the EU launched 'Operation Hera II', conducted by FRONTEX, the European agency for the security of the external borders of EU member states. As part of the operation, on 17 August the Portuguese corvette 'Baptista de Andrade' arrived on a 45-day surveillance mission in Cape Verde and to train the local coast guard.

The closer cooperation with the EU on immigration issues was reflected in an attempt to restrict immigration from the neighbouring continent. On 14 June, President Pires did not participate in the ECOWAS summit because the organisation had rejected the government's proposal to put clandestine immigration from member states to Cape Verde on the agenda. On 7 September, the government announced it would introduce stricter visa requirements for the citizens of all other ECOWAS member states.

In early November Prime Minister Neves attended the **Sino-African summit** in Beijing, together with a large delegation, including the then minister of the economy, Pereira Silva, and the minister of foreign affairs and cooperation, Victor Borges. During the meeting, China signed an agreement on the construction of a cement factory in Santa Cruz, Santiago island.

On 8 November, the US Millennium Challenge Corporation (MCC) declared Cape Verde eligible to apply for Millennium Challenge Account funds in the 2007 fiscal year as part of a newly created lower-middle income category of countries with per capita income above $ 1,576. The ongoing $ 110 m MCC programme for Cape Verde, signed in 2005, included water management and soil conservation, improved transport networks and private sector support.

Socioeconomic Developments

On 16 May, an IMF team concluded a mission to Cape Verde to assess the country's economic and policy performance. It also discussed with government a new programme under the Policy Support Instrument (PSI) developed for countries such as Cape Verde that have made significant progress towards economic stability and do not need IMF financial support, but would like ongoing **IMF advice** for their economic policies. The mission considered the archipelago's economic policies sound, as economic growth driven by private and public investments continued and inflows of both development aid and private foreign investments had further increased.

On 11 July, the government submitted to the IMF the policies it intended to implement in the context of a three-year PSI. The policies to consolidate economic stability included medium-term reduction in domestic debt, increased international reserves, as well as structural reforms such as improved budget management, reduced fiscal risks in public enterprises and a restructured system of tax incentives. On 31 July, the IMF formally approved the PSI for Cape Verde. The first IMF review mission of the PSI, conducted in early November, concluded that the country's economic and policy performance remained strong. Due to significant increases in foreign direct investment and tourism inflows and favourable agricultural prospects following good rainfall, annual GDP growth was expected to reach 6%.

On 27 June, the National Assembly approved the overdue annual **budget** for 2006 that had been considerably delayed by the legislative and presidential elections. The budget included total expenditures of CVEsc (Cape Verdean Escudo) 40.7 bn (€ 369.1 m), of which CVEsc 24.4 bn (€ 221.3 m) was current expenditures and CVEsc 16.3 bn (€ 147.8 m) was capital expenditures, with the major part of the investments in basic infrastructure improvements and rural poverty-reduction programmes. Foreign donors were expected to finance 75% of the state budget. The 2007 budget approved by the National Assembly on 27 November envisaged total expendidures of CVEsc 40.2 bn (€ 364.6 m), slightly less than in the 2006 budget. Current expenditure was CVEsc 23.6 bn (€ 214 m), while capital investment accounted for CVEsc 16.6 bn (€ 150.5 m), particularly for the modernisation of infrastructure. Total revenue was expected to increase by 5.3% to CVEsc 37.5 bn (€ 340 m), leaving a deficit of CVEsc 2.7 bn (€ 24.5 m), equivalent to 2.5% of GDP.

On 3 July, Prime Minister Neves inaugurated the Poilão dam on Santiago island, the country's first dam constructed by China. The **dam** is 26 metres high and 153 metres long, with a capacity 1.2 million m^3 of water, sufficient to irrigate an area of 64 ha. At the ceremony, the Chinese ambassador, Sun Rongmao, promised the continuation of his country's development assistance to Cape Verde.

On 17 March, the Cape Verdian Tecnicil Group announced the € 130 m Vila Verde golf resort tourism project on Sal island, which would be concluded within ten years. In late November, Cape Verde Development, an Irish company, announced an ambitious € 2 bn investment in a tourist resort and golf courses on a 425 ha site on Sal island, the island which dominates the **tourism sector** accounting for two-thirds of tourist nights spent in the country. Tourism represented the bulk of the investment projects, worth $ 300 m, approved by the government until the end of the year.

In late December, Veríssimo Pinto, the president of the board of Cape Verde's Stock Exchange (BVC), which inaugurated financial activities in December 2005, was satisfied with his institution's performance in its first year. BVC achieved a capitalisation above CVEsc 6 bn (€ 54.4 m), which generated transactions of CVEsc 500 m (€ 4.5 m) for the institution. According to Pinto, the results had been even better if the instruments traded on the BVC had increased as expected. Instead, the BVC traded only treasury bonds and the equities of the three listed companies 'Sociedade Cabo-Verdiana de Tabacos', 'Banco Comercial do Atlântico' and 'Caixa Económica de Cabo Verde'.

Gerhard Seibert

Côte d'Ivoire

For Côte d'Ivoire and its people, 2006 was – once again – a wasted year marked by exhausting uncertainty, many twists and turns, little hope and many fears. Yet the previous year had ended well with the implementation of an internationally mediated solution aimed at ending the deadlock that had arisen out of the impossibility of organising presidential elections at the end of President Laurent Gbagbo's five-year mandate (31 October 2005). A transitional period began with the extension of the presidential term by a maximum of one year and the nomination of a new prime minister – Charles Konan Banny, governor of the BCEAO – with extended powers (4 December 2005). This, however, did not end the impasse during 2006 as a result of the lack of political will among Côte d'Ivoire's politicians. When the new deadline for presidential elections drew closer, the Ivorian people and international community were provided with a remake of 2005: continuation of political deadlock and an exit option devised by the AU and UN, which proposed another one-year transition period.

Domestic Politics

As the main stumbling block of **eligibility for the presidency** had been resolved in 2005 by the provisional suspension of article 35 of the constitution concerning the nationality of presidential candidates, the peace process focused on and failed on two major issues: the recurring theme of disarmament of pro-Gbagbo 'Young Patriots' (12,000 militia members) and 'rebels' (42,500 'Forces Nouvelles' (FN) – troops), and the voter identification process. The latter, specifically the provision of identity papers and voting rights to second and third generation immigrants and many northern Ivorians, represented a shift from the article 35 issue to another aspect of the same problem, the definition of **national identity**. This issue had contaminated Ivorian politics since the beginning of the 1990s (the 'ivoirité' debate) and was the main trigger for the civil war in 2002.

The first crisis of the year was over the **status of parliament**. On 15 January, the 'Groupe de Travail International' (GTI) charged with overseeing the UN peace plan recommended that the parliamentary mandate, which had expired on 16 December 2005, not be renewed. In response, thousands of Gbagbo supporters took to the streets of Abidjan on 16 January and gathered outside the headquarters of the **UN mission**. On 17 January, the protesters (almost 300) vainly attempted to enter the UN compound, which was closed off by barricades. UN camps in Daloa and Guiglo in the western region were also attacked. UN Secretary-General Kofi Annan reacted sharply and called for an immediate end to what he called "orchestrated violence".

The same day, President Laurent Gbagbo's ruling party – 'Front Populaire Ivoirien' (FPI) – announced it would **withdraw** from the **peace talks** and end its participation in the transitional government. FPI leader and former Prime Minister Pascal Affi N'Guessan asked that a 'government of national liberation' be set up and announced that FPI could no longer tolerate recolonisation of the country under UN supervision. He called for the departure of all UN peacekeepers, the Licorne force (French troops under UN mandate) and other "forces of occupation, exploitation and enslavement of Côte d'Ivoire." However, on 27 January, President Gbagbo contravened the GTI's recommendation with a decree retaining the National Assembly with all its powers. In this explosive context, Prime Minister Banny, just returning from Pretoria, took the initiative to re-engage the peace process during the third cabinet meeting, held on 2 February. He proposed a plan of action for the transition focusing on the recurring issues of disarmament, reunification and presidential elections. Guillaume Soro, the FN leader and second-in-protocol in the transitional government in charge of reconstruction, chose not to attend.

The UN decided to maintain pressure and announced **sanctions** in terms of resolution 1572 of 15 November 2004. These came into force on 8 February and banned foreign travel by and froze the foreign assets of the two main leaders of the Young Patriots – Charles Blé Goudé and Eugène Djue – in retribution for the orchestrated violence of mid-January against UN personnel. The same steps were taken against the rebel commander of the Korhogo sector, Fofie Kouakou, who was sanctioned for violations of human rights and the use of child soldiers. Goudé and Djue mocked the decision, saying they had no foreign assets and did not travel much, but they avoided any verbal escalation. The Gbagbo side responded to these developments with a special session of parliament on 13 February with only half the representatives attending, mainly from FPI and under the leadership of the president's wife, Simone Gbagbo, the party whip. The GTI met again in Abidjan on 17 February, against a backdrop of Young Patriots, who served as a reminder of the consequences of the last GTI meeting in January.

Nevertheless, there was some movement when Konan Banny succeeded on 28 February in organising the **first meeting on Ivorian soil** since the eruption of civil war of the country's main political leaders. After days of hesitation about his personal security, Guillaume Soro met with President Gbagbo in the capital Yamoussoukro as well as with the two principal civilian opposition leaders, Henri Konan Bedié (former president and leader of the 'Parti Démocratique de Côte d'Ivoire', PDCI), and Alassane Ouattara (former prime minister and leader of the 'Rassemblement des Républicains', RDR), who had returned home on 26 January after three years of exile in France. Even if no decisive initiatives resulted, the meeting was presented as an **historic summit** and started a peace momentum welcomed by the international community. The first official military talks between FAFN ('Forces Armées des FN') and FANCI (the Ivorian army, 'Forces Armées Nationales de Côte d'Ivoire') started in Yamoussoukro on 2 April with Prime Minister Banny in the chair. In addition, the university in Bouaké, the northern rebel-held town, reopened on 3 April after three years of closure. Finally, on 9 April the AU chairman, President Denis Sassou-Nguesso, convened a meeting where the four main leaders – Gbagbo, Soro, Bédié and Ouattara – agreed with Prime Minister Banny to a disarmament programme and a census leading to elections by the end of October. The question of which should come first (disarmament or establishing voter identity for up to 3 m disenfranchised Ivorians) had been the major stumbling block between Gbagbo and the FN.

This fragile peace-building was disturbed when President Gbagbo announced on 16 April that the FN had to hand in its arms before voter cards would be issued. New **violence** broke out in the west with fighting near Bangolo at the end of April, leading to the deployment of UN blue helmets in early May. In response, Banny tried to recapture the initiative by announcing on 14 May that disarmament would start simultaneously with voter registration on 18 May in seven localities, both in rebel- and government-controlled zones. Banny hoped to capitalise on the support he had encountered among donors (EU, IMF, World Bank) when touring Europe and the US at the end of April. However, on 18 May nothing happened. After new talks on disarmament and demobilisation on 31 May, which supposedly led to a new agreement, rebels again demanded that pro-government militias be disbanded before they would lay down their arms. Disarmament was postponed yet again.

Pressure mounted on the prime minister when FPI leader Affi N'Guessan denounced the government's failure in the disarmament process and the pilot (voter) census. Nguessan warned on 4 June that if no elections were possible, Laurent Gbagbo would remain president and the FPI would defend him against any coup d'etat. The opposition answered on 6 June by floating the idea of a new type of political transition that would not include Gbagbo and be limited to 18 months. A new attempt to restart the peace process was made on 29 June at a meeting in Bouaké where all parties decided to form a **steering committee** to supervise voter registration. During his talks with the country's principal leaders in Yamoussoukro on 5 July, the UN secretary-general strongly supported this step and urged the country to speed up the peace process. According to the joint communiqué, the independent electoral commission was to set up offices across the country before 31 July while the identification process was expected to start in parallel with the implementation of the disarmament plan. Yet the peace process stalled again when the nationwide registration scheme, supposed to start on 13 July and based on public hearings, was delayed due to poor preparation and participants' fear of attacks by Young Patriots. A new round of peace talks gathering the 'four big men' (Gbagbo, Soro, Ouattara and Bedié) was organised by the prime minister on 5 September, but the talks broke down without a breakthrough.

This routine of failed commitments was halted when the government resigned on 6 September over a **pollution scandal** in Abidjan. President Gbagbo accepted the resignation the same day and asked Banny to form a new government. The toxic waste caused several deaths, huge contamination and panic across the city and led to protests and riots. These culminated on 14 September in an attack on Transport Minister Anaky Kobenan, who was dragged from his car and beaten up, and the burning of the house of port director Marcel Gossio.

The vacuum created by the resignation of the government made discussions with the GTI scheduled for 8 September impossible. The UN-appointed group confirmed what everyone knew – the election deadline could not be honoured. It called for a new framework with expanded powers for the prime minister, greater involvement by the international community and new sanctions. However, on 14 September, Gbagbo made his own move by announcing that the UN roadmap had failed and that he would not attend the UN meeting on Côte d'Ivoire scheduled for 20 September in New York, on the margins of the UN General Assembly. He also declared he would submit his own measures for a new peace process to be discussed by the AU. Hence, the **New York meeting** was a golden opportunity for the opposition, which proposed to invest the prime minister with full executive powers and charge him with leading the country during what it called the 'second transition'. This provoked a strong reaction from the Gbagbo camp. At the same time, pressure and nervousness mounted as ECOWAS announced the convening of a special summit on Côte d'Ivoire in the following weeks.

On 3 October, the FN proposed its own plan and called for the appointment of a transitional president, to be assisted by two vice-presidents, and the elimination from the transitional government of all persons known to be interested in running for president. On 4 October, the Gbagbo camp reacted with **threats** issued by Affi N'Guessan against citizens of ECOWAS member states, leading to sharp denunciation by the international community. The same day in Bouaké, the FN stronghold, protesters demanded Gbagbo's departure. However, the next day Nguessan escalated the situation further and called for the departure of all French troops and members of GTI, in which ECOWAS participated.

Simultaneously, Gbagbo unveiled an **eight-point plan** for peace ahead of the ECOWAS summit in Abuja, indicating that the plan was in response to the failure of foreign-inspired peace plans and to the need for Ivorian ownership of the process. Gbagbo's main points were strict application of the constitution; eliminating the buffer zone patrolled by UN and French troops; setting up a national unity government; restoring the president's powers to appoint the prime minister of his choice; and starting direct discussions with rebel leaders.

On 15 October, more than 10,000 people supporting the opposition took to the streets of Abidjan calling for President Gbagbo to step down. However, the inconclusive outcome of the ECOWAS meeting on 6 October coupled with the explicit outcome of the AU summit in Addis Ababa on 17 October consolidated Gbagbo's position by recommending a **new one-year extension** of the **presidential mandate**. This outcome was immediately condemned by the FN. At the same time, strong disagreements surfaced between the two camps regarding the definition of the 'extended powers' granted to the prime minister. The ECOWAS and AU recommendations were backed by resolution 1721 of the UN Security Council on 1 November, after heated debates among Council members. In a speech broadcast on 2 November, President Gbagbo announced he was pleased with the resolution which, he claimed, confirmed his mandate and respected Côte d'Ivoire's constitutional order.

A few weeks later, on 27 November, Gbagbo tried to test his room for manoeuvre by reinstating officials suspended by the prime minister in the wake of the toxic waste scandal. At the same time, he fired the general manager of the daily 'Fraternité Matin', recently appointed by the prime minister. This led to renewed tensions, while another GTI meeting on 1 December expressed deep concern about the delay in implementing UN resolution 1721 and expressed support for the prime minister in opposition to the president. The GTI also urged resumption of the roadmap, including voter identification and census, DDR and a move towards elections. However, attempts by Prime Minister Banny to find a **compromise** with Gbagbo were **unsuccessful**. On 4 December, he warned of the consequences for the peace process. The following day, the opposition staged protests in many cities, which were violently dispersed by police. Two people were killed in Agnibilékrou (in the north-east) and the Abidjan suburb of Koumassi. Forces loyal to the president continued with the strategy of maintaining tension by alleging that a coup d'etat was imminent (12 December).

In this volatile context, Gbagbo chose to move ahead by unveiling **another plan for peace** on 20 December. His proposal included five principal measures: direct discussions with FN rebels; an end to the buffer zone; creation of a national civic service providing jobs and skills to 40,000 youngsters; an amnesty and a repatriation scheme for displaced people. It was received as a non-starter.

Foreign Affairs

Côte d'Ivoire stayed high in the hit parade of crisis meetings and benefited from continuous efforts by the international community. Specifically, UN Secretary-General Kofi Annan tried all year long to keep Côte d'Ivoire on the agenda by increasing **UN support** and trying to find a definitive solution for the divided country. He closely followed the crisis, officially intervened several times in the debate through public statements and visited the country in early July to meet the political leaders. He also drafted five progress reports on the UN mission (as against three in 2005 and in 2004), plus a report on children and armed conflict in the country (25 October).

Following the events of mid-January, Annan took a **firm line** with President Gbagbo. He sent a letter on 2 February reminding him that by treaty the government was responsible for the safety of UN personnel and facilities in the country. Annan also mentioned he was "particularly concerned" that Côte d'Ivoire's security forces had largely failed in their commitments. The secretary-general pushed for the vote on sanctions against extremist leaders on 8 February. On 10 February, the UN sent a $ 3.5 m bill to the Ivorian government for the damage to **UN installations** during the January protests.

Of a total of 86 Security Council resolutions adopted in 2006, seven related to Côte d'Ivoire (as against eight in 2005, three in 2004 and four in 2003). The country thus remained one of the main concerns of the world body, together with Sudan and the Middle East. The United Nations Operation in Côte d'Ivoire (UNOCI) was the fifth UN **peacekeeping operation**, behind those in the DR Congo, Liberia, Sudan and Lebanon. All year long, the secretary-general together with France urged the Security Council to temporarily increase the peacekeepers in order to see through the transition process. Resolution 1652 (24 January) approved the extension of the mandate of UNOCI and the French forces, but only until 15 December. In response to the events of mid-January, resolution 1657 of 6 February authorised the redeployment of troops from Liberia until 31 March "in order to provide extra security coverage for UN personnel and property." UNOCI's personnel were significantly boosted by resolution 1682 of 2 June, allowing an increase of up to 1,500 more military and civilian police. At the end of the year, UNOCI totalled 9,029 peacekeepers (including 7,847 troops). The main troop-providing countries were Bangladesh (35%), five ECOWAS member states (Benin, Ghana, Niger, Senegal, and Togo, 25%) and Pakistan and Jordan (around 15% each). French forces were slightly reduced to 3,500.

The **GTI**, created by the AU on 6 October 2005 and endorsed by UN resolution 1633 of 21 October, met nine times in Abidjan. It represented the tangible expression of deep international involvement The first eight meetings were held monthly between January and September and the last on 1 December after the UN decision for a new transition period. At the same time, the **AU** continued its strong commitment to resolving the country's crisis. Olusegun Obasanjo, Nigeria's president and AU chairman, travelled to Côte d'Ivoire on 18 January to meet with Gbagbo and the transitional prime minister after the protests against the UN headquarters. The AU-backed South African mediation was reactivated when Prime Minister Banny travelled to Pretoria on 28 January to meet with President Mbeki and the new AU chairman, President Sassou-Nguesso, to discuss the worsening crisis. On 9 April, Sassou-Nguesso convened a new meeting of Côte d'Ivoire's leaders to consolidate recent progress, but the compromise lasted only seven days.

In this context, Banny decided to seek **international support**, starting with an official visit to France on 12–13 April, which included **meetings** with President Chirac, Defence Minister Alliot-Marie and donors. Then he went to Washington (24 April), where he met with World Bank and IMF management, the World Cocoa Foundation, the US trade representative and senior White House advisors charged with African affairs. President Gbagbo did not travel much and was mostly isolated on the international scene. He made a working visit to Chad on 15 June where he met President Déby.

In mid-August, the UN was forced to admit that its 31 October deadline for the presidential elections would be missed. These growing concerns, in addition to Gbagbo's decision on 14 September not to participate in the UN meeting on Côte d'Ivoire in New York, led to **renewed diplomatic activity**. AU Chairman Sassou-Nguesso flew to Côte d'Ivoire on 17 September but failed to break the deadlock. In New York, on 20 September, the opposition and the FN representatives had ample opportunity to denounce Gbagbo's obstructionism and urged the international community to strengthen the prime minister's powers. Mbeki planned to visit Abidjan but the final choice was to hold a meeting in Ouagadougou on 26 September with Gbagbo and Burkina's leader, Blaise Compaoré, chair of the AU's peace and security council. It was decided to continue to work at both ECOWAS and AU levels and Gbagbo announced he was ready to negotiate, not just to talk, and promised to table an alternative peace plan for review by his AU peers.

The **ECOWAS** meeting in Abuja on 6 October limited itself to making 'secret' recommendations to the next AU gathering. Rumour had it that this involved prolonging the transition for another year, with President Gbagbo and Prime Minister Banny retaining their respective roles. The recommendations of the AU meeting in Addis Ababa – attended by Gbagbo and Banny – on 17 October echoed and confirmed the ECOWAS position, for want of realistic alternatives. A statement to be transmitted to the UN Security Council proposed the extension of Gbagbo's term for a period not to exceed 12 months. It also confirmed the prime minister in his position with all the necessary authority to employ Ivorian armed and security forces to enforce the peace. The blurred formulation of the final communiqué was criticised by many as it was open to various interpretations. The Addis summit was also marked by a major change in **AU mediation**, as Mbeki requested to be relieved of his duties in response to accusations by the Ivorian opposition that he had sided with Gbagbo. Mbeki was replaced by the troika of Sassou-Nguesso, AU Commission President Alpha Oumar Konaré and the ECOWAS chair, Niger's President Mamadou Tandja.

The next international step was the **UN Security Council** discussions. These started on 23 October with a draft resolution circulated by France and supported by most of Africa's representatives on the council. The draft resolution took a strong position and reaffirmed the pre-eminence of international law over the Ivorian constitution during the transition period. It agreed with the AU and ECOWAS resolutions that President Gbagbo would retain the presidency for another year. It entrusted full command of Ivorian armed and security forces to the prime minister, including authority to lead the restructuring of these forces, to organise elections, and the possibility of ruling by decrees adopted by the cabinet and promulgated by him. The discussions took days and the vote was delayed because the Security Council appeared divided between supporters of a strong resolution granting extensive powers to the prime minister (France and many AU members) and another group that recognised the president as the principal authority until elections (mainly China, the US, Russia and Tanzania).

Resolution 1721, adopted on 1 November, unanimously decided to maintain Gbagbo and Banny, extend the transitional government for a final year and give new powers to the prime minister to implement a peace plan and prepare for elections. The resolution also gave the prime minister a new mandate to implement the roadmap. On the constitution, the resolution adopted a moderate position requiring "full compliance by all Ivorian parties and that no legal provisions should be invoked by them to obstruct the process." The resolution was backed by the GTI early in December when renewed tensions were increasing, leading to new warning signals to the international community.

The year ended with **two new resolutions** by the Security Council. Resolution 1726 authorised the extension of the mandate of UNOCI and French troops until 10 January 2007 and resolution 1727 extended the mandate of the group of experts in charge of following-up on the arms embargo (resolution 1572, 15 November 2004) for a further six months (it had previously been extended by three months by resolution 1708 on 14 September).

Socioeconomic Developments

Despite the closure of more than 100 small- and medium-scale French-owned enterprises in the wake of the events of November 2004, Côte d'Ivoire seemed to remain just above the waterline. As noted by an IMF mission in May, economic actors as well as government had shown surprising **resilience**. However, much of this appeared due to Côte d'Ivoire's 45% share of world cocoa production and the high taxation of this industry, in addition to its booming oil exports. The government was able to extract sufficient revenue to pay for civil servants' wages. Yet, with real GDP growth estimated at 1.2% – the previous 2005 growth rate was revised to 1.8% as a result of oil production – economic expansion did not keep pace with population growth (2%).

The international community's objective for Côte d'Ivoire remained 'good governance of public resources', something at which the country dismally failed. With **crude oil exports overtaking cocoa** exports in value for the first time, both sectors remained non-transparent, permitting the same corrupt practices, the build-up of a war chest and funding of off-budget military equipment.

Social violence was encouraged by the **proliferation of light weapons**, which reached worrying proportions. About 10,000 illicit small arms were believed to be in circulation, leading to a significant increase in **armed robberies**, drug trafficking and violence in local disputes.

The main socioeconomic sector, cocoa, was hit by a **farmers' strike** in October. Farmers protested low retail prices and high export taxes and took action the day after authorities had officially opened the harvesting season (16 October) by announcing a retail price far below farmers' expectations. Union leaders threatened to stop lorries carrying cocoa and other farm produce in order to paralyse and starve the country until the price was raised. The proposed price – CFAfr 400/kg – represented only 35%–40% of the FOB export price, while cocoa producers in other parts of the world received 70%–80%, as a consequence of a nearly equivalent taxation of CFAfr 313/kg (including export customs duties and CFAfr 53/kg of miscellaneous levies for development and stabilisation funds, cocoa sacks, etc.).

The paradox of the situation was that **cocoa exports taxation** provides an annual CFAfr 280–300 bn to the government and also CFAfr 80 bn to the farmers' associations, especially the 'Association Nationale des Producteurs de Café-Cacao de Côte d'Ivoire' (ANAPROCI), which are in charge of the private bodies introduced in the course of institutional sector reforms. As ANAPROCI and its president, Henri Amouzou, are direct supporters of Gbagbo's regime, the strike looked like a three-card trick when the presidency announced the release of CFAfr 10 bn to ANAPROCI to help fund cocoa producers' organisations.

The economic situation in **the north**, mainly based on cotton production, continued to decline as a result of shortages of inputs, deteriorating infrastructure and marketing difficulties. Cotton production fell from 320,000 tonnes in 2004 to an estimated 220,000 tonnes for the 2006–07 marketing year. 'La Compagnie Cotonnière de Côte d'Ivoire' (LCCI), one of the three cotton processing companies resulting from the privatisation process, declared bankruptcy in September. Public infrastructure in the rebel-held zone became really critical as social and sanitary conditions deteriorated, leading to an increase in disease and a severe risk of epidemics. UNICEF pointed to growing instances of typhoid and the start of a cholera epidemic in the west as well as in Abidjan.

Côte d'Ivoire was the seventh country affected by **avian flu**, with two disease epicentres discovered in the Abidjan region in April. Poultry culling took place in May in the Abidjan district, where the poultry industry is concentrated. This affected some 15,000 people directly or indirectly employed in the industry.

Abidjan's **toxic waste scandal** was one of the most tragic and spectacular events. Nine people died and close to 14,000 people fell ill, while 44,000 requested medical help when over 400 tonnes of toxic mud, mostly made up oil refinery waste, were unloaded from the 'Probo Koala', a Panamanian-registered ship, and dumped by a local company – 'Tommy'

– in about 10 landfills around Abidjan on the nights of 19–20 August. The ship had been hired by a Dutch company, Trafigura BV. Two senior (French) company officials were arrested. Based on the results of a commission of inquiry mandated by the prime minister, the head of the port, the head of the customs service and the governor of Abidjan district were accused of corruption and neglect. As a result, they were suspended – then immediately reinstated by Gbagbo. The clean-up operations took two months.

As to Côte' d'Ivoire's relations with the **donor community**, the emergency post-conflict assistance programme discussed in April with the IMF director-general was never approved as donor re-engagement was dependent on the usual set of preconditions, i.e., significant progress with disarmament, continuation of the voter identification process, elections and payment of arrears estimated at $ 400 m to the World Bank and other bilateral donors. However, all year long donors reaffirmed their commitment to immediate programmes involving emergency reconstruction assistance, disarmament support and general budgetary support.

Bruno Losch

Gambia

The five-party coalition, the National Alliance for Democracy and Development (NADD), which was formed in 2005 to contest the 2006 presidential elections, disintegrated on 1 February, following Ousainou Darboe's resignation from the executive. Darboe resigned over perceived hostility from other NADD executive members. This was a major disappointment to Gambians, albeit not a surprising one given the differences in political interests, ideology and personality among the leaders of the NADD executive. Another event that had an impact on the presidential election was the allegedly foiled coup attempt on 21 March, which shook the confidence of President Jammeh and his ruling APRC (Alliance for Patriotic Reorientation and Construction) to the core. It also set off a wave of arrests and alleged killings of coup leaders and civilian accomplices. Consequently, when elections were advanced to 22 September from their anticipated date in October, President Jammeh won a third five-year term, beating a poorly financed and fragmented coalition. Jammeh's victory was aided by anger and apathy of voters over the NADD's break-up as well as by the benefits of the incumbency. In addition, the run-up to the presidential vote was marred by violence and intimidation of the opposition and its supporters.

Domestic Politics

The September presidential election was held against the backdrop of a Commonwealth-brokered memorandum of understanding for political parties, concluded on 2 September 2005, and presided over by Nigerian President Olusegun Obasanjo. The MoU sought primarily to create an atmosphere conducive to a peaceful and orderly vote, which it achieved. Yet it was also clear that the APRC government did not fully adhere to the MoU, primarily because of unfolding political events and irregularities in the run-up to polling day. Following the disputed presidential elections on 18 October 2001, Jammeh changed the constitution in that year to a 'first-past-the-post' electoral process in order to avoid future run-off options, in addition to passing media laws by which the press could be muzzled and harassed by the National Intelligence Agency (NIA), the state's repressive arm. This forced the splintered opposition, together with several diaspora-based organisations, to unite, after a summit in Atlanta in 2003, into the **NADD** in May 2005. NADD comprised five political parties – United Democratic Party (UDP), National Reconciliation Party (NRP), People's Progressive Party (PPP), People's Democratic Organisation for Independence and Socialism and National Democratic Action Movement.

While the NADD generated high expectations because of the political threat it posed to Jammeh's continued rule, its creation led the president to react against opposition leaders with threats and invective, followed by arrests and detentions. On 1 February, Ousainou Darboe, the UDP leader, **resigned** from the NADD executive after allegations of 'mistrust', 'insincerity' and 'hate' within its ranks. The NADD chairman, Alhaji Assan Musa Camara, and a handful of PPP members of the NADD executive also withdrew and threw their weight behind Darboe. Darboe's resignation in February, contrary to his initial pronouncement to support NADD's chosen candidate, was the severest blow against NADD and seemed to confirm the regime's calculations that an alliance comprising 'self-interested politicians', with divergent political views and strategies, could never set its differences aside to sustain a coalition, much less remove Jammeh.

NADD's split emboldened President Jammeh and his ruling APRC, and they seized this opportunity to further discredit Darboe, Omar Jallow (OJ), Sallah and the other opposition politicians. In Jammeh's view, the choice was now clear because the disintegration of the NADD, which only a few months before had posed a major threat, made the election outcome a **foregone conclusion**. Apparently, Darboe was unwilling to accept a selection process for NADD's presidential candidate that seemed likely to nominate OJ, while he also had objections to some of his political colleagues as well as to the legal basis on which the alliance was built. Political disputes, perhaps personal ones as well, between him and Lamin Waa Juwara, (a.k.a. 'Mbarodi', meaning 'lion' in Fulani) the UDP's former propaganda secretary, further muddied the waters within NADD.

Amid the rancour, a UDP/NRP alliance crystallised and shortly thereafter, on 1 March, NADD selected Halifa Sallah as its presidential candidate to stem a deepening political and leadership crisis. While Gambians reeled from Darboe's resignation and the realignment in its wake – mostly defections to the ruling APRC – the military's top brass allegedly staged an **aborted coup d'etat** on 20 March. The alleged take-over exposed the army's internal cleavages as well as the dwindling support for the APRC within its ranks. It also pointed to a crisis of confidence in the political process and disappointment over the splintering of NADD.

President Jammeh's confidence was severely shaken by this incident and he reacted with characteristic vengeance. A wave of arrests, 'disappearances' and alleged killings of coup leaders, civilian co-conspirators and key security officers ensued. Daba Marenah, once Jammeh's right-hand man and head of the NIA, was allegedly killed. Other coup plotters were said to have been brutally tortured to extract confessions, which they then read on state-controlled radio and television. On 2 June, amid the **bloodletting**, the Independent Electoral Commission (IEC) chairman, Ndondi Njie, announced snap presidential elections for 22 September. He justified the new September date by pointing to the start of the Muslim holy month of Ramadan later that month.

Many Gambians vainly hoped that a UDP/NRP alliance and Halifa Sallah's selection as NADD's presidential candidate would lead to a new and stronger alliance. However, on **nomination day**, 2 September 2006, there were three candidates: Jammeh stood on the APRC ticket, while Darboe headed the UDP/NRP alliance and Sallah ran as the NADD flag bearer. The Gambia Party for Democracy and Progress's (GPDP) presidential aspirant Henry Gomez was disqualified and subsequently threw in his lot with the UDP/NRP alliance.

Meanwhile, President Jammeh's 'unofficial' campaign received a big boost from the seventh AU summit on 1–2 July in Banjul, despite adverse press coverage by journalists belonging to Reporters without Borders and other web-based Gambian newspapers. Following the summit, Jammeh's **intimidation** machine was once more set in motion. On 2 August, he dismissed and detained the IEC chairman, Njie, and commission member Sulayman Mboob over a controversy centring on a supplementary registration exercise. Alhaji Mustapha Carayol was named as the new IEC chairman. Two weeks before the poll, Dodou Sanneh, a state-employed television journalist assigned to cover the UDP/NRP/GPDP campaign trail, was arrested by the NIA and sacked for what was perceived as his sympathetic coverage of the alliance. This political environment shaped both the campaign and the ensuing elections.

In the end, Jammeh scored a **resounding victory** over his opponents. He received 67.3% or 264,404 votes out of a total of 670,000 registered voters. Darboe received 27% (104,808 votes), while NADD's Sallah won 6% (23,473 votes). Less than 60% of the electorate – 392,685 voters – turned out. This contrasted sharply with the 88.3% and 90% turnouts in the 1996 and 2001 presidential elections.

Foreign Affairs

Relations with **Senegal** remained frosty, even following the fence-mending over the two-month border closure in August–October 2005. Relations took a turn for the worse when a senior official in the Senegalese high commission in Banjul was implicated in the alleged coup of 20 March. Moreover, the coup's ringleader as well as several ex-military leaders, including ex-vice-chairman Sana Sabally, were resident in Senegal. Senegal's President Wade also pressured Jammeh to offer an amnesty and release all military personnel and civilians accused of participating in the plot. In addition, increased tensions between Senegal's central government and its secessionist southern province of Casamance led to a flow of 6,000 refugees into Gambia on 26 October. Consequently, scepticism in Dakar grew over Jammeh's capacity to remain neutral in the Casamance conflict, especially given the fact that the bulk of the secessionists belonged to Jammeh's own ethnic group, the Jola. Despite frequent meetings between Wade and Jammeh, relations between the two heads of state remained strained, notwithstanding what on the surface appeared to be cordial ties.

Relations with Taiwan, one of the regime's major financial supporters, continued to be good, as with many other African countries, including Mauritania and Nigeria. Ties with Arab/Islamic states improved as well. On 1–2 July, Gambia hosted the seventh AU summit, which was attended by 33 African heads of state as well as UN Secretary-General Kofi Annan and the presidents of Iran and Venezuela. Jammeh increasingly allied himself with these leaders in response to strained relations with the US. More significant, however, was the fact that Jammeh's legitimacy abroad grew somewhat, despite growing domestic repression. Relations with the **Commonwealth**, soured since the 1996 presidential elections, improved. Improving strained relations with Western donors and international financial institutions has been a major objective since 2001, and paid off somewhat in the form of modest EU and US financial assistance.

There were clear signals of change in the regime's relationship with the US. Rather than business-as-usual, pressure mounted for change in the sphere of human rights. On 15 June, US Congressman Adam B. Schiff expressed grave concern over the 2004 murder of newspaper editor Deyda Hydara and the slow and unproductive results from the government-led investigation. Speaking in the US house of representatives, he called for an end to "impunity" for "predators of press freedom". Schiff strongly urged the Gambian government to appoint an independent board of inquiry to investigate Hydara's murder. In response to increased human rights violations, on 19 June the US government **suspended Gambia** from its list of eligible countries to receive economic assistance from its Millennium Challenge Account. The reasons given were poor and deteriorating human rights, economic mismanagement and hostility toward journalists.

Socioeconomic Developments

While government data indicated macroeconomic stability, with a growth rate of 7.1%, up from 6.9% in 2005, this must be viewed with caution as previously reported data were suspect. Poverty, which prior to the coup of 1994 hovered at 65% of the population, has increased to almost 70% or more. Fiscal policy implementation remained one of the biggest policy failures. Unbudgeted expenditure was the main cause of this poor performance, combined with lack of capacity in the civil service, limited coherence between government departments and corruption. Transparency was low and scrutiny of government expenditure by parliament and civil society limited. The fiscal deficit has been consistently high, peaking at 15% of GDP in 2001, owing to large unbudgeted payments and AU summit-related expenditures. The government has always failed to adhere to pledges to tighten **fiscal policy**. At year's end, the domestic debt stock stood in excess of $ 130 m, while foreign debt stood at approximately $ 1 bn.

In his yearly budget speech, the minister of finance conceded that this level of debt was not sustainable and that it had a detrimental impact on efforts to alleviate poverty. Despite construction of several new high and middle schools, large rural hospitals and the construction of a new television station and a university, Gambians were clearly worse off than in 1993. To add insult to injury, mounting food and **fuel prices** reduced Gambians' standard of living. Workers, on average, earned less than $ 50 a month. Tourism and private **remittances**, however, continued to be a major source of foreign exchange. Private remittances grew to approximately $ 75 m – considerably higher than the combined annual economic assistance from donors and the inflow of foreign direct investment. The relative stability of the dalasi against major international currencies was attributed to an imposed exchange rate, tight controls over exchange bureaus and the almost complete elimination of 'behind the market' unofficial foreign exchange dealers. Yet, according to government data, the dalasi depreciated marginally against the euro, pound sterling, Swiss franc and the CFA franc by 3.8%, 4.2%, 2.1% and 5.9% respectively, but appreciated against the US dollar by 0.5%.

Despite these putative macroeconomic improvements President Jammeh's neo-liberal economic strategy, called 'Vision 2020', remained ambitious and poorly implemented. Instead of improving living standards, it continued to jeopardise short-term economic recovery and future economic prospects.

Abdoulaye Saine

Ghana

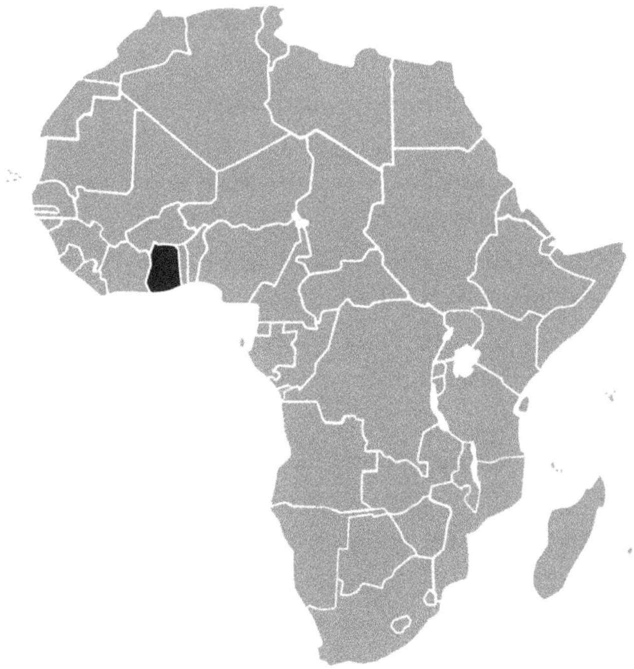

There were encouraging signs that economic growth was gathering momentum. The International Development Association of the World Bank was among those that saw Ghana as the emerging success story in Africa, stating that the country was on track to achieve middle-income status by 2015. The government actively continued to offer inducements to the private sector and solicited additional aid from East Asia, specifically China, for telecommunications and infrastructural development. On the political front, all eyes were fixed on the campaign for leadership of the two leading parties, the New Patriotic Party (NPP) and the National Democratic Congress (NDC), as the 2008 elections loomed. The main parties traded accusations about their respective records of involvement in corruption and drug trafficking, while the smaller parties struggled to set an agenda of their own.

Domestic Politics

There were five issues that dominated politics over the course of the year. The most hotly debated in the early months was the passage of the Representation of the People (Amendment) Act or ROPAA. The government maintained that Ghanaians in the **diaspora**, who contributed so much through remittances (allegedly 14.4% of GDP in 2005), should enjoy the right to vote with effect from 2008. The NDC was opposed, for the reason that the NPP had its greatest concentration of support in the Akan areas that accounted for the greater part of the Ghanaian community abroad. It therefore seemed as if the NPP was seeking to alter the rules of the game to its advantage. The minority leader in parliament, Alban Bagbin, avoided making this point on the floor of the house on 2 February, resorting instead to a catalogue of inconsistencies in the government case. He highlighted the difficulties the electoral commission would face in verifying who had the right to vote. However, his deputy's attempts to secure a legal writ restraining the Speaker from permitting further readings failed on 6 February. Three days later, the NDC started a **boycott of parliament**. The other opposition parties were divided. Within the People's National Convention (PNC), John Ndebugre supported ROPAA and was suspended from the vice-chairmanship of the party for doing so. On 14 February, the parties opposed to the legislation, united under the banner of Concerned Citizens, took to the streets of Accra to demonstrate in the first of a series of rolling protests. However, the government passed ROPAA on 23 February. Having lost this battle, the NDC returned to parliament on 2 March, hoping that it might still win the war.

The second salient issue was that of **corruption**, which had become a matter of concern during the previous year. The president reiterated his stance of 'zero tolerance' and on 27 July the Whistleblower Bill was finally passed, enabling individuals to disclose malpractices in the public interest. Nevertheless, the opposition and some newspapers alleged that graft was endemic at all levels of government. The annual Transparency International ratings placed Ghana 70th out of 163 countries in terms of perceptions of corruption. The country-specific index indicated that such perceptions had returned to where they had been in the last year of the NDC administration. To impartial observers, that sounded about right. The allegations that had been levelled in 2005 against Dr. Richard Anane, the roads transport minister, were investigated by the Commission on Human Rights and Administrative Justice (CHRAJ) through a series of public hearings. His former mistress, and mother of his illegitimate child, gave evidence in camera by satellite linkup. She claimed that she had been advised that it would be unsafe to come to Ghana to testify. She confirmed that she and Anane had conspired to use kickbacks to pay for the upkeep of their son, and that she had only decided to blow the whistle when Anane had stopped returning calls. To the consternation of many, Anane was not sacked in the April cabinet reshuffle. However, on 15 September, CHRAJ recommended his dismissal on grounds of conflict of interest, perjury and abuse of power, even though there was insufficient evidence to establish actual corruption. On 2 October, Anane reluctantly resigned. On 4 May, CHRAJ also issued its report on preliminary investigations into allegations of corruption and **conflict of interest** made against President Kufuor. These related to the purchase of a hotel by his son. CHRAJ declared that there was no evidence to suggest that the president was a stakeholder, although many critics pointed out that the foreign woman who had implicated Kufuor had not been given a similar chance to testify.

Members of parliament have relatively few chances for enrichment, but on 28 March the Ghana Aids Commission claimed that 122 MPs who had received money for HIV/AIDS campaigns had failed to account for the money. On 23 March, it was announced that MPs would in future no longer have direct access to their share of the district assemblies' common funds for local development projects, but would have to pass through the district chief executives in order to **minimise abuses**. This coincided with a dispute in Abuakwa South constituency where the foreign minister, Nana Akuffo-Addo, reacted to claims that executives had misdirected money from the common fund by demanding an audit. An enquiry later exonerated the officials.

The chief justice was himself accused of abuse of office and an inquiry was instigated by the president on the basis of a specific allegation. But on 13 July, the supreme court ruled that the president's intervention had been unconstitutional. Meanwhile, the vendetta against the former NDC government continued. On 12 April, the former first lady, Nana Agyeman Rawlings, and a number of senior ex-officials were put before the Fast Track Court for causing financial loss to the state. This related to the divestiture of the Nsawam cannery. The NDC sought to turn the tables whenever it could. On 26 May, work began on the construction of a new presidential palace and questions were soon raised about monitoring of expenditure. At the same time, the ministry of defence became embroiled in a public row over the exchange of the presidential jet, which had been purchased by the previous NDC regime, in return for military aircraft.

The third issue, which dominated the second half of the year, was a series of **cocaine** seizures, indicating that Ghana had become a transit country for hard drugs. Even more worrying was the evidence that government officials were implicated. This unfolded against the backdrop of the trial of an NPP parliamentarian in the US for cocaine trafficking. Following the discovery that a haul of 2,300 tonnes of cocaine had mysteriously disappeared from a vessel that docked at Tema harbour and the disclosure of a taped discussion between a senior police officer and alleged traffickers over the whereabouts of the drugs, the Justice Georgina Wood inquiry was set up in July. There were many calls for the inspector-general of police, Patrick Akyeampong, to be dismissed and hard questions were asked about immigration procedures at the airport when it transpired that there were incomplete records of the movement of suspected traffickers. Meanwhile, five 'drug barons' were put on trial. Kufuor tried to deflect the blame on to the NDC, claiming that the **Venezuelan traffickers** had been brought to Ghana by a stalwart of the former government, Robert Mettle-Nunoo. On 8 September, his assets and those of a number of people whose names cropped up in the Wood inquiry were frozen by the serious fraud office. But bizarrely, the question at issue was whether they had paid their taxes. Even more controversially, someone from the Asantehene's palace was mentioned on the tape, leading the king to fulminate against tribally motivated attacks against the Ashantis. On 25 November, the relevant minister, Albert Kan-Dapaah, declared that the police inspector-general would not be sacked, while the legal case against the accused began to implode.

The fourth issue concerned the **burial** of the **Ya Na**, the king of Dagomba (who had been murdered by the rival Abudu faction in 2002) and the appointment of a successor. On 18 March, the Abudus promised to cooperate with the Andanis in ensuring that the Ya Na was properly buried, but with conditions attached, notably their refusal to accept the appointment of a regent. This provoked a vigorous riposte from the Andanis on 28 March, just as the Tamale Central by-election was starting to heat up. However, on 1 April a mediating committee of eminent kings, headed by the Asantehene, announced an accord that seemed to have satisfied both parties, thereby permitting the burial to go ahead nine days later. On 21 April, an Andani regent and acting Ya Na was peacefully installed, but on 25 August there was a clash between the two sides that led to fatalities in Yendi, suggesting that this dispute was not yet over.

Finally, this was a year in which Ghanaians woke up to the realisation that they would be electing someone to replace Kufuor in 2008. Covert **campaigning** for the succession within the NPP gathered pace. Some argued that the eastern region's turn was overdue. The names that were touted as possible candidates included that of Yaw Osafo-Maafo, whose movement from finance to the education and sports ministry after the 2004 elections was deemed fortuitous because of unfolding good-news stories. The other key name was that of Akuffo-Addo. On 15 March, the 'Statesman' newspaper (founded by the latter) noted that the failure to fix a date for the leadership contest was creating unnecessary uncertainty. Among the non-easterners, the president's own brother, Kwame Addo-Kufuor, recurred in press reports about undercover campaigning. However, this was doubly problematic for the NPP because it would involve both an Ashanti and a **dynastic succession** that was bound to be unpopular in the country at large. As the only northerner in the race, Vice-President Aliu Mahama used the facilities that his office afforded him to maximum effect.

The president allegedly had to warn his cabinet colleagues on more than one occasion of the fact that they all had jobs to perform. On 28 April, Kufuor embarked on a major **cabinet reshuffle**, justified in terms of 'downsizing'. Several prominent ministers were dropped, among them Osafo-Maafo. Kofi Apraku's ministry of regional co-peration and NEPAD was subsumed under Akuffo-Addo's portfolio, with the result that Apraku, too, lost his job. By June, the lobbying of groups calling themselves 'Friends of Akuffo-Addo' and 'Friends of Kofi Konadu Apraku' was a clear indication that the leadership campaign had begun in earnest. On 25 July, Akuffo-Addo finally made his intentions explicit in the course of a canvassing tour in the Upper East, followed by Kwame Addo-Kufuor on 5 August. However, the choice of candidate was not expected to take place until well into 2007.

Following a rancorous NDC convention at Kororidua in December, at which Dr. Obed Asamoah was ousted as national chairman, the man who had effectively founded the party resigned on 5 January citing 'violence and hooliganism' by Rawlings supporters. A few days later, Asamoah announced the formation of a Democratic Freedom Party, which proceeded to win endorsements from some prominent ex-NDC stalwarts in the Volta region. Asamoah's exit left Jerry Rawlings firmly in control of the NDC, even if **ongoing resig-**

nations threatened to damage the party's future prospects. A prominent defection to the NPP came in early January when Wayo Seini, who had previously accused the government of complicity in the murder of the Ya Na, resigned his NDC parliamentary seat. He announced his intention to rejoin the NPP. However, his application could not be processed in time for the Tamale Central **by-election**, forcing him to contest it as an independent. The NPP decided not to put up a candidate, citing tensions in Dagomba, and gave a belated endorsement to Seini. However, the by-election was comfortably won by the NDC with 68% of the vote, making it three out of three wins since the 2004 polls.

On 24 October, the NPP comfortably retained the Offinso South seat (Ashanti) in a by-election, breaking its apparent jinx. However, the reality remained that the NDC was a force to be reckoned with and that lent added significance to the leadership question. Dr. Ekwow Spio-Garbrah, a former Rawlings minister, made the early running and was widely seen as the most serious challenger to John Atta-Mills. The only others to file nominations were Alhaji Mahama Iddrisu, also a former minister, and Eddie Annan, a businessman. On 21 December, the NDC party congress met to choose its candidate. On this occasion, Rawlings refrained from backing anyone explicitly. However, this did not prevent Mills from winning by a very large margin. The other candidates accepted defeat graciously and the party celebrated its **new-found unity**.

On 23 October, the cold war between Kufuor and Rawlings heated up again when the president accused his predecessor of soliciting funds from an oil-rich country to destabilise the government. The press took this to be a reference to the Venezuelan president, Hugo Chavez, whereas Rawlings thought it was a reference to the Middle East. On 26 September, the country went to the polls to elect unit committees and district assembly members. The candidates stood on individual non-party platforms as before, which made it an unhelpful guide as to the strength of the parties.

In February, alleged government plans to remove the preventive aspects from the Customs, Excise and Preventive Service (CEPS) and to reallocate them to the Ghana Immigration Service (GIS) caused ripples of open dissent in CEPS. On 15 February, the government denied that CEPS would lose any of its existing functions or undergo retrenchment. But when on 16 July, Minister of Interior Albert Kan Dapaah announced that a sum of Cedis 1.9 bn was being allocated to a border control programme – to deal with smuggling, human trafficking, passport fraud and cross-border crime – the task of implementation was allotted to the GIS. The latter would set up a border patrol unit that clearly encroached on CEPS terrain.

Finally, there was one issue on which Ghanaians were united and that was the pride that the national team, the 'Black Stars', instilled at the **World Cup finals** in Germany. A decisive defeat at the hands of Italy, the eventual winners, dampened hopes, but clear wins against the Czech Republic and the US put Ghana into the knockout stages. Although Ghana lost to Brazil on 27 June, team members were hailed as returning heroes and provided with national medals on 3 July.

Foreign Affairs

Ghana took up a **non-permanent seat** at the UN Security Council and in August it served as the rotating chair. This gave an enhanced profile to President Kufuor. On 1 May, Japanese Prime Minister Koizumi arrived on a state visit to drum up support for a permanent Japanese seat.

Kufuor has been criticised for the excessive number of foreign trips he has made and, if anything, these increased in 2006. The primary focus was East Asia, which the government regarded as the most likely source of concessionary aid. On 19 June, Chinese Prime Minister Wen Jiabao arrived in Ghana on a two-day visit. In return for various trade and aid deals, the government issued a communiqué stating Ghana's support for a united **China**. A Chinese business delegation followed in short order, promising to make Ghana the conduit for Chinese cars to the sub-region. On 2 November, Kufuor arrived in Beijing for the third Sino-African summit. On arrival, he repeated his wish that the Chinese assist with the construction of the Bui dam, rural electrification and telecommunications. Wen Jiabao promised that China would buy more processed goods from Ghana. But the reality was that by 2006, China was the second largest exporter to the country. Chinese companies were also awarded a number of high-profile contracts. Construction of the Sekondi sports stadium, to be completed in time for the 2008 African Nations Cup, ran into controversy when the 'Ghanaian Chronicle' alleged on 8 February that Chinese convict workers were used while local youth were ignored.

While courting China, the government also sought to make the most of its favourable image in Washington. President Bush invited Kufuor to visit in early April. Their joint press appearance emphasised Ghana's reward for good governance in the form of disbursements under the **Millennium Challenge Account**. A grant of $ 547 m was approved for a five-year programme targeted at poverty eradication and development interventions in the rural sector. The social projects were expected to cover water, sanitation and electricity ($ 100 m), while the agricultural development component ($ 240 m) would assist farmers with access to credit and promote land reform. A further $ 143 m would be channelled into infrastructural improvements. However, the list of regions that were expected to benefit excluded Upper East and Upper West, which were manifestly the poorest of all. Rather implausibly, the president claimed that 2 m new jobs would be created.

At the start of June, the president embarked on a foreign tour that took in the US, the UK, Nigeria and a visit to the football World Cup finals in Germany. The fact that his absence coincided with a strike by doctors, health workers and teachers provoked some adverse comment. On 4 July, having just returned from an AU summit in Banjul, he left for a state visit to Brazil with a stop-off in Britain. This was reckoned to be his 31st foreign visit in 18 months, provoking renewed press complaints about the expense of such **presidential globetrotting**. More was to come. In July, Kufuor travelled to Liberia for the independence celebrations before flying back to Washington for the signing of the Millennium Challenge

Account agreement on the 28th. On 12 September, he flew to Cuba to attend a summit of the Non-Aligned Movement and on 15 October he left again for Italy. He then rounded up the year with a state visit to Mali.

The African dimension of Ghana's diplomacy concentrated mostly on cementing peace in neighbouring **Côte d'Ivoire**. On 5 July, Nana Akuffo-Addo attended a meeting in Yamoussoukro chaired by Kofi Annan and attended by a number of heads of state. Ghana also sought to bolster the fledgling Liberian government. Whereas the Togo front was quiet, relations with Burkina Faso improved greatly. On 11 March, the Ghana-Burkina Faso permanent commission for cooperation met in Ougadougou to advance cooperation on a number of fronts, including border demarcation, which AU states are supposed to have completed by 2012. Akuffo-Addo conceded that progress on closer cooperation had been slow, but claimed that the Kufuor years had brought renewed urgency. On 2 April, a meeting between the Upper East administration and its Burkinabè counterpart ensued at which it was agreed that the number of checkpoints should be decreased to facilitate freedom of movement. In June, the newly elected Benin president, Yayi Boni, visited the country. Here again, the presidents agreed on the need to reduce customs and immigration restrictions and the importance of binding together Ghana, Togo, Benin and Nigeria, which would soon be linked by a new gas pipeline and an improved coastal road. On 28 September, Ghana joined the **Francophonie** group of countries, to the surprise of many.

Socioeconomic Developments

The current population of Ghana was estimated at 19 m, with an average growth rate of 3%. With Greater Accra growing at 4.4% and the poorer northern regions coming in at significantly below the national average, the pace of **urbanisation** was very apparent. The phenomenon of street children was regarded as a growing problem in Accra and Kumasi. The trafficking of children, within and across borders, also received growing publicity.

The Growth and Poverty Reduction Strategy II Report (GPRS II, 2006–09) was debated in parliament in March, with a number of MPs claiming that cost recovery was contributing to impoverishment in rural areas. However, on 4 September the IMF claimed that Ghana was making such strides that it might halve **poverty** by 2012, three years ahead of the deadline set under the Millennium Development Goals. However, the HDI, released on 10 November, placed the achievements in context. The report ranked Ghana 136th in the world out of 177 countries. It estimated life expectancy at birth at 57 years and the adult literacy rate at 57.9%. Those without access to improved water stood at 25%.

On 19 January, the deputy minister for **health**, Samuel Owusu-Agyei admitted that the projected coverage of 50% for the national health insurance scheme had not been met in 2005. The actual figure was 30%, but he said he expected the figure to rise to 55% in 2007. The brain drain remained a problem, with almost as many Ghanaian doctors residing in the

US as were working in Ghana. Whereas WHO recommended one doctor per 5,000 people, the figure in Ghana was one per 11,000.

Under the education sector plan (2003–15), the government remained committed to free universal primary **education** by 2015 and made a start by abolishing a range of school charges. Although education through the first nine years is supposed to be compulsory, the figures for 2005 suggested the enrolment was 87.5% at the primary level (90.5% boys and 84.4% girls), falling to 72.8% for junior secondary school (77.3% boys and 68.1% girls).

In August, the question of whether **homosexuality** should be legalised came to the fore when the president of the gay and lesbian association of Ghana took to the airwaves to present its case. Minister of Information and National Orientation Kwamena Bartels insisted that there would be no change to the law.

The government received praise for its handling of the economy, but questions were raised about whether the regime was really committed to its 'Golden Age of Business'. The state actually reasserted its control over the two fixed telephone companies (Ghana Telecom and Westel). However, the real expansion was in mobile phone uptake, with 2.6 m subscribers, of whom 60% belonged to the Areeba network. On 7 August, the minister of communications, Mike Oquaye, announced that the government intended to dispose of the majority of the shares in Ghana Telecom once again. More symptomatic was the crisis in the **aviation industry**. Against the backdrop of the withdrawal of South African Airways to Dakar, a struggle for control of Ghana International Airlines (GIA) – the former national airline that is 70% state-owned – became symptomatic of government interference. On 7 April, the presidential chief of staff, Kwadwo Mpianim, acted on a decision to dismiss the GIA management by sending security personnel to lock out the chief executive. He, in turn, complained to the American embassy. The vice-president of GIA, Sammy Crabbe, who happened to be the Greater Accra regional chairman of the NPP, mobilised his own party associates to defend the GIA offices. This was all deeply embarrassing, not least because it happened as Kufuor was in Washington at the invitation of President Bush. The Centre for Democratic Development (an independent think-tank) criticised the lack of transparency surrounding the creation of GIA as well as the manner in which positions had been filled. In October, the American partner company took the Ghana government to the international court of arbitration in the Hague.

Again, the government's commitment to free markets wavered in relation to the **textile industry**, where cheap Chinese imports wreaked havoc. The government's ruling that all textile imports should pass through Takoradi port brought the phenomenon of overland smuggling through Togo into sharp relief. Kufuor committed the regime to the reopening of Juapong Textiles, which had closed in 2005 due to financial losses. Indeed, more money from the Presidential Special Initiative was channelled into the garments sector, in the belief that Ghana could export to Europe and North America.

The government did seek to allow market forces to determine the domestic price for **petroleum**. Prices increased by 32.6% over the first seven months of the year, providing the Committee for Joint Action, a united front of opposition politicians, with the chance to widen the scope of its public protests. But the government insisted that it had no option but to pass on rising prices on the global market. However, after a rise in July, it announced the abolition of the 15% ad valorem tax on petroleum in order to bring pump prices back down a bit. This was not as profound as it sounded because the government found other ways of taxing petroleum. However, lower global prices made it possible to reduce the pump price on 25 September.

On 27 March, Dr. Paul Acquah, governor of the Bank of Ghana, predicted that the rate of **inflation** would fall to single-digit levels by December, despite higher fuel prices. The statistical service reported that this had indeed been achieved in the month of March, but a 20% public sector wage increase alongside a swingeing petrol price hike at the start of May, and again on 20 July, had an inevitable inflationary effect.

On 13 July, Minister of Finance Kwadwo Baah-Wiredu put a supplementary budget before parliament. This amounted to requesting areas of additional expenditure to cover aspects of GPRS II. The minister promised further improvements in **revenue collection**. He explained that a higher budget deficit in the first four months of the year was no cause for alarm because the spending year now began from January.

On 15 November, in advance of the 2007 budget reading, the Ghana statistical service declared that the **GDP growth** rate for the current year was estimated at 6.2%. When Baah-Wiredu introduced the budget the next day, he cited this figure as vindication for the claim that the economy was robust. His figure for industrial growth was 7.3%, but agriculture grew at 5.9%, below the target of 6.6%. The minister also stated that inflation stood at 10.5% at the end of October. Baah-Wiredu was explicit about the search for new sources of development assistance. He said that $ 482 m had been raised by the end of September, of which 65% came from multilateral institutions. The minister noted that the total public debt had declined from $ 8.4 bn in 2005 to $ 4.8 bn in September 2006, largely due to **debt cancellations**. The projections for 2007 included a 6.5% GDP growth rate and single digit inflation. Baah-Wiredu also claimed that Ghana would no longer require IMF loans but would enter the international capital market. The NDC claimed that the figures did not add up. Most sectors had registered growth rates below the projected targets. Baah-Wiredu had attributed the countervailing gains to rapid expansion in the water and electricity sub-sectors, but low water levels in the Volta lake had necessitated a spell of power-cuts and water shortages. Although the NDC questioning of the figures sounded plausible, international financial institutions vindicated government claims about a vibrant economy that was starting to make a dent on unemployment and poverty. Hence, the poverty headcount index was estimated by the IDA to have fallen from 42% in 2001 to 32% in 2005.

Paul Nugent

Guinea

The year 2006 was a tumultuous one, with signs that autocratic leader Lansana Conté might be losing his grip on power. Two general strikes organised by labour unions showed new life in civil society circles, forcing the government to make a series of socioeconomic concessions. The president's health continued to be a topic of debate and interest, especially when he was twice medically evacuated to Switzerland. An April government reshuffle first saw reformist Prime Minister Cellou Diallo's hand strengthened. However, within 24 hours he had been sacked, and all-powerful Minister for Presidential Affairs Fodé Bangoura appeared to be the second most powerful figure in the new premier-less government. The economic situation remained dire for most Guineans, and provision of water and electricity was the exception rather than the rule. Despite this, when he visited in November, EC Commissioner for Development and Humanitarian Aid Louis Michel said he was "very favourably impressed" by government reforms.

Domestic Politics

In January, the ruling 'Parti de l'Unité et du Progrès' (PUP) welcomed the results of the December 2005 elections, which had given it control of most regions of the country, including all of Conakry's municipalities. However, the risks of governing Guinea's increasingly unruly and dissatisfied population soon became apparent, as youths rioted on numerous occasions to protest power cuts during the televised matches of the African Nations Cup, in which Guinea continued to the quarter-final round before being eliminated.

In February, the country's two most powerful trade unions, the 'Confédération Nationale des Travailleurs de Guinée' (CNTG), and 'l'Union Syndicale des Travailleurs de Guinée' (USTG), called for a **general strike** after months of negotiations with the government yielded no results. Guineans overwhelmingly observed the general strike for five days, shutting Conakry down entirely. The organisers of the strike were keen to emphasise the non-political nature of their movement and unilaterally called the strike off, stating that they wanted to avoid the possibility of violence between the population and the security forces.

Immediately after the strike ended, President **Conté was evacuated** to Geneva for medical treatment for what was described as a combination of leukaemia, diabetes and high blood pressure. Conté, who had previously refused to receive medical treatment in the West (allegedly fearing the same end as his predecessor, Sékou Touré, who died in an American heart clinic), spent one week being treated. The combination of the new-found unanimity of the population, demonstrated by the general strike, and the evident frailty of the president opened the floodgates of debate, criticism and discussion of a post-Conté dispensation.

On 5 April, the national radio broadcast news of a cabinet reshuffle that appeared to settle the **stand-off** between the reformist Prime Minister Cellou Dalein Diallo and the powerful Minister for Presidential Affairs Fodé Bangoura in favour of the prime minister. Diallo, an ethnic Fulbe and long-time member of Conté's government, had been appointed in December 2004 and for over a year had struggled with the several ethnic Soso-dominated **cliques** around Conté who resisted any reforms that might diminish their influence. The 5 April government appeared to have given him the opportunity, finally, to name his own government over the objections of Conté's inner circles, in which Bangoura played a key role. But during the second broadcast of the ministerial changes, members of the presidential guard broke into the studio and stopped the broadcast. By the next day, Guineans learned that not only had the set of changes been annulled, but Diallo had been sacked.

This melodramatic reversal gave credence to rumours that had long circulated to the effect that Conté was no longer exercising any effective oversight over affairs of state, despite the fact that he was unwilling to delegate those responsibilities to anyone else. The April reversal was also consonant with accounts suggesting that Conté acted on the basis of the latest advice whispered in his ear, with little interest as to whether it was consistent with existing policy. This dynamic of **court intrigue** also gave inordinate power to Bangoura, who effectively acted as the gatekeeper to the president. The two most senior of Conté's four wives also entered the fray, with first wife Henriette seemingly losing favour in relation to second wife Kadiatou Seth, who lobbied on behalf of her brother-in-law Ibrahima Keira.

Although the shift marked a victory for Bangoura over the forces of reform, it probably marked the end of whatever limited legitimacy the government retained in the eyes of its citizens. From April onward, Guineans no longer seemed constrained by the kinds of reserve and cautiousness they had learned under the repressive socialist regime of Sékou Touré and that they had carried over into the Conté period. In a 30 May **cabinet reshuffle**, Conté fell back upon a variety of figures from former governments, many of them described as "dinosaurs" in the Guinean press. Foreign Minister Fatoumata Kaba Sidibé was replaced by former Foreign Minister Mamady Condé. Powerful Interior Minister Kiridi Bangoura was demoted and replaced by former Interior Minister Moussa Solano, while Ibrahima Keira was promoted to minister of transport.

Noting the simultaneous weakness and hardening of the position of the Conté government, the CNTG-USTG unions called for a **second general strike** of unlimited duration to begin on 8 June. This strike, also called because none of the promises made in the wake of the February–March strike had been respected, coincided with the exams for passage from primary to secondary school, and from secondary school to university. Students, enraged at their inability to take these exams, on 12 June flooded the streets of Conakry and provincial capitals of Labe and N'Zérékoré, where they clashed with security forces, who killed at least 11. The strike ended on 17 June.

Over the following months, the political situation stabilised, but the economic woes of the population only increased. Petrol, which had cost FG (Guinean francs) 1,500 as recently as August 2004, jumped from FG 5,000 to 5,500 on 11 May 2006. This meant that even government employees found themselves in a position where their salaries barely covered the cost of transport to and from work for a month. The level of suffering of average Guineans had become an acutely political issue, as evidenced by the two general strikes. In an apparent response to mounting resentments, President Conté revoked ministerial 4×4 vehicles to replace them with Toyota Corollas in September. Conté quietly made a **second medical visit** to Switzerland in mid-August. Whereas his return in March was greeted by an organised (some said forced) manifestation of support, this time he returned in the middle of the night, without even television coverage of his arrival.

By October, the political scene heated up again, particularly over the issue of a sum as much as $ 21 m taken from the Guinean central bank and given to close Conté associate Mamadou Sylla. The then vice governor of the central bank, Fodé Soumah, was accused in 2002–03 of having overseen the transfer and was removed from his position, only to be made minister of youth and sports. Investigating judge, Mamady Diawara, indicted Sylla in October, after the case had been long-dormant. This was seen by many as a symptom of the growing **rivalry** between Sylla and Fodé Bangoura for pre-eminent position in relation to the president. In the context of Sylla's indictment and the probability that the co-accused Soumah would follow, there was yet another small cabinet reshuffle in October, replacing Soumah at the ministry of youth and sports with former Interior Minister Kiridi Bangoura.

October also saw a large but **peaceful demonstration** in the capital of the forest region, N'Zérékoré. Suffering severely from the rise in prices, which because of the high cost of transport meant even greater increases for the inhabitants of N'Zérékoré, people also criticised the government for not having repaired a collapsed bridge that had turned the two-day trip from the capital into a five-to-seven day trip. As a result, petrol cost three times its price in Conakry (FG 17,000 versus 5,500 per litre), and rice twice as much (FG 200,000 versus 85,000 to 120,000 per 50 kg sack). The thousands of marchers demanded a response to their complaints within 72 hours, or threatened that they would block all roads going in and out of N'Zérékoré, an important crossroads town. A ministerial delegation promised to repair the bridge and the road leading to the forest region, starting immediately.

In November, investigating Judge Diawara ordered the arrest of both Soumah and Sylla in the central bank affair. When informed of his friends' arrests on 16 December, Conté went to the central prison in person and ordered the guards to release both men. Even in a country where the **separation of powers** was widely understood to be a working fiction, Conté's act stirred up virulent criticism. Decrying the president's contempt for the Guinean constitution, on 9 December the labour unions announced a new general strike for the second week of January.

The end of the year saw progress on the political front, with **draft laws** prepared to create an independent electoral commission (as opposed to the 'autonomous' commission that was overseen by the ministry of interior), public funding for all political parties, and changes to the electoral code and the legal status of political parties. In another small change in the government, powerful telecommunications Minister Jean-Claude Sultan lost his job at the end of the year.

Foreign Affairs

Aside from his medical evacuations, President Conté had not ventured outside Guinea for several years. In the first part of the year, the government was represented abroad by Prime Minister Cellou Diallo, who attended the January inauguration of President Ellen Johnson-Sirleaf of Liberia along with over a dozen African heads of state, US first lady Laura Bush and others. After Diallo's April departure, Guinea was represented abroad by its foreign ministers – Fatoumata Kaba Sidibé until May and Mamady Condé thereafter.

Guinea maintained cordial relations with Liberia, where President Conté had backed Johnson-Sirleaf on the advice of Aisha Keita, patron of the LURD rebel group (Liberians United for Reconciliation and Democracy). Its relations with Sierra Leone, though based on the personal friendship between Conté and President Ahmad Kabba, were tenser, because of continuing incursions by Guinean soldiers into Sierra Leonean territory. Relations also remained strong with Guinea-Bissau, where long-time Conté associate Nino Viera was president. On 14–15 December, President Ellen Johnson Sirleaf of Liberia and Ahmad Kabba of Sierra Leone travelled to Conakry to discuss peace and security in the **Mano river region**.

The peace that had come to Sierra Leone and Liberia, and the ceasefire and military impasse in Côte d'Ivoire, meant that many former fighters from across the region were now out of work (as roving warriors, at least). With relative stability prevailing in Sierra Leone (strengthened by the British 'over the horizon' promise to intervene in the case of armed conflict) and imposed by 15,000 peacekeepers in Liberia, Guinea's forest region remained one of the most attractive zones for **ex-combatants** to circulate in relative freedom.

As a result of the same regional peace, **refugees** continued to return home. On 6 September, the UN high commissioner for refugees closed its Kissidougou office, having repatriated 16,000 of the remaining 18,000 Liberian refugees from the camps in that area. The remaining 2,000 moved to the camps around N'Zérékoré, reducing the overall number of refugees in Guinea to 33,000.

Guinea's relations with countries beyond Africa were shaped by three factors: the scramble for Guinea's **mineral wealth**, China's continuing diplomatic/aid offensive, and European alarm over West African emigration, particularly by boat to the Canary Islands. The growing interest in Guinea's bauxite and iron ore seemed ironic in the face of profound political instability, but rapidly growing Chinese demand for these metals made the prize worth greater risks. Interest had grown to such an extent that a symposium on the Guinean mining sector was held in Düsseldorf in October.

South Africa also stepped up its diplomatic overtures, most likely with a dual view to increase its stature as a continental political and diplomatic actor, and to help ease the way for South African mining interests in the country. In July, President Thabo Mbeki made his second visit in a year, and Foreign Minister Zuma visited Guinea twice in 2006. The two countries agreed to drop the requirement for visas in the case of those holding diplomatic passports, and in December Guinean and South African officials discussed the possibility of starting a jointly owned airline.

China also stepped up its engagement with Guinea from what was already a significant level. In August, Guinean Foreign Minister Condé travelled to Beijing where he met Chinese Foreign Minister Li Zhao Xing. In September, China annulled the equivalent of $ 45 m of Guinean debt, erasing a further $ 25 m equivalent in November. In December, China pledged $ 9 m for Guinea's communications sector, shortly after the national radio and television stations moved into the Chinese-built and furnished studios at Koloma, a Conakry suburb. Also in December, the chief executive of the Chinese aluminium company CHALCO, visited Guinea, where the company has obtained 21 bauxite exploration concessions. China's Exim Bank agreed to invest the equivalent of $ 1 bn so that Chinese company Sinohydro could build a hydroelectric dam in the region of Telimélé. China also signed an agreement with the Guinean government to build a 50,000-seat stadium in the capital, and proposed building a new central hospital. There were also reports of China sending a boatload of rice to Guinea to help President Conté contain political unrest in October.

Much of this activity appeared to leave the US, a traditional Guinean ally, far behind. However, the **EU** worked hard to bring itself back into view. Just before Louis Michel's November visit, the EU announced that it would give € 25 m for repairing roads in the isolated forest region. After his visit, the EU released money that had been blocked for three years, totalling € 118 m. Among European countries, France worked hard to improve its relations with the Guinean government, and Spain made special efforts to promote development in Guinea as part of its offensive to diminish the number of West Africans attempting to reach the Canary Islands by boat. In addition to offering € 25 m to the Guinean government in development aid, Spain announced that it would open an embassy in Conakry in 2007.

Socioeconomic Developments

Despite Michel's positive November assessment, Aboubacar Somparé, president of the Guinean National Assembly stated in September that during the period 2002–06, the economic situation in Guinea had degraded considerably and that most Guineans had been plunged into distressing poverty as a result. Paradoxically, this slide took place while Guinea experienced another year of strong **macroeconomic growth** – 5% in real GDP, according to the IMF. Despite this, few Guineans saw any benefit. Only 19% of Guineans have access to electricity and Conakry residents had electricity and running water only about 20% of the time. Regional capital N'Zérékoré, which had once enjoyed electricity during evening hours, lived through its sixth straight year without any electricity because of a broken generator. Although most of West Africa's major rivers begin in Guinea, piped water was difficult to find. Families of patients in Conakry's main Donka hospital had to bring buckets of water for their relatives to drink, bathe in and have their bandages cleaned and changed.

Telecommunications have also posed an acute problem. The three existing companies – Sotelgui, Intercel and Spacetel – could not provide reliable service to their customers, at least in part because of oversubscription of limited infrastructure. Competition for a fourth GSM license was fierce and became a flashpoint in 2005 between then Prime Minister Diallo and Minister of Telecommunications Sultan. In 2006, the field opened considerably, with Senegalese Sonatel entering the fray as well as Celcom, an American company owned by Yoram Cohen, chief executive officer of Liberia's lucrative shipping registry. Still, by the end of the year domestic networks were poor and international calls extremely difficult to make.

As inflation rose, the value of the Guinean franc fell. The currency, which traded at FG 2,600 to $ 1 in June 2004, began 2006 at FG 4,335 to $ 1 and fell steadily to FG 5,662 to $ 1 at the end of December – a slide of almost one-third in its value. The IMF measured a 27% rise in consumer prices. Combined with the rising world cost of petrol, this led to catastrophic price rises in many areas: petrol rose from FG 4,400 to 5,500 per litre, imported

Asian rice hovered around FG 120,000 per 50 kg sack in the capital, while Guinean rice cost FG 150,000 for the same amount. Meat and smoked fish cost about FG 11,000 per kg. Given that most salaried workers earned between FG 150,000 and 250,000 a month, it was possible to see why many Guineans said that wealthier families often ate only one meal each day while those less lucky could go as many as three days without a meal. While those based in villages could escape the worst effects of **inflation**, fewer and fewer Guineans lived on the margins of the cash economy, and even subsistence farmers were affected when decisions involved, for instance, the cost of transporting family members with life-threatening illnesses to hospital.

There was reason to worry that the pillage of state revenues worsened the state of **education and health care**. During periods of poor or non-governance, such as 2004 (where eight months of the year passed without a prime minister to coordinate government activities), education spending as a percentage of GDP fell to 1.5% and health to 1.7%. These figures improved in 2005 under the leadership of Prime Minister Diallo, rising to 2% of GDP for education and 3.8% for health. Still, these figures fell far short of the sub-Saharan African average of 3% of GDP spent on education and Guinea's stated goal of spending 10% of GDP on health. Worrying trends included a rising student-to-teacher ratio (45 to 1, according to the most recent figures) and the fact that only 20% of non-salary expenditures in the health sector actually reached the health centres meant to receive them. After giving grants of $ 19 m for the electricity sector and the environment in November, the World Bank sent a joint mission with the IMF to explore the possibility of restarting a formal programme with Guinea, which had been dissociated from the IMF HIPC programme (as well as the Paris Club and the ADB) since 2003.

In this context, it was difficult to know whether the interest of **oil companies** and mining giants would contribute to reinstating the health of the Guinean economy or produce little wealth that would benefit the average Guinean. In August, American oil company Hyperdynamics made public its exploration rights to Guinea's entire offshore shelf – a highly unusual exclusive agreement. The company's president, Kent Watts, visited in the company of Herman Cohen, the former US assistant secretary of state for Africa and lobbyist. In November, the company announced that it planned to begin drilling in "the very near future".

Australian mining company BHP Billiton decided to enter Guinea's **alumina refining** fray. BHP Billiton, which already held rights to exploit the iron reserves in Nimba mountain at the border with Côte d'Ivoire and Liberia, now agreed to build a refining plant near Boffa. Also involved in the competition for Guinea's bauxite (one of the world's two biggest reserves, along with Australia's) were Russia's RUSSAL, Chinese CHALCO and US-based Global Alumina. Canadian ALCAN partnered with American ALCOA to propose an alumina refinery at Kamsar, present site of the longstanding Canadian-American-Guinean consortium CBG.

In a major potential shift, the World Bank and ADB met to consider funding a Trans-Guinean **railway** stretching from Guinea's forest region to the coast. This had been a non-negotiable demand of the Guinean government for decades, while mining companies wanted to ship ore out via the Liberian port of Buchanan, far closer to the mining sites. If the project does receive outside funding, Rio Tinto, Euro Nimba (largely BHP Billiton, with a small portion belonging to Mittal Steel) and newcomer Beny Steinmetz Global Resources group could start mining within six years.

The mining sector accounted for approximately 25% of the government's public revenues. The extractive industries **transparency** initiative committee, made up of 24 members from the Guinean government, the mining companies doing business in Guinea and civil society, issued its first report in 2006. It stated that mining companies had paid the equivalent of $ 123 m to the government in 2005. This cross-tabulation of what mining companies said they had paid to the government and what the government said it had received was one step in addressing the crisis of confidence in a country ranked last in Africa (and tied for second-to-last worldwide) in Transparency International's Corruption Perceptions Index.

Mike McGovern

Guinea-Bissau

Political tension and social turmoil remained the most prominent features of Guinea-Bissau, and determined the slow progress of political and personal reconciliation in the wake of the 2005 presidential elections. Governance problems and disputes over parliamentary legitimacy marked the political agenda, while the lack of funds hampered state institutions in their ability to discharge their administrative and security functions and to provide services. The need to contain expenditure on the oversized army and restore political control over the armed forces necessitated urgent reform of the security forces. Economic difficulties persisted: problems in the production and export of cashews along with an appalling rice harvest caused incomes to decline, especially in the south. The restoration of donor funds depended on political stability. Nevertheless, donors saw some progress and pledged significant contributions to help the government in carrying out its duties and proceeding with reform.

Domestic Politics

The election of João Bernardo **'Nino' Vieira as president** of Guinea-Bissau in late 2005 marked the end of the transitional period, during which the civilian and much respected businessman Henrique Rosa had held office as interim president following a military uprising in September 2003. After the 1998–99 civil war and six years of political unrest, Rosa's mission was to re-establish state institutions on a regularly functioning footing and reinstate democratic rule by organising parliamentary and presidential elections that could restore confidence in public institutions in this western African country, ranked sixth poorest in the world.

In his end of year speech, President 'Nino' Vieira expressed the hope that 2006 would be the year of **unity and reconciliation** for all Bissau-Guineans, and stated it was time to heal the wounds from the troubled electoral campaign of June 2005. Vieira, who declared unilateral independence from the Portuguese colonial power in 1973 as leader of PAIGC ('Partido Africano para a Independência da Guiné-Bissau e Cabo Verde'), had ruled the country as an autocrat until 1999, when a coup forced him into exile. Now Vieira was back in the presidential office, but this time following elections declared free and transparent by the international community. One of the major challenges facing the new president was the restoration of political and social stability in the country.

Appeasement of the military elite and bringing the military back under political control was identified as one of the major factors that had contributed to his election. Also known as 'the General', Vieira had the charisma of the liberator who had fought for independence and he had been, in fact, the commander in chief from that time up to his exile in 1999. The **reform** of the **armed forces** and the painful but unavoidable reduction of the burden of former combatants' wages and privileges, which weighed heavily on the state budget, were therefore a major challenge for Vieira, since the last two military uprisings had mainly arisen from the frustration of the military elite over unpaid salaries. The negative impact of ethnicity on the armed forces also gave rise to a need for reform and it was necessary to include in the reconciliation process (and the reform process) the former combatants in the ranks of the colonial power, Portugal. The UK provided a security sector development advisory team, which studied the situation and made recommendations that were welcomed by the government. A national security sector reform strategy document was approved by the council of ministers on 30 October. This document called for an expenditure of $ 184 m and envisaged a reduction of the military from 9,650 to 3,440 members.

On 28 November 2005, in one of his first acts as president, Vieira replaced the democratically elected prime minister, Carlos Gomes Júnior, the leader of the ruling PAIGC since the 2004 parliamentary elections, with Aristides Gomes, a former PAIGC member excluded from the party for supporting 'Nino' Vieira's presidential campaign. Since Aristides Gomes was no longer a member of the party in power, his appointment as prime minister was unsuccessfully rejected by the PAIGC. On 19 December 2005, the supreme court was called to intervene but upheld the president's claims and kept Aristides Gomes in office. At this point, the political **balance in parliament** tilted towards the coalition that had sustained Vieira's candidature, the 'Fórum de Convergência para o Desenvolvimento', a platform that included not only the second and the third most popular political parties, the Partido da Renovação Social (PRS) and Partido Unido Social Democrata (PUSD), but also dissidents from the PAIGC. This shift in the balance of power, distorted by the defections from PAIGC's and PUSD's ranks, triggered a period of instability that put the realisation of national reconciliation on hold, crippled the regular functioning of parliament and hampered the capacity of the government to push for economic and structural reform to meet international donors' conditions.

Nevertheless, there was some evidence of political and democratic maturity, with political stability being considered as a national priority to be placed above party disputes, if only for the restoration of donor confidence. Therefore, on 16 March the government pushed for approval by the National Assembly of the government workplan for 2006. In its fourth session, held between 26 June and 26 July, the assembly approved the **state budget** for 2006.

The stability of the alliance supporting the government was threatened by the return to the country of **Kumba Yala**, former and historical leader of the PRS, who had held office as president after the 2000 elections and ruled the country until being deposed in the military coup of 2003. Kumba Yala had left the country and abandoned the PRS leadership after losing the first round of the 2005 elections and giving his support to Vieira in the run-off against PAIGC's Malan Bacai Sanhá. Returning from his exile in Morocco on 28 October, Kumba Yala regained the PRS leadership with 70% of the votes at a party congress. Then he threatened to withdraw his support from the government and demanded dissolution of the executive and new elections. However, the PAIGC, Carlos Gomes Júnior and Malan Bacai Sanhá did not support Yala's actions and used the opportunity to press for the formation of a government of national unity in which the PAIGC would be represented. However, no such government materialised.

Foreign Affairs

The holding in Bissau of the sixth **summit** of the CPLP on 17 July was a major landmark and a triumph for Bissau-Guinean diplomacy. Donors provided funds for the accommodation of dignitaries and Bissau got a facelift. Roads and street lighting were repaired, along with public sanitation. Water and electricity ran without interruption, something many people had not experienced for several years. Despite the absence of Presidents Luis Inácio 'Lula' da Silva of Brazil, Xanana Gusmão of East Timor and Fradique de Menezes of São Tomé and Príncipe, the presence of José Sócrates and Aníbal Cavaco Silva, respectively the prime minister and president of Portugal, and of José Eduardo dos Santos, the Angolan president, provided a clear signal of confidence in the country's future and was a sign that CPLP partner countries and particularly Portugal were paying special attention to Guinea-Bissau. As the summit coincided with the tenth anniversary of the CPLP, member-states decided to align their strategies to attain the MDG pledge to eradicate poverty and hunger by 2015 and to fight illiteracy and HIV/AIDS.

Crucial to the country's near future was the **donor's roundtable** that was held in Geneva on 7 and 8 November, after several postponements. The international community had been very clear over the last few years that funds were conditional on the restoration of peace and stability and the resumption of regularly functioning democratic institutions. The new government appointed by Vieira prepared a 'Documento de Estratégia Nacional de Redução da Pobreza' (DENARP), the national PRSP endorsed by the World Bank and IMF, as the conceptual basis for the alignment and coordination of donor contributions. Along with the PRSP, the government made a huge effort to have the national budget approved by the end of July, despite its precarious power base in parliament. Donors welcomed the endorsement of the security sector reform strategy.

In Geneva, the prime minister pleaded for $ 538 m in donor funds to implement the PRSP, reform the security sector and restore administrative capacities. Far from meeting his expectations, however, the government managed to secure **financial pledges** for up to $ 262.5 m over the next five years for the implementation of development projects, and another $ 178.5 m for reform of the delicate security sector, once the government presented a 'good governance' programme. Despite assistance from donors and multilateral agencies, the budget deficit for 2006 was 28% of GNP and debt servicing alone reached 24%. At the previous donors' roundtable held in 2000, the government had requested $ 200 m worth of assistance, but this was never disbursed because of bad management.

At the end of March, based on performance assessments under the 2005 staff monitored programme, the IMF decided to include Guinea-Bissau in the emergency post-conflict assistance programme and renew its confidence in the country's leaders by continuing with the programme until December 2006. This enabled the government to come up with arguments to convince the EU to give some € 6 m in direct **budget support** and increase the financial contribution under the national indicative programme with Guinea-Bissau for the period 2002–07 by € 10.7 m. The EU will also finance a new bridge over the Cacheu river in the north of the country, estimated at € 31 m, a project that should be concluded in 2009. Moreover, the ADB opened an office in Bissau in late September to manage its $ 71 m package for the next eight years.

However, early in December a $ 15 m **World Bank package** directed at multi-sector rehabilitation of infrastructure was suspended due to a council of minister's order to acquire a 15 megawatt power generator through a negotiated contract, instead of following the procedures for international bidding. A high-level delegation from the World Bank was expected in Bissau in early 2007 to assess the situation and the future of the programme.

On 14 March, the army attacked **rebel bases** of the Senegalese separatist 'Mouvement des Forces Démocratiques de la Casamance' (MFDC) in the north of Guinea-Bissau. The attack resulted in heavy material damage to the civilian population. It also demonstrated the closer ties between Guinea-Bissau and Senegal, whose President Wade had supported Vieira's election as head of state in a bid to weaken the MFDC by cutting off external support. The international community appealed for an end to hostilities, which stopped a few weeks later when MFDC forces were dislodged. According to UN figures, some 10,000 internally displaced persons were affected. The planting of landmines negatively impacted economic activities, such as the cashew harvest in the areas of São Domingos and Suzana, thereby putting food security at risk.

Socioeconomic Developments

Against a background of simmering political instability and limited steps towards national reconciliation, Guinea-Bissau's economic and social problems continued. Thus, a 25% reduction in **rice production** as a result of drought and breaches in sea dykes represented another blow to food security. On 26 April, the government was forced to make an urgent appeal for international assistance for the affected communities in the south, the most important rice-producing area in the country. By the end of the year, the impact of the drought was lessening, owing to interventions by WFP and FAO with financial support by countries in the sub-region.

The price set by government for raw **cashew nuts**, a major export crop, was increased by 40%, but traders rejected the increase, thereby paralysing exports. In the wake of the rice crisis and facing a food scarcity, farmers had no choice but to settle for selling at half the price set by the government. According to the UN, by the end of the year only 60% of the crop had been exported.

On 22 November, confronted with a structural economic crisis and the simple lack of funds, the government faced social unrest from **civil servants**, **who protested** at the four-month arrears in their salaries. Teachers, too, were once more forced to take to the streets because salaries were not being paid.

The **fishing agreement** with the EU, granting fishing licences to European fishers, was extended until 2007 and delivered $ 8.5 m to the national budget. However, delays in the negotiations affected the arrival of these valuable revenues.

Rising oil prices made **oil exploration** cost-effective and led to offshore prospecting. It was hoped oil could provide much-needed revenue in the long run. Some observers alleged that the 2005 presidential election campaign had benefited from funds from foreign companies with an interest in this valuable resource.

Given the government's limited ability to patrol the country's borders, the United Nations Office on Drugs and Crime (UNODOC) warned against a rise in international organised crime and **drugs trafficking**. According to the UN, on 24 September 674 kgs of cocaine and stockpiles of weapons and communications equipment, with a street value of more than $ 25 m, were discovered. UNODOC put forward a strategic programme framework for Guinea-Bissau, which contained recommendations for action in this area. In December, Kofi Annan declared Guinea-Bissau a crossroads for drugs.

Nuno Vaz

Liberia

Liberia briefly became world news – for once, not on account of violence – when on 16 January it became the first country in Africa to have an elected female head of state. This was the result of the victory of Ellen Johnson-Sirleaf in presidential elections in November 2005. President Johnson-Sirleaf was formally inaugurated in the presence of a number of international authorities and representatives, including the American Secretary of State Condoleezza Rice and the US first lady, Laura Bush. Johnson-Sirleaf will serve a six-year term of office, and faces problems of staggering size.

Domestic Politics

The new president embarked on a series of initiatives with impressive speed and determination. Broadly speaking, her first weeks were dominated by the need to form a new government and to signal her wish to act against corruption, which had run amok under the National Transitional Government of Liberia (NTGL) that existed for two years after the collapse of the government of the warlord-turned-president Charles Taylor in 2003. Later in 2006, Johnson-Sirleaf was able to make some headway on a number of issues related to the economy, finance and infrastructure.

The first appointments to the new administration were announced on the day following the inauguration. The composition of President Johnson-Sirleaf's administration generally met with international satisfaction, although some Liberians remarked on the return of some old faces. At the end of the year, **the cabinet** had 21 members, of which five were from the president's own party, six from a variety of opposition parties and ten were independents. Five cabinet members were women, including at the key portfolio of finance (held by a former World Bank employee, Antoinette Sayeh). Taking into account deputy and assistant ministers, the proportion of women in the administration reached some 40%. Of the county superintendents – the key officials at provincial level, appointed by the head of state – five of 15 were women. While the high number of female officials attracted international support for the new government, Liberian analysts also noted the return of officials from families that had enjoyed a prominent role in national life prior to the coup of 12 April 1980 that is often regarded as the real start of the country's period of chaos and violence. For example, the new information minister, Johnny McClain, held precisely the same position on the eve of the 1980 coup. The same is true of John D. Woods, managing director of the forestry development authority, a key economic post. One of the deputy ministers at finance, Elfreda Stewart Tamba, is the daughter of Frank Stewart, the budget director who was executed in 1980. Also included in the cabinet were some of the president's own relatives, such as National Security Advisor Fomba Sirleaf (stepson) and Interior Minister Ambullai Johnson (cousin).

Outside the executive, other branches of government continued to contain large numbers of members of the **opposition**, including some who had played significant roles during the wars that wracked Liberia from the late 1980s to 2003. Significant examples included the former warlords or generals Prince Johnson and Adolphus Dolo, both of whom now sat in the senate, and Jewel Howard Taylor, former wife of ex-President Charles Taylor. It is notable that Senator Johnson ran his successful election campaign in 2005 largely on a platform of protecting the people of Nimba county against the Krahn of Grand Gedeh county, an indication that the bitterness of past decades had not disappeared. Another leading opponent of President Johnson Sirleaf was Edwin Snowe, former son-in-law of Charles Taylor. As speaker of the house of representatives, he held the third-ranked position in the state apparatus.

The new government's intention of taking action against **corruption** began almost immediately after 16 January, when among President Johnson-Sirleaf's first acts was the wholesale sacking of civil servants. The government identified more than 17,000 'ghost workers' or non-existent employees in its drive to clean up the state bureaucracy. By the end of the year, the government had moved to arrest some senior officials of former governments on charges of corruption. On 2 December, police arrested Lusinee Kamara and Tugbeh Doe (formerly minister and vice-minister of finance under the NTGL), former chairman of the ways, means and finance committee Tapple Doe, and Samuel Wlue, an ex-minister of commerce. These arrests followed an audit of the NTGL administration by officials of ECOWAS and the EU that had revealed the extent of corruption.

Meanwhile, other prominent former politicians were held outside the country. The most important of these was former President Charles Taylor, who was detained in Nigeria on 29 March while he was trying to escape from the country, where he had lived in exile since 2003. He was subsequently transferred to the custody of the special court for Sierra Leone, which had charged him in regard to crimes allegedly committed during the civil war in Sierra Leone that lasted from 1991 to 2002. For security reasons, Taylor was **flown to the Netherlands**, where he was expected to be tried by the court in 2007. On 30 March, the day following the arrest of the ex-president, his son 'Chuckie' Taylor (also known as Charles McArthur Emmanuel and as Roy Belfast Jr.) was arrested in the US and charged first with passport offences, and, later, under the terms of an anti-torture law. The offences related to a period when he headed the Liberian anti-terrorist unit. In the Netherlands, a former close associate of Charles Taylor, the Dutch businessman Guus Kouwenhoven, known in Monrovia as 'Mister Gus', was sentenced on 7 June to eight years of imprisonment for selling weapons to President Taylor's government in defiance of a UN embargo.

Wider questions connected with the country's violent past were entrusted to a **Truth and Reconciliation Commission** (TRC) that was established by law in June 2005, but which did not commence operations for some months. On 6 April, the UNDP signed an agreement to provide the TRC with $ 600,000 towards its operating costs. The TRC is mandated to investigate back to 1979 and has the power to recommend prosecutions. Its director is a lawyer and human rights activist, Jerome Verdier.

General aspects of **law and order** continued to pose serious problems. Less progress was made than hoped on the constitution of a new police force some 3,500-strong. In the absence of an effective police force, officers of the United Nations Mission in Liberia (UNMIL) continued to take responsibility for a great deal of police work. Monrovia, a desperately overcrowded city after the population displacement caused by years of war, was infested with armed robbers locally known as Issaka Boys. Perhaps more worrying in a longer-term perspective was the continuing animosity shown by many Monrovians, and also by people in Nimba county especially, towards the Mandingo section of the population. Mandingoes, who are generally Muslim, have a reputation as resourceful entrepreneurs and business operators. Throughout the war years, successive militias were led by Mandingo warlords or politicians and the latest of the militias, Liberians United for Reconciliation and Democracy (LURD), was instrumental in the overthrow of Charles Taylor in 2003. Many observers thought that anti-Mandingo sentiment represented the germ of future political difficulties.

Foreign Affairs

Notwithstanding the success in ending bloodshed in Liberia since 2003, many observers remained concerned by the country's underlying problems and believed that a premature abandonment by the international community could have serious consequences. The 15,000-strong UNMIL mission continued to play a leading role in stabilising the country under a mandate that was extended to March 2007. President Johnson-Sirleaf made a number of highly **successful international visits**, including several to the US. On 15 March, the highlight of the president's successful US visit was a 40-minute speech to a joint session of the US congress. In May, a presidential visit to Chicago was sponsored by a television production company owned by the star producer and celebrity Oprah Winfrey, who had revealed on air that her own roots can be traced to the Kpelle, Liberia's largest ethnic group. On 31 May, President Johnson-Sirleaf was received in London by Queen Elizabeth. The UK was the first country to officially recognise the Republic of Liberia as a sovereign state, in 1848. On 19 September, the president addressed the UN General Assembly in New York. These events were all important in marking the international community's faith in Liberia's new government and could translate into a degree of much needed diplomatic and financial support.

More prosaically, President Johnson-Sirleaf made efforts to normalise the relations with **neighbouring countries** that had become so disturbed during the years of war. These included meetings on 14 and 15 December with the heads of state of Sierra Leone and Guinea, fellow-members of the Mano River Union. On 27 December, ECOWAS foreign ministers meeting in Ouagadougou called for all sanctions on the Liberian government to be lifted in order to enable the country's recovery. The main centre of destabilisation in the wider West African region is now Côte d'Ivoire, where a condition of no peace/no war continued. Côte d'Ivoire hosts a significant number of Liberian war veterans, who had now joined various militias in Liberia's eastern neighbour.

In June, the speaker of the Liberian Congress, Edwin Snowe, caused a major controversy when he met with Taiwanese officials during a trip to Gambia. He is alleged to have signed a number of accords regarding recognition of **Taiwan**. This was in contravention of government policy, the NTGL having been the first government of Liberia to recognise the People's Republic of China. Prior to that date, Liberia had recognised Taiwan.

Socioeconomic Developments

The social and economic problems facing President Johnson-Sirleaf's government were enormous. The state had debt arrears of some $ 3.7 bn, compared to a population of just 3.4 m and a state budget amounting to a mere $ 129 m. In fact, approval of the 2006–07 budget was delayed until April by disagreement in the legislature, where the opposition wields considerable influence. Liberia is reckoned to be one of the world's three poorest countries, with 80% of the population living on less than $ 1 a day. Life expectancy is just under 39 years. According to UN figures published in February, the country's GDP is $ 543.3 m, or $ 151 per capita. The UN also estimated urban **poverty** in Monrovia at 50.6% and rural poverty at 86.3%. Of rural dwellers, 81.2% were reckoned to depend on subsistence agriculture. Up to two-thirds of the income of poor families was spent on food, and more than 800,000 people were in need of food aid. The justice system had effectively collapsed during the war, with no court cases at all being heard in some counties since the late 1980s. The education system, too, is in a lamentable state. The UN estimated school enrolment at 69.1% for boys and 39.9% for girls, but noted that many of those registered did not actually attend school because of lack of money.

The government proceeded on several fronts at once with the support of the Governance and Economic Management Assistance Programme (GEMAP). This programme, which had effectively been imposed on the NTGL by aid-donors who were alarmed by the rampant corruption of the transitional government, provided for **international control** of key posts within the Liberian financial and economic management structure. In May, the UN and the World Bank published an important paper on GEMAP. Although the scheme has been opposed by a number of Liberian politicians (and President Johnson-Sirleaf was lukewarm in her support), other Liberians welcomed it. Observers were keen to learn from the experience. It remained unclear whether GEMAP, or any similar scheme, could play a future role in Liberia's recovery or in other countries recovering from similar catastrophes.

Total **government revenue** during the year rose to $ 114 m, compared with $ 77 m in 2005. Official expenditure for the same period amounted to $ 93.5 m, compared with $ 81.8 m for the previous year. The balance of trade deficit increased from $ 98.5 m to $ 292.9 m.

A highlight of the year for many Monrovians was the return of mains electricity to at least part of the city in July. However, the return of electricity immediately resulted in a fire at the executive mansion, the presidential offices. This appears to have been due to a short circuit in the wiring at the mansion, but the occurrence was widely regarded as an ill omen. There was also some demonstrable progress in road repair, in the provision of water and in other **infrastructure facilities**. The improved political climate also helped persuade the one-tenth of the population who were officially registered as displaced to begin the move back from camps. At one stage, 314,096 people were registered as displaced, living in temporary shelters in 35 camps run by the government and by aid agencies. The largest single camp was at Salala, which, at its height, had a population of 30,000. By April, most of the inmates of Salala had departed.

There was particular attention given to the matter of **rape** as one of the legacies of the war. Accurate figures on the number of rapes were unavailable, but evidence suggests that the incidence of rape during the war was very high, and that this scourge continued. Clinics reported treating rape victims as young as five, and even having seen babies who had been raped. Although rape has long been a criminal offence, the Liberian Association of Women Lawyers reported in February that just one case had been prosecuted since 1999, a measure of the degree of impunity that in fact exists. On 17 January – just one day after the inauguration of the president – a new rape law came into effect that made rape a non-bailable offence. However, this was of largely symbolic importance, owing to the continuing inadequacies of the police and the court system.

During the year, the administration submitted 11 bills to the legislature in regard to the forestry sector, the revenue system and the customs service, among others. One such move that attracted considerable international attention was the renegotiation of a number of contracts signed by previous governments, and notably by the disastrous NTGL administration. Executive Order Number One – the first formal executive act by the incoming government – concerned dozens of **timber concessions** signed by the previous administration. So chaotic was this that timber concessions extended to some 26 m acres, whereas the actual area of exploitable timber was only about one-quarter of that figure. Many contracts had been signed by dishonest officials purely to obtain a bribe. Under a new forestry law, three distinct types of management regime would apply, dividing forests into protected areas, community areas and commercial areas. Liberia was estimated to be losing some 2% of its forest cover per year. On 20 June, the UN lifted sanctions on Liberian timber that had originally been imposed in 2003. The Security Council explicitly linked this decision to the reforms undertaken by the Liberian administration, including the appointment of an internationally recruited financial controller at the forestry development authority. Implementation of the government's policy on timber involved police action in regard to areas illegally occupied by former combatants. The best-known such case, although concerning another natural resource, was that of the Guthrie rubber plantation some 20 miles northwest of Monrovia, which was illegally occupied by some 3,000 ex-fighters, most of them from the defunct LURD militia. The plantation was successfully repossessed by the authorities. However, by the end of the year, illegal rubber-tappers continued to live on the massive Firestone rubber plantation and were intermittently engaged in violence in an effort to resist eviction.

As an indication of the government's list of priorities, Executive Order Number Two dealt with government policy on the per diem allowances given to officials travelling on government business, while Executive Order Number Three concerned a mechanism for control of government revenues.

In spite of the government's efforts in regard to timber, **economic sanctions** continued in other key sectors of the economy. On 20 December, the Security Council decided to renew its existing restrictions on arms sales to Liberia and on travel for a further 12 months, and extended measures on diamonds for an additional six months, also re-appointing a panel of experts to monitor compliance. In regard to diamonds, the UN determined that internal controls were not yet in place in conformity with the standards of the Kimberley Process, intended to prevent the marketing of 'blood' diamonds, associated with armed conflict.

Of all the attempts at renegotiation of contracts signed under dubious conditions by the NTGL, the most significant concerned the **Mittal steel** company. This is the world's biggest steel conglomerate. On 17 August 2005, in one of its last acts, the transitional government had signed a contract with Mittal giving the company rights to iron ore deposits in Liberia. The contract was widely regarded as very one-sided: in 2006, on 3 October, the non-governmental organisation Global Witness published a report strongly criticising the Mittal contract. It argued that the agreement virtually gave Mittal the right to ignore Liberian law, and that its provisions on the pricing of iron ore exports would allow Mittal to avoid payment of most taxes and royalties. In conformity with its stated intention of reviewing the contracts signed by the NTGL, the government began negotiations with Mittal in September and announced on 12 December that the two sides had reached agreement on a new document. The government regained control of the port of Buchanan, the port from which iron ore mined in Nimba county is exported, and of the railway line that links Yekepa, a town close to the iron ore mine, to the coast. Moreover, it was specified that the company's security force must operate in conformity with Liberian law, and that operations would generally be subject to Liberian laws on human rights and environmental issues. Importantly, in the renegotiation it was specified that the transfer price of iron ore – that is, the price at which it is transferred from one Mittal subsidiary to another – would be geared to the world market price of steel and could not be fixed arbitrarily by Mittal. Mittal also announced that it would increase its total investment in Liberia to $ 1 bn.

Stephen Ellis

Mali

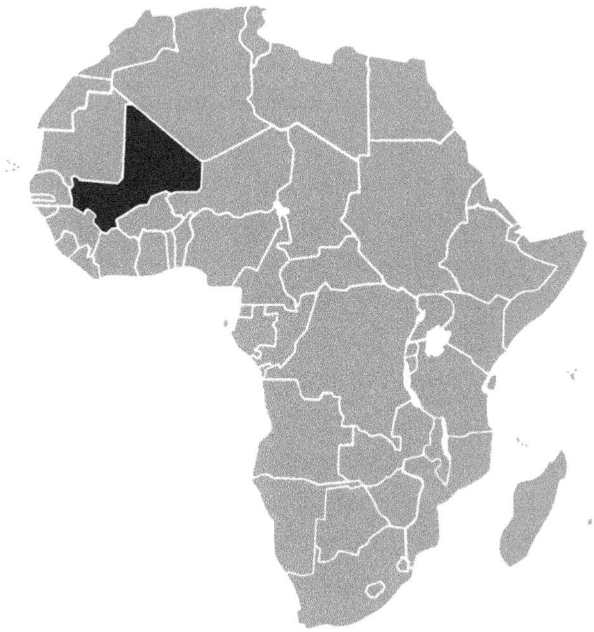

The state of Malian consensus democracy and the question of whether it should be continued was an important political issue throughout the year. The consensus model was instituted following the 2002 elections, when all major parties rallied around (independent) President Amadou Toumani Touré (ATT). Providing for a stable political climate and a smooth decision-making process, the consensus model has also been based on a rather small (and closed) group of elite politicians with links to ordinary citizens, thus weakening the functioning of political parties. In addition, the lack of parliamentary opposition led to a reduction in the quality of political debate and the checks and balances within the political system.

Domestic Politics

In light of the upcoming presidential and parliamentarian **elections in 2007**, all major parties were obliged to determine their electoral positions and reassess the consensus model. Following regional consultations, the 'Alliance pour la Démocratie' (ADEMA) – the former ruling party and the second force in parliament – publicly announced its continuing support for incumbent President Touré. Other important political parties such as 'L'Union pour la République et la Démocratie' (URD) and the 'Comité National d'Initiative

Démocratique' (CNID) also announced that they would not put forward presidential candidates for the elections in April 2007, but would mobilise their members behind the incumbent. Almost half a year of negotiations followed and on 8 December these three parties together with 11 others publicly launched the 'Alliance des Forces Démocratiques pour le Progrès' (ADP). This political platform was designed to support the re-election of Touré but also aimed at strengthening political cooperation after the elections.

The 'Mouvement Citoyen', a broad but loose **network of civic associations** that supported President Touré in the run-up to the 2002 elections, faced severe internal wrangles throughout the year. The main point of controversy was whether to institutionalise itself as a political party or to maintain its civic profile and loose organisational structure. A subsequent break-away group gave birth to the 'Parti Citoyen pour le Renouveau' (PCR), but both the political and civil factions of the 'Mouvement Citoyen' were expected to continue providing support to the president.

Most of the above parties experienced internal disputes regarding the electoral position taken by their leadership. Local branches, supported by some members of the national executive committees, aspired to a presidential candidate from their own party and accused the leadership of "[selling] the party to the incumbent in order to fulfil personal ambitions." In the case of ADEMA, the first Vice-President Soumeylou Boubèye Maïga (known as SBM) together with other senior members were **suspended** after they publicly distanced themselves from the official party line. Controversy about the consensus democracy had already been fuelled by the publication of a 'Manifeste pour la Démocratie' on 9 June. This document – signed by more than 100 individuals (members of various political parties and independents alike) – highlighted the negative consequences of the political consensus and argued for a working representative democracy with open debate and a healthy opposition. The debate on the weaknesses of Malian democracy became even more heated with the publication of the book 'ATT-cratie: la promotion d'un homme et de son clan' by unknown author(s) using the pseudonym 'Le Sphinx' – after a weekly newspaper – in September. The **book** described the autocratic and regionalist nature of ATT's regime in such detail that the author(s) must clearly have come from the country's inner political circles. People who felt offended by the book filed legal complaints against the publisher, Harmattan.

One politician hoping to capitalise most on these events was Ibrahim Boubacar Keïta (IBK), speaker of parliament and leader of the largest parliamentary party, the 'Rassemblement Pour le Mali' (RPM). He managed to regroup a limited number of parties around his ambitions (the most important being the CDS, 'Convention Social-Démocrate', and PARENA, the 'Parti pour la Renaissance Nationale') and alongside the political movement that supports the former vice-president of ADEMA and the network of politicians that signed the 'Manifeste pour la Démocratie'. This **reshuffling of elites** and parts of their support networks brought to the fore the two main electoral coalitions competing for presidential office in April 2007, with parliamentary elections to follow in June.

A **new electoral law** was passed in July 2006 and subsequently signed by the president in early August. A 30% quorum for female representation on electoral lists, as proposed by government, was rejected by parliament. Regulations on public funding of political parties that were introduced in 2005 did, however, to some extent encourage parties to increase the number of women on their lists, since additional funds would be provided for those parties with a high number of female MPs or local councillors. Parliament approved the mechanisms proposed by the government to limit the number of presidential candidates (a formal endorsement by 10 MPs or 45 local councillors spread equally over the various regions in favour of each candidate, together with a fee of CFAfr 10 m). According to the new electoral law, the number of polling stations for the 2007 elections would increase significantly from one station per 700 people to one station per 500.

An issue of contention proved to be **party funding**. Following poor financial reporting of the public funds received in 2005, the audit office advised the ministry of the interior to suspend public funding to political parties in 2006. The funds were only released after severe pressure on the president and after concrete steps had been taken to improve financial management within the parties.

Mali faced a small but threatening **revival of rebellion** in the northern provinces after Colonel Hassan Fagaga deserted and attacked government barracks in the northern towns of Kidal, Menaka and Tessalit on 23 May. Following an intervention by the army, the government signed a much disputed agreement with the rebels, which became known as the Algiers accord and promised – among other things – renewed socioeconomic investments in the northern provinces. In July, President Touré launched a $ 21 m programme known as 'ADRE-NORD'. Although government officials elaborately defended the agreement on state television, many newspapers criticised the fact that rebellion could apparently bring economic gain, a development which might in the long run harm political stability. After the agreement was signed, the military situation improved, although security remained problematic. This became all too apparent when two stages of the Paris-Dakar rally were cancelled later in the year. Also, a research delegation gathering data on behalf of the health department had to cancel its visits to three localities in the Kidal region as the government was unable to guarantee its safety. A local observer said the current situation in this region could be best described as "a precarious stability".

In early July, journalist Hamidou Diarra of 'Radio Kélédou' was beaten up in Bamako, an attack that attracted much attention from human rights activists and media associations as the journalist is known for his radio programmes criticising a number of Malian politicians. He was dragged into a car by unknown men and **assaulted**. While press freedom has been generally high, the incident accelerated the establishment of a 'Conseil Consultatif des Droits Humains' with a mandate to examine human rights and the progress made by government in implementing international human rights treaties.

The 'Association des Droits de l'Homme' and other institutions revitalised the debate on the formal abolition of the death penalty, which had not been used for over 25 years. In

December, another 'Espace d'Interpellation Démocratique' was held, an occasion at which ordinary citizens could directly present their complaints to members of the government. In Transparency International's 2006 ranking, Mali was classified 99th out of 163 countries with a mere 2.8 out of 10 points as regards the perception of **corruption**, a modest decline compared to previous years. In relation to other African countries, Mali ranked 18th out of 45 countries.

There was controversy when the **electoral commission** (not a permanent institution and composed of representatives of both civil society and political parties) was set up in September. Problems arose when parties assembled in the coalition called 'Espoir 2002' could not agree on who would represent them in the commission. Once that issue was to some extent settled, the commission had difficulty securing the funds from government necessary to execute its mandate. It was expected that after the 2007 elections, the model of the electoral commission would be evaluated and possibly adapted.

Foreign Affairs

The conflict in **Côte d'Ivoire** continued to negatively affect Mali's society and economy. The country remained obliged to use ports that are much further away (such as Cotonou), with the augmented transport costs having a severely negative impact on its international trade.

Besides the Ivorian refugees still to be found in the Sikasso region, the many Malians who used to reside in Côte d'Ivoire were forced to return and now placed a heavy burden on their families. In addition, traditional seasonal migration to Côte d'Ivoire has diminished, with obvious economic consequences. Low cotton prices together with a rising oil bill proved to be other important external factors weakening the economy.

On the international scene, Mali continued to present itself as host for important international events. The first African version of the **World Social Forum** (WSF) took place in Bamako between 19–23 January. Other events were the 24th regional conference of the FAO for Africa (30 January–3 February) and the 'People's Forum'. The latter conference took place on the eve of the G8 summit in St Petersburg in the remote city of Gao. It grouped more than 600 participants mostly from Africa and Europe to discuss international trade, debt cancellation and emigration. Between 6–8 December, the 4th international conference on avian flu took place in Bamako.

With thousands of illegal **Malian migrants** caught by police in Spain during the first three-quarters of the year alone, Malians represented the largest group of Africans trying to enter Europe illegally, even though many more migrated within the West African region. In September, the EU promised additional aid to the country in order to stimulate social development and diminish migration flows. According to an EU statement, an additional € 426 m would be made available between 2008 and 2013.

Among the various international leaders to visit Mali were regional colleagues such as Presidents Kufuor of Ghana, Wade of Senegal and Compaoré of Burkina Faso. During a one-day visit, Venezuela's President Chavez signed a number of agreements in the oil and cotton sectors. A much disputed visit was undertaken by Nicolas **Sarkozy**, who arrived in Bamako the day a controversial immigration law was passed in the French National Assembly. Local associations, mainly from the Kayes region, took to the streets.

Leaders of **UEMOA** met in Niger in March to elect a new governor for the regional bank (a post held by Côte d'Ivoire for decades). The economic and monetary union also created a regional solidarity bank with departments in all member states. Furthermore, Mali held the presidency of another regional body, CEN-SAD.

As for Amadou Toumani Touré, he attended the **Sino-African summit** on 3–5 November and travelled to Washington and Brussels to sign development agreements. Speaker of parliament Ibrahim Boubacar Keïta undertook a long visit to Angola in September.

Socioeconomic Developments

Mali's first PRSP (2001–06) set out with the ambition to reduce poverty by 25%. In urban areas, poverty figures dropped from 26.2% in 2001 to 20.1% in 2006. However, rural **poverty** remained almost unchanged (73%). Real GDP expanded by almost 5%, the effect of which was substantially reduced by demographic growth and an inflation rate of over 2%. On a positive note, Mali's external debt-to-GDP ratio was expected to fall to 25% in 2007.

Gold remained the most important export product, and Mali ranked third among all African gold-producing countries behind South Africa and Ghana. Gold contributed more than 10% to total GDP and generated almost 70% of total export revenues. President Touré inaugurated the new Tabakoto gold mine in May and, a few months later, the African Gold Group started a research programme in the mines of Kobada. In addition, investigation started on 11 potential gas and oil fields.

Cotton production did not significantly grow due to managerial problems in the 'Companie Malienne pour le Développement des Fibres Textiles' (CMDT) and low world market prices. It remained, however, one of the few products that could generate substantial profits for local farmers. Total production for the 2005–06 season did not attain 550,000 tonnes and the price awarded to producers declined from CFAfr 210/kg to CFAfr 160/kg. In a tactical move, privatisation of CMDT was delayed until 2008, i.e., until after the 2007 elections. The same happened to the national telecommunications company Sotelma and oil company UCOMA. For CMDT, strategic partners were identified who would assist government with the privatisation process. The ADB, together with the World Bank, the French department of international cooperation and the EU would be involved as technical and/or financial partners.

While the 2005 locust plague reduced overall **agricultural productivity**, this year sufficient rains led to a good harvest in most parts of the country. Improving food security for citizens remained the government's number one priority. In addition, a large programme focused on intensified and permanent agricultural land use. Parliament passed the important 'Loi d'Orientation Agricole', defining the broader framework of agricultural policy and specifying the roles of the various actors involved. It also set a deadline of five years for the elaboration of government policy on the contentious issue of land titles involving, among other things, the conflict between traditional entitlements and modern legal instruments, many of which are not implemented in rural areas. In contrast to the problems cited in the cotton sector, cereal production (corn, millet and sorghum) improved significantly. Finally, a factory was established for agricultural equipment in Sikasso.

The government signed a number of important **development treaties** with various partners. In March, seven large donors signed an agreement for direct budgetary support. The EU invested more than € 70 m in a programme aimed at reforming (mainly decentralising) state structures. Preparations for the 10th European Development Funds – such as defining Mali's governance profile – were also embarked upon. Next to the large amount of funds granted by the EU, the US admitted Mali to its list of countries that may benefit from the Millennium Challenge Corporation (MCC). From these funds, Mali would receive a total of $ 461 m. A great share of these resources would be invested in irrigation projects, infrastructure, improved market access and assistance to small enterprises.

At the university level, Mali faced yet another **turbulent educational year**. University did not start in October as it should have as a result of a strike by teachers protesting against continuing poor working conditions and the non-implementation of previous commitments made by government. The crisis was unresolved at year's end. The education sector suffers from lack of infrastructure at all levels, overcrowded classes and a lack of human resources (especially sufficiently qualified teachers). However, following an agreement signed in September, the sector became one of the first in which some progress was made with the transfer of responsibilities and funds from the national state to lower levels.

In view of an illiteracy rate of 75%, however, the sector continued to pose an enormous social and economic problem. The ministry of education and Mali's international financial partners had jointly developed a ten year 'Programme d'appui à l'Education' (PRODEC) in order to address the main challenges. The first phase ended in 2005, and the second started in April 2006. The main objective of the programme, in line with the Millennium Development Goals, was to ensure that everyone aged below twelve would have **access to education** by 2015. Although much progress had been made in recent years on such access (27% in 1990, 40% in 1995 and 69% in 2004), only 34% of pupils complete the first six years and a mere 20% continued further. At this primary level, an average of 73 pupils still had to share one teacher while one textbook was available per two students (although many schools were identified with no books at all). On a positive note, the number of training centres for teachers increased from five in 2000 to 12 in 2004. The number of schools has also grown during recent years, but this was mainly due to the increase in private schools and 'madrassas'. Within PRODEC, access to and quality of primary education had been identified as the single most important priority. Besides this, attention was paid to secondary and technical education. At this level, too, private schools have increased in importance in recent years (educating 55% of students in 1996 versus 75% in 2004). An important objective for this educational level from 2006 onwards, as for universities, was to better connect labour market needs to the educational system. Decentralisation is the last important area of intervention highlighted in the ten-year programme. In this respect, regional 'Academies d'Enseignants' were created as well as local committees. However, communication between the various levels remained problematic, frustrating real participation by the lower levels.

Large investments were made to improve **road infrastructure** and provide rural areas with access to markets. The government was able to finalise the long-awaited bridge over the Niger River at Gao, which was expected to have a considerable impact in reducing the isolation of the northern provinces. In addition, roads to the northwestern town of Kayes improved, as did the connection between Kati and Kita and between Koulikouro and Banamba.

In the field of **health care**, Malian citizens remained one of the most disadvantaged peoples in the world, with a life expectancy of 41. The country experienced an outbreak of meningitis in August and also in that month a yellow fever epidemic broke out in Kayes. Following the heightened risk of an outbreak of avian flu, a worldwide concern, the first regional office of the World Organisation for Animal Health in Africa was established in Bamako in July.

The government initiated a substantial social **housing programme** in different towns. Various categories of citizens (formally employed but with low wages, without formal employment, Malians now residing outside the country) could apply for such accommodation and, once accepted, pay a monthly fee for many years after which they would become legal owners.

Institutions were put in place to investigate the longer term environmental impact of gold mining. In the **cultural field**, Mali mourned the death of artist Ali Farka Touré. Apart from his musical career, he was also involved in local politics, being mayor of the northern town of Niafunké. Much international attention was paid to the film 'Bamako' released in November, with its severe criticism of the social impact of World Bank and IMF policies. Rising numbers of tourists visited the country, among other reasons for musical events, of which the 'Festival du Dessert' as well as the 'Festival sur le Niger' were the most prominent. The city of Timbouctou hosted the celebration of Prophet Mohammed's birth, in which several leaders from neighbouring countries participated.

Martin van Vliet & Walter van Beek

Mauritania

The 'Conseil Militaire pour la Justice et la Démocratie' (CMJD) led by President Vall, which overthrew President Maaouiya Ould Taya on 3 August 2005 after he had held power for 20 years, was strongly condemned by the international community (including the UN, AU, France and the US) from the beginning, even as most Mauritanians welcomed the coup. By 2006, however, the CMJD had been largely accepted internationally because it formed an interim government charged with organising legislative and presidential elections within 19 months and had granted a general amnesty to political prisoners. Parliamentary elections took place in November–December in the presence of a large number of international observers and were regarded as relatively free and fair. Although the human rights situation generally improved, there were reports of ill-treatment of detainees, ethnic tensions among the country's Arab, Berber, Moor and sub-Saharan African groups, and some evidence of the persistence of slavery. The economy received a boost with the commencement of oil exports in February. However, agriculture, on which most Mauritanians depend, was affected by drought and locust invasions. Mauritania has least developed country status and qualified for debt relief under the HIPC initiative. Poverty reduction programmes continued.

Domestic Politics

A referendum held on 25 June led to acceptance of an amended constitution that included a limit of two five-year terms for the president and an age limit of 75 years. The constitution also prevents the head of state from holding a leading position in a political party. The referendum took place after a nationwide registration that ended on 30 April. According to the official records, turnout was 76%, of whom 97% approved the new constitution.

Municipal and legislative **elections** took place on 19 November (first round) and 3 December (second round). The turnout was 70%. 25 political parties took part, among them many that had been banned before the military coup. Women took 17 seats and would make up 18% of the National Assembly. No party won an overall majority in the parliamentary polls. The 'Coalition des Forces du Changement Démocratique' (CFCD), a coalition of 11 opposition parties, took 41 seats (of a total of 95), and in the municipal elections CFCD won a majority, thus providing it with control of many cities, including the capital, where it won eight of nine seats. The CFCD comprises the 'Alliance Populaire Progressiste', 'Front Populaire', 'Flam/Rénovation', 'Mouvement de la Démocratie Directe', 'Parti Mauritanien de l'Union et du Changement', 'Parti Unioniste Démocratique et Socialiste', 'Rassemblement des Forces Démocratique', 'Rassemblement pour la Mauritanie', 'Réformateurs Centristes', 'Parti du Renouveau Démocratique' and the 'Union des Forces de Progrès'. The former ruling party, 'Parti Républicain pour la Democratie et le Renouveau' – in power from 1992 until the military coup – won only seven seats. A large number of **independent candidates** won a total of 39 seats. Some opposition politicians alleged that these independent candidates, considered loyal to the political elite, were encouraged to stand by the interim military government to ensure that the National Assembly continued to be an ineffective political force. While officially an Islamic republic, Islamist parties and movements have been banned in Mauritania. This resulted in many Islamist candidates standing as independents.

In May, a national committee for **human rights** was established in line with the commitments of the ruling military council. Several Mauritanian non-governmental organisations, including 'SOS Esclaves' and the 'Association Mauritanienne des Droits de l'Homme', which for years were illegal and had survived with great difficulty, were officially recognised in June. Even if **slavery** had been officially abolished several times (the last time in 1981), further evidence emerged of the persistence of this practice. Two organisations, 'SOS Esclaves' and 'El Hor' ('The Free'), both led by ex-slaves, work to free slaves at great risk to themselves, while pressuring the government for change and assisting escaped slaves. The majority of **political prisoners** were released after the military coup. However, ill treatment of detainees, during arrest and in police custody, continued to be rife. During the old regime, many leaders of Islamist movements were imprisoned and charged with imaginary coup plots. After the 2005 coup, events demonstrated that the Islamist movement had next to no popular support. Even so, several Islamists were arrested in 2006. On 30 April, two spokeswomen for Islamist prisoners' family committees were arrested, while 30 Islamists were arrested in Nouakchott in May and June. On 27 December, the CFCD urged the government to release all of the students still held in police custody.

New independent media were established, press freedom having been curtailed during the old regime of President Ould Taya. In March, a new **media law** was adopted and newspapers were no longer required to obtain permits before publication. The military council also announced that it would allow the creation of private radio and television stations. On 5 October, a bill on further liberalisation was examined and presented and provided for the creation of a 'Haute Autorité de la Presse et de l'Audiovisuel'. This authority is to manage the issuance of licences and authorisations for broadcasting networks. This was seen as an important step towards full liberalisation of the media sector.

Foreign Affairs

During the year, Mauritania remained under AU sanctions. Immediately after the 2005 coup, the **AU** had suspended Mauritania's participation in all AU activities "until the restoration of constitutional order in the country." The AU sent a ministerial delegation to Mauritania "to reiterate the AU's positions to the perpetrators of the coup d'etat and to engage them on the modalities for a speedy restoration of constitutional order." However, after the elections on 19 November and 3 December 2006, the 'l'Assemblée Parlamentaire de la Francophonie' began to consider the country's readmission into the organisation, which could occur at the next general assembly in July 2007.

The government continued to work in accordance with the EU's **Cotonou agreement**, which provides for political dialogue and requires fulfilment of 24 undertakings in the fields of good governance, human rights, democratic principles and the rule of law. The successful conclusion of the article 96 negotiations opened up the possibility of resumption of development projects that had been temporarily suspended in the wake of the August 2005 coup. Mauritania also expressed interest in participating in the EU's 'Barcelona process'.

France remained Mauritania's most important European partner, and was strongly involved in development and cultural cooperation. On 30–31 August, the French cooperation and development minister, Brigitte Girardin, visited Mauritania and President Vall visited Europe in September, including a working visit to Paris and Bucharest, where he attended the Francophonie summit on 28–29 September.

On 23 March, the European Commission decided to contribute € 2.45 m in **refugee aid**. In this field, cooperation between Spain and Mauritania was intensified. In May, Spain offered Mauritania patrol boats to help tackle illegal refugee boats en route to the Canary Islands, and to assist in the establishment of camps in Nouadhibou. During the summer, the Spanish minister for internal affairs and the foreign minister, Miguel Angel Moratinos, visited Mauritania in order to discuss the massive migration to the Canary Islands. Spanish authorities claimed Mauritania had become a new launching point for illegal migration to

Spain after Morocco had stepped up its security. The International Organisation for Migration (IOM) estimated that more than 30,000 West Africans were shipped from Mauritania's northern fishing ports in 2006 and that more than 500 migrants died at sea. Spanish immigration authorities came with a much higher figure (see the chapter on Sub-Saharan Africa). While Mauritania has 63 police checkpoints and 37 gendarmerie checkpoints along its borders with Mali and Senegal, the possibility of stopping mass migration is limited. Nevertheless, the government established cooperation on border security with Mali and Senegal. President Vall visited Mali and the Malian president reciprocated with a visit to Nouakchott. The Senegalese president visited Nouakchott on 30 January. A fishing agreement with Senegal was signed in February, and President Vall visited Senegal in March. The question of resettlement of an estimated 25,000 **black Mauritanian refugees**, expelled to Senegal in 1989–90 without identity papers, remained to be resolved.

The government supported the UN efforts to solve the **Western Saharan conflict**, maintaining a strictly neutral position despite its frequent contacts with the Polisario Front and Mauritania's numerous tribal connections with the territory. Bilateral ties with **Algeria** improved. On 6 May, President Vall visited Algeria, leading to a decision to increase and intensify cooperation. The role of Israel in the Middle East conflict led to a series of protests in June, with most political parties calling for the breaking of diplomatic relations, which had been restored in 1999.

Relations with the **US**, which have improved in the course of the latter's 'war on terror', continued to make progress, notably after the constitutional referendum on 25 June. In January, the Mauritanian foreign minister visited Washington and in February a US delegation came to Nouakchott. Cooperation with **China** so far has been rather marginal, but Chinese interest increased, especially in relation to oil. Thus, in April an agreement with the Chinese oil company Sinopec was signed. Sino-Mauritanian cooperation has involved fisheries, farming, infrastructure development and health care. On 4–5 November, President Vall visited Beijing in the context of the Forum on China-Africa Cooperation (FOCAC) and had a separate meeting with Chinese President Hu Jintao. Further cooperation on telecommunications, science and technology was discussed. In December, China also allotted Mauritania an interest-free loan estimated at 2.52 bn ouguiyas (€ 1 = 357.21 ouguiya) to fund poverty reduction projects.

Socioeconomic Developments

On 26 February, Mauritania became Africa's latest **oil-producing nation** when it exported its first crude from the Chinguetti oil field, which, with an estimated 95 m barrels of reserves, was still small by international standards. Daily production, estimated at 75,000 barrels, is in the hands of a consortium consisting of five companies: Hardman (based in Perth, Australia), which has a 21.6% stake; Woodside Mauritania (35%); AGIP Mauritania (35%); Fusion Oil and Gas (6%); and Rock Oil (2.4%). Production was expected to increase in the near future, even if the reserves are hardly comparable to those of Nigeria or Angola.

In January, former Oil Minister Zeidane Ould Hmeida was arrested and charged with "serious crimes against the country's essential economic interests", according to an official statement. This referred to amendments to four offshore production-sharing contracts with Woodside signed by Hmeida in February 2004 and March 2005. It was claimed that the deals cut the state's share of **oil revenue**, lowered taxes and removed bank guarantees that were part of the initial contract. It was estimated that the amendments could cost Mauritania up to $ 200 m a year. The dispute ended in March when Woodside Petroleum signed an agreement stipulating payment to Mauritania of $ 100 m in compensation, the return of 50% of its oil acreage and an annual allocation of $ 200 m to cover environmental risks.

In July, a new **fisheries** partnership agreement with the EU was signed, covering a period of six years from 1 August and providing fishing opportunities for EU vessels. The EU's financial contribution would amount to € 516 m and include improvements to port facilities, strenghtening scientific capacity related to fisheries research, and monitoring and control of fishing activities. The payments from the fishing licences were estimated at $ 80 m a year.

Accounting for 56% of Mauritania's imports and 61% of its exports, the EU is the country's most important trade partner. It is also Mauritania's largest donor, the total amount disbursed from the EU's European Development Fund totalling € 191 m, including support for structural adjustment, food supply and compensation for fishing rights. Improvements to infrastructure constituted the main focus of this assistance, including renovation of Nouadhibou harbour and, for an amount of € 66 m, the repair of the Kaédi-M'Bout-Selibaby-Gouraye road. The latter initiative was aimed at improving the living conditions of communities in southern Mauritania and followed the decision on 29 May to fully resume **EU aid** in response to the progress by Mauritanian authorities in implementing democracy and the rule of law. The EU also provided support for the reform of transport and finance and € 7.5 m was disbursed for combating the locust invasion. These funds were in addition to the € 13.6 m already allocated to Mauritania in support of political reforms undertaken by the new authorities.

When in June Mauritania paid back the last instalment of the $ 18 m credit it had received from the IMF on the basis of false figures concerning central bank reserves, the country qualified for debt relief as decided at the G8 meeting in July 2005. On 18 December, the IMF approved a three-year arrangement under the **PRGF** for $ 24.2 m. The government's efforts to implement the dual policy goals of economic development and improved fiscal accountability continued. Further reforms, particularly in the area of governance, were considered necessary.

The fiscal surplus was 7.6% of GDP, mainly due to large inflows of oil revenue. Efforts were made to guarantee the transparency of figures for natural resource revenues. However, the ADB country strategy paper, released in November, emphasised the need for further reforms in order to safeguard the changes already made. This also included strengthening state capacity to fight money laundering and the financing of terrorism. The inflation rate was 6.5%, almost entirely due to food prices, which make up over 50% of the consumer price index. As a result of the locust outbreak in September and flooding in some areas, food prices did not decline after September as they usually do. **GDP per capita** was $ 2,600. Real GDP growth was 14.1% (including oil income). The current account deficit was 6.9% of GDP, a clear improvement over the 2005 deficit of 49.9%. This was mainly due to oil, iron ore and gold exports.

On the UNDP's **Human Development Index**, Mauritania ranked 153rd out of 177 countries, while on the Economist Intelligence Unit's 'Index of Democracy' it stood at 133 out of 167 countries. During the year, **trade policy** was liberalised through the lifting of price regulations, liberalisation of the exchange rate and continuing privatisation of state-owned companies. Plans were made to introduce foreign exchange auctions in 2007. In June, the government established an agency for **environmental issues**, appointed its own minister of rural development and the environment and announced a national action programme for environmental issues and sustainable development.

Claes Olsson & Helena Olsson

Niger

Abundant rains, though late, improved the country's food situation substantially, thus breaking the downward spiral that started with insufficient rains and a locust plague in 2004 and led to famine conditions in 2005. Social tensions caused by precarious economic conditions continued to characterise life in the urban areas, where new protests peaked in early summer. The stability of the government was not as seriously jeopardised as in 2005. Tensions between the president and prime minister, which had worsened over the famine controversy, nevertheless increased in the wake of the prime minister's decision to run for the presidency in 2009. Relations with the media remained problematic. Security in remote areas was precarious, in part because of spill-over effects from Chad. Economic prospects brightened somewhat with new interest in Niger's uranium reserves and growing Asian commitments. This improvement was not enough to end Niger's status as the world's poorest country.

Domestic Politics

Relations between leaders of Niger's political class were marked by shifts and strains. The announcement by Prime Minister Hama Amadou on 29 December 2005 that he would **run for president** in 2009 had the potential to open a three-year campaign involving speculation about rival candidates, political manoeuvring and the deterioration of Amadou's relations with President Mamadou Tandja, already damaged by their disunited response to the famine crisis. Both are members of the ruling 'Mouvement National pour la Société du Développement' (MNSD), but Tandja has been constitutionally barred from standing for a third term. There was speculation that he might want to change the constitution or support another candidate, thus countering previous expectations that he would support Amadou.

Early in the year it was rumoured that Tandja would support the **candidature of Mahamane Ousmane**, chairman of the National Assembly and leader of the 'Convention Démocratique et Sociale' (CDS), the government's minor coalition partner. However, the press accused Ousmane of duplicitous dealings in the 2004 presidential elections with Tandja and Mahamadou Issoufou, leader of the opposition 'Parti Nigérien pour la Démocratie et le Socialisme' (PNDS). This was followed by the suspension of Ali Maman, CDS mayor of the third district of the capital Niamey, for 'serious errors' (i.e., corruption) on 21 February, making him another Ousmane loyalist to be struck by MNSD power holders. Other mayors, too, got into trouble. President Tandja began to distance himself from Ousmane, as did Mahamadou Issoufou, who met the president several times, fuelling rumours that Tandja might support the PNDS leader, his rival in the 2004 contest. It was rumoured that Tandja incited Issoufou to campaign against Amadou and Ousmane, although several MNSD leaders wanted the president to stand himself.

Consequently, relations between Tandja and Prime Minister Amadou remained difficult, with the president rumoured to have demanded the latter's resignation in an impending **cabinet reshuffle**, a demand that Amadou would have claimed was the prerogative of the National Assembly. The prime minister struck back by nominating several supporters to important regional positions. While he was reported to have clashed with the influential minister of economy and finance (and presidential associate), Ali Mahaman Lamine Zeine, both retained their positions in a cabinet reshuffle of 27 June. At year's end, there were again reports of strains and potential reshuffles.

The reorganisation of the cabinet ended the tenures of the ministers of health and of education, who, according to an EU audit report on the ministry of education, were involved in embezzlement of donor funds to a value of $ 7.8 m over a five-year period. On 1 October, the Assembly decided that the minister of education would be prosecuted for financial mismanagement in the 'Haute Cour de Justice'. The **massive embezzlement** reflected badly on the prime minister and provided President Tandja with a means to reinforce his position at Amadou's expense. In February and March, he threatened financial controllers at ministerial departments with dismissal if corruption and mismanagement was not halted. Tax raids took place in Niamey on 20 March but targeted small fry, such as street traders, and should hence be seen as symbolic. In another case, the state was reported to have been defrauded of millions of CFA francs through a racketeering scheme involving customs declarations for government vehicles.

The embezzlement of education funds was politically explosive as a result of **social protests**, spearheaded by university students, who complained of non-payment of grants and poor facilities. In June, they forced the closure of the university. This was the culmination of months of unrest that began in February, when students boycotted classes and Niamey's hospital was hit by strike action. Medical personnel intended to go on strike from 7 to 9 March. Generally, these protests should be seen against the backdrop of declining living standards that over the years have made the pre-harvest rise in food prices as well as the reduction in public services, partly IMF-induced, insupportable. Fresh vegetable prices in June rose by 54%.

On 15 March, 50,000 people walked through the capital to protest against high food prices and falling incomes. In May and June, tax collectors went on strike, while students declared a state of permanent protest and complained that scholarship fees had not been paid since January. **Riots** erupted when the government ordered the evacuation of the university campus by 29 May, with more than 40 people being injured and 300 arrested. No courses could be given during the following month. On 20 June, 3,000 to 4,000 students, teachers and angry citizens marched to the National Assembly to protest against mismanagement and the lack of university funds. As in the previous year, when tax riots led to the empowerment of a new citizen's movement, different groups were banding together against the government. The volatility of political life was not limited to the capital either, as shown in the town of Birni N'Konni, where riots erupted in late May and early June after police tried to clamp down on petrol smuggling from Nigeria. Events in the capital quickly recaptured national headlines, however. On 15 June, the 'Coalition Contre la Vie Chère' (CCVC), made up of union and consumer groups and led by Nouhou Arzika, as well as the 'Coordination Démocratique de la Société Civile du Niger' (CDSN), organised another **'Pays Mort' campaign** that brought Niamey to a standstill. The demonstrations involved civil servants as well as taxi drivers. Arzika accused the government of pursuing IMF-dictated policies, arbitrary increases in petrol prices and increased charges, all of which put basic utilities beyond the reach of the poor. His coalition demanded a reduction in telephone, electricity and water tariffs of between 30% and 50%. On 22 June, there was a similar day of protest, and the go-to-work call of the governor of Niamey was ignored. No violence was reported. A third 'dead country' campaign was held on 6 July, but a fourth scheduled for 29 July was called off to avoid clashes with cadres from government parties.

As in other matters, the country's leadership was divided in its responses. On 10 July, Tandja released cereal reserves to be sold at reduced prices or handed out free of charge to the poor. Three days later he established a negotiating committee, promising dialogue with citizens' groups. The prime minister, however, denounced the campaign organisers and went so far as to organise a **counter-demonstration** by tens of thousands of MNSD supporters in front of the National Assembly on 29 July. A social forum of NGOs scheduled for 27–30 October was banned.

With food availability such a sensitive issue, the government persevered in its defensive attitude towards international media coverage of famine and malnutrition. When a BBC team reported food shortages in the Maradi region, one of the worst hit in the 2005 famine, it was summoned to Niamey. On 3 April, the government banned accreditation of foreign journalists covering the food story. This decision was taken at the behest of Tandja himself and lent credibility to complaints by foreign aid workers of a **culture of denial** at the highest levels of government. Yet, the prime minister had been more open about the 2005 famine and had led a swift response to an outbreak of avian flu in February. On 5 June, moreover, Finance Minister Lamine Zeine sent a memorandum to the IMF admitting that up to 25% of the population had been affected by the famine of the previous year. Tandja thus took it upon himself to lead his cabinet in a national prayer meeting on 28 June to pray for the seasonal rains, which by then were late in coming. When they did arrive, they were abundant and resulted in good harvests, easing the food situation. With a predominantly rural electorate, this could only reinforce the government's position.

The country was reminded of the risks of political instability when on 21 February the **trial of 70 soldiers** implicated in the 2002 mutiny commenced. Prosecuted for a mutiny over better pay and conditions in Niamey and the eastern towns of Diffa and N'Guigmi, six men were sentenced after a two-week trial. Two men were sentenced to seven years in jail, four others to four years each, which meant that they were immediately released, since they had spent that amount of time in provisional detention. Human rights groups expressed concern over the time the soldiers had spent in jail. This has been a normal occurrence in Niger, with people spending years in incarceration awaiting trial for even minor offences, a predicament that could often only be ended by having family bribe prison staff or members of the judiciary, an option that left those without relations in dire circumstances. The mutineers of Diffa, who had taken hostages in 2002, leading to fighting and two deaths, were still awaiting prosecution.

Another event with implications for stability was a meeting between Tandja and Rhissa Ag Boula, the former Tuareg minister of tourism who was jailed for the murder of an MNSD militant but released in 2005. He was now asked to help prevent the spill-over of a conflict between **Tuaregs** and the government of neighbouring Mali (2 June). This allowed Rhissa to press for the rehabilitation of his comrades, who have been confined to special camps since 1995. In April, Tandja announced a $ 1.6 m programme to help them integrate into society. It was not clear whether this was part of the same programme launched in 2005 and funded by the US, Libya and France.

Chronic trafficking in the northern regions contributed to insecurity. On 11 August, a goods convoy escorted by the army was attacked and robbed near Agadez. The assailants captured five vehicles containing cigarettes destined for Libya. One soldier was killed, another abducted. Local radio reported that the attackers were rebels from Chad, although the military refused to speculate. In December, a customs official was killed and five people were wounded in an exchange with smugglers just north of the mining town of Arlit.

In the **border region with Chad**, 23 tourists were kidnapped between Agadem and Bilma (14 August). The group entered Niger from the Chadian town of Mao – a route known for its banditry. What made the authorities angry was the fact that the convoy of 11 four-wheel-drive vehicles and one lorry did not go to the city of N'Guigmi to report to customs, but travelled northwards to Bilma along a dangerous desert track parallel to the Chadian frontier. In a premeditated move, they were ambushed by armed men claiming to be members of the 'Front des Forces Armées Révolutionnaires du Sahara' (FARS), a group of Toubou rebels active during the 1990s. One German managed to escape, after which the rest of the party was released, with the exception of two Italians. The kidnappers demanded a dialogue with the authorities, insisting on establishing why their leader Chahaye Barkaye had been killed in clashes with the army in 2001, despite a peace accord concluded in 1997, and demanding implementation of the accord's development provisions. On 12 October, a Libyan charity close to President Kadhafi secured the release of the Italians. Though this was denied, it is likely that money was paid. Some of the captors would have been Chadian. Apart from the travelling party's apparent irresponsibility, satellite telephones have increased the attack capabilities of local groups.

Politically more dangerous was the deterioration of relations with **Chadian immigrants**, notably nomadic Mahamid Arabs who migrated to the Diffa region in the 1970s and 1980s to escape drought and conflict. The 2001 census pointed to growing tensions over grazing land and access to wells. On 24 October, the government announced the expulsion of 100,000 to 150,000 Mahamids, who themselves claimed to number 30,000. It was rumoured that a political motive might be involved, as many Mahamids would back a presidential rival to Tandja, who himself hails from the region. The Mahamids originally registered with local chiefs and in several cases obtained Nigérien identity papers along with the right to vote. Many became wealthy, controlling substantial parts of the local economy or occupying positions in the civil service or the security forces. Local grassroots pressures were apparently responsible for the government's action, which led to protests from Niger's wider Arab community and neighbouring countries. After security forces started rounding up people, the government backtracked. On 27 October, the operation was suspended. It was claimed that only those without papers would be expelled, estimated to number 3,000 to 4,000. A special commission of officials of the interior ministry and environmental and veterinary experts were to consider alternatives to expulsion. The rescinding of the expulsion order led to protest marches in Diffa on 28 and 31 October. Nigérien human rights groups condemned the politicisation of the issue.

As in previous years, relations with **the media** were difficult. On 20 February, the director of 'L'Autre Observateur' was fined after spending 25 days in provisional detention for defamation of an entrepreneur close to Tandja. In April, the composition of the state media regulator, the 'Conseil Supérieur de la Communication' (CSC), was changed to the advantage of its government representatives. The CSC suspended the newspaper 'l'Opinion' and warned 'Radio Ténéré' for biased reporting on the 'dead country' campaigns. On

1 September, two journalists of 'Le Républicain', arrested on 4 August, were jailed for 18 months for defamation and spreading 'false news'. They published an admittedly tendentious article on the prime minister and his supposed courting of relations with Iran, anti-Western bias and disrespect for human rights. The editor and publisher were heavily fined. On 28 August, a reporter of 'L'Enquêteur' was arrested for a story on ritual killing and on 18 September he was sentenced to a six-month prison term. The partisan reporting of many media channels aside, part of the problem continued to be the broad definition of the media laws and the powers of the CSC, which invited the sustained intervention of (international) media watchdogs.

Foreign Affairs

On 12 January, Tandja was re-elected chairman of ECOWAS at a meeting of government leaders in Niamey. This was followed by the **UEMOA** conference, which ended in Niamey on 27 March after deciding to defer the date for economic convergence of the eight member states until late 2008, the second postponement since 1999 when the convergence pact was signed. Niger had not achieved the four primary convergence criteria for economic integration (balanced budget, 3% inflation maximum, maximum public debt of 70% GDP and no debt repayment arrears).

US involvement continued in the framework of 'anti-terrorism' collaboration. A small presence of **US troops** was reported at In Abangharit, an oasis southwest of Arlit and ideally located for keeping watch on transborder migration from Mali. Troops were also spotted in Maradi, known for its Islamist groups, and at Abrik, a transit point between Niger, Algeria and Libya. Niger's 'anti-terrorist' units are often sent to Louisiana in the US for training.

France financed a project worth € 11 m for water provision to villages in the Tahoua area. Relations with **Algeria** were boosted by an agreement signed on 23 January that awarded the Algerians oil exploration rights in the Bilma, Djado and Tamesna regions. In addition, Niger agreed to participate in the NEPAD-sponsored project for a 4,500 km trans-Saharan gas pipeline for exporting natural gas from Nigeria to Algeria, reported to cost some $ 7 bn. **Asian countries**, too, showed renewed interest. On 13 February, it was announced that India would provide $ 500 m for funding the extension of the railway from Parakou in northern Benin to Niamey – an old plan that would now cost $ 1.5 bn. China on 18 July agreed to build and finance the second bridge across the Niger river in the capital. Active in oil exploration in the Ténéré desert, the Chinese also announced the discovery of major coal reserves in the Tahoua region. Three Chinese companies alongside two Canadian ones were granted concessions for the exploration of uranium, thus potentially challenging France's domination of Niger's uranium industry.

Socioeconomic Developments

Niger's problem continued to be its inability to deal with short-term crises alongside long-term development needs. The decisions of the G8 summit of 2005 led the IMF in December of that year to cancel Niger's IMF debts incurred before January 2005 ($ 111 m). Shortly before, it had significantly increased its financial assistance under the PRGF. In 2006, on 19 June, the IMF completed its second review of Niger's PRGF and released $ 8.7 m, bringing the total amount drawn under the programme to $ 26.1 m. The IMF provided waivers for the non-compliance with tax reforms due to the 2005 food crisis. In April, the ADB announced it would write off debt, while on 29 June the World Bank provided multilateral debt relief of an annual $ 20 m over a 37-year period. Total **debt relief** was expected to halve external debt.

During the summer, the EU and France provided $ 47 m in food and healthcare support. Saudi Arabia, the ADB and the World Bank announced decisions worth a total of $ 35 m to improve **water supply** systems (26 May, 6 and 28 July). The global bank on 13 June also announced a credit of $ 50 m to increase government service delivery to the poor. The West African Development Bank committed itself to a loan for improving the water supply in towns west of the capital and south of Maradi. The Chinese were similarly active in Zinder.

Niger's gold mine at Samira Hill began to increase export receipts, with gold overtaking **cattle exports** as the country's second most important export earner. This was partly due to the fall in cattle exports in the wake of the 2005 famine. Uranium exports were expected to rise due to interest from various companies and soaring prices. The 2005 inflation rate was finally estimated to have averaged 7.8%. In the course of 2006 it fell, reaching 6.4% in April. GDP growth, closely following agricultural output, was forecast during the year to reach between 3% and 4%.

The BCEAO estimated that the 2005 harvest was 37% higher than in 2004. Niger thus entered 2006 with modest food surpluses, although pockets of **food deficits** persisted. Prices for cereals, fish and vegetables continued their downward trend in the first months of the year. Millet and sorghum prices fell 50% compared to the mid-2005 peak, but worries persisted about whether this would be enough to allow for the replenishment of stocks. While food shortages during the lean season (starting in March) have been a fact of life, the result of the 2005 famine was that people had little to fall back on to withstand hardship. Household indebtedness was high, since people had bought food or seeds on credit or sold off cattle. Peuls and Tuaregs – mostly pastoralists – were expected to face difficulties. Still thought to be vulnerable were 1.8 m people, notably in the Tillabéri, Dosso and Tahoua regions. On 28 March, the UN launched an appeal to buy food stocks for the Sahelian countries, including Niger. USAID warned that food shortages would increase until the autumn harvest and Niger's government appealed for aid in replenishing food reserves, which as a result of the famine were significantly below the desired 110,000 tonnes.

Rains finally started in mid-July and developed into **torrential downpours** in many places. In the north, 10,000 people were hit, especially in the Saharan town of Bilma, which received more rain than during the entire previous decade and was practically destroyed. Between 30,000 and 50,000 people in 5,000 villages in the north, south and west were affected as downpours swept away mud houses and vegetable gardens, and the government was forced to provide lodging in administrative buildings, as well as food and medicine. WFP provided food aid, while Libya sent tents and blankets. Nevertheless, the rains led to good harvests. Even if there were localised deficits, overall there was a **cereal surplus** of an estimated 457,237 tonnes.

Food security was complicated by an outbreak of **avian flu** of the dangerous H5N1 strain. Coming from Nigeria, it was first discovered in Magaria and then spread to Gouré and N'Guigmi in the far east. With WHO funds amounting to CFAfr 2 bn, a programme of forcible culling was launched, with owners receiving compensation. The torrential rains later in the year also led to cholera outbreaks in the central region and the east, with a few dozen people succumbing to the disease. An outbreak of **meningitis**, three times greater than in 2005, proved potentially more serious as the strain, diagnosed among 1,500 children (late March), was resistant to existing vaccines. There was controversy about uranium contamination in Arlit, where NGOs claimed radioactive mine waste constituted a danger to public health. On 3 May, thousands of people marched through the desert town demanding action. A government committee met with local groups. Niger retained its position at rock bottom on the Human Development Index.

Klaas van Walraven

Nigeria

In 2006, the failed third-term campaign by supporters of incumbent President Olusegun Obasanjo coincided with a deep constitutional and political crisis in four states that threatened the political system and endangered the run-up to the forthcoming election marathon in April 2007. These events may have far-reaching repercussions for the democratic transition to a new leadership. The contentious and even dubious impeachments of four state governors caused nationwide uncertainty and raised serious constitutional and legal questions about Nigeria's federal system. It even highlighted the arbitrariness with which elected and appointed bodies tried to break legal rules whenever they saw fit. In relation to the domestic security situation, there was a frustrating paradox between an increasing number of police, expanded organised crime and the re-emergence of a deep social and ethnic-religious divide, demonstrated by the Danish cartoon controversy. Notwithstanding the general security decay, thanks to soaring oil prices the government accumulated huge foreign reserves, which paved the way for a possible exit strategy with the London Club of creditors and remarkably stabilised macroeconomic performance.

Domestic Politics

An anti-third term campaign inside and outside the National Assembly and the ruling People's Democratic Party (PDP) successfully placed in question President Obasanjo's almost undisputed leadership position. Despite months of public discussion, the senate put an end to the extremely contentious constitutional issue at the commencement of the legal process on 16 May by halting any amendment of the **constitution**, which stipulates that presidents and governors should serve a maximum of two terms. Although the president had never publicly said he wanted to stand for re-election, maintaining he would make his decision if the constitution were amended, he was nevertheless aiming for a third term. Moreover, incumbent and former governors would have benefited from such an amendment as well.

The failed third-term bid also highlighted the intense factional struggles within the political class (particularly within the PDP) in the run-up to the 2007 election to secure access to the immense financial resources generated by oil and gas revenues. These struggles increased because the governors receive and administer huge statutory allocations to states and local governments, thereby enjoying considerable powers. On 7 July, the **supreme court** actually strengthened these powers by declaring legislation unconstitutional that empowered the federal government to monitor the statutory disbursement of local government allocations by state governments.

The federal government's **anti-corruption campaign**, mainly executed by the Economic and Financial Crimes Commission (EFCC), had recovered some $ 5 bn in illegally acquired monies within just three years. In addition, the commission also took aim at several incumbent and former governors. In the case of Diepreye Alamieyeseigha, former governor of Bayelsa state, for example, British police handed back about £ 1 m to the Nigerian government, while his South African mansion was auctioned. However, gubernatorial immunity prevented the commission from taking legal action against governors while in office. This contrasted starkly with the position of legislators at all levels, who enjoyed such protection only with regard to proceedings on the floor of the house. Several governors were, nonetheless, under investigation, and the EFCC regularly fed legislators with information on corruption charges and sometimes put pressure on those who were under scrutiny to cooperate with the commission. Once again, dubious impeachment proceedings, which were in fact power struggles within the ruling PDP, brought to light the widespread culture of political deviousness among the political class.

The **impeachment saga** began in Oyo state in the northern Yoruba heartland on 12 January, when the state legislators impeached Governor Rashidi Adewole Ladoja (PDP). His deputy, Christopher Alao-Akala, took over. After ten months of vigorous legal battles, a unanimous judgment by the court of appeal nullified the impeachment of Ladoja as unconstitutional. On 7 December, the supreme court upheld the ruling and Ladoja returned to the governor's house in the state capital, Ibadan.

The political crisis in Anambra state in the Igbo heartland continued unabated, despite the fact that Peter Obi of the All Progressive Grand Alliance (APGA) was sworn in as governor on 17 March, thereby ending the long-lasting legal contest with the then PDP governor, Chris Ngige. Against the background of a deeper crisis that cost many lives, involving militias such as the banned Movement for the Actualisation of a Sovereign State of Biafra (MASSOB) and the Bakassi Boys, Peter Obi could not maintain his leadership position. From the day he took office, he was locked in a power struggle with Andy Uba, a close advisor of the president and a PDP aspirant for the next governorship of the state. Under dubious circumstances, the PDP-dominated state assembly finally impeached the incumbent, and his deputy Virginia Etiaba reluctantly took over on 3 November, just 24 hours after declining to be sworn in. Thus she became the first **female governor** in the history of the country. Nevertheless, on 28 December, the high court in the state capital of Awka declared the impeachment of Peter Obi null and void, but this had no immediate political impact.

Governor Joshua Dariye (PDP) of the crisis-ridden Plateau state in the volatile minority area in the Middle Belt was the next impeachment victim. In the wake of increasing turmoil and violence in the state, testimony by a detective from the Metropolitan Police in London detailing the circumstances leading to the arrest and questioning of the governor in Britain in 2004, caused the state house to impeach Dariye on 13 November with just eight of the 24 legislators present. Notwithstanding this **illegal act**, his deputy, Chief Michael Botmang, took over the same day.

With the impeachment of another PDP governor, Ayodele Fayose of Ekiti state in the eastern part of Yorubaland, on 16 October and the declaration of a **state of emergency** three days later by President Obasanjo, the impeachment saga reached its climax. The political and constitutional crisis in the state escalated after the former speaker of the state house, Friday Aderemi, became governor after he had supervised the impeachment of Fayose and his deputy, Mrs. Biodun Olujimi. While the impeached governor did not accept the verdict and went into hiding, his deputy claimed to be the acting governor. The upshot was that there were three potential governors in the state.

The federal government took the view that the whole impeachment process was **unconstitutional** and used the ridiculous situation of having three governors as the main argument to declare a state of emergency. The president suspended the office of governor and the legislature for six months and appointed a former head of the West African peacekeeping force in Liberia, retired Maj. Gen. Adetunji Olurin, as administrator. After a long and controversial debate, the National Assembly eventually endorsed Obasanjo's decision with the required two-thirds majority of both chambers on 26 October.

By the end of December, the National Judicial Council (NJC) had suspended the chief judge of Anambra state, a high court judge in Plateau state and the chief judge and a high court judge in Ekiti state. In the view of the NJC, they had not followed due process during recent impeachments of state governors. However, on 14 July, the court of appeal finally resolved the last case arising from the 2003 gubernatorial elections and confirmed the validity of James Ibori's governorship (PDP) in Delta state, which had been challenged by Chief Great Ogboru.

The failed third-term bid paved the way for several rounds of fierce contest within the ruling PDP. Despite his own defeat, Obasanjo was still able to steer the selection process in a particular direction. Vice-President Atiku Abubakar and former military dictator Ibrahim Babangida, both considered as strong potential successors, were the most prominent victims on the PDP platform. The vice-president was suspended from the party over **corruption allegations**, which were orchestrated by the presidency. Obasanjo finally sacked his vice-president on 23 December while the latter was on a private visit in the US, thereby executing a long-awaited but constitutionally contentious decision. Babangida, however, reluctantly withdrew from the race in the run-up to the convention in December, realising that he would face public humiliation at the convention.

In the aftermath of this political manoeuvre, the election of Umaru Musa Yar'Adua, governor of Katsina state, as **PDP presidential candidate** came as a surprise to many analysts. With no real military background but backed by Obasanjo, he thus succeeded as the consensus candidate on 17 December. Most delegates saw him, even as a Muslim, as someone who would probably be acceptable to large parts of the Middle Belt and of the establishment in the south and southwest. The son of one of the richest and most famous Hausa-Fulani families in northern Nigeria's Muslim establishment, Umaru Yar'Adua grew up under the shadow of his older brother, retired Maj.Gen. Shehu Musa Yar'Adua, number two under General Obasanjo when the latter was junta chairman from 1976–79. The Yar'Adua family was one of the very few Hausa-Fulani families who spent much time in the then capital of Lagos and were familiar with Yoruba politics and culture. Because of that, the general was able to establish and sponsor a powerful nationwide political network with the ultimate aim of being elected president. Imprisoned in 1995 and assassinated by military dictator Abacha in 1997, Shehu Musa Yar'Adua's network eventually served as the main platform for the PDP. Hardly had Umaru Yar'Adua been elected PDP presidential candidate than he named Goodluck Jonathan, governor of the southern oil state of Bayelsa, as his running mate. Obasanjo, however, convinced the delegates to amend the party rules in his favour, thereby becoming PDP chairman of the board of trustees after leaving office.

During the year, Vice-President Abubakar, who also belonged to the pre-PDP network, strategically established a new political platform made up of factions of other parties. Supported by an alliance of prominent politicians, such as former PDP chairman Innocent Audu Ogbeh and Bisi Akande of the Alliance for Democracy (AD), Abubakar was chosen by the Action Congress (AC) as presidential candidate at a convention in Lagos on 20 December. The former junta chairman, retired Maj.Gen. Muhammadu Buhari, runner-up in the 2003 presidential election, became the consensus candidate of the All Nigeria People's Party (ANPP).

As in previous elections, the **electoral commission** was not able to live by its own rules and regulations. The Electoral Act stipulated that the electoral register was to be completed 120 days before the start of elections for governors and state assemblies and for president and National Assembly (14 and 21 April 2007 respectively). The exercise began on

25 October, but because of poor logistics as well as serious technical, administrative and managerial problems, only some 20 m of an estimated 60 m eligible voters were registered by the 14 December deadline. INEC, the Independent National Electoral Commission, had no choice but to extend the exercise and set a new deadline of 30 January 2007. This legally contentious decision was made possible after the National Assembly began the procedure to amend the Electoral Act before 30 January 2007.

During the second half of the year, several ministers and special advisors resigned or were relieved of their posts. The first major **cabinet reshuffle** took place on 1 June. The most prominent figure among those removed from the cabinet was the national security advisor, retired Lt. Gen. Aliyu Gusau, who was replaced by retired Maj. Gen. Sarki Murktar. Finance minister, Mrs. Ngozi Okonjo-Iweala, who had taken credit for the debt agreement with the Paris Club in 2005, reluctantly replaced Oluyemi Adeniji as foreign minister. The latter was moved to the ministry of internal affairs. Okonjo-Iweala's deputy, Mrs. Nenadi Usman, became minister of finance and after a short and bitter power struggle with her former superior took over the powerful presidential economic team as well. After Ngozi Okonjo-Iweala claimed to have uncovered alleged fraud at the ministry, the presidency dismissed her claims, clearing her predecessor of any wrongdoing. On 3 August, she resigned and Joy Ogwu, director-general of the Nigerian Institute of International Affairs (NIIA), took over her portfolio.

In November, the second major cabinet reshuffle included the resignation of the defence minister, Rabiu Musa Kwankwaso, a former governor of Kano state, who again had political ambitions in his home state. Minister of State Thomas Aguiyi-Ironsi, son of Nigeria's first military ruler, took over. In addition, Babalola Borishade (aviation) swapped his portfolio with Femi Fani-Kayode (culture and tourism) after a **devastating air disaster** on 29 October, which left some 100 people dead, among them Muhammadu Maccido, Sultan of Sokoto, his son and other dignitaries. On 12 June, Justice Salihu Modibbo Alfa Belgore replaced Chief Justice Muhammad Uwais, who had reached the mandatory retirement age of 70.

By the end of December, the government announced the pruning of federal ministries from 27 to 19. Accordingly, it merged aviation, transport and works into the ministry of transport, while the ministry of police affairs was taken over by the ministry of internal affairs. The most important decisions affected the oil and power portfolios, which were merged into the energy ministry, and the ministry for information, which assumed the functions of the communications ministry.

The decision regarding personnel affected the **military** as well. On 30 May, the president retired General Alexander Ogomudia (chief of defence staff) and Air Marshal Jonah Wuyep (chief or air staff) and replaced them with chief of army staff Lt. Gen. Martin Agwai and Air Vice Marshal Paul Dike respectively. Lt. Gen. Owoye Andrew Azazi was appointed chief of army staff, while Vice Admiral Ganiyu Adekeye retained his position as chief of naval staff. Agwai was promoted to the rank of general and Dike to that of air marshal. Dike became the first ethnic Igbo to rise to that position, while Azazi was the first ethnic Ijaw to head the army.

However, an air disaster hit the top military brass of the army when a Dornier **military aircraft crashed** on 17 September, leaving only five survivors. The officers had been en route to the Obudu cattle ranch in Cross River state for a meeting ordered by the chief of army staff to discuss the future of the military in the next decade. Four days later, 23 senior officers, including eight major generals and two brigadier generals, were buried with national honours in the capital Abuja.

The **Danish cartoons** of the Prophet Mohammad led to the re-emergence in their worst form of deep ethnic and religious divisions in the world's largest Christian-Islamic country. The cartoons even triggered several bloody clashes, namely in Shendam and Namu in Qua'an Pan local government area, Plateau state and in Ihima, Kogi state in April, and in Offa and Enrinle, Kwara state in June. Although the cartoons had been published in Denmark in September 2005, the worldwide protests against the publication reached the predominantly Muslim north only in early February 2006. The Kano state house of assembly immediately banned all Danish goods and cancelled negotiations with a Danish company over the building of a power station. The issue escalated when members of the state house set ablaze Danish and Norwegian flags within the assembly's premises on 7 February. On 18 February, the issue got out of hand and exploded in Maiduguri, the Borno state capital, in the northeast. A mob of Muslims turned on local Christians, mostly ethnic Igbo, after police had broken up a rally against the cartoons. Several people were killed and a number of churches and shops looted and set on fire. Thousands of Christians sought sanctuary in army barracks and police stations while bloody clashes spread to other cities in the north. The arrival of the first corpses in the southern commercial city of Onitsha, Anambra state, sparked two days of riots (22–23 February) against the tiny northern Muslim community, mostly Hausa-Fulani. At least 80 died during the massacre before the governor imposed a curfew. Notwithstanding this action, reprisal attacks spread to neighbouring Enugu state, causing more deaths. In total, the riots over the cartoon cost some 130 Nigerian lives, by far the highest number worldwide.

At the same time, the inspector-general of police banned the activities of **religious marshals**, known as 'Hisbah', in Kano state: they were entitled by the state government to enforce shariah law. However, the state government refused to abide by the ban, maintaining that the 'Hisbah' volunteer group had been properly established by state law. In January, the southern Abia state had passed a similar law, which brought back the outlawed Bakassi vigilante group. In a swift reaction, however, the federal government accused the Kano state government of turning the 'Hisbah' vigilante group into a parallel police force and of seeking foreign sponsorship to train religious militants, thereby posing a threat to national security. On 9 February, the police arrested two of its leading figures, Yahaya Faruk Chedi and Abubakar Rabo Abdulkareem, and charged them in court in Abuja. After a three-month legal battle, the court of appeal overturned the verdict of the federal court and granted the detainees bail. Notwithstanding this, the Kano state government had already filed an application in the supreme court in February demanding that the court stop the federal government from disbanding 'Hisbah'. The federal government filed a counterclaim in April, asking the court to dismiss the constitutional case, and the court adjourned the case till 2 March 2007. In view of the cartoon and 'Hisbah' incidents, the public increasingly lost interest in archaic shariah court verdicts, which were becoming less frequent anyway, while several had been overturned or deemed to be pending.

On 2 November, because of the fatal air disaster that cost the life of Sultan Maccido, his younger brother Muhammad Sa'adu Abubakar, then a serving colonel, emerged as the 20th sultan of Sokoto. He immediately retired from the army and was subsequently promoted to the rank of brigadier general.

Anambra state and the Niger Delta were the most volatile parts of the country. The predominantly ethnic Igbo state in the southeast, centre of the banned militia MASSOB, the outlawed Bakassi Boys and the Anambra vigilante service, experienced another wave of violence between May and August. The multidimensional struggle for power and local revenues, in which militias, vigilantes, the state government, political parties and organised transport owners and transport workers were involved, escalated almost day by day. The prelude to this crisis began in late May when policemen from Abuja arrested more than 200 people, claiming them to be members of MASSOB. On 18 June, Governor Peter Obi imposed a one-week **dusk-to-dawn curfew** in the commercial capital, Onitsha, after a crowd had gone on the rampage the previous day and burned down two police stations. MASSOB claimed that police had killed eight of its members in a raid, a charge the police denied. However, the acts of violence increased when militants stormed Onitsha prison and set some 240 inmates free. That action forced the governor to extend the curfew to six neighbouring communities. Notwithstanding the curfews, clashes between police, militias and the feuding groups continued, leaving about 20 dead, including policemen. With good reason, the state government extended the curfew in Onitsha until mid-August.

MASSOB leader Ralph Uwazuruike, who had been arrested and detained the previous year, faced new **treason charges** and was denied bail. Mujahid Dokubo-Asari, the leader of the Ijaw militia, the Niger Delta People's Volunteer Force (NDPVF), suffered a similar fate. By contrast, Frederick Fasehun, leader of the banned Yoruba militia, the O'odua People's Congress (OPC), was granted bail because of serious health problems, with the federal government eventually dropping the treason charges against him, while Ganiyu Adams, factional leader of OPC, was released on bail on 19 December.

The continuing crisis in the oil- and gas-producing Niger Delta at times turned into **local warfare**, cutting annual oil production by more than 20%. Shoot-outs between soldiers and militias, military bombardments, car bomb explosions, kidnappings for ransom, armed robbery and the killing of innocent people were the order of the day. In the course of the year, some 160 foreign oil workers from Europe, Asia and the US were taken hostage. In several statements, militant groups gave the continued detention of militant leader Mujahid

Dokubo-Asari and former Bayelsa state Governor Diepreye Alamieyeseigha as factors driving their actions. In most cases, hostages were released unharmed within hours or days, usually after a financial deal was struck, in several cases mediated by the rather moderate Federated Niger Delta Ijaw Communities (FNDIC) under the leadership of Chief Bello Oboko or the state government. In short, **hostage-taking** had become a flourishing business. Consequently, these payments, which were kept secret, fuelled the violence and the proliferation of armed groups almost by the day. One US citizen was assassinated on 10 May in Port Harcourt, while a Briton lost his life during a rescue attempt on 22 November.

The military lost about 40 soldiers during several **gun battles** with militia forces, including the Movement for the Emancipation of the Niger Delta (MEND), the Joint Revolutionary Council (JRC), Coalition for Militant Action in the Niger Delta (COMA), Movement of the Niger Delta People (MONDP), Niger Delta Vigilante (NDV), Iduwini Volunteer Force (IVF) and, last but not least, the NDPVF. Security services, however, had a reputation for overkill in executing crackdowns, with the result that local communities, which the government needed on its side, were further alienated and made allegations of army brutality. The replacement of Brigadier Elias Zamani by Brigadier Alfred Ilogho in March as head of the military task force, which had been demanded by militia groups for some time, did not really change matters. The number of militia and civilian casualties was several hundred at least. Estimates by local observers put the figure even higher. Whatever the accurate figure, the bloodiest battles took place at Shell's Benisede flow station on 15 January and its Cawthorn Channel gas-gathering plant on 7 June and 2 October. On 15 February in Warri, the **military task force** bombarded the Ijaw community, who were suspected of harbouring militant youths. According to community leaders, 20 people died. At year's end, four foreigners who were taken hostage on 7 December by members of MEND were still being held and only a small number of militants had been arrested and charged.

In November, despite widespread hostilities, the chief of army staff opened a rare **dialogue with militants**. In addition, more stakeholders, such as the Nobel laureates' commission comprising Wole Soyinka and 64 other laureates, UNDP and USAID got involved to reverse the longstanding neglect of development of the Niger Delta. The commission was established to address injustice, mitigate suffering and prevent conflict from escalating and spilling across Nigeria's borders, and presented its comprehensive report on 1 December.

While cult and gang violence went on almost unabated, Nigeria experienced a wave of hitherto unknown organised crime and **politically motivated killings**. In the run-up to the elections in 2007, several well-known politicians at state and local level were assassinated. Governorship aspirants Jesse Aruku in Plateau state (end of June), Funso Williams in Lagos state (27 July), Ayo Daramola in Ekiti state (14 August) were killed by unknown assailants, and Sa'adatu Abubakar Rimi, wife of a former Kano state governor, was hacked to death in Kano city on 14 January. On 14 February, Shuaibu Sabon Birnin, director in the ministry of internal affairs, fell victim to gunmen wearing military uniforms. On 7 March, a former attorney-general of Kaduna state, Muhammadu Sani Aminu, was gunned down, and on

18 December, Ibrahim Bakare, a PDP campaigner in Lagos state, suffered the same fate. Segun Enrile, a former top civil servant in Ekiti state, was murdered on 22 October; Godwin Agbroko, chairman of the editorial board of the national daily 'This Day', was shot dead on 22 December; and Vincent Makanju, lecturer involved in peace education at Obafemi Awolowo University in Oyo state, was killed on 11 October. Local observers estimated that contract killings could be arranged cheaply and could cost as little as naira 100,000, equivalent to $ 775, depending on the victim's reputation.

As in previous years, **armed robbers** targeted long-distance buses, but the number of bank raids, raids on bureaux de change and armoured personnel carriers also increased significantly. An unknown number of retired and active security service staff were involved in these activities. Although most robberies took place in the southern part of the country, especially in Lagos and Port Harcourt, the crime wave also penetrated Abuja and bigger cities in the far north, such as Sokoto, Kaduna and Kano.

On 4 December, about 30 robbers targeted the international airport of Lagos just after midnight. In a four-hour operation, the gang took naira 150 m from the bureau de change and got away unscathed. On this particular occasion, no one was killed. On 17 November and 14 December, the famous Alaba international market along the Lagos-Badagry expressway was raided, leaving at least 26 persons dead, including some policemen. In fact, armed robbers raided no fewer than 12 banks during December alone. In the face of this **crime wave**, Nigeria's 25 banks decided to spend $ 15 m in upgrading security. However, for the first time security staff discovered explosives in the luggage of a passenger, one Samuel Dickson Adima, who was about to check in for an Abuja-bound flight in Lagos on 18 November. He was arrested and later four other suspects were taken into custody by security personnel.

Some 100 policemen lost their lives on duty – 67 alone within the fourth quarter of the year. Despite this unprecedented loss, the police retained their reputation for corruption and ongoing **extra-judicial killings**. The ugliest incident happened in crime-ridden Abia state on 10 August, when the police paraded 12 robbery suspects who had survived a deadly shoot-out with security forces. The following day, the 12 suspects were found dumped in a mortuary. The police did not comment on the incident and started an internal investigation. The federal government's reaction to the incessant crime, however, was just a major shake-up of the police in August, with the appointment of ten new deputy and assistant inspectors-general and the promotion of several officers within the top echelons of the police force in September. Nevertheless, in a remarkable verdict, the supreme court confirmed the death sentences against three policemen sentenced in 2001 for culpable homicide and armed robbery. In a highly symbolic gesture, 1,520 ethnic Igbo officers who were dismissed from the police force shortly after the civil war of 1967–70 were issued retirement letters by the police service commission with effect from 29 May 2000. This was in compliance with the approval of a presidential amnesty for police officers affected by the civil war.

Because of the worsening security situation, Nigeria's overall **human and civil rights** record was rather mixed. Harassment of journalists decreased slightly. In early February, charges were dropped against two broadcasters from Rhythm FM in Port Harcourt who were standing trial. Klem Ofuokwu and Cleopatra Taiwo were detained and charged in December the previous year with airing a news item that was later found to be false. TV presenter Mike Gbenga Aruleba of the private Africa International Television (AIT) and Rotimi Durojaiye, correspondent of the 'Daily Independent', were arrested in June and charged with sedition over a report questioning the airworthiness and cost of the new presidential jet, but the charges were eventually dropped. On 14 May, two days before the third-term bid was put to rest in the senate, the State Security Service (SSS) ordered AIT to immediately stop broadcasting a documentary on the extension of the tenure of officeholders and removed the master tape. In March, the Nigeria Broadcasting Commission (NBC) imposed a partial ban on Radio Freedom in Kano, the first privately owned radio station in the far north, for an alleged violation of the broadcasting code. On 16 June, the Nigerian navy detained an American photographer of the 'National Geographic', Ed Kashi, in Bayelsa state for photographing gas flares at a flow station. After three days in detention, however, he was released by the SSS. On 10 February, Bekololari Ransome-Kuti, member of the famous Kuti family and one of Nigeria's staunchest human rights and pro-democracy leaders, passed away at the age of 65.

A new law, the Advance Fee Fraud and Other Related Offences Act 2006, which came into effect on 5 June, forced all internet service providers to register with the EFCC. In July alone, the EFCC raided more than 20 cyber cafes. In August, as part of **prison reforms**, the federal government announced the release of 10,000 of some 40,000 inmates, those released having spent up to a decade in jail awaiting trial. Another 15,000 similar cases were to be considered in 2007. Large numbers of non-convicted inmates remained in jail because of delays in the justice system, missing police files, absent witnesses and poor prison management. On top of that, more than 400 convicted inmates had been waiting on death row for years.

Throughout Nigeria's colonial and postcolonial history the **national census** has always been a highly political and consequently contentious issue. The 2006 census was no different. Violence (which cost several lives), poor logistics, lack of material, widespread confusion and rows over payments to officials characterised the ambitious exercise (24–25 March). In fact, counting had to be extended by two days. At year's end, the national population commission released the provisional results, a figure of 140 m. In other words, Nigeria's population would have grown by 51 m since the last official census in 1991, meaning that the annual growth rate stood at 3.2%, with the ratio of males to females at 105 to 100.

Foreign Affairs

Nigeria's foreign policy focused on maintaining good relations with the US, which received more than 50% of all Nigerian exports; expanding existing relations with China; further increasing cooperation with Britain; leading African states in establishing closer ties with Latin America; and putting the Bakassi conflict with neighbouring Cameroon to rest.

Top-ranking politicians, military personnel and personalities from the US visited Nigeria during the year. George W. Bush's wife Laura arrived on 16 January on her three-nation West African tour and announced that the US was providing $ 163 m in 2006 to combat HIV/AIDS in the country. Former US President Bill Clinton joined the 7th biennial Leon Sullivan summit in Abuja (17–20 July), together with World Bank President Paul Wolfowitz and several African heads of state. On 16 July, North American Airlines opened a new chapter in direct US-Nigeria flights and flew in several summit delegates. **Cooperation with the US** was again confirmed by the visit in March of the commander of the allied joint force command in Naples, Admiral Henry Ulrich, and the arrival of a missile destroyer at the end of May to join the Nigerian navy's golden jubilee celebrations. In addition, security personnel from both countries took part in two high-level rounds of talks on security and safety issues in the Gulf of Guinea in May and July, while the US significantly increased its naval presence in the region. In December, Military Professional Resources Incorporated (MPRI), which works for the US government and comprises former top-ranking US military personnel, submitted a blueprint for a new defence policy to Nigeria's military top brass, both serving and retired. Ever since the end of military dictatorship in 1999, MPRI has acted as consultant to the Nigerian military leadership and provided special courses.

Bilateral relations got a boost after the federal government approved the extradition of war crimes suspect and former Liberian President Charles Taylor to his home country on 16 March. The decision paid off and Obasanjo was invited to the White House on 29 March. The close cooperation in combating financial crimes, money laundering and fraud was strengthened, and the US department of justice trained more than 130 Nigerian anti-corruption officials in February. In a joint action by the Nigerian and US **drug enforcement agencies**, some 14 metric tonnes of cocaine were intercepted at the port of Lagos in June. While the US Exim Bank approved $ 300 m for 14 of the 25 Nigerian banks to support US exports to Nigeria, it committed $ 15 m to promote the conduct of proper elections.

Nigeria extended and consolidated its **relations with China** on the economic front. In January, the China National Offshore Oil Company (CNOOP) bought a $ 2.3 bn stake in a Nigerian oil and gas field. Interestingly, India's largest oil and gas company had won the bidding in December 2005, only to have the purchase blocked by its government, which considered the bid commercially unviable and too risky. However, China's massive investment drive went on unabated, supported politically by the visit of its foreign minister in January, President Hu Jintao's two-day state visit on 26–27 April and the visit of the vice-president of China's Exim Bank in November. The Chinese president even addressed a joint session of the National Assembly, pointing out that China would forge a new type of Sino-African strategic partnership. In April, work spanning over 10 years commenced in Lagos on the Lekki free zone project. In addition, China agreed to finance the rehabilitation of the dilapidated railway system, build the Mambilla hydro power plant, which would cost some $ 2.5 bn, and to continue with the national rural telephone project. In August, Huawei Technologies, a leading private Chinese high-tech network equipment vendor, won a contract worth $ 100 m to provide the local Multi-Links company with sophisticated and state-of-the-art technology for multiple communication services in six core cities, namely Lagos, Ibadan, Port Harcourt, Abuja, Kaduna and Kano. After Obasanjo attended the three-day forum on Sino-African cooperation in Bejing (3–5 November), China Southern Airlines began direct air services to Nigeria on New Year's Eve. The temporary closure of the Chinese village in Lagos by the Nigerian customs service and the trial of some Chinese who had allegedly imported prohibited items caused some friction, but eventually proved to be a rather minor matter.

The strong orientation towards Asia did not stop there. With the three-day state visit by President Roh Moo-hyun (9–11 March), **South Korea** increased its engagement and investment by signing two wide-ranging agreements on energy cooperation and oil exploration. Obasanjo paid a return visit on 6 November. In October, the Malaysian-Nigerian Global Formwork joint venture started to build the $ 600 m 'Malaysian Gardens'residential housing scheme in Abuja, partly financed by Malaysia's external trade development corporation. His trips to Asia took President Obasanjo to the D8 summit in Indonesia (12–13 May) and to the annual meeting of the IMF and World Bank in Singapore in September, where he met consultants from JP Morgan and Fitch Ratings on 17 September and discussed his plan to pay back all debts of the **London Club** of private creditors. The president also met members of the global business community and assured them that elections would be peaceful, free and transparent. Then he stopped over in Japan to hold talks with Japanese Prime Minister Junichiro Koizumi and the president of Chubu Electric Power Company, one of the world's largest users of liquefied gas.

Top British politicians visited Nigeria as well, underlining growing **British interest** in its former colony. On 14 February, the secretary of state for foreign and Commonwealth affairs, Jack Straw, delivered a lecture on the role of the late junta leader, Gen. Murtala Ramat Muhammed, in nation building. Britain donated £ 250,000 for the retraining of policemen and fighting corruption, while £ 230,000 was given to the EFCC to strengthen its war on money laundering and other related crimes. Chancellor of the Exchequer Gordon Brown took part in an international conference on financing development in Africa in Abuja in May. In addition, Prince Charles went to northern Nigeria on a three-day visit (28–30 November) where he was treated to a traditional durbar similar to the one held 50 years ago for his mother, Queen Elizabeth II. The main purpose of the visit was, however, the inauguration of a peacekeeping training centre at the military college in Jaji, Kaduna state, which was built with £ 500,000 of British government funding. The government's aid agency, the Department of International Development (DFID), had already opened an office in Kano to manage the increased support to the Islamic north and to indicate a long-term commitment to Britain's former colony. President Obasanjo, along with several top ministers and Nigerian business tycoons, attended the Nigerian investment forum organised under the auspices of Baroness Linda Chalker in London (15–16 June).

The long lasting **Bakassi peninsula** and land border conflict with neighbouring Cameroon was finally put to rest in Archibong town on 14 August. In compliance with a ruling by the ICJ in 2002 and a UN-brokered deadline, authority over Bakassi was transferred, the Nigerian flag lowered and the Cameroonian flag hoisted in its place. The 12 June Greentree agreement paved the way for the final withdrawal of Nigerian troops. On 14 June, Obasanjo informed the public and defended the decision in a nationwide broadcast. Interestingly, the outcome of this costly and unnecessary legal and political battle exactly matched the findings by the late attorney-general of the federation, Taslim Olawale Elias, in 1970.

Nigeria's efforts to mediate and conclude the peace talks on the **Darfur crisis** in Sudan produced only mixed results. With the US deputy secretary of state, Robert Zoellick, and Britain's secretary of state for international development, Hilary Benn, in attendance as international mediators, an agreement with the main faction of the Sudan Liberation Movement (SLM) was signed on 5 May in Abuja. However, a splinter group of the SLM walked out of the signing ceremony and the other rebel group, the Justice and Equality Movement (JEM), also refused to join the accord. On 4 January, Maj.Gen. Collins Remy Umunakwe Iherike took over command of the AU intervention force in Darfur from his colleague Festus Okonkwo. However, on 19 August, three Nigerian peacekeeping soldiers were shot dead in an ambush.

Apart from Bakassi, Sudan, an African cocoa producers' summit in Abuja in May, an AU conference on security in the capital in September, and the extraordinary ECOWAS summit on Côte d'Ivoire on 6 October at the same location, the Nigerian leadership did not pay too much attention to continental or sub-regional politics. Obasanjo focused rather on getting the necessary support from the AU for the inaugural **Africa-South America Summit** in Abuja (26–30 November). A number of African and Latin American heads of state and government attended, among them Luiz Inácio 'Lula' da Silva from Brazil, Bolivian President Evo Ayma Morales, Blaise Compaoré of Burkina Faso and Muammar Kadhafi from Libya. The summit adopted a declaration that contained a plan of action intended to implement a wide-ranging cooperation programme. In addition, it was agreed that future summits would be held every two years and would alternate between Africa and Latin America, with the next summit scheduled for 2008 in Venezuela.

Nigeria's relationship with the **EU** was more or less defined by the financing of traditional development projects and projects that would strengthen democratic institutions. Accordingly, the EU provided funds to combat corruption and promote democracy. During a three-day visit (19–22 November) to Nigeria, the president of the European parliament,

Josep Borell Fontelles, donated $ 50 m to the electoral commission, INEC, and the anti-corruption agency, EFCC. On 26 June, a delegation of the EU commission, in collaboration with the national planning commission, launched two major programmes worth some $ 20 m aimed at institutional and economic reform of state and local governments as well as water and sanitation projects in six states, Anambra, Cross River, Osun, Kano, Jigawa and Yobe. In July, the Nigerian ministry of defence signed an $ 84 m contract with the Italian aircraft manufacture Alenia Aermacchi for the maintenance of 12 jet trainers.

After the meeting of **OPEC** in Abuja on 14 December, it was announced that Nigeria's minister of state for petroleum resources, Edmund Daukoru, would assume the OPEC presidency on 1 January 2007. In addition, on 17 November, Minister of Justice and Attorney-General Bayo Ojo was elected to the UN's prestigious International Law Commission.

Socioeconomic Developments

As in the previous year, socioeconomic developments were dominated by continually **soaring oil prices**, thereby stabilising the economy at the macroeconomic level. These developments were, however, overshadowed by the insurgency in the Niger Delta, which at times was akin to civil war, and devastating air and oil pipeline disasters.

Oil and gas prices on the international market rose sharply to historic heights. The price of light sweet crude and Brent, comparable to Nigeria's high quality crude, rose from the high $ 50 mark per barrel at the start of 2006 to $ 78 in August, before it fell to the $ 60 mark towards the end of the year. The permanent upheaval in the Delta region forced all oil companies to cut production, which cost Nigeria $ 4 bn in fiscal 2006. Nevertheless, the losses were to some extent offset by the extraordinarily high oil prices, which actually enabled the federal government to accumulate foreign reserves of an unprecedented $ 41 bn. Thus, the government appointed **external asset managers** to manage its foreign reserves and assets, including JP Morgan Chase and Credit Suisse from abroad and the local First Bank of Nigeria and Zenith Bank. At the end of May, President Obasanjo informed the senate that his government would negotiate repayment of some $ 2.3 bn owed to the London Club of creditors. By year's end, $ 1.4 bn had been paid back. Notwithstanding Obasanjo's ambitious aim to get rid of the debts owed to the Paris and London Clubs before leaving office, **domestic indebtedness** still amounted to $ 12 bn at the end of June. In a remarkable political move, the federal government commenced the payment of naira 75 bn in retirement arrears to an estimated 200,000 pensioners across the country in August. In July, it had already disbursed naira 4.5 bn of some naira 150 bn debts owed to local contractors.

Although it is a major oil producer, Nigeria showed that its gas production was becoming more important, indicated by the fact that liquefied natural gas production stood at some 22 m tonnes, which was delivered to the huge US market and the Mediterranean countries in the EU and Turkey. Thus, with **gas reserves** of some five trillion cubic metres, it had one of the largest reserves in the world at its disposal, more than double its oil reserves.

Notwithstanding the prosperous outlook, fuel scarcity prevailed most of the time, even disrupting international flights and leading to power failures. As in previous years, most petroleum products had to be imported and were still subsidised to the tune of almost $ 1.4 bn. The black market rate for fuel rose to naira 130–250 a litre in urban centres, although the official pump price was only naira 65.

A side effect of the huge reserves of foreign currency was the merger of the official and parallel market exchange rates for the local currency in May, which resulted in an exchange rate of naira 129 to the dollar. In recognition of Nigeria's general financial reforms, the country received its first credit rating by Fitch as well as by Standard & Poor's, two international rating agencies, in January and February. On 23 June, the Paris-based international finance task force even removed Nigeria from a list of countries that do not cooperate in the fight against money laundering. On 22 February, Obasanjo signed the naira 1.9 trillion ($ 14.5 bn) **budget** for 2006, which was related to a benchmark of $ 35 per barrel. Of the $ 4.2 bn capital budget, 40% was appropriated for key infrastructural areas such as power, roads, water supply and railways.

As in the previous year, Nigeria experienced devastating air disasters, which demonstrated again that the country's **air safety** was far below reasonable standards, although some $ 150 m was made available in April to improve safety at airports. On 14 November, President Obasanjo signed the new Civil Aviation Authority Act 2006 into law, which established flight safeguards, improved security checks and laid down tougher eligibility rules for air transport licences.

In the greater Lagos area, two petrol pipelines exploded on 12 May and 26 December, killing about 200 and 500 persons respectively. In early November, no fewer than 20 **pipeline vandals** were burnt to death in northern Adamawa state while tapping fuel. The blasts were probably ignited by sparks or candlelight shortly after the thieves had punctured the high pressure pipelines and tapped the fuel in order to sell it on the lucrative black market. This crime often attracts ordinary and poor people living next to the pipelines, who try to get fuel free of charge, ignoring the extreme dangers.

At the end of 2005, the federal government had within days cancelled the poor deal with the Egyptian Orascom Telecom Holding, which had offered a paltry $ 256 m for controlling shares in Nigerian Telecommunication Limited (NITEL). To put an end to the NITEL saga, the bureau of public enterprises **privatisation agency** dropped further competitive bidding in favour of a negotiated sale. On 3 July, the Nigerian Transnational Corporation Limited (Transcorp) took over 75% of NITEL and its mobile subsidiary M-TEL for the sum of $ 750 m. British Telecom, the operator and non-equity-holding technical partner, seconded Steve Brookman and John Weir to become chief executive officer of NITEL and head of M-TEL respectively. The booming Nigerian mobile phone market, with some 32 m subscribers towards year's end, saw another major takeover in May/June when Celtel, a subsidiary of Kuwait's MTC, acquired a controlling 65% share in V-mobile for $ 1.5 bn.

The second half of the year saw the retrenchment of thousands of civil servants under the public service reform programme. According to the president, the downsizing of the bloated service of some 1.5 m civil servants would enable government to spend more on the hitherto poor provision of services and infrastructure. Given the generally volatile political and socioeconomic situation, the National Industrial Court Act 2006 was passed in July, stripping federal and state high courts of jurisdiction to adjudicate suits relating to labour disputes in favour of newly established **industrial courts**. However, the high courts were granted one year to dispose of or decide all pending cases.

After South Africa and India, Nigeria was the third highest **HIV/AIDS**-infected country, with some 4 m persons living with the deadly virus. According to WHO, Nigeria topped the international polio list, with almost 1,000 cases in the northern part of the country. On 3 July, a five-day **polio immunisation** campaign in 11 endemic northern states was completed, but health officials were seriously concerned about the low turnout. Shortly thereafter, however, local health authorities, in collaboration with the UN, launched the 'Immunisation Plus' campaign to immunise 10 m people with the aim of eradicating the disease by the end of 2007.

The H5N1 **avian flu** virus reached Nigeria in January, causing health authorities to cull some 700,000 of an estimated 140 m poultry by October at a cost of more than $ 4 m. In early March, the government started to pay some compensation to poultry farmers, although 'backyard' poultry farmers accounted for an estimated 60% of business. On 29 March, however, the World Bank supported Nigeria's fight against the virus with a low-interest loan of $ 50 m.

In September, the **World Bank** emphasised that Nigeria was not a fragile state but had made rather good progress in addressing conflict and corruption. In December, the **IMF** commended the strong macroeconomic performance and the sustaining reforms in a difficult policy environment. In this context, the World Bank approved a $ 200 m loan for the Lagos metropolitan development and governance project on 6 July.

Heinrich Bergstresser

Senegal

Although one could hardly speak of electoral fever, it was quite obvious that the presidential elections scheduled for February 2007 affected the attitudes and manoeuvring of the country's principal political players. The designation of a presidential contender was the main preoccupation of political parties, leading to realignments and turmoil. In addition, cabinet reshuffles took place on two separate occasions, while the publication of politically motivated books about the government of President Abdoulaye Wade helped to heat up the political climate. Press freedom was marred by the confiscation of some of these publications, while libel suits hit local journalists and political leaders, some of whom were sentenced to prison terms. Foreign affairs were dominated by the rising tide of Senegalese migrants trying to gain entry into the EU, an issue that had implications for the country's ties with Spain and France. Compared to previous years, economic growth witnessed a noticeable decline. This affected large numbers of citizens, who expressed mixed feelings about the government's performance. The Casamance region remained a source of concern.

Domestic Politics

The domestic political scene was completely dominated by the preparations and campaign for the presidential elections scheduled for February 2007. President Abdoulaye Wade, nearing the end of his first seven-year term as head of state, publicly confirmed on 28 July that he would run for a new term in the **upcoming presidential contest**. In October, the ruling 'Parti Démocratique Sénégalais' (PDS) backed Wade to stand for a second term. According to a constitutional amendment introduced in 2001, this term is limited to five years.

The first event marking the unofficial start of the election campaign was the **release** on 7 February of **Idrissa Seck**. The former prime minister had spent six months and 17 days in custody on charges of threatening state security and misappropriation of funds allocated to renovation works in the town of Thiès, of which he was mayor. No evidence was found for the major accusation of threatening state security, but Seck was warned that he could still face legal action for fraud. Upon his release, Seck and his family left for Paris. Speculation began as to whether he would try to reconcile himself with Wade and support the president in the election campaign or decide to challenge his former political father and stand as candidate himself. At the beginning of April, Seck returned to Dakar and on 4 April, Independence Day, he at last made public his decision to run for president.

The impending elections also gave rise to much movement within the opposition parties. Particularly the 'Parti Socialiste' (PS), which was defeated in the 2000 presidential election after 40 years of ruling the country, faced a serious crisis. Its first secretary, Ousmane Tanor Dieng, commonly known as Tanor, was blamed for this defeat and a battle broke out for the PS candidature between Tanor and one of the other leading figures in the party, Ziguinchor's mayor Robert Sagna. This was the beginning of various **political realignments** that took shape over the course of the year and ultimately resulted in the nomination of three other opposition members as presidential candidates. Ousmane Tanor Dieng became the official candidate of the PS. In December, a new group of ten opposition parties created the 'Coalition Alternative 2007' (CA-2007) and elected Moustapha Niasse, former prime minister and leader of the 'Alliance des Forces du Progrès' (AFP) as their presidential contender. Robert Sagna became the candidate of the 'Takku Deferat Senegal' coalition (Rally to Develop Senegal).

The publication of certain **books** definitely formed part of the pre-election campaign. In March, a book was published on the economic thoughts of President Abdoulaye Wade. Entitled 'Abdoulaye Wade, sa pensée économique. L'Afrique reprend l'initiative', it was written by a journalist, Mamadou Alpha Barry. This was followed in May by another book on the president, also written by a journalist, Cheikh Diallo, under the title 'Si près, si loin avec Wade'. But the most discussed publications were again those by Abdou Latif Coulibaly. His book 'Sénégal Affaire Sèye: un meurtre commandé' published in 2005, in which he alleged that Wade was involved in the death of Babacar Sèye, achieved high sales figures in Dakar, but was unofficially banned in April when the new stock was confiscated by customs at the airport, as were copies found in the luggage of passengers. Coulibaly continued his crusade against the regime of Abdoulaye Wade with a new publication: 'Une démocratie prise en otage par ses elites', published in November.

In February and March, two minor **government reshuffles** took place. On 1 February, two ministers left the government and two others changed portfolio. Mamadou Seck, minister of infrastructure, equipment and transport, quit and was replaced by Habib Sy, until then minister of agriculture. The then minister of national solidarity, Farba Senghor, became the new minister of agriculture. The head of the ministry of small and medium sized enterprises, women's entrepreneurship and micro-finance, Maïmouna Sourang Ndir, had to step down in favour of her successor, Marie-Pierre Sarr. In May, a mini-crisis between the prime minister, Macky Sall, and the minister of local communities and decentralisation, Aminata Tall, lead to the dismissal of the latter. Her portfolio was added to the ministry of home affairs, headed by Ousmane Ngom. A more important reshuffle occurred on 24 November with the appointment of five new ministers, mostly drawn from the opposition in order to create a national unity government. The new ministers were the leader of the 'Parti des Travailleurs et du Peuple' (PTP), El Hadj Diouf, at the ministry for the national hydrographical network; Oumar Khassimou Dia of the 'Rassemblement pour le Peuple' (PR) as minister of Senegal's expatriates; Abdourahim Agne, leader of the 'Parti de la Réforme' (RP), who was appointed minister of microfinance and decentralised international cooperation; and Abdoulaye Babou, previously member of the 'Alliance des Forces de Progrès' (AFP), who became the new head of the ministry for labour, civil service and professional organisations. Finally, Khoreyssi Thiam, member of the PDS, was named minister of craft industries. This new cabinet shake-up was definitely part of the campaign for the presidential polls slated for 25 February 2007.

There was little progress towards ending the more than two-decade-old conflict in the southern **Casamance** region. The year started with an attack on 2 January by armed assailants: Gorgui Mbengue, the number-two government official in the district of Diouloulou, died in hospital and two other passengers travelling with him were injured. In April, one of the main rebel factions led by Salif Sadio moved to the border area with Gambia, the forested region of Koreck, after his base in southern Casamance had been attacked and destroyed by the Guinea-Bissau army. This resulted in clashes with another rebel faction led by Ismaïla Magne Dieme for control of this area. Forest resources such as timber, palms and charcoal were used to fuel the rebellion in this part of the Casamance. In December, Sadio's fighters attacked Dieme's base, killing most of his fighters and razing several villages in the vicinity of Koreck. On 4 December, about 20 men ambushed five vehicles on a road in this area and robbed the occupants of their possessions. One of the passengers died and five others were injured. In the same month, gunmen also ambushed a Senegalese army convoy involved in de-mining operations, killing two and injuring 14. To escape the fighting among the rebels and with government troops, thousands of people crossed into neighbouring Gambia. In November, President Wade met with more than 100 Casamance elders and asked them to broker a peace deal with rebels from the Movement of Democratic Forces of the Casamance (MFDC). He pledged an allocation to the elders of some CFAfr 60 m ($ 122,000) and logistical support to conduct their mission. Some factions of the MFDC, however, accused the elders of treachery and opportunism.

There were also some **institutional changes**. On 30 January, the number of members of the 'Conseil de la République pour les Affaires Economiques et Sociales', an advisory council, was increased from 100 to 110. Similarly, a law adopted on 7 November increased the number of deputies in the National Assembly from 120 to 150. The opposition criticised both measures as being too expensive and as an electoral stunt to give well-remunerated jobs to political clients of the president. On 9 November, the government amended the penal statutes by introducing sanctions against acts of terrorism. Finally, the National Assembly approved the government's proposal to grant voting rights to the military and paramilitary forces. This was the first time in the country's history that soldiers were allowed to vote.

The country celebrated the centennial of the birth of its first president, Léopold Sédar Senghor. The year 2006 was declared **Senghor year** and was marked by the publication of countless books about the 'président-poète' and more than 2,000 events all over the world, including the inauguration on 25 November by his successor Abdou Diouf of a Boulevard Senghor in Porta-Vila, the capital of Vanuatu. In Senegal, the official celebrations took place on 7 October in his birth place, Joal-Fadiouth. The local population and opposition parties criticised the national authorities for the lack of interest shown in this event. The presence of only one minister at the event was labelled 'a real insult for Senghor'. Although the Senghor year was announced by President Wade on the occasion of Independence Day, the government had endowed local authorities with limited funds for the celebration. A minor event took place on 7 February to celebrate the 20th anniversary of the death of Senghor's political opponent, Cheikh Anta Diop.

With regard to **freedom of expression**, a controversial bill was signed by the president on 4 January creating a 'Conseil National de Régulation de l'Audiovisuel'. The new body – a nine-member panel appointed by the president – was given the power to monitor media behaviour and impose punishments ranging from temporary closures to exorbitant fines of up to $ 18,000. On 22 November, Nancy Ndiaye Ngom was appointed the president of the new council. Despite continued promises by President Wade to decriminalise several press offences, no changes were made to article 80 of the penal code and other laws that impose criminal penalties for defamation and the publication of materials that compromise national security. Indeed, several people were arrested and charged with defamation. On 23 March, the director of the daily newspaper 'Il est Midi', Ndiogou Wack Seck, was sentenced to six months imprisonment, a fine of CFAfr 5 m and a two-year ban on practising his profession. He was found guilty of defaming a journalist working for the weekly 'Jeune Afrique'. On 18 April, the leader of the opposition party 'Parti de l'Indépendance du Travail' (PIT), Amath Dansoko, was summoned by the police crime squad ('Division d'Interrogation Criminelle', DIC) for spreading false information, and in August both Jean-Paul and Barthélemy Dias, father and son, got into trouble with the authorities. Jean-Pierre Dias, the leader of the 'Bloc des Centristes Gaïndés' (BCG) was sentenced on 15 August to three months imprisonment and his son Barthélemy, affiliated to the PS, to six months a week later. Both had made malicious statements with regard to President Wade and the public prosecutor, Lamine Coulibaly. Finally, the government restricted freedom of expression by seizing books considered too critical of the regime. Publications with titles such as 'L'Affaire Sèye' by Latif Coulibaly, 'Qui est cet homme qui gouverne le Sénégal' (Mody Niang), and 'Les Scandales Politiques sous la Présidence d'Abdoulaye Wade' (Mamadou Seck) were no longer available.

Despite this, a number of **new publications** were launched. In addition to the 20 existing daily newspapers, a new one, 'Place Publique', started in May and the seven existing weeklies were enriched with two new ones, '52' and 'Hebdomadaire Gratuit', the latter, as a paper free of charge, was quite a novelty on the African continent. Also, the three major private broadcasting stations with national reach, were joined by a new one, 'Océan FM'. Finally, in February, a private news agency was established in Dakar, Apanews, equipped with an English and French website.

Foreign Affairs

It was quite a busy year for the octogenarian Wade. The president not only received countless heads of state and other foreign VIPs, but also toured several countries himself. One of the most striking visits to Senegal was paid by the **Libyan leader Kadhafi** from 3–6 April. Kadhafi, together with four other African heads of state, attended the festivities marking the celebration of the 46th anniversary of Senegal's independence (4 April). He also held talks with President Wade on bilateral, African and international issues, addressed the National Assembly and laid the foundation stone of Kadhafi Tower, a 50-storey edifice funded by the Libyan Investment Fund for Africa at an approximate cost of $ 250 m.

Other remarkable **visits** were those by the two major rivals in the French presidential elections, Ségolène Royal and Nicolas Sarkozy in September. The French minister of home affairs, Sarkozy, signed an agreement with his Senegalese counterpart on 23 September in order to tackle the problem of Senegalese migrants to France. For Ségolène Royal, who was born in 1953 in Dakar, where her father was an officer in the colonial army, it was a two-day journey to her roots. Official candidate of the French 'Parti Socialiste', Royal was warmly welcomed at the headquarters of the Senegalese PS. Finally, on 2 December, President Ellen Johnson-Sirleaf of Liberia held talks in Dakar with Wade and female African foreign ministers gathering in the capital.

President Wade's foreign tours started on 30 January with a visit to his colleague in neighbouring Mauritania. On this occasion, President Vall and Wade discussed bilateral cooperation on energy and fishing issues and agreed to build a trans-Saharan motorway from

Tanger via Nouakchott to Dakar. In May, Wade visited Paris, mainly to receive the Houphouët-Boigny Peace Prize from UNESCO (16 May), an **award** won in 1991 by Mandela and De Klerk. The prize was given to President Abdoulaye Wade "for his contribution to democracy in his country and for his mediation in political crises and conflicts in Africa", said jury president Henry Kissinger. However, the award to Wade was much debated outside UNESCO headquarters, although the Sorbonne granted him an honorary degree at the end of the year (15 December).

The month of June was dedicated to **Asia**. Wade first made a six-day state visit to China (21–26 June) to further improve Chinese-Senegalese relations and sign a series of agreements, including an agreement on economic and technical cooperation. He continued his trip by paying an official three-day visit to Iran, where he met his counterpart President Mahmoud Ahmadinejad. The two presidents signed several cooperation agreements. At the beginning of August, Wade made a trip to Sudan and Chad to mediate between the two neighbours and help promote peace in Darfur, where a Senegalese contingent of about 7,000 soldiers is deployed. In November, Wade returned to China to attend the third Sino-African summit in Beijing.

Senegal particularly hit the international headlines because of the rising tide of **illegal migrants** heading for Europe. At least 31,000 Senegalese undertook the dangerous voyage to that continent, either by sea in small boats or through the burning desert, and many of them perished. On top of this, many Senegalese succeeded in entering Europe on tourist visas or with false documents. The massive increase in migrants (a fivefold increase reaching the Canary Islands compared to the previous year) was attributed to Spain's legalisation in 2005 of a huge number of illegal immigrants. In Senegal, the issue provoked diplomatic clashes with Spain and France. In May, the Senegalese government called off its assistance in the forced repatriation from Spain of the first contingent of Senegalese immigrants, protesting the fact that they were handcuffed. Abdoulaye Wade demanded treatment of his compatriots in accordance with international conventions and asked for large sums of aid to patrol the Senegalese coast and intercept migrant vessels. In the course of the next months, relations with Spain improved. An agreement on combined patrols was signed, Senegal sent police officers to the Canary Islands to assist their counterparts with the identification of more than 4,000 Senegalese awaiting repatriation, and in September the Spanish government adopted a plan focusing on the development of the agricultural sector in Senegal. Finally, on 4 December the prime minister of Spain, José Luis Zapatero, and Abdoulaye Wade signed an agreement providing for 4,000 temporary visas until the end of 2008 that would allow Senegalese to work in Spain. With France there was initially a dispute over the concept of 'selected immigration' put forward by the French government, which aimed at facilitating visas for Senegalese businessmen and artists. Ultimately, both countries signed an agreement providing for bilateral cooperation on immigration issues (23 September). In addition to selected immigration, this involved joint efforts to repatriate clandestine Senegalese and French agricultural projects worth some € 2.5 m. On the basis of the Spanish and French funds, Abdoulaye Wade initiated a programme ('Retour vers l'Agriculture', REVA) with the object of keeping youngsters at home by stimulating agriculture.

The case against the former dictator of Chad, **Hissène Habré**, who had been living in Senegal since 1990, gained momentum on 2 July when the AU called on the country to prosecute Habré 'in the name of Africa'. Exactly four months later, the government announced that it would revise its laws to permit Habré's trial and establish a governmental commission under the minister of justice to oversee the legal changes. In addition, it intended to establish contact with Chad, create a witness protection programme and raise money to carry out the investigation and trial.

Socioeconomic Developments

Economic performance was weak, with GDP growth projected at around 3.3% (the average growth rate in preceding years was about 6%) and a significant increase in the fiscal and external deficits. The decline mainly reflected the impact of higher oil prices, frequent disruption in electricity supplies and a temporary interruption in the operations of the chemical company, 'Industries Chimiques du Sénégal' (ICS). **Foreign assistance**, in the form of grants, loans and debt relief, amounted to about half of the external current account deficit in 2005–06. In addition to the aid promises made during official visits, the World Bank had approved 158 loans and credits totalling about $ 9 bn as of August. An amount of $ 35 m (approved on 28 February) was lent to increase agricultural production. Another credit line of $ 80 m was approved on 18 July to strengthen the capacity of the 67 urban municipalities and increase access to infrastructure and service in the urban areas. This Local Authorities Development Programme (LADP) is a five-year undertaking and was scheduled to start in November.

ICS, one of the largest firms in the country that used to make handsome profits from **phosphate** production, had now run into debts of approximately CFAfr 200 m. In August, its outstanding electricity bills led to a temporary power cut, including to the houses of its workers. In December, the Indian consortium Iffco/Oswal – holding 20% of ICS shares – brought some relief with its decision to invest CFAfr 60 m in the firm and support efforts for improved management. By contrast, **cement** production reached record levels, amounting to 2.8 m tonnes. This peak was merely the result of a construction boom in the country. In December, the International Financial Corporation granted a € 20 m loan to one of the two cement works, Sococim, to enable it to increase its daily production capacity. In the **ICT** sector, Senegal continued its success story: most important administrative forms could henceforth be downloaded from the internet, while in another sphere the number of call centres operating from Dakar increased to 18, providing many better paid jobs to well-trained youngsters.

In general, harvests as well as pasture conditions were relatively good. This was also true for the **groundnut** sector. However, as in preceding years, the recently privatised marketing company Sonacos ('Société Nationale de Commercialisation des Oléagineux du Sénégal') faced serious problems and had to interrupt its operations for several months, leading to the loss of export receipts of up to CFAfr 70 bn. Again, peasants complained about the tardiness of the authorities in fixing retail groundnut prices. The decision to maintain the price at CFAfr 150/kg offered by retailers, implying a state subsidy of CFAfr 8.2 bn, came through on 15 December. **Onions**, an important ingredient for the Senegalese consumer, were in short supply, leading to excessive prices on the local market. This was merely the effect of a measure taken on 6 January to 'rationalise' imports. The measure was revoked in August and producers reached consensus on fixing the selling price at CFAfr 175/kg.

A year before the elections in 2007, a **survey** of 8,000 inhabitants of Senegal was conducted in order to gauge public opinion on the achievements of the Wade regime since the president had taken office in 2000. The results showed reasonable satisfaction with regard to access to water and schools and great satisfaction about freedom of religion, women's rights and security. On the other hand, people expressed their concerns about issues such as unemployment, electricity cuts and problems of mobility, the latter due to bad roads and traffic jams in Dakar. Wade was also criticised by some for focusing on the problems of the capital and neglecting rural areas. He was further blamed for not being able to end the problems in the southern region, the Casamance.

The high **unemployment** rate (about 48%) affected the youth particularly (the median age being about 19 years), impelling millions of them to undertake the dangerous journey to Europe. The **energy sector** was a cause for unrest in the country, with frequent cuts in electricity service, a situation unheard of several years ago. Indeed, the number of days per year with electricity cuts was estimated at more than 31. To become less dependent on ever more expensive oil, the minister of agriculture, Farba Senghor, decided in November to start a project in collaboration with Brazil and India to produce more ecologically friendly energy, such as rapeseed oil, bio-ethanol and biogas. Brazil will provide scientific and technological skills, India promised investments and Senegal offered farmland and manpower. To relieve the overcrowding at the international airport in Dakar, the government took the first step towards the long-heralded **new airport** 45 km from Dakar by creating a public company on 26 February, the 'Société Anonyme de l'Aéroport International Blaise-Diagne' (AIBD-SA). This company has the task of searching out private funds. Construction was scheduled to start at the end of the year.

In **the health sector**, President Wade announced on 10 April an ambitious project, called Sesame, providing free medical care for all the elderly people of the country. He promised to make available CFAfr 700 m to cover this project. Although the polls had resulted in rather positive opinions about **education**, there was some unrest. Firstly, in January there were strikes by teachers at colleges and secondary schools complaining about their career prospects. Secondly, from February to April students protested against the bad conditions at the university campuses, particularly in Dakar. The government announced the creation of regional university centres in Bambey, Thiès and Ziguinchor in order to relieve the overcrowding at the University of Dakar.

Gerti Hesseling

Sierra Leone

For the first time in many years, it seemed that the political landscape was undergoing significant changes. Milton Margai's Peoples Movement for Democratic Change clearly established itself as a potential force in the presidential and parliamentary elections in 2007. His rise was linked to widespread dissatisfaction with the ruling party and the president, which related in part to the continued activities of the Special Court for Sierra Leone (SCSL), for which President Kabbah was held responsible. The court continued with its highly unpopular trial of Hinga Norman, who was perceived by the general population as a war hero rather than a criminal. Again, Sierra Leone's economic performance was sound, and this could be credited to massive debt relief and increasing mining activities. However, this performance did not translate into a decrease in the high unemployment rate. This, together with widespread corruption, remained the country's most prominent concern.

Domestic Politics

Towards the end of July, President Kabbah announced that **presidential and parliamentary elections** would be held in July 2007. Traditionally, the political landscape was divided between the All Peoples Congress (APC), mainly drawing its support from the northern part of the country, and the Sierra Leone Peoples Party (SLPP), having its support base in the south and east. This year, Charles Margai's Peoples Movement for Democratic Change (PMDC), which was established in October 2005 after Margai lost the SLPP leadership contest, proved to be a more than temporary phenomenon and became a serious player in the presidential elections. Margai was particularly popular among the youth of Sierra Leone, who form a large part of the electorate. Whether this support will be sufficient to deny the SLPP's candidate and current vice-president, Solomon Berewa, his anticipated victory is still open to speculation. APC supporters hoped that their candidate, Ernest Koroma, would be able to benefit from these divisions.

In December 2005, Margai had been arrested for an 'unauthorised campaign rally', but his party was provisionally registered on 19 January 2006 and so became the first one to sign up at the political parties' registration commission, headed by former Chief Justice Abdulai Timbo. On 11 April, the commission granted full registration to the PMDC, which brought the total number of political parties in Sierra Leone up to 28, although not all parties were expected to participate actively in the elections. Already at his first press conference, Timbo, who was aware of the possibilities for election-related violence, urged political parties not to create tensions. On 23 March, the National Electoral Commission (NEC) allocated the seats among the 14 electoral districts. In July and September respectively, the NEC started with the boundary delimitation and voter registration. Total costs of the elections were estimated at about $ 26 m, with donors expected to provide two-thirds of this sum and the government the balance.

The **Anti-Corruption Commission** (ACC), after having indicted several high-profile persons in 2005, failed to prosecute them fully. In early August, the ACC presented its annual report to President Kabbah. Since this report covered the year 2004, the ACC was already more than a year behind schedule. Even more negatively, ACC's aggressive investigation style into what probably were fabricated accusations of corruption, was found to have caused the eventually fatal decline in the health of the recently appointed chief immigration officer, Gloria Newman-Smart, in October 2005. This was the main conclusion of a report produced by the government's commission of inquiry headed by the chairman of the parliamentary committee on human rights, Dr. Alusine Fofanah. In May, Frederick Carew, minister of justice, presented the findings of the committee, and stated that, "The former Chief Immigration Officer, Gloria Newman-Smart died of stress caused by actions of the ACC which was investigating her of alleged corruption . . . The government is satisfied that there was no credible evidence establishing the truth of the allegations that were made." While many welcomed this conclusion, human rights activists expressed their concern that the government could use ACC's folly to compromise its investigation of other cases.

Arguably, the most significant contribution in addressing the corrupt practices of politicians and the like came from musicians rather than journalists or opposition parties. Last year's 'Borbor Bele' by Emmerson Bockarie, which had an enormous impact and reached the top 10 charts in the US and the UK, was now followed by songs like 'Faya for Faya' by Daddy Saj and 'Same Soup' by the Jungle Leaders. In early March, the Independent Media Commission (IMC) presented its first annual report to President Kabbah. Part of IMC's mandate was the promotion of **media pluralism** and freedom of expression throughout the country. So far, the commission has registered 39 newspapers, 31 radio stations, four international radio relay stations, four agents for the South African-based company MultiChoice DStv, which provides direct-to-home digital television, and six television stations, although only three of the latter were actually operational.

On 27 May, Justice George Gelaga King was appointed and joined the team of the other five judges on the **SCSL**. He became the first Sierra Leonean to preside over the court since its creation in 2002. One of his first priorities was to secure continued and additional funding for the court, which relied on voluntary donations. Critics had pointed to the huge payroll, including the tax-free salary of $ 250,000 for each judge, and more generally questioned the judges' lack of suitable experience. King stated that he did not expect the trials to be completed in 2007. It was, indeed, unlikely that the Charles Taylor case would be completed, since on 17 May his defence was served with a first batch of over 32,000 pages of material by the prosecution, which continued to gather evidence throughout the remainder of the year. Charles Taylor was arrested by Nigerian officials on 29 March, two days after he escaped from his house in Nigeria, where he was granted asylum in 2003. Taylor was indicted by the UN-backed SCLC in 2003 for war crimes and crimes against humanity in relation to his alleged help to and support for the main rebel faction, the Revolutionary United Front of Sierra Leone, during the war. After his arrest, he was deported to Liberia and then to Sierra Leone. There, on 3 April, he pleaded not guilty. He was then deported to the Netherlands to stand trial. Because of safety concerns expressed by the special court, the trial, scheduled to start on 2 April 2007, is to take place on the premises of the International Criminal Court in The Hague, but in a specially created trial chamber for the SCSL. If found guilty, Taylor will serve his sentence in a British prison.

The defence lawyer for Hinga Norman, former deputy defence minister under the Kabbah government and leader of the Civil Defence Forces (CDF), had lined up several **high profile witnesses** to give testimony. These included Peter Penfold, former British high commissioner, Albert Joe Demby, former vice-president, and David Richards, the British general who had worked on the disarmament of fighters in Sierra Leone between 2000 and 2001. In June, despite the request and a subpoena by Norman's defence lawyer, two of three judges of the special court ruled that President Kabbah did not need to appear as a witness. On the last three days of November, the final arguments in the trial of accused CDF members, Norman, Moinina Fofana and Allieu Kondewa were presented by the prosecution and defence, effectively bringing this phase of the trial to a close. However, the trial of Armed Forces Revolutionary Council (AFRC) members Alex Tamba Brima, Brima Bazzy Kamara and Santigie Borbor Kanu continued throughout the year, as did the trial of Revolutionary United Front (RUF) members Issa Hassan Sesay, Morris Kallon and Augustine Gbao. Concerns about the SCSL's functioning persisted and many, including the UN Integrated

Office in Sierra Leone (UNIOSL), pointed to the possibly negative effect of the court's activities on the country's stability.

On 12 January, ex-RUF spokesman Omrie Golley and former ex-combatants Mohamed Bah and David Kai-Tongi were arrested. Ten days later, they were charged with treason over their alleged involvement in a coup d'etat attempt and a plan to assassinate Vice-President Berewa. Some interpreted this as a politically motivated move by a government that was taking an increasingly heavy-handed approach to dealing with the opposition. Omrie's arrest took place only a day after he had paid a one-hour visit to Hinga Norman in his cell. Equally, people started to question the independence of the **judiciary**, since the evidence brought forward by the prosecution seemed to be extremely weak and the trial itself was postponed several times, with charges withdrawn in mid-May, only to be immediately followed by other charges.

Since the ending of the war, the government has made several attempts to reclaim illegally occupied **government land**, mainly in the eastern part of the capital Freetown, where the poor who had fled from the interior occupied many plots. This year, the government turned its attention to 'Hill Station', once a smart district in western Freetown. Rather unexpectedly, it met with strong opposition from the occupants that resulted in the death of Kenneth Moore, a senior official in the ministry of lands, housing and environment. Moore's body was found on 10 June with the letter x carved into it, similar to the sign normally used by officials to indicate which illegal structures were to be demolished.

Foreign Affairs

While the improved security situation in Liberia was a source of relief, both the political situation in Côte d'Ivoire and neighbouring Guinea remained potential security threats. Nevertheless, the **British government** declared that Sierra Leone had at last became 'a secured African state'. In April, the British foreign office announced that "we are no longer advising against travel to areas of Sierra Leone." On 4 February, 450 police recruits went through their passing-out ceremony. The police force had been a major target for all armed groups during the war and these new recruits were part of a wider strategy to a achieve a safer and better Sierra Leone. On 20 April, outgoing British High Commissioner John Michiner announced that the International Military Advisory and Training Team (IMATT) would have a presence in Sierra Leone until 2010 and beyond. IMATT, with its staff of about 100, including 80 British nationals, continued to train the Sierra Leone army. In addition to the presence of IMATT, there were rumours that a Royal Navy vessel was just beyond the ocean's horizon with another 3,000 marines on it.

On 10 March, the Chinese ambassador to Sierra Leone presented a naval patrol boat to the government to be used by the maritime wing of the army to safeguard maritime resources and the coastline. On 28 August, the Dutch government presented 57 new vehicles for use by the armed forces. On 16 September, Libya too made substantial donations, including buses, trucks and garbage collectors worth some $ 11.1 m.

The first report by UNIOSL was presented on 28 April. UNIOSIL, the first such UN office in the history of the world body and working with a $ 23 m budget, started operating in January to support the peace consolidation process. It represented a **continued UN presence** in the country after UN peacekeeping troops were withdrawn at the end of 2005. According to the report, the high and increasing youth unemployment was the main threat to the country's stability. It also criticised the government for failing to deliver clean drinking water and electricity in most regions, including Freetown. Most households could not afford to buy even the most basic commodities. In the eyes of the general public, according to the report, this was mainly because of mismanagement and corruption. The report indicated that the continued downsizing of the army, as proposed by IMATT, was creating growing dissatisfaction in army ranks. Relations between UNIOSL's chief Victor Angelo and President Kabbah were soured by the report and only a phone call by UN Secretary-General Kofi Annan prevented Angelo from being declared *persona non grata*.

During the year, several **high-level visits** took place. In early February, 51 judges from the UK visited Sierra Leone for two days, including a visit to President Kabbah, as part of their tour of the West African region. In Britain, the judges were mainly involved in immigration matters. On 10 May, the British high commissioner to Sierra Leone John Michiner took his leave of President Kabbah. During the first two days of June, the president attended the eighth ordinary session of the community of Sahel-Saharan states, held in the Libyan capital Tripoli. One month later, in early July, the UN secretary-general paid a one-day working visit to UNIOSL and to President Kabbah and a cross-section of ministers and government officials. Later that month, on 17 and 18 July, the British Secretary of State for International Development Hilary Benn and the president of the ADB, Donald Kaberuka, visited Sierra Leone. This was followed by a two-day visit from Paul Wolfowitz, president of the World Bank, starting on 20 July. Less than a week later, on 26 July, President Kabbah, together with Presidents Kufuor of Ghana and Gbagbo of Côte d'Ivoire, were guests of the president of Liberia, Ellen Johnson Sirleaf, to celebrate the country's 159th independence anniversary.

In early October, the president visited Botswana and Lesotho. Kabbah was particularly interested in Botswana's diamond industry and in how this valuable mineral could be used for constructive ends instead of destructive objectives, as was the case with the country's 'blood-diamonds'. Kabbah had a bilateral meeting with Chinese President Hu Jintao at the Sino-African summit in Bejing in November. **China** expressed its interest in continued and increased cooperation with Sierra Leone and donated the equivalent of $ 2.5 m. Finally, the Prince of Wales was in Sierra Leone on a two-day official visit, arriving on 27 November, and met with President Kabbah.

The border town of Yenga in the far eastern district of Kailahun remained a source of tension with neighbouring Guinea. **Guinean troops** still occupied the town and its inhabitants complained about forced labour practices. Despite the fact that the governments of both countries commissioned British and French experts to help in the demarcation of the common border, dialogue stalled. In addition, early in the year Guinean troops ordered a bauxite mining company in Sierra Leone's Kambia district, along the Guinean border, to stop its prospecting activities.

Socioeconomic Developments

On 27 March China donated tractors and agricultural equipment. In addition, it trained 50 Sierra Leoneans in food processing techniques and agriculture. At the start of 2006, self-sufficiency in rice stood at 69%, while cassava and sweet potato production yielded a surplus. Despite average **GDP growth** of 7%, 82% of the population still lived below the poverty line of $ 2 a day and it was unlikely that the country would achieve the 2015 MDGs. Sierra Leone took 136th position on the UN Human Development Index.

Three referral **hospitals** – Connaught, Princess Christian Maternity Hospital and the Children's Hospital at Fourah Bay Road – and five western area health centres were officially reopened to the public on 27 March after several months of rehabilitation work. The multimillion dollar rehabilitation project also included the training of staff. On 14 December, Kissy Mental Hospital, now renamed the National Psychiatric Medical Hospital was officially reopened after major reconstruction work, following a loan of $ 2.5 m by the Islamic Development Bank. The hospital, headed by Sierra Leone's only psychiatrist, Dr. Nahim, was still the sole mental institution in a country that had undergone massive trauma as a result of the decade-long civil war.

The country was able to drastically cut its **external debts**. As a result of its governance measures, macroeconomic stability and the beginnings of the implementation of the Poverty Reduction Strategy Paper, the country reached the enhanced HIPC completion point, which translated into total debt reduction of nearly $ 700 m by, among others, the IMF, IDA and bilateral creditors. Sierra Leone became eligible for debt relief of another $ 550 m under the Multilateral Debt Relief Initiative proposed by the G8 summit at Gleneagles in 2005. The fiscal space created by this debt relief would be used to reduce poverty and promote economic growth, in order to achieve the MDGs, according to the government. In total, Sierra Leone's debt was reduced – in 2000 net present value terms – from $ 1,197.6 m to only $ 110 m.

The mining sector was in full swing, with three-quarters of the country now licensed for mineral exploration. Rutile (titanium dioxide) production started in 2005 and the first shipments occurred in May 2006. Bauxite production recommenced as well. A particular advantage for bauxite mining companies was the relative accessibility of the resource, with deposits located close to Freetown and the deep-water port of Pepel. In addition, mining could also benefit from the proposed rehabilitation of the railway network. According to preliminary findings of a Russian research project into the viability of revitalising the long-abandoned railway network, presented to the president on 18 May, rehabilitation could be sustainable if railway-use involved freight as well as passengers. Diamond production continued to increase. Traditionally concentrated in the eastern part of the country, a series of reconnaissance surveys took place in the northwest after several reports of diamond findings in that region. By the beginning of the year, it was estimated that about 50% of mining operations were taking place through official channels. Gold mining also grew significantly, with several mining companies actively engaged.

Still, about 90% of alluvial diamond mining, and probably an even higher percentage for gold, was undertaken by **small-scale prospectors**. While diamond mining mostly involves men, with an estimated 120,000 alluvial miners, women make up about 90% of those involved in alluvial gold mining. Although not a very lucrative undertaking, gold mining generates at least some money for those involved, which cannot be said of the majority of alluvial diamond miners. Since there was no official gold market, prices remained low and did not reflect high prices on the international market. Gold smuggling to Guinea was rampant. It was estimated that diamonds to the value of between $ 30 and $ 160 m are still smuggled out of the country.

Krijn Peters

Togo

The political accord between the government and major opposition parties in August was welcomed internationally as a major breakthrough, in view of the aftermath of rigged presidential elections and subsequent political turmoil in 2005. The formation of a transitional government of national unity under Yawovi Agboyibo, renowned opposition leader, gave rise to optimistic forecasts concerning the preparations for early free and fair parliamentary elections in June 2007, which would be the first after decades of autocratic rule.

Domestic Politics

The **inter-Togolese dialogue**, sponsored by the EU to overcome the political crisis, recommenced in Lomé on 21 April, after lengthy discussions, dogged by controversy, over the agenda, the venue and presence of an external mediator. The political dialogue, which had aleady commenced in May 2004, had been interrupted by the illegitimate usurpation of power by Faure Gnassingbé in the aftermath of the death of his father President Eyadéma on 5 February 2005 and the ensuing bloody suppression of political opposition. The resumption of the talks was in line with the 22 democratic commitments made by the Togolese government to the EU within the framework of the accord of April 2004. The talks constituted one of the preconditions for continuing development cooperation with the EU and other major donors, suspended in 1993. Yawovi Agboyibo, leader of the opposition party 'Comité d'Action pour le Renouveau' (CAR), was on 22 April elected as chairman of the resumed dialogue, in which all major political parties as well as delegates from two women's organisations (traditionally in favour of Eyadéma) were meant to participate. However, two of the largest opposition parties, the 'Union des Forces du Changement' (UFC) led by Gilchrist Olympio and the 'Convention des Peuples Africaines' (CDPA), presided over by Léopold Gnininvi, boycotted the reopening of the dialogue because they had vainly demanded the presence of an impartial foreign mediator, as already conceded by the president in 2005. The major aim of the negotiations was the preparations for early legislative elections. To guarantee an impartial poll, additional items placed on the agenda were the revision of the electoral code, the voters' register and the constitution; the reorganisation of the independent electoral commission ('Commission Électorale Nationale Indépendante', CENI), the constitutional court and the army – all biased in favour of the ruling 'Rassemblement du Peuple Togolais' (RPT) party and the Gnassingbé clan; and last but not least, an end to impunity for perpetrators of violence and politically motivated killings.

As a sign of compromise, the head of state consented to the celebration of the anniversary of Togolese independence (27 April) for the first time in decades, instead of his father's coup d'etat on 13 January 1967. On the eve of independence day, a coalition of international human rights organisations (among them Amnesty International and the 'Fédération Internationale des Ligues des Droits de l'Homme', FIDH) denounced the blatant impunity that had reigned in the country since the accession to power of Gnassingbé Eyadéma in 1967 until the violent conflicts in the aftermath of the rigged presidential elections of 2005. Week-long negotiations behind closed doors resulted in a **compromise** by seven of the nine parties engaged in the dialogue, involving a political draft agreement to hold free and fair elections before October 2007. The settlement was rejected by the leading opposition groups, UFC and CDPA, because it was limited to the immediate aim of organising legislative elections and achieving the resumption of aid, rather than addressing the major undemocratic features of four decades of despotic rule.

The deadlock was finally broken by the mediation of President Blaise Compaoré of Burkina Faso. After a ten-day meeting in Ouagadougou, all parties signed a comprehensive political agreement on 20 August. This **Ouagadougou accord** provided for a transitional government of national unity and the organisation of early free and fair parliamentary elections by a truly independent CENI before October 2007, i.e., before the mandate of parliament, based on an undemocratic election in 2002 that had been boycotted by the opposition, ran out. CENI proposed 24 June 2007 as the provisional polling date. It remained unclear, however, whether the agreement on credible legislative elections would also apply to the next presidential elections. This would have been of special importance to the UFC in view of another key part of the Ouagadougou accord, namely the abolition of the rigid residence requirement and of the exclusion of dual nationality for eligible candidates. These had been imposed in the election law and the constitutional amendments of December 2002 in order to prevent the election of Gilchrist Olympio as president. The government and ruling RPT for the first time accepted a minority position of nine within CENI, which was composed of 19 members from all major parties, the cabinet and civic groups.

The deal opened the way for the formation of a new transitional government of **national reconciliation** headed by Yawovi Agboyibo, the veteran leader of CAR, the second largest opposition party. His nomination as prime minister by the head of state on 16 September was strongly contested by the UFC, which believed it had the rightful claim to the post, being the largest opposition party. Again, Faure Gnassingbé had fallen back on the tactics of his father, who had split the opposition with a similar trick in 1994 when, in violation of the parliamentary rules, he had nominated Edem Kodjo, head of a minority opposition party, as prime minister, instead of Agboyibo, the leader of what was then the largest opposition party, CAR. Agboyibo now replaced Kodjo, who had been reappointed as head of the first nominal government of national unity (boycotted by the major opposition parties) in June 2005. The national press lauded Agboyibo's appointment as a positive measure to seal the Ouagadougou deal.

The new transitional government, nominated by the prime minister on 20 September, comprised 39 members (five more than the old cabinet), with representatives of all major players in the Ouagadougou accord, apart from the UFC, which again refused to take part, although it participated in the new CENI set up in October. The government was more balanced than the old one, with 19 ministers from the ruling RPT, ten from opposition parties and four from civil society groups. The number of **women** in the new cabinet increased to six, compared with four in the old cabinet. Zarifou Ayéva of the opposition 'Parti pour la Démocratie et le Renouveau' (PDR) remained foreign minister; Léopold Gnininvi, leader of the CDPA, was given the ministry of mines and energy; while the second vice-president from the UFC, Amah Gnassingbé – who had defected from his party – became minister of state.

However, the most powerful portfolios remained in the hands of the RPT and the **Gnassingbé clan**. Kpatcha Gnassingbé, elder half-brother of the head of state and head of the militia that had contributed to the bloody conflicts of April 2005, was appointed defence minister. Col. Atcha Titikpina (RPT), former head of the presidential guard (the so-called 'Green Berets') and equally accused of masterminding the atrocities of April 2005, became minister of security. Payadowa Boukpessi (RPT) remained finance minister and Kokouvi Dogbé (RPT) minister of telecommunications. The latter was of particular importance in the organisation and monitoring of the forthcoming elections, as shown by the crucial role of telecommunications in rigging the last presidential elections of 2005. To guard his rear, the head of state formed a sort of parallel cabinet directed by Pascal Bodjona (RPT), former Togolese ambassador in Washington. Other members were the former minister of security and RPT hardliner, Col. Pitalouna-Ani Laokpessi, who was compensated for the loss of his portfolio by his nomination on 16 December as special councillor for security at the presidency, where he rejoined other old hands like Edem Kodjo, nominated as minister of state at the presidency, and former minister of foreign affairs Kokou Tozoun, promoted to the post of rapporteur of CENI, a post of some strategic importance in view of the upcoming elections.

The most important, yet unresolved point of the Ouagadougou accord remained the **reform of the army** ('Forces Armées Togolaises'), at the heart of the empire around the Gnassingbé clan, to which it was bound by family and ethnic ties and personal loyalties. It has acted more as a praetorian guard and been responsible for gross human rights violations and has been protected by a long-standing culture of impunity, as demonstrated most recently in the 2005 turmoil. In view of this clouded image, the army chief, General Zakary Nandja, on 28 August assured both the head of state and the international community that he backed the Ouagadougou accord and would abstain from interfering in the political arena. Nothing was less certain, however. Apparently, there was a fragile equilibrium between different factions within the Gnassingbé family and among competing clans in the army, all of them jealously guarding their prerogatives. It remained to be seen whether the head of state had sufficient authority and determination to effect the required changes. In April, the draft code of conduct for the armed forces and security services of West African states, a joint project of ECOWAS and the Centre for the Control of the Armed Forces in Geneva, was approved during a meeting in Lomé, serving as a reminder to the army about its supposed new role.

While the code of conduct was intended to improve civilian control of the army within a framework of regional protocols on good governance, democratisation and conflict resolution, it remained a dead letter. At the end of November, retired Gen. Assani Tidjani, a Muslim from northern Togo, former army chief and ex-defence minister under Eyadéma, **challenged the authority** of the head of state by openly supporting the rebel 'Forces Nouvelles' of Guillaume Soro in northern Côte d'Ivoire against the country's President Laurent Gbagbo. He thus undermined the cordial relationship between the Togolese and Ivorian heads of state. The acting army chief, Kpatcha Gnassingbé, went on an urgent mission to Abidjan on 11 December to reassure President Gbagbo, who had declared that the presence of the Togolese contingent in the United Nations Operation in Côte d'Ivoire (UNOCI) was now undesirable. Five days later, Tidjani was given a two-month prison sentence.

The human rights situation remained precarious. According to UNHCR, up till October less than half the 40,000 refugees who had fled the post-electoral violence and persecution in 2005 had voluntarily returned or been repatriated from neighbouring Benin and Ghana. A total of 16,500 remained in exile, fearing political reprisal. About 6,500 were in Ghana and 10,000 in Benin, among whom 6,000 in the Agmé refugee camp near the Togolese border, with the remaining 4,000 staying with relatives or host families in Cotonou. The influx of such considerable numbers of migrants caused stresses and strains in some host communities, not least because locals resented the fact that 'foreigners' were provided with better amenities than nationals. Thus, the Lokossa camp in Benin, where some 9,300 **refugees** had originally been accommodated, appeared to be almost deserted after fierce clashes between refugees and residents of neighbouring villages in February. In spring, the eastern and Volta regions of Ghana were 'invaded' by a second wave of migrants. Despite assurances from the Togolese government, several returning refugees had been arrested or harassed and were forced to flee a second time, now in the company of additional relatives. They remained in the transit and refugee camps of Abotase, Digya and Manchere or scattered across 114 villages in the Volta region, where they faced acute shortages of food, water and shelter. In December, the EU granted Togo € 14.6 m to assist in the strengthening of reception and reintegration facilities.

On 18 May, the FIDH, based in Paris, and 'Comité Contre la Torture' (Geneva) published a **human rights** report denouncing the generalised culture of impunity, notably for acts of torture, disappearance, rape and arbitrary arrest by military and security personnel. In addition, Amnesty International drafted a report entitled "Togo: I Want to Know Why my Son was Killed", containing the testimony of victims of the 2005 turmoil. The report, based on a research mission in July, was originally to be published in November but was delayed because the government demanded time to prepare an adequate response. Nevertheless, by December the draft report was circulating among the opposition in Lomé and abroad and attracted international attention.

On 22 December, parliament liberalised the restrictive abortion law of 1920, which allowed **abortion** only to save the life of the pregnant woman. Under the revised law, termination was now also possible in cases of rape, incest or a severely handicapped foetus. With this law, Togo adopted the most liberal abortion regime in Francophone Africa, although it still fell short of the more progressive stands taken by other African countries such as Tunisia, Cape Verde or Zambia.

Foreign Affairs

The EU welcomed the resumption of the national dialogue for reconciliation and kept a close watch on the process. Filiberto Ceriani Sebregondi, who headed the EU delegation meant to assess its progress in the first weeks of May, backed the demands of the 'radical opposition'. He recommended an external facilitator to prevent setbacks, which would endanger the badly needed resumption of **EU development aid**. It was envisaged that the latter would involve up to € 60 m. The Ouagadougou accord triggered the clearance of € 15 m of previously allocated Stabex funds, thus extending EU aid for the current year to over € 36 m. A further € 41.6 m was promised if a date for the legislative elections was fixed. EU Development Commissioner Louis Michel again reminded President Faure Gnassingbé, during the latter's official visit to the EU in early September that took him to Brussels, Rome and Paris, that development cooperation would not be normalised without the establishment of a legitimate National Assembly. However, EU and ACP monitoring missions in October and November reported considerable progress. On 15 November, the EU council of ministers dangled the clearance of € 40 m of the 9th EDF as well as the inclusion of a further € 110 m in the programming for the 10th EDF (2008–12).

The resumption of EU aid was most important, as it was considered as a precondition for continuation of IMF negotiations on poverty reduction and growth facilities, which, in turn, would allow for seeking debt relief with the Paris Club under the HIPC scheme and the new multilateral debt relief initiative. **France's President** Jacques Chirac, who still regarded himself as a personal friend of the family of late Eyadéma Gnassingbé, rewarded the progress made in the national dialogue with an additional € 5 m of French aid. In November, the signatories of the Ouagadougou accord established a nine-member international monitoring committee to evaluate the progress of the democratisation process. It was composed of one delegate from each of the major political parties, in addition to representatives of the EU, ECOWAS and the Burkinabé presidency. The committee met for the first time in Lomé on 16 December and was meant to have monthly meetings up to the elections in June 2007.

President Blaise Compaoré of **Burkina Faso** played a decisive role in mediating the national dialogue. On 26 July, he accepted the renewed request of the protagonists to act as a facilitator. This was also welcomed by Paris, which considered Compaoré as an advocate of its policies in Francophone Africa. He had already mediated in the Togolese crisis before – though in vain – during the crucial transition phase in 1992–93 and the ensuing Ouagadougou I, II and III accords. After prolonged quarrelling between the government and opposition about other possible candidates, Prime Minister Edem Kodjo solicited the help of Compaoré in February. Both heads of state met in the hometown of the Gnassingbé clan, Kara, in northern Togo, on 21 March to confirm the deal. The leaders of the opposition UFC, CAR and CDPA first opposed Compaoré, whom they considered too close to the Lomé government. They endorsed him after further consultations in the Burkinabé capital. On 15 August, President Faure Gnassingbé completed his own consultations with Compaoré, who had previously held talks with representatives of the Togolese political parties, civil society, traditional chiefs and religious authorities. The results of these deliberations were presented in Ouagadougou on 17 August.

The growing competition between China and Western powers, all of them keen to enlarge their resource base in Africa, was also felt in relations with Togo. Faure Gnassingbé visited Beijing in January. He and Chinese President Hu Jintao vowed to enhance their long-standing bilateral ties in such fields as agriculture, trade, telecommunications and infrastructure on 13 January. In April, the new multimillion dollar presidential palace in Lomé, with over 40 offices and banqueting halls and already contracted and built by the **Chinese** under the late President Eyadéma, was inaugurated. The cordial relationship was confirmed by his son's attendance of the Beijing Sino-African summit on 3–5 November. On 22 July, Chinese Vice-President Zeng Qinghong signed a number of technical cooperation agreements in Kara, including grants and interest-free loans from the Chinese government for funding projects and a framework agreement on preferential loans for the realisation of the Adjarala hydro-electric project. During the China Business Days in Lomé in November, organised by the 'Banque Ouest Africaine de Développement' (BOAD) with the help of UEMOA and the BCEAO, BOAD signed two cooperation agreements, one on Chinese technical assistance with BOAD (approx. € 1 m) and another for a credit line of € 70 m between BOAD and the Chinese Exim Bank for development of infrastructure, exploitation of energy resources and construction projects in West Africa, including Togo.

In August an **Indian** investment holding company signed an agreement with the government in Lomé for investments worth € 40 m in the mining sector. In particular, this covered iron ore deposits at Bassar in the Kara region (estimated at 600 m tonnes), besides chromite ore (1 m tonnes) at Farendè (Kara) and Mont Ayito in Plateau region and manganese (13 m tonnes) at Naéga (Savannes region). The agreement would also involve the construction of a 100 km railway and development of energy and water supplies.

Socioeconomic Developments

In view of the economic crisis triggered by the political turmoil and decades of bad government, in 2005 Togo had met only one of UEMOA's eight convergence criteria, namely the share of wages in total domestic revenue, which fell to 30.4%. In 2006, the problem of public sector salary arrears persisted and, with it, strike threats by Togo's major labour union, the 'Intersyndical des Travailleurs de Togo' (ISTT). To mitigate labour unrest, parliament adopted a new labour code in December. Its stipulations offered, at least formally, greater protection and better employment conditions, including a 40-hour week and equal pay for equal work. The stock of external debt increased to $ 1.8 bn at the end of 2006, overwhelmingly due to the accumulation of repayment arrears (some $ 100 m). For the first time ever, Togo was included in the **Corruption** Perceptions Index of Transparency International, being ranked the third most corrupt UEMOA state or 130th of 163 countries worldwide. In December, the council of ministers proposed the budget for 2007 with a deficit of CFAfr 13 bn (about 1.6% of GDP), despite optimistic forecasts of increased revenue. Improvement in the budget situation depended to a great extent on the resumption of development assistance, conditioned by success in the democratisation process.

Togo's participation in the world **football** cup in Germany in June had mixed results. It aroused national pride, but also bitter feelings among the Togolese team and population, which attributed the defeat of its heroes at least partially to mismanagement and allegedly gross corruption by officials of the country's football association, notably its president, Rock Gnassingbé, brother of the head of state.

Dirk Kohnert

V. Central Africa

The sub-region was arguably still the most unstable part of the continent, particularly when taking into account the spill-over effects of the Darfur crisis on Chad and the Central African Republic (CAR). Major new outbreaks of older armed conflicts in both Chad and CAR counterbalanced the positive developments in DR Congo, while widespread violence continued throughout different zones of the biggest country of the sub-region. The growing interest in Africa's mineral resources also had an impact in Central Africa, where major oil and gas deposits are located. Visits by Chinese officials confirmed this growing interest and were welcomed by national governments. However, only a few countries could yet claim steady economic growth.

Elections

National elections were on the agenda in Chad, DR Congo, Gabon and São Tomé and Príncipe. Calls by the opposition to postpone presidential elections in **Chad** in light of numerous outbreaks of violence were not heeded by President Déby. The opposition failed to present a strong alternative to the incumbent, who won the contest in the first round on 3 May, officially with 64.7% of the votes. No international observers were fielded and it was difficult to confirm allegations of widespread fraud and of an inflated turnout (officially 53.1%).

The single most important electoral event in the sub-region for decades was the presidential and legislative elections in **DR Congo** on 30 July. About 50,000 national and over 1,700 international observers were deployed to monitor technically difficult elections that mobilised more than 70% of the electorate. UN and EU troops had to guarantee the security of the operation. The expected outbreaks of violence were at first limited to two provinces, but serious incidents were to follow shortly before the announcement of the results, when security forces and the guardians of opposition candidate Jean-Pierre Bemba exchanged shots. This was only the beginning of a series of clashes. The two best-placed candidates, incumbent Joseph-Désiré Kabila and Bemba, had to contest a second round after no candidate received an absolute majority. It came as no surprise that Kabila was in the end credited with 58% of the votes and was declared winner in the elections. In parliament, the Kabila camp controlled 224 of the 500 seats. Although the elections went off in a much more orderly way than most analysts had expected, serious doubts remained about the preparedness of numerous players to respect the rules of the democratic game.

Legislative elections in **Gabon**, held on 17 December, did not alter power-relations. The presidential majority received 98 seats (with President Omar Bongo Ondimba's 'Parti Démocratique Gabonais' taking 81 seats), while a divided opposition could claim only 16 seats, with most of the successful independent candidates (five) being considered close to Bongo.

São Tomé and Príncipe held legislative elections on 17 April, in which the 'Movimento Democrático Força de Mudança – Partido de Convergência Democrática' (MDFM-PCD), close to President Fradique de Menezes, won a plurality of seats and had to form a minority government. On 30 July, Menezes won the presidential elections more comfortably with 60.6% of the votes. Despite bitter infighting among the small elite, the island republic remained the only true democracy in the sub-region. Once again, São Tomé and Príncipe was the only 'free' country in the sub-region, according to Freedom House. The US-based NGO noted some smaller changes, with only Congo changing its overall category from 'partly free' to 'unfree'. Four other countries continued to fall into the worst 'unfree' category of states (Cameroon and Equatorial Guinea were unchanged, while DR Congo got a slightly better rating in 'political rights' due to the elections held, while Chad was rated worse in 'civil liberties'). CAR and Gabon remained 'partly free'.

Human Rights

Human Rights Watch issued a report on the spill-over effect from Darfur on the human rights situation in **Chad** ("Violence beyond borders. The Human Rights Crisis in Eastern Chad") after issuing photographs documenting cross-border raids on Chadian villages. In November, the NGO drew attention to the fate of Chadian Arabs, who were among the victims of an escalating cycle of violence in southeast Chad. Chadian officials were asked to cease support to armed groups responsible for abuses. Overall, the poor human rights record of the Chadian government deteriorated further during the year as security forces committed numerous serious human rights abuses, mostly during flare-ups in the armed conflict. In **CAR**, the government's respect for human rights deteriorated overall in the course of the intensification of the rebellion. Following rebel attacks on military targets, members of the presidential guard conducted reprisal attacks on numerous villages near the Chadian border, during which they indiscriminately killed up to 100 civilians in two northwestern prefectures. In a report ("Government tramples on the basic rights of detainees"), Amnesty International criticised the arbitrary arrests of more than 40 men and women and urged the government to respect its own laws.

The picture drawn by the US state department in its yearly country reports on human rights practices again showed a problematic record for the entire sub-region. The department recorded some positive developments in **Gabon**, where, unlike previously, there were no reports of government agents committing arbitrary or unlawful killings. In **Cameroon**, by contrast, security forces continued to commit unlawful killings throughout the year. The report noted a problematic upward tendency in mob violence, including the burning to death of people suspected of theft and of practising witchcraft.

The official anti-corruption campaign in Cameroon made some progress, while civil society campaigners in neighbouring Congo had a difficult time. Christian Mounzéo, president of the the NGO 'Rencontre pour la paix et les droits de l'Homme' and country coordinator of the Publish What You Pay campaign, was arbitrarily arrested and detained by authorities after criticising the government's misuse of oil revenues. Mounzéo had travelled abroad before to attend several meetings of the Extractive Industries Transparency Initiative (EITI).

Arguably, **Equatorial Guinea** had the worst human rights record. Four activists from the banned Popular Party were arrested in October and only released more than a month later after beatings as well as deprivation of food and water for several days. They were threatened with death if they did not confess to having formed an illegal association. Possessions taken by police were not returned.

A major cause of concern was the human rights violations by the newly formed armed forces of the **DR Congo**. Physical violence, including rape, occurred almost routinely when official forces were deployed. The international peacekeeping mission, MONUC, had to investigate allegations of abuses by its personnel.

Militia leader Thomas Lubanga (DR Congo) was transferred to the **International Criminal Court** (ICC) in March and subsequently charged with the recruitment and use of child soldiers. His first appearance before the pre-trial chamber was on 20 March, when he presented himself as "a politician by profession". A trial was expected to begin in early 2007. No progress was made in the case of former President Patassé of CAR and others accused of crimes against humanity: the ICC prosecutor still had not decided whether and when to conduct an investigation into the case.

Instability, War and Peace

Armed conflict occurred in **CAR** and **Chad**, while election-related violence in the DR Congo was also recorded. On 14 March, an attempt was made to shoot down the plane of Chadian President Déby upon his return from the CEMAC summit in Equatorial Guinea. This was only the beginning of a series of dangerous events. After the failed attempt to take N'Djaména in a surprise attack in April, various rebel groups staged further attacks in the east of Chad. The government launched its own counterattacks, and both sides claimed invariably heavy losses for the other side. As obscure as the situation was, it was clear that rebels had intensified their struggle against the regime. Massive French military support came to the rescue of President Déby. The situation on the frontier with Sudan was unstable, with the governments of both Chad and CAR accusing their mighty neighbour of being behind destabilisation efforts in their countries. CAR saw the worst escalation of violence since the capture of Bangui by Bozizé in 2003. Various rebel groups launched attacks, the most serious of which led to the temporary capture of a number of northern towns, including the provincial capitals Birao and Ndélé. Reprisal attacks by government forces were no less ferocious and resulted in civilian victims. The recapture of the rebel-held towns necessitated the use of French air fighters. By year's end, it was unclear whether a much-debated UN peacekeeping operation to secure the frontier zone (Sudan-Chad-CAR) would be deployed: logistical difficulties were cited among the major constraints.

The announcement that parts of the Ugandan Lord's Resistance Army (LRA) could not only find refuge in DR Congo's Ituri province but also on CAR soil underlined the fact that frontiers and the capacity to uphold national sovereignty were often more virtual than real in the sub-region.

Several provinces in the **DR Congo** were not entirely pacified. In Ituri, a number of armed groups were still active and insecurity persisted, while the situation in the southern province of Katanga improved after the deployment of additional troops. Most serious were the activities of renegade General Nkunda in North Kivu, where new clashes occurred at the end of the year. Neither the Congolese army nor MONUC dared to arrest Nkunda. Violence erupted occasionally during the election campaign, but the most serious incident was in the capital Kinshasa following the announcement of the election results: the house of second-placed candidate Jean-Pierre Bemba was attacked while he was receiving foreign ambassadors. UN and EU peacekeepers had to evacuate the diplomats. Bemba interpreted the assault as an attempt to kill him. Confidence-building measures only succeeded to some degree but at least permitted the completion of the electoral process. In the aftermath of the second round of elections, new skirmishes between government troops and Bemba's guards erupted leading to an uneasy situation in Kinshasa. The election results confirmed the major east-west divide, and the earlier xenophobic propaganda of a number of the candidates (including Bemba) raised fears about overall stability in years to come.

A final initiative by the retiring UN secretary-general brought the border dispute between **Cameroon and Nigeria** to an end. Nigeria had at first failed to hand over the Bakassi peninsula but drew back its troops after the high-level mediation on 12 June 2006 between Annan and presidents Biya and Obasanjo.

No major progress was recorded in the maritime border dispute over Mbane island between **Equatorial Guinea and Gabon**. However, the oil-rich zone became an issue of intra-elite quarrels in Gabon when rumours circulated that the interior minister wanted to sell it to the neighbouring country. An ad hoc commission involving both sides held talks in Malabo with a view to defining a zone of joint exploitation but failed to reach consensus (26–29 May). Gabon's President Bongo Ondimba cancelled a mini-summit between him, Obiang Nguema and UN Secretary-General Kofi Annan scheduled for 2 October in Geneva after all three had met in Switzerland on 27 February. Annan's efforts to settle this dispute before the end of his mandate were therefore unsuccessful. Another trial at the International Court of Justice was to be expected since both countries had closely followed the Bakassi affair.

A preparatory ministerial meeting attended by 200 participants from 16 countries as well as UN, AU and EU delegations was held in Bangui on 20–23 February and decided to again postpone the second summit of the International Conference on Peace, Security, Democracy and Development in the **Great Lakes region**. The conference was finally held in Kenya on 14–15 December and led to the signing of a security, peace, stability and development pact. The concern to strengthen sub-regional peacekeeping capabilities remained high on the agenda. A UN-led military exercise dubbed 'Barh El-Gazel 2006' was initially scheduled to take place in Chad in February, but had to be postponed owing to the prevailing security situation in that country. The 24th ministerial meeting of the UN standing advisory committee on security questions in Central Africa was hosted in Kigali, Rwanda on 25–29 September with all member-states attending.

The repatriation of **refugees** of DR Congo origin from neighbouring countries started slowly. According to UNHCR, from January to September only about 25,000 Congolese refugees were repatriated, mainly from Tanzania and Congo, while some 350,000 still awaited repatriation. It was expected that the holding of elections and the formal ending of the transitional phase would accelerate the pace of return. New refugee populations were building up both in Chad and CAR. The total number of CAR refugees in southern Chad at year's end was close to 50,000. While refugees from Darfur, Sudan received regular care, the highly variable estimates of new Chadian IDPs – maybe 100,000 – made it unlikely that appropriate measures to feed and house them were taken. To complete the grim picture, there were an estimated 150,000 IDPs all over the northern part of CAR.

Socioeconomic Developments

Economic development in the sub-region was more homogeneous than in preceding years, as the booming economy of Equatorial Guinea fell back to an estimated 1% growth rate (according to the IMF in its Global Economic Outlook) after crude oil production dropped by an estimated 4.4% because of temporary technical factors. The best performers on a macro-level were the oil economies of Congo with a growth rate of 6.4% and, above all, the tiny newcomer to the oil bonanza São Tomé and Príncipe, with 8%. After years of destruction and overall low-level growth, the respectable growth rate of 5.1% in DR Congo (down, however, from 6.5% in 2005) did not contribute much to the reversal of the overall bleak situation. Cameroon and CAR recorded an estimated 3.5% growth. Very modest growth occurred in both Gabon and Chad (1% and 1.3% respectively). In sum, the sub-region again fared far worse than Sub-Saharan Africa as a whole: for the entire sub-continent growth was projected at 5.7% in the IMF's Global Economic Outlook. At a joint economic forum in Brazzaville on 19–21 June organised by CEEAC, ECA and 'Organisation Internationale de la Francophonie', among others, the sub-regional ECA director pointed to the sub-region's "world record of the least attractive investment climate", despite existing opportunities for growth and private initiative. Climatic problems and the weak transport, telecommunications as well as energy infrastructure were mentioned as root causes, but political factors such as instability and institutional constraints were also considered important. Difficult access to credits for the private sector was a more immediate factor hampering growth while the increasing foreign direct investment was overly concentrated on the exploitation of mineral wealth.

Minerals were also the main driving force behind China's growing interest in the sub-region, an interest attested to by the numerous visits by officials. Likewise, representatives of all the countries of the sub-region – save São Tomé and Príncipe – travelled to the 3rd Sino-African summit, the Forum on China-Africa Cooperation (FOCAC), held in Beijing on 3–5 November. As AU chairman, Congo's Sassou Nguesso gave a keynote speech. Biya, Bongo and Obiang were also present in person.

Countries in the sub-region fared differently in respect of **public finances**. Cameroon stood out for planning a 20% budget increase arising from both high oil and cocoa prices and substantial debt relief under the HIPC initiative after it had finally reached completion point. The Equatorial Guinean budget at year's end projected an increase in domestic revenue of more than 100%, but all figures provided by the government must be dealt with cautiously, since about three-quarters of earlier expenditures were reportedly off-budget. Chad's budget constantly changed and had to be revised because of new revenues from oil-related payments by major oil companies. The Economist Intelligence Unit suspected that most additional revenues would be used "to finance higher military spending and other extra-budgetary expenditure." Even though the expected oil bonanza in the small island republic of São Tomé and Príncipe had not yet fully materialised, it proved possible to increase the budget by about 10%. The Congolese budget was enlarged even more, by about 11%, thanks to growing oil income. Much worse was the situation in neighbouring DR Congo, where fiscal indiscipline added to opaque operations and a soaring inflation rate. Donors provided more than half the country's budget. Public finances in CAR remained under enormous pressure as debt arrears and outstanding public sector salaries continued to undermine stability. Gabon's budget for 2007 adopted in October remained practically at the same level as the revised 2006 budget.

Inflation in the CEMAC area was on the rise at year's end. According to BEAC figures, the level had passed from 2.5% in 2005 to 3.3% as an annual average and to 5.1% at year's end. Rising oil prices were considered a major source of inflation. More dramatic figures were provided by the IMF, which recorded very high inflation rates, particularly for DR Congo and São Tomé and Príncipe, both Non-CEMAC countries: DR Congo's rate was 13.2% and São Tomé and Príncipe's 21.4%, the latter being certainly related to the sudden arrival of oil money. Other sources of inflation varied from country to country, e.g., the insufficient supply of staple foods in CAR or rising beef prices connected to fears about the effects of avian flu in Gabon and Chad.

The poor ratings for the sub-region in the 2006 **Corruption Perceptions Index** (CPI) of Transparency International changed little. Chad's ranking – in the last index labelled the most corrupt country in the world – improved to 156th, on an equal footing with DR Congo, which declined by 12 ranks. In this year's CPI, 163 countries were rated, including for the first time CAR. The country was immediately ranked 130, better than most others in the sub-region (Cameroon 138, Congo 142, Equatorial Guinea 151). Gabon again received a relatively positive rating (rank 90).

The UNDP's human development report saw Equatorial Guinea (rank 120), Gabon (124) São Tomé and Príncipe (127), Congo (140) and Cameroon (144) in the range of 'medium human development', while DR Congo, Chad and CAR fell into the 'low' category (167, 171 and 172 respectively, out of 177). This meant that the two last-mentioned countries had swapped their sub-regional positions. The overall **poverty** situation in the sub-region saw no major change. Here Chad retained its sad position of 100th out of 102 on the Human Poverty Index (HPI-1: CAR 91, DR Congo 80). Chad had recovered from the repercussions of the 2004 locust invasion and recorded better harvests in 2005 and 2006, but the armed conflict resulted in difficulties for the production and delivery of food. For the same reasons, serious concerns were also raised about the situation in CAR.

New UNAIDS data on **HIV/AIDS infection** (2005 estimates published in 2006), showed that there were significant variations in the sub-region. While rather low figures were recorded in Equatorial Guinea, Chad and DR Congo (3.2%, 3.2% and 3.5%

prevalence rate respectively), the situation was far more serious in Congo (5.3%), Cameroon (5.4%) and even more so in Gabon (7.9%) and CAR (10.7%).

Regarding epidemics in 2006, the sub-region enjoyed a comparatively good record. A suspected **pneumonic plague** outbreak was reported in four health zones in DR Congo's Oriental province in the northeastern part of the country, with local authorities indicating 1,174 suspected cases (and 50 deaths). In March, Cameroonian authorities detected the first case of the deadly **H5N1 avian flu** virus in a duck and thereby became the fourth African country to report the pandemic. A further spread was feared.

The massive inflow of Chinese investments had not only positive effects. Ecological concerns were voiced when Chinese oil company Sinopec prospected illegally in Gabon's Loango National Park, constructing roads and building a workers' village in an area meant to protect endangered species. These activities were eventually halted.

Sub-regional Organisations

At the request of Chadian President Déby, an **extraordinary CEMAC summit** was held in N'Djaména on 4 January focusing on the situation on the frontier between Chad and Sudan and on the rebellion in Chad, which also extended to other insecure frontier regions, including the Chad-CAR-Cameroon triangle. The presidents of CAR, Congo and Gabon participated, as well as high-ranking representatives from Cameroon and Equatorial Guinea. The reform of Chadian oil legislation was also discussed, leading to an appeal for dialogue between N'Djaména and the World Bank. The ordinary summit followed on 14/15 March in Bata, Equatorial Guinea, in the presence of presidents Obiang (host), Biya, Bongo, Bozizé, Déby and Sassou. President Menezes of São Tomé and Príncipe as well as DR Congo Foreign Minister She Oktitundu attended as observers. Biya had to leave early, reviving speculation about his health. Outgoing **CEMAC chairman Obiang** gave a keynote speech touching on problems of resource management. He made highly critical remarks on the pace of the integration process. A committee charged with accelerating the process to reform CEMAC was established after audit reports had painted a dark picture of its organisational capacity: the lack of implementation capacity, lack of respect by member-countries of decisions jointly taken, delays in implementing a common market, etc. The committee consists of ministers and representatives of donor, private sector and civil society organisations under the presidency of Obiang and is to deliver a report by 2008. One important background factor was the fact that Equatorial Guinea had grown in financial, economic and political importance but had no leading role in BEAC and CEMAC. Obiang asked for at least one vice-governorship in BEAC, a request that in itself was felt to necessitate a change in the statutes. In an interview with the Paris-based weekly 'Jeune Afrique', he asked for a complete 'plastering' of the CEMAC house, with the EU as a model. The summit also prolonged the mandate of the multinational CEMAC force in CAR until 30 June 2007, and extended it significantly to include contributing to the re-establishment of free movement on four major road axes and control of three particularly unstable regions.

On 7 August, a **second extraordinary CEMAC summit** was held, again in N'Djaména, and was attended by all the persons present at the first one plus Obiang. Bongo, as the 'doyen' of the heads of state, and Sassou, as acting AU chairman, were charged with finding solutions so that the sub-region could live in peace, stability and security. Two decisions were taken: first, the community's parliament was to be installed in Malabo before the end of the year (this could not be achieved); and second, the CEMAC passport should be brought into immediate circulation. One major change in personnel occurred when the CEMAC executive secretary, Jean Nkuete, joined the Cameroonian government in September. He had served in the CEMAC position since 1999. Vice-secretary Mouiri Boussougou (Gabon) replaced him.

The longstanding dispute over the sub-regional airline **Air Cémac** was again on the agenda. At the CEMAC summit in N'Djaména the heads of state charged presidents Déby and Bongo to do everything they could to make the company operational by the end of the year. This goal was not achieved and new doubts about the political will to replace ailing national airlines with a community-wide one were raised.

The EU signed a funding agreement with **CEEAC** worth € 4 m to support the community in crisis-reaction capacities and to support the rudimentary early warning system 'Mécanisme d'Alerte Rapide en Afrique Centrale' (MARAC). A new joint military exercise, baptised Sawa 2006, was held in Cameroon as part of the French-led initiative 'Renforcement des Capacités Africaines de Maintien de la Paix' (RECAMP). Eleven countries participated in this operation for about a month. The final goal of the AU associated with the programme was to have 18,000 trained troops for peacekeeping purposes at their disposal.

CEEAC became more involved in observing elections. About 20 observers were deployed to monitor elections in DR Congo under the chairmanship of Burundi's former president, Pierre Buyoya. Legislative elections in Gabon were also observed. The final report noted some irregularities (late opening of voting centres, insufficient voting material in some places, etc.) as well as a declining and weak participation rate. However, the mission concluded by lauding the peacefulness of the exercise and the maturity of the Gabonese voters. The credibility of this kind of peer review in a generally undemocratic context was considered limited.

CEEAC and ECOWAS, with the help of the United Nations Office on Drugs and Crime (UNODC), elaborated a joint plan of action against trafficking in persons, which was adopted in Nigeria in July. UNODC also organised a ministerial round table of West and Central African countries on a counter-terrorism legal framework in Madrid on 25 and 26 May.

Heads of state and government ministers of the **Gulf of Guinea Commission** countries met on 25 August in Libreville and designated São Tomé's Fradique de Menezes as executive secretary of the Commission for three years. This was considered the start of the functional phase of the organisation, which would deal with conflict resolution and peace monitoring in a region where disputes over oil and aquatic resources had multiplied in recent years.

The 'Commission des Forêts d'Afrique Centrale' **(COMIFAC)** tried to consolidate its organisational basis. The executive secretariat gave a report to the council of ministers held in Malabo on 19–21 September that listed numerous activities (mostly sub-regional and national workshops), but concluded by drawing attention to the problematic financial situation. The modest yearly contributions of CFAfr 31 m per member country agreed in 2005 were, at best, paid late. The cumulative arrears of member states at the time amounted to CFAfr 420 m. Four member countries had not paid anything at all up to this point. This meant that the biggest part of the organisation's funding continued to come from bilateral donors (France and Germany) as well as FAO and the World Bank. The host and new acting chairman of the organisation, President Obiang's son Teodoro, was absent from the council's meeting, leading to sharp criticism by his peers. An extraordinary meeting of the council of ministers held on 24 March in Libreville had already opted for a funding mechanism for the organisation based on an additional tax of 0.1% on imports from third countries outside COMIFAC. This should also lead to harmonisation of funding for all sub-regional cooperative institutions (i.e., also CEEAC and CEMAC).

Andreas Mehler

Cameroon

The year 2006 was marked by two landmark events. First, there was the country's attainment of the completion point under the enhanced Heavily Indebted Poor Countries (HIPC) debt-relief initiative. One of its immediate consequences was the heightening of expectations among ordinary Cameroonians of a rapid end to their precarious living conditions, which the government felt obliged to dampen. Second, there was the achievement of an equitable agreement with Nigeria on the modalities of Nigerian withdrawal from the Bakassi peninsula, in accordance with the October 2002 International Court of Justice (ICJ) verdict.

Domestic Politics

The political situation in Cameroon was relatively stable. The ruling party, the 'Rassemblement Démocratique du Peuple Camerounais' (**RDPC**) consolidated its grip on power in the face of a divided and ineffective opposition. On 21 July, the Cameroonian president, Paul Biya, was re-elected president of the RDPC at the party's third extraordinary congress in Yaoundé. In his acceptance speech, he sought to mobilise party militants ahead of legislative and municipal elections scheduled to take place in 2007. He called for tolerance and dialogue to promote debate, and promised to open the party to new ideas, with greater participation by youth, women and intellectuals. Despite such promises, many party members felt disappointed. They had hoped for an overhaul of the party's central committee and political bureau, the members of which were last elected in 1996.

Bitter internal disputes within the main opposition party, the Social Democratic Front (**SDF**), exploded in mid-February when the party split into two rival factions, one led by the long-serving SDF 'chairman', John Fru Ndi, and the other led by Professor Clement Ngwasiri, an SDF parliamentarian who was one of the party's founding fathers and chairman of its National Advisory Council (NAC). There were various reasons for Ngwasiri's dissent, but one major factor was undoubtedly the growing unease among a number of the party's executive with Fru Ndi's style of leadership: they accused him of running party affairs in a dictatorial fashion and of instituting a personality cult. On 26 May, the two rival factions held simultaneous party conventions, albeit in different locations: the Fru Ndi faction in Bamenda and the Ngwasiri faction in Yaoundé. The Bamenda convention re-elected John Fru Ndi as leader, conferring on him the power to appoint an 18-member shadow cabinet and the party's secretary-general. The Yaoundé convention elected as SDF leader Bernard Achu Muna, a renowned lawyer and erstwhile close ally of Fru Ndi, who pledged to end Fru Ndi's personality cult. The Yaoundé convention also repealed the controversial article 8.2 of the SDF constitution, under which many of Fru Ndi's opponents had been expelled from the party. Subsequently, the two factions became embroiled in a battle for recognition as the 'authentic' SDF. Many SDF militants feared that this factional rivalry would split the SDF vote in the 2007 polls and increase the influence of the ruling RDPC in the regions from which the SDF used to draw its core support.

A few days after the Yaoundé convention, 23 members of the SDF faction loyal to Fru Ndi were arrested. They were part of a larger group of SDF 'vanguards' who had stormed the party's headquarters in Yaoundé in an attempt to prevent the Ngwasiri faction from holding its own convention. During the clashes, one leading member of the Ngwasiri faction, Grégoire Diboulé, was brutally murdered and 30 others were injured, five of them seriously. Among those arrested for the murder was a retired army colonel, James Chi Ngafor, who had recently been appointed by Fru Ndi as SDF coordinator for the Centre province. Events took another dramatic turn on 22 August when prosecutors summoned Fru Ndi to answer questions about the murder. Afterwards, Fru Ndi constantly denied that he had been formally charged with murder or that he had ordered the attack.

Some **other opposition parties** also organised congresses to prepare for the 2007 polls. The 'Union Démocratique du Cameroun' (UDC) of Adamu Ndam Njoya held its congress from 31 November to 2 December, while the 'Union des Populations du Cameroun' (UPC) faction of Augustin Frédéric Kodock held its congress on 30–31 December. As was the case with the RDPC and the SDF, their leaders were re-elected too.

A **cabinet reshuffle** carried out by President Biya on 22 September did not lead to major changes, although some minor ministers were sacked and several others exchanged portfolios. The cabinet reshuffle tended to strengthen the position of the prime minister, Ephraim Inoni, since some of those sacked were known to have had previous confrontations with him. Those who were looking forward to a more dynamic, younger team of ministers were disappointed, because the president brought back a number of former ministers. The president was also careful to preserve an ethnic balance, a characteristic of all his cabinets since his coming to power in 1982. The opposition parties dismissed the changes as cosmetic and criticised the president for maintaining the size of the cabinet at more than 60, a number they considered too costly for the country.

On 22 February, the government announced its intention to amend the electoral laws to enhance transparency in the electoral process. The announcement fuelled speculation that an **independent electoral commission** would be created in line with the demands of the Commonwealth as well as the opposition and certain civil-society organisations. The government's decision in September to ban the initiatives by civil-society groups, such as the Roman Catholic church, to debate the issue publicly dampened hopes that such a body was being seriously considered. In response, the opposition parties threatened at the beginning of November to boycott the forthcoming legislative elections unless an independent electoral commission was established. Prime Minister Inoni then started inviting opposition groups and civil-society groups in late November to discuss the structure of the new institution. Subsequently, on 14 December, he summoned parliament to an extraordinary session to examine a bill concerning the introduction of an independent electoral body called 'Elections Cameroon' (ELECAM). SDF and UDC parliamentarians immediately boycotted its examination for two main reasons. First, the bill largely empowered the president of the republic to nominate ELECAM members and second, article 42 of the bill stipulated that ELECAM would be introduced only progressively. In the end, however, government agreed that ELECAM would come into operation within 18 months of approval of the bill.

On 4 January, four days after pledging to renew **the fight against corruption** in his new year speech, President Biya sacked two local magistrates for corruption and abuse of trust – this being the first time that the president had publicly sacked members of the judiciary for graft. Between 11 and 24 February, the former heads of three state-owned companies and several of their subordinates, as well as a number of senior government officials, including the energy and water minister, Alphonse Siyam Siewe, were arrested and detained on charges of corruption. The arrests were made with considerable fanfare, supporting claims that the president was mounting a show to convince donors of the seriousness of his intentions and to improve Cameroon's chances of reaching completion-point status under the IMF-World Bank's enhanced HIPC initiative. Some newspapers tried to fuel the so-called 'opération épervier' (Operation Sparrow-hawk) by publishing lists of the wealthiest Cameroonians. Several members of the political and administrative elite featured on the lists, including the finance minister, Polycarpe Abah Abah, who successfully filed lawsuits against the newspapers for defamation.

Several new, often somewhat overlapping institutions and laws were launched to curb corruption. On 25 January, there was the inauguration of the 'Agence Nationale d'Investigation Financière' (ANIF), which was charged with investigating financial crimes, such as misappropriation of public funds, counterfeiting, illegal capital flight and money laundering. A few months later, on 11 March, President Biya established a new anti-corruption commission, the 'Commission Nationale Anti-Corruption' (CONAC) to replace the 'Observatoire National de Lutte contre la Corruption' (created in 2000 and reporting to the prime minister), which was to report to him directly. CONAC would be responsible for the monitoring and evaluation of the government's anti-corruption and good governance programme. In addition, it was mandated to investigate cases of corruption. On 22 March, the National Assembly adopted a law that made it compulsory for public officials to declare their assets and property in accordance with article 6.6 of the 1996 constitution. Apparently, in a deliberate effort to maintain the confidentiality of this information and allow officials to avoid public scrutiny, the law stated that the declaration would be made to an assets and property declaration commission, whose members were to be appointed by the president of the republic. Despite all these anti-corruption measures, the Corruption Perceptions Index of Transparency International (TI) showed no improvement in the country's level of corruption. While the 2005 TI report ranked Cameroon 137th in a survey of 159 countries, the 2006 TI report ranked Cameroon 138th in a survey of 163 countries.

Activists of the **Anglophone secessionist movement**, the Southern Cameroons National Council (SCNC), continued to be subjected to various forms of repression. On 27 March, for instance, some 30 activists of the militant Southern Cameroons Youth League (SCYL) were arrested by gendarmes in the towns of Mutengene and Muea in the South West province and detained. They were charged with recruiting members into the so-called Southern Cameroons Defence Force. On 27 April, 65 SCNC activists were arrested and detained in Oku in the North West province for holding an illegal meeting in a private home. They were later released, but two weeks later rearrested and detained in Bamenda. Notwithstanding an administrative ban on SCNC activities and heavy troop deployments during the celebration of the Southern Cameroons independence day on 1 October, SCNC activists were once again able to hoist flags in several Anglophone towns.

A temporary setback in the improvement in the country's **human rights situation** occurred on 30 June when parliament adopted a bill postponing the implementation of the new Criminal Procedure Code from 1 August 2006 to 1 January 2007. This code, which constituted an attempt to harmonise the Anglophone and Francophone judicial systems, was thought to stop arbitrary arrests and detentions, to better protect human rights during criminal proceedings, to curb judicial delays and ensure the rapid execution of judgments.

One of the most significant events on the **media scene** was a government attempt to curb what it described as media excesses. In March, the government introduced a bill in the National Assembly to tighten press laws. The bill sought to increase the powers of government officials to shut down newspapers for up to six months, but was quickly abandoned when the government realised that it could damage Cameroon's democratic credentials. This attempt to clamp down on press freedom occurred after three relatively unknown local newspapers, 'Le Méteo', 'L'Anecdote' and 'Nouvelles d'Afrique' had published lists of presumed homosexuals among the national political, economic, religious and cultural elite. Many of those named by the newspapers came out publicly to strongly deny the allegations of homosexuality, which in Cameroon is a crime punishable by a jail term. Others, such as the parliamentary affairs minister, Grégoire Owona, went to court to clear their names, eventually leading to the conviction of the publishers. Another significant event on the media scene was what was generally seen as a revolt among the staff of the state-owned Cameroon Radio-Television Corporation (CRTV). On 24 August, 68 CRTV employees wrote an open letter to the newly appointed general manager, Ahmadou Vamoulké, accusing him of mismanagement and neglecting their interests.

There were again a number of confrontations between **students** and university and government authorities. The most violent incident started at the University of Buea (UB) on 27 November. UB students protested against what they considered to be grave fraud. Their vice-chancellor, Cornelius Mbifung Lambi, had previously signed a list of candidates who were to participate in the oral entrance examination of the newly created UB medical school, all of them Anglophone. However, shortly afterwards the minister of higher education emerged with another list with 26 names added, all of them Francophone. This sparked off a riot on the campus that lasted for two weeks, during which security forces shot to death two students and severely wounded several others. Besides calling for the immediate implementation of the original list of candidates, in a memorandum the students denounced the hike in fees for postgraduate courses, the payment of CFAfr 1,000 for the provision of transcripts and the poor quality of food in the UB restaurant. They also demanded the immediate publication of the findings of the presidential commission into the killing of two UB students during the April-May 2005 university strike.

Foreign Affairs

Relations between Cameroon and **Nigeria** could improve following a landmark agreement between the heads of state of both countries on the modalities of the Nigerian withdrawal from the Bakassi peninsula in accordance with the October 2002 ICJ judgment and with due respect for the well-being of the Nigerian inhabitants. The agreement was concluded on 12 June at a summit meeting on the Greentree estate in Manhasset, New York under the auspices of the UN secretary-general, Kofi Annan, and attended by representatives of four witness states (the US, UK, France and Germany). The so-called Greentree agreement, which was widely commended as a shining example of peaceful conflict resolution in Africa, contained the following main provisions. First, Nigeria would withdraw its estimated 3,000 troops from the territory within 60 days and formally cede the territory to Cameroon. Second, the islands of Atabong and Akwabana, which were populated almost exclusively by Nigerians, would be administered by Nigeria for two years. Third, Nigerian inhabitants of Bakassi would have two years to decide whether to remain on the peninsula as Nigerian citizens, take Cameroonian nationality or be relocated to Nigeria. Fourth, a special transitional provision granting Nigerians free access to the Bakassi region would be in force for five years. Fifth, a follow-up commission composed of 10 representatives – two each from Cameroon, Nigeria and the UN plus one from each of the four witness states – would be set up to implement the agreement.

In the weeks leading up to the handover, local Nigerian chiefs and their subjects organised into the so-called Bakassi Movement for Self-Determination filed a suit in the federal high court in Abuja, Nigeria, to demand a halt to the process, rejecting the Greentree agreement and vowing to fight their relocation. According to BBC, they even proclaimed the independence of Bakassi on 27 July. Nevertheless, Nigeria began to withdraw its troops from the peninsula on 1 August, and on 14 August Nigerian and Cameroonian officials took part in a ceremony at Akwa village formally marking the handover of the territory to Cameroon. Soon afterwards, however, a new source of conflict arose. During the 15th session of the Cameroon-Nigeria mixed commission – a body set up by the UN to implement the ICJ ruling – held in Yaoundé on 6–7 September, Nigerian representatives alleged that Nigerian citizens living in Bakassi and other parts of Cameroon were returning to Nigeria with awful stories of maltreatment by Cameroonian gendarmes. Between 22 and 30 August, more than 6,000 Nigerians had been shipped from Douala and Limbe to Nigeria. The commission then resolved to send an observer mission to the peninsula to be made up of 15 UN representatives and five delegates each from Nigeria and Cameroon.

Cameroon's relations with **regional and continental organisations in Africa** continued to be marked by the absence of active diplomatic initiatives. There were two CEMAC summit meetings. President Biya, renowned for his regular absence from meetings of African organisations, did attend the first CEMAC meeting at Bata in Equatorial Guinea from 14–16 March, a move widely interpreted as a gesture to improve Cameroon's strained relations with its neighbour arising from the latter's alleged mistreatment of Cameroonian migrants and its continuing support for Nigeria in the border dispute with Cameroon. During this meeting, President Biya fell ill, causing panic in Cameroonian government circles. He decided to send the president of the National Assembly, Cavaye Yegui Djibril, to the second CEMAC meeting, which was held in N'Djaména, Chad, on 7–8 August. Both CEMAC meetings aimed at overcoming what the president of Equatorial Guinea, Obiang Nguema, called during the Bata meeting "the catastrophic balance of CEMAC". Djibril also represented Cameroon at the sixth AU summit in Khartoum on 23–24 January, which dealt with education and culture. Prime Minister Inoni participated in a meeting of heads of state from the Gulf of Guinea region in Libreville on 25 August, held to discuss the structure of a newly established commission for the peaceful resolution of conflicts in this strategic oil-rich region. Since Cameroon had failed to ratify the treaty that had instituted the Commission of the Gulf of Guinea, it was not granted any function in the new organisation.

Cameroon's relations with **Western countries**, the major donors to its development programmes, were generally good. Most Western countries continued to believe that they could exert a positive influence on good governance and democratic reforms through cooperation. France remained Cameroon's foremost ally in the West. President Biya visited France from 26 to 28 July. During his visit, French President Jacques Chirac expressed the hope that the new 'contract of debt relief and development' signed between France and Cameroon in June, which made Cameroon the primary beneficiary of French aid, would open a new chapter in mutual cooperation (see below). Many observers, however, underscored the growing orientation of Cameroon's foreign policies towards the US. On 15–16 February, the US assistant-secretary of state for African affairs, Jendayi Frazer, visited Cameroon to open the new $ 57 m US embassy at Bastos in Yaoundé and to strengthen US relations with Cameroon. Prime Minister Inoni, in turn, went on a predominantly economic mission to the US on 19 October. This was his third mission to the US since his nomination as prime minister in December 2004.

Cameroon continued to maintain close relations with a number of international **organisations**, in particular the 'Organisation Internationale de la Francophonie' (OIF) and the Commonwealth, membership in both of which reflected the 'bilingual nature of the country'. President Biya participated in the conference of OIF heads of state and government in Bucharest from 28–29 September. The Commonwealth once again demonstrated its persistent interest in political reforms in Cameroon. Following a meeting on 20–22 February with a Commonwealth delegation led by Joe Clark, the ex-prime minister of Canada, the government announced its intention to establish an independent body to manage future elections in the country.

Cameroon was eager to intensify its relations with some **Asian countries**, notably Japan and China. President Biya visited Japan from 16 to 22 April, where he had an audience with Prime Minister Koizumi. Japan then allocated CFAfr 8.5 bn to Cameroon to be used to construct schools, provide rural water and rehabilitate Ahmadou Ahidjo stadium. President Biya was also among the large number of African heads of state who attended the third meeting of the forum on China-Africa cooperation in Beijing from 3 to 5 November. On that occasion, China agreed to grant Cameroon tourism-destination status and to provide it with a gift of CFAfr 2.5 bn for social projects.

Socioeconomic Developments

On 28 April, the World Bank and IMF announced that Cameroon had finally reached the **completion point** under the enhanced HIPC initiative. As a result, Cameroon benefited from generous debt relief, including $ 1.3 bn under the enhanced HIPC initiative, $ 1.1 bn under the Multilateral Debt Relief Initiative (MDRI), and additional Paris Club write-offs on a bilateral basis, amounting to about $ 2.6 bn. In a related development, on 22 June Prime Minister Inoni signed the 'contract of debt relief and development, (C2D) with the French minister-delegate for cooperation and development, Brigitte Girardin. The agreement covered the period 2006–11, and granted Cameroon total debt relief worth $ 680 m, which would be awarded in five equal annual disbursements. The funds had to be used for poverty alleviation and would be focused on five areas: health and the fight against AIDS; basic education; infrastructure; agricultural development and food security; and the environment. According to an IMF-IDA report, published in April, Cameroon's total public external debt was expected to fall from an estimated $ 6.2 bn at the end of 2005 to just $ 525 m at the end of 2006.

The announcement that Cameroon had reached completion point, which was described by government officials as an historic event in the country's struggle for development, raised **high expectations** among ordinary Cameroonians of an immediate improvement in their living conditions, and civil servants started demanding substantial salary increases. Taken aback by the heightened expectations, the government sought to dampen them. In an address to the nation on 12 May, President Biya recognised that debt relief provided an unprecedented opportunity to combat poverty effectively and improve standards of living, while highlighting that it would not solve all the country's problems. He urged Cameroonians to work hard and to expect to make further sacrifices. Delegations of senior government and RDPC party officials held numerous meetings throughout the country in August to explain the prospects and challenges that the country was facing after reaching the completion point.

In the three-year, $ 26.8 m poverty reduction and growth facility (PRGF), which was awarded in October 2005, the government had committed itself to reinvigorating the stalled **privatisation and restructuring programme** for public enterprises. However, an IMF mission visiting Cameroon in late August noted little progress in public-enterprise reform. On 29 June, the government announced the winning bidder for the troubled national airline, Cameroon Airlines (CAMAIR), namely First Delta Air Services, a consortium comprising the Belgian national airline, SN-Brussels, and a Cameroonian venture-capital fund, Central Africa Investments (CENAINVEST). A few months later, on 12 September, a Cameroonian newspaper, 'The Post', reported that President Biya had halted CAMAIR'S privatisation following a better offer from a US company. In July, the government launched the tender for the privatisation of its fixed-line telephone company, Cameroon Telecommunications (CAMTEL), and plans were once again advanced for the privatisation of two huge agro-industrial parastatals, the 'Société de Développement du Coton' (SODECOTON) in northern Cameroon and the Cameroon Development Corporation (CDC) in Anglophone Cameroon. The government also promised to increase its efforts to restructure the national refinery, the 'Société Nationale de Raffinage' (SONARA), the national postal company, Cameroon Postal Services (CAMPOST) and the national water utility, the 'Société Nationale des Eaux du Cameroun' (SNEC). In addition to ranking low on public-sector reforms, the government undertook few initiatives to boost private investment. On 6 September, the World Bank and the IFC published a report,

"Doing Business in 2007" that ranked Cameroon 152nd out of 175 countries for ease of doing business. This represented a drop from 147th in their previous report.

On 21 November, Prime Minister Inoni presented the **budget for 2007** to the National Assembly, amounting to CFAfr 2,251 bn, an increase of CFAfr 390 bn compared to the 2006 budget. The increase in the 2007 budget was mainly due to the expected high oil and cocoa prices and the substantial debt relief under the HIPC initiative. The budget aimed at real GDP growth of 4% and an average inflation rate of 2%. It sought to consolidate government's tight fiscal policies as stipulated in the three-year PRGF arrangement. It made provision for only a slight reduction in the value-added tax (VAT) on some food items, such as rice and fish. Agricultural output could even be badly affected by the introduction of VAT on agricultural inputs.

In June, the primary education minister, Haman Adama, announced a programme to improve provision of **education at primary level**. This included the hiring of 3,000 new teachers each year between 2006 and 2015, and the construction of 40,000 new classrooms by 2015. The programme's estimated CFAfr 500 bn cost was expected to be financed by donors, the government and funds freed up by the recent debt write-off under the enhanced HIPC initiative. The government's growing attention to educational expansion at primary level was largely responsible for the slight improvement in Cameroon's ranking on the Human Development Index published by the UNDP in its "Human Development Report 2006". Its position rose from 148th out of 177 countries in the previous year to 144th this year.

On 31 May, Cameroon's National Institute of Statistics (NIS) published the results of the first phase of its national survey on employment and the informal sector. As expected, the survey revealed high levels of **unemployment and underemployment**, with an estimated 9.3% of the working-age population unable to find work and 75% classified as underemployed. The worst affected included those aged from 20 to 29, women and university graduates, 36.5% of whom were unable to find work after finishing their degree. The report highlighted the importance of the informal sector in providing jobs – it employed an estimated 90% of the workforce – with only 20% of workers having a formal contract and 7.9% having regular salaries.

Workers in various sectors of the economy resorted to **strike action** to protest either against their lay-offs during the privatisation and restructuring of state enterprises or their precarious living and working conditions. The most protracted and violent strikes took place in the Tole and Ndu tea plantations, which had been sold in October 2002 by the CDC to Brobon Finex of South Africa. The Tole strike lasted from 26 February to 15 September. The Ndu strike started on 28 August and had not been called off by year's end. The workers complained of unpaid wages and social benefits, the withdrawal of the healthcare and other social services they had enjoyed prior to privatisation, and what they described as inhuman treatment by management. On 1 December, security forces killed two strikers and wounded several others at Ndu.

Cameroon's poultry industry fell into deep crisis after a government announcement in March that the deadly **avian flu virus** had been detected in a small village close to the northern provincial town of Maroua. This triggered a slump in sales throughout the country. Consumption of chickens and eggs fell dramatically and market prices collapsed.

Trading began at the Douala **Stock Exchange** (DSX) on 30 June – more than three years after it was inaugurated – with the listing of 9,200 shares of the bottled water company 'Société des Eaux Minérales du Cameroun' (SEMC).

On 25 September, almost a year after signing a memorandum of understanding with the government, a US transport company, Parker Transnational Industries (PTI), launched its urban service in the capital, Yaoundé. PTI became the majority owner of a joint-venture company – 'Le Bus' – in partnership with the government. By the end of October, the company had put 16 buses into service.

Piet Konings

Central African Republic

Some major reform steps by Prime Minister Elie Doté's government secured the award of a much-needed PRGF with the IMF in December. This could not immediately benefit the population, which has suffered through ten years of instability and insecurity. The entire northern part of the country was not safe from incursions by rebel groups and indiscriminate counter-attacks by government forces. In October, the outright capture by rebel groups of the provincial capital of Birao in the northeast sent a strong signal to Bangui. Security concerns dominated public debate during the year.

Domestic Politics

President Bozizé undertook **two government reshuffles**, while retaining Prime Minister Doté. On 31 January, three ministers left the cabinet, five others changed their positions. The second cabinet reshuffle on 2 September increased Doté's influence, since he additionally assumed the finance and budget portfolio. Some heavyweights exchanged positions: Charles Massi, for example, moved from transport to rural development, while Lt.Col. Parfait-Anicet M'bay moved in the opposite direction. Interpretations of the event were divided. While hopes were expressed that Doté, who was seen as a driver of the reform processes, would finally be in a key position of power, some observers warned that the departure of Foreign Minister Jean-Paul Ngoupande (replaced by Côme Zoumara) from government could destabilise the coalition of forces behind Bozizé. Ngoupande had recovered from serious health problems at the beginning of the year. His 'Parti de l'Unité Nationale' (PUN), an essential backer of Bozizé in the second round of the 2005 elections and part of the KNK alliance ('Kwa na Kwa', literally 'work, nothing but work'), was no longer represented in government. In August, the constitutional court, upon the request of the speaker of the National Assembly, ruled that members of parliament nominated as ministers would lose their popular mandates. Ngoupande, Massi and two others decided to give up their seats in parliament. The head of state continued to retain the defence portfolio for himself. He appointed Ngoupande as presidential advisor.

The **climate of insecurity** continued to haunt citizens in the northern part of the country. Several violent incidents were recorded in the capital Bangui. The most serious of these related to the murder of an army officer by Claude Sanze, a former bodyguard of the transitional legislative assembly's president Nicolas Tiangaye, believed to have been cheated in last year's parliamentary elections. Sanze fled to the UN peace-building mission's premises before being surrendered to the gendarmerie. He was subsequently murdered by army personnel. During Sanze's burial, security forces fired into an angry crowd, killing three. Much more serious were the armed incursions by various rebel groups into northern CAR. On 29 January, the town of Paoua in the prefecture of Ouham-Pende (hometown of former President Patassé) was attacked by rebels whose identity was unclear. Worse yet were the actions of the republican guard under the command of Bozizé's nephew Lt. Eugène Ngaïkoïssé, which led to a massacre (81–104 dead, according to different unconfirmed reports) and the flight from the town of half the local population. Five days later, three members of parliament, among them former Speaker Luc-Apollinaire Dondon Konamabaye, accused the government of responsibility for the massacre. The current speaker, Célestin Gaombalet, also repeatedly criticised the government for the continuing insecurity in the north. A second wave of rebel attacks followed in May. Two members of the armed forces (Forces Armées Centraficaines, FACA) were killed close to the provincial capital of Birao (Vakaga prefecture). Demonstrations against widespread violence took place in Bangui in April and May. At the end of June, the 'Union des Forces Républicaines' (UFR) launched new attacks on Gordil and Tiringoulou (Vakaga), and some 12 FACA elements were killed, as were two Chadian peacekeepers from the 'Force Multinationale de la CEMAC' (FOMUC). Responsibility for this operation was claimed by Lt. Florian François Ndjadder, son of a former head of the gendarmerie who had been killed during the attempted coup d'etat of May 2001. Ndjadder headed the rebellion by the UFR, which had announced in January already that it was working to bring about the downfall of the Bozizé regime. The different **rebel groups** were not easily distinguishable. In September, three smaller movements claimed to have formed the 'Union des Forces Démocratiques pour le Rassemblement' (UFDR) in Kigali, Rwanda. A 'Mouvement Populaire pour la Renaissance du Peuple Centrafricain' (MPRPC) claimed responsibility for murdering the mayor of Bossangoa in March. Finally, the 'Armée pour la Restauration de la République et la Démocratie' (APRD) abruptly lost its leadership when on 24 February, its Lt. Larmasoum was arrested in Bangui while reportedly hiring a commando to assassinate Bozizé. He was later condemned to forced labour for life. A former deputy minister for education from 2001–03 under Patassé, André Ringui, was later presented as the leader of APRD. The Patassé-friendly warlord Abdoulaye Miskine, who headed his own 'Forces pour la Démocratie du Peuple Centrafricain' (FDPC), was variously reported to be close to the APRD, UFR and the UFDR.

After the June attacks, Bozizé reacted by changing the entire **FACA leadership**, including the chief of staff, Gen. Antoine Gambi, on 4 July. A week later, France decided to provide more logistical, material and tactical help, including the provision of one C130 aircraft to transport troops. This did not improve army morale and on 11 August Bozizé again heavily criticised the army after 80 soldiers deserted their positions in the northeast of the country, the third such occurrence. They were immediately arrested.

On 30–31 October, UFDR rebels attacked Birao, killing ten FACA soldiers and taking the town. Subsequently, other towns (Sam Ouandja, Ouanda Djallé in Vakaga, Ouadda in Haute-Kotto and provincial capital Ndélé in neighbouring Bamingui-Bangoran) fell to the rebels. This meant that a quarter of all provinces were at least partly in the hands of rebels or faced the prospect of sliding into violent conflict. Surprisingly, on 20 November the rebel leader Michel Djotodia and his spokesman Abakar Sabon were arrested and held in Benin. A week later, Birao was recaptured with massive French help, and the other towns soon followed. The extreme vulnerability of the regime – indeed, of the whole state – was laid bare by these events.

The number of **refugees** and internally displaced persons steadily rose. In October, 50,000 displaced persons from 122 villages in four districts in the Ouham prefecture were counted. On 8 December, UNHCR gave out a new figure of 150,000 internally displaced persons. In addition, by year's end there were 50,000 refugees in Chad along with a smaller number of forgotten refugees living unattended in southeastern Sudan.

While the UFDR rebels asked for negotiations under international mediation, Bozizé was more than reluctant. The only noteworthy signal was when the head of state held a one-day forum in the National Assembly on 28 July as a limited form of dialogue with all "vibrant parts of the society", during which he at least did not rule out direct talks with rebels. The meeting was snubbed by several opposition leaders.

Numerous **human rights violations** were committed by both rebels and state agencies, particularly the presidential guard. This was most evident in the zones of insecurity in northern CAR (including Paoua, Kaga-Bandoro), but sporadic acts of indiscriminate violence and murder by security forces occurred even in Bangui. Dissident wings of the 'Mouvement pour la Libération du Peuple Centrafricain' (MLPC) and the 'Front Patriotique et Populaire' (FPP) were barred from holding public rallies in mid-2006 and even, temporarily, from gaining access to the media. Some leading members of both parties were detained without proper indictment, including Florence Ndouba, president of the women's wing of MLPC and sister of Patassé's spokesman. Prominent FPP member Claude Yabanda was also arrested, but it was unclear whether this was related to a power struggle inside his party over the succession to party founder Abel Goumba (who favoured his own son as party chairman) or to alleged coup plots.

In June, **Bozizé supporters** created a new party 'Union pour un Mouvement Populaire en Centrafrique' (UMPCA), headed by Bozizé's cousin Yvonne M'boïssona (later appointed minister of tourism). This was seen as an attempt to build a more solid power base following the earlier formation, in April, of a loose 'Groupe des Partis Politiques de la Majorité Présidentielle' (GPPMP). About 80 of 105 seats in the National Assembly belonged to the presidential majority.

The **power struggle** inside the MLPC continued. During a meeting on 22–24 June of the national political council that was swiftly declared to be an extraordinary congress, Patassé – in exile in Togo – was suspended by persons sympathetic to the new party president, Martin Ziguélé. Dondon Konamambaye, leader of the pro-Patassé wing of the former ruling party, immediately declared this session illegal. Bozizé received Ziguélé upon the latter's arrival from Paris on 18 August. Ziguélé, his most serious challenger during the 2005 elections, declared that he was alarmed at the level of violence in the country. He declared that he would only return to CAR in 2007 for the ordinary MLPC congress.

In August, Patassé and an advisor were sentenced *in absentia* to 20 years of forced labour and a fine for fraud, and ordered to reimburse the treasury about € 10.7 m. Additionally, the court ordered that the former president lose his civic rights. A second charge of embezzlement was separated from this action. However, the appeals court declared itself unable to pursue the case against him and several other personalities for **crimes against humanity** committed in 2001. The prosecutor at the International Criminal Court (ICC) had not taken a decision by year's end as to whether and when to conduct an investigation in the case against Patassé and others submitted by the government to the ICC as early as December 2004. One reason given was the continued violence in the northern part of the country. This could be interpreted as a willingness to include ongoing crimes against humanity.

A second high-profile trial in the so-called **Raikina affair** ended with the acquittal of all indicted citizens on 12 September, as the charge of a coup plot could not be proven. However, the acquitted were not immediately released but were transferred to a prison in the interior, leading to widespread protest. The Central African Human Rights League (LCDH) called attention to the dangers involved in the activities of human rights workers.

Towards the end of the year, Bozizé personally ordered the burning of the houses of two Baptist pastors, after they had set fire to the home of another pastor in a row over the use of a chapel for Christmas services in Bangui.

Foreign Affairs

The escalation of armed encounters in October-December between rebels and a coalition of pro-government forces consisting of FOMUC peacekeepers, French troops and the army, revived the spectre of civil war and of a regional war transcending the borders with Sudan and Chad. Relations with **Sudan** soured after Chadian rebels transited from Sudan through CAR territory to attack the Chadian capital of N'Djaména in April. In reaction, the authorities closed the border with Sudan on 14 April. In November, Bozizé accused Sudan of backing rebels in the northeastern part of the country. The Sudanese embassy in Bangui denied these allegations.

At their summit in Libreville on 29 June, **CEMAC** heads of state decided to prolong the stay of the 380-man FOMUC force, drawn from Chad, Congo and Gabon, until 30 June 2007. The mandate itself was extended to cover the protection of key roads in the north and additional support tasks for FACA. Patrols around provincial capitals of Bria, Bozoum and Kaga-Bandoro, with logistical support from France, were meant to contribute to the security of the population.

The **UN Security Council** held deliberations on CAR on 7 July and condemned the earlier rebel attacks. On 31 August, the Security Council adopted resolution 1706 in which it decided that the mandate of the UN mission in the Sudan should include improvement of the security situation in regions bordering on Chad and CAR. The AU's Peace and Security Council subsequently issued a supportive communiqué on 20 September. A UN technical assessment mission was sent to Chad and CAR, meeting with the heads of state of both countries. Bozizé called for the deployment of UN troops as soon as possible. However, in a report at year's end UN Secretary General Kofi Annan pointed to the considerable risks and logistical problems facing a peacekeeping force in eastern Chad and northeastern CAR. The AU sent a multidisciplinary mission whose report was released in Addis Abeba in December. It suggested that the country needed a "patriotic reawakening on the part of its elite".

Relations with France were crucial. In January, Paris deployed two helicopters to help the FACA in transporting troops. Cooperation intensified after the rebel conquest of northern towns in November. In a dramatic radio message, the government appealed to the international community and "friendly nations, in particular those linked by specific treaties, particularly France, to work for the restoration of the territorial integrity." The response was immediate. France used six Mirage fighter jets to combat rebels in accordance with the military pact linking both countries. About 300 French soldiers took part in the operation. Nine years after the closure of her two military bases in CAR, France was back.

Diplomatic ties were re-established with **Cuba** after 23 years of interruption. Incidentally, Cuba was suspected of having played played a role in the attempted coup d'etat of Bozizé against former President Kolingba in 1982. Japan re-established economic cooperation in March, having suspended disbursements following the 2003 coup d'etat.

Socioeconomic Developments

Under Prime Minister Doté, some major efforts have been undertaken to bolster the revenue base of the state, which should help to achieve overall stability goals. The **Emergency Post-conflict Assistance** (EPCA) programme concluded in 2005 (worth some $ 10.2 m) was considered a success and paved the way for a three-year **PRGF** on 22 December (of about $ 54.5 m) to support the government's economic programme into 2009. According to the IMF, the country had made advances in structural reform in such areas as public financial management, tax and customs administration and governance and transparency. The World Bank and the ADB gave equally positive assessments at the end of the year. However, all major steps undertaken were under tight supervision by foreign experts. The new goal to reach the decision-point under the enhanced HIPC debt-relief initiative early was rated as highly optimistic by observers.

Growth rates have improved gradually since 2004 to an estimated 3%. This cannot hide major problems, however. The national economy continued to be shaped by traditional **agriculture**, while cash crop production has suffered enormously during the last years of instability (with the cotton sector close to collapse). Agro-pastoral producers particularly in the north continued to hide in the bush or in semi-urban areas, because of the risk of attacks. Sufficient subsistence production was at risk.

The **mining sector** showed further high potential, with diamond production at around 350,000 carats: BEAC even expected production of 441,000 carats. Newly discovered uranium deposits will have to be exploited in a transparent manner to have any positive effect on the overall bleak situation. The authorities in this resource-rich country continued to have difficulty in administering the sector, which, nevertheless, represented the only hope for quick recovery of the whole economy. On 17 October, Bozizé inaugurated the first uranium-mining project at Bakouma, which had been developed by the South African mining company UraMin (owning 90% of shares, 10% remaining with the government). Canada's Axmin signed the first gold mining convention in January.

In September, Bozizé decreed the dissolution of the notoriously ineffective and corrupt **customs service** after a disastrous evaluation report by French experts. This was seen as an opportunity to clean-up a particularly problematic sector. An increase in state revenues was considered crucial to any development effort. Most donors appeared to be broadly satisfied with the emergency post-conflict assistance (EPCA) programme, but debt arrears and the belated disbursement of public sector salaries remained serious concerns.

The notorious inability of the government to pay **public sector salaries** continued, leading to several strikes and low productivity. Even CAR's judges staged a sit-in at the court of appeals on 20 April and demanded payment. Bozizé publicly condemned several strikes, while Doté at least agreed to negotiate with the teachers' branch of the powerful 'Union Syndicale des Travailleurs en Centrafrique' (USTC) during the autumn. University and school teachers again went on strike in September-October demanding an improvement in their status and the payment of salary arrears. The USTC called off strike action after the government committed to further negotiations.

The **humanitarian situation** remained highly problematic, although the international community had at least taken notice of the crisis. Compared to 2005, when only some $ 11 m came in, the UN office for the coordination of humanitarian affairs registered about $ 27 m in commitments of humanitarian aid by different donors. The entire northern part of the country was for a substantial period connected only sporadically with the capital. After the October attacks, the first UN humanitarian flight reached the city of Kaga-Bandoro (only 333 km north of Bangui) on 1 November.

Andreas Mehler

Chad

As in 2005, the Darfur crisis dominated domestic and foreign politics during 2006. Insecurity mounted in the east and southeast of Chad. The number of refugees continued to rise. Now included among them were refugees from the Central African Republic (CAR), where a fresh rebellion had broken out in the northeast, and from Chad itself, with masses of new IDPs feeling compelled to leave their homes in the affected areas in the east of the country. There were numerous battles between three rebel groups and the Chadian army culminating in a surprise attack by the 'Front Uni pour le Changement Démocratique' (FUCD) on N'Djaména, the Chadian capital, on 13 April. Domestic issues were dominated by the presidential elections on 3 May, which resulted in the re-election of Idriss Déby Itno. The conflict with the World Bank over the allocation of oil revenues ended in July with a Memorandum of Understanding specifying new conditions for spending oil revenues. Food security improved somewhat following a record harvest in both 2005 and 2006 and sustained emergency aid efforts by the international community in the east and south of the country.

Domestic Politics

Mounting tension characterised the political scene in Chad for the first six months of 2006. Rebel attacks in the east of the country increased in frequency and severity. There was a direct **attack on President Déby**: on 14 March, an attempt was made to shoot down his plane as he returned from a summit of Central African leaders in Equatorial Guinea. According to the government, the plotters were neutralised. It identified the brothers Tom and Timan Erdimi, former members of the regime who had joined the opposition abroad, as the instigators of the attempted coup. A week later, the Chadian army launched an offensive against the headquarters of the rebel movement 'Socle pour le Changement, l'Unité et la Démocratie' (SCUD) in Hadjer Marfaine, a mountainous area on the border with Sudan. This movement mainly comprised deserters from the Chadian army. During the fighting, the army chief, a cousin of Déby, General Abakar Youssouf Mahamat Itno, was killed. According to observers, this was an indication that the command structure in the Chadian army was on the verge of collapse.

On 11 April, a column of another rebel movement, the FUCD, a coalition of 13 rebel groups led by Mahamat Nour Abdelkarim, entered the country from Sudan through the CAR, and launched a **surprise attack on the capital N'Djaména** two days later. En route to the capital, they briefly seized the towns of Goz Beida, Am Timan and Mongo. This attack could only be countered with French intelligence and logistical support, which enabled the Chadian army to annihilate the rebel advance columns. A French fighter jet also fired a warning shot over the rebel forces. The fighting in N'Djaména left more than 200 combatants and civilians dead and many more wounded, among them the military commander of FUCD, Mahamat Issa Mahamat. The rebels claimed that they had made a tactical retreat and disappeared across the borders to Sudan. Analysts agree that the attack was a military blunder by the rebels, though it did much to undermine the political credibility of the Déby regime. It also showed that the opposition were not a united front, as the other two main rebel groups, SCUD and the 'Rassemblement pour la Justice' (RPJ), made no move to support FUCD.

In the same period (mid-April), a violent confrontation took place between alleged Janjaweed horsemen, coming from Darfur, plus allied villagers on the one hand, and Daadjo villages in the southeast of Chad on the other. The fighting left 75 Daadjo dead and many more wounded. Earlier attacks on the same village were regarded as cattle theft, but this attack could be termed planned murder. The Daadjo, relying on machetes and spears, were nearly defenceless. There were probably more attacks such as these on villages with 'African' populations. The ethnic character of the incident is undeniable, though economic motives should not be overlooked. On 25 December, the government could claim major success when a peace accord was signed in Tripoli with Mahamat Nour, the leader of FUCD.

These violent episodes loomed large over the **presidential elections**, which were planned for 3 May. Opposition parties called on President Déby to postpone the elections as safety and freedom could not be guaranteed in large parts of the country. The opposition did not field a strong candidate to oppose Déby, since most opposition parties and candidates boycotted the elections. Eventually, the elections were held as planned and took place without violence. The opposition consisted of four straw candidates who could not prevent

Déby from achieving victory in the first round. According to the official results, he won 64.7% of the votes, with a total turnout of 53.1%. The opposition claimed the elections were fraudulent and that only 20% of the electorate had made its way to the polling stations. The elections were held without external observers, so there was no independent confirmation of these allegations.

In a bid to appease the opposition, President Déby organised a **national dialogue** from 28 July to 2 August, but he did not invite the rebel movements. The main opposition leaders refused to participate, while 54 political parties and civil society organisations did take part in the debates. Because of the unrest, the legislative elections were postponed by one year. On 14 August, the government was reshuffled to give the losing presidential candidates ministerial posts. The main positions in the government remained unchanged.

Attacks by rebel groups of various origin and counterattacks by government in the east continued throughout the second half of the year, with both sides claiming to have inflicted heavy losses on their opponents. In September, a major offensive was launched against rebels in the Aram Kolle mountains, 150 km north of Abéché. There was also fighting in Adre and Birak, close to the border with Sudan. Rebels briefly captured Goz Beida, a major aid-agency hub, in October. There were more reports of rebels temporarily occupying towns in the east and looting the army's weapon stocks. The Déby regime probably survived because of the arrival of large number of new recruits with new weaponry following an agreement with the World Bank and the oil companies over the management of oil revenues and the payment of tax arrears.

Whereas initially the attacks could be associated with specific rebel movements, in the last three months of the year the east was the scene of increasing chaos. At least 20 villages were attacked and burned by unidentified bands of armed men riding horses and camels, resembling the situation in Darfur. In some reports, mention was made of attacks with machetes. The clashes had an increasingly localised character, with reports of local militia participating in the looting, raping and killing. As a result, the government felt compelled to declare a **state of emergency** on 14 November in the east of the country and in N'Djaména, curtailing press freedom, among other things. The security situation deteriorated further on 20 November, when a relief worker from MSF was killed. On 25 November, the WFP's warehouses were looted when Abéché, the hub of emergency aid for refugees from Sudan, was attacked. In the southeast, more than 50,000 refugees arrived from the CAR. In December, the fighting reached Guéréda, also a major hub for emergency aid for Darfurians.

Estimates of the number of internally displaced Chadian citizens varied widely, with the Chadian government claiming that 600,000 Chadians had left their homes, but converged on a number of approximately 100,000 people. This situation worsened the already grave humanitarian crisis in eastern Chad. As aid agencies came under increasing attack as well, there was discussion of suspending aid operations and withdrawing expatriate personnel.

Strikes and protests, mainly in N'Djaména, were expressions of the discontent of civil society groups and continued to cripple social life. In January, retired civil servants protested to obtain arrears pension payments. In July, Chadian oil workers protested against the discrimination in remuneration between expatriates and Chadian workers. In June and July, there was a two-month general strike in government hospitals, effectively jeopardising health care for the poor. In both cases, the government finally capitulated, paying the salaries being sought and improving employment conditions.

Foreign Affairs

Early on, N'Djaména called on other African leaders to support Chad against what President Déby called the "subversive plots" of neighbouring **Sudan**. Déby used the opportunity provided by a special summit of the six-nation CEMAC in the Chadian capital on 4 January to air his views. The continuous tensions with Sudan were one of the central elements in Chadian foreign affairs in 2006. The Chadian government constantly accused Sudan of deliberately destabilising it by supporting Chadian rebel movements and by directing the violence in Darfur into eastern Chad.

Several attempts were made by, among others, **Libya** and the AU to mediate between President Déby and President al-Bashir of Sudan. An initial agreement to end hostilities was signed on 8 February in Tripoli. However, this did not last: Janjaweed militias in the Andjerene zone launched an attack on 6 March and operations by Chadian rebels operating from Sudan resumed during March and April. The **AU** tried to calm the situation on several occasions. The **UN** Security Council (UNSC) and the UN secretary-general expressed their concern over the situation in Chad on a number of occasions. Darfurian rebels also continued to operate from their Chadian bases into Sudan. Two days after the attack of 13 April on the capital, Chad severed diplomatic ties with Sudan and closed its borders. On 26 July, a new deal was struck to discontinue hosting each other's rebel groups. At the margins of the **CEMAC** summit on 7 August and President Déby's inauguration on 8 August, an agreement was signed to reopen the borders between both countries. Despite all these agreements, cross-border attacks from both sides of the Chad-Sudan border continued and violence spread through the whole region during the last three months of the year. On 28 November, Chad declared that it was in a state of war with Sudan and accused both Sudan and Saudi Arabia of instigating armed rebellions from Sudanese territory.

The opposite accusation, that Chad was supporting Darfurian rebels, was also expressed several times by the government of Sudan, especially after the Abuja peace accords, when some of the rebels made peace with Khartoum while the others decided to fight on. Relations between the Chadian government and the Darfurians fighting against Sudan grew closer. There were unconfirmed reports that Darfurian rebels participated in joint operations with the Chadian army against Chadian rebels. Aid agencies alleged that the Darfurian rebel groups recruited young boys in the refugee camps of eastern Chad.

The situation in the northeast of the **CAR** remained highly unstable, leading to new waves of refugees across the border into Chad when fighting broke out in June. With violence spreading into southeastern Chad, the Chadian army offered support to its CAR counterpart. Both countries accused Sudan of instigating rebellion in the CAR. By the end of the year, UN Secretary-General Kofi Annan had sent a multidisciplinary technical assessment team led by the department of peacekeeping operations to Chad and the CAR to investigate the possibilities for a peacekeeping mission. Because of the high level of violence, the mission was not able to visit the affected areas. It further noted that, given the state of infrastructure and the lack of political will, a peacekeeping mission would face almost insurmountable problems and would be very costly. As a result, the UNSC deferred a decision on the deployment of this mission.

Another security problem with international dimensions manifested itself in the border triangle with **Cameroon** and CAR, where banditry and looting by armed groups reached such heights that 20,000 people from CAR sought refuge in Chad. These refugees arrived without possessions and camped in the open air in the forest for weeks before aid arrived. The armed bandits probably originated in the former rebel groups and probably also comprised Chadian mercenaries. The latter had been hired in 2003 to help CAR President François Bozizé to power. After Bozizé's successful coup, they were disbanded without proper compensation.

Relations with neighbouring **Niger** underwent stress when Niger decided to expel a group of Mahamid Arabs originating in Chad on 24 October. This group had moved into Niger during the droughts of the 1980s. According to the government of Niger, the Arabs were causing unrest in eastern Niger and were behaving in a racist manner towards the local population. Some observers said that Niger wanted to get rid of them because they supported the opposition against President Mamadou Tandja. The expulsion decision was suspended on 27 October.

After secret negotiations in New York and Paris, Chad established diplomatic ties with the **People's Republic of China** on 6 August. A day before, Taiwan severed its diplomatic ties with Chad. At that very moment, a Taiwanese government delegation was on its way to attend President Déby's inauguration. All collaborative projects between Chad and Taiwan were immediately ended, except the exploration project in three oil fields in a concession held by a Taiwanese oil company. According to the Chadian government, the rebels who attacked N'Djaména in April used mainly Chinese weaponry. It was speculated that China had promised to suspend its support for Chadian rebels in return for diplomatic recognition.

Despite the military turmoil, there was relative silence on the diplomatic front. France and the US, Chad's major Northern allies, remained utterly mute on the conflicts with the rebels. Neither did they comment on the results of the presidential elections either positively or negatively. **France** maintained its military presence in Chad and even sent in more troops in April following the attacks on the capital. Part of the French contingent was stationed in Abéché in the east, officially to secure the border with Sudan and counter incursions by bandits. Chadian rebels accused France of direct involvement in the fighting in support of the Chadian army and threatened to turn against French citizens. There were a few visits by French ministers and President Déby visited France in September, a month after his inauguration.

Socioeconomic Developments

Oil continued to dominate economic development in Chad, representing 22% of non-oil GDP. Contrary to expectations, economic growth slowed over 2006. Real GDP growth was reduced to 1.3%, because of falling revenues from the oil sector (–7.7%), though GDP growth did surpass expectations at the beginning of 2006, when it was set at 0.1%. Non-oil GDP increased by 5.1%. Inflation was high at 15%, due to skyrocketing meat prices (up 67%) following increased livestock exports to neighbouring countries affected by avian flu. Charcoal prices soared as political tension mounted. Economic growth was expected to decline over 2007 and even to become negative, with a projected decrease in oil revenues of more than 20%. On the one hand, this was due to a decline in oil production, which stabilised at around 150,000 b/d, against expectations of 200,000 b/d. By developing a new oil field and intensifying production at existing fields, oil multinational Esso hoped to increase production again to 200,000 b/d. On the other hand, oil prices were expected to decline in 2007.

The government also faced a major setback when the **World Bank** suspended its operations and payments from the government's oil escrow account after a unilateral revision of the Petrol Revenue Management Law (PRML) in December 2005. The Chadian government argued that it needed more money for the ordinary budget (30% instead of 13.5%) and security-related expenses such as the police, territorial administration and the judiciary, instead of reserving capital for the future and spending 80% of the revenues on the four priority sectors, health, education, infrastructure and rural development. After tedious negotiations, a memorandum of understanding was concluded on 13 July specifying the provisions of a new PRML that reduced the share of revenues set aside for development and increased the Chadian government's manoeuvring space. Agreement was also reached to establish a mechanism for saving excess oil revenue. There was increasing concern over the capacity of Chad's economy to absorb and spend oil revenue efficiently because of the weak infrastructure, the lack of management capacity and the isolated character of the oil sector. During the year, a total amount of more than $ 336 m was transferred from the escrow account at London's Citibank to the Chadian government.

On 26 August, the government forced two foreign oil companies (Chevron and Petronas) to suspend their operations because of alleged tax arrears of $ 450 m (CFAfr 250 bn). The Chadian government also demanded a 60% share in the pipeline project, without further specification. It held at that time only an 8% share in the Chadian section of the pipeline (and 3% of the Cameroonian section), through a new national oil company, the so-called 'Société des Hydrocarbures du Tchad' (SHT). The dispute was settled on 6 October, and unconfirmed reports stated that the oil companies had paid $ 280 m. Allegedly, agreement was also reached on a 12.5% share for SHT in the oil project, but by the end of 2006 no action had been taken to establish SHT.

Total tax revenue from oil companies was estimated at 8% of non-oil GDP. According to the World Bank's website, a cumulative amount of $ 458 m had been paid in taxes by the end of the year. The 'Collège de Contrôle et de Surveillance des Ressources Pétrolières' (CCSRP), the body responsible for the allocation of oil revenues, could only begin to approve government projects by July, after settlement of the conflict with the World Bank and the oil companies. By October, only part of the budget had been approved. The International Advisory Group, an independent group of experts that monitors the oil project, could not get confirmation from the ministry of finance on how much money had been disbursed to the ministries, and whether these ministries were able to absorb these budgets.

Exports of non-oil products declined. The production and export of **cotton** especially slowed down, as insufficient investment was made in the sector.

Food security improved somewhat in most of the country without changing the basic condition of the poor. Following a record harvest in 2005, prices of main staple grains dropped significantly on the markets of the four major towns, and the number of kilograms of cereals relative to the price of livestock improved. The harvest in 2006 was also good, 2% higher than in 2005. Nevertheless, food security in specific parts of the country (Kanem, Batha) remained precarious, especially for the very poor. The security situation in the east (Salamat, Abéché, Biltine) entailed great risks for food production. An unknown number of displaced persons were not in camps. More generally, the situation of refugees settled in camps was quite stable. However, there were grave concerns over the refugees from the CAR and IDPs in Chad, who had yet to find a stable place to settle.

Trade in these areas was disrupted because of insecurity and because people no longer dared to cultivate in remote areas. Cereal prices remained stable because of the good harvests, with the lowest prices in Abéché, the hub of emergency aid to the refugees from Darfur and Chadian IDPs. Insecurity made it increasingly difficult for aid organisations to do their work properly, with storehouses plundered by rebels in Abéché and other major towns in the east.

According to IMF estimates, the military efforts in the east and southeast of the country would have accounted for approximately 4.3% of GDP in extraordinary spending. However, given the size and frequency of the operations and the stock of arms pouring into the country, this may well have been an underestimate. It is probable that clandestine sources have been used for additional military spending.

The **health situation** of the population left much to be desired. There were several outbreaks of cholera in April, October and November, not only in the countryside but also in N'Djaména.

Mirjam de Bruijn & Han van Dijk

Congo

The year 2006 was marked by paradoxical political developments: reinforcement of the power of the president and intensification of the contradictions between his oldest and most powerful supporters inside his party. Internationally, Sassou Nguesso profited from his position as AU president, while his legitimacy at home suffered seriously from the widening gap between rich and poor.

Domestic Politics

Domestically, reports of **the precarious health of the president and his daughter** dominated behind-the-scenes discussions. Many key actors speculated about Sassou's possible disappearance from the political scene. Two scenarios were advanced: the first saw Sassou succumbing to illness, while the second foresaw his removal from office through a state coup and his subsequent killing by his own (former) supporters. Based on those speculations, political actors, be they from opposition or from the presidential sphere of influence, sought to reinforce their positions ahead of the 2007 legislative elections.

The president took advantage of this situation both to normalise his relationship with the external opposition to his **'Parti Congolais du Travail'** (PCT) and to confirm his family members as the cornerstones of the established machinery for reproducing political power. In fact, relationships were regularised between the president and certain powerful opponents who had gone into exile after being removed from power at the end of the civil war in 1997. This political readjustment was convincingly consecrated when the former Brazzaville mayor and the main opponent of former President P. Lissouba from 1992 to 1997, Bernard Kolélas, came back in 2005. Other opponents also returned and reorganised their parties. This action created the illusion of credibility in favour of the national opposition. The president encouraged the rallying of opponents to his cause. Illustrating this reconciliation, Kolélas invited his followers to support "the presidential action in favour of peace and reconciliation".

The **'family system'** was concretely embodied in the political arena through organisations already managed by Sassou's sons and nephews. One of them, Chrystel Sassou, controlled the 'Pôle des Jeunes Républicains' (PJR). At first, this was an association of young men supporting the presidential sphere of influence, but it tended increasingly to become a political party. As for his nephews, Wilfried Nguesso led the 'Club 2002'. This club had been aimed at rallying a generation of progressive intellectuals and young executives since the end of the war in 1997 in order to encourage them to think of ways to stabilise the country. In fact, the club looked more and more like a melting pot for ambitious young leaders who wanted to replace the PCT. Additionally, Jean Dominique Okemba became the special advisor in charge of the presidential security council. Finally, Edgar Nguesso led the 'Agir pour le Congo' ('Acting for Congo') association, another youth association that tended to become a party.

This double process was a strategy to counterbalance the strong influence that some **PCT factions** had in the political arena or maybe even to eliminate this party entirely. In fact, the dominant party controlled the parliament and the senate and participated in the decision-making process. The intensification of the internal crisis culminated in a fracture and the birth of two groups in the PCT, 'rénovateurs' (recasters) and 'reformateurs' (reformers, also known as the 'refondateurs'). The second group was closer to the president of the republic and to the PCT secretary-general, Ambroise Noumazaly. This group controlled the majority in the politburo (21 members of 24) and intended to renew the party in order to adapt it to the evolution of the country and to the international order, i.e., getting rid of certain Marxist symbols while also extending the platform to smaller political parties close to the president. As for the 'rénovateurs', led by Justin Lékoundzou, they dominated the central committee and seemed to be 'guardians of the orthodoxy', and pretended that adjustment of the founding texts of the party while preserving its structure was sufficient.

Trench warfare developed between the two factions and extended beyond the party. Tension between the two groups worsened when on 31 January Lékoundzou was evacuated to France suffering from a cerebral affliction. Popular perceptions were that he would not survive. To make matters worse, his principal private secretary, Marcel Akourawa, had similar symptoms. The rumour was that both had been poisoned. Six months later, Lékoundzou returned to Brazzaville and was warmly received like a head of state by his supporters and by a section of the population. Buoyed by this success and pressed by his supporters, he issued an ultimatum to the politburo to immediately convene the 5th extraordinary PCT congress by 12 October or he would organise one of his own. The 'reformateurs' counter-attacked, considering this initiative a coup attempt. They then took Lékoundzou to court. On 20 September, the president of the court of justice decided to discharge Lékoundzou for lack of evidence. On 11 October, the state minister and president's principal private secretary, Aimé Emmanuel Yoka, and General Pierre Oba were officially appointed intermediaries to heal the rifts within the party. They succeeded in getting a memorandum of understanding signed by the two factions.

Despite this, the 'rénovateurs' held their congress on 12 October. This was in turn soon interpreted by the 'refondateurs' as a pretext to overthrow the regime, because the president of the republic had been in Paris since 9 October to attend the UNESCO general assembly. Sassou, who is also the army's supreme commander-in-chief, instructed the military command through the head of the army's headquarters, General Mondjo, to mobilise the police services, the national gendarmerie and the army to prevent the two factions from any public demonstrations. Nevertheless, 1,384 delegates took part in the 'rénovateur' congress. Opposition political parties, e.g., former President Pascal Lissouba's 'Union Panafricaine pour le Développement Sociale' (UPADS) and former Prime Minister André Milongo's 'Union pour la Démocratie et la République' (UDR)-Mwinda were invited as friends and brother parties. UPADS took advantage of the opportunity to demand more democracy and transparent elections.

Two days later, congress participants stopped their meeting at the moment they were about to vote on the party's leadership positions. The official reason was that they wanted to be respectful of the central committee president's instructions and to conform to the memorandum of understanding. However, they instructed participants not to leave Brazzaville in order to be ready to vote and close their congress if the memorandum was not respected. In fact, this document called for a unitary congress by 31 October. On that day, the leadership of the 'reformateurs' reacted on behalf of the commission preparing for the 5th extraordinary congress. Ambroise Noumazalay's supporters broadcast a communiqué stating that the memorandum was outdated and that the 'rénovateurs' wanted to weaken the president of the republic politically.

In the end the PCT held its 5th extraordinary unitary congress in December. A **central committee** of 513 members was set up and Lékoundzou became a member of the politburo.

The 'rénovateurs' lost their majority in the central committee and were weakened in the composition of the party's leadership. However, the 'rénovateurs' retained a majority among the rank and file of the party. Thus, while purification at the leadership level had taken place, the crisis continued to loom.

Foreign Affairs

Despite his weak legitimacy in the country, President Denis Sassou Nguesso preserved his influence internationally. Still executive president of CEEAC, in January he was appointed president of the AU when the originally designated Sudanese president was invited to stand down because of the Darfur war. **Sassou's declared ambitions** were numerous: He wanted to solve the crises in Côte d'Ivoire, Darfur, DR Congo and especially the crisis between Sudan and Chad. In March, UN Secretary-General Kofi Annan paid an official visit to the Congo. The country is a non-permanent member of the Security Council for 2006–07 and held the presidency of that institution from 1 to 31 March, thereby giving its government considerable influence. The UN Security Council dealt at that time with African conflicts and Iranian nuclear questions, peace in the Middle East and in Haiti.

In April, the Congo adopted a law authorising adhesion to the international convention for the suppression of terrorist bombings. This entailed enlargement of the field of legal investigation, pursuit and extradition, and establishing international jurisdictional sanctions against such crimes. The international convention had come into force on 23 May 2001, and was aimed at implementing a uniform cooperative mechanism.

To consolidate peace in the country in the aftermath of the civil war, the Congo continued with the implementation of **demobilisation operations** during the year. These were financed by international organisations through a national programme for disarmament, demobilisation and reintegration of ex-fighters.

Bilateral relations were strengthened with Asian and European countries. In June, the Chinese prime minister visited the Congo and in August, parliament examined a memorandum of understanding between the two countries. In September, **China** started financing community projects. In September, Italy cancelled debts amounting to $ 27 m and in December, **France** cancelled debts of € 782 m. It also gave a grant of € 24 m to help Congo repay its debts to the ADB. In addition, Congo and Cameroon initiated the construction of the Ouesso-Sangmelima route, a major infrastructure project, without having secured the necessary funding. In October, the remains of former colonial explorer **Pierre Savorgnan De Brazza** and his four family members, formerly buried in Algiers, were transferred to a newly built mausoleum in Brazzaville. It was rumoured to have been built for $ 28 m, an amount confirmed by well informed people. By this act, Congo inaugurated a new phase in the life of a postcolonial African country – the official celebration of a colonist. The government's official explanation was that De Brazza had been a humanist. A polemical response was unavoidable given that Congo had formerly been a Marxist-Leninist country that had lashed French 'imperialism'. The implication that part of the Françafrique members' network had been involved (some prominent Gaullists, Freemasons and oil businessmen), provided further food for thought. Apparently, the celebration was intended as a critique by members of the network of the French government for lacking consideration for very important persons, Europeans or Africans, who had acted in France's name in Africa. However, as a reminder it is important to note that the late Senegalese president and member of the French Academy, Leopold Seder Senghor, had been given a much less glorious funeral when he died in 2001. The Françafrique network obviously influenced Congolese policy. Public rumours spoke of the affiliation between De Brazza and the Freemason network. It was also rumoured that President Sassou Nguesso belonged to the Great French National Lodge (GLNF). The same rumour suggested that through this transfer of the remains, President Sassou Nguesso wanted to weaken the influence of another famous Freemason, Gabon's President Omar Bongo, who was also his son-in-law. Strategically, Sassou wanted to become a more important element than Bongo in the Françafrique network.

Socioeconomic Developments

The parliament and senate adopted a provisional **budget** for $ 2,874 bn, versus $ 2,582 bn in 2005. The share of oil income represented CFAfr 1,113 bn (about $ 2.4 bn) or 82.3%, as against only $ 478 m for non-oil income. The allocation for debt servicing was $ 672 m, for staff expenditures $ 268 m, goods and services $ 290 m, transfer expenses $ 322 m and for investment $ 570 m.

These figures demonstrated that the **oil sector** still dominated economic life. This strategic resource continued to provide about 60% of the global GNP and represented 90% of exports. Moreover, forecasts about reserves were very optimistic. Murphy Oil, in partnership with the state-owned Congolese oil company 'Société Nationale des Pétroles du Congo' (SNPC), announced at the end of August an important deep water discovery, the first in the Congolese offshore. Additionally, French Total declared that Boabou field, which has been known for many years, was richer than expected. Finally, Cuba's Prestoil, in partnership with SNPC (50% of shares), launched an accelerated development programme to start production at the beginning of 2007.

Apart from his political activities (see above), the president's son Chrystel Sassou was in charge of the commercialisation of oil and director of COTRADE ('Congolaise de Trading'), a society based in London that sold Congolese oil directly. Another company, SNPC Holding, directed by Denis Auguste Marie Gokana, and its subsidiary company 'Congolaise de Raffinage' (CORAF), were some of the lynchpins in the system of companies created by the president's immediate circle as a shield before being made public in 2005, when the Congo was taken to court by the Congo's. On 24 February, SNPC had its ordinary administrative board meeting in Brazzaville. Its chairman and managing director reported that his policy would be to carry on with cleaning up accounts and fostering transparency in management. He also revealed that the SNPC group had an annual profit of $ 13 m and that SNPC alone had realised $ 50 m. This latter amount was used to fill a shortfall in CORAF's finances.

Under **IMF** and **World Bank** pressure, measures to clean up oil management were taken. On 26 January, the president signed a decree obliging every administrator involved in the management of all state oil companies or of the subsidiaries to report every year, from the moment he is appointed and before he takes office, his other involvements and investments to the court of account and budgetary discipline. In March, the World Bank and the IMF decided to make Congo eligible for further debt relief through the enhanced **HIPC initiative**. The executive boards of both institutions made their decision conditional on the strengthening of transparency in the management of oil revenues and the organisation of two audits in the oil sector. Consequently, the president announced on 12 August, when addressing parliament on the eve of the 46th anniversary of independence, that a stabilisation account for receiving the budgetary surplus from rising oil prices would soon be opened at the regional central bank, BEAC. He emphasised that the account would be audited yearly and the results publicised. However, this decision had no immediate effect. Finally, the government decided to stop the system of cashing money in advance of oil sales. In similar vein, Congo promised to begin with the certification of oil revenues, start an assessment of SNPC's oil trading policy and to implement an accountability system inside SNPC in conformity with international norms. These measures had no effect during the year and no steps to counter corruption were implemented.

Over the years, the system for the **redistribution of oil rents** had resulted in the reinforcement of state power in the society. The increasing share of oil income taken by the state had no productive effect and did not lead to any diversification or modernisation of social and economic infrastructures. A closer look at the state's budget revealed that only the state's core personnel, the staff from political institutions and those elements in the public administration in charge of transferring budgets received a share of oil revenue. Others were left behind. According to an official enquiry made into the Congolese poverty reduction strategy within the HIPC framework, in 2006, 56% of an official 3 m inhabitants lived on less than $ 1 per day.

Given the lack of distribution of oil rents and the precarious circumstances under which everybody lived, certain civil servants, executive and other, extorted money from inhabitants and small business owners daily. Abrupt 'power cuts' and 'water cuts' helped to increase servicing costs. To **deal with these shortages**, citizens left taps and switches on. The result was that nobody could control their consumption rates. Despite the cuts, consumers were obliged to pay bills, otherwise they could be disconnected from urban networks: taps and meters would be shut off. Unjustified and threatening demands on traders by finance officers or policemen for taxes, including small business taxes, represented another form of racketeering.

The contrast between the poverty of the majority and the wealth of the rulers increased. This contrast became more explosive because of the **conspicuous consumption** exhibited in the new lifestyles of the beneficiaries of oil rents. They drove their brand-new prestigious cars through the rutted streets of the town while specialised garages to repair such cars did not exist in the country. They quickly built luxurious houses and wanted to expropriate the properties of the inhabitants of Brazzaville's long-established districts of Bacongo in the short term and of Poto-Poto in days to come in order to build so-called social lodgings that will be granted to the *nomenklatura*. The cost of the lodgings was estimated to be around $ 140,000 each. These new residential areas were built in unhealthy surroundings. Tensions exploded during a **transport strike**, when taxis and buses refused to pay the taxes (coats of arms, various technical checks) collected by municipal authorities through a company belonging to the presidential family. The strike disturbed the authorities since it took place at a time when the social truce had to be renegotiated with unions. The authorities were forced to suspend the payment of these taxes temporarily. By the end of the year, a solution had not been found.

The government began implementing projects financed by international organisations in order to open up the hinterlands. The Congo received from the World Bank a grant of $ 500,000 for agricultural development projects and the rehabilitation of rural tracks. Additionally, in May, construction began on national route No. 1, linking Nganga-Lingolo-Kinkala-Ngambari. This project, financed by the EU, would last 24 months and involved costs of $ 46 m. The entire southern part of the country should benefit from the road.

The EU's **sugar market** reform affected the Congolese company SARIS Congo negatively. In fact, the EU stopped its annual importation of 13,000 tons from this company. Financial aid of $ 16 m over six years was offered as indemnity. The company sought to invest in the CEMAC market to secure alternative and more reliable outlets.

Rémy Bazenguissa-Ganga

Democratic Republic of Congo

The long-awaited presidential, parliamentary and provincial elections, the first democratic polls in over four decades, were the main focus of attention for both domestic and foreign actors. Against many odds, the elections took place in a fairly peaceful and orderly manner. As had been widely expected, incumbent Joseph Kabila was elected as the head of state. Although the electoral process was an extremely remarkable achievement, its completion did not alter the fact that the war-ravaged country continued to face enormous challenges in terms of peace-building, security and socioeconomic recovery.

Domestic Politics

In mid-January the 'Commission Électorale Indépendante' (CEI) published the **results of the constitutional referendum** of December 2005. A clear majority of the voters (84%) had approved the new constitution. After considerable delays, the country had thus taken an important formal step in preparation for the 2006 elections and the post-transitional period in general. President Kabila promulgated the new constitution on 18 February in the presence of South Africa's President Thabo Mbeki and the EU's commissioner for development, Louis Michel.

Among the issues keeping the country in suspense during the pre-election period was whether one of its main political parties, the 'Union pour la Démocratie et le Progrès Social' (UDPS), would take part in the ballots. Having boycotted the voter registration process in the previous year because of a variety of grievances, the party's leader, Etienne Tshisekedi, announced in January that the UDPS would participate in the elections on condition that the CEI would reopen voter registration for UDPS supporters. Arguing that this would lead to another postponement of the elections, the CEI rejected the demand with the apparent approval of the 'Comité International d'Accompagnement de la Transition' (CIAT), a body comprising Congo's most important external backers. It was widely perceived that the intransigent Tshisekedi had overplayed his hand and that domestic and international efforts to convince him to join the electoral process had reached their limits.

Yet, **further postponements of the elections** followed, with the initial deferment of the date for the parliamentary election and the first round of presidential elections from 29 April to 18 June. The reasons for the renewed delay were, firstly, that the National Assembly and President Kabila were slow to pass the electoral law. Secondly, only a limited number of parliamentary candidates had submitted their candidacy to the CEI, and the registration period was extended by ten days. In the end, more than 9,406 candidates registered to run for the 500 parliamentary seats (of those, 748 were registered as independents) and some 10,500 contenders ran for the senate and the provincial governorships. Thirty-three people registered as candidates for the presidential elections. Of those, four registered as independents. There were four women registered as presidential candidates while 1,305 (13.5%) ran for parliament. Thirdly, a number of key political and logistical tasks posed significant challenges, including the verification of the electoral register and the designation of electoral districts. As a consequence, CEI's chairman, Abbé Malu Malu, announced that the 19 June date would be rescheduled too. It was only on 1 May that CEI disclosed that 30 July would be the new election date. The date for a possible second round of the presidential election (29 October) was only announced in late July.

The **mounting problems** leading to the further deferment of the elections and CEI's decision itself triggered a heated debate in Kinshasa, mainly, but not exclusively because the new election date contravened the provision that the transition period was to end on 30 June, thus effectively prolonging the tenure of the transitional government. A coalition of 19 political parties, along with the mighty Catholic Church criticised the CEI's 'unilateral' decision and called for negotiations involving political parties and civil society groups to discuss both the electoral calendar and the substantive problems surrounding the transparency of the elections. Yet even within this group there was little agreement that more thorough preparation for the elections would justify further postponement of the polls. The group included Vice-President Azarias Ruberwa of the 'Rassemblement Congolais pour la Démocratie' (RCD), who threatened to withdraw from the elections unless Minembwe (South Kivu), a stronghold of the Banyamulenge which the RCD had elevated to the status of a territory (or administrative unit) during the war, would be designated as an electoral district. However, after a meeting with UN Secretary-General Annan, Ruberwa retracted his threat. In an effort to allay some of the anxieties about the lack of impartiality and transparency, the UN mission in the DR Congo (MONUC) facilitated the establishment of the **international committee of eminent persons** headed by Mozambique's former president, Joaquim Chissano. The body, first proposed by the International Crisis Group (ICG), was to play a mediating role in case of conflicts over the electoral process.

At any rate, the Kabila camp objected to the suggested negotiations. In this it was strongly supported by the international donor community. Like Kabila, the donor community did not send representatives to a gathering of political forces to discuss unsettled electoral issues (30 June). This clearly suggested that the international community, which also footed the bill of $ 430 m for the most expensive and largest election operation ever conducted by the UN, was running out of patience and was willing to push the elections through regardless of the deficits and concerns that had the potential to disrupt the whole process.

Unsurprisingly, the upcoming elections set in motion a plethora of **political manoeuvres and realignments**. Shortly before the election, for example, Mbusa Nyamwisi, the president of the 'Rassemblement Congolais pour la Démocratie – Mouvement de Libération' (RCD NGO – ML) and himself a presidential candidate, cast his lot in with Kabila. Further related to the approaching ballot was the continuing turbulence in the 'Mouvement pour la Libération du Congo' (MLC). As in 2005, Vice-President Jean-Pierre Bemba's movement continued to lose prominent figures to rival political movements, particularly the Kabila camp. Following last year's expulsion of then Secretary-General Olivier Kamitatu by the MLC, Bemba's party obtained a supreme court verdict stating that Kamitatu would have to give up his post as president of the National Assembly. Kamitatu, long rumoured to be in close contact with other political parties, joined the newly formed 'Alliance pour le Renouveau du Congo' (ARC) as its leader, and subsequently became spokesman for Kabila's coalition alliance, the 'Alliance pour la Majorité Présidentielle' (AMP). Shortly thereafter, Alexis Thambwe-Mwamba, the minister of planning, announced his resignation from both the MLC and his cabinet post. Running as an independent candidate, he later won a parliamentary seat in his hometown of Kindu (Maniema) before joining the AMP too.

The **election campaign** officially started on 29 June and was marred by a number of worrying incidents, including frequent intimidation of journalists, violent clashes between supporters of rival candidates and/or the police (i.e., in Kinshasa, Rutshuru and Mbandaka) and the obstruction of campaigning candidates by local and military authorities. In mid-June, the police shot dead nine people during a demonstration of the political-religious group Bundu dia Kongo in Matadi (Bas Congo), though it remained unclear whether the incident was related to the upcoming polls. The single most serious incident occurred during Bemba's rally on 27 July. Clashes between Bemba's guards and the police resulted in four deaths, with 17 people being injured, the looting of several police stations as well as the ransacking of the offices of the 'Haute Autorité des Medias' (HAM), a body under the transition process that was to act as watchdog and regulator of the media.

Much of the rising tension could be attributed to the **media**, many of them aligned with one or the other candidate. With balanced reporting extremely rare, fierce and highly personal attacks on contenders were a trademark of the campaign, despite a code of conduct signed by the political parties. It appeared that particularly Bemba's strategy was focused on making up for Kabila's control of the national radio and TV stations by spreading radical ethnic and even xenophobic messages. Bemba's main campaign slogans were 'Congolité' and '100% Congolese', insinuating that President Kabila was in fact a foreigner and/or a pawn of foreign interests. HAM's efforts to rein in hate speech met with limited success. The agency lacked the means to enforce its suspension orders, which were repeatedly ignored by media outlets across the political spectrum.

Bemba was by no means the only candidate to resort **to hate speech**. Xenophobic rhetoric was also used by Vice-President Yerodia Ndombasi, a close ally of Kabila, who called on people to chase Rwandophone groups out of eastern Congo. Given Congo's recent and not so recent history, it was not surprising that virtually no candidate presented a credible political programme, or that money and power politics shaped a campaign dominated by those who were part of the transitional government. It was widely speculated and rumoured that President Kabila's war chest was several times larger than those of his contenders. This, and his control of much of the state apparatus and the media suggested that Kabila, who ran as an independent (not as the candidate of his 'Parti du Peuple pour la Réconstruction et la Démocratie', PPRD) was the leading contender. However, other candidates mounted large campaigns as well. These included Pierre Pay-Pay, a former Mobutu associate and leader of the 'Coalition des Démocrates Congolais' (CODECO) and Oscar Kashala, a Harvard-educated medical doctor and candidate for the 'Union pour la Réconstruction du Congo' (UREC). Little known before his return from the US in 2005, Kashala came into the limelight in May when the government arrested 26 South African and US citizens, accusing them of being mercenaries with ties to Kashala and of planning to topple Kabila. The quick release of those arrested seemed to indicate that the mercenary coup had been fabricated by the Kabila camp.

The **logistical preparations** for the polls went as smoothly as possible in the context of a vast war-torn country lacking in infrastructure. Highlighting the logistical challenges, Ross Mountain, deputy special representative of the UN secretary-general in the DRC and previously in charge of the elections in Iraq, famously observed, "Compared to Congo, organising elections in Iraq was a walk in the park." Thanks largely to MONUC, 50,000 polling stations were established, with some 260,000 electoral staff and 72,258 Congolese security forces deployed across the country. These included 12,000 crowd-control elements trained by the EU, MONUC and other foreign partners. They were stationed in particularly sensitive cities such as Kinshasa, Lubumbashi, Kisangani and Mbuji-Mayi. The ballot papers were printed in South Africa and arrived in the DRC in late June.

Given the high risk of escalation during the electoral process, foreign-sponsored **security arrangements** were beefed up. After the US had repeatedly rejected Annan's pleas to the UN Security Council to increase MONUC's troop levels during the potentially risky election period, the UN sent a request to the EU to provide a "visible and credible force that could enhance MONUC's quick reaction capabilities in the DRC during and immediately after the electoral process." In response, and after considerable haggling among the UN, the EU and EU member states, the EU decided to deploy a German-led military mission, EUFOR R.D. Congo, mainly comprising forces from Germany, France, Poland and Spain. With some 1,000 soldiers in Kinshasa and 1,500 stand-by troops in Gabon, the mission's main mandate was "to support MONUC to stabilise a situation, in case MONUC faces serious difficulties in fulfilling its mandate within its existing capabilities." According to UN Security Council resolution 1671 of 25 April, the mission was to cease four months after the date of the first round of the presidential elections and would be concentrated in Kinshasa, allowing MONUC to focus its attention on eastern Congo. In addition to EUFOR, MONUC's troop levels of 17,000 were finally increased. Security Council resolution 1669 of 7 April 2006 authorised the temporary deployment of one battalion and 50 military observers from the United Nations Mission in Burundi (ONUB) to the DRC. On 22 December, the Security Council mandated the deployment of an additional 916 troops until the end of MONUC's current mandate on 15 February 2007.

Election day, 30 July, was generally peaceful and the presidential and parliamentary elections took place in a largely orderly manner, as noted by nearly 50,000 national and over 1,700 international observers. Popular enthusiasm for the elections was reflected in a fairly high voter turnout of 70.5% of the more than 25 m registered voters. The main exception to the generally positive picture was the two Kasai provinces, where violent clashes among supporters of competing candidates delayed delivery of ballot papers and the ransacking of polling stations occurred. As a consequence, polling at more than 200 voting stations was deferred to 31 July and 1 August. Unlike the polling itself, the counting process was marred by significant problems and there were scenes of chaos at some compilation centres. Nevertheless, the CEI compiled the results fairly effectively and announced the provisional results on 20 August. Meanwhile, tensions rose amid allegations of irregularities. The initial climax came on 20 August, only a few hours before CEI announced the poll results, when security forces, including the presidential guard, and members of Bemba's security detail had a shoot-out in Kinshasa, leaving six people dead. After mediation efforts by the international community, the situation was calmed and CEI chairman Malu Malu announced the provisional **results of the first round of presidential elections**.

With 44.8% of the votes, incumbent President Kabila was the winner of the elections. A little more surprising was the good result of Jean-Pierre Bemba, who won 20%, followed by Antoine Gizenga of the 'Parti des Lumumbistes Unifiés' (PALU), a veteran politician and one-time leader of Lumumba's government in Kisangani in 1960–61, who won 13%. No less astonishing was the strong showing of Nzanga Mobutu, son of former President Mobutu, who received 4.8%. Kashala came fifth with 3.4%, followed by Ruberwa (1.7%)

and Pay-Pay (1.6%). Since no candidate had an absolute majority, Kabila and Bemba were to contest a second round of elections.

No sooner had the results been published when **post-election violence** erupted in Kinshasa. On 21 August, police forces sought to shut down Bemba's media stations. In the afternoon, several hundred presidential guards launched an attack on Bemba's offices and residence. At the time of the attack, 14 members of CIAT and MONUC boss William Swing were holding talks with Bemba at his residence. After hours of heavy fire, MONUC and EUFOR forces were able to evacuate the diplomats. They also deployed in the vicinity of Bemba's premises and at intersections in downtown Kinshasa while negotiations under Swing's leadership led to a cessation of hostilities and the subsequent withdrawal of the presidential guard. Some 30 people were killed during the fighting. The causes of the confrontation remained unclear, but many observers held that it was implausible for the attacks against Bemba to have taken place without the consent of Kabila. In a report, the ICC convincingly argued that the attack was launched in the context of the Kabila camp's disappointment at its failure to win an absolute majority. This hope had been fostered for weeks by the incoming results from eastern Congo, where Kabila had won overwhelming majorities, but was dashed by the results in the west of the country, which were compiled late in the counting process. In Kinshasa, for example, the incumbent won only 14.7% of the vote.

In the wake of the August crisis, MONUC and CIAT diplomats took steps to establish a wide range of confidence-building measures. In addition to a commission of inquiry into the fighting, these included memoranda of understanding on a code of conduct for the second round of presidential elections, agreement to establish a weapons-free zone in Kinshasa, regular meetings between representatives of both parties and the establishment of joint patrols, also comprising MONUC and EUFOR, to verify troop movements in the capital. On 13 September, Kabila and Bemba met to discuss the post-election violence. A day later, the supreme court confirmed the validity of the election results.

On 7 September, the provisional **results of the parliamentary elections** were published. According to the CEI, the PPRD, Kabila's party, came first in six of the 11 provinces, winning 111 seats, followed by Bemba's MLC with 64 seats. Gizenga's PALU won 34 seats, coming first in its heartland, Bandundu province, followed by a relatively new party, the 'Mouvement Social pour le Renouveau' (MSR), which took 27 seats and the 'Forces du Renouveau' with 26 seats. RCD's somewhat unexpectedly strong showing gave it 15 seats in parliament, while Pierre Pay-Pay's 'Coalition des Démocrates Congolais' (CODECO) and the 'Convention des Démocrates Chrétiens' (CDC) each won ten seats. The 'Union des Démocrates Mobutistes' of Nzanga Mobutu took nine seats, with the remaining 104 seats going to independent candidates and representatives of 60 other parties. In terms of the coalitions of political parties that had been formed prior to the polls, the Kabila camp and its AMP won 224 of the 500 seats, while Bemba's coalition, the 'Regroupement des Nationalistes Congolais' (RENACO), took 116 seats in the new National Assembly.

Given the surprisingly strong showing of **Antoine Gizenga** and his PALU, the octogenarian Gizenga found himself the object of political overtures from both Kabila and Bemba. Had Gizenga thrown his weight behind Bemba in the second round of the presidential polls, the election could have been an extremely close call. However, in mid-September, Gizenga announced the establishment of an alliance with Kabila, thus giving Kabila's AMP a comfortable majority in parliament. In return, Kabila promised Gizenga the job of prime minister. Kabila scored another success when Nzanga Mobutu joined AMP, while Bemba obtained the support of Kashala and Joseph Olenghankoy of the 'Forces Novatrices pour l'Union et la Solidarité' (FONUS), who had won a mere 0.6% of the votes in the presidential elections. Subsequent to this, Bemba renamed his coalition 'Union pour la Nation' (UN). Disappointingly for Bemba, Tshisekedi's UDPS, which could have swayed the result of the second round of elections, was apparently immersed in an internal dispute whether to align itself with one camp or the other. While some elements in the party seemed willing to re-enter the political fray, rumours suggested that Tshisekedi categorically refused to do so. Still, it appeared that a sizeable percentage of UDPS supporters cast their ballots for Bemba. For its part, RCD under Ruberwa declared its neutrality.

Perhaps the most remarkable characteristic of the second round of elections was the almost complete lack of campaigning by the two candidates. On the Kabila side, the most active campaigner was his wife Olive, whom he had married shortly before the elections. Bemba did not travel either, citing security concerns and the destruction of his helicopter by the presidential guard during the August confrontations. As with the first round, the election on 29 October took place in a peaceful and orderly manner. The counting and compilation process was significantly improved over the first round, gaining the CEI hard-won praise from international observers. However, and like the period following the first round, tensions flared up again amid claims by either side to victory in the elections, allegations of vote rigging by Bemba and growing evidence that new weapons were entering the capital of Kinshasa. On 11 November, fighting erupted briefly between Bemba's fighters and the presidential guard. More tension ensued when the Archbishop of Kinshasa, Frédéric Etsou, issued a statement that serious vote rigging in favour of Kabila had taken place.

Four days later, on 15 November, the CEI announced the preliminary **results of the second round of the presidential election**, giving Kabila 58% over Bemba's 42%. Turnout (64.9%) was lower than during the first round. Bemba immediately filed an unconvincing protest against the results in the supreme court. Elements within Bemba's entourage, notably Olenghankoy, seemed to place their bets on mobilising the streets of Kinshasa. On 21 November, Bemba's forces stormed the supreme court and set parts of the building alight. However, the population, tired of political conflict and anxious about the tight security in the capital, remained largely quiet. The reservations of Bemba's followers may have also resulted from the fact that the presidential guard in Kinshasa, believed to number up to 6,000 soldiers, largely outnumbered the estimated 800 fighters on Bemba's side. On 27 November, the supreme court rejected Bemba's claim of substantial irregularities. The following day, Bemba eased the nerve-racking situation by publicly declaring that he accepted the ruling and that he would lead a 'republican opposition', while still insisting that the election had been rigged.

Overall, and similarly to the first round, the election results showed a fairly **strong geographical divide**, or what some perceived as a fracture between the Swahiliphone east and the Lingalaphone west. Indeed, the vast majority of voters in the eastern provinces voted for Kabila (Katanga: 93.8%; Maniema: 98.3%; South Kivu: 98.3%; North Kivu: 96.4%; Oriental: 79.5%). Thanks to Gizenga's support, Kabila was also able to significantly improve his showing in Kinshasa (32%) and to a lesser extent in Bandundu (39.5%). This suggested that voters who had cast their ballot for Gizenga in the first round had followed the advice to switch their vote to Kabila, though this was more evident in Kinshasa than in Bandundu. This was not the case for Nzanga Mobutu, since the vast majority of his supporters in the province of Equateur voted for Bemba. In the west, north and parts of the centre of the country, Bemba had a clear, albeit not as impressive a lead (Kinshasa: 68%; Bas Congo: 74%; Bandundu: 60.5%; Equateur: 97.2%; Kasai Occidental: 76.6%; Kasai Oriental: 67%).

There was little agreement among national commentators on the **causes of the divide**, but the most frequent explanations noted that Kabila's eastern Congolese descent as well as his would-be image as a peacemaker struck a chord in eastern Congo, the region most affected by war and by ongoing insecurity. In addition, Bemba's campaign, with its leitmotif of *Congolité*, certainly prevented immigrant communities in the Kivus and elsewhere from voting for him. Perhaps the most significant implication of the election result was the perception, particularly in Kinshasa, of a power shift in Congo's politics, arising from the fact that the new president's political and electoral base was in eastern Congo, thus marking a possible end to the traditional political dominance of Lingala speakers from western Congo.

On 6 December, Kabila was sworn in as Congo's president in the presence of a large number of foreign dignitaries, among them South African President Thabo Mbeki and Belgian Prime Minister Guy Verhofstadt, who arrived in Kinshasa at the head of a large delegation. In his speech, Kabila announced the "end of the period of re-creation" and called upon his compatriots "to get down to work in peace and tranquillity." He spelt out his intention to spark off of a veritable "revolution" in the country to foster security, development and democracy, and to work for the public good by surmounting partisan interests. On 30 December, **Kabila nominated Gizenga as the future prime minister**, tasking him with initiating the extremely difficult negotiations with the more than 30 parties comprising the AMP to form a government. How the various political and economic interests were to be accommodated was difficult to fathom.

On 4 December, CEI published the preliminary results of the **elections to the provincial assemblies**, which had been held jointly with the second round of the presidential elections. Kabila's AMP won the majority of seats in seven of the country's 11 provincial assemblies, including Bandundu, the Kivus, Katanga, Maniema and Kasai Oriental. Kabila's own party, PPRD, won 132 of the 632 seats, followed by Bemba's MLC with 104 seats, which thus held 16.4% of the seats as against 12.8% in the National Assembly. The pro-Bemba UN coalition won the three provinces of Kinshasa, Equateur and Bas Congo. Subsequent to this, Bemba announced his intention to run for a seat in the senate. A strong performance by the RCD gave it 42 seats, whereas PALU achieved a result far below that for the parliamentary election (1.9% vs. 6.8%). In addition to the elected 632 seats, 58 members of the provincial assemblies were to be designated among traditional chiefs. By year's end, the selection process had not been completed amid haggling over the positions. The provincial elections constituted a significant step towards a more decentralised political system in the DRC, as enshrined in the new constitution. Most importantly, the provinces, which are to be divided into 26 provinces within the next three years, would retain 40% of the resources they generate. Furthermore, the members of the new provincial assemblies elect the provincial governors and the members of the senate. These elections were scheduled for January.

With a solid majority in both chambers of parliament, Kabila gained a strong mandate, but the dangers of his majority rule came quickly to the fore. On 28 December, members of parliament elected the members of the bureau of the National Assembly. Given AMP's absolute majority in the lower house, its candidates won all the posts. Vital Kamerhe, secretary-general of the PPRD, was elected president of the Assembly and Christophe Lutundula of the MRS became first vice-president. The AMP swiftly began to use procedural rules to ensure that all parliamentary commissions, elected by majority vote, were controlled by the Kabila coalition, including commissions of inquiry and the committee on parliamentary finance. The supreme court rejected an appeal by 55 opposition MPs against AMP domination, leaving opposition parties with virtually no space to exercise even moderate influence.

Notwithstanding the generally successful electoral process, the situation in **eastern Congo** remained extremely precarious. Particularly severe were the ongoing activities of former RCD general and renegade commander **Laurent Nkunda** in **North Kivu**. Hostilities between Nkunda's troops and the Congolese army ('Forces Armées de la République Démocratique du Congo', FARDC) resumed in January in Rutshuru territory and continued intermittently throughout the year. Nkunda, who claimed to defend the interests of Kivu's Rwandophone population, benefited from numerous defections from the 83rd Brigade in North Kivu, many of the defectors being Congolese Tutsi. As elsewhere in the country, the slow pace of demobilisation and the divided loyalties of armed units posed a significant challenge. The government re-issued an international arrest warrant for Nkunda but neither MONUC nor the hapless Congolese army dared to arrest Nkunda at his headquarters in Masisi territory, where Nkunda frequently met the national and international press. Nkunda did not disturb the election process but struck again in late November. Citing a string of recent Tutsi killings in North Kivu, Nkunda's troops took the town of Sake, 15 km west of Goma. After FARDC units supported by MONUC staged a counter-attack, the rebels withdrew, but fighting continued in the following weeks, particularly in nearby Rutshuru, and a military solution seemed out of the question.

The seriousness of the situation was underlined when a series of military and political leaders were detached to Goma, including General Gabriel Amisi, commander of the FARDC land forces, General Kisempia Sungilanga Lombe, head of the chiefs of staff, as well as the ministers of the interior and defence. Most notably, President Kabila himself travelled to Goma. Despite the bellicose utterances of the government, credible rumours suggested that behind-the-scenes negotiations had been started to bring about a political solution to Nkunda's insurrection. However, by year's end sporadic fighting continued, resulting in the displacement of more than 80,000 people.

The presence in the DRC of the **Lord's Resistance Army** (LRA), a Ugandan rebel group, was confirmed in January when an LRA ambush on MONUC troops resulted in the death of eight Guatemalan peacekeepers, bringing the total number of MONUC military fatalities since the start of its mission to 70. Subsequently, the Ugandan government claimed that Joseph Kony, the LRA leader, had moved into the DRC. In April, Congolese troops clashed with Ugandan soldiers in pursuit of the LRA, though this was denied by Kampala.

The situation in **Katanga** remained relatively calm throughout the year, following the deployment of an additional battalion to the province and the capitulation of a number of armed groups. These included the infamous Mai Mai leader Gidéon in Katanga, who surrendered to MONUC on 12 May in Mitwaba along with some 750 fighters. At year's end, it was unclear whether he would be put on trial or given a post in the army.

In northeastern Congo's **Ituri** district, an extremely insecure climate persisted as armed groups continued to operate. MONUC, in concert with FARDC units, conducted numerous operations to pressure the militias into disarming. In mid-July, the government promised Peter Karim, leader of the 'Front des Nationalistes et Intégrationnistes' (FNI), a high-ranking position in the national army and full amnesty for his troops in return for surrender. A similar agreement was reached with Mathieu Ngudjolo of the 'Mouvement Révolutionnaire Congolais' (MRC). However, these deals raised tough questions about the consistency of this buy-in approach and the dangers of immunity.

In contrast to Karim and Ngudjolo, for example, Chief Kahwa Mandro ('Parti pour l'Unité et la Sauvegarde de l'Intégrité du Congo', PUSIC) was sentenced to 20 years in prison for crimes against humanity by a military court in Bunia in August. The most publicised case regarding a militia leader involved Thomas Lubanga. Following his transfer to the International Criminal Court (ICC) in March, **Lubanga was charged** in late August for the recruitment and use of child soldiers by his 'Union des Patriotes Congolais' (UPC) militia in Ituri district. Subsequently, the ICC conducted pre-trial hearings. These were expected to result in a trial in January 2007. Though this was welcomed inside the DRC and out, there was widespread consternation that Lubanga had only been charged with the use of child soldiers. This approach seemed to arise from the ICC's intention to move ahead speedily with solid charges against Lubanga rather than charge him with even more serious crimes that could be more difficult to substantiate. However, ICC's chief prosecutor, Luis Moreno-Ocampo, stated that he planned to investigate further charges against Lubanga as well as other militias. Still, there was little doubt that the handling of human rights abusers was extremely uneven.

The ongoing insecurity in much of eastern Congo attested to the insufficient progress being made in **reforming the security sector**, i.e., the formation of integrated national police and military forces and the disarmament, demobilisation and reintegration of combatants (DDR). At the end of the year, the 'Commission Nationale de Désarmement, Démobilisation et Réinsertion des ex-Combattants' (CONADER) reported it had disarmed 182,468 of an estimated 330,000 combatants, with 100,000 to 120,000 weapons being handed in. More than 53,000 combatants were voluntarily integrated into the army. More than 99,000 combatants of the envisioned 150,000 were demobilised, including 2,500 woman and almost 30,000 children. More than 85,000 fighters registered for the reintegration process. Some 150,000 combatants still awaited demobilisation. At year's end, CONADER had run out of funding, but financial problems were only one aspect of the intricate and difficult process. For one thing, the various external actors involved in DDR had still not harmonised their efforts, thereby creating inefficiencies and overlaps. Secondly, the reinsertion dimension of DDR was not taken into account sufficiently, leaving tens of thousands of restless fighters across the country in an extremely precarious situation.

As regards the formation of the national army, the well-known problems reported in the previous year persisted. In addition to corruption in government and the military hierarchy, these included the essentially political problems arising from the divided loyalties among former warring factions, which inhibited a coherent chain of command, and a lack of funding for even the most basic operational needs of the integrated brigades. As a consequence, the mere creation of 14 integrated brigades (about 50,000 soldiers) did not reflect their military capabilities in any meaningful way. Indeed Nkunda's attack on Sake, where the integrated FARDC units quickly collapsed, was an obvious demonstration that not even a nucleus of a national army worthy of the name yet existed. The unexpected death of Maj.Gen. Sylvain Buki, former RCD officer and commander of Congo's ground forces (4 July), was a further setback. Buki was believed to be one of the few generals in Congo's military not to be involved in large-scale corruption and seemingly willing to move forward with the formation of an integrated army. Human rights groups in Kinshasa suggested that this was exactly the reason for his premature death, the cause of which remained unclear.

Aside from the army's poor military performance, FARDC soldiers routinely committed **human rights violations**, including sexual violence, in the course of military operations. More generally, MONUC reported physical violence against civilians and serious human rights abuses "wherever the army [was] deployed." MONUC also observed that in the first six months of the year, FARDC soldiers and police were the source of 81% of all human rights violations in the country (compared to 12% perpetrated by non-state armed groups), making the forces supposed to protect the population the single most important security threat in the country. As a result, MONUC repeatedly threatened to stop cooperating with the FARDC, with little discernible effect. Meanwhile, the UN had to admit that it was conducting more **investigations into sexual exploitation** and abuse by its peacekeepers in the DRC than in any other country. Of the 313 investigations of civilian and military staff since 2004, 202 cases concerned personnel in MONUC, the UN's largest peacekeeping operation worldwide.

Foreign Affairs

Significant improvements in **Congo's relations with its eastern neighbours** appeared to take root as Rwanda and Uganda adopted a more constructive stance towards Kinshasa. As an example, the incursion of Ugandan LRA insurgents into eastern Congo was not allowed to serve as a pretext for escalation, in spite of the seriousness of the problem. On the sidelines of the **summit of the International Conference of the Great Lakes Region** (ICGLR) in Nairobi (14–15 December), President Yoweri Museveni of **Uganda** hailed Congo's elections as a significant step towards peace, going as far as to note that the polls would "solve 50% of the Great Lakes' problems."

After three years, the ICGLR culminated in the adoption of the **Pact on Security, Stability and Development**. The pact consists of ten protocols, including one on non-aggression and mutual defence, as well as 33 concrete projects in the fields of conflict prevention, democracy and governance, economic development and regional integration. The implementation of this ambitious agenda by the 11 core ICGLR countries remains to be seen. However, the presence of newly elected President Kabila in Nairobi was an encouraging sign.

Relations with **Rwanda** improved significantly. In contrast to previous years, no alleged incursion by the Rwandan army into eastern Congo was reported, although the demobilisation and repatriation of the Congo-based Rwandan Hutu rebels of the 'Forces Démocratiques pour la Libération du Rwanda' (FDLR) made limited progress. Most notable were unprecedented statements by Rwandan President Paul Kagame, who publicly noted that FDLR no longer posed a significant threat to Rwanda's security, though he did not exclude future military action. It more and more appeared that Kagame had decided that an election victory by Kabila would serve Rwanda's best interests, at least compared to his opponents, whom Kagame seemed to trust even less. Although no concrete evidence materialised, a number of rumours suggested that Kabila, Kagame and the hardcore of the RCD in Goma, including North Kivu Governor Eugène Serufuli, had cut a mutually beneficial deal to accommodate their respective interests. In early August, Rwanda announced that it would open an embassy in Kinshasa after the elections.

The **international community** was heavily engaged throughout the year to shore up the electoral process militarily, financially and politically. In addition to regular and frequent visitors such as Thabo Mbeki, the EU's special representative to the Great Lakes, Aldo Ajello, and EU commissioner for development, Louis Michel, myriad luminaries travelled to the DRC in a show of support. These included UN Secretary-General Kofi Annan, the president of the EU commission, José Barroso, the high representative for the common foreign and security policy of the EU, Javier Solana, US assistant secretary for African affairs, Jendayi Frazer, the president of the AU commission, Alpha Konaré, and a delegation of the UN Security Council. To the extent that elections had been the central objective of international intervention since the 2002 peace accords, and given the large investment that had been made in this effort (the costs of MONUC alone exceeded $ 1 bn in 2006), this was hardly surprising. However, casting the elections as a make-or-break affair was not free of ambiguity. While the strong international pressure on Congolese actors probably contributed to the relatively smooth unfolding of the ballot, the depth of interference raised some awkward questions. In particular, a significant segment of Congolese society, certainly in Kinshasa, suspected the international community – probably correctly – of a pro-Kabila bias. This also extended to the EUFOR mission until its joint intervention with MONUC during the crisis in August, which probably saved Bemba's life and encouraged a change of popular attitudes towards the Europeans in Kinshasa.

The UN's group of experts on Congo's **arms embargo** issued two reports in 2006. Once more it documented the intricate relationship between the violent competition for natural resources and the illegal trans-border flow of arms. According to the group, the key problem in the ongoing violation of the embargo were Congo's weak state administration, the porosity of its borders, continued lack of air surveillance and poorly monitored financial flows, resulting in what the group described as a "permissive environment for embargo violations." By resolution 1698 (31 July), the Security Council extended the mandate of the group of experts until 31 July 2007.

Socioeconomic Developments

Compared to 2005, the number of **refugees and internally displaced persons** (IDPs) dropped slightly. The UN office for the coordination of humanitarian affairs reported that 1.1 m Congolese people were still displaced in their own country more than three years after the war had officially ended. Over 400,000 Congolese living in neighbouring countries were still to be repatriated, most of them in Tanzania (130,000) and Uganda (73,000).

With an expected annual growth rate of 5.7%, **GDP growth** was by and large the only macroeconomic indicator that did not disappoint Congo's donors. However, this was hardly surprising in a year in which elections were to decide the distribution of power among former warring factions, most of which had access to state coffers as part of the 2002 power-sharing deal. For many members of the transitional government, 2006 was the last chance to fill their pockets. A report by ICG claimed that government spent less than 2% of its budget outside Kinshasa. The costs of campaigning contributed further to the slide in the macroeconomic indicators. According to some estimates, Kabila and Bemba spent $ 50 m and $ 22 m respectively in the run up to the first round of elections alone. Between June and November, the budget deficit jumped from $ 10 m to $ 54 m. While much of this expenditure was the result of outright theft from state coffers, the printing of fresh money may also have occurred. With **fiscal discipline abandoned**, the Congolese franc (CDF) lost 20% of its value in less than six months and inflation soared to 20% in December. The average annual inflation rate was thus likely to be 16%, far above the 10% the government had predicted. Election-related expenditures also impacted the exchange rate, which stood at CDF 535 to $ 1 in December compared to CDF 433 to $ 1 at the start of the year.

However, the fiscal and monetary slide had already started in late 2005. In March, the IMF suspended its PRGF and the government had to accept a six-month staff monitored programme until the IMF could re-establish the government's commitment to previously signed agreements with lenders. In October, an **IMF delegation visited Kinshasa** to assess the macroeconomic situation. Although they put on a brave face, a leaked report by the bankers condemned in no uncertain terms the government's performance, citing **overspending, printing of money and increasingly lax revenue collection**. As regards the post-election period, donors, who provided 57% of the 2006 budget, faced a dilemma: either limiting their financial support to the incoming government and thus imperilling the overall political and economic achievements to date or continuing to support the DRC in spite of unrelenting corruption and mismanagement. To make matters worse, a fresh macroeconomic start in early 2007 seemed unlikely in the face of the political horse-trading in Kinshasa over the formation of a government in which dozens of parties expected pay-offs in return for their support for Kabila. The central bank, under its governor Jean-Claude Masungu, promised to reduce transfers to government and for other fiscally detrimental measures, but he was unlikely to keep his promises in the face of political pressure from the presidency. For example, between September and October alone, the bank's foreign exchange reserves diminished by $ 14 m.

Even so, the poor economic performance in 2006 was unlikely to change the country's new image as a haven of investment opportunity, mainly though not exclusively in the **mining sector**. UNCTAD reported a record $ 1.3 bn foreign direct investment in 2005, far higher than the total amount of FDI in previous years. The upward trend was expected to continue as foreign mining companies stepped up their involvement in the DRC in 2006.

At the same time, the **opaque nature of transactions in the mining sector**, Congo's principle source of income, came once more to the fore. In February, the long-awaited parliamentary report examining mining contracts signed by government between 1996 and the end of the second war in 2003 was published. It highlighted a number of exploitative contracts between foreign and Congolese state companies that amounted in fact to a sell-off of state assets. By year's end, the report had not been discussed by parliament and probably will never be considered by the new Kabila-dominated legislature. The commission's chairman, Christophe Lutundula, joined AMP. In November, a **World Bank memo**, leaked to the 'Financial Times' (17 November), observed that mining deals worth billions of dollars between state-owned companies and three international mining groups had been signed with a "complete lack of transparency" in 2005. It alleged that the deals transferred 75% of the enormous reserves of the state-owned Gécamines ('Générale des Carrières et des Mines') to the foreign mining companies and questioned the economic rationality of the deals. They were signed before a French consultancy firm, Sofreco, had taken over the management of Gécamines in early 2006 to restructure the heavily indebted company.

The disclosure of the shady deals was particularly embarrassing to the World Bank, which has been heavily involved in efforts to promote good governance in Congo's mining sector since 2002. Indeed, the World Bank memo warned that the bank's reputation could be severely tarnished as a result of "perceived complicity and/or tacit approval" of the mining contracts. To add insult to injury, the bank's department of institutional integrity started investigating allegations of fraud and corruption in World Bank operations in the Congo. All of this suggested that the Congolese government, elected or not, would remain an extremely difficult partner for outside actors, with President Kabila announcing his determination to deal with donors bilaterally in the aftermath of the elections and the end of the CIAT mandate.

Denis M. Tull

Equatorial Guinea

With his re-election as chairman of the ruling party, the confirmation of his candidature for the next presidential elections scheduled for 2009 and a government reshuffle, President Obiang reaffirmed his tight grip on power. In foreign policy, the government continued to exploit the rivalry between China and its traditional trading partners and investors from the US and Europe. All sides were eager to gain greater access to the country's oil and gas resources. The economy entered into a more moderate growth pattern. The government announced increases in public spending, but it remained to be seen whether these would really trickle down to benefit the great majority of the population, still stuck in appalling poverty.

Domestic Politics

At the **fourth ordinary congress of the** ruling 'Partido Democrático de Representantes del Pueblo' (**PDGE**) that took place in Malabo from 8–10 July, President Obiang was re-elected as the head of his political party for another five-year term, along with the confirmation of his candidature for the next presidential election in 2009 on behalf of the PDGE. Obiang's apparent and reaffirmed grip on power swept aside speculation about his supposedly fragile health for the time being.

Apparently as a prelude to an anticipated **government reshuffle**, and rather unusual for the ruling political party, the delegates to the PDGE congress were outspokenly critical of the performance of the government of then Prime Minister Miguel Abia Biteco Borico. Consequently, President Obiang's announcement on 10 August that the two-year-old government had been sacked did not come as a major surprise. The **new government** saw the number of its members increase from 51 to 59, with most key officials holding on to their portfolios, including the two eldest sons of President Obiang and the main contestants for his succession, Minister of Agriculture and Forestry Teodorín Nguema Obiang Mangue and Deputy-Minister of Mines and Hydrocarbons Gabriel Mbegha Obiang Lima. The major surprise was the appointment of Ricardo Mangue Obama Nfubea as the **new prime minister**. Although Prime Minister Mangue fitted the usual pattern in that he had served in government for more than ten years, his appointment marked a break with the past. Whereas all prime ministers had come from the minority Bubi ethnic group indigenous to the island part of the country, he is a Fang from the mainland, although from the Ebibiyin rather than from President Obiang's Esangui clan. The move was interpreted as an attempt to broaden the country's elite ahead of the eventual transition in the presidency. The appointment also exemplified a further setback for the Bubi minority, even if the prime minister's role was always rather symbolic, given that political control has always remained firmly in the hands of the extended family of President Obiang.

Prime Minister Mangue set out with a new priority to improve public administration and to **control corruption**, leading in November to minor sentences for five public servants for embezzling public funds. President Obiang had acknowledged the pertinence of this issue and announced new legislation. Equatorial Guinea continued to figure prominently among the most corrupt countries in the world in the Corruption Perceptions Index released by Transparency International on 6 November. The country ranked 151st out of a total of 163 countries surveyed. While there might be new efforts to control corruption in the lower echelons of the public administration, the president's eldest son and minister of agriculture gave a rare insight into the **endemic corruption among the country's elite** in an affidavit filed with the South African high court in Cape Town in August, as part of a law suit against him over a $ 7.8 m commercial debt. 'Teodorín', as he is commonly known, who received an official annual salary of $ 60,000 in 2006 but who owned, among other things, mansions in South Africa, Europe and in California as well as a fleet of luxury and sports cars, testified that cabinet ministers in Equatorial Guinea were allowed by law to set up companies that, in consortium with a foreign company, can bid on government contracts. If successful, a cabinet minister would end up with a sizeable part of the contract price in his bank account.

In a move to comply with the ratification of the UN convention against torture in 2002, President Obiang approved **legislation against the use of torture** and released four political prisoners on 2 November. The new legislation was a novelty in a country commonly accused of widespread abuse of human rights, including torture by the security forces at all levels. It remained to be seen, however, whether the new legislation was merely symbolic. The new law coincided with President Obiang's visit to Spain later that month and was clearly intended to divert the considerable criticism among the public of the former colonial power.

Foreign Affairs

At the beginning of the year, on 27 February, a solution to the longstanding **maritime border dispute with Gabon** seemed imminent when the presidents of the two countries met with UN Secretary-General Kofi Annan. Annan paid another visit to Equatorial Guinea on 24 March, stating he was confident that a solution could be achieved before the end of the year. Later developments, however, provided a **major setback**. Bilateral talks scheduled for early October were cancelled at the last minute by Gabon's President Bongo and both countries seemed to be ready to refer the dispute to the international court of justice in The Hague, thereby pushing aside previously favoured bilateral negotiated solutions, such as a joint management zone or the purchase from Gabon of one of the three contested islands in Corisco bay off the southern coast of the mainland. Implicitly backed by Spain, the authorities in Equatorial Guinea came to believe that they would win sovereignty over the island without having to make major concessions. Further substantial delays on the issue were obvious and hence prevented further expansion of oil exploration in the contested areas.

President **Obiang travelled extensively** to all major partners, thereby demonstrating both his apparently more robust health and his confidence in the security situation at home. He visited the US on 11–12 April. Secretary of State Condoleezza Rice called him "a good friend" in public, although her own department's annual human rights report released on 6 March accused officials from Equatorial Guinea of committing substantial human rights abuses and of tolerating widespread torture. President Obiang signed a **memorandum of understanding with the US** on 11 April to establish a social development fund in the country, implementing projects in health, education, women's affairs and the environment. At the beginning of the year, on 13 February, US Assistant Secretary of State for African Affairs Jendayi Frazer paid a visit to Equatorial Guinea. She held a series of meetings with the country's officials and launched the new consular section at the US embassy in Malabo. On 14 February, she was hosted by President Obiang in Bata on the mainland.

For the past decade, there had been no resident US ambassador in the country and the US chiefs of mission in Cameroon had managed US relations with Equatorial Guinea during that period. The **US ambassador-designate**, Donald C. Johnson, who was officially appointed ambassador to Equatorial Guinea shortly afterwards, explained in testimony before the US senate foreign relations committee in Washington on 3 August that the Bush administration believed an ambassadorial presence in Equatorial Guinea to be important. There was more than $ 10 bn of US foreign direct investment in the country, mainly in the oil industry, and this represented the fourth-highest level of US direct investment in sub-Saharan Africa. As a classic strategy to counter a predominant position by one major partner, President Obiang continued to play the Chinese card as well. His foreign minister visited China and South Korea in July. After a prior visit to Japan, President Obiang attended the **Africa-China summit in Beijing** from 4–5 November, his third trip to China over the last five years. A number of economic agreements were signed between the two countries, including a $ 2 bn interest-free and oil-backed loan aimed at improving the country's transport, housing and energy infrastructure. Upon his return to Malabo, and intended as a signal to the country's partners from the West, President Obiang praised the Chinese policy of non-interference in domestic affairs, with no prior conditions on democracy or human rights.

After a long gap of 15 years, President Obiang paid an **official visit to Spain** from 14–16 November. The way for the visit had been prepared by the Spanish foreign minister, Miguel Angel Moratinos, who paid an official visit to Equatorial Guinea together with the justice minister, Juan Fernando Lopez Aguilar, on 23 October. The delegations reached several cooperation agreements to reinforce dialogue between the two countries. However, due to heavy criticism from the Spanish press and public, who accused their own government of violating its commitment to an ethical foreign policy, President Obiang's visit to Madrid was downgraded from an official visit to simply a working visit. Government officials from Equatorial Guinea made their protests known and President Obiang was able to meet the Spanish Prime Minister Zapatero and to dine with the Spanish king. Spain settled for a policy of constructive dialogue aimed at promoting human rights and political reforms, thereby keeping up the hope of gaining greater access to Equatorial Guinea's oil and gas wealth.

Socioeconomic Developments

Owing to different outlooks for the hydrocarbons sector, the forecasts for **GDP growth rates** fluctuated between only 1% and a moderate expansion of 5.3%. The former forecast was made by the IMF, whereas the latter, covering the first half of the year, came from the sub-regional central bank BEAC in December. **Crude oil production** was expected to contract by 4.4% as a result of technical factors and the periodic shutting down of certain offshore platforms for maintenance. The situation may improve by 2008 when the latest field, which began producing in December, will reach peak production. The hydrocarbons sector at large continued to benefit from the **significant expansion in methanol gas production**. This expansion was further boosted by an agreement signed with Nigeria on 11 December providing for a substantial supply of natural gas to the projected second line of the liquefied natural gas plant at Punta Europa on Bioko. Cameroon had announced on 27 November that it planned to export gas to Equatorial Guinea as well.

For the time being, however, the economy's double-digit growth rates so characteristic of the decade since 1995 seemed to be over. The **inflation rate** reached more than 5% by the middle of the year, prompting government to revert to **price controls on basic commodities** in October to divert mounting public protests over rising fuel, food, transport and housing prices. The **budget** for 2007, approved in late November, foresaw an increase in domestic revenue by 131% compared to the 2006 budget. Expenditures were set to rise to CFAfr 2,313 bn, with half of that going into recurrent and capital expenditure, with ambitious investments in public infrastructure, and the other half earmarked for debt repayment and for flowing into the intergenerational equity fund at BEAC. Although the budget did show **some improvement in transparency**, the details provided remained of little use. A report by the Banque de France had found that 76% of recurrent expenditure was off-budget in 2005. **Foreign direct investment** continued to rise from $ 1.66 bn to $ 1.86 bn, reconfirming the country's role as the third-largest recipient of foreign direct investment inflows in sub-Saharan Africa. The deficit on the **current account** continued to narrow after the peak reached in 2004 and the country's **foreign exchange reserves** rose by more than 40% to $ 2.9 bn at the end of September.

Characteristic of a country with one of the highest per capita national incomes in the world but where most **citizens continued to live in appalling poverty**, data from the latest HDI released in November highlighted the growing scarcity of water in the developing world showed Equatorial Guinea to be the worst off country in Africa: 57% of the population had no access to clean water. So far, the ambitious investments in public infrastructure have failed to trickle down to the majority of the population. More than a decade of rapid economic growth has led to **little or no improvement in social indicators**. Oil and gas dominated everything while the national agricultural sector was unable to meet the basic needs of the people. The IMF highlighted the social weaknesses of the country's performance in its annual Article IV consultations, but the Bretton Woods institutions had no real leverage on a government flooded with oil and gas revenues. Although the **IMF** managing director, Rodrigo de Rato, signed a service agreement with President Obiang for a **two-year technical assistance project** in Malabo on 15 March, such non-lending projects will not have a significant impact.

Meanwhile, the government tried to demonstrate its maturity in dealing with the all-dominant oil sector by promulgating a **new hydrocarbon law** in November. The royalty tax was raised from the 10% to a minimum of 13% and the possibility of imposing a windfall tax by the state was included as well. Whereas the laws and contracts of the early 1990s were interpreted as overwhelmingly favourable to the oil companies, the new law included a number of hardships for the oil companies. However, compared to regional norms, Equatorial Guinea's new oil and gas legislation continued to make further exploration a worthwhile endeavour for the oil companies.

Cord Jakobeit

Gabon

President **Omar Bongo Ondimba**, the longest-serving African head of state, whose ruling 'Parti Democratique Gabonais' (PDG) won another landslide in this year's legislative elections, remained in patrimonial command of politics, government and business. After 39 years of pro-French orientation, Bongo has opened his country's natural resources to Chinese state companies. Asian countries were steadily becoming more important as lenders, investors and trading partners. Emblematic of this new partnership was the signing of the multibillion-dollar Bélinga iron ore project, heralded as 'the operation of the century'.

Domestic Politics

President Bongo named **Jean Eyéghé Ndong** as the **new prime minister** on 20 January, following an unwritten tradition that the post be held by a Fang originating from the Estuary province. Ndong was a former deputy finance minister who had overseen the privatisation of several important state companies. The appointment of a new prime minister was seen as a way of fulfilling Bongo's re-election campaign promise for renewal. But on 23 October, Bongo announced on Radio France Internationale that he intended to stand for re-election in 2012, "if God gives me the strength." Ndong presented his government policy to PDG lawmakers in the National Assembly on 6 March. Based on Bongo's 2005 campaign manifesto entitled 'Mon Projet, des actes pour le Gabon', Ndong's policy ostensibly sought to improve the conditions of the poor, the status of women and the future of youth.

On 9 April, the number-two man in the regime, **George Rawiri**, died in Paris as a result of gastroenteritis. The long-time president of the senate (a key post, with the incumbent serving as interim head of state if the president dies) was a Myène, a journalist by profession and founder of Radio Télévision Gabon. Several times cabinet minister and named as the country's first senate president in 1997, his most memorable achievement was the construction of the Transgabonais railway, which reputedly made him the second wealthiest man in Gabon. In memory of his lifelong friend, Bongo baptised the airport in Lambaréné, the region from which Rawiri originated, in his name.

On 24 May, Rawiri was replaced by Senator René Radembino Coniquet, also a Myène, and a political dinosaur who had served under the French colonial governor and the first president of independent Gabon, Leon Mba, before joining Bongo's cabinet and holding various cabinet portfolios. The ruling PDG, which held 53 out of 91 seats in the senate, opted for Coniquet because of his lifelong loyal collaboration with Bongo and also to avoid any new quarrels between the ruling party's two major factions, the 'rénovateurs', who rally around defence minister (and the president's son) Ali Ben Bongo, and the 'appelistes', who rally around finance minister (and the president's son-in-law) Paul Toungui. Rawiri was a long-time friend of the Bongo family, and his death was interpreted as a loss for Ali Bongo's reformers.

Before the 17 December **legislative elections**, 110 of 120 deputies in the National Assembly belonged to the presidential majority. The PDG alone held 86 seats. Over 850 candidates presented themselves to the electoral commission, a record number, more than half of whom came from the 40 parties that make up the presidential majority. The only party represented in every electoral district was the ruling PDG. Former opposition leader, now Bongo loyalist, Paul Mba Abessole, of the 'Rassemblement National des Bûcherons-Rassemblement pour le Gabon' (RNB-RPG) presented candidates in 60 districts. Zacharie Myboto, a former Bongo loyalist, now opposition leader, who founded 'Union Gabonaise pour la Démocratie et le Développement' (UGDD) and challenged Bongo in the 2005 presidential elections, also put up candidates in 70 districts.

Pierre Mamboundou, charismatic founder of the 'Union du Peuple Gabonais' (UPG), was one of the rare opponents to have never succumbed to the temptation of a cabinet position. A Punu from Ndgendé, where he was elected mayor, Mamboundou has twice run for president, winning second place both times, with 16.5% of the vote (1998) and 13.6% (2005). After strongly contesting the results of those elections, his headquarters in Awendjé were sacked on 21 March and he sought refuge in the South African embassy in Libreville. Eventually the page was turned and he was invited on 19 April to Bongo's presidential palace in Libreville where the two men, who had not spoken face-to-face in 20 years, reached an agreement to begin constructive dialogue before the legislative elections. Eventually the UPG ran candidates in 80 districts.

Almost all of the PDG heavyweights were re-elected in the December races, but divisions within the presidential super-majority were expressed by Prime Minister Ndong's defeat of Vice-Prime Minister Mba Abessole in a highly symbolic contest for a seat in Libreville. In the end, the **presidential majority coalition held 98 seats** in the lower house, with the PDG winning 81 seats, and the remainder being held by seven other allied parties in the presidential coalition, including seven seats for Abessole's RPG. Meanwhile, five opposition parties managed to take 16 seats, including eight for the UPG, which is now the second largest party in parliament, and four for the UGDD. There were also 'independent' candidates, close to the presidential majority, who took five districts. Finally, the constitutional court annulled the results of one election in the Ogooué-Lolo district because of gross irregularities.

Foreign Affairs

Within the region, President Bongo continued to enjoy good relations with the governments of CAR (where he helped broker the peace), DR Congo (where he received representatives from different political parties two days before the July presidential elections) and Congo. Bongo, however, has not enjoyed such good personal relations with either Paul Biya of Cameroon or Teodoro Obiang Nguema of Equatorial Guinea. So it was encouraging to see Gabonese Trade Minister Paul Biyoghé Mba meet with his counterparts from **Equatorial Guinea and Cameroon** on 7 April to discuss the free exchange of people, goods and services in the 'three border zone'. It was also encouraging to see Gabon and Equatorial Guinea prepare a joint dossier to hold the football cup of African nations in 2012.

But more important were the 1–5 October talks in Geneva held under the aegis of the UN to settle the longstanding dispute over **oil-rich Mbane**, a 30-hectare sandy island in the Bay of Corisco straddling the border between Gabon and Equatorial Guinea, located above a vast offshore petroleum reserve. A scandal erupted on 13 September when the interior minister, Andre Mba Obame, was rumoured by the daily newspaper 'l'Union' to have tried to convince President Bongo to sell the island to Equatorial Guinea, a charge formally denied by both Bongo and Nguema. One newspaper, 'L'Echo du Nord', which questioned Gabon's sovereignty over the island, was shut down for three months by the Gabonese government. The talks came to a standstill when Gabon refused to accept Equatorial Guinea's demands for recognition of its sovereignty. The island remained occupied by a handful of Gabonese soldiers.

Bongo's relations with **France** remained strong. Six new military cooperation conventions were signed with France by Jean-Marc Simon, French ambassador, and Ali Bongo, defence minister, during a summit from 20–23 May. French military advisors ran 11 training projects in Gabon and 430 Gabonese soldiers received training in France. In

August, Bruno Leclerc of the 'Agence Française de Développement' (AFD) finished his three-year mission, during which bilateral development aid increased from € 16 m to € 64 m. The AFD aid was essentially concentrated on urban water and power, AIDS and new national parks. Over the next three years, the AFD will give priority to the poverty reduction and strategic growth document (signed in 2005) which privileges forestry, infrastructure and education. But despite several decades of French neocolonial cooperation, many believed that France was losing influence. On 30 October, at any rate, Bongo declared in a keynote speech at a business convention in Shanghai, "Gabon is not anybody's private game reserve." This was interpreted as a stern warning to Paris.

On 3 May, Bongo visited **India** before opening Gabon's first embassy there and met with the Indian mining minister to discuss various projects, including the exploration permits of Coal India Ltd. From 9–11 October, the commerce minister, Paul Biyoghé Mba, travelled to New Delhi with a delegation representing the 11 CEEAC member states.

The most important new actor in Gabon was undoubtedly **China**, which has penetrated the forestry and mining sectors at a startling rate. On 7 September, Wu Guanzheng, a member of the Chinese communist party's politburo, signed an agreement with Prime Minister Ndong for the exploitation of the **Belinga iron reserves** in northeastern Gabon, along the border with neighboring Congo (see below). The total cost of the project was an estimated $ 3 bn, dwarfing by far all other foreign direct investment. President Bongo was personally involved in the new partnership, which he said would create 30,000 new jobs. According to Bongo at the signing ceremony, "This is the biggest operation since the Transgabonais" (railway). On this occasion, he lauded the policy of cooperation with China in general terms.

President Bongo was also invited to travel to Beijing to participate in a meeting of African heads of state being hosted by the People's Republic. He arrived first in Shanghai on 29–30 October to host the Sino-Gabonese economic forum. Then he attended the **China-Africa summit** in Beijing on 4–5 November. On the margins of the summit, China organised a business fair (6–7 November), in which 35 Gabonese enterprises participated. Before returning to Libreville, Bongo stopped in Paris to meet with French businessmen operating in his country. This suggests that, despite all the pronouncements to the contrary, it would be overly hasty to deduce the end of French influence in Gabon.

Socioeconomic Developments

Gabon remained the fifth largest oil-exporter in sub-Saharan Africa, but the IMF estimated that its reserves would be exhausted in 30 years. Gabon's oil reserves were estimated at 760 m barrels. After peaking at 18.5 m tonnes in 1997, oil production fell to 13 m tonnes in 2006. The Rabi Kounga field, which at its apogee supplied 60% of national oil production at 220,000 b/d, barely produced 50,000 b/d in 2006. Despite declining production, oil still represented over 50% of GDP, 65% of public finance and more than 80% of export revenues. **Skyrocketing oil prices** of an average $ 45.3 per barrel generated CFAfr 1,057 bn in government oil revenue in 2006, compared to CFAfr 570 m at an average price of $ 28.9 per barrel in 2003.

In 2006, there were 106 **oil permits** held by 22 operators, of which 41 were exploratory and 65 were producing crude. The active oil companies were Total, Shell, Perenco, Vaalco, Marathon and PanOcean, which extracted an average of 238,000 b/d. In January, Mitsubishi Petroleum Development Co. of Gabon signed an exploration contract for the Moabi and Nguma basins. The Japanese firm has been actively operating in partnership with the French Total since 1974 and the American Amerada since 1999, but this was to be its first solo operation. The company also intended to invest in a joint-venture with Irish Tullow Oil, declaring that Gabon was the country they knew best geologically.

Systematically driven out of Angola and Nigeria by their fellow Asian competitors, **Indian oil groups** also made several acquisitions in Gabon. Oil India, Indian Oil Corporation and ONGC Videsh obtained a 3,700 km^3 permit to explore the banks of the Ogooué southeast of Libreville, between Ndjolé and Lambaréné. Also, in March, ONGC Videsh negotiated the purchase of 10,000 b/d from PanOcean producing fields.

Non-oil mineral exports were expected to increase as oil reserves steadily decline. In 2006, Gabon produced 25% of the world's **manganese** exports, averaging about 255,000 tonnes per month. Through its 'Compagnie Minière de l'Ogooué' (Comilog) the French group Eramet was the second largest producer of manganese in the world. If increased production continues as planned and new reserves in Okondja, Franceville and Ndjolé can be exploited, the country is set to become the world's largest manganese exporter.

The **Chinese-Brazilian consortium** to exploit the Belinga **iron** reserves was delayed by disputes between the China National Machinery & Equipment Import & Export Corporation (CMEC) and the Brazilian 'Companhia Vale do Rio Doce' (CVRD) over who would control the $ 600 m project. This dispute split the Gabonese government, with one faction led by Foreign Minister Jean Ping supporting the Chinese and another led by Mining Minister Richard Onouviet supporting the Brazilians. Belinga, discovered in 1895, is one of the last great unexploited iron reserves in the world, with estimated reserves of 1 bn tonnes of iron ore. CMEC eventually was awarded the entire reserve on 7 September, after promising to build a 250 km conveyor belt between Belinga and Boué; another 30 km belt from Ntoum to the port of Santa Balara; to double the existing section of the Transgabonais railway with 500 km of new track; to build a hydroelectric dam on the Ivindo river (where CVRD had only proposed to build a thermal power plant); and to construct a deep-water 8-km jetty at the port of Santa Clara, with a treatment plant, a train station and a giant storage plateau. Finally, the Chinese government promised to guarantee the project, reducing the risk of bankruptcy in a way the totally private Brazilian CVRD could not. In December, CVRD laid off 200 employees and announced its would freeze new manganese projects after the fall in world manganese prices.

In January, the monopoly of the 'Société Nationale des Bois du Gabon' (SNBG) over okoumé and ozigo (the two principal Gabonese **wood** export species) came to an end, allowing foresters to earn an additional CFAfr 15,000–20,000 per m^3. SNBG was still the largest and oldest forestry company in the country and had enlarged its activities to negotiate exports of the ensemble of other Gabonese wood species. Still, profitability in the forestry sector was not good. The 'Union des Forestiers Industriels du Gabon et Aménagistes' (UFIGA) complained in July of being confronted with builders from the dollar zone. A sheet of Gabonese okoumé plywood made in China would be sold in Holland for 25% to 35% less than a sheet of plywood made in Europe with the same material.

On 29 March, the World Bank approved a $ 10 m project for management of the **national parks** and their biodiversity, funded by the World Wildlife Fund. This contrasts with the announcement (18 March) by Emile Doumba, minister of forests, water, fishing and national parks, that wood exports had increased from 241,000 m^3 in 2003 to 411,000 m^3 in 2005, and that his ministry planned to bring the contribution of the forestry sector up to 10% of GDP by 2015. Of 14 m hectares held by the government, he said, 10 m would be forested and 4 m protected. With 85% of its territory covered by forests, Gabon represents around 15% of the total Congo basin rainforest.

In summer, the Wildlife Conservation Society reported that **Sinopec**, the Chinese oil company, had been illegally damaging **Loango National Park** while prospecting, including a plan for 16,000 dynamite explosions in lagoons filled with endangered species, the unauthorised construction of roads, the building of a workers' village and a host of other activities destructive of the flora and fauna. These activities were strictly illegal, as Sinopec's environmental impact report had been refused by the government as grossly inadequate. After donor nations addressed the forestry minister, Emile Doumba, Sinopec was forced to withdraw its teams from the reserve at the end of September. The affair revealed serious divergences within the government between those who support aggressive Chinese extractive industry investments and those who seek sustainable development through eco-tourism.

In February, the government announced the dissolution of Air Gabon and concluded an agreement with Royal Air Maroc (RAM) to continue international service under the guise of Air Gabon International (51% RAM, 49% government of Gabon). The company announced the definitive end to all inter-African flights, leaving only flights to Paris. National links between the capital city and Franceville, Oye and Port-Gentil would be maintained with rented aircraft. However, after interminable disagreements between RAM and the government over ownership and operational control, the decision was made instead to create **Gabon Airlines**, entirely owned by private banks and investors and headed by **Christian Bongo**, one of the president's sons.

Douglas A. Yates

São Tomé and Príncipe

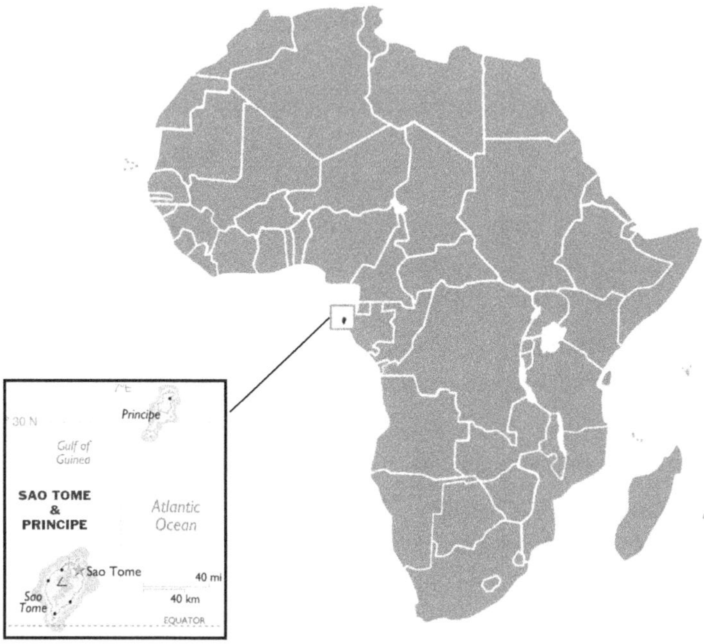

Politically, the year was marked by three consecutive elections, all of them won by President Menezes and his allies. The 'Movimento de Libertação de São Tomé e Príncipe/Partido Social Democrata' (MLSTP/PSD), in power since 1994, lost its position as the party of government to the 'Movimento Democrático Força de Mudança – Partido de Convergência Democrática' (MDFM-PCD), the party alliance close to the president. Menezes won the presidential elections, but the presidency lost its executive powers at the beginning of his second term. On the economic front, the disappointing results from the first exploratory drilling provoked uncertainty in the oil sector. Production-sharing contracts for three oil blocks awarded in 2005 were signed. However, because of outstanding debts, Nigeria delayed the release of São Tomé's share of signature bonus payments.

Domestic Politics

Early in the year, several events indicated that Menezes's position was far from comfortable. In January, the president abandoned the referendum **on the government system** that he had been pursuing during the preceding months. As the National Assembly rejected the holding of the referendum agreed on in a memorandum of understanding signed in January 2003, he lacked the constitutional power to enforce one.

In mid-January, following accusations that € 407,000 in Moroccan bilateral aid had been spent on the purchase of cars and goods for the presidency and the foreign ministry outside the budget and without the consent of Prime Minister Silveira, **Foreign Minister Ovídio Pequeno resigned**. President Menezes had refused the prime minister's request that he dismiss the foreign minister. In March, Menezes appointed Pequeno ambassador to Washington.

On 16 January, about 50 disgruntled policemen of the rapid reaction force seized the police headquarters and demanded higher salaries and the dismissal of police commander Armando Correia, whom they accused of corruption and maltreatment. The conflict was resolved after one week of negotiations, when the government dismissed Correia, who was subsequently appointed advisor to the defence minister. It was only in October that the government appointed Gilberto Vaz de Andrade as the new police commander.

Eight parties and two party alliances participated in the **legislative elections** of 26 March. The campaign was marked by persistent reports of vote buying. In 13 localities, some 9,600 of the 89,850 registered voters were prevented from voting by roadblocks erected by local demonstrators protesting poor access roads and the lack of other basic infrastructure. In these places, the elections were repeated on 2 April.

Subsequently, the constitutional court decided to recount all ballots to reconfirm the results announced by the national electoral commission. The MDFM-PCD fiercely criticised this decision as a possibly fraudulent attempt to favour the MLSTP/PSD electorally, arguing that by law only contested ballots could be recounted. Shortly afterwards, on the order of the defence minister, Óscar Sousa, who is considered close to President Menezes, for an hour heavily armed military forces surrounded the court building where the recounting occurred, supposedly to protect the court from threats against the public order. The outgoing MLSTP/PSD government accused Sousa of intervening militarily without its consent and demanded his dismissal.

According to the final election results announced by the supreme court on 17 April, the MDFM-PCD won 23 seats, the MLSTP/PSD and the 'Acção Democrática Independente' (ADI) obtained 20 and 11 seats respectively, while the newly established party Novo Rumo gained one seat. In April, the MDFM-PCD formed a **minority government** headed by Prime Minister Tomé Vera Cruz, the MDFM leader. Although the ruling party alliance has only 23 seats in the National Assembly, on 18 May Francisco Silva (PCD) was elected speaker of parliament with 30 votes, while the opposition candidate Carlos Tiny (MLSTP/PSD) gained only 25 votes. Apparently, Tiny lacked sufficient support from his own party and the ADI.

On 30 July, the incumbent Fradique de Menezes won the **presidential elections** with 60.6% of the votes. His main opponent Patrice Trovoada, son of former President Miguel Trovoada and ADI leader, gained 38.8% of the ballots. Trovoada was also supported by the former ruling MLSTP/PSD, which did not put forward its own candidate, and seven small parties. The third candidate, Nilo Guimarães, obtained 0.6% of the votes. Voter turnout was

65%. On 3 September, Menezes was sworn in for his second five-year term in the presence of the heads of state of Congo, Gabon, Equatorial Guinea and the Central African Republic, and the prime ministers of Angola and Chad. Simultaneously, the constitutional amendments approved in January 2003 that reduce the executive powers of the president came into effect.

Preparations for the long overdue local elections were marred by one incident, which must be seen in the light of recent history. The previous local and regional elections had been held in December 1992 and March 1995 respectively. Thereafter, consecutive governments failed to organise local elections due to a lack of political will. On 5 June, a local court declared null and void the ten candidacies put forward for the local elections that had finally been scheduled for 9 July on the grounds that they had been submitted after the 25 May deadline. Following a huge outcry in Príncipe on 12 June against the court decision spearheaded by the opposition movement 'União para a Mudança e Progresso do Príncipe' (UMPP), the head of the island's regional government, Zeferino dos Prazeres (MLSTP/PSD), was forced to step down. The MLSTP/PSD accused government of having orchestrated the rebellion. However, the demonstrators denied this. Subsequently, the MDFM-PCD government appointed João Paulo Cassandra, leader of the revolt, as head of a provisional regional government until the regional elections.

The **local elections** were finally held on 27 August. The MDFM-PCD party alliance won the majority in five of São Tomé's six district assemblies, while the MLSTP/PSD obtained the majority in Lembá district. Because of lack of funds, the MLSTP/PSD had not participated in Água Grande and Mé-Zochi, the two most populous districts. The independent UMPP movement, headed by Tozé Cassandra, won an absolute majority in the regional elections in Príncipe.

Because of the three consecutive election defeats, the leader of the MLSTP/PSD, Guilherme Posser da Costa, resigned on 28 August. He declared that his party had experienced its worst crisis ever and admitted to having made errors. However, he said he was not the only culprit. The party's vice-president, Dionísio Dias, became acting leader until the election of Posser's successor.

Two key officeholders were replaced during the year. Following the government's decision in May to cancel the extension of the central bank building, budgeted at $ 8 m and planned by the former executive, in late June the government dismissed the central bank's governor, former prime minister Maria do Carmo Silveira, and the bank's administrative board on the grounds that the planned construction had not been included in the bank's budget for 2006. The opposition MLSTP/PSD fiercely condemned the dismissal as politically motivated. In July, the government appointed Arlindo Afonso de Carvalho (PCD) as new bank governor.

On 11 August, President Menezes appointed Roberto Raposo as attorney-general to replace Adelino Pereira, who had resigned after less than four years in office to continue his studies in the US. In September, after local auditors discovered the disappearance of

$ 2 m from the accounts of the food aid agency 'Gabinete de Gestão da Ajuda' (GGA), which had already experienced the embezzlement of $ 3 m in 2004, Raposo demanded the end of impunity for and the trial of the two deputies Maria das Neves and Arzemiro dos Prazeres charged in the first scandal. On 30 October, the government decided to dissolve the corruption-plagued GGA.

Foreign Affairs

In February, the **US navy** donated a nine-crew patrol boat to São Tomé's coast guard. In June, the US navy selected São Tomé as regional centre for its Marine Domain Awareness, a surveillance radar programme for the identification and monitoring of maritime traffic in the Gulf of Guinea. The installation of the system started in early December.

On 26 May, the EU renewed the fishing agreement with São Tomé for the period 2006–10. In return for an annual payment of € 663,000, 43 trawlers were allowed to fish in territorial waters. Half of the amount was destined to support artisanal fishing.

In early May, President Menezes visited Libya to seek budgetary assistance from Colonel Kadhafi. Libya promised to provide financial aid and sent an expert team to assess technical needs in São Tomé. On his return, Menezes paid a visit to Abuja to ask President Obasanjo to extend the deadline for the repayment of Nigerian loans worth $ 15 m.

On 8 July, the Taiwanese foreign minister, James Huang, paid an official visit to São Tomé. Huang thanked São Tomé for its diplomatic support for **Taiwan**'s readmission to the UN. On 14 October, São Tomé participated as an observer in the economic cooperation forum between **China** and Portuguese-speaking countries held in Macao. However, São Tomé did not take up Beijing's invitation to participate in the China-Africa cooperation forum in November.

On 25 August, the summit of the heads of states and governments of the eight-country **Gulf of Guinea Commission** in Libreville designated São Tomé as executive secretary to the commission for a three-year period, while Luanda was chosen as the headquarters of the organisation. Menezes appointed Carlos Gomes, former chairman of the Joint Development Authority (JDA) in Abuja, as the commission's secretary.

During a three-day visit to **Angola** in October, Prime Minister Tomé Vera Cruz invited local business people to invest in the archipelago and promised fiscal incentives on investments. Vera Cruz signed a protocol on cooperation in oil exploration in his country's exclusive economic zone.

On 30 November, the Senegalese president, Abdoulaye Wade, paid a three-day visit to São Tomé. President Wade promised scholarships in his country and to send Senegalese teachers to São Tomé.

From 4–6 December, a **round-table donor conference** on infrastructure, education and good governance was held in São Tomé. The government expected to raise funds worth $ 121 m, but donors pledged only $ 52 m.

Socioeconomic Developments

In early March, the National Assembly approved the 2006 **national budget** totalling dobras (Db)1,061.4 bn (= $ 87 m), of which 65% was capital investment, including debt service payments. Foreign donors provided Db 475.8 bn ($ 39 m), while Db 190.3 bn ($ 15.6 m) stemmed from the national oil account. The budget included indemnification payments for some 3,600 former public sector workers, who received a total of Db 23 bn (approx. $ 1.89 m).

In the same month, the IMF concluded the first review of the PRGF signed in August 2005. The IMF considered performance under the arrangement satisfactory and released $ 600,000. The second review was completed in August, enabling the release of another $ 600,000. After the country had established a court of arbitration and approved new fiscal legislation, as demanded by the IMF, in November the IMF declared that the country was close to the **completion point for debt relief**.

In January, ChevronTexaco started drilling the **first exploration well**, located in some 1,700 metres of water in Block 1 of the Joint Development Zone (JDZ). The well was finished at a cost of $ 37 m in mid-March. However, Chevron announced the discovery of hydrocarbons only in May, but stressed that it was premature to say if the deposits were commercially exploitable. Chevron announced that a second exploratory well out of a total of eight selected in the block would be drilled in late 2007.

Due to the controversial investigation report into the second licensing round of the JDZ, the signature of the **production sharing contracts** (PSC) for the awarded blocks suffered considerable delays. On 15 March, the JDA signed PSCs for Block 2 with the operator Sinopec (Chinese), Addax Petroleum (Swiss) and the Nigerian-owned Environmental Remediation Holding Corporation (ERHC) (65% stake) and other companies; for Block 3 with Anadarko (51%) and ERHC/Addax (25%) and other parties; and with Addax/ERHC (60%) and other consortium winners in Block 4. The signing of PSCs for Blocks 5 and 6 was postponed. The signature bonuses for Blocks 2–4 were $ 71 m, $ 40 m and $ 90 m respectively. Because of ERHC's bonus-free options, São Tomé was entitled to only $ 28.6 m of the total amount. In May, the contractor companies paid the signature bonuses to the JDA. However, Nigeria delayed the transfer of São Tomé's share and demanded the repayment of the bilateral debts of $ 15 m. São Tomé argued that the oil revenue management law did not allow debt payments from signature bonus payments, although the country had once promised Nigeria to settle the debts with the signature bonus money.

On 23 May, Air São Tomé's only airplane, a 12-seat Twin Otter, crashed into the sea near the airport during an instruction flight, killing all four persons aboard. Subsequently, the government dissolved the deficit-laden company created in 1993 and on 1 October established a **new national airline**, STP Airways. The Angolan airline TAAG was invited to take a stake in the company. Following the bankcrupty of Air Luxor in September, the weekly flight connection to Lisbon operated by this private airline ceased. On 14 December, TAP

Air Portugal threatened to suspend its weekly flight to São Tomé from 13 January, if government would not undertake the necessary repair work on the damaged runway of the local airport. Later that month, Taiwan donated $ 900,000 for these repairs.

On 8 July, the South African Falcon Group announced that it would construct a $ 350 m tourist project at Lagoa Azul. The ambitious project includes a quay for cruise liners, an 18-hole golf course, a conference centre and a hotel with a health spa. Local director of Falcon is Alércio Costa, a former soldier in the South African Buffalo Battalion who in July 2003 had been one of the leaders of the military coup in São Tomé.

On 12 July, Prime Minister Vera Cruz laid the cornerstone for a $ 10 m free trade zone at São Tomé's airport, a project of the 'Sociedade de Desenvolvimento de São Tomé' comprising two Portuguese construction companies.

Gerhard Seibert

VI. Eastern Africa

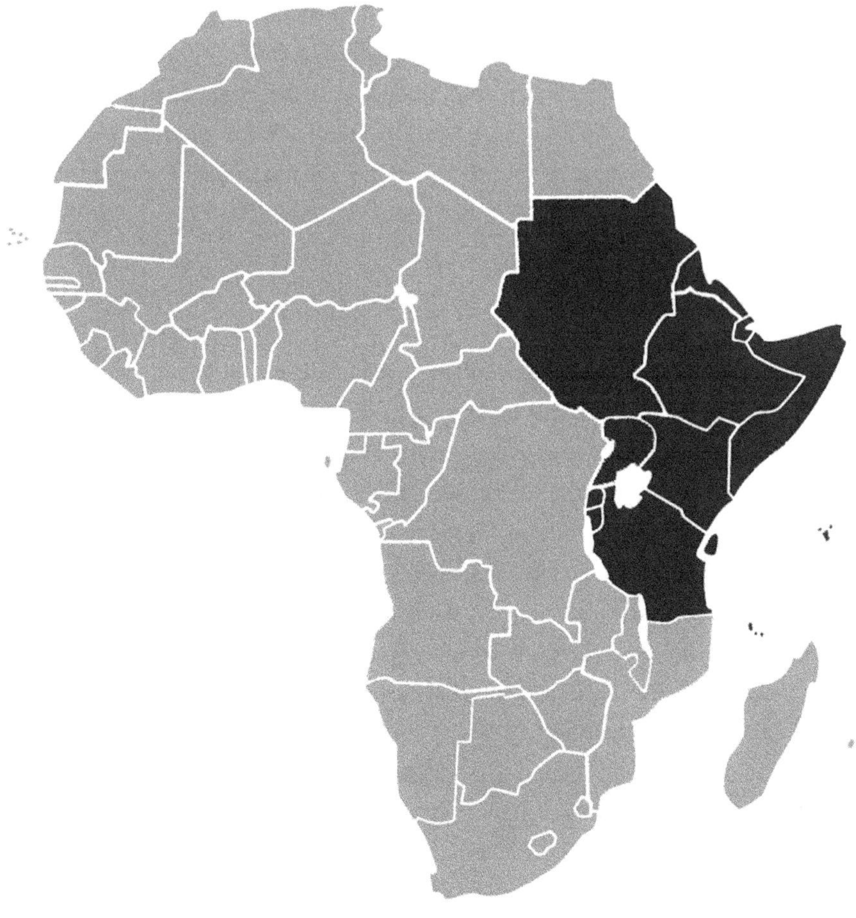

Substantial parts of the sub-region continued to be characterised by the armed conflicts and belligerent confrontations that had already been in evidence for years (Darfur region of Sudan, northern Uganda, Somalia, Eritrea-Ethiopia), but no new theatres of open conflict emerged during the year. Burundi and southern Sudan experienced a somewhat shaky consolidation and reconstruction under peaceful conditions that had been brought about only in 2005 after long years of conflict. Important national elections were held in Uganda and in the small island nations of Comoros and Seychelles. In Tanzania, a new president established his imprint on an exceptionally stable political environment. In Djibouti, Eritrea, Ethiopia, Kenya and Rwanda the domestic political scene remained largely unchanged. The year ended with renewed heavy fighting and the incursion of Ethiopian troops into Somalia.

Continuing from the previous year, large parts of the sub-region, both in the Horn of Africa and in the core of East Africa, suffered from the effects of severe drought during the first half of the year. This raised fears of partial famine among particularly vulnerable social groups and necessitated appeals for food aid from external sources, but also entailed prolonged power shortages with negative effects for the economies.

All countries of the sub-region managed to achieve positive, although mostly modest macroeconomic growth rates. Sudan and Ethiopia were the outstanding performers, with GDP growth rates above 10%; Kenya and Tanzania were just slightly above the sub-Saharan average of 5.7%; and all the other countries did not measure up to this yardstick. Burundi and Rwanda were admitted as new members of EAC.

Political Developments

The **Sudan** continued to attract much international media attention as a result of the unrestrained armed conflict and civilian tragedy in its western Darfur provinces, already into a fourth consecutive year without any sign of a lasting peace agreement. Temporary hopes for an end to the humanitarian suffering raised by the signing of a peace agreement in May, after protracted rounds of negotiations under international mediation, were almost immediately dashed when it became clear that not all the relevant groups had signed the agreement and that it had hardly any noticeable effect on the unabated violence on the ground. The situation degenerated into an increasingly fragmented pattern, with various local leaders and groups, offshoots of the original rebel movements, pursuing their own narrow interests without any clearly identifiable political objectives. The AU monitoring force of 7,000 soldiers remained too small and too poorly equipped to be able to protect the civilian population fully and to prevent many ongoing atrocities, while the Khartoum government successfully blocked moves for larger international intervention under UN auspices. At the same time, some further difficult progress was made with the establishment of new administrative structures by the semi-autonomous government in southern Sudan that had been created in 2005 upon the conclusion of the comprehensive peace accord. While in this formerly war-torn part of the country difficult reconstruction slowly got under way, President al-Bashir's national government felt sufficiently secure to resist outside pressures to take concrete steps against the perpetrators of the massive human rights violations in Darfur.

The domestic scene in **Ethiopia** was still largely influenced by the aftermath of controversial 2005 elections and the ensuing confrontation between government and different opposition parties and civil society groups. The state authorities continued to exert their power in a highly authoritarian fashion, and there were no signs of possible national reconciliation or of a softening of political repression. Despite a prevailing atmosphere of clearly discernible tension, the government of Prime Minister Meles Zenawi had the upper hand and appeared to be in no danger of losing control. Some international criticism of government for civil and human rights violations was raised, but generally only in a rather restrained fashion, since Ethiopia was widely perceived by Western governments as a pillar of stability in a region threatened by potential Islamist terrorism. The continued intransigence in the border conflict with Eritrea and the active military involvement in Somalia at the end of the year rather boosted the government's popularity at home.

In **Eritrea**, there were no signs of change or of improvement in the repressive political situation. Any hopes for gradual democratisation remained as elusive as ever. The entire society was subjected to the military exigencies of the autocratic leadership. No open political dissent was possible and many young people opted to leave the country. Internationally, Eritrea remained rather isolated and insistent in its confrontation with Ethiopia.

In **Djibouti**, the ruling party of President Ismail Guelleh won a landslide victory in controversial local and regional elections in March and thus secured full political control of all administrative levels of the country. There were, however, some signs of a possible resurgence of ethnic confrontations and of limited activities by armed rebel groups. Attempts to mediate in the difficult conflict processes in Somalia did not prove successful.

The already extremely precarious situation in **Somalia**, which had been without a recognised national government since the fall of the Barre regime in 1991, underwent a few more unexpected twists and a return of open war at year's end. The transitional federal institutions (parliament and government) created in 2004 in Kenya were only able to relocate to Somali soil in February, when they established themselves in Baidoa. Although recognised internationally, they had barely any effective grip on the country and certainly not on Mogadishu, which was still controlled by a number of competing warlords and their clan factions in different sections of the city. With American backing, in February these faction leaders formed a coalition against the growing influence of armed religious leaders joined in a network of Islamic courts. After months of fighting, the Islamic courts gained full control of the city in June and eventually of large parts of southern Somalia, forcing the factional leaders to retreat to a few remaining strongholds. The victory of the Islamic courts brought a period of relative security and tranquillity for the civilian population, but uncertainty over the degree of enforced Islamist orientation of all aspects of life. Western observers, but also Ethiopia, saw the strength of the Islamist forces as a threat for the entire sub-region, while the transitional government initially tried to reach a peaceful agreement with the Islamic courts. When this proved to be unrealistic and the Islamic courts further expanded their zone of influence, Ethiopian troops (with tacit American support) started a massive military intervention in late December, ejected the Islamic courts from Mogadishu and thus enabled the transitional government to take control of the city for the first time. This sudden turn of events once again left Somalia faced with turmoil and an uncertain future. The authorities of **Somaliland** insisted on keeping out of all these conflicts and maintained their claim for international recognition as a sovereign independent state. Despite some tensions between the president and his government on the one hand and the opposition-controlled parliament on the other, the political climate remained pragmatic and largely cooperative.

Presidential elections in **Seychelles** confirmed the incumbent President Michel and the political domination of a party that has been ruling the country for almost 30 years, while the relatively well established opposition managed to make no further gains. In **Comoros**, the election of a new president, Abdallah Sambi from Anjouan island, was seen as a test of the fragile unity of this island nation, with its three semi-autonomous island governments and with a constitutionally stipulated rotating presidency. The installation of an Islamic cleric as president brought a new leadership style, but did not help to overcome the deep-rooted mistrust and confrontations between the Union and the separate island authorities.

Kenya experienced another year full of political speculation and of intricate manoeuvres by the leading political actors and their parties and factions. Despite a crushing government defeat in a constitutional referendum in late 2005 and the subsequent break-up of the then ruling coalition, President Kibaki managed relatively easily to maintain a functioning government with support from different political camps. This was possible given the situation in parliament where the conventional order of government and opposition had become rather blurred: strict party loyalties had been significantly eroded amid attempts to forge new political coalitions ahead of the crucial next elections, scheduled for December 2007. The situation remained extremely fluid throughout the year and the shape of the most likely future political alliances remained unclear. No substantial progress was made in the long-debated issue of changing the constitution. Despite the constant flurry of political excitement, political life took place within the existing institutional space without recourse to unconstitutional means.

In **Tanzania**, a new president, Jakaya Kikwete, took office after a landslide victory for himself and the ruling 'Chama cha Mapinduzi' (CCM) party in the December 2005 elections. This was confirmation of Tanzania's extraordinary political stability and further prolonged CCM rule, dating back uninterruptedly to independence in 1961. Kikwete introduced a new popular leadership style, but there were hardly any substantial changes and the political opposition remained quite weak. **Zanzibar**, with its semi-autonomous political status, had a relatively unproblematic year with less open political antagonism and confrontation between CCM and the opposition than in most previous years, despite continued disagreement over the validity of the controversial 2005 elections.

Uganda held its first multiparty elections in many years in February, after the long ban on unrestricted party activities under the so-called 'movement system' had finally been lifted in the previous year and a constitutional referendum permitted President Museveni to run again for another term. The run-up to the elections was marred by some obstructions for the campaign activities of the opposition parties, but the conduct of the elections was judged by most observers to have been largely proper. Museveni was convincingly re-elected, albeit by a reduced margin, and his NRM party secured a comfortable majority in parliament, thus allowing them practically uninhibited continuation of their 20-year rule. In August, a formal ceasefire agreement was reached to end the long rebel war in the north, but the subsequent peace negotiations dragged on until the end of the year without achieving a lasting agreement. Nevertheless, armed hostilities practically ceased in the northern areas, which had for many years been greatly affected by the war. A slow return to normality now appeared possible.

The domestic situation in **Rwanda** remained largely unchanged, with the government in full control and hardly challenged by a weak civil society or any substantial opposition forces. This lack of political pluralism was, however, beginning to be viewed more critically by some parts of the international community, which had for years been extremely supportive of reconstruction efforts after the 1994 genocide. A major focus during the year was the implementation of far-reaching local government reforms. The government refrained from intervention in the DR Congo during its crucial election year, and after years of waiting Rwanda was admitted as a new member of the EAC.

In **Burundi**, the new government, democratically legitimised by the 2005 elections, was faced with the extremely difficult task of reconciling a partly divided society after long years of civil war and of reconstructing the shattered economy. The first year of the post-transition period was, however, largely characterised by high-handedness on the part of the government and the ruling party vis-à-vis the political opposition and civil society groups, raising concerns about the beginnings of a new authoritarianism. At the same time, major cracks within the inner circles of the new power elite began to emerge. With the help of external African mediation, a ceasefire agreement with the last remaining rebel group was concluded, but negotiations for a comprehensive peace agreement dragged on beyond the end of the year. Burundi was also formally admitted to the EAC.

In the widely used, although not undisputed judgment of **Freedom House**, with its worldwide assessment of political rights and civil liberties, there were very few changes in the sub-region during 2006. Most country ratings remained the same, the only exceptions being Comoros, whose index for political rights was raised to category 3 (out of 7), and Burundi (lowered to 4) and Somalia (lowered to 7). While no sub-regional country was listed in the top category as 'free', four countries (Somalia, Sudan, Eritrea and Rwanda) remained in the 'not free' category. Even from an overall global perspective, Somalia, Sudan and Eritrea belonged to the group of worst rated countries. Another eight sub-regional countries (plus Somaliland) were considered 'partly free', i.e., in the intermediate category, with both political and civil liberties in the range of 3–5 index points, with Kenya and Seychelles ranking highest, followed by Comoros and Tanzania.

The Corruption Perceptions Index of **Transparency International** for 2006 also revealed wide discrepancies between the countries of the sub-region. Among the 163 countries listed (Comoros, Djibouti and Somalia were not covered), Seychelles again easily achieved the top position, ranking 63 and scoring 3.6 points (out of 10), but nevertheless indicating some slippage, while Sudan was listed near the bottom in rank 156 with only 2.0 points. The remaining countries were grouped with most other African countries with scores between 2.9 and 2.2 points: Eritrea and Tanzania (jointly ranked 93), Uganda (105), Rwanda (121), Burundi and Ethiopia (130) and Kenya (142).

Another valuable comparative yardstick is the degree of press freedom as regularly assessed by **Reporters Without Borders**. In its 2006 Press Freedom Index, 168 countries were listed with scores ranging between 0.5 and 109, again indicating a very broad spectrum for the countries of the sub-region. Eritrea was again considered by far the worst offender against freedom of the media and ranked 166 with a 97.5 score, followed relatively closely by Ethiopia (rank 160), Somalia (144) and Sudan (139). Tanzania (rank 88, score 19.8), Comoros (rank 93) and Seychelles (95) obtained the best marks for the degree of press freedom permitted, with the remaining countries occupying intermediate ranks with scores in the 30–41 range: Uganda (rank 116), Kenya (118), Djibouti (121), Burundi (125) and Rwanda (128). In comparison to 2005, the most discernible slippage in the ranking was experienced in Ethiopia, Burundi, Uganda and Seychelles.

A similar ranking system to assess the general **human rights situation** in different countries is impossible, since this comprises a fairly wide range of different phenomena and cannot easily be compressed into a quantitative scale. However, based on the regular reporting of Amnesty International, Human Rights Watch and other NGOs it was patently obvious that the worst politically motivated offences against human rights during 2006 occurred once again in Sudan, Eritrea, Ethiopia and Somalia, i.e., in the larger Horn of Africa area. Serious human rights violations were also recorded in all the other sub-regional countries, but not on the same scale and were often connected to uncontrolled brutal interventions by state security agents and deplorable prison conditions. Moreover, they either related to very specific issues or were largely confined to limited territorial areas (e.g., northern Uganda).

Transnational Relations and Conflict Configurations

The precarious domestic situation in the **Sudan** continued to have important direct or indirect implications for all neighbouring countries. Ever since the outbreak of rebel activities in Darfur in 2003, there had been strong and very evident repercussions for the eastern parts of **Chad**, the result of close inter-ethnic linkages across the border, the influx of large number of Sudanese refugees into the neighbouring territory and the need to mount substantial international humanitarian relief operations in their support. There had all along been pointed accusations by both sides of active interference in each other's political affairs, specifically the alleged support of rebels by either side and permission for them to operate across the border. This state of affairs escalated further during the year with the deteriorating internal situation on both sides, and in November the Chadian government declared it was in a state of war with Sudan. In a new development, northeastern parts of the **Central African Republic** were also drawn into the Darfur conflict with cross-border refugee and rebel movements.

The establishment of the autonomous government of **Southern Sudan**, on the other hand, contributed significantly to the initiation of a process that was expected to bring an end to the longstanding rebel war in northern **Uganda**, although no conclusive agreements were reached by year's end. The movements of the rebel Lord's Resistance Army (LRA) on Sudanese territory had been severely curtailed, and LRA was forced to partially retreat into the **DR Congo** and the **Central African Republic**. With the mediation of the southern Sudanese government, a protracted round of negotiations between the LRA and the Ugandan government got under way in Juba.

Sudanese relations with **Eritrea** improved considerably after years of tension due to the reciprocal support given to each other's internal opposition groups. Eritrea helped to mediate in the process that led to a peace agreement between the Khartoum government and the Eastern Front opposition active in the border region with Eritrea.

No tangible progress was made towards a mutually acceptable solution for the border conflict between **Eritrea** and **Ethiopia**. There were a number of isolated skirmishes along the border, but no resumption of major armed hostilities, as was intermittently feared as a result of the exchange of belligerent statements by both sides and the added confrontation over the situation in **Somalia**.

This volatile situation created a new element of insecurity with potentially far-reaching implications for large parts of the entire sub-region, and drew in practically all neighbouring states in one way or another. Several observers expressed fears about the danger of igniting a conflict with much wider sub-regional implications and even interference by outside forces. During the first half of the year, the transitional federal institutions were at last relocated to Baidoa in Somalia, while a new US-supported alliance of clan faction leaders engaged in heavy fighting with militia forces of the Union of Islamic Courts (UIC) for control of Mogadishu. The latter's victory in June brought some months of relative peace to the city, but international obsession with the UIC's feared extremist Islamist orientation and alleged inclination to terrorism, as well as the confrontation with the transitional institutions, provoked a military invasion by **Ethiopia** (with US backing) in December. The defeated UIC forces retreated from Mogadishu, but were helped by **Eritrea**. A plan discussed earlier to deploy an IGAD peacekeeping contingent from neighbouring countries did not materialise. **Djibouti** tried without discernible success to mediate between the warring Somalian groups, while the **Somaliland** authorities by and large managed to keep their country out of the new Somalian turmoil, which was left absolutely open-ended at year's end.

Inter-state relations in the **Great Lakes region** proved much less confrontational than they had been for years, while all attention was focused on the outcome of crucial elections and anticipated new political arrangements in the **DR Congo**. Both **Rwanda** and **Uganda** largely refrained from active interference in the Congolese electoral contest and did not openly prop up proxy forces in adjacent Congolese provinces as they had previously done. The three countries, plus **Burundi**, under their 'tripartite plus' grouping continued to cooperate in the search for common solutions aimed at defusing the precarious situation of insurgencies and armed militias in the entire Great Lakes region. Although some progress was made, the rebel groups hostile to the Kigali and Kampala governments that had long been present in the eastern DR Congo could not be neutralised and remained at least a nuisance factor. Bilateral relations between Rwanda and Uganda, strained for several years, also improved considerably, with Uganda actively supporting Rwanda's and Burundi's long-awaited admission to the EAC.

The 2nd **international conference on the Great Lakes Region** was held in Nairobi on 14 and 15 December, one year later than originally scheduled, as a follow-up to the first summit in Dar es Salaam in November 2004. At a number of preparatory technical meetings and a 3rd inter-ministerial meeting on 20–22 February in Bangui, the ground was prepared to create a permanent institutional structure for the ambitious task of tackling the intertwined issues of peace, security, democracy and development in the vast sub-region, made up of 11 core member countries plus another six co-opted countries. In order to stabilise peaceful development of the sub-region, it was decided to establish a secretariat in Bujumbura under the direction of Tanzanian diplomat Liberata Mulamula; to set up national coordinating committees in all member states; to institutionalise regular ministerial and parliamentary meetings; and to initiate concrete programmes with the assistance of international donors. The conference culminated in the signing of a regional security, stability and development pact, accompanied by a fund expected to amount to $ 2 bn.

In 2005 and 2006, **Tanzania** was a non-permanent member of the **UN Security Council** and tried as best it could to focus that forum's attention on the particular problems of the sub-region, specifically during its tenure in the presidency in January.

UN peacekeeping activities in the sub-region again presented a mixed picture of successes and failures. In **Burundi**, the 'Opération des Nations Unies au Burundi' (ONUB) had played a significant role in the successful political transition process, allowing it to be gradually reduced during 2006 and closed down by December. The new UN Peace Building Commission, on the other hand, selected Burundi as one of its first two countries for special post-conflict support. The UN Mission in **Ethiopia** and **Eritrea** (UNMEE) again experienced a complete lack of progress in the resolution of the border conflict between the two countries, and the continued enmity of the Eritrean authorities necessitated an extension of its mandate beyond the end of the year. The UN Mission in **Sudan** (UNMIS) continued to monitor the implementation of the peace process in southern Sudan without any outstanding obstacles, but it still had to struggle against the constant bureaucratic hurdles on the part of the central government in Khartoum. In contrast, no progress was possible in the deployment of UN peacekeeping forces to **Darfur**, given the staunch resistance of Khartoum and the continued lack of united determination among the members of the UN Security Council. A Security Council resolution in August called for the deployment of 20,800 UN peacekeepers to Darfur, but its implementation proved impossible. During the prior deliberations, some thought had even been given to extending the mandate to the war-affected areas of Chad and the Central African Republic. However, no concrete activities eventuated.

In the absence of a UN mission, the **AU Mission to Sudan** (AMIS) continued with its very limited resources to have at least some influence in containing the violence against the civilian population in Darfur by different militia and rebel groups. AMIS, with a strength of 7,000 peacekeepers, remained severely underfinanced and underequipped in relation to its enormous task. Intermittently, it appeared that AMIS would have to be terminated without replacement, but its mandate was then extended into 2007 after more international funding had been mobilised. Discussions about mounting a combined hybrid peacekeeping operation by the AU and UN also met with stiff resistance from the Khartoum government and came to naught.

Despite earlier discussions, no AU or IGAD peacekeeping missions were set up during the year to contain the escalation of military confrontation and general violence in Somalia. A relatively small AU Mission for the Security of the Elections in the Comoros (AMISEC), deployed for two months, helped to provide a safe environment for crucial elections in that conflict-ridden country.

In 2005, the **International Criminal Court (ICC)** had commenced investigations into the leading perpetrators of violence and human rights violations in Darfur, but it was still unable to collect enough hard evidence to start prosecutions against and issue arrest warrants for specific individuals. These difficulties prompted some international criticism of the ICC's practical limitations. The Darfur investigations were the first such case opened against the will of the country concerned. In the Ugandan case, the ICC warrants issued in 2005 against five leaders of the LRA rebel movement became a major stumbling block in the protracted peace negotiations between the government and the LRA, since the implicated leaders did not want to surrender without the lifting of these warrants, a course of action clearly beyond the government's competence.

The **International Court of Justice (ICJ)** ruled on 3 February that it had no jurisdiction in an application filed by the DR Congo in May 2002 regarding Rwandan armed activities on the territory of the Congo. This was a reference to Rwanda's invasion of the Congo and the looting of local resources during the second Congo war, which started in 1998. In a similar case, the ICJ had in December 2005 ruled against Uganda and ordered payment of reparations.

The sub-region continued to be more severely burdened by the problem of **refugees** and **IDPs** than almost any other part of the world. Based on UNHCR assessments for the end of 2006, Sudan had by far the highest number of IDPs (estimated at almost 5 m), due to the dual conflicts in the south and in Darfur. However, IDPs were also much in evidence in Uganda (with 1.1 m remaining, while 500,000 had already returned home) and in Somalia (400,000). Tanzania still hosted by far the greatest refugee population, an estimated total of about 680,000 (registered and unregistered). In response to the new post-conflict situations in Burundi and DR Congo, substantial repatriation exercises were begun, but refugees were likely to remain a heavy burden for some time to come. Kenya (270,000) and Uganda (260,000) were also hosting very substantial numbers of refugees, while an estimated 240,000 people from Darfur had taken refuge in Chad.

Socioeconomic Developments

The countries in the sub-region showed rather divergent, modestly satisfactory **macro-economic performance**, although in most cases this was still not strong enough to achieve a substantial breakthrough in overcoming structural poverty and kick-starting a sustainable growth pattern. Only two countries achieved a markedly higher **GDP growth rate** than the average of 5.7% for the whole of sub-Saharan Africa (according to preliminary 2006 figures in the IMF's World Economic Outlook of April 2007). Ethiopia had a third exceptionally good year, with 10.6% growth despite continued drought problems for the agricultural sector, and Sudan achieved a record 12.2% growth as a result of its booming oil sector. Kenya (6%), Tanzania (5.9%) and Uganda (5.4%) all performed relatively close to the sub-Saharan average, but somewhat below earlier expectations and below their recently achieved rates (except for Kenya). Burundi (5.1%) experienced a noticeable recovery in its first post-conflict year, and Seychelles (4.5%) earned the fruits of a firm reform orientation after years of stagnation. Djibouti (4.5%) had its highest growth in many years, while Rwanda (4.2%) was faced with an unexpected slowdown. By far the most disappointing results were those for Eritrea (2%) and Comoros (1.2%), in both cases at least partly the result of unresolved political issues.

Most countries continued their cautious monetary policies and thus contained **inflation** at comparatively modest levels, markedly lower than had long been the case in earlier periods. Only Eritrea (17.3%), Kenya (14.1%) and Ethiopia (12.3%) had inflation rates beyond the 10% threshold, whereas Seychelles even experienced a decline in consumer prices by 0.5%. The remaining countries had average price increases of between 3% and 7%.

All countries of the sub-region had a negative **balance of payments on current account** (including grants) in excess of the relatively low sub-Saharan average of -1.3% of GDP (due to substantial surpluses of major oil and mineral exporters). The largest deficits (as a percentage of GDP) were recorded in Seychelles (-23%), Sudan (-14.5%, despite its oil revenues), Burundi (-13.6%) and Ethiopia (-11.6%), and the smallest in Eritrea (-2.1%) and Kenya (-3.3%).

There were also extremely wide variations in the capacities of countries to raise **government revenue** domestically for executing state functions. The ratio of government revenue (excluding grants) as a percentage of GDP (sub-Saharan average 26.2%) fluctuated between extremes of 50.9% for Seychelles and only 13.2% for Tanzania and Uganda, with the rest in an intermediate range between 14.2% (Comoros) and 28.3% (Eritrea).

The UNDP's 2006 **Human Development Index** (based on 2004 data) also pointed out clearly the wide variations existing between countries in the sub-region. Only Seychelles was included in the high human development category and ranked number 47 (out of a total of 177 countries). Comoros (ranked 132), Sudan (141) and Uganda (145) appeared in the lower portion of the medium category, with index values somewhat above the sub-Saharan average, while all other countries remained in the low human development category, with Burundi and Ethiopia almost at the bottom, with ranks 169 and 170.

In continuation from 2005, large parts of the sub-region (the four countries of the Horn of Africa plus northern and eastern parts of Kenya and some areas in Tanzania) were still strongly affected by exceptional **drought conditions** during the first half of the year, triggering temporary problems of famine for particularly vulnerable groups in various localities. Despite the well-known problem of delay in mobilising special relief efforts by national governments, international agencies and NGOs and only a limited international response, the situation was by and large contained without major humanitarian catastrophe. **Heavy floods** in the latter part of the year in Ethiopia and parts of Kenya and Somalia caused substantial destruction and again necessitated relief activities.

Except for Sudan, with its booming oil sector, and Tanzania, which had for years been attracting substantial mining investments (mainly for gold), the sub-region had so far not been able to benefit much from growing global demand for **mineral resources**. Many new exploratory activities (particularly for oil and natural gas) were, however, undertaken throughout the sub-region (e.g., Ethiopia, Uganda, Tanzania, Seychelles) amid high expectations of early progress into the production stage.

Sub-regional Cooperation and Sub-regional Organisations

EAC, despite some unavoidable friction and delay over specific issues, by and large made good progress towards consolidating and expanding its ambitious longer-term goals. A key event on 30 November was the long-pending admission of **Burundi** and **Rwanda** as **new members**, expected to become effective on 1 July 2007 after the signing of an accession treaty and ratification by the parliaments of the two countries.

The presidents of the three EAC countries met twice on 5 April and 30 November in Arusha for the 7th and 8th regular **EAC summits**, and were on the latter occasion joined by the presidents of Burundi, Rwanda and Zanzibar. In April, in compliance with the rotation principle, ambassador Juma Mwapachu from Tanzania was appointed the new secretary-general, with Julius Onen (Uganda) as deputy for finance and administration and Beatrice Kiraso (Uganda) in the new post of deputy specifically charged with pursuing the political federation, while Kipyego Cheluget (Kenya) remained the deputy for projects and programmes. It was noted that all three countries had in the meantime appointed ministers specifically responsible for EAC affairs as a measure to improve the day-to-day functioning of the community. Progress on the technical verification exercises regarding Burundi's and Rwanda's applications was reviewed, but a widely expected formal decision was again postponed. As part of a generally satisfactory review of various ongoing projects and programmes, the East African Development Bank was directed to undertake a reorganisation to enable it to become a lead agency in further economic integration and development. The concept of fast-tracking East African integration and of pursuing a political federation was again reiterated. This was to be accompanied by a wide-ranging consultation process with the general population, a process that was simultaneously started with a fanfare on 13 October by all three presidents. It was expected to last six months and to come up with recommendations and an understanding of public opinion on the issue. Mwapachu stressed the need for re-branding EAC in the eyes of the public.

The November summit finally approved the admission to EAC of the small francophone neighbouring countries Burundi and Rwanda, but a number of technical and formal issues remained to be solved before the entry could become fully effective. Both countries had already participated as observers in some activities and had been subjected to a technical verification process. Special arrangements for a gradual adjustment to long-established East African procedures and habits still needed to be thrashed out, presenting the old EAC partners with a considerable challenge. The summit further approved the 3rd EAC development strategy for the period 2006–10, a staff expansion in the secretariat and salary increases as of January 2007. Under consideration was the creation of a new development fund for financing regional infrastructure projects and the elevation of the status of the East African Business Council to that of accepted EAC institution.

Considerable confusion arose in regard to the expected swearing-in of new members of the **East African Legislative Assembly (EALA)**, after the five-year mandate of the initial group had lapsed on 29 November. While the nine members from Tanzania and Uganda had been duly elected by their national parliaments (in accordance with the relative strengths of parties), in the Kenyan case they had, as a result of the volatile situation in the Kenyan parliament, been appointed by the political parties. In response to an injunction by a Kenyan MP, the **East African Court of Justice (EACJ)** had ruled this procedure illegal, thus preventing the swearing-in of all new EALA members and delaying this into 2007, when a legally acceptable solution was expected to be found. This infuriated the presidents, who were not ready to accept the curtailment of their national sovereignty. Assembled for an **extraordinary EAC summit** on 14 December in Nairobi (on the sidelines of the Great Lakes conference), they agreed to amend the EAC treaty by creating a new East African court of appeal, by allowing national courts to override the EACJ and by permitting the recall of EACJ judges by the presidents, the supreme EAC organ. This move, which had no parliamentary approval, was heavily criticised by the Law Society of Kenya and other legal spokespersons, and an injunction was sought in the Kenyan high court. No solution to the legal wrangle was in sight by year's end.

Some disputes continued about the regulations of the **EAC customs union** since its start in 2005. In November, Uganda was eventually granted a temporary waiver on the application of the agreed common external tariff on a range of imported inputs deemed essential for local industries, after specific concessions had also been made to Kenya and Tanzania.

The **overlapping membership** of the partner states in other sub-regional organisations (Tanzania in SADC, Kenya and Uganda in COMESA) with plans to move to higher forms of economic integration continued to present a confusing scenario, since simultaneous membership in two customs unions is not possible. No immediate political solution was, however, in sight. The problem also complicated the protracted negotiations with the EU on the formalisation of **Economic Partnership Agreements (EPAs)**. These were still expected to come into force in 2008, although not much tangible progress had been made for the sub-regional Eastern and Southern Africa (ESA) configuration under the technical coordination of the COMESA secretariat.

In a number of ministerial and summit meetings, **IGAD** was largely preoccupied with the unfolding Somalia crisis, repeatedly urging genuine dialogue among the different feuding groups, but essentially to no practical avail. The possible deployment of an IGAD peace support mission to Somalia, first mooted in 2005 as a measure to assist the Transitional Federal Government (TFG) created under the aegis of IGAD, was again discussed by the 11th summit on 20 March and an extraordinary summit on 5 September in Nairobi, but in the end did not materialise. This underscored IGAD's continuing institutional weakness, with only a limited range of concrete activities and deep-seated animosities between several of its members.

While IGAD had initially been coordinating the establishment of the **Eastern Africa Standby Brigade (EASBRIG)**, one of five sub-regional components of the AU's envisaged African Standby Force, a meeting of defence ministers from the 11 participating countries on 26 April in Nairobi confirmed the institutionalisation of an independent EASBRIG coordination mechanism and the selection of Addis Ababa as headquarters, and of Nairobi as seat of the secretariat for the planning elements. Tanzania had chosen to join the SADCBRIG for southern Africa.

COMESA held its 11th summit on 15–16 November in Djibouti, reiterating the plan to create a customs union for its 19 member countries by December 2008. Meanwhile, the existing FTA had been joined during the year by Comoros and Libya (bringing its membership to 13). It was decided to relocate the Trade and Development Bank (formerly PTA Bank) from its longstanding temporary premises in Nairobi to Bujumbura in early 2007. Angola had practically withdrawn from COMESA, but without giving formal notice of ending its membership.

The 22nd council of ministers meeting of the **Indian Ocean Commission (IOC)** was held on 16–17 March in Antananarivo. The rotating presidency for the following year was passed from Madagascar to the foreign minister of Mauritius and the secretariat's annual budget was raised by 13% to € 365,000. The 6th council of ministers meeting of the **Indian Ocean Rim Association for Regional Cooperation (IOR-ARC)** in its regular two-year cycle was convened in Teheran (Iran) on 21–22 February, and focused on the promotion of trade and investment, maritime cooperation and the establishment of early warning systems.

Technical preparations for reviving the **'Communauté Economique des Pays des Grands Lacs' (CEPGL)** of Burundi, Rwanda and DR Congo continued with particular support from the EU's development commissioner, Louis Michel, but a formal ministerial re-launch was postponed until early 2007. This revival of institutional cooperation with Kinshasa would provide a francophone counterweight to Burundi's and Rwanda's closer integration into the anglophone EAC.

Representatives from all ten riparian states of the Nile river basin met as part of the **Nile Basin Initiative (NBI)** from 3–6 May in Bujumbura for the 14th council of water ministers and a series of technical and donor meetings. After years of acrimonious exchanges about the validity of colonial-era treaties (from 1929 and 1959), which required Egyptian approval for any water utilisation by other countries, and in response to stronger demands from East African politicians, some progress was made towards agreement on their repeal and replacement by a new treaty. However, a formal conclusion remained elusive. The rapid fall in Lake Victoria's water level and fears about overuse of its water resources underscored the urgency of finding new cooperative solutions.

Rolf Hofmeier

Burundi

Burundi's new government led by the 'Conseil National pour la Défense de la Démocratie-Forces pour la Défense de la Démocratie' (CNDD-FDD) was faced with a Sisyphean task in 2006, namely reconstructing a country whose physical, economic and social infrastructure had been destroyed by 12 years of civil war, with limited resources and against a backdrop of ongoing conflict with the **last remaining rebel movement**, the 'Parti pour la libération de Hutu-Forces Nationales de Libération' (Palipehutu-FNL). In the **post-transition period**, however, the country's democratisation process was marred by political gaffes and abuses by the new government and the ruling party, raising fears of a reversal towards authoritarianism. The erstwhile rebel movement often governed in a high-handed and populist manner, coming under fire from the media, civil society and the opposition. The regime's authoritarian drift and high levels of corruption were also a source of friction with the international community.

Domestic Politics

The Burundian political landscape was dominated by the consolidation of the CNDD-FDD's electoral feat and by tensions within the ruling party on the one hand, and between the government and the opposition parties, private media and civil society on the other. The

CNDD-FDD made **far-reaching personnel changes** in state institutions to equilibrate the existing ethnic imbalance in order to gratify party militants and to capitalise on electoral gains. CNDD-FDD members replaced 'Front pour la Démocratie au Burundi' (FRODEBU) and 'Union pour le Progrès National' (UPRONA) directors of state companies, directors-general of ministries and heads of diplomatic missions. Many of the new appointees were ill-equipped for technocratic work, unsurprisingly given the CNDD-FDD's brief experience in the transitional administration. The executive and legislative branches were dominated by the CNDD-FDD and the judiciary was closely tied to the executive, which replaced judges of the supreme and constitutional courts with CNDD-FDD adherents. Furthermore, the CNDD-FDD co-opted members of other political parties, who were motivated by the 'politics of the belly' rather than political conviction. In July, five elected FRODEBU local administrators were dismissed by the CNDD-FDD governors of Bujumbura-Rural and Bujumbura Mairie (in breach of the communal law) and were replaced by CNDD-FDD administrators.

CNDD-FDD's leading figures further **abused the party's dominant position** in the state for individual enrichment, leading to cracks in the ruling party. The party chairman, Hussein Radjabu, was accused of meddling in the executive and of sidelining President Nkurunziza, increasingly perceived as the former's puppet. In April, CNDD-FDD parliamentarian Matthias Basabose implicated leading figures of the ruling party and government officials in embezzlement, corruption and rent-seeking activities in the allocation of public tenders. Basabose admitted to receiving a 120 m Burundian franc (FBu) bribe for his party for a tender. His parliamentary immunity was lifted on 4 May and a judicial inquiry was launched into his involvement in fraud. On 17 May, Radjabu recalled second Vice-President Alice Nzomukunda to Burundi from an official visit to Belgium, because she had accused him of corruption to World Bank officials in Washington.

Despite the president's proclaimed tough stance on corruption and the adoption of an anti-corruption law in January, the **criminalisation of the Burundian state** risked setting in. In February, the marketing of sugar was given to seven CNDD-FDD members (among them four parliamentarians). Burundian businesspeople complained that contracts for key products were awarded to party supporters without opening tenders. The sale of the presidential plane in June at $ 2 m lower than the price offered by the highest bidder, left room for speculation over shady dealings by Finance Minister Dieudonné Ngowembina and Radjabu, who were handling the sale. On 8 July, the 'Observatoire de Lutte contre la Corruption et les Malversations Économiques' (OLUCOME) reported 400 cases of public procurement fraud. No parliamentary commissions of inquiry probed the cases of corruption, as all eight parliamentary commissions were headed by CNDD-FDD parliamentarians.

Electoral antagonisms continued in 2006; 'winners' and 'losers', particularly within the Hutu political family, emerged. The two political parties that had led the political transition between 2001 and 2005, the Hutu-dominated FRODEBU and the Tutsi-dominated UPRONA were represented in the government. Their position changed significantly in the **post-transition period** and they wavered between their role as government coalition parties and as opposition parties. The 'Conseil National pour la Défense de la Démocratie' (CNDD) (the original rebel movement led by Léonard Nyangoma) had been excluded from government and constituted the main opposition party. Historical politico-ethnic competition declined because of military integration and CNDD-FDD anti-ethnic discourse. The Tutsi political class lost control of the army and was considerably weakened. Nevertheless, small Tutsi parties, the 'Mouvement pour la Réhabilitation du Citoyen' (MRC)-Rurenzangemero and the 'Parti pour la Redressement National' (PARENA), were content with their inclusion in the executive, while many Tutsi individuals were at ease in the ruling party.

FRODEBU's main electoral success in 2005 was in Bujumbura-Rural, the stronghold of the Palipehutu-FNL. During the elections, the CNDD-FDD had accused FRODEBU of connivance with the rebels. During much of 2006, security forces harassed FRODEBU members on suspicion of their being FNL supporters and party meetings were obstructed in the western provinces, where FNL activity continued. FRODEBU saw this as a CNDD-FDD attempt to weaken it. It pressed for greater representation in the government, demanding five rather than the appointed three ministers in the cabinet, in proportion to its representation in the National Assembly. In March, FRODEBU **withdrew from the government**, officially entering the opposition. UPRONA also showed signs of frustration with its under-representation in the executive (it held one instead of the two due ministerial posts) and with insufficient participation in government decision-making. Nevertheless, it remained outside the official opposition. The CNDD consistently scrutinised the CNDD-FDD's governance and was quick to point out slips. In so doing, it became a chief government target: public meetings were hampered, Nyangoma and CNDD Secretary-General William Mumyembabazi were harassed by security forces, and in August Nyangoma was **stripped of parliamentary immunity**. CNDD members were apparently bought off by the ruling party to subvert the leadership, culminating in a sham party congress that suspended the directors' committee. In September, the CNDD headquarters in Bujumbura were ransacked by the 'Police Nationale' (PN) and were shut down.

The principal political parties were weighed down by **internal conflicts**. UPRONA was ostensibly divided between supporters of the (Hutu) champion of Tutsi rights, Charles Mukasi, and those of Aloys Rubaka, who demonstrated a conciliatory approach towards CNDD-FDD. The latter was elected president of the party at its January congress, a result Mukasi rejected. FRODEBU's withdrawal from government was both an outcome and cause of internal factiousness. In 2005, FRODEBU's former president, Jean Minani, had gained ministerial positions for his supporters and drifted closer to the CNDD-FDD at the expense of a party bloc led by the president of the transition, Domitien Ndayizeye, and Léonce Ngendakumana. Ngendakumana assumed the party's presidency but failed to unify the two groups. The three FRODEBU ministers were instructed to resign, but refused and were sacked from the party amid protest from 14 parliamentarians led by Minani. A significant number of FRODEBU MPs did not generally follow the party line in voting, and three disrespected a joint boycott between FRODEBU, UPRONA and the CNDD of much of the second parliamentary session, in protest against the adoption of an anti-corruption brigade.

The **private media** and **civil society** assumed functions of a democratic opposition and reported critically on government activity, mismanagement and unconstitutional acts. The government thus developed an uneasy relationship with civil society and chose a mix of reticence and suppression of criticism. Basic **civil liberties were curbed**: journalists and civil society activists were frequently harassed and arrested. Journalists who attended a press conference by Basabose on 17 April were detained for hours by the PN, some were beaten and their recordings seized. Journalist Aloys Kabura was arrested on 31 May for 'insulting public authorities' over comments on government corruption in a local tavern. On 16 August, OLUCOME President Gabriel Rufyiri was arrested for voicing similar criticism. Activist Térence Nahimana was arrested on 15 May on charges of 'threatening state security', after deploring the government's intentional delays in negotiations with the Palipehutu-FNL and for the stalemate in transitional justice talks. This was symptomatic of a broad mistrust by the former rebels (particularly the uneducated) of intellectuals.

On 6 March, the government announced that it had uncovered a **coup plot** by three high-ranking 'Forces de Défense Nationales' (FDN) officers, three PN officers and three politicians, but no evidence was provided. On 1 August, the government claimed that a conspiracy to assassinate the president and to 'destabilise the democratic institutions' had been thwarted. Alain Mugabarabona, president of the 'Forces Nationales de Libération' (FNL)-Incanzo, was arrested on 31 July. He provided a list of 'co-conspirators', leading to a string of arrests without following correct legal procedures: vice president of the transition Alphonse-Marie Kadege of UPRONA, Déo Niyonzima of the 'Parti pour la Reconciliation du Peuple' (PRP), and ex-Forces Armées Burundaises (FAB) Colonel Damien Ndarisigaranye and Popon Mudugu, members of the Tutsi association 'AC-Génocide Cirimoso'. Kadege's and Niyonzima's lawyer, Isidore Rufikyiri, was arrested, following his inquiries into his clients' medical condition. Finally, former President Ndayizeye's senatorial immunity was lifted and he was arrested on 21 August. FRODEBU spokesman Pancrace Cimpaye, who was in Tanzania, and Ndayizeye's former chief of protocol, Isaïe Simbare, who went into hiding, escaped arrest.

The government claimed it possessed recorded telephone conversations of the plotters. Yet the case relied on the confession of Mugabarabona, who rescinded his confession in an interview with three radio stations from his prison cell on 24 August, stating that it was made under duress. Mugabarabona claimed that he was given a list with names of people to incriminate, including Alice Nzomukunda and the minister of defence during the transition, Vincent Niyungeko. The preventive detention period of the suspected plotters expired on 22 September. The supreme court ordered their release on 6 October but the attorney-general blocked this. The supreme court then prolonged their detention in a new ruling. At year's end, seven of the detainees remained in custody. The government also clamped down on journalists who questioned the conspiracy's authenticity. The opposition denounced the coup claims as a ploy to eliminate opposition and Nyangoma, also fearing arrest, went into hiding.

The conspiracy allegations threw the government into disarray. On 4 August, the minister for national solidarity, human rights and gender, Françoise Ngendahayo, told the press that three of the detainees had been tortured, while the government spokesman, Ramadhani Karenga, refuted her claims. The defence minister, General Germain Niyoyankana, also departed from the government line, asserting that the military intelligence services had no evidence to support the plot allegations. Radjabu was generally pinpointed as concocting the plot allegations. According to some observers, this was a manoeuvre to take full control of the CNDD-FDD, enmesh it with the state and press on with a de facto single party state. The second vice-president resigned on 6 September, protesting government abuse of the law, graft and lack of separation of government powers. Nzomukunda was irregularly replaced (the senatorial confirmation vote fell short of the quorum) by Radjabu ally Marina Barampama. Nzomukunda reproved Radjabu's de facto role of head of state and in a press conference with Basabose in Brussels on 26 October, the two CNDD-FDD dissidents claimed that a 'parallel [to the state] power base', dubbed the '**Radjabu system**', was being established.

The coup plot appeared to be a fabrication. Some of the alleged would-be plotters were disgruntled with CNDD-FDD abuses. But the 'co-conspirators' came from extreme poles of the Burundian ethno-political spectrum during the post-1993 troubles (e.g., Niyonzima was a Tutsi youth militia member, while Mugabarabona was an ex-Palipehutu-FNL member) and during the transition (Ndayizeye had sacked Kadege in November 2004 as a result of disagreements over the constitution). While the CNDD-FDD was on its guard, possibly fearing a repetition of 1993, the structure of the FDN (50% ex-FAB, 50% ex-belligerent forces) served as a safeguard against partisan involvement by the new army.

The strength of the CNDD-FDD was its **proximity to the rural population**, with which the party was at ease. As President Nkurunziza indicated in his address to the National Assembly in December, the government reached a rapprochement between the leadership and the population. Nkurunziza visited 12 communes throughout the year and each government member spent at least two days per week in the countryside listening to the people. Whereas in the past, politics centred on the capital Bujumbura, the CNDD-FDD took politics across Burundi. However, this was widely criticised in political and diplomatic circles, which attributed government ineffectiveness and inaction to distraction by populist trips.

Burundi was engaged in an **armed conflict** between Agathon Rwasa's Palipehutu-FNL and the government forces. The FNL stretched the conflict out of its traditional areas of attack (Bujumbura-Rural and Bubanza) into Bujumbura Mairie and Cibitoke and the government stepped up its military campaign in response. The civilian population was trapped between the two forces, both committing crimes against it. In June, **peace negotiations** began in Dar es Salaam between the government and the FNL, while fighting continued. In an 'agreement of principles' signed on 18 June, the government offered the FNL limited amnesty and the right to exist as a political party, should a ceasefire follow. The negotiations subsequently stumbled over FNL demands to dissolve and restructure the FDN and PN, reducing the Tutsi quota. The government rejected this, as it would sap the power-sharing agreement on which the new politico-military status quo is based, and would remove the safeguard to the Tutsi minority of equal representation in the army, a cornerstone of ethnic reconciliation. A **comprehensive ceasefire agreement** was concluded on 7 September, notwithstanding. Its implementation was delayed, however, because the FNL demanded the release of its head of military and intelligence operations, Jean-Berchmans Ndayishimiye, captured in July by the FDN.

Though significant progress was made in **security sector reform**, challenges remained. Cohesion among the fused elements of ex-government and ex-belligerent forces in the FDN and the PN was reinforced. The FDN officer corps remained Tutsi-dominated, but Hutu were receiving military and academic training in order to assume higher ranks. The former adversaries also received training in collaborative decision-making and team-building. Despite the Arusha Agreement's stipulation for a human rights-based security sector reform, agents of the **intelligence services** – the 'Documentation Nationale', renamed 'Service National des Renseignements' (SNR) – FDN, PN officers and civilian informers (often demobilised ex-FDD) were responsible for **human rights abuses**, mainly in the context of the conflict with the FNL. The SNR was responsible for arbitrary arrests (800 cases were reported), abductions, summary executions, beatings and torture of FNL rebels and suspected civilian collaborators. SNR personnel also tortured three of the suspected coup plotters, who were forced to sign confessions. According to Niyonzima, this was with the knowledge of the SNR administrator, ex-FDD General Nshimirimana, and his deputy, ex-FAB Colonel Kiziba, who were nominated by and were required to report directly to the president. PN officers and FDN soldiers also committed common crimes. Such crimes were in part due to weaknesses in command and control (some remained attached to their wartime leaders), a mind-set hardened to excessive use of force, impunity and low pay. The 'Opérations des Nations Unies au Burundi' (ONUB) gave basic training to FDN and PN officers in human rights practices, while in July the government doubled FDN wages, which may have contributed to fewer cases of FDN exaction and theft against civilians. Nevertheless, the security forces had not yet internalised civilian protection and their professionalism was wanting.

The **demobilisation process for ex-combatants** was almost concluded, with some 5,000 remaining. Demobilised ex-combatants received reinsertion cash benefits. The 'Commission Nationale du Démobilisation, Réinsertion et Réintégration' (CNDRR) assisted some in finding employment and engaging in income-generating activities. However, long-term reintegration assistance was generally problematic and demobilised ex-combatants engaged in banditry and sexual violence in rural areas. **Civilian disarmament** was another unsettled issue. By October, the 'gardiens de la paix' and the 'militants combattants' (civilian militias) were dismantled. But small arms and ammunition circulating freely among the civilian population remained a grave security concern. Between July and September, scores of people were killed and wounded in Bujumbura in grenade attacks. The government launched a civilian disarmament campaign to address the issue on 13 April, requiring civilians to register arms in their possession for government collection. Because of persistent insecurity and pending the disarmament, demobilisation and reintegration of FNL, public response was limited.

In the domain of **justice**, some positive steps were made in addressing human rights abuses. An SNR civilian informer was arrested in August over killings in Kinama in northern Bujumbura. In September, the head of the Muyinga branch of the SNR and two military officers were arrested and charged with participating in the disappearance and possible summary execution of 31 people in the province. These arrests notwithstanding, most cases of human rights abuse were not investigated, general **accountability was lacking** and **impunity** endured.

A first round of negotiations on the question of justice for past crimes began in March between the Burundian government and the UN office of the legal advisor. The talks centred on the establishment of a national **Truth and Reconciliation Commission** (TRC) and a **special tribunal for Burundi**. The neutrality and independence of the two mechanisms; principles of immunity; and amnesty for genocide, crimes against humanity and war crimes were sticking points in the negotiations. Due to the gap between the idealist position calling for accountability for past crimes (held by the UN and Burundian civil society) and the realist position favouring stability (held by most existing political formations, given their role in crimes committed in Burundi), no transitional justice mechanisms were installed.

An ad hoc commission that had been set up in November 2005 identified 4,000 **'political prisoners'**. On 3 January, a presidential decree ordered the release of 'political prisoners' who had been imprisoned for more than two years without charge and those who had served a quarter of their sentence, and gave them **provisional immunity**. The 3,614 released prisoners would be answerable to the TRC and judged again by the special tribunal. The decision aimed at bolstering inter-ethnic reconciliation and decongesting overcrowded prisons. Nevertheless, the decree sparked an extensive debate over the lack of transparency in the commission's work and its criteria for identifying those prisoners. While

FRODEBU and CNDD took a positive view of the prisoners' release, UPRONA opposed it, claiming that it did not recognise that genocide had taken place against the Tutsi. Three civic associations maintained that the prisoners' release was unconstitutional and on 9 May filed a petition against the government in the constitutional court, but were overruled.

The reintegration and resettlement of **refugees and IDPs** remained a challenge for the government. Many returning refugees and IDPs found their land occupied by others and their livestock stolen, exacerbating conflicts. On 31 August, the president launched a **national land commission** to resolve land-related issues. Some 120,000 IDPs remained in 160 camps, which assumed certain features of permanent towns and villages. By late November, just over 38,000 refugees had been repatriated of a targeted 50,000. This was attributed to lack of infrastructure, continued insecurity, food insecurity and an upsurge in human rights abuses. However, large-scale voluntary repatriation was anticipated following the implementation of the ceasefire agreement between the government and FNL.

Foreign Affairs

Burundi received $ 126 m in **foreign aid** from multilateral and bilateral donors. While $ 168 m was pledged for the year at a conference held in Bujumbura on 28 February, the donor community became sceptical about engagement with Burundi because of high levels of corruption and mismanagement. The World Bank did not disburse its second tranche of budgetary support to the government, insisting on an independent audit of the bidding procedure for the sale of the presidential plane. In June, the EU representative in Burundi exposed the misappropriation of an estimated € 5 m of aid by administration officials. In view of aid conditionality by Western donors, the government sought alternative sources of financing and cooperation, turning to oil-rich Muslim countries, namely the Sudan, Saudi Arabia and Libya. However, these countries' potential influence on Burundi amplified Western donor scepticism. Burundi joined the EAC on 30 November, which increased its trade and investment prospects.

The government's poor record on human rights and its unsubstantiated coup allegations strained relations between the government and ONUB, international NGOs, the EU and the Belgian government. The government was suspicious of international human rights organisations, which pleaded with donors to tie aid to respect for human rights and the rule of law. The ONUB human rights unit constantly tried to monitor security force actions and to keep government on track with its democratic obligations. On 29 August, the government asked the UN to recall the ONUB head, Nureldin Satti, after he described the political and security situation in Burundi as 'catastrophic' to diplomats in Bujumbura (which the UN declined). The EU presidency warned the government of its impatience with the deteriorating political and human rights situation, while the Belgian foreign minister signalled that the Burundian democratisation process was threatened.

In January, the government asked for the **withdrawal of ONUB**. This was completed on 31 December. The 'Bureau Intégré des Nations Unies au Burundi' (BINUB) would take over UN activities in Burundi on 1 January 2007. Burundi was one of two countries chosen in June to benefit from the new UN Peacebuilding Commission.

Uganda, South Africa and Tanzania remained engaged in the **regional peace initiative for Burundi**. South African Minister of Public Security Charles Nqakula facilitated the peace talks between the government and the FNL and played a significant role, together with President Mbeki, in prodding both sides into signing the ceasefire. The regional peace initiative and AU delegates formed a joint verification and monitoring mechanism (JVMM) with the Burundian government and FNL to oversee the implementation of the ceasefire. The mechanism was supported by 1,500 South African troops redeployed from ONUB to the AU.

In December, the alleged coup plot became a source of friction between Burundi on the one hand and Rwanda and Uganda on the other. A Burundian government source cited the Rwandan chief of general staff, General James Kabarebe, and the Ugandan president's brother, Salim Saleh, as accomplices of the Burundian conspirators, aiming to destabilise Burundi and use it as a rear-base to infiltrate the DR Congo to bolster Congolese rebel Laurent Nkunda's rebellion. Relations with the **Rwandan government**, however, remained cordial. Rwanda and Burundi formed technical subcommittees of the Tripartite Plus Joint Commission (also comprising the DR Congo and Uganda) on closer military cooperation to dismantle 'Forces Démocratiques de Libération du Rwanda' (FDLR) and FNL rebels active in the DR Congo, on refugee issues and on asylum seekers. Hussein Radjabu confirmed Rwando-Burundian ties after the publication of a report by French Judge Louis Bruguière incriminating Rwandan President Paul Kagame and nine top officials of shooting down the plane carrying the former Rwandan and Burundian presidents in April 1994. Burundi agreed to represent Rwandan interests in France after Rwanda severed ties with that country.

Socioeconomic Developments

Poverty remained widespread. Burundi ranked among the ten countries with the lowest HDI. Moreover, 68% of its population lived below the international poverty line of $ 1 (purchasing power parity) per head. On the other hand, Burundi was on track to implement its first PRSP. It thus received highly indebted poor country assistance. Further, Burundi profited from the PRGF.

In 2006, inflation fell significantly. Yet unfavourable weather decreased gross agricultural production by 1% compared to 2005, possibly affecting the 6% growth target. In 2006 (season A), drought resulted in food shortages, estimated to have affected 1.5 m people, mostly in the northern provinces. Seasons B and C were adequate and partly made up for the loss. Nonetheless, the majority (65%) of the Burundian population survived on less than 2,100 Kcal per person, the minimum standard of daily calorie intake. Chronic malnutrition was widespread and estimated at 43%. Even a good harvest in 2007 would not compensate for food deficits.

The IMF envisages a major role for the private sector that should be attracted by a better investment climate and by privatisation policies for public enterprises. This was a major action point in the third and fourth reviews of its 2006 PRGF programme. In the agricultural sector, IMF recommendations stressed the importance of increasing productivity by focusing on the efficient use of arable land and improved techniques. The crops identified by Burundian authorities as most favourable for growth were coffee, tea, cotton, sugar and palm oil. According to IMF estimates, the resulting primary growth would spill over into non-agricultural growth, specifically 0.7% for each 1% of primary growth, due to increased demand in the off-farm sector (mostly services).

Another major issue was **whether primary growth would be pro-poor**. The 2006 policy documents departed from the observation that over 80% of the labour force depended on agricultural revenues. The majority of small-scale farmers faced institutional barriers, such as a lack of purchasing power, credit and insurance mechanisms against setbacks, which prevented them from investing in more profitable activities.

Other action points were public service delivery to guarantee primary health care and education. The Burundian government had announced free primary education in August 2005 and free health care for children under five and pregnant women in May 2006. However, the budgetary challenge to meet these objectives remained. Public health expenditure represented 0.7% of GDP – among the lowest in the world – and education expenditure represented 5.2% of GDP, which is comparable to Uganda but not enough to sustain free primary education, since primary school enrolment doubled.

Marina Rafti & An Ansoms

Comoros

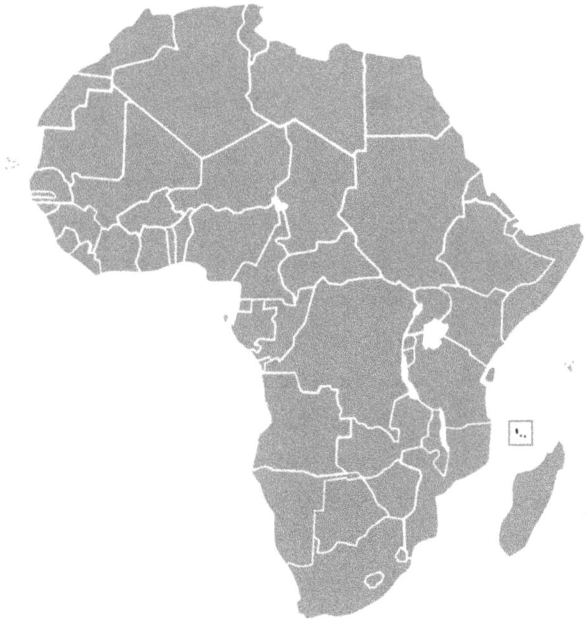

Presidential elections in April and May resulted in the installation of **Ahmed Abdallah Sambi** from Anjouan island in the highest office, in compliance with the constitutional requirement that the presidency rotate among the three semi-autonomous islands of the 'Union des Comores' (Comorian Union). The peaceful elections and hand-over of power provided initial hope of an end to almost a decade of political crisis and disunity. However, fundamental disagreements over the respective competencies of the Union and island authorities soon re-emerged and continued to threaten the delicate unity of the country. External mediators and donors remained sceptical about a genuine return to normality and the economy remained depressed.

Domestic Politics

The scheduled presidential elections were seen as the first major test of adherence by all political players to the complex 2001 federal constitution. Contrary to widespread speculation, President **Azali Assoumani** (from the main island **Ngazidja/Grande Comore**) and his followers did not attempt to interfere with the laid-down procedures and the schedule for electing a new Union president from **Anjouan**, the second-largest island, whose attempted secession in 1997 had precipitated the crisis. As a first step, the Anjouanese electors (117,000) had to choose three front-runners from among 13 candidates in **primary elections** on 16 April. These front-runners would become the candidates in the subsequent national electoral contest on 14 May. The favourite was Caabi Elyachroutu, who had held many top political positions and had resigned as vice-president on 27 February to run as an independent, to avoid being seen as a candidate of Assoumani's 'Convention pour le Renouveau des Comores' (CRC) party. CRC support was thus split and officially given to Ibrahim Halidi, also a former prime minister. Other strong contenders were Mohamed Djaanfari, a Union MP, and Sambi, a businessman and cleric, nicknamed 'Ayatollah' because of his past as a student of Islamic theology in Iran. There was a 55% voter turnout. Elyachroutu won only 9.6% of the votes and was eliminated, with Sambi (23.7%), Djaanfari (13.1%) and Halidi (10.4%) qualifying for the next round. Elyachroutu complained of some irregularities, but the constitutional court confirmed the results. An AU mission (AMISEC), with 462 soldiers and policemen, mostly from South Africa and also funded from there, was deployed throughout April and May to ensure the safety of both elections.

The **national elections**, contested by the three remaining candidates, each with two vice-presidential running mates from the other two islands, resulted in a **clear victory** for 48-year-old **Sambi**, with 58% of the votes, as against 28.3% for Halidi and 13.7% for Djaanfari. The conduct of the elections, with a 57% turnout, was adjudged by several external observer groups (mainly AU and Francophonie) to have been generally free and fair and was validated by the constitutional court without controversy on 20 May. Much had been made during the campaign, particularly by outside observers, of Sambi's alleged Islamist orientation, but he had clearly proved to be the most popular candidate by far, particularly among the youth and women. He had been co-founder in 1990 of the 'Front National pour la Justice' (FNJ), a party advocating adherence to Islamic virtues, had become an MP in 1996, was then accused of supporting Anjouanese separatism and had become a businessman after leaving politics. In his first official announcements, Sambi made it clear that he considered himself a moderate Islamist, but that he had no intention of turning the country into an Islamist state, since the society was clearly not ready for such a move. Sambi's election was, nevertheless, an important turning point in Comorian political history: he was himself formerly a secessionist from Anjouan, and the Assoumani regime that had initially usurped power in a military putsch in 1999 had been brought to an end. Expectations were high that these circumstances would allow for a return to more consensual national political affairs, particularly in view of the fact that all three island presidents had advised their followers to vote for Sambi.

Immediately after his inauguration (26 May), Sambi nominated a new and considerably smaller **government** of eight ministers (including two vice-presidents with ministerial portfolios, one a woman) as compared to 13 before, and also a smaller personal advisory staff ('cabinet'). Most of the appointees were middle-aged technocrats, in contrast to the traditional seasoned politicians that had long dominated the political landscape. The particularly delicate responsibility for the military was not given to a minister, but to Sambi's trusted 'directeur de cabinet'.

Sambi moved quickly to announce publicly the priorities of his intended **green** (i.e., Islamic) **revolution** in running the country. The focus was on an enhanced fight against corruption, more attention to social spending, efforts to ensure the functioning of schools (threatened by teachers' strikes arising from several months of unpaid salaries), better consultation with local leaders and notables and the reassertion of Union institutions on Anjouan. On 10 August, a government conclave of the most senior leaders (but boycotted by Ngazidja authorities) was convened to discuss the priorities for an action plan. In early June, 36 senior officials and ministers from the previous administration were ordered not to leave the country, in the expectation of investigations for corruption. In July, some of these persons were remanded in custody. **Tensions** soon developed **between the new leadership and the entrenched bureaucracy** of the old elite on Ngazidja. A rapid flurry of new appointments in the civil service, judiciary, parastatal entities and the diplomatic staff also created frictions with the island presidents, who saw their own turf being encroached upon and referred some of these cases to the constitutional court. On 16 June, a new chief of staff (from Mohéli island) of the 'Armée National de Développement' (AND) was appointed. His priority was to ensure the unity of the military and its presence on Anjouan. On 17 September, five judges were suspended for releasing several government officials charged with corruption. This action in turn led to protests from the syndicate of magistrates.

Sambi held **national day celebrations** on 6 July on all three islands consecutively, along with military parades. On Anjouan, this constituted the first presence of the AND and the singing of the national anthem since 1997. However, it soon became apparent that Sambi's authority on Anjouan was still extremely tenuous, when island authorities on 3 August again celebrated the 1997 secession and on several occasions turned back Union officials.

A **major conflict** arose on 26 August when the Union government awarded a 15-year management contract for the ports of Moroni (Ngazidja) and Mutsamudu (Anjouan) to a company from the United Arab Emirates without consulting the island authorities and after revoking existing concessions. This provoked sharp protests from both island governments and brought the question of island/Union jurisdictional competencies into focus.

At the root of this unresolved conflict was the long delay in agreeing on the so-called **organic laws**, discussed at length in 2005 but blocked and never signed by Assoumani. Sambi finally promulgated these laws on 7 September after another two-week round of tough negotiations between Union and island representatives. The laws are meant to specify the respective competencies mainly in the areas of homeland security, the judiciary, management of parastatals, health care and social policies. Sambi repeatedly denied any intention of centralising power and insisted that henceforward responsibility for any shortcomings in their areas of competency would rest squarely with the island authorities. The island presidents were to be responsible for local security forces (with restrictions on heavy weapons, to prevent the emergence of parallel armies), the appointment of tribunal judges (with a supreme court at Union level), running schools and health facilities (except hospitals) and appointing island managers of parastatal companies (with national directors being appointed by a joint national board). This complicated compromise was intended to overcome the deep-rooted distrust between the key players that had not fundamentally changed after the handover from Assoumani to Sambi, who insisted on defending the country's unity against parochial island interests.

Tension escalated again in mid-December when drawn-out negotiations over the concrete implementation of the organic laws (specifically regarding security and the types of weapons allowed) were broken off and the island presidents declared a definitive rupture in the dialogue with Sambi. On 23 December, Sambi landed on **Anjouan** in defiance of a ban by island President **Mohamed Bacar** and two days later held a public meeting in Mutsamudu, at which he stressed the authority of the Union and accused Bacar of renewed separatism and of preventing any AND presence on the island. On 30 December, a small regional AND unit was officially installed, while conflict still simmered over an AND arms shipment that had been seized by the Anjouan gendarmerie on the grounds of an alleged putsch against the Bacar regime. The year thus ended with a recurrence of heightened tension.

This may have been partly attributable to uncertainties and political posturing ahead of the **next elections** for the **island presidents** due in **April 2007**. It was not yet clear whether the current presidents intended to run again, and there was speculation about many other possible candidates. On **Ngazidja**, President **Abdou Soule Elbak** had reshuffled his government on 15 July, retaining only three incumbents in a nine-member cabinet, with the clear intention of displaying new vigour. In December, the first-ever municipal elections since independence were held on Ngazidja. On **Mohéli**, a motion to censure President **Mohamed Said Fazul** in late October was defeated, but it did show the dissatisfaction with the socioeconomic conditions and alleged extent of corruption.

Foreign Affairs

During his last months in office, **Assoumani** took time off for **extensive travels** abroad: in January to the AU summit in Khartoum, in February/March on a long trip to the US, Italy (FAO), Togo and Senegal; and at the end of March to Tanzania (to sign a bilateral trade agreement). Representatives of the island presidents, using forged travel documents, tried unsuccessfully to present a position to the AU that contrasted with Assoumani's. In March, the US ambassador reiterated continuing American concerns about the allegedly unrestricted movements of Mohamed Abdallah Fazul, a key suspect in the 1998 terrorist attacks on US embassies in Kenya and Tanzania. Similar fears were later expressed about the apparent strengthening of general Islamist tendencies in the country.

Sambi quickly showed a penchant for activating external contacts and expressed his intention to undertake many trips abroad with the aim of attracting foreign investors. Not surprisingly, the first initiatives indicated a discernible (but by no means exclusive) shift towards the **Middle East**. On 18 August, a visiting delegation from **Iran** signed a cooperation agreement (covering agriculture, education and defence), followed in November by a memorandum of understanding (covering fisheries and industry, among other matters). After attending his first AU summit in Gambia, Sambi undertook an extended foreign tour (Libya, UN general assembly, Francophonie summit in Romania) in September, then visited Saudi Arabia in October (obtaining a $ 5 m grant for his high-priority habitat project) and China in November. A Sudanese delegation in August and substantial investor interests from Kuwait were further indicators of his preferred orientation.

Nevertheless, the traditionally close links with **France** continued to be very important. A visit by the French cooperation minister, Brigitte Girardin (26–27 November), resulted in a new partnership agreement entailing a grant of € 88 m for the 2006–10 period. This was a major step after a seven-year interruption (in reaction to the 1999 putsch) and the initial resumption of the mixed Franco-Comorian commission in 2005. The delicate question of the status of **Mayotte** (the fourth Comorian island administered as part of France) was, however, left unresolved. The government cautiously expressed its resolve to uphold the claim for the eventual reintegration of Mayotte into the Comorian state and to raise the issue again in the 2007 UN general assembly, but without jeopardising cordial relations with France. As a symbolic gesture, 12 November (commemorating the accession of Comoros to the UN in 1975) was declared a national Mahorais holiday.

The **international community** that had been engaged in the difficult national reconciliation process over the last few years (primarily represented by the AU, Francophonie and EU) remained apprehensive about the continued political distrust, despite the installation of a new government. The long-serving special AU representative, Francesco Madeira (from Mozambique), warned that the international community would not support the country indefinitely. Donors were keen to see the achievement of a socioeconomic environment that would allow the substantial aid pledges that had been made at the donor conference in December 2005 to flow. The government repeatedly singled out praise for France, China and Saudi Arabia as by far the most important providers of aid.

The **accession** of Comoros to the **FTA** of **COMESA**, originally scheduled for January, took effect after some delay in July, although the potential benefits of this move were not altogether clear.

Socioeconomic Developments

Mainly as a result of political uncertainties and pre-election laxness, but also of low world-market vanilla prices and of meagre tourism receipts, the country experienced a general **economic slowdown** and a sharp **deterioration in public finances** during the first half of 2006. Although the new government started introducing important remedial measures, the overall result for the year was still expected to be disappointing (1.2% GDP growth; budget deficit inclusive of external grants 0.3% of GDP; huge negative balance of trade with an import-export ratio of only 7%, down from 12% in 2005). Membership in the franc zone provided a stabilising anchor, containing the inflation rate to 3.8%. Despite this dismal performance, the comparative standing of the country was still relatively good (ranked 132nd in the HDI with a per capita income in 2004 of $ 623 and of $ 1,943 in PPP terms). However, 45% of the population was estimated to be below the national poverty line of $ 700, with significant variations among islands (Anjouan was worst affected due to years of isolation).

The 2006 Union **budget** (expected expenditure $ 85.2 m, with 31% externally financed) was passed in early January, but was immediately called into question by external advisors as unrealistic. During the first half, fiscal revenue declined by 13% because of pre-election governance problems and was expected to reach 4.2% of GDP for the full year. In conjunction with a supplementary budget in August, the government introduced an improved inter-island **revenue-sharing mechanism**. All government revenues were to go into a single account at the central bank, which would retain 25.6% for external debt service and for pension payments, while the remainder was shared among the four governments (Union 37.5%, Ngazidja 27.4%, Anjouan 25.7%, Mohéli 9.4%). The IMF expected this mechanism to function much better than had been the case up to now.

The economy continued to be highly dependant on **remittances** (estimated to account for 18% of GDP and more than half of all imports) from the **diaspora** and on external aid inflows to counterbalance the increased and extremely high trade deficit (estimated exports of $ 11.9 m as against imports $ 92.5 m). Only this level of remittances, the highest in Africa, kept the current account deficit at a moderate level, while rapid accumulation of **external debt** in recent years has led to substantial arrears to external creditors and an unbearable debt situation well above the general HIPC threshold.

During the year, several **IMF missions** assessed the progress of the **staff monitored programme**, concluded in 2005 and extended in February until December 2006. The reviews revealed a mixed picture, with non-achievement of most original targets, but with signs of gradual economic improvement and of government determination to pursue reforms largely in line with donor-prescribed policies. An interim PRSP (completed in October 2005) was submitted to the World Bank's board on 16 May and will serve as the basis for any future engagements by the IMF and World Bank. However, contrary to earlier expectations, no PRGF was concluded before year's end. This was now expected to occur in 2007, assuming further progress on the agreed SMP targets. The PRGF is a prerequisite for the badly needed inclusion of the Comoros under the enhanced HIPC and multilateral debt relief initiatives.

Rolf Hofmeier

Djibouti

During the year, Djibouti held elections for the communal and regional assemblies. The electoral process and the results prompted serious protests by some opposition parties, posing a threat to the country's domestic political stability. The government continued to play a significant role as mediator in the Somalia conflict, although with little progress, especially after the setback in December when Ethiopia sent troops into Somalia. The year witnessed the launch of the first phase of the port extension project as part of a long-term strategy to enhance economic growth. Cooperation efforts between Djibouti and Ethiopia grew. In the northern districts, armed conflict continued to escalate. In response, the government adopted a severe strategy of clamping down on the militia groups before the situation escalated into full-blown conflict.

Domestic Politics

The political scene was dominated by **local elections and the resurgence of armed conflict** between the Afar-dominated group and the Djibouti army in the northern region. In March, elections for the three communal assemblies in Djibouti city and the five regional assemblies were held, despite the failure of the government to compile an electoral register based on a new national census as a precondition for free and fair elections. The

'Rassemblement Populaire pour le Progrès' (RPP), the dominant partner in the ruling Union for a Presidential Majority (UMP) coalition, won 161 of 204 seats and secured control of eight local assemblies for the next five years. This overwhelming victory gave President Ismail Omar Guelleh almost total power from the national to local spheres, a potentially ominous development that may lead to the undoing of the country's political stability since the signing of the peace agreement in 2001. The **ceasefire agreement signed in 2001** was a compromise between the Isaas and Afars. It stipulated the formation of an alliance between the RPP and 'Front de la Restauration de l'Unité et de la Démocratie' (FRUD). The overwhelming victory of the ruling party led to dissatisfaction within FRUD. This may lead to a weakening of the alliance that is crucial to peace in the country.

In the 2001 peace agreement, the government pledged to improve local democracy, increase decentralisation and introduce an electoral register. However, **the elections** took place without the government having kept these promises or achieved the targets set out in the peace accord, hence the fear of the resurfacing of conflict. The elections were condemned and boycotted by the main opposition alliance 'Union pour l'Alternance Démocratique' (UAD). In contrast to the UAD boycott, independent local alliances contested the elections in two of Djibouti city's districts and two of the regions. The most prominent of these was the Citizens List ('Liste Indépendante Citoyen'), which won 12 seats in the Boulaos commune of Djibouti. The List is led by former RPP figure Idriss Gouled, a nephew of former president Hassan Gouled Aptidon. Gouled criticised the way in which the elections were conducted, citing electoral irregularities.

In May, the government launched an **operation to weaken the growing power of the underground opposition** in Tajurah and Obock in the north. Two thousand troops were reportedly despatched. The operation led to the arrest of up to 50 people. According to government sources, these arrests were of criminals, mostly foreigners, who had attacked the nomads in both districts. However, the Paris-based exile movement 'Alliance Républicaine pour la Démocratie' (ARD) claimed that the arrests targeted their supporters.

The army operation led to a **virtual sealing off of the northern region**, with caravans bringing essential food supplies being turned away. According to ARD, a militant faction that had split from FRUD in 1994, the operation caused major food shortages and the isolation of families. In its public statement, ARD complained that the international community had failed to intercede and curb serious **violations of human rights**, for instance where local communities were denied access to food supplies and elderly people were unjustly imprisoned. ARD asserted that the strategic significance of Djibouti to the US was the reason alleged human rights violations could continue unnoticed by the international community. In June, the US government handed over four newly refurbished vessels to patrol Djibouti's territorial waters. Meanwhile, Amnesty International reported that Djibouti was one of the countries where prisoners were allegedly abducted, held and mistreated by the US in the course of its 'fight against terrorism'. The UAD coalition planned demonstrations during the COMESA heads of state summit that took place in

Djibouti from 6–16 November to highlight the suppression of democratic politics and human rights in the country.

Despite mounting international condemnation, the government took a series of steps to **restrict the activities of independent trade unions and foreign observers**. In February, the International Confederation of Free Trade Unions (ICFTU) published a report on labour standards in Djibouti. On 1 April, the government expelled a joint mission of ICFTU and the 'Federation Internationale des Ligues des Droits de l'Homme' (FIDH). This was followed by the deportation of a diplomat from the International Labour Office. The diplomat had presented the case of a detained trade unionist to the minister of justice. Growing concerns about the failure of the government to uphold international labour laws was only one aspect of the dark human rights situation in a country where **freedom of the press and media was constantly curtailed**. For example, the Radio France Internationale transmissions were cut in January 2005 because of their reporting on the investigation into the killing of a French judge in Djibouti.

Foreign Affairs

In an attempt to increase the country's share of economic activities in the East African region, the government had identified the strengthening of its **relations with its neighbours** as a key component of its strategy. A large share of Djibouti's national income derived from the port services it provided Ethiopia. The government is interested to see these services being extended in the future to other neighbouring countries.

Following the lifting of **Saudi Arabia's** five-year ban on livestock imports from the Horn of Africa region, the government sought to capitalise on the new opportunities, as livestock is traditionally one of the country's main exports. The **government of Somaliland**, however, expressed displeasure at some of the actions of the Djibouti government, such as the statement by a Djibouti government minister publicly crediting his government's diplomatic interactions with Saudi Arabia for the progress that had led to the lifting of the ban. The government of Somaliland viewed such claims with concern, suspecting that neighbouring Djibouti wanted to secure a monopoly for its exports to Saudi Arabia. This disagreement finally led to the expulsion of Somaliland diplomats on 26 December. This was the second time that Djibouti had closed down Somaliland's diplomatic offices since 2000.

Diplomatic **relations with Ethiopia** and Eritrea took a more positive turn. On 9 April, Seyoum Mesfin, the Ethiopian foreign minister, and his Djibouti counterpart, Hawa Ahmed Youssouf, signed a new memorandum of understanding (MoU) designed to enhance the growing ties between both countries. The two governments agreed to work together on infrastructural development as well as on the interconnection of telecommunications and electricity projects. The new MoU is aimed at introducing new procedures and forms of cooperation and to serve as an acceleration mechanism. It was felt that joint initiatives between both countries had suffered to this point from the slow pace of implementation. The

MoU received a boost with the signing of an agreement to connect Djibouti to the Ethiopian grid and with the recent progress on the long-awaited railway line between the two countries, for which a contract was finally awarded to the South African Comazar company.

Djibouti also attempted to repair its **relations with Eritrea**. This was evident from the visit to Eritrea by a Djiboutian delegation that was led by the head of Djibouti's military staff. The visit was followed by a reciprocal visit at ministerial level by the Eritrean minister of defence, who also led a delegation to Djibouti to meet with President Guelleh and members of government to discuss diplomatic relations. The talks also involved enhancing military cooperation.

Djibouti assumed an important role in **sub-regional diplomacy** when it offered to mediate in the conflict between the Transitional Federal Government (TFG) and the Union of Islamic Courts (UIC) in **Somalia**. Guelleh also invited the leaders of Ethiopia and Eritrea to come to the table in an effort to seek an agreed solution for Somalia. The attempted mediation failed with the Ethiopian military intervention in December.

Outside the sub-region, Djibouti maintained its good relations with its established partners, the **US and France**. The French and the Djibouti governments signed a framework partnership in terms of which Paris pledged an additional € 53 m to € 67 m over a five-year period. This aid complemented the loan made by France to the Djibouti army as a result of an agreement signed in 2003. The loan, estimated at € 30 m per year, is to be paid over 10 years. In total, France will give the tiny country € 200 m between 2006 and 2010. The framework partnership document clearly outlined the three main sectors this new aid money would focus on, education, health and infrastructural development. However, the decision by France to issue arrest warrants on 2 October against senior Djibouti government officials alleged to have involved in covering up the murder of the French judge may strain the long-standing alliance between the two countries.

Socioeconomic Developments

Macroeconomic figures on Djibouti are not easily accessible. IMF estimates suggest GDP growth of 4.2%, up from 3.5% in 2005. In an attempt to bring growth to the economy, the government undertook several **infrastructural development** projects aimed at enhancing trade. The expansion of the port in Djibouti continued to be the major enterprise. The first phase of the harbour upgrade, the **Doraleh oil and petroleum terminal**, which will have a capacity of 370,000 km^3, was launched in February. This expansion is envisaged to improve access to the region, especially for Africa's main trading bloc, COMESA.

There was progress on the long awaited **joint railway project** between Ethiopia and Djibouti. The Ethio-Djibouti railway line, until now jointly owned by the two countries, runs for 781 km. The railway construction contract was awarded to the South African company Comazar in March. The line originally handled 240,000 tonnes of freight per year. The privatisation aimed at achieving a higher efficiency thereby increasing this figure to 1.5 m tonnes a year.

These major projects, however, are temporary and therefore had limited impact in stimulating the economy and attracting further investment into the country. After visiting Djibouti in June, a joint delegation of the IMF and World Bank stressed its dissatisfaction with the government's progress in tackling the **budget deficit** and structural economic reform. The revised data for the budget for 2005–06 showed that the budget deficit had grown from Djiboutian franc (Dfr) 6.3 bn ($ 35 m) in 2004 to Dfr 7.3 bn in 2005 and was expected to increase to Dfr 9.3 bn in 2006. Without long-term strategies, the government would fail to bring the country back on a growth path.

A report by the WTO on Djibouti highlighted the main structural constraints facing the country in attracting **Foreign Direct Investment** (FDI). These included weaknesses in the judicial system, lack of transparency in the taxation system and poor infrastructure. The report further singled out the high costs of energy, telecommunications and water as some of the more fundamental challenges to attracting FDI.

Current development projects also faced the challenge of recurrent **drought**. The recent drought and famine phase gripping the Horn of Africa hit Djibouti very hard. It was estimated that between 70,000 and 150,000 people were affected by food shortages in the rural and coastal areas. The famine early warning system operated by USAID upgraded Djibouti's alert status from warning to the highest emergency level. Japan made a direct pledge of $ 700,000. The US contributed $ 1.1 m to Djibouti in an attempt to mitigate the impact of the drought. This was in response to the appeal made to the international community by the UN. However, these contributions fell short of the $ 9 m requested by the government of Djibouti.

The World Bank also announced that an **Industrial Development Abstracts credit** of $ 2 m would be spent on the rehabilitation and recovery of the economic and social assets damaged during the April 2004 floods, improving living conditions in the resettlement zone and supporting employment generation. The current natural challenges have also made the IMF adopt a less stringent approach to dealing with the government's failure to meet some of its commitments to financial reform. Djibouti remains in 148th position on the UN's Human Development Index. According to the latest figures (for 2004) published in the World Bank's 'Global Development Finance', Djibouti's external debt grew strongly for the third consecutive year, by 8.2%, which was 63% higher than in 2001. Although Djibouti's debt-service ratio appears sustainable at 7.5%, payment arrears grew again in 2004. Interest arrears increased to $ 8.7 m, and accumulated principal arrears increased to $ 20.3 m.

Qinisile Delwa

Eritrea

An oppressive political situation and very poor human rights, including the arbitrary arrest of thousands of people, prevailed in the country. There were no steps towards democratisation. The policy of militarisation of the educational system and of state control of the economic sector prevailed, leading to a mass exodus of young people. There was no break in the stalemate in the border conflict with Ethiopia, and both countries engaged in the conflict in Somalia on opposing sides. The humanitarian situation did not improve, while the economy was characterised by a lack of hard currency and a shortage of basic goods and energy.

Domestic Politics

During the year, no major changes in the political system occurred. Since independence, the **People's Front for Democracy and Justice (PFDJ)** has remained the only legitimate party, and no national elections were held. The National Assembly remained defunct for the fourth consecutive year. The **president, Isaias Afeworki**, spent extended periods in the port city of Massawa, from where he conducted state business. It remained unclear if this change of residence was due to health problems or the alleged lack of security for him in the capital city, Asmara. The cabinet met in Massawa from 6 to 8 April. There were no major changes in the cabinet. Mohamed Omer, head of the Middle Eastern desk at the ministry of foreign affairs, was apparently appointed acting **minister of foreign affairs**, but was largely inactive politically. Clearly, foreign affairs continued to be run from the president's office. The same was true of internal affairs. The lack of democratic institutions involved in the legislative process remained unchanged, and the constitution remained unimplemented. The **poor state of the judicial system** persisted. As in previous years, arrests frequently occurred without formal charge and trial, and there was no due legal process. There was a new tendency to release people only on bail, in order to prevent them from leaving the country. The **human rights situation** continued to be extremely worrying. The **PFDJ dissidents** (G15), as well as the journalists of the free press arrested in 2001 remained in custody without being brought to court. There were unconfirmed reports that they were being held in solitary confinement at Eiraeiro, a remote place in the northern Red Sea region, and that three of the journalists and three of the dissidents, namely General Oqbe Abraha, former armed forces chief of staff, Mahmoud Sheriffo, former minister of local government and vice-president, and Saleh Kekya, former minister of transport, had died in detention.

As in 2005, the arrest of **parents whose children failed to report for military service** or had left the country continued. Especially during the summer months, thousands of parents were jailed. They had to forfeit an amount of between Nacfa 50,000 and 100,000 ($ 3,500–$ 7,000) in order to be released. Starting in late October, more than 90 members of the **business community** were arrested, 30 of them for allegedly being involved in illegal money transfers, and the others for importing undeclared goods. Owing to the lack of hard currency, it was difficult to import goods or spare parts. Customs duties were exceptionally high, making contraband trade attractive. Those arrested had to pay fines and part of their savings were confiscated. Some private companies were taken over by military officers without compensation. There were also numerous arrests, related to corruption, involving engineers and contractors accused of bribery, as well as bank and customs employees. Another **wave of arrests** occurred when teachers suspected of facilitating the escape of school children to neighbouring countries were imprisoned. This included some serving at the secondary school centre at the Sawa military training camp.

In spite of the government's efforts to control the borders, the **mass exodus of young people** to evade military conscription and national service continued. The Sudanese authorities forced more than 2,500 Eritreans back home when they were found to be without valid residence status. This happened especially after relations between the Sudanese and the Eritrean governments had improved (see below). Nevertheless, from March to September, 7,148 Eritrean refugees were officially registered in Sudan. The number of those who did not report to Sudanese authorities was estimated to be much higher by refugee organisations, which calculated that each month approximately 700 Eritreans fled their country to Sudan and about 400 to Ethiopia. After a popular state TV news presenter, Temesghen Debessai, did not return from a seminar abroad in early October, nine journalists of the **state media** were temporarily arrested. In mid-December, journalist Aklilu Solomon managed to escape to Ethiopia. He had been arrested in 2003 after he had reported for the Voice of America that parents were mourning the deaths of their children during the Eritrea-Ethiopian war. He had spent 18 months in prison and had been under house arrest since his release. The crew of an Eritrean air force aircraft applied for political asylum in Saudi Arabia on 23 December. There were also defections of several **sports teams** during competitions abroad, even though the government required bonds equivalent to $ 700 for members of such teams before granting them exit visas. During a PFDJ festival held in Australia in December, a famous Eritrean band sent there by the government defected.

The persecution of **members of minority churches** continued, and Eritrea was considered a 'country of particular concern' under the International Religious Freedom Act, according to the US state department's International Religious Freedom Report 2006. Many members of minority churches (evangelical and Pentecostal) remained in detention without formal charge or access to legal counsel. Many of them were pressured to renounce their faith. As in preceding years, Jehovah's Witnesses suffered particularly harsh treatment for refusing to undergo mandatory military service. More than 1,700 Christians of evangelical or Orthodox persuasion were in custody. Some forms of Islam considered 'radical' by the government remained forbidden, as were the activities of foreign Muslim preachers. Generally, **government involvement in religious affairs** remained high. The patriarch of the Orthodox church, Abune Antonios, who was dismissed in August 2005, remained under house arrest. His suspension was officially acknowledged for the first time in February by the minister of information, and he was unofficially replaced by Dioscoros, who was not recognised by the Coptic Orthodox pope in Cairo. The government continued its attempts to control the financial assets of the legal churches (Orthodox, Catholic and Lutheran) and the Muslim institutions, both of which had to declare all their financial resources and real property. From December, all tithes collected by the Orthodox church had to be deposited directly into a government account. Members of both the Orthodox and Catholic clergy above a certain number were no longer exempted military service, but the Catholic church declined to send its pastors to the military. The government confiscated assets of the **Muslim community**. These included areas in Asmara formerly granted to *awqafs* (charity organisations). A member of the department of religious affairs was arrested after protests against this policy. Starting from January, members of the Muslim clergy were arrested for preaching about the socialisation of children (especially girls) according to Quranic rules as this ran counter to the government's strategy of placing the youth in their militarised educational system. Teachers and under-age students at Quranic schools were also arrested in Asmara, Keren and Senafe on suspicion of radical Islamist tendencies. The exact number of those arrested is unknown, but in Keren alone about 90 Muslims were detained during the first months of the year. About 70 persons have remained in custody since November 2005 for opposing the government-appointed mufti.

In the port city of **Massawa**, an area within the historical centre was cleared of residential houses during the summer months for the purpose of building infrastructure connected with the city's free trade zone. The inhabitants were displaced without compensation and were left without shelter during the extremely hot summer. After many of them opted to resettle in Sudan, compensation was provided to some in order to secure their return to Eritrean territory.

The **Eritrean opposition in exile**, the Eritrean Democratic Alliance **(EDA)**, did not play a significant role throughout the year and remained unable to produce a convincing plan of action against the government. The alliance, which consists of 16 member organisations, held a press conference on 28 July addressed by its chairperson, Husein Kelifa, and vice chairperson, Abella Adem, as well as Eritrean Liberation Front-Revolutionary Council (ELF-RC) chairman Weldeyesus Amar. They admitted to the weakness of the EDA in lobbying its case in the international arena. Simultaneously, the **ELF-RC** held its 6th congress, involving 156 delegates, in Addis Ababa, after Sudanese authorities withdrew permission to hold the congress in Khartoum, owing to the improved relations between the Eritrean and Sudanese governments. ELF-RC urged the international community to put as much pressure as possible on the Eritrean regime. A leadership cadre of 33 members was elected. The **Eritrean Democratic Party (EDP)**, formed by former PFDJ dissidents, concluded its 2nd congress in Milan on 29 July. Some changes were made to the party's political programme and constitution, and it elected a leadership group of 25 'parliament members'. Some independent civic organisations continued their activities on a small scale. Generally, the Eritrean diaspora became increasingly disillusioned with government at home. PFDJ fundraising festivals were less well attended than in previous years.

Relations between the **Eritrean government and the UN's Mission to Eritrea and Ethiopia (UNMEE)** remained extremely poor. The government refused to cooperate with the UN secretary-general's acting special representative, Azouz Ennifar, who had replaced Legwaila Joseph Legwaila after he stepped down on 5 April. Restrictions on UNMEE activities, such as the ban on helicopter flights over the Temporary Security Zone (TSZ) remained in place and ground patrols were even further restricted. Starting from 4 May, 11 members of the local staff of UNMEE were arrested for alleged evasion of national duties, but more likely for having assisted persons to leave the country. At the end of the year, five local UNMEE personnel remained in detention. On 25 September, five non-Eritrean UNMEE personnel were declared *persona non grata* for 'involvement in spying activities'. From June, existing travel restrictions on foreigners were tightened, and they now required a travel permit when leaving the capital.

Foreign Affairs

The **conflict with Ethiopia** remained unsettled. While Ethiopia continued to refuse to implement the Ethiopia Eritrea Boundary Commission (EEBC)'s decision, which had determined that the disputed village of Badme belongs to Eritrea, President Isaias declared the border issue as 'settled', thus rejecting involvement in further discussions. On 27 November, the EEBC indicated its willingness to provide assistance by placing boundary markers, but neither party responded to this offer. At the end of the year, **UNMEE** comprised 2,285 personnel (2,004 troops, 56 headquarters staff and 225 military observers). The military situation between the countries remained tense and volatile. In October, over 2,000 Eritrean troops entered the TSZ. Subsequently, on 22 December, further incursions occurred when a force of 350 militia (according to UNMEE, these were more probably regular troops) headed towards Senafe in the centre sector. Near the border town of Tsorona, there were increased activities by armed Eritrean personnel. On the Ethiopian side, an increased military presence, including artillery, could be observed from October in sectors west and centre. There were several exchanges of fire along the border, leading to a number of casualities. On 16 December, an UNMEE patrol was stopped at gunpoint near Adi Quala and temporarily detained by Eritrean militia. The military coordination commission of Eritrea and Ethiopia did not hold its 38th regular meeting because of differences between the parties. In March, the UN Security Council extended UNMEE's mandate for only one month, and again in mid-April for a further month. Consideration was also given by the Security Council to turning UNMEE into an observer mission or to withdrawing it completely. This followed an unsuccessful meeting of both parties in London with the EEBC on 10 March that yielded no concrete result. On 29 September, the Security Council extended UNMEE's mandate until 31 January 2007. According to observers, there was a dangerous stalemate in the peace process with no willingness by any party to break the impasse. This was considered to be a serious source of instability, especially in connection with developments in Somalia.

The **conflict in Somalia** between the Union of Islamic Courts (UIC) and the provisional government could be considered as a proxy-battlefield for Eritrea and Ethiopia. While Ethiopian troops marched into Somalia with US backing to reconstitute the provisional government, Eritrea sided with the UIC. As the Eritrean government strongly opposed Islamist activities in its own country, its support for the UIC could be interpreted as an effort to weaken Ethiopia, albeit with limited success because of the rapid retreat of UIC troops in December following the Ethiopian occupation of Mogadishu in order to reinstate the provisional government in the capital. The exact extent of Eritrean involvement in the Somali conflict remained unclear. It seems plausible that Eritrea supported the UIC with artillery and ammunition sent via Yemen and Djibouti. The government strongly denied the involvement of Eritrean troops in the conflict, but there were indications that about 2,000 Eritrean troops were deployed.

Eritrean relations with the **US** deteriorated further due to both countries' engagement in Somalia on opposing sides. Eritrea blamed the US for its open support of Ethiopia, not only in the Somali conflict, which it interpreted as an invasion of sovereign Somali territory by Ethiopia acting as a US 'mercenary', but also in the conflict between Eritrea and Ethiopia.

A US mediation effort in the border conflict between Eritrea and Ethiopia launched in January produced no results and Eritrea held the US government responsible for the failed implementation of the EEBC boundary decision. The US government imposed travel restrictions on Eritrean diplomats in retaliation for restrictions placed on US diplomats in Asmara. The US withheld non-humanitarian assistance, since the government refused to bring to trial the employees of the US embassy arrested in 2001, and USAID's activities remained suspended.

Relations with **EU** member states continued to be poor, as the Europeans condemned the human rights situation in the country, the government's restrictive behaviour concerning NGOs, the lack of transparency in economic issues and the restrictions placed on UNMEE. In September, the fifth anniversary of the arrest of the political dissidents and journalists (see above), the EU urged the government to disclose the details of their whereabouts. On 6 March, the first secretary at the Italian embassy in Asmara, Ludovico Serra, was declared *persona non grata* for 'having broken the law'. He was arrested in an Italian-owned building in Massawa then occupied by the president's bodyguards and was told to leave the country within 24 hours. The exact circumstances of this event remained unclear, but Eritrean relations with Italy were severely strained. The president made a visit to **Italy** during the first week of December. This was dubbed a 'working visit' by Eritrean media, but a 'private visit' by the Italian news agency. He visited representatives of the Toscana region and Parma district to talk about possible investment opportunities for Italian companies. On 4 December, he held talks with Prime Minister Romano Prodi, who expressed his preoccupation with the political situation in Eritrea.

Eritrean relations with **Sudan** improved significantly and in March an agreement was reached to exchange ambassadors and reopen the border, which had been closed in 2002. In February, Sudan's first vice-president, Salva Kiir Mayardit, held talks in Massawa with President Isaias, and on 27 August a memorandum of understanding was signed between the two governments. During his stay in Eritrea, Salva Kiir also met with the designated leader of a Darfur rebel group, the Sudan Liberation Movement (SLM). Later in the year, Darfur rebel leaders grew more sceptical of Eritrean mediation in the Darfur crisis, as they feared an Eritrean bias in favour of the Sudanese government. Eritrea was actively involved in the mediation between the Sudanese government and the Eastern Front (Al Sharq), an opposition movement active in the regions bordering Eritrea. On 14 October, a peace agreement between the Front and the Sudanese government was signed. Eritrea also continued its close relations with **Libya** and President Isaias visited the country several times. On 22 November, he took part in a summit on the Sudan crisis held in Tripoli, hosted by Muammar Kadhafi, along with the presidents of Sudan, Egypt, Chad and the CAR. All participants were strongly opposed to the deployment of UN troops in Darfur and suggested Isaias as a mediator in the conflict, a proposal strongly opposed by both the AU and the UN.

China continued to provide development aid and maintained its commercial activities in Eritrea, while President Isaias and several members of the cabinet took part in the China-

Africa summit in Beijing from 3–5 November. There were attempts by Eritrea to establish closer ties with **Iran**. In early December, a government envoy travelled to Teheran to lobby for improved bilateral ties and received a positive response, including an invitation to establish an embassy in Teheran. **Pakistan** planned to set up an office of its main oil company in Asmara, but there was no visible outcome. It can be assumed that Eritrea's primary motive for strengthening relations with Iran and Pakistan was to secure military equipment from these countries.

Socioeconomic Developments

On 24–25 April and 14–18 October, the UN's special humanitarian envoy for the Horn of Africa, Kjell Magne Bonderik, visited Eritrea and met with the president. He stated that the humanitarian situation was serious, and that there were high malnutrition rates, especially in rural areas. The government's lack of transparency made it increasingly difficult to assess the **humanitarian situation** in the country, as no official data on the 2005 and 2006 harvests were released. Relations with the donor community were poor. Travel permits for aid workers to the southern and western regions were extremely hard to obtain. There was no change in the government's **hostile attitude towards NGOs**. During the year, eight organisations had to leave the country, among them Irish-based Concern, US-based Mercy Corps, the International Rescue Committee and Samaritan's Purse (nine of whose local employees had been arrested), as well as ACCORD, a British charity with a substantial number of programmes in the country. WFP distributions remained suspended, since the government had banned free food distribution in favour of food-for-work programmes. The only exception made was for the approximately 70,000 **internally displaced persons** in camps: they received food aid from the government.

Foreign aid was basically limited to humanitarian assistance because of the country's unsupportive policy in dealing with foreign aid agencies, its poor human rights record and the border stalemate with Ethiopia. In August, the **EU** announced it would give $ 6 m in humanitarian aid to provide urgent food and water supplies. The money was to be channelled through UN agencies, whose areas of operation within the country were restricted. The World Bank had several projects in the country, amounting to $ 254.3 m, mainly in health care, electric power distribution and demobilisation. In May 2002, $ 60 m had been approved for the emergency demobilisation and reintegration programme, but only a small number of persons had been demobilised, casting doubt on the practical outcome of this project.

On 11 April, **China** agreed to lend $ 23 m to develop Eritrea's telephone network. In September, two agreements were signed between Eritrea and China regarding investments in air transport and mining exploration. In early February, a joint venture in the agricultural sector between the ministry of trade and industry and an Italian enterprise was announced. A new plant in the Gash Barka region should be established to produce fruit for export.

Generally, military involvement in plants producing cash crops remained high, including the confiscation of commercial farms by military officers.

Eritrea's **economy** was characterised by ever-increasing **government intervention**, continuing **high levels of mobilisation** of people of productive age, and a severe lack of hard currency, which could be partially attributed to the decline in diaspora remittances. Basic goods such as milk and bread continued to be difficult to obtain. Generally, the economy suffered from a lack of funds in order to import even basic inputs. From March, the **electricity supply** was rationed and the capital remained without power several hours a day, while provincial towns received electricity for only a few hours. **Private investment** was further discouraged when the government seized several private business companies, arrested business persons and restricted private companies from operating in, for example, the construction sector. The illegal holding of foreign currency continued to be liable to severe punishment (two years in prison and a fine of two million Nacfa).

The **militarisation of the educational system** continued. In summer, the only university in the country was closed for an unspecified period, leaving technical colleges near Asmara (Mai Nefhi), Keren (Hamalmalo) and Massawa, and a so-called 'centre of excellence' at Embatkala as the only sources of higher education. Another college was supposed to be opened at Adi Keyh (Zoba Debub), but this plan did not come to fruition. Students were not able to obtain BA degrees at these colleges, such as had formerly been offered by the University of Asmara, and thereby qualifying for further studies. The government had been unhappy with the failure of the majority of students to return home after concluding studies abroad in recent years. The colleges were administered by the president's office and not by the ministry of education, and the facilities were run by military commanders, while all students were forced to live under military conditions. The secondary school at the Sawa military camp, where all students nationwide must go to pass their final examinations after the 12th school year, was also run like a military institution. Students had to undergo military training and were obliged to work in agricultural and construction projects on a regular basis. After the examinations, they were either accepted for further education at a technical college or immediately conscripted into the army, and, after six months of military training, were supposed to do their indefinite national service under the framework of the '*warsay-yikealo* development campaign', which remained the centrepiece of the country's development strategy. Party-controlled companies continued to make use of conscripts by employing them without payment except for pocket money and basic nutritional items.

In spite of the IMF's demand, the government again published no **national budget**, and the lack of transparency and reliability of the sparse available data continued. Eritrea ranked 157th on UNDP's Human Development Index, GDP per capita was estimated at $ 219 and the economic growth rate at 2%. Official development assistance decreased to $ 61.3 per capita. The UNDP report gave no numbers for military spending by the government, but it is improbable that there was a decline given the unresolved border conflict with Ethiopia and Eritrea's involvement in the Somali conflict. Conventional arms imports amounted to

$ 276 m in 2005, but actual figures could be significantly higher. State spending on health and education declined to 3.8% of GDP (2003) and 2% (2002–04), respectively. Of the population, 73% were undernourished, and HIV prevalence was estimated at 2.4%. The IMF estimated the inflation rate in 2006 to be 16.5% in 2006. The current account balance was minus $ 345,3 m (-28.8% of GDP). A solution to Eritrea's **foreign exchange crises** was not in sight.

Preparations by Canadian-based Nevsun resources company at Bisha in western Eritrea to commence **gold mining** activities continued, but exploitation of the mine was not slated to start before the end of 2008.

Nicole Hirt

Ethiopia

Ethiopia struggled with the aftermath of the controversial 2005 parliamentary elections and with enduring economic, environmental and food security problems. It was involved in a short but intense war with a new Somali Islamist movement active in southern Somalia. Economic growth and infrastructural investment was registered, but poverty and unemployment did not undergo notable reduction. The legitimacy and popularity of the incumbent political leadership appeared to decline, coupled with a tendency to political repression and intolerance of opposition. The political process showed no meaningful signs of opening up or conciliatory effort and took on a grim character. International human rights agencies heavily criticised the human rights record. Donor countries and the World Bank slowly resumed development support to the government, although they tried to avoid direct funding to the federal government. There was no solution to the border dispute with Eritrea. Ethiopia maintained stable relations with its other neighbours (Somaliland, Djibouti, Sudan and Kenya).

Domestic Politics

Ethiopia's domestic politics was marked by the continued **political crisis** that emerged after the 2005 elections. These elections had led to a dramatic stand-off and to massive repression of opposition groups, notably the Coalition for Unity and Democracy Party (CUDP, formerly CUD), and this continued in 2006. The government, dominated by the former insurgent movement, the Ethiopian Peoples Revolutionary Democratic Front (EPRDF), remained in power, had a large majority in the parliament and continued to implement its economic and political programmes uninfluenced by opposition ideas or calls for compromise. While the opposition had almost a third of the parliamentary seats, its influence was marginal, as EPRDF and its allies block-voted on all issues brought to the parliament, the House of Peoples' Representatives. In addition, some opposition leaders and activists, including MPs, claimed that they were the target of repression and sometimes persecution. In the countryside, dozens of people sympathising with, or members of the opposition disappeared or were on occasion killed under mysterious circumstances. Opponents often made the accusation of targeted killing. One case in point was the assassination in October by police or militia of a CUDP-affiliated youth activist, the 16-year old Wondwossen Gutu, in Addis Ababa. Another was the mysterious death of a top airforce instructor, Daniel Beyene. As with past killings, the culprits were not found and judicial proceedings were not initiated, feeding the idea of the impunity of the security forces. The EPRDF tried to tighten its grip on the rural population by continuing to organise people in administrative units with a duty to report to higher levels.

The **mass trial against opposition leaders** and civil society members that had started after their arrest in November 2005 continued. Convincing evidence against the accused (who included diaspora activists and academics critical of the government but not known for violent agendas) was not produced, and a series of inconclusive court meetings and appeals dragged on. All the prisoners were denied bail. The Ethiopian political leadership made frequent prejudiced remarks about this trial, confirming the impression that it was a political trial meant to silence key opponents. Few if any independent observers continued to speak of Ethiopia as a country 'on the road to democracy'. The leadership mostly ignored pleas for national dialogue and the release of the accused made by the EU, US and the visiting UN commissioner for human rights, Louise Arbour.

At the beginning of the year, in the aftermath of the violent repression in November and December 2005, **anti-government protests** were only carried on via demonstrations, strikes and symbolic actions by high school students in several towns, resulting in frequent beatings, several deaths, arrests, intimidation of parents and teachers and the closure of schools. In January, a Christian religious celebration ('Timqet') went awry when people began to chant anti-government slogans. Police responded with force, killing three people, among them a 12-year old child, beating up dozens of others and making 42 arrests.

During the course of the year, opposition parties further fragmented into factions due to disunity, the divisive activities of government supporters and harassment in the countryside. The CUDP, in the absence of its major leaders, was taken over by new people more favourably disposed towards the government. This was denounced by the diaspora branches of the party. Many observers noted that the party had now been co-opted and was no longer 'opposition'. The second-largest opposition party, the United Ethiopian Democratic Front (UEDF) more or less held its own, but the Oromo National Congress, one of its constituents, was the target of consistent subversion. The opposition voice in parliament was therefore much weakened.

Opposition demands that the National Electoral Board of Ethiopia (NEBE), which had overseen the elections of 2005 but had not satisfactorily resolved outstanding problems, be depoliticised and its membership evenly balanced between government loyalists and independents or opposition members, were rejected by the government.

Early in the year, the formation of a new and somewhat unexpected alliance of opposition parties was announced: the **Alliance for Freedom and Democracy** (AFD), made up of the CUDP (its diaspora section), the Oromo Liberation Front (OLF), the Ogaden National Liberation Front (ONLF), the southern Sidama Liberation Front (SLF) and the Ethiopian Peoples Patriotic Front (EPPF). This alliance, formed among the diaspora, was received with mixed feelings both in Ethiopia and among Ethiopian communities abroad. It gathered groups that advocated peaceful democratic struggle (CUDP) and those that did not exclude violence and had combat groups in the country (OLF, ONLP, EPPF). Its position on the unity of Ethiopia was not clear. The OLF and the ONLF perspectives seemed to dominate this alliance. Its formation in Utrecht, the Netherlands, was reputedly 'witnessed' by a major political figure from Eritrea (a presidential advisor), which further prevented the AFD from gaining substantial support in Ethiopia. The second big Ethiopian opposition party, the UEDF – a mixed coalition of democratic ethno-regional parties – was also invited into the AFD but ultimately refrained from becoming a member. The AFD called on government to take up dialogue. Predictably, the government refused.

All this meant that the political scene in Ethiopia remained frozen. There was continuation of rhetoric on 'democracy' but in reality a hardening of positions. The attitude of the ordinary population moved towards a mixture of cynicism, despair and disdain for politics, augmented by growing anti-Americanism due to the US's perceived indifference towards domestic repression and injustice.

As with other African countries, **debates in cyberspace** on Ethiopian politics and society were increasingly prominent. Websites of opposition groups and Ethiopian diaspora communities continued to be vocal and influential, although apart from furnshing valuable first-hand information on developments in the country some of them also provided forums for exaggerated rhetoric and even insults across political, ethnic and community lines. The Ethiopian government blocked several of the critical websites and web-logs.

This was also the 'year of **defections**': dozens of diplomats, army personnel, civil servants, judges and journalists left or fled the country. This could further erode the standing and legitimacy of the government. The high number of defecting diplomatic personnel (more than 60) was remarkable. The defectors cited repression, bad governance, corruption or personal intimidation and dissatisfaction as their motive. Several defecting diplomats also revealed secrets of the regime in memos of internal meetings at embassies and ministries. Revealing also was a 52-page document (in Amharic, published on some diaspora websites) with instructions for Ethiopian embassies on how to pressurise or neutralise diaspora opposition voices abroad. According to some observers, these concrete plans of action could lead to interference in the internal affairs of the states where the embassies are located.

The **human rights and civil liberties** situation remained bad. Throughout the year a constant stream of reports and news items on the abuse of rights by police, militia and army was published. The annual US state department report on human rights in Ethiopia was very critical. Politics and the legal system continued to be marked by unpredictability, lack of transparency, difficult access to justice and lack of timely and fair judicial process. Constitutional rights were often ignored. According to documented local human rights reports, hundreds of people were arrested on vague charges (or none at all), shot, extra-judicially killed, abused, allegedly tortured or made to 'disappear'. Few of the cases of this and past years were brought to a court of law, meaning justice was often denied to the victims and the bereaved. Leaders of the Oromo Mecha-Tulama Association, arrested in 2004, remained in prison without being charged.

The planned reform of the **legal sector did not make much progress**. The justice system was not free from political (government) pressure or intimidation and also struggled with the case load. A verdict was passed in the 12-year 'Red Terror' trial against 57 (27 *in absentia*) former leading officials of the Mengistu regime: all were found guilty of 'genocide, treason and murder'. Final sentences would come in early 2007. In December, a first verdict *in absentia* was also passed on former dictator Mengistu Haile-Mariam – he was sentenced to life imprisonment. This was later appealed by the state prosecutor. Mengistu remained in Zimbabwe under the protection of President Mugabe.

Overall, the regime's rhetoric was still full of references to 'democratic values', 'rule-of-law', 'justice', 'progress', etc. and some work was done to realise these ideals. In the eyes of most Ethiopians, however, the record was very disappointing. A revealing example of undue government pressure was the case of the **inquiry commission** into the 2005 post-election violence. This commission was handpicked in January 2006 by government and headed by two reputable, independent judges with no political connections. They had to report on the question of whether government forces had used excessive force in the June and November 2005 disturbances. After extensive research based on documents and on interviews with all parties, including eye-witnesses and police and army people, they concluded that 193 people, many of them uninvolved bystanders, including women and children, had been killed, six policemen had died, 763 people had been injured (often seriously) and that about 30,000 mostly young people had been arrested and put into remote prison camps. In its 3 July judgment, the commission decided (by a vote of eight in favour and two against) that government had indeed used excessive force and abused its powers. The report was not accepted by government. Even before its final version was ready, the commission had experienced serious intimidation while it was reviewing the evidence and writing its report. This led the chairman and the vice-chairman (and later some other members) to flee the country. Then the remaining commission members revised their opinion under pressure and collaborated in 'rewriting' the report, this time with conclusions absolving the government of blame. Although the rewriting happened outside the legal mandate and time frame of the commission (until 7 July), this report was duly 'approved' by parliament in late October.

The CUDP leadership arrested in November 2005 remained behind bars the entire year. Their trial on 'treason' and 'genocide' charges made little progress, with constant delays in court sessions and hearings. The prisoners' health deteriorated owing to bad conditions and inadequate medical attention. There was no credible evidence against them. It was feared in Ethiopia that false witness statements and forged papers (a trusted practice in past trials in Ethiopia) were being prepared. Western donor countries continued their criticism of this political trial, which has done the government much damage.

The **mass media** suffered from continued pressure and unpredictable harassment. The independent press endured further intimidation and arrests of journalists and newspaper vendors. At least 14 journalists were on trial on various charges ranging from 'defamation' to 'attempted overthrow of the constitutional order'. In a preposterous move, the government in June dismissed the TV presenter of the nation's popular children's programme, the aged *Ababba* Tesfaye, who was held responsible for one derogatory 'ethnic' utterance by a young child in his programme. While the urban population had at least some, although declining, access to independent information, the majority of Ethiopians had little or none to news or opinions other than those of the government.

Local-level **group conflicts** were evident in some areas of the country, notably Gambela and the Somali and Oromiya regions. In Gambela, an unsolved conflict between Nuer and Anywaa people again led to looting, displacement and killings in January and March. On 11 June, some 25 people were killed in an ambush on a bus by armed rebels near Gambela. In the Oromo and Somali areas of southern Ethiopia, resource and border conflicts re-emerged in which several dozen people were killed. For instance, in Oromiya clashes in early June took place between the Guji and the Boran (approx. 150 people killed), and on 29–31 May, 39 people were killed in the Somali region (Daroor area) in a dispute between two Garhaji subclans. There were also smaller clashes in the southern region: violent riots in the southern towns of Dilla on 3–4 April (killing 11 people) and in Bule (3 April). Clashes between students and police occurred in Meqele (in early June), Nazreth (on 2 June, with one student killed) and Asella (on 7 June, again with one student killed). Government troops kept the lid on further communal clashes, but they often came too late and were sometimes also claimed to be taking sides. On 3 January, the government through the ministry of justice announced that it would seek to develop alternative dispute resolution mechanisms based on local community structures. In urban areas in the first few months of the year there were a dozen bomb attacks, which killed 12 people and injured 100 more. No one claimed responsibility for these attacks.

As in previous years, **regional or ethnic rebel movements** were active in the Oromo, Somali and Amhara regional states, reflecting continued discontent with policies, political interference and repression by the central government as well as socioeconomic problems. No significant attempts to negotiate or address the underlying grievances were made. Among the most important movements were the OLF, the ONLF and the EPPF, a small and shady nationalist group operating in northern Ethiopia. An assessment of their field strength is difficult to make, but as in previous years the nuisance value of these movements was significant. Their programmes did not always have a clear national vision, and appeal to certain sections of the Ethiopian public. Some of these movements have their own problematic political and human rights records.

The Somali Region 5, a large territory with 3.9 m inhabitants, remained unstable, with the central government frequently changing personnel and clan groups clashing with each other, e.g., in September, under the impact of resource competition, internal disunity and partly due to divisive state politics. The separatist ONLF has some support in rural areas but followed a risky strategy of armed confrontation and had no constructive, inclusive programme for either the Somali region or for Ethiopia in general.

A relatively recent type of conflict – at least for Ethiopia – was **religious clashes**, some between Ethiopian-Orthodox and Pentecostal-Evangelical believers, others between Christians and Muslims, with Muslims increasingly showing antipathy toward Christians living in their midst. On 15 April, a church in Jijiga town was bombed, injuring five people. In incidents similar to those reported in 2004 and 2005, some Christians were killed, among them several Muslims converted to Christianity, and their property destroyed. For example, in Dembi town in western Ethiopia on 1–2 October a violent clash caused the death of five people and the destruction of two churches. Another clash occurred in mid-October in Bora and Beshesha in western Ethiopia, where 11 Christians were hacked or burnt to death allegedly by militant, Wahhabist-inspired Muslims. Security forces were not decisive in suppressing or preventing such violence, but reconciliation efforts started after the incidents.

For unclear reasons, more and more foreigners and tourists reported stone-throwing incidents and acts of harassment, notably by children and young male adults in villages and towns, suggesting that anti-foreigner feelings were on the rise in Ethiopia.

The three main religious denominations remained Orthodox Christianity (45%), Islam (38%–40%) and Protestant-Evangelical Christianity (about 10%). Adherence to Evangelist-Pentecostal Christianity and to Islam continued to grow. The number of people belonging to traditional religions declined, although as part of political, ethnic-nationalist movements in some places, indigenous religion seems to have made a modest comeback (e.g., the 'Waqefeta' belief among Oromo in central Ethiopia).

Foreign Affairs

The Ethio-Eritrean 'border conflict' was not solved: no movement of any kind was registered in the two positions. Eritrea, however, kept up rejectionist rhetoric, insisting on literal execution of the 2003 decision of the Ethiopia-Eritrea Boundary Commission (EEBC) at the Permanent Court of Arbitration (PCA) in The Hague without talks on implementation and adjustments on the ground. Ethiopia did not concede anything either. While Ethiopia is legally in a weak position since it had committed itself to the PCA decision beforehand, it insisted that the mandate was not properly carried out and mistakes in the decision should be rectified. The stalemate continued, despite another round of international efforts by the UN and the EU to mediate. No compromise could be reached on any talks, with Eritrea further isolating itself diplomatically and Ethiopia refusing to acknowledge a controversial border line and the impending loss of Badme town, where the fighting in 1998 had started. Ethiopia remained vigilant in the border zone, while Eritrea further restricted the activities and movements of the UN Mission for Ethiopia and Eritrea (UNMEE) teams and patrols. The Temporary Security Zone (TSZ) along the border was frequently penetrated by Eritrean soldiers. In October, some 1500 soldiers with 14 tanks moved into the demilitarised security zone, officially to 'harvest crops'. The mandate of UNMEE was renewed by the UN, but its forces were further reduced from 3,373 to 2,300 people. Meaningful patrolling of the zone became impossible, also because of Eritrea's prohibition since 2005 of UN helicopter flights.

In the **Somali conflict**, the Eritreans supported the rising Islamist movement, the Union of Islamic Courts (UIC), with training, advisors and weaponry. The rise of the UIC caused great concern in the region, notably in Ethiopia, because of repeated threats made by the UIC towards Ethiopia, Somaliland and Puntland: they openly clamoured for a forceful 'reunification' of all Somali-inhabited areas and for an 'Islamic state' as well as calling for Muslim revolt within Ethiopia. The Ethiopian government, pursuing its long-term policy, supported the Transitional Federal Government (TFG), the legal government of Somalia since November 2004 seated in Baidoa and threatened by military assault from the UIC. When the UIC forces – taken over by a radicalising 'jihadist' leadership originating in the former 'Al Ittihad al Islami' movement – attacked Baidoa in December, the Ethiopians and TFG forces retaliated and war ensued. In one week of fighting the UIC was defeated and melted away but it later regrouped elsewhere, developing a radical/terrorist agenda under Islamist leadership. The military defeat of the UIC was a setback for the Eritreans but did not change their rhetoric or practice and their continuing support for UIC and other Ethiopian opposition movements elsewhere. A few days after the start of its military operations in 21 December, Ethiopia announced it would leave Somalia on condition that an AU peacekeeping force was installed.

Ethiopia had the **support of the US government** despite its worrying political and human rights record, obviously because of its pro-US international stance notably in the anti-terror campaign. Military and intelligence cooperation continued, for example with the US combined joint task force stationed in Djibouti. In the US congress, scepticism about Ethiopia's domestic policies gained momentum and a number of congressmen tried to get a critical bill on Ethiopia drawn up in late 2005, the Ethiopia Freedom, Democracy and Human Rights Advancement Act (H.R. 5680), on the agenda. This bill suffered delay, being put on hold in July, and it had not been adopted by the house of representatives by year's end.

The EU and the Ambassadors' Donors Group continued to express its misgivings on Ethiopia's political record, especially on the so-called 'treason/genocide' trial against the democratic opposition, but did not interrupt attempts at crisis diplomacy or halt economic support. In January, however, the UK said it would suspend $ 88 m in direct budgetary aid. In the course of the year, EU countries as well as the World Bank (in July) resumed aid programmes in an adapted format, e.g., trying to divert the flow to other, lower-level targets, such as the protection of basic services programme via local governments and NGOs, instead of to the federal government. During a visit to Ethiopia on 15–17 February, EU Commissioner Louis Michel called for renewed political dialogue and democratisation. Two EU diplomats were expelled after being arrested on 19 October near the Kenyan border with an Ethiopian human rights lawyer working with the EU Commission who was fleeing to Kenya to avoid persecution. This lawyer, Ms. Yalemzewd Beqele, was still in prison at the end of the year.

Relations with China intensified, especially in the economic sphere (information technology, trade, investment) and in military cooperation. In May, a Chinese company started drilling for oil in the Gambela area. Politically, China did not engage the Ethiopian government in any sense.

The Nile question continued to be controversial, with Ethiopia (the source of the Blue Nile, the main tributary) pushing for a greater role and share in its use of the waters for irrigation and power generation. The Nile Basin Commission (NBC), founded in 1999 by the relevant countries, did not make significant progress. Two points of controversy were not resolved: the status of the old Nile treaties concluded before 1999 and the giving of prior notification by a member country of any national development project to the other member states.

Socioeconomic Developments

Food security in Ethiopia was not achieved and, as in any good year (with sufficient rainfall), 2–3 m people required food aid. Structural problems in Ethiopia's agricultural economy relating to land tenure, insecurity of title to land, low productivity, taxation, population pressure and lack of arable land persisted. Some experiments were made – on the basis of studies by various ministries – in adapting the policy of state ownership of all land. But as controlling the rural population remains vital to the current government, fundamental changes were not in the making, despite a move towards defining more possession and use rights (e.g., via registration and transfer to children). In order to combat recurrent food insecurity, the government went on with a 'safety nets programme', supported by the World Bank, in which people do food-for-work projects such as building wells, small irrigation systems or soil erosion prevention schemes. In February, the FAO called for $ 18.5 m of food aid for some 1 m people affected by severe drought in the Somali region and in parts of Oromiya.

Urban unemployment was around 30–40% and rural unemployment went unregistered. Job creation in a few economic sectors such as the flower business, construction and small enterprises continued, but could not address the magnitude of the problem. In the farming areas, for instance, unemployment aggravated generational tensions, with young men demanding money and the premature partition of the land by their parents.

The **public health situation** remained critical, despite an extension of health facilities across the country. Continued population growth (2.5%–2.7% per annum with a fertility rate of 5.5 children per woman) offset investment gains. Major diseases were HIV/AIDS, malaria, diarrhoea and TB. Several outbreaks of meningitis (in January in Wolaitta region) and cholera (in April, leading to 52,000 cases) were registered. Due to low salaries and substandard working conditions in many hospitals and clinics, Ethiopia suffered from a lack of doctors and other qualified medical personnel, many of whom emigrated.

The HIV/AIDS crisis continued, with 4% (almost 3 m) people infected and probably another 100,000 estimated deaths (ill-recorded, owing to incomplete statistics and public shame about the disease). New treatment and prevention initiatives were tried, one of them under the the 2005 US-funded emergency plan for AIDS relief ($ 20 m annual budget) under which several hundred thousand people were tested and counselled, and a slight decline in the infection rate was noted. Other NGOs and some civil society groups were also engaged in anti-AIDS programmes. For rural women, a major health risk remained birth complications, which often went untreated. Local food scarcity and famine caused additional deaths from malnourishment or infectious diseases. In early August, in parts of the Amhara, Southern, and Somali regional states, the worst flooding in decades caused the death of at least 600 people and made more than 10,000 destitute, notably in and around Dire Dawa.

The **education sector** continued to grow in terms of facilities, number of schools and number of pupils enrolled. Whether overall progress in the qualitative sense was made remained unclear. As with other Millennium Development Goals, the measurement is difficult if not inadequate. The building of many regional universities went on, but funding to make them into mature centres of learning was strained. In February-March, teachers across the nation were obliged to follow a series of cadre lectures on EPRDF policies in education and afterwards had to sign that they would implement them. This was not popular and was seen as a party control measure. In view of the still widespread abuse of children and the custom of 'forced marriage' (by abduction), notably in the rural south of the country, the government in October released a 'national action plan on sexual abuse and exploitation of children'.

Economic growth in Ethiopia, as in previous years, was significant. Estimates of GDP growth ranged from 5%–9%. This is difficult to determine in view of different figures given by government spokespersons, shaky statistics and lack of a visible rise in overall wealth levels. The World Bank in March 2007 mentioned a figure of 5.5% growth for 2006. The grain harvest was comparatively good because of sufficient rains. Foreign direct investments also increased. Exports rose, infrastructural works were carried out, entrepreneurial activities were on the rise and new housing projects were completed in urban areas (slum clearance in Addis Ababa was halted for the time being after the 2005 elections). Still, productive industrial investments lagged and did not absorb the swelling number of school leavers and unemployed in the towns and the rural sector. Neither did the urban formal sector have the capacity to provide jobs to the many higher education graduates. Most of the unemployed disappeared into the large informal economy or went into hawking or petty crime. Remittances by Ethiopians abroad represented largely invisible foreign investments, of which the annual amount was estimated to be some $ 400–$ 450 m in the past two to three years. This money went to relatives of the migrants, helping them survive, improve housing and make small business investments.

Tourism was a growth sector and was reported to have earned more money than in the previous year, but the figures were unknown. It is the third largest foreign exchange earner after coffee and oilseeds. In the new 2006 Plan for Accelerated and Sustainable Development to End Poverty (PASDEP), the government announced its goal to make the country one of the top-ten tourist locations in Africa by 2012.

Ethiopia continued negotiations on WTO admission, but opinions, including in high political circles, were divided on the balance of benefits and drawbacks of membership. Some felt it might open the door for global capitalism – especially via the financial sector (banks) and in tourism – to add another African country to its hunting ground. This would lead to the national economy being dominated by international capital, to profits being repatriated abroad, to socio-cultural problems and to the growth of a small trading and entrepreneurial elite linked to the political leadership to the detriment of ordinary Ethiopians and the middle class.

The growth figures and the government's cautious financial management are in fact what prevented donors from giving up on or backing out of Ethiopia. Despite its major political and economic problems, the country is still seen, notably by EU diplomats, as a test case in Africa that 'must succeed'. In addition, Ethiopia is protected against serious pressure or sanctions by its close association with the US campaign against global terrorism. The new US ambassador, D. Yamamoto, stated on 20 September that Ethiopia was seen as an "important strategic partner". This became evident during the Ethiopian military campaign in Somalia in December, condoned by the US.

The Ethiopian **state budget** in 2006 (the budget year is from 7 July to 6 July) was approximately ETB (Ethiopian birr) 35.4 bn ($ 4.1 bn). State revenues were $ 2.65 bn, 53% of which was to be domestically generated by taxation and 34% by foreign aid and loans. On 23 June, the auditor-general noted in his report that $ 83 m of the 2006 budget was unaccounted for. In November, the auditor-general was dismissed.

Ethiopia's **GDP** stood at $ 13.3 bn. Agriculture contributed some 48% to this, the service sector about 40% and industry only 13%. The agricultural sector employed, as in previous years, about 80% of all productive workers, while industry was slightly up at 8% due to an industrial growth of some 7%. Annual inflation was 12% and was reflected in the significant rise not only of prices for imported consumer items, but also in the prices of food staples, cooking oil, meat, cereals, butter, fruits and fuel (petrol and kerosene for cooking). Poverty in both the urban and rural sectors was widespread, with income inequalities rising, but some reduction in the percentage of the poor was registered, albeit with an estimated 40% still living below the 'poverty line' of $ 1 a day. It is still not clear what the exact impact and overall results of GDP growth are for the country. Ethiopia remained the seventh-poorest country in the world.

Ethiopia again had to pay more for its oil imports, an estimated $ 800 m. A growing volume of oil imports came from Sudan. The development of the huge natural gas fields in the Ogaden (Kalub and Hilala) did not see any progress. In August, after a new round of bidding by international companies to develop the reserves, Malaysia's Petronas won the contract.

Coffee exports earned some $ 350 m, but the world market price was faltering and many farmers switched to other products such the stimulant leaf *ch'at*, and to petty trade. Flower exports grew by 70%, generating earnings estimated at $ 35 m. Horticultural products earned about $ 32 m. Other foreign currency earners were the traditional export products such as hides and skins, *ch'at*, leather products, gold, livestock and oilseeds.

Overall annual exports brought in $ 1.085 bn, a milestone, because for the first time the $ 1 bn mark was passed. But imports were again much higher at $ 4,105 bn. The national debt rose to $ 6,038 bn, despite another round of debt cancellation with, notably, the World Bank, Russia and the IMF (which wrote off $ 161 m in January). The national debt was about 80% of annual GDP. Debt service payments amounted to almost 7% of GDP. Military expenditure – at least the figure publicly known – was about $ 296 m, or almost 4% of GDP. In reality, considering the substantial and growing security apparatus and the cost of the war in Somalia in December, it was probably much higher. There was a balance of payments deficit of – $ 3,384 bn. This was closed with foreign aid to the tune of $ 1.6 bn and with various domestic and international borrowing schemes.

In **infrastructure**, progress was made in road building, electrification of towns and villages and in the installation of telephone lines as well as cellphone network coverage. Internet connections grew slightly, but access to the Web was seriously restricted. In

September, the monopolistic Ethiopian Telecommunications Corporation (ETC) signed a contract of $ 1.5 bn with three Chinese companies for all telecom investments in the country for the period 2007–11. The relevant 'suppliers credit memorandum of understanding' envisaged a loan by China repayable in ten years. The deal, implying exclusive reliance on Chinese telecom technology, drew criticism especially among workers and expert technicians with the ETC. This company also came in for much criticism from customers due to its grave mistakes in billing, bad management, waste of equipment, poor services and corruption. Disgruntled employees created a website to air their grievances. In a rare move, the new general manager appointed in October admitted mistakes and promised improvements.

Throughout the year, problems of **corruption** and other abuses of public office at all levels of state institution were regularly reported. Most common was embezzlement of state funds, preferential treatment in business deals and bribes under contracts with foreign companies and development aid. The situation has not reached the unmanageable proportions known elsewhere in Africa, but corruption did not diminish either. Ethiopia was ranked in the 130–138 bracket (on a scale of 158) on TI's Corruption Perceptions Index, roughly the same position as in 2005.

The economy continued to be dominated by a few big businessmen and by companies led by government party members. Dozens of big private enterprises remained in the hands of shareholders and managers closely affiliated with the EPRDF. Several banks, such as the Wegagen, Nib and Dashen banks, were also party-affiliated.

Migration was substantial, both internal in response to to local ethnic conflicts, lack of opportunity, poverty and instability, as well as trans-border to the Middle East or further abroad. The port of Bossaso in Puntland, Somalia was a magnet for many Ethiopians trying to get to the richer shores across the Red Sea. The risks of the sea voyage in ill-equipped fishing boats, managed by human traffickers, were great and often led to human casualties: dozens of people drowned during the crossing and an uncertain future awaited them once they arrived. As in previous years, there were also refugees from neighbouring countries in Ethiopia: some 75,000 Sudanese, 15,000–20,000 people from southern Somalia and a growing number of Eritreans. Towards the end of the year, it was reported that dozens of young Eritreans were crossing the border into Ethiopia (as well as into Sudan) every month. By late 2006, their number was upwards of 10,000. The internally displaced (from previous wars, 'ethnic' clashes and the Somalia campaign) were estimated to be between 150,000 and 200,000 (mostly in Somali, Tigray and Gambela, and to a lesser extent in Oromiya and the southern region). This reflected the overall instability in the country and in the wider region.

Continued population pressure contributed to **environmental problems**, conflicts over land and water and food insecurity. While in the cities there were slight indications that birth rates were stabilising and in some cases slightly declining, in the countryside the average number of children born to a woman was still close to six. Land scarcity was getting worse and was aggravating food insecurity as well as communal conflicts.

Due to population growth, conversion to farmland and the drying out of rural areas, forest cover in Ethiopia this year further diminished by some 140,000 ha, falling below 13 m ha (including coffee and other plantations) of the total land area of 109 m ha. Since 1990, an estimated 14% of forest cover has been lost. Ongoing deterioration of the environment was a dangerous process undermining the basis of Ethiopia's livelihood and was not adequately tackled.

Jon Abbink

Kenya

Ahead of the 2007 general elections, it was back to the drawing board for all political strategists to refashion the political landscape after the major blow to the ruling National Rainbow Coalition (NARC) in the 2005 referendum that saw the Orange Democratic Movement (ODM) successfully oppose the new constitution. The result for the year was the creation of two major new parties, NARC-Kenya and ODM-Kenya. Kenyans saw ministers stepping down over corruption allegations and being reinstated some months later and wondered how and when the substantial 6% growth in the economy would start trickling down. On 21 April, all Kenyans received a one-off public holiday of national prayer to end a series of disasters that included famine, ethnic clashes and a plane crash.

Domestic Politics

On 21 March, seven months after the November 2005 constitution referendum turmoil, parliament resumed. During the break, President Kibaki had **reshuffled** his **cabinet** twice (the first reshuffle occurred in 2005). The first realignment was necessary to replace the ODM ministers who had opposed the new draft constitution. The second reshuffle occurred on 15 February, after Finance Minister David Mwiraria resigned over corruption allegations. Lands Minister Amos Kimunya replaced him. President Kibaki appointed Environment

Minister Kivutha Kibwana as acting minister of lands. Noah Wekesa, minister for science and technology and Henry Obwocha, the minister of planning, were appointed as acting ministers for education and energy respectively after George Saitoti (education) and Kiraitu Murungi (energy) resigned on 13 February over two major corruption scandals, namely Goldenberg and Anglo Leasing respectively. Vice-President Moodi Awori (Liberal Democratic Party, LDP), though, withstood pressure to resign over his role in the Anglo Leasing affair. On 24 February, a constitution review committee, led by Bethuel Kiplagat, was installed to evaluate the constitutional review process and propose the best way forward.

The next indication that NARC might be falling apart came in May when a new party was launched named NARC-Kenya and composed of Kibaki supporters such as Raphael Tuju (foreign affairs), Mukhisa Kituyi (trade) and Kivutha Kibwana. On 21 June, it was announced that members linked to Secretary-General William Ruto of the opposition Kenya African National Union (KANU) had struck a deal with LDP to team up in the 2007 elections and in the July **by-elections** in five constituencies. These polls had become necessary after a military plane crashed killing 14 people, among them assistant ministers Mirugi Kariuki, Titus Ngoyoni and MPs Bonaya Godana, Abdi Sasura and Guracha Galgalo. LDP leader Raila Odinga declared the by-elections 'a test run for 2007', which forced former President Moi back into active politics to block a united stand by KANU and LDP. Another veteran in Kenyan politics, Charles Njonjo, led the Central Kenya Initiative, operating under ODM, which intends to make inroads into Kibaki's backyard. President Kibaki, who persistently avoided revealing for which party (among the Democratic Party, NARC or NARC-Kenya) he would seek re-election in 2007, gave a slight indication when he campaigned for the NARC-Kenya candidates. The party scored three seats (Nakuru Town, Saku and North Horr), leaving KANU with Laisamis and Moyale. Although it held only three seats, a total of 85 MPs signed up for NARC-Kenya, making it virtually the biggest party in parliament. In November, the Kenyan National Commission for Human Rights (KNCHR) released a report implicating ministers John Michuki (security) and Mutua Katuku (water) and four MPs, among them KANU chairman Uhuru Kenyatta, in the bribing of voters in the July by-elections.

Although the state machinery assisted Kibaki's campaign, the by-election outcome was a firm warning that he would again be a formidable candidate in 2007 unless LDP and KANU united. On 16 August, the ODM leaders met and agreed to register the Orange movement as a political party incorporating LDP, part of KANU and the Labour Party of Kenya. Uhuru Kenyatta did not attend the meeting. In September, ODM-Kenya was formally registered. Several ODM politicians declared their candidacy for the presidency in the 2007 elections (William Ruto, Najib Balala, Julia Ojiambo, Musalia Mudavadi, Fidelis Gumo, Kalonzo Musyoka, Raila Odinga). **Opinion polls** released in October showed ODM-Kenya as being the most popular, at 32%; NARC scored 21%; and NARC-Kenya 17%. ODM-Kenya led in six of the eight provinces leaving, Central province to NARC-

Kenya and North Eastern province to KANU. Among ODM-Kenya supporters, Kalonzo Musyoka scored 49%, ahead of Raila Odinga (30%), William Ruto (5%), Musalia Mudavadi (5%) and Uhuru Kenyatta, who had since joined ODM-Kenya (1%). Kibaki did well among NARC (74%) and NARC-Kenya (77%) supporters. Of more importance, 68% of Kenyans rated the president's performance as satisfactory by late 2006.

A **third cabinet shuffle** in November saw the reappointment of Saitoti and Murungi and brought in many more assistant ministers from strategic regions in the country thought to be needed to win the 2007 election. Whether the election will become a two-horse race or not is not yet clear. At the end of September, another party, 'Chama Cha Mwananchi' (CCM) was registered. The head of CCM is the assistant minister for information and communications, Koigi wa Wamwere. Rumours also circulated that the remnants of NARC, most prominently those linked to Charity Ngilu's National Party of Kenya, Paul Muite's Safina and other political parties, such as the Democratic Party, FORD Asili, Sisi Kwa Sisi, Shirikisho Party of Kenya and political parties not represented in parliament, were trying to construct a **third force**. Whether FORD-Kenya and KANU remnants will be able to play that role is unclear, especially as both parties experienced internal coups aimed at their respective chairpersons: in surprise moves, KANU's Biwott replaced Kenyatta and Housing Minister Soita Shitanda took over Local Government Minister Musikari Kombo's position within FORD-Kenya.

And the question stands if the **constitutional dialogue** will be revived after five parties walked out on 16 November, blaming Justice and Constitutional Affairs Minister Martha Karua for obstructing the acceptance of minimum reforms agreed upon. Karua claims the government wants a comprehensive review by September 2007.

The year 2006 witnessed a number of legal steps by the Kenyan government to fight **human rights abuses**. On 13 March, it launched the parliamentary human rights handbook to help MPs better fulfil their role as protectors of human rights. On 14 July, President Kibaki signed the Sexual Offences Act 2006 which criminalises rape, defilement, child pornography and sex tourism. Amnesty International, however, lamented the new law's failure to recognise marital rape. Nor did it criminalise forced female genital mutilation.

Moreover, the conduct of **security forces**, the police in particular, created serious **human rights problems** such as unlawful killings, torture, arbitrary arrest and prolonged pre-trial detention. The Independent Medico Legal Unit (IMLU) reported that 287 extra-judicial killings occurred during the year. For example, on 14 March, police shot and killed seven would-be mattress thieves in Kisumu while on 21 December, five suspected bank robbers were shot dead in Nairobi. No action was taken against the perpetrators. Police also killed civilians at checkpoints. The IMLU attributed the increase in killings to the March 2005 'shoot-to-kill' directive. The police claimed that the 'shoot to kill' policy was necessary because of the large number of firearms in the hands of criminals.

There were also reports that persons died while in police custody or shortly thereafter, occasionally as a result of **torture**. During the year, 380 cases of torture by security officers, compared to 397 allegations in 2005, were reported: 13 cases resulted in death. On 21 July, a court ruled that the 2004 deaths of five prisoners at Meru G.K. Prison were the result of inhumane prison conditions. Kenyan prisons are severely overcrowded, up to three times their intended capacity. The government tried to improve the situation by releasing nearly 8,000 detainees in July. In September, it also established a health unit for inmates.

The **Kenya Anti Corruption Commission** (KACC) found that 86.3% of citizens considered the police the most corrupt government institution. The KNCHR issued a report that noted that street children regularly paid into a collective fund to bribe police. In August, the police commissioner deployed a special undercover police squad to combat corruption in the police force during traffic stops.

Reforms in the judiciary had begun in 2003, but seemed to fall short. In August, the ministry of justice announced it would form a public complaints unit, noting that corruption had contributed to the judiciary's inability to protect human rights adequately. In December the APRM reported a "visible lack of independence of the judiciary" in the country.

Violent conflicts over natural resources caused the loss of many lives. The increasing proliferation of guns, the growth of a modern bandit culture, unresponsive local-level political leadership and the inability of security forces to quell the violence seemed to worsen this trend. In June, a major conflict erupted in western Kenya near Mt. Elgon that lasted for six months. Land claims exacerbated by rivalries among political leaders were at the root of the conflict. The ongoing violence in northern Kenya between Gabra and Borana left more than 200 people dead and thousands of head of livestock were stolen. Some pointed to the drought that killed as much as 80% of domestic animals and caused famine for some 4 m Kenyans. Others claimed the involvement of the Oromo Liberation Front from Ethiopia.

Approximately 11,000 **squatters** were **forcibly evicted by the authorities** from forests in Uasin-Gishu and Marakwet districts and a slum in Nairobi, and their property destroyed. Notice was sometimes, but not always given. The government pledged to develop national guidelines on evictions, and in May set up an inter-ministerial task force to finalise them.

Communal violence around Likia killed eight persons and injured ten while on 20 September, four persons were killed and 12 injured in inter-ethnic clashes near Nakuru. Fights occurred between rival Luo and Kikuyu gangs in Nairobi slums, claiming more than ten lives. On 13 January, the government stated it would continue to crack down on members of the outlawed Mungiki sect. Police arrested more than 250 suspected members on 30 January, approximately 100 on 3 February and some 800 in December. Mungiki members engaged in criminal activities and harassed and intimidated residents.

Internal Security Minister Michuki escaped death when gangsters sprayed his house with bullets. Other ministers, MPs and foreign diplomats were robbed, including the Russian ambassador. **Violent robberies** sometimes triggered mob violence and vigilante justice. The government rarely arrested the perpetrators. A second-time arrest, though, was made of Tom Cholmondeley, a grandson of Lord Delamere, this time accused of killing Robert Njoya on the Delamere ranch on 10 May. On 19 April 2005, Delamere had killed game warden Samson ole Sisina, but the attorney-general had terminated the case.

In 2006, there were serious reports of increased intimidation and **harassment of media** workers and journalists by the authorities. The press freedom index of Reporters Without Borders placed Kenya at 118 (out of 168) down from 109 (out of 167) in 2005. On 1 March, police, acting on government orders, raided 'The Standard' newspaper and the studios of KTN television, both owned by the Moi family. Three 'Standard' journalists had been arrested earlier and were accused of producing 'alarming' articles (falsely) reporting that the president had held secret talks with opposition leader Kalonzo Musyoka. On 29 September, the charges were dropped.

The raid on 'The Standard' cropped up again in what came to be known the **Armenian brothers saga**. Artur Margaryan and Artur Sargasyan, claiming to be 'investors', came into the limelight when MP Raila Odinga stated there were assassins in the country hired to eliminate opposition politicians. The duo was hurriedly deported after they caused a security scare at Jomo Kenyatta international airport on 9 June. A subsequent police raid on their well-guarded estate revealed automatic weapons, forged passports and government papers identifying them as deputy commissioners in the Kenya police force. Journalists claimed that the house contained computers and videos thought to have been raided from 'The Standard'. Journalists also reported that Winnie Wangui, daughter to Mary Wambui, Kibaki's second wife, was in a business partnership with the two men. The incident cost the powerful director of the criminal investigation department, Joseph Kamau, his job. A commission of inquiry headed by former Police Commissioner Shedrach Kiruki was appointed to probe the activities of the Armenians. Leaked details of the report accused the Arturs of drug smuggling and money laundering. The report also mentions tax evasion and corporate fraud by Winnie Wangui.

In April, Royal Media House was banned from covering parliament's proceedings after Citizen Radio broadcast a programme that unfavourably depicted MPs. The Radio Hope office of the Pentecostal church, based in Nairobi, was attacked during the night of 12 May by a gang of nine Muslim extremists. They killed a watchman, injured others before firebombing studios and taking the station off air. The assault followed the broadcasting of a programme that promoted conversion to Christianity for Muslims.

In November, the constitutional court upheld the dismissal by the chief magistrate of a 2005 suit filed by Clifford Otieno, a television journalist from the 'Daily Nation', against first lady Lucy Kibaki for assault and damaging his camera. In January, he had to flee the country after threats and harassment.

A draft bill – the Media Council of Kenya Bill 2006 – proposed a statutory media council to replace the existing voluntary council. The bill was criticised for imposing restrictions on the work of journalists through an annual licensing system and limiting the right of appeal against the council's decisions. By the end of 2006, the bill had not been passed.

In January, John Githongo, former ethics and governance permanent secretary who remained in self-imposed exile in Europe, released a report providing details of a massive **corruption** scandal, **Anglo Leasing**. Vice-President Moodi Awori and two cabinet ministers, Mwiraria (finance) and Murungi (energy), were among 30 people summoned by the KACC in connection with this scandal. Murungi was dropped from the cabinet after a tape implicated him in blocking an inquiry into the fraud. He was heard coercing Githongo to drop his investigations in return for cancellation of an outstanding debt of Kenyan shillings (KSh) 30 m owed by Githongo's father to businessman Anura Pereira, one of the key players in the € 250 m scandal. However, the attorney-general, Amos Wako, decided not to prosecute the 15 suspects, including Mwiraria, indicted by the KACC.

On 15 February, the Bosire report on the **Goldenberg** scandal, which involved the loss of $ 1 bn in false gold and diamond exports in the 1990s, was published. It recommended corruption charges against businessman Kamlesh Pattni, Education Minister George Saitoti, former President Daniel arap Moi and several others. The following day the police ordered 20 prominent Kenyans implicated in the scam, including Gideon and Philip Moi and lawyer Philip Murgor, to surrender their firearms and passports. In March, five people, including Kamlesh Pattni, were charged. The others were former chief spy James Kanyotu, former Kenya Commercial Bank general manager Elijah arap Bii, former Central Bank of Kenya Governor Eric Kotut and his former deputy Eliphaz Riungu. However, the case was stopped pending an appeal lodged by Pattni. In August, a panel of three high court judges declared Saitoti immune from prosecution in the Goldenberg case due to protection from double jeopardy. In November, both Saitoti and Murungi were reinstated as ministers.

In February, the KNCHR and Transparency International published a report, 'Living Large', which detailed wasteful government expenditures, in particular the purchase of luxury vehicles. In another 'big money' case it was revealed how the government paid six lawyers KSh 72 m to act in two referendum cases in 2005. Key players were Solicitor-General Wanjuki Muchemi, the then Justice Minister Kiraitu Murungi and lawyer Gibson Kamau Kuria, representing a law firm closely linked to the minister. In March, KACC visited the Kenya Pipeline Company and the East African Portland Cement Company to find evidence in relation to allegations of corruption in construction contracts, meddling in tendering and non-competitive recruitment of senior staff. The KACC was dealt a blow when the constitutional court quashed a charge against former Transport Minister Chris Murungaru, who had been forced to resign in 2005. Another big name in court was suspended Central Bank of Kenya Governor Andrew Mullei for a KSh 9 m abuse of office charge in hiring four consultants, among them his son, without following procedures. In September, the chairman of the KNCHR, Maina Kiai, was summoned by the KACC for an investigation into allegations of abuse of office. Forty civil society organisations came to his defence and accused the government of using anti-corruption mechanisms to silence critics.

In March, a new scam emerged implicating the police in tampering with the burning of 1.1 tonnes of **cocaine** confiscated in late 2004. The Dutch police had tipped their Kenyan counterparts about a deal involving six Dutch citizens and a Kenyan. The police waited almost a week, enabling the dealers to escape, albeit without the drugs. This gave rise to the rumour that flour had been burned and that corrupt officials had sold the real stuff to Europe. That rumour gained credibility with the arrest of Kenya Airways flight attendants found carrying cocaine on the Amsterdam and London routes.

Foreign Affairs

Relations with foreign donors sunk to a low. The **British government** issued a ban on former President Moi's sons Gideon and Philip and 22 others under investigation by KACC. The **US** also issued a ban on Kibaki's former aide Alfred Getonga and three businessmen, Kamani, Pereira and Wanjigi, named in the Anglo Leasing scandal. Tense relations with the US over the refusal by Kenya to reject the international criminal court eased when the US government, for geopolitical reasons, partially lifted the ban on military aid to Kenya imposed in 2005.

Mau Mau fighters went to court seeking compensation for being tortured by British authorities during detention in the 1950s. The first formal demand to the British government was filed in mid-October. At the beginning of the year, the UK and Kenya had reached a new five-year agreement that enabled British troops to continue training in Kenya.

Attempts by Finance Minister Mwiraria to have a KSh 449 bn debt partly cancelled failed when the **World Bank and IMF** directed the country to the Paris and London Clubs for rescheduling its external debt. A possible alternative to Western donors is **China**. President Kibaki was among the 48 African leaders who attended the **Beijing summit** of the Forum on China-Africa Cooperation in November. China's presence in Kenya in both development cooperation and trade is on the rise.

The Anglo Leasing scandal impacted upon the **Kenyan embassy** in the Netherlands when in March a Dutch company, Nedermar, filed a KSh 2.7 bn claim relating to the construction of a military facility in Nairobi, also known as **Project Nexus**. The Kenyan government responded that the contract was under scrutiny by the KACC. On 25 July, the district court in The Hague rejected the request by the Kenyan government to lift the attachment of the embassy buildings, but ruled that the embassy's bank account should not be used for security.

In October, the government appointed former President Daniel arap Moi as special envoy to help in the resolution of conflicts in the region. Shortly before, Kenyan troops had been on high alert after renewed fighting erupted in Somalia, sending a new wave of refugees into Kenya. In November, the **EAC's membership** comprising Kenya, Tanzania and Uganda was expanded to include Burundi and Rwanda. The two countries are supposed to become full members in July 2007. In November, the Nairobi and Uganda stock exchanges signed an agreement and announced plans to merge in two years to form the East Africa Stock Exchange. On 15 December, African leaders from the **Great Lakes** area signed a treaty in Nairobi ending two years of negotiations between 11 countries on issues of security, democracy and economic development in the region. A reconstruction and development facility was created to finance projects for which $ 2 bn was sought from member states as well as international donors and the ADB.

Socioeconomic Developments

Real GDP growth was 6.1%, up from 5.8% the previous year. As in 2005, agriculture and tourism were the key drivers of the economy. On Madaraka Day (1 June), President Kibaki reported the creation of 469,000 jobs, compared to 458,900 jobs in 2005, mostly in the informal sector, equivalent to the number of annual entries into the job market. The surprise closure of Uchumi supermarkets that same day, affecting 1,200 employees, underlined the huge task of reducing unemployment. The growing economy, though, enabled the government to fund public projects such as free primary education to over 7.6 m children, rehabilitation and creation of new health centres and roads. The government also increased the minimum pension for retired public servants from KSh 500 to KSh 2,000 per month. Still, the president acknowledged that the country's growth is not shared equitably.

By December, overall **inflation** stood at 15.6%, significantly up from 10.3% in 2005. This was mainly caused by high international oil prices and drought. The Kenyan shilling appreciated against the dollar but depreciated against the euro. It traded at the beginning of the year at KSh 72.2 and KSh 87.5 to the dollar and euro respectively, while at year's end these figures stood at 69.6 and 92. On the regional front, the shilling gained against the Ugandan and Tanzanian currencies to trade at USh 26.1 and TSh 18.6 against the Uganda and Tanzania shillings respectively in December, compared with USh 25.2 and TSh 16.3 in January.

The government's **budgetary operations** resulted in a budget deficit of 3.6% of GDP in fiscal year 2005–06. This reversed the trend of a surplus of 0.1% of GDP in the previous period. The **public debt** stood at $ 10.3 bn at the beginning of 2006. This was equivalent to almost 53.3% of GDP. At year's end, total public debt had increased to $ 11.4 bn, yet down to 47.9% of GDP due to faster growth in GDP than in debt. Kenya's **overall balance of payments** improved to a surplus of $ 691 m compared to $ 275 m in 2005. This was due to an improvement in the capital and financial account surplus of $ 1,677 m (up from $ 1,359 in 2005), which offset the $ 986 m deficit in the current account balance. The latter account widened following a worsening of the trade deficit from $ 2,462 m to $ 3,874 m, the result of a 28.2% increase in merchandise imports (mainly machinery and transport equipment, petroleum, chemicals, manufactured goods). Kenya sourced most of its imports from the United Arab Emirates (14.7%), UK (6.5%), US (4.7%), South Africa (6.4%), Japan

(5.6%), China (5.5%), Saudi Arabia (5%) and India (7.1%). The value of imports from the UK and US was significantly reduced compared to 2005, whereas those from Japan, Singapore, China and India increased.

Export earnings continued to grow following higher export volumes in some sectors (horticultural products) and higher prices in other sectors (coffee and tea). The value of Kenya's exports stood at $ 3,437 m, up $ 197 m from 2005, an increase of 6.1%. Coffee and tea exports increased by 7.8% and 16.9% and stood at $ 138 m and $ 656 m respectively. The value of horticultural exports increased by 17.3% to reach $ 509 m. The manufactured goods sector also performed well, up 20.6% to $ 422 m, while re-exports saw a 52.4% decline to $ 316 m. Kenya's exports to African countries dropped from 49.2% in 2005 to 43.5% in 2006. Uganda (11.2%) remained the main destination for merchandise exports, but its share dropped significantly, down from 17.4% in 2005. Other major destinations were the UK (11%), the Netherlands (7.4%) and Tanzania (7.4%). The US (7.1%) and Sudan (4.1%) showed a strong rise in prominence as export destinations.

Agriculture, forestry and fishing remained the most important economic sector (over 24% of GDP). Except for tea (-5.5%), all sectors increased output. Growth figures for coffee and horticulture were 6% and 2.2% respectively. The increase in the horticultural sector was mainly in cut flowers, whereas output of vegetables and fruits declined by 3.8% and 17.5% respectively. Profitability in the sector was hampered by the high cost of implementing stringent phyto-sanitary conditions, expensive input and increased competition from low-cost producers elsewhere (especially Ecuador and Ethiopia).

Deliveries in the **coffee** sub-sector improved, partly because prices improved from $ 2,329 per tonne in 2005 to $ 2,649 in 2006. Plans were launched by government to address restrictive marketing laws. Agro-industrialist Sasini was among the beneficiaries of the new law that allows farmers to market their coffee abroad directly. The company also built its own coffee mill, but some argue that a boost in quality not in output is needed for Kenya to be competitive on the world market.

Although coffee output was affected by failing rains, it was mainly **tea** that suffered from a major drought, with harvests down 70% on the previous year. Some multinational companies, such as Unilever, were forced to close down their factories temporarily in early 2006.

By contrast, the Kenya meat commission slaughterhouse reopened with a slaughtering capacity of 1,000 cattle per day. An outbreak of Rift Valley Fever in northeastern Kenya in December killed over 25 people and affected the livestock trade. Milk deliveries in the formal dairy sector increased by 5.9%. Fears over the possible outbreak of avian flu among Kenya's 50 m chickens affected the business of Kenchic, East Africa's largest integrated chicken business. The threat eventually passed.

There were mixed fortunes in **manufacturing**. As in the previous year, improvements were recorded in cigarette and beer production, albeit with lower increase rates of 12.2% and 5.3% respectively, while soda ash production increased by 2.7%. Sugar production, however, declined by 3.1%. With the gradual reduction in tariffs in the EAC and the emerging new market in southern Sudan, the Central Bank of Kenya expects the growth momentum in the manufacturing sector to accelerate in the medium term.

After signing a 21-year lease in Kwale on 3 February 2005 to mine **titanium**, used in aircraft, pacemakers and watches, Tiomin Kenya commenced a process of compensating and relocating over 600 families on five-and-a-half-acre plots. Eight farmers, holding over 100 ha, did not accept the KSh 80,000 per acre compensation and refused to move. On 21 December, however, the high court ruled that the state could take the land in matters of urgency through a provision in the Land Acquisition Act.

Hopes for Kenya becoming an **oil producer** gained momentum in November when a consortium indicated it had found found over 30 prospecting leads off the Kenyan coast in the Lamu basin. Other potential oilfields are in the Turkana and Mandera regions, both part of the Anza basin, a geological formation Kenya shares with Chad and Sudan. China's state-owned China National Offshore Oil Company (CNOOC) controls more than a quarter of the total exploration area in the country. President Hu Jintao of China visited Kenya and signed a deal to this end in April. Apart from allocating blocks to CNOOC, Kenyan authorities have granted exploration rights to other firms, including Australia's Woodside Energy.

Electricity generation increased by 5.5% in 2006 to 5,823 m kw hours, of which 51.8% was generated from hydro sources. Thermal and geothermal sources accounted for 30.3% and 18% respectively. A major development was the initial public offer of Kenya Electricity Generating Company (KenGen), responsible for 80% of the country's energy supply. This turned out to be the largest IPO in the history of capital markets in East Africa, and realised KSh 26.4 bn ($ 366 m) from investors worldwide and was oversubscribed three times. In July, KenGen announced plans to increase generation from 58.8 watts an hour to 130.3 in 2008, increasing the percentage of Kenyans with electricity from the current 15% to over 40%. Expansion will be in the traditional sources as well as in alternative energy, such as windmills and biogas. With improved economic growth during the year, consumption of electricity grew by 5.3%. In August, the management of the Kenya Power and Lightning Company (KPLC) was taken over by a team of managers seconded by the Canadian firm, Manitoba Hydro International. The KPLC performance is to be significantly improved and the promise was made to connect at least 120,000 new subscribers every year.

The **telecommunications sector** continued its recent vibrant performance. The number of mobile telephone subscribers increased to 7.34 m by December, up from 5.26 m in 2005. In October, Safaricom officially became the region's most profitable company, reporting a 44.6% increase in pre-tax profits to KSh 12.8 bn. Safaricom is said to be owned by Vodafone of the UK (35%), Telkom Kenya (60%) and a mystery firm called Mobitelea Ventures (5%), apparently linked to former President Moi's inner core. The company signed a KSh 12 bn loan facility to expand its network. National telephone operator Telkom Kenya is reorganising to deal with a huge debt. Plans were launched to offer 60% of its shares on the stock exchange. The company started negotiations to sell another 9% stake in Safaricom to Vodafone. Mobile phone competitor Celtel introduced the 'one network' facility for its customers in East Africa, which significantly lowered the cost of cross-border communication in the region.

The issue of a third mobile operator, Econet Wireless Kenya, licensed in November 2004, dragged on in 2006. It failed to come into operation allegedly due to government's failure to provide the necessary frequencies. More trouble arose after the Communications Commission of Kenya (CCK) approved Vtel consortium, a Dubai-based company, as a second national operator. The authorisation would allow both fixed lines and mobile phone services. However, in late December a court stopped the CCK from awarding the licence. Telkom Kenya, referring to Vtel's plans, decided to roll out its own mobile network. Vodafone announced it would oppose this move since Telkom is the majority shareholder in Safaricom.

Fixed lines stood at 303,905 as of 30 June. China extended a KSh 1.8 bn credit line to provide a minimum of 2,000 fixed lines to each district headquarters in the country. Improved communication is hurting the postal corporation. In response, Posts Kenya, in collaboration with US-based Afripayments, launched PostaPay, a much cheaper way of sending money than traditional players like Western Union and MoneyGram. Safaricom and Celtel Kenya, however, have also applied for money transfer service licences. The Kenyan community abroad and their relatives will be the main beneficiaries: remittances reached some $ 750 m in 2006.

In April, Eastern Africa's **submarine cable** system (Eassy) ran into trouble. The KSh 15 bn project had failed to secure funds and stakeholders disagreed over the ownership model. Later in the year, enough countries signed on to begin the project. By June, however, local firm Kenya Data Network announced it had secured the services of an Indian telecommunications company, FLAG, to set up a rival fibre optic network. In November, Telkom Kenya signed a deal with Etisalat from the United Arab Emirates to build a $ 110 m rival connection known as The East African Marine Systems (Teams). The cable will connect East and Horn of Africa countries to the rest of the world at drastically reduced costs.

Cargo handled by the Kenya Ports Authority (KPA) increased by 8.6% to 14.4 m tonnes from 13.3 m tonnes in 2005. The volume of petroleum products transported by the Kenya Pipeline Company (KPC) grew by 8.5% to 3.83 m m^3 units, up from 3.53 m. Upgrading of the **Mombasa port** continued. Japan is a major financer of the 25-year plan that will provide new cargo handling equipment, staff training and computerised systems.

Cargo handled by the Kenya Railways rose by 9.4% from 1.79 m to 1.96 m tonnes for the fiscal year 2005–06. Further improvements were expected from the takeover scheduled for 1 April by the **Rift Valley Railways** (RVR) consortium, led by Sheltam Rail Company from South Africa. Financial problems resulted in several postponements till 1 November. RVR had announced it would provide reliable and faster delivery of goods at lower costs.

In Kenya, just over 3,000 workers were retained and 5,000 sacked, while salaries were slashed by up to 25%. More worries arose when it was revealed that the company had lost its South African partner, Grindrod, and had failed to pay an entry fee of $ 3 m to Kenya.

Air passengers through Nairobi increased by 8% in the fiscal year 2005–06 to 1,401,225, while outgoing passengers increased by 5.6% to 1,401,482. Kenyatta airport is undergoing major overhaul to improve safety and increase its capacity to 9 m passengers a year. At the end of May, **Kenya Airways** announced a pre-tax profit of KSh 6.9 bn. Total revenue stood at KSh 52.8 bn, up 25%. The cost of jet fuel and security remained the greatest threats, while competition in the region also intensified. At the end of 2006, low-cost carrier Fly540 launched two daily flights between Nairobi and Mombasa. Other routes within the East African region are planned.

Tourism continued its strong growth of recent years, albeit at a lower pace. Visitors to the country increased by 14.5% to 954,335 in 2006, compared with 831,959 in 2005. Tourists from Europe accounted for 56.3% of total arrivals, followed by Africa (19.8%) and America (11.6%). In 2005–06, cumulative earnings from tourism were estimated to be $ 608 m, up from $ 482 m. Officials attending a UN climate conference in Nairobi in November warned that global warming might negatively affect Kenya's tourism industry. Climate change threatens biodiversity treasures such as the Maasai Mara national reserve and Mount Kenya, as well as cultural heritage sites such Lamu, in the latter case through rising sea levels. The drought that hit hard in 2005 continued into early 2006. In the last months of 2006, floods troubled these same regions.

On 31 March, President Kibaki announced that the government had taken specific measures to combat HIV/AIDS, malaria and tuberculosis. It distributed over 3 m insecticide-treated mosquito nets either free (to pregnant women) or at minimal cost. Success was reported in the fight against HIV/AIDS, which was said to have been reduced to 6.1%, down from 13% in five years. In Kenya, malaria is the leading cause of death of children under five years, resulting in an estimated 34,000 deaths annually. In March, a new more effective anti-malaria drug known as Duo-Cotecxin, an artemisinin-based combination therapy (ACTs), was introduced into the country, replacing sulphur-based drugs that are no longer effective.

Marcel Rutten

Rwanda

The political climate continued to be strongly influenced by security developments in the region and the complex internal situation. Reforms and institution-building played a key role in the government's efforts to manage the precarious balance between survivors and perpetrators of the 1994 genocide and society-at-large in order to achieve reconciliation and post-conflict rehabilitation. Trials in the semi-traditional 'gacaca' courts started in July. The international community continued to give recognition to the development efforts of the government, but became somewhat more critical of the lack of political pluralism. Rwanda became a member of the EAC, froze relations with France and applied to join the Commonwealth. Per capita growth improved slightly in 2006.

Domestic Politics

The number of provinces was reduced from 12 to four and the number of districts from 106 to 30 from 1 January, as part of **local government reform**. The aim was to use scarce human resources more efficiently in order to improve capacity at district level, decentralise power and responsibilities and improve service delivery. All officials were supposed to have at least a secondary school education. The reform also aimed at breaking eventual local (government) patronage networks. The senate approved the nomination of the new governors on 5 January.

Elections for the new cell, sector and district levels began on 6 February with the election of 12 people for each of the 2,150 cells. The cells constitute the electoral college for the 146 sectors. Elections at the sector level took place on 13 February. The sector leaders in turn elected the new district leaders and mayors on 24 February. Cell leaders were not allowed to contest the elections on a party political ticket and parties were not allowed to campaign at cell level, but could hold rallies at district level. The candidates themselves could, however, campaign. Election day was a public holiday and the population of the cells of voting age were supposed to assemble to listen to the different candidates' presenting their agendas, discuss these and then line up behind the candidates of their choice. Turnout was high and the elections were peaceful. Apart from minor logistical challenges, few irregularities were reported. Even if the open process compromised the secrecy of the ballot, this was the most democratic election ever held at local level in Rwanda.

The **new mayors** where sworn in on 4 April and had to sign a performance contract in order to improve accountability at local level. On 22 August, an election was held for executive committees at the cell level and members of the 'mediation committee'. Participation in all local elections was high. The national electoral commission estimated registered voter turnout at 80%. Intimidation by authorities to get people to vote was reported from a few localities.

In a **cabinet reshuffle** on 11 March, Minister of Finance Manasseh Nshuti was demoted to minister of public service and labour, just six months after he had replaced long-serving Finance Minister Donald Kaberuka, who had been elected president of the ADB in August 2005. James Musoni, the minister of commerce and former head of Rwanda revenue authority, replaced Nshuti. The liberal economic policies promoted by Kaberuka had earlier been criticised by Nshuti, who had argued for a more interventionist development strategy inspired by South East Asian examples. Musoni was regarded as closer to Kaberuka's position. Sheikh Moussa Fazil Harerimana, former governor of Western province, replaced Christopher Bazivamo as minister of security. Bazivamo was demoted to minister of lands. Romain Murenzi, the minister of education, science and technology was demoted to a new ministry of science and technology in the president's office. Jeanne d'Arc Mujawamariya became the new minister of education.

President Paul Kagame continued to take a tough stand on **governance issues** and in the **fight against corruption**. Several top leaders were dismissed during the year and taken to court on corruption and embezzlement charges. These included the minister of justice, Edda Mukabagwiza, who in early August was replaced by Tharcisse Karugarama, a former chief justice of the high court. Allegations that the minister had handled property belonging to Rwandans in exile in an improper way lay behind the reshuffle, but the evidence against her was weak. On 6 November, **TI** released its 2006 annual Corruption Perceptions Index (CPI), which pointed to a "strong correlation between corruption and poverty." Rwanda got 2.3 marks out of 10, down from 3.1 in 2005 and ranked 121st out of 163 countries worldwide with regard to corruption perceptions. Tito Rutaremera, the ombudsman, as well as the government, strongly contested the downgrading of Rwanda, and requested TI to reveal the criteria used. According to Rutaremera, corruption cases have declined as a result of Rwanda's zero tolerance policy, the removal of corrupt leaders, training and supervision and the decentralisation process.

Civil service reform continued. Parliament reviewed a civil service law. The review of the civil service's wage structure, which was to be completed by the end December, was expected to be delayed until March 2007.

Legal sector reforms resulted in expedited trials and increased judicial independence. The recruitment of better-qualified staff to the judiciary was concluded. However, the huge backlog of cases persisted. The judiciary still faced challenges, including lack of capacity, inappropriate premises, corruption and poor legal understanding. The independence of the judiciary was questioned by human rights organisations, but the government dismissed the criticism.

On 17 February, the supreme court ruled against the **appeal by former President Pasteur Bizimungu**. He was sentenced to 25 years imprisonment for treason and divisionism. In April 2005, he had been found guilty of embezzlement of public funds, spreading malicious rumours with intent to cause disturbance and the creation of a rebel group. In Rwandan law, divisionism means promoting ethnic division and is forbidden. Human Rights Watch claimed that the trials were marked by insubstantial evidence and many violations of due process. Six co-defendants were acquitted, as the evidence was considered too weak.

Most international observers viewed the **human rights situation** with concern but acknowledged that Rwanda was making progress. Rwandans in the political diaspora and some observers, among them a few human rights organisations, claimed that the **'political space'** had narrowed. This was rejected by government and by some researchers and observers in Rwanda as conspiratorial and as exaggerating the homogeneity of the political elite, as well as the possibility of maintaining such a small circle of power. The debate continued as to whether the vague concept of 'divisionism' reflected a strategy by the executive to control the political opposition or whether it genuinely reflected, as parliamentary commissions in 2003 and 2004 had reported, the continuing deep divisions in society and the continued prevalence of the political ideas that had led to the genocide. The APRM noted that "the government faces an uncomfortable dilemma – how to promote political pluralism in a country where political parties have in the past been organized along two main ethnic lines." The report stated that there were some positive trends in the country but that government had to increase its efforts in areas such as political pluralism.

Parliament was assessed in, for instance, the APRM report to be weak in relation to the executive. Its performance had, however, improved and it had on a number of occasions called on ministers to debate ongoing reforms or had taken the initiative to monitor the executive. Other institutions, such as the auditor general (AG), human rights commission and the ombudsman also monitored political developments. In his 2005 report, released in

March, the ombudsman called on government to pay its debts to local suppliers or risk being sued. The AG's report for 2005, presented to the senate in November, reported that ministries, parastatals and institutions of higher learning were not keeping proper and balanced accounts, that tendering procedures were not followed and that Rwanda francs 3.6 bn were unaccounted for. President Kagame criticised parliamentarians, at the fourth national dialogue meeting in December, for not following up on issues highlighted by the AG.

Political parties, apart from the **ruling Rwanda Patriotic Front (RPF)**, continued to be weak. The culture of **guided consultations** on policy issues continued, for example, in the form of the national dialogue on the new economic growth and poverty reduction strategy and the fourth national dialogue in December.

The **APRM** report for Rwanda was presented in Banjul, Gambia on 30 June, at the fifth AU APRM forum. The report noted a number of achievements in building institutions for good governance and socioeconomic development; managing the aftermath of the genocide; nation-building; effecting decentralisation through a participatory bottom-up approach and making progress in freedom of expression. It was more critical of other aspects, and was in turn criticised by the Rwandan government. In the final version in October, some statements were toned down, in particular the discussion on the limited political space in Rwanda. The June report noted that "political space for competition of ideas and power, voting system in local elections and the capacity of the NEC" was limited, and that "Rwandese political system or culture is characterised by absolute consensus rather than voluntarily participation by political parties." There was also concern about the independence of the judiciary, the weakness of representative structures vis-à-vis the executive, particularly at the local level, and the 'gacaca' process's "legitimacy and ability to win trust and confidence in dispensing justice, while strictly conforming to contemporary international human rights norms and standards." In its conclusion, it suggested the removal of all restrictions on political rights and freedoms, while ensuring that political parties are able to operate freely but along non-ethnic or racial lines.

On 15 July, the **'gacaca' courts** resumed trials in all the 9,013 cells and 1,545 sectors, after being in suspension for the first six months of 2006 while local government was being reorganised. In parallel, work continued in identifying victims and perpetrators and in recording preliminary testimonies and destroyed property. 'Gacaca' is a hybrid institution aimed at providing a bridge between restorative and retributive justice, namely "justice that reconciles". 'Gacaca' courts derive from traditional Rwandan jurisprudence, in terms of which communities were directly involved in solving their conflicts. The courts can impose different penalties, including compensation, but most importantly they emphasise the two aspects of confession and forgiveness as a way of healing the wounds of the genocide and forge a nation. In October, the National Service of Gacaca Jurisdictions (NSGJ) estimated that up to 766,489 Rwandans – one-tenth of the population – were due to testify in 'gacaca' courts. Of these, 72,539 are category I suspects (genocide planners, reputed killers and rapists), 397,103 category II and 296,847 category III. Category I suspects will be handed over to conventional tribunals. At the end of the year, NSJG reported that **around 40,000 accused had been tried**. NSGJ had reported at the end of 2005 that the number of **leaders implicated** in acts of genocide was 28,477, including MPs and senior military, political and religious figures. This included 26,752 'gacaca' judges. Major-General Laurent Munyakazi was the first prominent leader to be arrested in the 'gacaca' process. The ruling RPF was accused of shielding Hutu persons accused of genocide.

There was **concern about the process**, not least among genocide survivors, who argued that it was much too lenient on the perpetrators and unsafe for witnesses. At least seven **witnesses and judges were murdered** during the year, in some cases triggering reprisal killings. This caused fear among genocide survivors and 'gacaca' witnesses. IBUKA, an umbrella association for genocide survivors, criticised government during the year for not doing enough to prevent the killings of witnesses and stated that this inaction encouraged additional killings. Others feared the 'gacaca' process had shifted from fostering restorative justice to retribution, with an emphasis on revenge. The limited capacity to handle the reawakened traumas of the victims giving testimony as well as of the perpetrators was a cause of concern.

The immense scale of the 'gacaca' process raised logistical and juridical challenges. More important was how the 'gacaca' process might affect the fragile peace in the country, to what extent witnesses would dare to provide evidence and the judges rulings, and if there were alternatives to managing the enormous case load. The minister of justice, Tharcisse Karugarama, declared on 19 December that the 'gacaca' tribunal proceedings would be concluded by the end of 2007.

The APRM report on Rwanda in October was concerned that 'gacaca' courts lacked the independence, objectivity, impartiality, competence and equity specified for judicial processes in international human rights conventions. No defence attorneys or prosecutors were allowed – the public played both roles through their involvement in the process. The 'gacaca' law was reviewed at the end of the year, and it was proposed that the number of judges be reduced, witnesses safeguarded and the rights of the accused be respected.

There were continuing ups and downs in Rwanda's relations with **International Criminal Tribunal for Rwanda** (ICTR) in Arusha (Tanzania). Rwanda has criticised the ICTR for being slow, bureaucratic and expensive; for having little linkage to the reconciliation process in Rwanda and for neglecting rape and sexual torture. More than $ 1.6 bn had been spent on the tribunal since its inception 1994. For 2006–07, approximately $ 250.5 m was budgeted, compared to $ 17.9 m in the 2006 annual budget for the entire justice sector in Rwanda. The president of ICTR reported on 15 December that judgment had been passed on 32 accused and that the UN Security Council (UNSC) deadline of 2008 for completing the trials and of 2010 for appeals, involving between 65 and 70 accused, would be met, including the 59 concluded or ongoing cases. Rwanda would like to see the cases transferred to its national jurisdiction in order to speed up the processes. Dossiers on 30 genocide suspects had been handed over to Kigali by the end of 2006. The ICTR's reasons for not transferring cases has been the poor standard of prisons, doubts that the trials would be fair and Rwanda's death penalty. The reforms to the justice sector have improved capacity to manage trials with adequate standards, even if Human Rights Watch, for instance, is concerned that the system does not have enough capacity to handle the transferred cases.

In October, RPF decided to abolish the death penalty and a bill was supposed to be taken before the National Assembly in December. However, this was postponed to 2007. Genocide survivors protested, saying that capital punishment was an effective deterrent to similar crimes in the future.

ICTR made a landmark ruling on 16 June that all trial chambers take 'judicial note' that the genocide took place between 4 April and 17 July 1994. The implication of this ruling is that prosecution lawyers do not need to prove in each case that there was genocide, while defence lawyers cannot claim that it was a civil war.

Foreign Affairs

The situation in the eastern DR Congo continued to be of major concern, even if the progress made in late 2005 continued in 2006. The **UNSC and AU acknowledged that a comprehensive solution** had to be found to disarming and reintegrating all hostile forces. In nine resolutions in 2006, the UNSC urged countries in the region to continue their collective efforts to promote peaceful coexistence; agree to confidence-building measures; and institutionalise respect for human rights, good governance, the rule of law, democratic practices and development cooperation. The council strongly condemned the activities of militias and armed groups in the region, the **'Forces Démocratiques de la Libération du Rwanda'** (FDLR), the 'Parti pour la Libération du Peuple Hutu – Forces National de Liberation' (Palipehutu-FNL) and the Lord's Resistance Army (LRA). UNSC also called on countries to enforce the arms embargo in the DR Congo and reiterated its demands that Uganda, Rwanda, DR Congo and Burundi prevent their territories from being used by armed groups and militias in the region. The estimated 8,000–10,000 FDLR fighters, linked to the 1994 genocide, did not constitute a military threat to Rwanda. However, their propaganda and repeated ambushes in Rwanda and on civilians in eastern DR Congo continued to destabilise the region, the domestic reconciliation process and the elections in DR Congo. Limited disarmament did occur. FDLR conditions for disarmament, namely that it be allowed to transform itself into a political party and that FDLR returnees not undergo the 'gacaca' process, were unacceptable to the **Rwandan government**, which **refused to negotiate** with a group it considered to be criminal. FDLR leaders in DR Congo, for their part, had little incentive to return to Rwanda, where some would face trial and others lose status and assets. Rwandan intelligence estimated, however, that only about 50–60 individuals among the FDLR's officers were guilty of category I crimes and would have to face justice, while 80% of the force could return to Rwanda, but would have to go through 'ingando' (solidarity camps organised by the national unity and reconciliation commission) and 'gacaca'. FDLR leader Ignace Murwanashyaka was arrested by German police on 6 April as a result of a UN travel ban on FDLR leaders.

However, strong **international support for the Rwandan position** whereby Rwanda got guarantees that its external security would be respected in return for not intervening in the DR Congo's election process, was successful. Rwanda did not interfere in the **election process**, despite earlier fears that it would do so. Relations with the DR Congo improved during the year, with the presidents of both countries making several statements about improved relations and changed attitudes in domestic speeches.

Rwanda continued to develop its **international and regional** links. The deployment of 254 Rwanda Defence Force (RDF) soldiers to the UN Mission in Sudan (UNMIS) and of more than 2,000 to AMIS (AU Mission in the Sudan) made Rwanda the sixth largest contributor to peacekeeping operations in Africa.

Rwanda's (and Burundi's) admission as full members to **EAC** in December was an important step forward for Rwanda, particularly its plans to establish the country as a bridge between West African French-speaking nations and the anglophone countries of the east. It was also a step towards further integration into regional and international anglophone communities. A discussion unfolded about the extent to which the move was anchored in peoples' minds and whether Rwanda, with its small and undiversified economy, could compete with the original members with their larger and more developed economies. However, EAC membership contributed to enhanced relations with Uganda and Tanzania.

After extensive consultations and preparations, the second summit of the **International Conference on the Great Lakes Region** was held in Nairobi in December under the auspices of the UN. A pact on peace, security and development in the Great Lakes region was signed by Rwanda, Burundi, Uganda, Tanzania, Kenya, DR Congo and Zambia, among others. It rested on the four pillars of peace and security; democracy and good governance; economic development and regional integration; and cooperation on humanitarian and social issues. Even if it lacked enforcement provisions, the pact was a further mechanism to manage the conflict-torn region.

The **Tripartite Plus** Joint Committee (TPC), the US-brokered tripartite agreement between Uganda, Rwanda, DR Congo plus Burundi to monitor border security and resolve disputes, recommended after its meeting on 21 April that the AU adopt provisions committing AU member states to enforce sanctions against the political and military leaders of the rebel groups operating in the TPC states. The 14th TPC sub-commission on security and defence meeting on May 27 resulted in agreement on a number of issues, including enhanced information-gathering and formalising a 'wanted list' of individuals and groups subject to travel restrictions and sanctions on assets. The **joint verification mechanism** set up in 2004 did not meet during the year. The UNSC called for the revitalisation of existing regional security mechanisms.

Relations with **Uganda** continued to be volatile, with mutual accusations of support for rival political parties or guerrilla groups. In April, a Rwandan diplomat in Kampala was arrested for having had an affair with a married woman. Rwanda reacted strongly about the way the issue was handled and expelled Uganda's first secretary. The permanent Rwandan-Ugandan commission, nevertheless, made some progress and an extradition treaty was signed in July. **Relations improved** after a series of high-level negotiations at diplomatic, political and military levels between Kampala and Kigali. President Kagame met President Museveni twice in Uganda, mid-year and at the end of September. The foreign ministers met in the Joint Permanent Commission (JPC) from 12–13 October and discussed border security, refugees, asylum seekers, trade and commerce, agriculture, public service, health, education and justice. Sector-specific joint technical committee meetings including police, the army, justice, education and security followed the JPC meeting. At the end of the year relations were cordial.

Relations with **Burundi** remained close. Of mutual concern was the alleged cooperation between FDLR and Palipehutu-FNL, the only Hutu rebel movement still at war in Burundi. Rebel attacks and recruitment among refugees destabilised the peace process in both countries, particularly in the border areas. A comprehensive peace agreement between the Burundi government and Palipehutu-FNL in September further strengthened Rwanda-Burundi relations. Border conflicts were discussed in a meeting in June.

Between April 2005 and March 2006, some 19,000 **Rwandan asylum seekers** arrived in Burundi, reportedly fleeing persecution under Rwanda's traditional 'gacaca' justice and/or for economic reasons. A joint technical commission, comprising UNHCR and government experts, started in December 2005 to analyse individual cases to determine the Rwandans' eligibility for refugee status. On 10 April, the Burundian government threatened to expel all Rwandan asylum seekers who failed to meet conditions for acceptance as refugees. Repatriation started on 12 April following a decision by the governments of Burundi and Rwanda to re-label the asylum seekers as 'illegal immigrants'. By the end of the year, some 17,000 had **been repatriated**. Few of the repatriated refugees returned to Burundi, according to UNHCR.

Other countries in the region also took a tougher stand on **Rwandan refugees**. In a move to evict 'illegal foreigners', Tanzania expelled 10,400 Rwandan immigrants up to November, and a further 60,000 were expected to be expelled in 2007. Deportees claimed that the process was crude and that Tanzanian authorities confiscated property. A joint commission of inquiry was set up by the two governments to investigate the claims and to suggest solutions. In June, the Zambian government started to revoke the status of around 6,000 Rwandan refugees.

The president of the national refugee commission, Frank Gatete, urged refugees in Rwanda to return voluntarily to countries that had regained peace and stability.

Relations with **France** changed drastically during the year. Three senior French military officers involved in the controversial 'Operation Turquoise' in 1994 were called to testify to the ICTR in the trial of Théoneste Bagasora, the cabinet director in the ministry of defence during the genocide and believed to be one of its key orchestraters. The testimony was expected to highlight France's controversial role in Rwanda during the build-up, course and aftermath of the genocide. On 22 November, two months before the testimony, French **Judge Jean-Louise Bruguière**, vice-president of the 'Tribunal de Grande Instance', signed an **international arrest warrant** for nine senior Rwandan government officials, including James Kabarebe, chief-of-staff of the RDF, and Charles Kayonga, army chief-of-staff, for alleged complicity in the shooting down of former President Juvénal Habyarimana's aeroplane on 7 April 1994, thereby setting off the genocide. President Kagame, the then commander-in-chief, was accused of having given the order. A sitting president could not, however, be prosecuted under French law, so Bruguière called upon ICTR to take up the case. The Rwandan government furiously rejected the charge and claimed that the action was part of the French government's longstanding efforts to undermine the RPF-led government and to divert attention from France's role in Rwanda during the genocide. Several observers pointed at weaknesses in the Bruguière case, including that it involved only a few witnesses, whose credibility could be questioned by virtue of their association with or closeness to the government that had carried out the genocide. Rwanda demanded an apology from the French government. The latter declined to do so and stated that Bruguière had acted independently. **Rwanda broke off diplomatic relations with France** and gave the French ambassador 72 hours to leave. All French-funded development projects were halted, as were all Radio France Internationale broadcasts, and the French cultural centre and Kigali's French school were closed. Rwanda's position was strongly supported by Uganda, Tanzania and several other African governments.

Rwanda strengthened its ties with the US, UK and Asia. In early December, President Kagame made his first state visit to the UK, Rwanda's biggest bilateral donor. A few days later, relations with France were cut. In mid-December, Rwanda formally applied to join the **Commonwealth**. President Kagame made a two-week business visit to the US in April and in October discussions were held on AGOA.

Kagame led a delegation to **China and Japan** from 2–8 November, concluding with the third China-Africa summit. He met Chinese President Hu Jintao and Japanese Prime Minister Shinzo Abe. Additional summits were held involving officials and business leaders. Among the issues discussed were development support and the strengthening of relationships.

Socioeconomic Developments

An external review of the first **Poverty Reduction Strategy** (PRS1), presented on 12 January, reiterated that the PRS had to be understood in the context of national unity and the reconciliation process. Among the points made were the need for a continued focus on rural development, but with clearer information on how the reforms affected the vulnerability and poverty of specific groups of poor people. Although **growth** had been **relatively high**, it appeared to **bypass the rural poor**. Implementation of the agricultural strategy had improved, but not sufficiently, while education and health policies were largely on track and had delivered results. The main challenge was the slow implementation of the decentralisation policy. Public expenditure in priority areas had increased from 37% in 2002 to 52% in the 2005 budget. PRS1 was extended to 2007. The preparation of a new PRS, with a stronger focus on growth and renamed Economic and Development and Poverty Reduction Strategy (EDPRS), started with a national workshop launched by President Kagame in January. Improved agricultural productivity through land reform was one key policy.

Economic development was positive at the aggregate level and reversed the downward trend of the last two years. Real GDP growth was estimated at 6% for 2006. The main factors were more favourable weather conditions at the end of the year and increased agricultural production, both of export and food crops. The mining, construction, transport and communication sectors also contributed to growth. The energy crisis was partially alleviated. Driven by declining food prices, inflation fell from 10% to an estimated 8.2%. However, most of the growth was confined to urban areas and inequality persisted.

The **trade balance** deteriorated in 2006 due to a 36% increase in costs for energy imports, despite improved tea exports and higher coffee prices. Mining export incomes declined while tourism rose to become the second highest foreign exchange earner after transfers.

The World Bank announced on 28 March that it would provide a $ 37 bn debt relief under the **Multilateral Debt Relief Initiative** (MDRI). The effect on the debt-service ratio was limited, as most loans were concessional.

The draft **budget** for 2007 went to the National Assembly on 3 October. After lengthy discussions, the final version was approved in mid-December. The budget was increased by 25% compared to 2006, the largest increases going to the social sectors: education up by 35%, health 42%, defence 30%, while expenditures on agriculture increased just 4%. Donors were expected to provide 54% of the budget. At the same time, tax collection was budgeted to increase by 23.2%. Collections of taxes in 2006 by the Rwanda revenue authority exceeded its targets.

The cabinet approved **a new aid policy** on 26 July intended to improve Rwanda's 'ownership' of programmes and policies supported by donors and the coordination of donors. The aim follows the Paris agenda to move from project to general budget support.

The World Bank signed an interim strategy note on 13 October for 2007–08, allocating $ 84 m for 2007. The Belgian minister of development cooperation announced on 23 October in Kigali that Belgium would scale-up the annual budget from € 25 m to € 35 m.

At the sixth annual government of Rwanda and development partners' meeting (22–23 November) further financial assistance was pledged.

The preliminary **poverty update report** for the period 2000–01 to 2005–06 noted in December that although poverty had declined, inequality had increased. Statistically significant reduction of poverty occurred in the eastern province, but fell at slower rates in other provinces, except in the southern province, where poverty rose modestly. Net enrolment in primary schools increased substantially over the period, from 74% to 86%. A small fraction of children go on to secondary education. The frequency of medical consultations increased only marginally, despite a reported rise in illness. These facts, plus the high initial level of inequality, moderated the impact of a reasonable growth performance over this period on poverty reduction.

Jonas Ewald

Seychelles

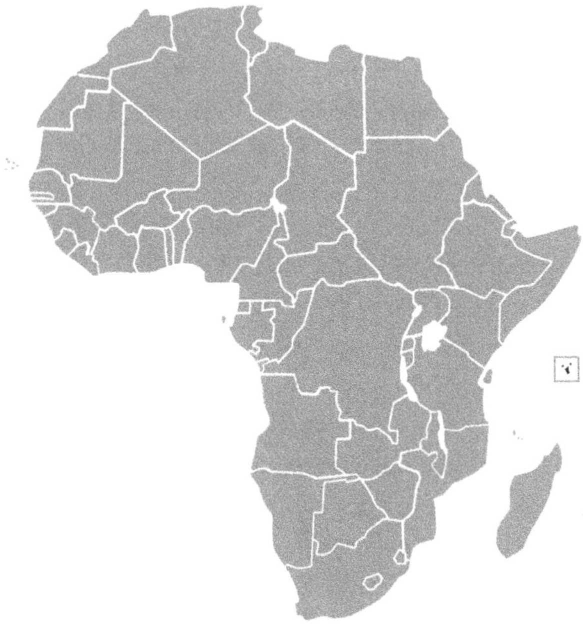

President **James Michel** was convincingly confirmed in office in the July presidential elections, with all hope of a united opposition front against the dominating role of the **Seychelles People's Progressive Front (SPPF)**, which had been in power since 1977, being dashed once again and with indications of a rise in a more confrontational style of politics. After several years of stagnation (albeit at a relatively high absolute level), the economy showed clear signs of recovery and renewed growth resulting from the continuation of cautious reform policies aimed at further liberalisation. Moreover, the country's international financial standing improved considerably and made possible the complete clearance of outstanding multilateral debt.

Domestic Politics

Presidential elections were held on 30 July (over the two preceding days on some of the smaller islands), just four days before the expiry of the presidential mandate under the constitution. For Michel, they constituted the first electoral contest since he had taken over as president in April 2004 from his long-serving predecessor, France Albert René. René was re-elected as SPPF chairman during the 22nd party congress in May and thus remained a highly influential political figure. Contrary to widely made predictions, the elections, with a high 88.7% participation rate, brought almost the same result as in 2001 – a clear victory for the incumbent SPPF candidate with 53.7%, as against 45.7% for **Wavel Ramkalawan** of the **Seychelles National Party (SNP)** and a mere 0.6% for the independent, lawyer Philippe Boulle. Michel won in 16 constituencies, Ramkalawan in nine (including a majority in the capital, Victoria). The SNP had for the first time also been supported by the **Democratic Party (DP)**, which had previously insisted on remaining separate. For Ramkalawan, it was his third successive election defeat since 1998, but he remained the undisputed opposition leader in the run-up to the 2007 parliamentary elections (due in December at the latest). For a while there had been serious speculation about bringing these elections forward to coincide with the presidential contest, but a formal motion by the SNP on 17 May to dissolve parliament was not in the end supported by the SPPF. Nevertheless, all parties had started making detailed preparations, with SPPF even nominating constituency candidates (half of them new) and SNP and DP trying to thrash out an opposition alliance by presenting joint candidates in each constituency.

The **pre-election period** witnessed increased **tension**, with some minor incidents of violence, prompting leaders from the three main churches to appeal for calm and a peaceful campaign. René stood out as having a particularly aggressive style against the opposition, including highly personal attacks against some of their leaders, while Michel was at pains to offset his somewhat sombre public image with a more consensual style. He also used the opportunities presented by a sequence of national holidays in June (5 June, liberation day; 18 June, national day; 29 June, independence day celebrating 30 years of independence) to outline his achievements in introducing cautious economic reforms and to promise an even better future by turning the country into a nation of shareholders, entrepreneurs and investors. Despite recent experiences of stagnation and some shortages, a majority of the population still apparently retained enough trust in the welfare-oriented social policies of the government. The SNP had wrongly expected to capitalise more on expressions of public anger and frustration. The election result, however, clearly showed that the two distinct political camps persisted largely unchanged in the country. Ramkalawan's relatively soft and non-aggressive campaign had obviously not paid off and was subsequently criticised by some of his followers as having been too timid. Several international observers (from the Commonwealth, Francophonie, SADC and the US) adjudged the elections to have been generally free and fair and to have credibly expressed the will of the electorate.

Since January, SNP and DP had begun to work on an **opposition alliance** against the all-powerful SPPF. Unlike in the past, this approach was also endorsed by James Mancham, the DP's former leader and the country's first president (deposed in René's putsch in 1977). In March, the **DP** executive council elected **Paul Chow**, a representative of the party's old guard, as **new leader** by a small majority (10 to 8 votes) over the interim leader Nichol Gabriel, who had been more reluctant about the alliance with the SNP. Gabriel remained DP secretary-general.

The election victory provided Michel with enhanced personal authority to pursue his cautious reform policies, to introduce some administrative changes and to move out of the shadow of his predecessor. The new **cabinet**, sworn in on 9 August, consisted of ten ministers (instead of seven). All previous ministers were retained (with some shuffling of portfolios) and three new faces brought in. Michel relinquished the finance portfolio that he had held for over 13 years. It went to Danny Faure. Michel retained the ministries of defence, internal affairs and economic planning.

In the aftermath of the election, **political** relations between government and opposition became more **confrontational** in style, primarily over the issue of **media control**. For years, this had been a point of serious contention for the opposition. In May, the SNP had unsuccessfully protested against a high-profile pre-election interview with Michel on the French TV 5 channel. In September, the SNP started a public appeal for money for a new radio station (Radio Freedom) not operated by the state, but the SPPF majority in parliament quickly amended the Broadcasting Act so that radio licences could not be granted to political parties or religious groups. A protest demonstration against this move outside parliament on 3 October was broken up by a paramilitary police unit. Twenty-five people were injured, including Ramkalawan and two other senior SNP officials. Charges against the SNP leaders were later withdrawn by Michel, another rally on 10 October was allowed to take place and an independent inquiry into the police conduct was launched, to be led by a retired police officer from Ireland. On 23 October, the opposition-leaning weekly 'Regar' newspaper was once again heavily fined (€ 50,000) in a dubious libel case, leading to the paper's immediate suspension as a protest measure. An appeal through the courts was expected to take quite a long time. In the press freedom ranking of 'Reporters sans Frontières', Seychelles fell from 17 to 24.5 points (from a ranking of 71 to 95 out of 168 countries). In response to the clear **deterioration in the political arena**, SNP parliamentarians declared a **boycott** of parliament and all committees (only interrupted by participation in the 2007 budget debate on 7 December, since this offered a chance for general radio coverage). Hard-line elements from both political camps started producing leaflets that threatened and attacked the opposing side, while a new committee on law and order with participants from both government and opposition was set up in an attempt to pacify the tense situation.

The independence of the **judiciary** also continued to be jeopardised by attempts to exert political influence. In March, the president of the appeal court, Michael Ramodibedi from Lesotho, resigned from this new position after less than two years, complaining that he had not been given the necessary resources to run the institution properly. There had also been a conflict over the respective responsibilities of himself and of the president of the supreme court, Vivekanand Allear from Mauritius. These conflicts had some underlying political dimensions, since the SNP would have preferred to strengthen the appeal court's role. According to TI's 2006 Corruption Perceptions Index, the country experienced some slippage in ranking (from 55 to 63), but still held a leading position (ranked 5th) in sub-Saharan Africa.

Foreign Affairs

In 2005, Michel's government had made public a new foreign policy orientation that stressed renewed support for regional organisations and the general strengthening of contacts with different parts of the world. A new application for membership in SADC (after withdrawal in 2003) was, therefore, made, but the SADC summit in August only took note of this without making a final decision. Particular efforts were made to improve the relations with all multilateral financial institutions (IMF, World Bank, ADB, EU, etc.) and to clear all outstanding debts, but arrears in contributions to the AU continued to curtail the exercise of full membership rights. After the cost-saving closure of several embassies in 2003, the reopening of new embassies in Beijing, Brussels, New Delhi, Pretoria and Rome was approved and plans to implement this decision were made. At the end of September, Michel made a trip to Europe for meetings with investors in London, participation in the Francophonie summit in Bucharest and a visit to Rome. In the European parliament, there were protests over the police brutality against the SNP demonstrations. In November, Michel combined participation in the China-Africa summit in Beijing with an official state visit to China, during which he signed an economic and technical cooperation agreement and attempted to attract Chinese investors.

Socioeconomic Developments

After several years of economic stagnation and as a visible result of the various reform measures undertaken since 2003 under Michel's leadership, the **economy** had clearly gained **new momentum** with a projected GDP growth rate of 4.5% in 2006, after having increased by 1.2% in 2005. Despite the recent slump years, Seychelles had in absolute terms always been far better off than any other country in sub-Saharan Africa, with a nominal per capita GDP in 2004 of $ 8,411 ($ 16,652 in PPP terms) and 47th overall position in the 2006 Human Development Index. In his state of the nation address in February, Michel reiterated the government's determination to continue with its cautious and gradual liberalisation and privatisation of the economy, which had long been hampered by the strong influence of René and the preponderant socialist welfare-oriented ideology. He even promised the considerable relaxation before year's end of the tight foreign-exchange controls (in force since 2001). In August, the creation of a new National Economic Planning Council (NEPC) was announced, indicating Michel's concern to find a viable longer-term strategy. The Seychelles Chamber of Commerce and Industry (SCCI), as representative of the private sector, protested their non-inclusion in the NEPC and the apparent inactivity of the existing Joint Economic Council (JEC).

A first step toward **privatisation** was made in January with the sale of a 30% share of the renamed Seychelles Assurance Co. Ltd. (SACL) to a joint venture involving the Seychelles pension fund and Swan Insurance from Mauritius. Subsequently, in March, stakes of 30% were offered to the general public and 20% to SACL employees. However, this initiative met with only limited interest. The next privatisations – of Nouvobanq, Seychelles Savings Bank and some units of the important Seychelles Marketing Board (SMB) – had been scheduled for August, but were postponed until 2007 because of procedural complications. The SMB's new role was to be trade facilitator and regulator rather than monopolistic economic actor. In February, the 60% share held by the US multinational Heinz in the Indian Ocean Tuna (IOT) cannery, by far the largest industry in the country, was sold to Lehman Brothers merchant bank, with the government holding on to its 40% share. The deal secured the immediate survival of the plant, but left its longer-term future uncertain. IOT continued to perform well and the **fishing sector** remained a major pillar of the economy.

Tourism, the economic mainstay of the country, experienced a strong recovery, despite worries about the potentially negative effects of the spread of chikungunya fever (similar to malaria) in various Indian Ocean islands. Tourist numbers in 2006 (140,627, an increase of 9.3%) were at an all-time high, and even led to a disproportionate increase in foreign exchange inflows (18%). Many new tourism projects, mostly in the luxury category, were financed by record inflows of foreign direct investment (projected at $ 114 m in 2006). These inflows also indicated renewed confidence in the economy following parliament's approval of a new investment code in December 2005.

During the election campaign, Michel had vehemently argued against depreciation of the Seychelles Rupee (SR), whose politically-motivated **overvaluation** (fixed at SR 5.50 per $ since 2003) had long been criticised by, among others, the IMF, although the strict foreign exchange controls had already been relaxed somewhat. Limited **liberalisation** of the **foreign exchange regulations** was nevertheless introduced in October by transferring the allocation mechanism to the commercial banks and applying a new basket of three major currencies in determining the exchange rate (which dropped slightly to SR 5.80 per $ by year's end). In July, the government started to obtain a **sovereign international credit rating**. Standard & Poor's gave the country a B rating with a stable outlook, which allowed the issuance in October of a bond on the international capital market, managed by Lehman Brothers. The bond volume of $ 200 m was heavily oversubscribed ($ 383 m), an indication of confidence among international investors. The proceeds from the bond were used to clear the outstanding commercial loan with the Bank of Tokyo-Mitsubishi and all arrears with multilateral finance agencies (IMF, World Bank, ADB, EIB), while the remainder was used to build up currency reserves. This new flexible and outward-looking approach gained positive commendation from an IMF team visiting Victoria from 8–21 November for regular article IV consultations. By the end of October, foreign exchange reserves had reached an all-time record of $ 133 m (161% higher than a year earlier).

The **2007 budget** presentation by Finance Minister Faure in parliament on 5 December revealed the remarkable fact that in 2006 a budget surplus had been achieved (5% of GDP) for the fourth consecutive year, allowing further reduction in the high internal debt built up earlier. Despite some election-related inducements, the surplus was practically on target, but lower than the extraordinary 9% achieved in 2005. For 2007, the aim was 7%. The austere fiscal policy was also reflected in a projected negative inflation rate of about -0.3% for 2006. The health and education sectors, the improvement of infrastructure and increased public sector efficiency continued to be budget priorities.

The liberalisation of **trade** precipitated a substantial increase in imports (32% until the end of October over 2005), thus further enhancing the traditional high structural deficit in the balance of trade (exports representing only about 55% of imports). Nevertheless, due to high tourism earnings, the 2006 **current account balance** was projected to be contained at slightly above 20%.

The **offshore business sector** continued to thrive, with about 32,000 companies being registered with the Seychelles International Business Authority (SIBA). In the Seychelles International Trade Zone (SITZ), 50 licensed companies (with IOT by far the largest) offered employment to about 2,800 persons (of whom 56% were Seychellois). With a record low **unemployment** rate of 2.9% in September and the continuing creation of new jobs (mainly in the tourism sector), the country faced the unusual situation of needing to import labourers from abroad.

Rolf Hofmeier

Somalia

The political crisis in Somalia reached the end of a cycle with the US-Ethiopian military intervention in late December. The year ended with a war in most of southern Somalia. The internal dynamics of the Somali crisis were not considered seriously by the international community. Instead, the war on terror became the sole framework for understanding the events that took shape in 2006. The fragile Transitional Federal Government (TFG), led by Abdullahi Yusuf Ahmed, which was contested by the Union of the Islamic Courts (UIC), won the battle.

Domestic Politics

From the very beginning of the TFG in October 2004, MPs were divided over the question of **foreign troops** and the status of the capital.

The situation in the Somali capital had grown more than ever difficult after 2002. Not only had the different factions fought each other, but **security had collapsed** with the appearance of gangs of delinquents and a veritable kidnapping industry. The city's inhabitants and businesses – large and small – confronted this situation by creating neighbourhood militias. In some zones of the capital, **Islamic courts** were created in 2004 and 2005, but their jurisdiction extended to only about ten blocks in the entire city.

With the return of the factional leaders and their inner circles to Mogadishu, city dwellers hoped for a return to normalcy. Initially, this did occur but it had swiftly collapsed by the summer of 2005, when the factional leaders were unable to rise above their self-serving interests and petty jealousy. Popular support for the **Islamic courts** took shape in the acute resentment of the city's inhabitants. These courts were initially local responses to the lack of security. Their creation followed more or less the same format. In a war-torn urban environment, some zones were dominated numerically by a particular clan. In several cases, because of gang violence the clan elders decided to form an Islamic court. In naming the court's members, they were careful to choose judges who represented the diverse spectrum of Islam in Somalia. The militias had no connection to a particular religious trend. Islamic and Islamist movements were obviously present in these institutions because their leaders had prestige and often had the organisational skills that were otherwise lacking. These courts, which numbered less than ten before 2006, led a determined struggle against bandits and gangs. The situation did not improve because of the return of the factional leaders in spring 2005. The improvement was the result of the actions of these courts.

In early January, the TFG president and the president of parliament met in Aden and reached **agreement** on the reunification of transitional institutions in the city of Baidoa (Baydhabo). The revolt of the factional leaders in Mogadishu was cut short. Early on, it was clear that they were unable to secure the capital and if they returned to Baidoa they would be politically marginalised. In this context, a **conflict** erupted in early February 2006 between what was soon called the Alliance for the Restoration of Peace and Counter-Terrorism and the Islamic courts.

Several wars merged into a series of extremely **violent confrontations** between January and June. First, there was the clan element: faction leaders tried to establish a local parliament in Mogadishu in the fall of 2005 but refused to give it an elected speaker. In the ensuing debate, threats were made against certain clans, which could explain their participation in the war against the factions. These tensions, however, were not enough to provoke such violence and the courts did not even take part in this dispute. Simultaneously, there was a violent conflict between two groups of businessmen, one led by an American ally (Bashir Rage) and one by an ally of the courts (Abuker Omar Adane). These two men were members of the same Abgal sub-sub clan. The increasingly violent skirmishes concerned a piece of land on the coast that was to house a port for exporting charcoal, one of the most profitable and environmentally destructive exports. This bloody competition began in 2005 but in 2006 the Islamic courts became involved. They had received substantial donations from Abukar Omar Adane and he requested their assistance. Bashir Rage used his American allies in the CIA and established the famous **alliance against international terrorism**.

American involvement changed the nature of the war. Anti-American sentiment brought the local population together, along with its hostility to a series of assassinations after September 2001 and kidnappings of religious figures. The **assassinations and kidnap-**

pings, carried out by the factions, were thought to have been ordered by the Americans and Ethiopians. American involvement mobilised Islamic movements well beyond Mogadishu. While these movements were very different in terms of rites, ideology and recruitment, they were united in their opposition to the US. Hundreds of combatants arrived from Somaliland and others from southern Somalia. In the less populated Puntland, there were fewer recruits but large donations were collected: the diaspora supporting the courts also made substantial donations. The heterogeneity of the war meant that support did not come solely from radicals and Islamists. Some factions, such as the Juba Valley Alliance based in Kismaayo, joined the combat.

When the **factional leaders fled the capital** in early June, the Islamic courts were the only agency that could take advantage of the victory, since the clans and the businessmen supporting the war effort were not organised. It was a victory by default and the leaders of the UIC, Sheikh Sharif Sheikh Ahmed and Hasan Dahir Aweys, were well aware of this from the start.

This victory inaugurated a **radical transformation of the political arena** in Mogadishu and, soon, beyond the capital. It also changed the balance and reshaped relationships between the courts and their component backers. Just as in 1991, when Mohamed Siyad Barre was overthrown and the militiamen close to General Aydid gained strength by looting barracks, some Islamic groups took control of factional arsenals and methodically consolidated their influence in the movement after June. 'Hizb al-Shabab', the Youth Party characterised by its radical Islamist populism, gained strength and appeal. The inhabitants of the capital had not appreciated the desecration of the Italian cemetery in February 2005 by the Youth Party leader, Adan Hashi Farah Eyro, when Italy was giving almost official and religious burial to Somali immigrants who had drowned during their Mediterranean crossing. But his involvements in the frontline and his control of a powerful arsenal changed public opinion for a time.

The influence of the courts spread rapidly beyond the borders of the capital. The first extension was linked to securing the capital: they could not leave the town of Jowhar in the Alliance's hands. The struggle to secure the town against the factions was, however, very minimal in late June and July. Second, courts rapidly appeared in other cities and called for UIC assistance during the summer. The **victory of the courts in Mogadishu** meant the end of the faction as a form for organising Somali political life, a role it had held since 1991. This victory also signalled the arrival of a new generation of political actors. Behind the old leaders and religious figures, a younger generation of men had stepped forward, most of them less than 40. Opportunism was also evident: the creation of an Islamic court could allow one to challenge those who had assumed power or who had directly or indirectly benefited from the power of a faction. For example, in Beled Weyne and Jowhar, as in Mogadishu, there was no 'religious revolution', just the dismissal of an unpopular administration by sectors of the population that took advantage of the Islamic courts' rise by joining them. These revolutions were fundamentally 'political'. Another form of expansion gave more credence to Ethiopian and American claims: military annexation, primarily in the lower Juba region with the capture of Kismaayo by the UIC in September.

The courts committed this major error as a result of several factors. The **Juba Valley Alliance** that controlled Kismaayo had been divided for months, not over interpretations of the Quran, but over the more secular distribution of money from the port and the future structure of the local administration. Initially, the courts did not wish to be involved in this affair, because they did not feel ready to extend their influence before coming to terms with serious internal problems. After several weeks of hesitation, however, they became involved in September. Eritrean advisers warned in early September that Kismaayo would be occupied by Ugandans and Ethiopians. Moreover, Hasan Abdullah Hersi 'al-Turki' and his followers in the Hizb al-Shabab and the courts were pushing to secure lower Juba and the border with Kenya. They won the debate on the strength of rumours of an American presence in northeastern Kenya. Kismaayo's capture was not without consequence. It gave rise to the first popular opposition to the courts, which sent one of their harshest leaders to the region. This action gave credence to the idea of the encirclement of the TFG after several earlier armed incidents provoked in and around Baidoa by Shabab commanders.

But the developments outside the capital contributed less to **the dysfunction of the UIC** than other obstacles: problems of internal organisation, ideological difference and clan troubles. Early in June, the courts established an executive committee that quickly grew to 20 members, presided over by Sheikh Sharif. The advisory committee, the *shura*, presided over by Hasan Dahir Aweys, ballooned to more than 90 members. Which of the two bodies had the final say? What were the decision-making procedures? Who had the mandate to do what? No one knew, including the courts themselves. Not only did they do nothing to eliminate these many ambiguities, but decisions were also often made by commanders in the field who had only relative respect for these two authoritative bodies and favoured their own contacts on each committee. Simply accepting fait accompli rather than debating decisions became a common occurrence.

The ban on *qat* in October and on charcoal exports in August, the requirement for women to be accompanied outside by a male family member (July), the proscription of cinema and sport, etc. (June), were all decisions made without a collective process at the top and had only local validity that spread through horizontal relationships between militia leaders. Ironically, the courts, which had wanted to preserve justice, renewed the arbitrary authority of the militias.

The terms of debate inside the country changed with the massing of **Ethiopian troops** on Somali territory from August onward, when unity became a question of life or death. Contrary to what some have called a 'Talibanisation', in many places in Somalia daily life continued without interference or coercion from court representatives. Yet, the prime minister of the TFG and the Ethiopians singled out examples of coercion to prove the al-Qaida influence within the UIC after June.

There were deep **ideological differences in the Islamic courts**. Somali Islam and Islamism are profoundly connected to global dynamics. There is no need to invoke al-Qaida to explain the extremism of some of the *tariqa* (Muslim brotherhood) and the moderation of others. Many thought that discussions should be held with the TFG, which would return to govern in the long term, while the courts would continue to use their prerogative to maintain order. Others wanted a power-sharing agreement and welcomed the negotiations sponsored by the Arab League in Khartoum in June, August and October. They did not contest the TFG president: however, the prime minister was unanimously opposed. The latter, who welcomed the losses of the factional leaders, held the most radical position against the courts, revealing his dependence on Addis Ababa and his desire to stay in his position no matter what the cost to Somalia. However, a radical and military popular element – oversimplified by those who say it was the Shabab alone – refused negotiations, seeing them as a betrayal and even trying at all costs to sabotage them until the last minute.

Given the lack of ideological unity and the pressure from foreign threat, this **Shabab movement** gained ground in the court-controlled regions. It sparked increasing resistance in court organisations, but also among the populace. The people began to protest the drastic rise in taxes in October, the ban on *qat* that punished thousands of people who earned their living in its trade and the normative coercion that saw young militia members with limited religious knowledge humiliating anyone in the street who did not seem sufficiently pious.

Given this context, the **negotiations mediated by the Arab League** between the TFG and the UIC were rife with problems. The first meetings in Khartoum on 23 June produced meagre results but could have gained some momentum. Not only was there mutual recognition, which is not negligible, but the parties declared a ceasefire However, the Arab League did not insist on the creation of a joint commission for verification. During the second round of discussions in August, this idea was included in the final document, but the TFG second-guessed its own delegates. The Europeans were on vacation and applied no pressure to immediately enact the principle of a joint commission for verification. The negotiations in Khartoum 3 in October did not even start and the courts made a further strategic mistake. By placing preconditions on the negotiations, they appeared to be the cause of their failure. The US and Ethiopia had their *casus belli*. War, once only probable, became certain. There were, however, two **glimmers of hope**. First, the speaker of parliament travelled to Mogadishu in early November following the failure of Khartoum 3 and made an agreement to return to real negotiations on 15 December. However, TFG once again turned a deaf ear. On 20 December, European Commissioner for Development Louis Michel went to Baidoa and Mogadishu to obtain signatures on a memorandum to return to negotiations, establish a joint commission and ensure European involvement. But his political success was swept aside by fighting between the Ethiopian army and the militias of the courts.

Before the intervention, the Security Council passed **resolution 1725** on 6 December. The text proposed by the US was very surprising. It authorised an organisation, the AU, to intervene in Somalia and asked the international community to finance the intervention. The UN would not be involved in any way! Predictably, after violently criticising the resolution, the UIC issued an ultimatum on 13 December demanding the departure of Ethiopian troops. They lifted their threat when Louis Michel's visit was announced. But skirmishes began on the night of 19 December and by 20 December war had begun.

The TFG was playing two cards after the intervention. On the one hand, it endorsed American and Ethiopian decisions, at least on a rhetorical level, to demonstrate its connections with its powerful allies. On the other, it told the international community that if it did not receive the support it deserved, chaos would emerge when all the Islamists in the world descend on Mogadishu. In short: send money and troops, reconciliation could wait.

Foreign Affairs

The **decision to intervene in Somalia** merged two different logics. On the one hand, there was the global agenda based on the vision professed by Washington concerning the war on terror and the hunt for members of al-Qaida. On the other, the Ethiopian regime, which is contested from inside the country, was trying to prevent a new power from emerging along its southern flank that would have cordial relations with its Eritrean enemies and armed Ethiopian opposition groups. The end result was a growing challenge to stability in Somalia and beyond, in the whole region.

The intervention that started on 20 December was Ethiopian, but **not exclusively Ethiopian**. It would not have been possible without **American consent** and, most of all, American funding. The intervention was American but not only American. If Ethiopia had refused to invade, the US would have returned to its policy of funding Somali groups to hunt down members of al-Qaida.

With a common frontier of more than 1,500 km, Ethiopia could hardly remain indifferent to the Somali situation. However, history and the situation in the region did not make the task any easier. Moreover, in 2005, the fatigue over authoritarianism brought the overconfident Ethiopian rulers electoral defeat.

Ethiopia's extreme response was all the more logical given the level of hostilities between Addis Ababa and Eritrea and the Eritrean regime's historic ties with the armed groups based in Ogaden to whom it had provided training facilities and weapons to the extent that it could afford them. As early as 1999, Eritrea had some success in sending Oromo fighters through Somalia. This project gained new currency with the rise of the Islamic courts and their direct nationalist opposition to Ethiopian policies. **Eritrean support for the courts**, which began in the spring of 2006, was aimed at weakening the position of the TFG, which in the eyes of Eritrean leaders was from the start an instrument of Ethiopian power. The leaders of the courts shared the idea of a strong, centralised and united Somalia. They saw the creation of Somaliland in 1991 and Puntland in 1998 as attempts by Ethiopia to balkanise Somalia and to weaken Somalis as well as the Muslims of the Horn of Africa. The courts issued several contradictory statements about pan-Somalism and their claims for Ethiopian territories inhabited by Somalis.

Islamism was not **Ethiopia's primary concern**, despite its public pronouncements. Addis Ababa had other priorities. The first was to block Asmara and maintain Eritrea's isolation in the region, especially at a time when relations between Eritrea and Sudan had been improving since the summer of 2006. The second priority was to ensure that Ethiopian armed groups would not have sanctuary in Somalia. The third was to secure its southern flank by controlling the emergence of a Somali government: instead of dividing Somalia into 'little republics', it could prevent the appearance of autonomous political agents. That is what it did by helping create the TFG. This imperial approach to security is problematic, but Addis Ababa has a strong diplomatic argument: the fight against terrorism.

Since 1998, **the US** has considered Somalia to be a security problem. Some reasons for this include the preparations in Somalia for the attacks against the American embassies in Kenya and Tanzania in the summer of 1998 and the attack on a Mombassa hotel and an Israeli plane in November 2002. Once the idea of entering Somalia was abandoned in December 2001, the US established a containment policy that was successful until the mistake of February 2006, when the CIA offered massive support to the Alliance for the Restoration of Peace and Counter-Terrorism. For several years, they had funded faction leaders, informers and gangs to enact their counter-terrorism policies. Adan Eyro narrowly escaped capture while the members of his inner circle living in his house were killed in 2003. The Islamists responded by executing officers or members of civil society who were suspected of working for American and Ethiopian intelligence services.

After the failure of the Alliance, the state department moved quickly to push for the creation of an International Somalia Contact Group. The group initially appeared to be an attempt by the US to rehabilitate itself and promote political solutions to the Somali question. By the fall, however, it became clear that it was just a manoeuvre to stave off criticism from the media and public opinion and that security concerns continued to dominate policy. On 14 December, US officials finally announced that the UIC was controlled by al-Qaida.

The **US-Ethiopian military intervention** in Somalia was a turning point in the fight against terrorism. In conformity with the priorities listed in the quadrennial defence review in 2005, American policy intends to grant certain countries the status of 'new regional power' in the fight against terrorism. This designation has several advantages in the case of Ethiopia: its army does not hesitate to respond to attacks and the regime has already dismissed the criticism of the international media. This strategy also gives an increased role to the Pentagon over the CIA and state department. Although international events argue for a police approach to fighting terrorism, this policy favours a military approach.

The regional organisation, **IGAD**, once more played no significant role except to endorse the Ethiopian priorities in Somalia. Uganda and Kenya sided with Addis Ababa in all major issues, while Eritrea and Djibouti were either silent or sidelined. More surprising, Khartoum kept a very low profile owing to the ongoing Darfur crisis and its wish to be chair of the AU after the one-year interim presidency of the Congo. The AU, as always in the case of Somalia, endorsed all decisions made by IGAD without any consideration for peace in the region: ignorance, disdain or US follow-my-leader attitude.

The **EU was split**. While Italy and France firmly supported the negotiations and questioned the war on terror rhetoric, Germany and the UK endorsed the US priorities or kept silent for their own reasons. The late involvement of Louis Michel, commissioner for development, was courageous and productive but too late to provide an international alternative to the US-Ethiopian intervention.

The **TFG was entering Mogadishu** thanks to foreign troops and this would weaken its already notional legitimacy. Reconciliation was the only cure but its core figures were not inclined to it. The terrorism issue was used as a justification for the whole invasion. Most of the international media adopted this explanation without asking simple questions. How many were those terrorists? What was the quality of the intelligence? Was it worth invading a country for an alleged couple of dozen terrorists and risk opening a new front in the Horn of Africa? US and Ethiopian behaviour looked increasingly like a self-fulfilling prophecy.

Socioeconomic Developments

The **reopening of the international port and the airport** in Mogadishu had an important positive impact on prices as it led to the reconfiguration of the supply networks in south and central Somalia, the improved security being another important factor. By a kind of 're-nationalisation' of operators, a new component in the telecom sector was established. Animal husbandry still dominated Somalia's economy. Saudi Arabia was the last of the Gulf states to lift its ban on the import of livestock from Somalia, which it did in early December. The opening of the Saudi Arabian market was expected to lead to a boom in exports, in particular from Puntland and Somaliland.

In March, the **food security and nutrition** report for Somalia, published by the FAO's food security analysis unit, sounded an early caution that Somalia was at high risk of famine because of shortage of rains. About 2.1 m Somalis faced a critical food security situation. Food prices rose vastly as a result of the lowest annual cereal harvest in more than ten years. Rains finally came and a major humanitarian crisis was averted, despite local pockets of serious difficulty. At the end of the year, prices of many basic food items had fallen noticeably in areas under the control of the UIC.

As a result of the expected armed confrontations between UIC and the interim government, a large number of **refugees** fled to Kenya, with the exodus increasing dramatically in October. Additionally, floods in November (affecting neighbouring countries as well) forced people to leave their homes.

Roland Marchal

Sudan

One year after the signing of the Comprehensive Peace Agreement (CPA) between the central government in Khartoum and the Sudan Peoples' Liberation Movement/Army (SPLM/A), the implementation of the agreement was moving forward only slowly. The crisis in Darfur reached a positive turning point with the signing of a peace agreement in May between the central government and a large part of the main rebel group, the Sudan Liberation Army (SLA). However, since other Darfurian rebel groups, such as the Justice and Equality Movement (JEM), refused to accept the agreement, fighting continued with heavy civilian losses. International concerns over the humanitarian situation in Darfur led to accusations of human rights violations and war crimes followed by pressure for sanctions and for the deployment of a UN peacekeeping force. Sudan's economic performance followed the positive trend of 2005 largely due to increasing oil production and oil prices and investments in the oil sector.

Domestic Politics

By the beginning of the year, it was estimated that as many as 300,000 people had died as a consequence of the **fighting in Darfur** and the number of IDPs was estimated at 2 m. On top of that were the refugees who had escaped into neighbouring Chad. The ceasefire agreement from April 2005 provided for an **AU Mission in Sudan (AMIS)**, which was to monitor the ceasefire and protect the civilians. The Sudan government, after mid-2005 known as **Government of National Unity (GNU)**, had agreed with the UN to disarm the Arab militia known as the **Janjaweed**, but apparently this did not happen. In fact, it was widely believed that the government supported the Janjaweed in their attacks on rebel groups, villages and innocent civilians. The UN received disturbing reports about human rights abuses and war crimes in Darfur, some even mentioned genocide and the pressure for an international UN force to be sent to stop the violence in Darfur increased in January-February. The AU was willing to leave the job to the UN, but the GNU, dominated by the Islamist National Congress Party (NCP), was strongly against the proposal and by the end of the year AMIS had not been replaced.

Peace negotiations between the GNU and the Darfur rebels began in **Abuja**, the capital of Nigeria, in 2005 but noticeable progress was made only from January 2006. At that time the two main rebel groups, SLA and JEM, agreed to unite as the Revolutionary Forces of Western Sudan. This looked like a positive step towards stopping the infighting and formulating a common political platform, but in practice the rebel groups persisted as factions with their own political agendas. In the negotiations, the Darfur rebels referred to the CPA and demanded similar rights for Darfur, for instance increased autonomy and political representation at the national level, something the GNU could not fully accept.

The negotiations culminated in a **Darfur Peace Agreement (DPA)** signed in Abuja on 5 May between a faction of the SLM led by Minni Minnawi and the GNU. However, the remainder of the SLM under the leadership of Abdel Wahid Mohammed Nur, as well as the JEM, refused to sign, and this contributed to more fighting. JEM was led by Khalil Ibrahim and was composed of people from the Zaghawa tribal group. They had an ambiguous position as they are ideologically linked to Hasan al-Turabi, leader of the Islamist Popular Congress Party (PCP).

It was also unlikely that the Janjaweed, who had not taken part in the Abuja negotiations, would let themselves be disarmed. Thus, on the ground there was increased violence following the peace agreement as the rebel groups moved from political disagreement to violent clashes, a situation the AMIS peacekeepers were unable to control. The GNU and the Janjaweed took advantage of the internal fighting among the rebels. A **conference in Brussels** in July, backed by the UN, gathered delegations from 70 countries and raised about $ 200 m for peacekeeping and humanitarian work in Darfur, but the meeting failed to persuade GNU to accept a UN peacekeeping force.

Those who signed the **Abuja agreement** were given positions within the GNU. For instance, Minni Minnawi was appointed assistant advisor to President Hasan Omar al-Bashir and became leader of the Darfur transitional authority. On the other side, SLM rejectionists as well as members of JEM united to form the National Redemption Front (NRF) with the assistance of Chad and Eritrea. NRF was led by the former Darfur governor, Ahmed Ibrahim Diraij (Fur), and Sherif Harir (Zaghawa). The NRF also included rebels from various elements opposed to the Abuja agreement, such as a splinter group from SLM/A representing smaller ethnic entities such as the Tunjur and Daju.

In August, the GNU started to move an estimated 22,000 **troops into Darfur**, probably in an effort to secure military victory over the rebels and to demonstrate to the UN that none of its forces were necessary to curb the violence there. At the same time, GNU announced that the AMIS mission was to end by 30 September, a deadline that was later delayed under strong UN pressure to mid-2007. However, AMIS continued to be understaffed and GNU continued to oppose any talk of the deployment of UN peacekeeping forces. Towards the end of the year, it was clear that the DPA could not be implemented: the local forces opposed to it were too strong and the GNU army had failed to disarm the Janjaweed as planned. In fact, there were rumours that the opposite had taken place, to the extent that Minni Minnawi considered withdrawing from the agreement. However, in August it was reported that Minni Minnawi's group and GNU forces had launched offensives against the rebel groups that had refused to sign. The humanitarian situation continued to deteriorate, causing serious international concerns.

The NRF **attacked an oilfield in Southern Kordofan** in November and threatened to attack al-Fasher in early December, causing great alarm there. **Factional strife** and political manoeuvring further divided the rebels and undermined the DPA, but this weakness did not bring the GNU closer to military victory. There were rumours that negotiations would resume, but at the end of the year no progress in this direction had been reported. A positive change was that a UN proposal to create a joint AU/UN peacekeeping force looked like gaining the support of the Sudanese president, Omar Hasan al-Bashir, although the size of the force remained unclear. The president later denied this.

On the **humanitarian front**, it became increasingly difficult for international organisations to bring aid to the IDPs: they were either hindered by GNU or attacked by the Janjaweed, who stole their cars and cargoes. Some aid workers were killed. The Janjaweed were also responsible for raping girls and women in villages and refugee camps, particularly when they were left unguarded while searching for firewood. The number of displaced and killed people rose throughout the year, but exact figures are difficult to obtain.

One year after the signing of the CPA between the Islamist government and the SPLM/A, the implementation of the agreement and the **interim constitution** was moving forward only slowly. In the South, the SPLM struggled to increase support for the CPA among groups traditionally opposed to the SPLM/A by offering positions in the new government structure in the South, the **Government of the Southern Sudan (GoSS)**. Similarly, in the North President Omar Hasan al-Bashir worked to make opposition parties endorse the agreement, but the National Umma Party led by Sadiq al-Mahdi refused. The Umma Party had left the National Democratic Alliance (NDA), formed after 1989 some years earlier, but the remaining parties in the NDA, the Sudan Communist Party (SCP) and the Democratic Unionist Party (DUP), accepted the CPA and, in terms of its allocations to the northern opposition parties, obtained in 2005 14% representation in the new National Assembly. It was clear that the two partners to the CPA agreement, the Islamist National Congress Party and the SPLM, did not have the full support of people either in the South or in the North. Opposition groups as well as peripheral populations felt they had been left out of the settlement and that the resources of the country were not equally shared. Darfur is a good example of such dissatisfaction, but also in the East and in parts of the South people turned to violence to notify GNU and the international community of their demands.

The sharing of the country's **oil wealth** was a particular source of anger. The CPA provided for equal division of the oil revenues between North and South, but SPLM suspected GNU of withholding information about the real revenues from the oil sector. The question of ownership of the oil in the disputed Abyei enclave only added to the tension. Similarly, peripheral regions accused GNU and GoSS of appropriating all the oil revenues for themselves and of leaving nothing for them. The unrest in the East and the West was clearly also connected to this issue. In the East, disturbances were set in motion by the newly formed Eastern Front (EF), a coalition of the Beja Congress and the Rashaida Free Lions. These groups demanded to be incorporated into the CPA and to be represented in Khartoum. A document on procedural issues was signed in Asmara, capital of Eritrea, on 25 May. On 13 June, peace talks between the Eastern Front and Khartoum were opened in the same city and the parties agreed to a ceasefire on 23 June and promised to work towards a comprehensive settlement. Finally, on 14 October, the Eastern Sudan Peace Agreement was signed. In terms of this agreement, the EF would get one assistant to the president, one presidential advisor and one state minister's position, in addition to ten parliamentary seats in Khartoum. At the end of the year, however, the agreement had not yet been implemented.

The **building of government institutions** in the North and the South moved forward in line with the interim constitution. For **Silva Kiir**, leader of the SPLM, president in the South and first vice-president in the North, it was particularly important to work out the power-sharing arrangements. By spring, it was reported that the main national, regional and local institutions were operational and that power had been transferred to GoSS. On 27 May, a three-day meeting between leaders of SPLA and NCP discussed and evaluated the implementation of the CPA. Silva Kiir criticised the delays and lack of Southern influence in Khartoum and voiced his concern that the GNU supported opposition groups in the South. The status of the border enclave of Abyei caused much heated debate. The international **Abyei boundary commission** had recommended drawing the borders in such a way that the oil-rich enclave would become a southern area, a proposal GNU rejected. No agreement was therefore reached. The **joint commissions** envisioned in the CPA, such as the human rights commission, had not been established by September, except for the ceasefire political commission and the national petroleum commission.

On the military front, an important step was taken in January when most of the South Sudan Defence Forces (SSDF) merged with the SPLM/A. SSDF were dominated by the Nuer tribe and often operated in alliance with Khartoum. They were thus rivals of the Dinka who dominated the SPLM/A. In this way, a dangerous source of division in the South had been eliminated. However, a splinter group from the SSDF continued to attack SPLM forces and allegations of NCP support for this and other groups opposed to SPLM continued throughout the year. SPLA/M and the Sudan Armed Forces (SFA) agreed to deploy joint forces in the three disputed areas of Blue Nile, Nuba Mountains and Abyei, but this had little effect on the ground. Thus, the situation in Abyei continued to be tense, particularly as the NCP refused to accept the Abyei boundary commission's recommendations. In general, security remained problematic for the new GoSS. The UN Mission in Sudan (UNMIS) was engaged in keeping the SPLM and the SAF from fighting each other in the South and had started to deploy forces in the disputed border areas between the North and the South. They could not, however, effectively hinder occasional attacks from groups outside the CPA settlement. Infrastructure and the settlement of returning refugees were other pressing issues for GoSS.

Gradually, the **GoSS** under the leadership of Silva Kiir established itself in Juba, the former southern capital, but progress was slow. **The South** lacked everything from roads, transportation systems, health services and schools, and even the houses were in ruins in most of the region. The political structures had to be re-built from scratch, not only in Juba but also in the ten states that make up the region. Consequently, people who expected rapid changes were disappointed. Lack of security and local clashes between armed groups remained a problem. The most serious incident occurred in **Malakal** in November when fighting broke out between the SSDF and the SPLA. When some fighters from the SSDF took refuge in a SAF garrison, the incident turned into a clash between SPLA and SAF, who were supposed to work together to maintain peace and stability and finally to merge into one national army. According to UN estimates, the fighting left 150 dead and 400 injured. It was reported that UNMIS dealt with this and other minor incidents in a constructive way so as to defuse the tension.

Sudan's human rights record remained abysmal in 2006. The national human rights commission specified in the CPA was not established. In the war zones, civilians were attacked, chased away, raped and killed. In other areas, critical journalists, human rights activists and political opponents might be arrested, tortured and killed. Freedom of expression was very limited. In fact, there was an increase in censorship, arbitrary arrest and harassment. At least 15 foreign and Sudanese journalists were arrested and detained. The International Criminal Court (ICC) continued to investigate crimes in Darfur and its officials visited Khartoum.

Foreign Affairs

Sudan's international relations were marked by foreign concerns about the government's performance in implementing the CPA in line with the interim constitution, and the government's inability or unwillingness to stop the violence in Darfur. The worsening crisis there brought accusations of **war crimes** and **genocide**. Sudan was threatened with UN intervention, severe international **sanctions** and of alleged war criminals being brought before the **ICC** in The Hague. Relations with **Chad** deteriorated when Darfurian refugees there were attacked by Janjaweed militia from across the border. In the South, the rebellion of the **Lord's Resistance Army (LRA)** in **Uganda** spilled over the border into Sudan, causing death and destruction.

Whereas Sudan's relations with the UN and the West deteriorated over several issues, relations with **China, Russia and India** were relatively good.

In Darfur, international humanitarian organisations were coming under increasing attack from militias and rebel groups or were caught in the fighting. NGO vehicles were stolen and sometimes adapted as military vehicles. On 4 April, the Norwegian refugee council was ordered out of southern Darfur by local authorities. The growing humanitarian crisis was repeatedly discussed in the **UN Security Council** and plans for more sanctions and a UN peacekeeping force were put forward. The situation in the refugee camps was particularly alarming, since aid agencies were prevented by warring factions from bringing in sufficient assistance. Sudanese President al-Bashir was particularly criticised. Chad accused the Sudan of supporting **Chadian rebels** against the government in January and tension between the two countries led to fears of a regular war breaking out between them. It was generally recognised that AMIS was not able to protect civilians. By January, AMIS had not yet reached its authorised strength of 6,171 military and 1,560 police personnel. The **UN's special representative for Sudan, Jan Pronk**, argued for a new and much larger UN peacekeeping force with the necessary mandate and equipment to keep the peace and disarm the militias. The US and Britain supported the proposal in the Security Council and started work on a resolution to authorise the deployment of such a force in Darfur. There was also talk of expanding UNMIS to cover Darfur. Jan Pronk was later, on 22 October, declared *persona non grata* by the GNU and expelled from the country. In March, the **AU** agreed to be replaced by a UN force in Darfur, but the Sudanese government was strongly against the idea. Their argument was that there had to be a peace agreement first, something the AU was currently working on. Another was that unilateral deployment would open the way for total war in Darfur and the possible establishment of **al-Qaida** there, according to the **Sudanese defence minister, Abdel-Rahim Hussein**. The UN therefore continued to pressure the government until the end of the year, but did not seriously envisage deployment of UN peacekeepers without Sudanese consent.

Another approach to the Darfur crisis was the imposition of **sanctions on the Sudan**. Previously, sanctions had been imposed on the supply of arms to Darfur. In addition, a panel of experts established in terms of Security Council resolution 1591 in March 2005 had examined the current problems, the effects of the sanctions and had worked out a list of individuals (among them 17 senior officials) who had either broken the arms ban or been responsible for human rights violations or war crimes and who might therefore be brought before the ICC. The experts' report, which also suggested additional sanctions against the Sudan, was discussed in the Security Council in February. It was strongly opposed by

China, Russia and Qatar, which meant that no comprehensive resolution would be passed and there would be no extradition of suspected war criminals. However, the Security Council in late April decided to impose sanctions on four Sudanese men suspected of human rights abuses, a move that led to stronger Sudanese opposition to any UN force in Darfur.

The threat of sanctions and constant international pressure were instrumental in achieving the DPA in Abuja on 5 May, a turning point that relieved the pressure for some time. The Security Council was satisfied with the agreement and repeated its offer of UN troops to replace AMIS, even suggesting using chapter VII of the UN charter, which would not require Sudanese consent. A resolution to this effect was passed on 16 May. The Chinese, however, put an end to that line of thinking. Instead, a **Security Council mission** was sent to Khartoum in June, where it met President al-Bashir and **Foreign Minister Lam Akol** and discussed a possible UN force in Darfur. However, although there was no breakthrough, the GNU agreed to the sending of a joint **UN-AU** team to Darfur to study the needs of a future peacekeeping mission, and there were plans for strengthening AMIS to 10,000 men, with logistical support from **NATO**. To the extent that UN peacekeeping forces were discussed, it was now a question of adding UN forces to AMIS some time in the future so as to keep the African identity of the peacekeepers. The key term here was hybridisation. This pushing of the arrival of UN forces into the future appeared to be only a temporary victory for the GNU: UN and international pressure continued to grow in the second half of the year. It seems clear that GNU calculated that local political dangers from giving in to UN demands were greater than the danger of rejecting them.

On 31 August, after weeks of negotiations, the Security Council passed resolution 1706 under Chapter VII, which provided for the deployment of a 20,800–strong peacekeeping force by the end of the year as an extension of UNMIS (China, Russia and Qatar abstained). Although this resolution did not require the consent of the Sudanese government, the UN continued to pressure it to accede to UN demands. Instead, the Sudanese president warned the UN in a letter to **Kofi Annan** of very strong civilian opposition to the idea in Darfur and that he should be left to implement the DPA according to his own plan, which, among other things, involved the deployment of 10,500 government troops. Shortly afterwards, the government instructed AMIS to leave Darfur by 30 September, an order that was later withdrawn after causing much international concern. On 29 November, the AU extended AMIS by a further six months.

The implementation of the CPA was of less concern internationally at the beginning of the year, but UN Secretary-General Kofi Annan called for the speeding up of the deployment of UNMIS troops in the South. With the assistance of GoSS, a ceasefire was reached between the **LRA** rebel group in Uganda and the **Ugandan government** on 29 August. This might improve the security situation in the border area and the stability of Sudan's southern neighbour. Diplomatic relations between the Sudan and **Chad**, broken off in April, were restored in August following an agreement to stop hosting each other's rebels. However, later in the year Sudan was again criticised for supporting attacks by Chadian rebel groups. Chad was gravely concerned about developments in Darfur. Many Darfurian rebels were from **President Déby's** own ethnic group, the Zaghawa, whom he might be tempted to support against the Khartoum government. Moreover, Darfurian refugees in Chad were pursued by the Janjaweed, who thereby brought the fighting on to Chadian territory. President Déby accused Khartoum of supporting an insurrection in Chad in April that reached as far as the suburbs of **N'Djaména**, the capital. Khartoum was also suspected of supporting a rebellion in the **CAR**, where **French troops**, supported by Chadian troops, were engaged in heavy fighting in December. Chad was concerned that the potential oil wealth of the region stretching from Darfur to Lake Chad was encouraging Sudan, backed by China, to destabilise the region.

On the eastern border, Sudan signed a memorandum of understanding with **Eritrea** on 27 August aimed at ending Eritrea's alleged support for the **Eastern Front** and the NRF. Eritrea brokered an agreement between the GNU and the Eastern Front on 14 October (the **Eastern Sudan Peace Agreement**) and thus contributed to both increased stability in the East and to better diplomatic relations between the two countries.

On the international diplomatic scene, the country was able to benefit from the lack of coherent approach to the Sudan question. The AU held its annual summit in Khartoum in January but Sudan was refused the leadership of the organisation on account of its record in Darfur. This was a blow to the prestige of the Sudanese president, who had actively sought the chairmanship. The US and EU and other countries were very critical of the Sudan government's responsibility for the violence in Darfur and some bilateral and multilateral sanctions were imposed. In October, for instance, **President Bush** signed a decree that tightened US economic sanctions on Sudan. The decree prohibited US companies from involvement in the energy or petrochemical sectors and renewed the sanctions on US trade. Southern Sudan, Darfur and some border areas were exempted. There were also EU sanctions, mainly in the defence sector. More serious sanctions, such as the call for a naval blockade of oil exports from **Port Sudan**, were not implemented, as they would hurt the rebuilding of the South. There was international disagreement on how much one could punish the Sudanese government. After all, the future of the CPA required a minimum of cooperation with the government and one could not risk expulsion of UNMIS from the South. On the other hand, Sudan counted on the support of China and Russia whenever really serious measures against it were proposed in the Security Council.

The **Arab world** was also likely to support Sudan against its international critics. Unilateral deployment of UN forces in Darfur was therefore not a realistic option. The Sudanese oil concessions to China paid back in the form of protection against Security Council sanctions. This support also meant that any extradition of suspected war criminals to face trial by the ICC was highly unrealistic. And any economic sanctions that might hurt the rebuilding of the country, particularly the South, could also be ruled out. This situation encouraged Sudan to continue its rejection of a UN peacekeeping force in Darfur. As noted above, Security Council resolution 1706 proposed a force of 20,800 men to take over from AMIS in Darfur. The Sudan government responded by threatening potential troop-contributing countries, saying that participation would be considered a hostile act. On 22 October, the UN envoy to Sudan, Jan Pronk, was expelled after a comment on GNU military losses in Darfur. However, Sudan's resistance started to pay off. The UN was now considering a **joint UN-AU peacekeeping force** to be developed in three steps, and in November Sudan extended the AMIS presence in Darfur to mid-2007. However, the GNU was not yet fully ready to accept UN troops even if they were combined with AMIS. There was also international concern that Khartoum would accept nominal UN participation in AMIS and thereby proclaim that it had complied with UN demands.

Socioeconomic Developments

Oil production and oil exports have become the mainstay of the Sudanese economy, due to both increased production and record high prices for oil. The **agricultural sector** also experienced positive development in 2005–06, thanks to plentiful rain and the return of many refugees to their fields. **Inflation** was kept under control through stricter credit and liquidity regulations, but there was some pressure on the price of consumer goods. Continuous appreciation of the Sudanese **dinar** was a sign of growing foreign currency reserves, but threatened to hurt Sudanese non-oil exports.

Sudan witnessed **growth in the production of oil**, new concessions were allocated and new fields started to produce. By the end of the year, total output was stated by the minister of energy and mining to be 500,000 b/d, compared to the earlier estimate of 650,000b/d. This difference was largely due to decreasing output in some fields, to the low quality of the crude in some new fields and technical difficulties. However, it was still an increase over the previous year, at the end of which output was estimated at 330,000 b/d. Production from blocks 3 and 7, operated by Petrodar, which started to produce in April, had a noticeable effect on output and government revenues. Petrodar is a consortium led by the Chinese National Petroleum Company (CNPC) (41%) and the Malaysian firm Petronas (40%), together with a Sudanese state oil firm, Sudapet (8%), Chinese Sinopec (6%) and Al-Thani Petroleum (UAE, 5%). A new pipeline to the Red Sea was constructed to convey the oil from 80 wells in the two blocks, which were estimated to produce 175,000 b/d, constituting 35% of total output. With rising oil prices, revenues from this sector reached new records, and it was estimated that the South would receive $ 1 bn as its share of the oil revenues, well above the budgeted $ 750 bn.

Greater Nile Petroleum Operating Company (GNPOC) operated a promising field in block 4 in Southern Kordofan. The White Nile Petroleum Operating Company (WNPOC) sent its first shipment of oil in August from the Thar Jath field in block 5A. However, by December construction of the new Bashayr 2 export terminal at Port Sudan, intended for the oil from the Petrodar concession, was not yet complete, and the GNPOC export terminal, used for oil from blocks 1, 2 and 4 (Nile Blend quality oil), had to take care of the Petrodar oil from blocks 3 and 7 as well. The oil from these two blocks was initially defined as **Dar Blend**, a quality lower than Nile Blend, but turned out to be even more acidic, which meant a very low price on the international market, $ 17–18 a barrel.

The **White Nile** firm started exploration of block Ba in southern Sudan, a concession given to them by GoSS. This concession was contested by the French firm **Total**, which claimed it had belonged to them for the past 20 years. GNU supported the French view, so the national petroleum commission was unable to reach an agreement. The case went to a British court, where Total won the first round in May. In the meantime, White Nile continued exploring the concession. This conflict convinced GoSS to press ahead with its plans to build a pipeline to Kenya both to supply that country and for export through the **Indian Ocean** port of **Mombasa**.

Expansion of the **Jeili refinery** northeast of Khartoum was announced by CNPC in July, increasing its refining capacity to 100,000 b/d. It was particularly designed to handle the heavy crudes, such as from blocks 3 and 7. The products from the refinery were both for domestic consumption and for export.

In December, Sudan applied to become a member of **OPEC**. Membership will give Sudan higher status as an oil producer and protect the country if or when it is threatened with sanctions against its oil industry. On the other hand, Sudan should be concerned about the level of the production quota that the country will be subjected to by OPEC. Sudan's production has doubled since 2003 and it is believed will double again by 2008.

At the end of 2005, FAO in collaboration with the WFP expected **cereal output** for the period November 2005 to November 2006 to be 55% above the previous year. **Sorghum (durra)** was the main crop, constituting about 80% of overall cereal output. Small-scale traditional rain-fed farms were expected to produce 40% of the estimated output, while mechanised farms also showed growth, whereas output from irrigated schemes was more stable. This general growth was due to good rainfall in the 2005 cropping season, which also made it possible to cultivate wider areas. The return of refugees (IDPs) and increasing security also had positive effects on output. Improved security made it possible to bring cereals to areas suffering from food scarcity. However, there were still areas in the South which remained largely outside the cereal distribution networks. The increasing number of returnees quickly led to **lack of food** in vulnerable areas and added to the number of people needing food aid, particularly in the South. Some 700,000 people from inside and outside the country were expected to return to the South during the year. Darfur particularly suffered from low or uneven local food production and a lack of security that hindered imports of food. In fact, FAO estimated that Darfur would need 530,000 tonnes of food aid. According to FAO, another problem in the agricultural sector was lack of access to credit because of low creditworthiness of farmers: this meant low levels of investment. This situation existed in spite of improved mechanisms for extending credit to the private sector in general.

In May, the FAO in association with WFP published a new report on cereal production in the Sudan. It confirmed the positive outlook of six months earlier by estimating an output of 5.5 m tonnes, 900,000 tonnes above the five-year average. A particularly positive projection concerned Darfur, where increased sorghum and millet production was estimated at 570,000 tonnes. But again, the report warned of highly **uneven harvests** that would leave large areas with very inadequate food and grain reserves. The WFP expected to feed 6 m people, but as both funding and food could not keep up with the need, they had to cut down on emergency food rations and the number of people they could feed.

At the end of the year, FAO/WFP estimated cereal production and basic food supply for the season 2006–07 to be very good, 22% higher than the harvest for the previous year and 36% above average annual production.

As for the Sudanese economy in general, real **GDP** growth remained strong throughout the year largely due to the growth in the non-oil sector, according to figures published by IMF. The **agricultural sector**, the largest single sector of the economy, was a big contributor here, as were increasing government spending and private consumption, which grew markedly. In spring, the growth in real GDP was estimated at 9%, but at the end of the year it had already reached 9.6%.

Similarly, estimates for **inflation** ranged between 7.5% to 9.5%, a marked improvement on earlier years. This was due to measures by the **Bank of Sudan** to tighten domestic liquidity, the easing of import procedures and the effect of a **strong dinar**. However, domestic consumer demand would keep the price level up. Following IMF recommendations, GNU cut subsidies on fuel and sugar in August, causing a jump in inflation in September to 15%, but the annual inflation did not rise above an average of 7–7.5%, which was within the IMF target range. Nonetheless, price pressure remained strong.

The dinar experienced marked appreciation against the US dollar. In May 2005, the rate was Sudanese dinar (SD) 249: $ 1, in February 2006 the rate was SD 230: $ 1 and in March SD 228: $ 1. The value of the dinar continued to appreciate, reflecting the growth in foreign currency entering the country (oil earnings, foreign investments and remittances).

At the beginning of the year, **oil revenues and taxation** were expected to rise by 40% to $ 8.2 bn. However, because of growing government expenditure, a small fiscal deficit was expected. The GNU put emphasis on reducing the deficit by keeping government spending under strict control in close cooperation with the IMF, which, however, agreed to increased spending in view of the projected high revenues from the oil sector. Thus, IMF expected a fiscal surplus of 1.2% of GDP. There are reasons to believe that GNU underestimated oil revenues in its budget and thus overestimated the fiscal deficit. It may also be that the GNU tried to hide real oil revenue so as to transfer to the South a lower amount than was its due. At least, this was how the GoSS interpreted the discrepancy between IMF and NGU estimates.

In spite of a **growing export trade**, Sudan carried over a trade deficit from 2005 and this deficit grew worse. However, capital inflow ensured a balance-of-payments surplus. By the middle of the year, the Bank of Sudan noted that the value of exports had risen by over 10% year on year, with crude oil constituting around 80%. Oil exports proceeds rose by 6.5%, in spite of a drop in the volume exported. This drop was caused by technical problems and delays. Among agricultural exports, **sesame** showed an increase of 107.4% year on year. On the other hand, the value of **cotton** exports dropped by 14.2%. However, the value of imports grew even more, by nearly 42% year on year. Imports comprised machinery and equipment, manufactured goods and raw materials, etc., largely a reflection of industrial and infrastructural developments. As a result, the first six months saw a very strong increase in the trade deficit of 241%, reaching $ 858 m.

The **current account deficit** in 2006 was offset by strong growth in direct foreign investments and a foreign currency reserve that in the third quarter amounted to $ 2,407 m, covering 2.8 months' worth of imports, according to IMF. This had shrunk to 2.6 months at the end of September and to 1.8 months at the end of the year, with a reserve estimated by IMF at $ 1.7 bn. The reason for this drop in currency reserves is unclear.

At the end of year, total **government revenue** was estimated at $ 7.5 bn, of which 50% came from the oil sector. Almost 90% of Sudan's export revenues came from this sector. Total export proceeds were $ 6.2 bn, compared to spending on imports of $ 8 bn, making for a trade deficit of $ 1.8 bn. When the non-merchandise deficit is added, resulting largely from income repatriation by foreign firms and payment for services, the current account balance showed an estimated deficit of $ 4.8 bn. This figure represented 9.5% of GDP. At the end of the year, it was closer to 10% as a result of growing imports.

Exports from Sudan went mainly to Asian countries, notably China (71% by value), Japan and UAE. Likewise, China was Sudan's most important source of imports: in the first six months, the figure was 20% of total imports by value. The value of trade between Sudan and China amounted to $ 2.9 bn. China, for instance, bought 65% of Sudan's exported oil and strengthened its position as Sudan's biggest supplier of weapons.

Anders Bjørkelo

Tanzania

The year marked the beginning of a new political era under the **newly elected president, Jakaya Mrisho Kikwete**, but under the continued undisputed leadership of the ruling party 'Chama cha Mapinduzi' (CCM, Party of the Revolution). Although this implied some change in leadership style, the general orientation of gradual reform policies remained practically unchanged. Neither the domestic political arena nor the foreign policy field presented any outstanding challenges. Despite the partial effects of drought and recurrent power shortages, economic performance remained satisfactory.

Domestic Politics

After his overwhelming election victory in December 2005, the **new president**, **Kikwete**, was expected to lead the country for the next ten years (two constitutional terms). Although fundamental changes were not expected, the 'fourth phase government' (in continuation of the Nyerere, Mwinyi and Mkapa governments) was likely to focus on different issues than its predecessors. Kikwete stated that he wanted to be judged according to the success of his government in tackling the country's many problems and set himself a three-year timetable. Inaugurating the Union parliament on 30 December 2005, Kikwete named **solving the Zanzibar crisis** and **fighting corruption** as his government's overarching priorities.

The first major challenges for the new government were the consolidation of its power and the healing of wounds within the **ruling CCM** after the severe infighting that had marked the nomination process for its presidential candidate. Although 12 cabinet members from the previous administration were re-appointed, **the new cabinet** reflected an even more reformist composition than that of Benjamin Mkapa. Kikwete was clearly able to impose his will on the party. Being a real CCM insider with a strong power base, he could expect support for most of his political projects and reforms. To avoid a serious split in the party, however, he had to reconcile those less reform-oriented CCM factions that had been defeated during the nomination process. These considerations may have affected some of the reform projects, especially the anti-corruption drive.

Like his predecessor, Kikwete had featured this prominently in his election campaign. Despite some success in reducing small-scale corruption, Mkapa's record in fighting corruption among high-profile politicians had not been very convincing. Kikwete initiated a second phase of the **national anti-corruption strategy and action plan** specifically focused on fighting corruption at local government level. It remained, however, unclear to what extent these plans and public statements were put into practice. Tanzania hosted two important international conferences on corruption issues: the second global conference of Parliamentarians against Corruption in Arusha from 19–23 September, with 300 delegates from 50 countries, and the pan-African journalists' conference in mid-September in Dar es Salaam.

Having appointed his close friend and long-time political ally Edward Lowassa as new prime minister on 29 December 2005, Kikwete announced the **composition of the new cabinet** on 4 January. Contrary to promises to reduce governmental expenses, the president **increased the number of ministries** from 19 to 22 and the number of ministers from 45 to 60 (including 31 assistant ministers). He justified this step on the basis of the need to adjust governmental design to better suit the requirements of the country. The move was, however, contested by the opposition, which questioned whether a poor country could afford such a costly extension of ministries.

A newly created **ministry of public safety and security** was given responsibility for the police, which had been under the ministry of home affairs. A widely perceived increase in crime and common discontent with widespread corruption among the police as well as with the involvement of officers in crime was apparently the motivation for this step. Both issues had been major themes in Kikwete's election campaign. In March, a number of high-ranking police officers were replaced and the structure of police organisation in Dar es Salaam was changed. In August, to reduce armed robbery, the authorities of several towns called upon the population to register small arms.

Improvement of the poor infrastructure was to be much more vigorously tackled through the creation of a new **ministry of infrastructure development** under the well-respected former finance minister, Basil Mramba. The former ministry of livestock and water development was split into two separate ministries. Also new were the ministry for East African cooperation and the ministry of planning, economy and empowerment. The inclusion of aspects of empowerment reflected a desired new emphasis on empowering people to start their own businesses instead of waiting for service-delivery by government or aid agencies.

The cabinet reflected a good blend of new and experienced ministers and a good balance between change and continuity. Several former deputy ministers were promoted and the number of **female ministers** was increased from three to six. Two key ministries were now headed by women: Asha-Rose Migiro was appointed minister of foreign affairs and Zakia Meghji minister of finance.

The new president started energetically to give effect to his **campaign slogan** 'new zeal, new vigour, new speed', but made it clear that this was not to be understood as complete change of his predecessor's policies but in terms of speeding up the ongoing reform process and of ensuring that all government institutions were committed to hard work. Shortly after his inauguration, Kikwete visited every ministry to make clear his expectations of them. A week-long retreat for ministers, deputy ministers and permanent secretaries in Arusha in mid-March served to inculcate Kikwete's agenda into all members of his government team and to strengthen cohesion among them. The primary aim of this approach was to commit top-ranking government leaders to work unselfishly for the interests of the country and its people. Both Kikwete and Lowassa were keen to demonstrate that the new government was actively tackling the most urgent problems. This also involved **various symbolic actions**. Cabinet representatives were repeatedly sent to the regions to demonstrate the government's concern and presence. Juma Akukweti, state minister in the prime minister's office, became a prominent victim of this activism. On 16 December, he was involved in a plane crash en route to Mbeya to inspect the extent of damage caused by a fire that had destroyed a major market. Three members of the delegation were killed instantly, while Akukweti died on 4 January 2007 in a South African hospital. Kikwete's new approach was also aimed at **improving the performance of civil servants**. The finance minister was given powers to punish wasteful civil servants. On 1 July, a presidential commission to investigate the need to increase civil service salaries began its work.

A number of projects decided in principle but never implemented under Mkapa were now put into practice. The **eviction of street vendors** ('machinga') from Dar es Salaam's city centre had been decided years before, but the changes came only after Lowassa instructed city authorities to take action. An estimated 40,000 'machinga' were evicted and kiosks and other property destroyed after a deadline set by Lowassa expired at the end of September. Despite government promises to provide the 'machinga' with small loans and to construct three new business complexes in the city (one in each district), the eviction was generally viewed with mixed feelings and also provoked criticism. Although both government and city council claimed to have plans for the further development of the 'machinga' sector, it remained unclear whether these plans could work out in practice and whether they would meet the needs of the 'machinga' and further their empowerment.

After only ten months, much of which had been used for reorganisation and to establish new working structures, a surprise **cabinet reshuffle** was announced on 15 October. Although no official explanation was given, this was most likely mainly prompted by public discontent with the long-standing electricity crisis. Ibrahim Msabaha, the minister of energy and minerals, was accused misleading the public by promising that the power crisis would be resolved by October, when in fact the problems had become even worse. Altogether **ten ministers and eight deputy ministers were transferred** to new portfolios, including key personalities like Mramba, who was transferred to the ministry of industry and trade. Given that Kikwete was seemingly dissatisfied with the performance of some ministers, it remained unclear why the cabinet was reshuffled without any of its members being sacked. This was particularly true of the transfer of the much criticised energy minister to another portfolio (East African cooperation). Observers more sympathetic to the new administration, however, described the reshuffle as a 'wake-up call', indicating the president's determination to react in cases of unsatisfactory performance. Whether the shuffle was an appropriate step or merely a publicity stunt to demonstrate governmental action, and the extent to which it had been constrained by CCM strongmen, were all subjects of public discussion.

The 7th **CCM national congress** held in Dodoma on 24–25 June (one year earlier than the regular five-year cycle) elected **Kikwete** as the new **party chairman** and successor to Mkapa, who relinquished the position before the end of his tenure. During its meeting on 29–30 April, the CCM national executive committee had unanimously nominated Kikwete as the sole candidate. The **CCM's secretary-general**, Philip Mangula, was replaced by Dar es Salaam's regional commissioner, **Yussuf Makamba**, who had strongly backed Kikwete's presidential candidacy. Other party posts as well as numerous district commissionerships were also filled with Kikwete supporters. The two important **CCM vice-chairman** positions remained, however, in the hands of old-guard politicians who could potentially create problems for the new leadership. **John Malecela**, vice-chairman for the mainland, had been the most prominent representative of the anti-reformist faction in CCM's internal contest for nomination as presidential candidate in 2005. Zanzibar President **Amani Karume** remained the other CCM vice-chairman.

The new **parliament** was just as heavily dominated by CCM as the previous one (with 276 of 322 MPs). Opposing views were mostly expected to come from within CCM's ranks. The new speaker, Samuel Sitta, encouraged more open debate with the apparent tacit approval of the president, who had been instrumental in the selection of Sitta. The creation of a ministry of parliamentary affairs also indicated that Kikwete was seeking to cooperate more closely with parliament and thus to increase its political importance.

As a result of their poor electoral performance, all **opposition parties** remained weak. The **Civic United Front (CUF)**, by far the strongest with 30 of the 43 opposition MPs, decided in January to form a shadow cabinet without including other opposition parties. This move was heavily criticised by these parties – especially since almost all CUF MPs came from Pemba Island (Zanzibar) and could hardly speak for the mainland opposition. Subsequently, CUF invited members from the other parties to join the shadow cabinet. Wilbroad Slaa, from the second largest opposition faction, **'Chama cha Demokrasia na Maendeleo' (CHADEMA** – Party for Democracy and Development) with 11 MPs, became deputy opposition leader.

On 6 May, the high court – in response to a petition by Christopher Mtikila, chairman of the small Democratic Party (DP) – ruled that **independent candidates** were allowed to run in presidential and parliamentary elections. This had for years been demanded by opposition parties, but had been persistently rejected by the government. Another high court ruling on 25 April declared illegal the use of **'takrima'** (traditional hospitality) during election campaigns. This practice of distributing free gifts to the electorate had been hotly disputed during the 2005 election campaign, since opposition parties and NGOs perceived it as a veiled form of corruption favouring the ruling party with its much better financial resources.

Expectations were high that Kikwete's government would start new efforts to find a lasting **solution to the political impasse in Zanzibar**. In his first address to the Union parliament, Kikwete promised to put this issue on top of his agenda. He expressed deep concern about the crisis on the islands and the deepening **political schism between Pemba** (dominated by CUF) and **Unguja** (held by CCM). CUF formed a 16-member shadow cabinet in the Zanzibar parliament on 15 January and criticised Zanzibar's President Karume for appointing just one of ten additional MPs from Pemba. CUF continued to refuse to recognise Karume's presidency because of alleged irregularities in the 2005 Zanzibar election, but nevertheless took part in all parliamentary proceedings. When visiting the islands for the first time as president in early April, Kikwete appealed in several public addresses for reconciliation and political tolerance. A positive indication of possible new moves was the government's decision to assign **responsibility for Union matters** to Vice-President Mohamed Ali Shein from Pemba. With Shein in this position and Hussein Mwinyi as new minister of Union affairs, two high-profile politicians were put in charge of the sensitive issue.

Whereas during Mkapa's presidency talks to resolve the crisis took place only between CCM and CUF, his successor involved the two governments. **Union Premier Lowassa and Zanzibar Chief Minister Shamsi Vuai Nahodha** met in May and November to identify the key issues to be tackled in reforming the complicated asymmetrical design of the Union. Other ministries and governmental agencies were also involved in this process, which reflected the insight that many of the islands' political problems derived not only from the competition between CCM and CUF, but also from the structure of the union and the unwillingness of Zanzibar's CCM leadership to subscribe to reforms. In late March, the Zanzibar government refused to ratify the **human rights and good governance commission that** had been established by the Union parliament in 2001. Zanzibar's attorney-general demanded amendments to the constituting act to enable Zanzibar to establish a separate commission, but this was rejected by the Union ministry of justice and constitutional affairs. Besides political talks, Kikwete proposed stronger efforts to boost Zanzibar's economy as possible steps to reduce tensions on the islands and in particular suggested greater diversion of national resources to Zanzibar as one measure.

It was, however, not clear to what extent CUF's concerns were also considered in the talks. CUF Secretary-General Seif Sharif Hamad in late October demanded a re-run of the 2005 Zanzibar elections and the formation of a government of national unity to organise and oversee new elections impartially. On 27 December, CCM Zanzibar's Publicity Secretary Vuai Ali Vuai stated that talks on the political impasse did not include the option of a coalition government. Zanzibar's President Karume even declared such a government unconstitutional. On 11 and 12 November, CUF staged demonstrations in Dar es Salaam and Zanzibar to protest Karume's statements that there was no political crisis on Zanzibar and to underscore the demands for new elections. These demonstrations were supported by the opposition Tanzania Labour Party (TLP) and National Convention for Constitutional Reform (NCCR).

CUF obviously viewed CCM Zanzibar and the Zanzibar government as its main adversaries, but closely cooperated with the new president on Union matters. The CUF's leadership praised Kikwete for his attempts to find lasting solutions, which were, however, dependent on CCM-Zanzibar's willingness to cooperate. The longer the talks continued without visible result, the stronger was the danger of radicalisation within CUF and the feared split within the party.

On 23 April, ten Zanzibaris submitted a petition in the Zanzibar high court challenging the **legality** of the **Zanzibar-mainland union**. Since this appeal appeared to be a relatively hopeless venture from the beginning and was eventually dismissed on 2 October, its probable intent was to bring the Zanzibar issue to international attention rather than to find a legal solution to a political problem. This view was supported by the fact that a number of high-profile witnesses, including UN Secretary-General Kofi Annan, were called before the court. Although the claimants lost the case, a new problem emerged from the proceedings: the original Union treaty, signed by both parties in 1964, was found to have been lost.

In August, Zanzibari members of the Union parliament pleaded for **separate representation of Zanzibar in the envisaged East African federation** and demanded at least associate membership for the islands. On 21 November, Lowassa made it clear that it was impossible for Zanzibar to join as a separate entity and that it should channel its interests in the EAC through the Union government.

The new government – contrary to prevailing sentiments towards the end of the 10–year Mkapa period – was initially supported by a **wave of public sympathy**. Expectations were high that the new administration would seriously tackle the country's various problems, especially corruption, the Zanzibar issue and poverty reduction. Public trust in the new administration was considerable throughout the year, but on the evidence of opinion polls dwindled significantly. Massive problems with the electricity supply, continued high crime rates, especially in Dar es Salaam, and a temporarily perceived economic crisis, mainly in response to the drought, contributed to a growing impression that the government's initial measures may have been merely cosmetic. Kikwete's frequent absences from the country and the fact that he and Lowassa were often accompanied by their families on state visits abroad fuelled critical views of the government's ability to find appropriate solutions for the country's problems.

Although the **refugee** population in Tanzania's western regions had been drastically reduced in recent years, it remained a concern. By year's end, about 290,000 refugees, more than 150,000 from Burundi and almost 130,000 from DR Congo, were still registered by UNHCR. In view of the improved situation in Burundi, Kikwete called on UNHCR and Burundian authorities to speed-up voluntary repatriation. While the government refrained from expelling Burundian refugees, several thousand alleged Rwandans, most of whom had lived for many years in Tanzania, were deported to Rwanda, causing annoyance on the Rwandan side. Both countries formed a team to resolve the issue. Tanzanian authorities also deported more than 1,000 Burundians, many of whom had stayed in Tanzania for more than 20 years. In talks with Kikwete at the AU summit in Gambia in July, UN Secretary-General Kofi Annan commended Tanzania for its immense contribution to hosting refugees from the Great Lakes region for extended periods.

The government further enhanced efforts to reduce the number of **illegal immigrants** and non-Tanzanians working in Tanzania. The major concern was the criticism that many foreigners came to work in Tanzania while citizens remained unemployed. Foreigners applying for work permits were screened more carefully and companies were told to look for Tanzanian workers first.

In July, the film **'Darwin's Nightmare'**, awarded the prize for best European documentary in 2005, caused massive public outrage. Although mainly aimed at criticising Western companies and globalisation for unscrupulously exploiting Africa's wealth and causing negative social effects in Africa, the film was perceived as damaging Tanzania's good reputation in the world. The film claimed that the planes used to transport fish from Lake Victoria to Europe brought weapons on their way to Mwanza, which were used to fuel the wars in the Great Lakes region. However, no clear evidence was provided to support these allegations. A local journalist who had contributed to the film later stated that most of the 'documentary scenes' had been arranged by the film's Austrian director. Also, accusations that Tanzanian authorities had threatened and even arrested journalists over the film proved to be false. Kikwete, as well as parliament and several ministers, strongly condemned the film. Several Tanzanian institutions, including the president, used this episode to accuse the Western media of painting a biased picture of Africa.

In February, the worldwide discussions about the caricatures of Prophet Mohammed published in a Danish newspaper prompted protests by some **Muslim groups**. Tanzania's highest-ranking sheikh, Mufti Shabani Simba, demanded that the Danish government withdraw the newspaper's licence and apologise to all Muslims in the world. On 16 February, thousands of Muslims took part in a peaceful demonstration demanding that Danish and Norwegian residents leave Tanzania, but the excitement soon died down and had no lasting repercussions.

The killing of a Dar es Salaam **'daladala' (commuter bus) driver** on 4 November by **Tabora Regional Commissioner** Ditopile Mzuzuri attracted much public attention. After a road accident between the 'daladala' and the regional commissioner's car and a subsequent argument, Ditopile shot the driver in front of his passengers. Two days later, he was arrested and charged with murder. The trial was expected to be watched closely, since Ditopile, a prominent politician, was one of Kikwete's strong supporters and longtime allies.

Foreign Affairs

As in previous years, relations with foreign countries were generally unproblematic. Having been foreign minister for ten years, Kikwete had excellent international contacts and undertook an intensive travel schedule. He justified this on the basis of the need to introduce the new government to many international partners. Usually accompanied by high-ranking delegations, the visits were also vindicated as providing an opportunity to promote new investment in Tanzania. Despite these explanations, Kikwete's frequent absences and the costs of these journeys prompted charges that he may have forgotten he was no longer foreign minister.

Pleased by the good and peaceful conduct of the 2005 elections, particularly in Zanzibar, and by expectations that the new government would follow the reformist course of its predecessor, **donor countries and international institutions** remained generally sympathetic and praised Tanzania as a deserving recipient of substantial aid.

Relations with the **East African neighbours** remained generally harmonious. The creation of a separate ministry of East African cooperation indicated the importance given to all aspects of the EAC. This was also underlined by the fact that Kikwete began his round of state visits by travelling to Kenya, Uganda and Rwanda. On 5 April, Juma Mwapachu, former Tanzanian ambassador to France, was sworn in as new EAC secretary-general at its seventh summit in Arusha. On 13 October, the process was started to gather the views of the population on the envisaged creation by 2013 of an East African federation with common political institutions. A 16-member committee was given the task of visiting the entire country to solicit the opinions of the Tanzanian population. The accession of Rwanda and Burundi to the EAC on 30 November was generally welcomed in Tanzania, despite some fears that this move might result in the 'importation' of the political problems of the two neighbours. Some quarrels over EAC customs union regulations continued and fears of Kenyan economic domination led several observers to doubt the genuineness of Tanzania's commitment to the goal of full EAC integration.

On 19 September, the signing of a ceasefire between the Burundian government and the Palipehutu-FNL, the last remaining Burundian rebel group, highlighted a series of **peace talks** hosted by Tanzania. The Palestinian ambassador requested the Tanzanian government to take a lead in peace negotiations between Israel and the Palestinians. The request was supported by the deputy head of the Israeli mission in East and Central Africa. A few Tanzanian soldiers joined the new UN mission in Lebanon. The Sudanese government and the UN requested Tanzania to support the AU peace mission in Darfur. Kikwete stated that the government would be willing to send soldiers to Darfur only when the Sudanese government and the rebels had signed a peace agreement and when the military equipment for the mission had been provided by the AU.

Cooperation with **China** received new impetus, building on earlier close relations in the 1960s and 1970s. A number of projects, such as the revitalisation of the TAZARA railway to Zambia, the construction of a new 60,000-seat national stadium in Dar es Salaam, primary schools and a loan to improve the power supply system were initiated. Chinese premier Wen Jiabao visited Tanzania in June and Kikwete spent a week in China and participated in the large Sino-African summit in Beijing in November.

In the second year of Tanzania's two-year membership of the **UN Security Council** (the second time after a lapse of 30 years), the country held the rotating presidency in January and used the opportunity to give particular attention to the problems of the African Great Lakes region.

Socioeconomic Developments

Despite an intermittent public perception of an impending economic crisis (resulting from the combined effects of drought, persistent power cuts, falling exchange rate and increased inflation), the overall **macroeconomic performance** continued to be quite satisfactory. The estimated **GDP growth rate** of 5.9% was below the original target of 7%, but still above the African average and reasonable under the circumstances. The average inflation rate for the year was 6.3%, with unusually high monthly fluctuations mainly as a result of changing food prices. The trade deficit widened considerably, with a 35% jump in imports to $ 4,070 m (largely due to high oil and food imports) and only a modest increase in exports to $ 1,898 m (further growth in mineral and manufactured exports, but a slump in traditional agricultural export crops). The structural current account deficit was, therefore, expected to reach a new record of about $ 1,600 m (13.6% of GDP), while foreign reserves grew by about 10% to $ 2,259 m by the end of December (6.5 months import coverage). The Tanzania shilling (TSh) fell sharply against the US dollar to a low in August (without attempts at intervention by the Bank of Tanzania), but afterwards recovered somewhat due to seasonal foreign-exchange inflows (harvest receipts, aid transfers). At year's end, the shilling had lost 8.3% against the US dollar. The external debt was substantially reduced from $ 8.1 bn (end of 2005) to $ 4.7 bn as a result of MDRI write-offs. Despite the generally good performance, Tanzania remained one of the poorest countries with a 2004 per capita GDP of $ 288 ($ 674 in PPP terms) and ranked 162 on UNDP's HDI.

On 15 June, Finance Minister Zakia Meghji introduced the 2006–07 **budget** in parliament after providing a review of the generally successful fiscal performance in the **2005–06 financial year**. Overall domestic revenue collection of TSh 2,060 bn had been practically on target owing to various measures to increase the efficiency of tax collection, thus meeting the targeted tax ratio of 14.3% of GDP (only 13.6%, however, on the basis of revised GDP data). External aid resources accounted for 43% of total expenditures. Not all originally estimated aid funds were, however, actually secured, thus causing a higher-than-expected overall budget deficit of 4.9% of GDP.

In the **2006–07 budget**, the domestic revenue target was set at TSh 2,451 bn (an increase of 19.1%), assuming the attainment of a tax ratio of 14.5% of GDP, a GDP growth rate of 7.3% in 2007 and inflation not exceeding 4% by June 2007. Total expenditures were budgeted at TSh 4,850 bn (64% recurrent, 36% development expenditures), of which 46% were expected to come from external concessionary loans and grants (including debt relief). Although efforts to reduce dependency on aid funds had been stated repeatedly, this was clearly not reflected in the budget figures. To accommodate a large rise of civil service salaries, the budgeted public wage bill was increased by 46%.

Harmonious cooperation with and support from many **bilateral and multilateral donors** continued to be of crucial importance to all governmental development endeavours. The substantial new debt relief that had been promised in 2005 under the MDRI became reality with the formalisation of ADB's debt cancellation in April and the World Bank's announcement on 1 July of the cancellation of $ 3.9 bn in outstanding debt. These steps reduced the remaining debt to $ 4.7 bn. On 9 May, the World Bank approved a fourth PRSC of $ 200 m for general budget support and later started preparing for a similarly sized fifth PRSC (expected to be an annual exercise). A new source of funding was expected to become available with Tanzania's selection as a recipient under the US Millennium Challenge Account. The existing IMF support through a three-year PRGF expired as scheduled in December (last review and disbursement in February 2007) and was not renewed. This indicated Tanzania's vastly improved status as a successful reform economy no longer in need of this instrument. Instead, negotiations began with the IMF to conclude a Policy Support Instrument (PSI), a new form of economic policy advice and monitoring without any provision of financial funds. The PSI was expected to focus on strengthening the private and financial sectors and on fiscal efficiency.

The government's **national strategy for growth and reduction of poverty** (Swahili acronym: MKUKUTA), launched in 2005 as a second-generation PRSP, continued to be the basis for all domestic and externally supported development activities. It's three main clusters focused on economic growth and reduction of income poverty, social services and improvement of quality of life and strengthening good governance. The Tanzanian PRS process was generally acknowledged to be on track, yet needing regular review and more effective prioritisation of investments and mobilisation of domestic resources. The **Joint Assistance Strategy** (JAS) for harmonised cooperation between the government and all donors (produced as a draft in 2005) became effective in July.

The general thrust of **economic policy** under Kikwete was the continuation of the reform policies pursued by his predecessor Mkapa, with some proclaimed emphasis on fighting corruption, furthering local empowerment and environmental protection and enhancing governmental efficiency. In contrast with Kikwete's 'new zeal, new vigour, new speed' campaign slogan, actual performance was largely characterised by a rather cautious approach to real changes. No new anti-corruption law was passed by November, as had been promised, thus triggering a reduction in Danish budgetary support. In April, an executive secretary of the national empowerment council (established in November 2005) was appointed and various statements stressed the importance of empowering local entrepreneurs through the formalisation of unregistered assets in the informal sector, also as a way to create more employment opportunities. This was formulated in a new **property and business formalisation programme** (Swahili acronym: MKURABITA). A new package of investment incentives (known as the 'Blue Book') apparently had a positive effect on the general business environment. In the World Bank's latest "Doing Business Report", Tanzania was praised as one of the top reforming countries, although in absolute terms it was still classified in a low rank (142 of 175).

There was continued prevarication about ending the **privatisation of parastatal enterprises**. On budget day, it was announced that the remaining 36 public corporations would be restructured and the Parastatal Sector Reform Commission (PSRC) be dissolved by December 2007, but doubts about meeting this deadline remained. Still no final agreement was reached to privatise the Tanzania Railways Corporation (TRC) and the National Insurance Corporation (NIC). In October, the PSRC announced the offering of a further 21% stake in the National Microfinance Bank (NMB) on the Dar es Salaam stock exchange in March 2007, and the Zanzibar government announced in December its intention to offer a 60% stake in the People's Bank of Zanzibar (PBZ) to a strategic investor. In view of the disappointing performance of Air Tanzania since the 2003 purchase of a 49% stake by South African Airways, it was agreed to reverse this deal and to restructure the airline for a new revitalisation.

There were also mixed signals about the **management** of existing **parastatals**. While the contract with a South African firm to manage the Tanzania Electric Supply Company (TANESCO) was terminated in December and responsibility was handed back into local hands, the management of the Tanzania Telecommunications Company (TTCL) was unexpectedly awarded to a Canadian firm. TANESCO had for years been severely criticised for bad service, exorbitant electricity tariffs and insufficient investment, and the foreign management had been unable to significantly improve the situation. In 2006, however, the **crisis** took on a new political dimension because of severe **power cuts** (resulting from prolonged drought conditions and low water levels in dams) and the inept handling of the situation by the political authorities, who gave misleading reassurances. Severe power rationing measures were applied early in the year, but contrary to official predictions had to be later reintroduced until the end of the year. This had a negative effect not only on private urban consumers, but also on all industrial activities due to production losses and significantly increased power costs resulting from reliance on generators.

Foreign direct investments have remained relatively constant in recent years ($ 473 m in 2005), considerably higher than in Kenya and Uganda, and went overwhelmingly into the **mining sector**. Gold was by far the most important export ($ 615 m in 2005) and Tanzania was the fourth-largest gold producer in Africa. In response to public allegations that many past contracts had been far too favourable to international mining firms, the new government promised to systematically review all existing mining contracts, but it turned out that the government did not possess much leverage.

The prolonged drought in parts of the country had severe negative effects on the **agricultural sector**. Most traditional export crops (except tea) experienced poor harvests, while many farmers shifted to the production of food crops in response to a significant rise in local food prices. In February, with 3.7 m people estimated to be at risk of food shortages, the government appealed for international food aid, but overall the country was able to avert a major famine. The national strategic grain reserve was run down to an extreme low of 3,165 tonnes in April, but had already been replenished (partly through imports) to 110,203 tonnes in December.

Some private sector business interests continued to lobby for a reconsideration of Tanzania's withdrawal from **COMESA** (in 2000), but opinions were divided and no immediate change of position was in sight. There was also some growing concern about potential problems arising from Tanzania's overlapping membership in the **EAC customs union** and in **SADC** (aiming to create a customs union in 2008), which also had repercussions for the ongoing negotiations with the EU about concluding economic partnership agreements by the end of 2007. In the **NEPAD** context, the first self-assessment stage of the **APRM** process was launched, and was entrusted to independent persons free from direct government control.

Kurt Hirschler & Rolf Hofmeier

Uganda

There were two major events with a considerable bearing on the future of the country: the re-election of President Yoweri Kaguta Museveni plus the gaining of a comfortable parliamentary majority for his ruling National Resistance Movement (NRM), and the beginning of peace negotiations with the Lord's Resistance Army (LRA). Relations with neighbouring countries showed some improvement. International concern over the situation in northern Uganda grew. The economy, by and large, did well, but faced obstacles caused by electricity shortages leading to power rationing, locally known as 'load shedding'.

Domestic Politics

The year began with the release on bail of **Dr. Kizza Besigye**, leader of the opposition Forum for Democratic Change (FDC), on 2 January. He had been held in prison since November 2005 in order to answer charges of treason, illegal possession of firearms and rape. Simultaneously he was charged by a court martial for the same offences, except rape. Even after he had left jail, he had to appear intermittently in court for trial, forcing him to repeatedly interrupt his presidential campaign.

For the **presidential elections** on 23 February, apart from incumbent Museveni and his main challenger Besigye, who had also opposed Museveni in the March 2001 presidential contest, there were two elderly candidates from the old parties and a young independent. John Ssebaana Kizito, a former mayor of the capital Kampala, stood for the oldest extant party, the Democratic Party (DP), founded in 1954. The Uganda People's Congress (UPC), in existence since 1960, fielded the widow of former President Apolo Milton Obote, Miria Kalule Obote. Born-again Christian Dr. Abed Bwanika, a newcomer to the political arena, was the independent candidate. On the same day as the presidential vote, the elections for parliament took place. Thus, all voters received three ballot papers: one for the presidential election, one for electing the local MP and the third to choose the district woman representative. About 65.8% of the 10.5 m registered voters cast their votes. The special seats (for army, youth, workers, people with disabilities) were decided in separate procedures.

Compared to the 2001 campaign, there was no high level of violence: there was no systematic intimidation and obstruction of the opposition. To a large extent this was due to the improved operation of the electoral commission, including the preparation of registers and voters' identity cards, and the transparency it ensured. Nonetheless, the incumbent president and the NRM parliamentary candidates benefited greatly from being able to use state structures. In the presidential election, **Museveni** received about 10% fewer votes than in 2001, but his 59.28% guaranteed him a comfortable lead over Besigye, who won 37.36%. The three other candidates combined received only 3.36% of the ballot. The leading candidate among them was DP's Kizito, with 1.59%, followed by Bwanika with 0.95% and UPC's Obote with just 0.82%. The 'old parties', UPC and DP, constantly singled out by Museveni and the NRM as the main culprits for Uganda's past problems, appear to have succumbed to two decades of ideological pressure. However, their real strength may have been underrated since many of their followers apparently voted strategically for Besigye as the only candidate with a realistic chance against Museveni.

The regional distribution of votes showed that though the percentage of votes for Museveni had declined in all four regions of the country compared to 2001, three regions again voted overwhelmingly for him. The western region (Ankole, Bunyoro, Kigezi, Toro) and the central region (i.e., Buganda, the central part of the country) together accounted for 59% of all voters. In these regions Museveni won 78.5% and 61.8% respectively. In the east (where 25% of the voters lived) he got 56%. The north, with 16% of Ugandan voters, had the lowest population: only 29.6% of its votes went to the incumbent. Here Besigye did best, with 62.9%. In the other regions, Besigye came second. In the west (home to both himself and Museveni) he took 20%, in the central region 34.7% and in the east 41.2%. Ssebaana did relatively well in the central region (2.7%) and in the north (2.4%), Bwanika in the north (2.2%) and the east (1%), Obote in the north (3%) and the east (0.8%).

Museveni won because there was no prevailing mood for change and people, especially in rural areas, were still grateful for 20 years of stability and reconstruction after the turmoil of the Amin and 'Obote II' years. There was, however, the notable exception of the capital and the special situation in the north. Here the safety and prosperity of the southern or western parts of the country were unknown.

The results of the **parliamentary elections** in the constituencies to a certain extent followed the same voting pattern, but generally the votes FDC parliamentary candidates received did not correspond to the percentage Besigye achieved in the presidential election. Instead, they lagged far behind, in part as a result of FDC's concentration on the presidential campaign. Most constituencies went to NRM candidates. There were some casualties among prominent politicians: former Amin General Moses Ali who had served as first deputy prime minister lost his East Moyo seat. Former UPC secretary-general, 'Iron Lady' Cecilia Ogwal, lost her Lira seat to Jimmy Akena, son of Obote and official UPC candidate, but afterwards was elected as the woman representative for the new Dokolo district in Lango.

Eventually, after taking into account the appointment of 13 ex-officio members by the president and the 28 August election of district woman representatives in ten of the 11 districts created after the February election, the eighth parliament of the Republic of Uganda had 332 members, of whom 99 (29.8%) are women. This group comprises 79 district woman representatives, 14 constituency MPs, one representative each for youth and disabled persons and two representatives each for army and workers. Total female representation rose by 5.1% in comparison to the previous legislature. Two hundred and eleven members (63.6%) belong to NRM, 41 (12.3%) are independents, 38 (11.4%) belong to FDC, 9 (2.7%) to UPC, 8 (2.4%) to DP, and there is one member each from the Conservative Party (CP) and the Justice Forum (JEEMA). The government's 13 ex-officio members hold 3.9% of the seats, whereas the officially non-partisan ten representatives of the army account for 3%. The NRM members, the ex-officio members, the government-leaning army representatives plus some of the independents close to NRM together account for roughly three-quarters of the seats in parliament. Among the prominent newcomers was the first lady, Janet Kataha Museveni, who captured the seat in the Ruhaama constituency in Ankole.

President Museveni was sworn in for a fresh five-year term of office on 12 May. At the beginning of June, the new 72-member **cabinet** took office. Constitutionally, in Uganda the head of state also heads the government. Since there is no provision for the office of prime minister, legally the prime minister and his three deputies are cabinet ministers like the others. Including the president, the vice-president, the prime minister, his deputies and the minister of parliamentary affairs, who is also chief whip, the cabinet comprises 28 members. To these the 44 ministers of state must be added. Ministers not reappointed included losers in the parliamentary elections. Among them were Moses Ali and compromised figures such as Brigadier Jim Muhwezi, who was cited in the scam over the misappropriation of money provided by the Global Fund to Fight AIDS, Tuberculosis and Malaria. Retained were Sam Kutesa (foreign affairs), Dr. Ezra Suruma (finance) and Dr. Ruhakana Rugunda (internal affairs). The previous minister of defence, Amama Mbabazi, was put in charge of security, whereas Dr. Crispus Kiyonga, hitherto the national political commissar, was given the defence portfolio. Among the new arrivals in cabinet was an old face, Eriya Kategaya, a former first deputy prime minister who had temporarily joined the opposition and then returned to the fold. He was appointed first deputy prime minister again and put in charge of East African cooperation. General Caleb Akandwanaho, better known as Salim Saleh, Museveni's popular younger brother with a somewhat chequered record in business and politics, became minister of state for microfinance.

Five of the top six positions are held by people from the western and the central regions. President Museveni and Kategaya hail from Ankole; second Deputy Prime Minister Henry Kajura comes from Bunyoro; Vice-President Gilbert Bukenya and Prime Minister Apolo Nsibambi come from Buganda. Home to third Deputy Prime Minister Ali Kirunda Kivejinja is Busoga, part of the eastern region but culturally quite close to Buganda. The north is poorly represented. Its most prominent representative is Lands Minister Daniel Omara Atubo from Lango, a former UPC member who won his seat in the eighth parliament as an independent candidate.

On the whole, the election that returned Museveni and established the eighth parliament was conducted properly and reflected the true will of the Ugandan people, according to domestic and international observers. However, they also noted that the elections did not take place on a level playing field. Despite the return to multi-party politics, the state structure still was geared towards the Movement, and NRM candidates were favoured in many ways. Judicial action against Besigye was another major point of criticism. It also led to a landmark decision on 31 January, when the constitutional court ruled that a military court procedure against civilians concerning terrorism and unlawful possession of firearms was inconsistent with the constitution. On 7 March, after pressure from donor countries, President Museveni assured diplomats that Besigye would not be tried by court martial. This was about two weeks after the elections and on the same day Besigye was acquitted of rape. The treason trial before the high court continued.

Given the general deficiencies of the election process, Besigye on 7 March lodged an election petition in the supreme court, citing acts of intimidation, lack of freedom and transparency, unfairness and violence, with a view to having the presidential elections declared invalid. The court ruled on 6 April that there had been serious irregularities but that they were not so great as to disqualify the whole exercise. By four votes to three, it dismissed the petition but expressed its concern about the continued involvement of the security forces in the conduct of elections. A number of complaints were filed by candidates who lost in the constituency elections.

The political developments in Southern Sudan after the implementation of the 2005 comprehensive peace agreement created new chances to get rid of the long-lasting **LRA menace**. Though the Khartoum government had since 2002 allowed Ugandan armed forces to pursue the LRA into the south of the country, campaigns such as the 'Iron Fist' operation failed. To some extent this appears to have been due to continued tacit backing of the LRA by elements of the Sudanese army or government, and it was only in early April that supplies originating from these sources ceased. The LRA had lost its main sponsor and found itself in an uncomfortable position in a territory now ruled by the same Southern Sudanese it had fought before on behalf of Khartoum.

International concern had grown in the meantime. In September 2005, part of the LRA, under its deputy leader Vincent Otti, had crossed from Southern Sudan into the DRC. The threat posed by the LRA to the whole region became evident when it killed eight Guatemalan soldiers of the UN peacekeeping force stationed in DRC on 23 January. There was also increasing pressure on the UN Security Council from civil society and also from the Canadian government to take up the matter. Council resolution 1663, adopted on 24 March, "strongly" condemned "the activities of militias and armed groups such as the Lord's Resistance Army" and requested the secretary general to include in a report already commissioned by resolution 1653 of 27 January "recommendations which would include proposals on how United Nations agencies and missions . . . could more effectively address the problem of the LRA." This report provided a concise summary of the situation: "For two decades, LRA has inflicted enormous suffering, mostly on the Acholi community, the very ethnic group on whose behalf it claims to be fighting. It has caused the displacement of around 2 million people, the majority of whom fled within their own sub-counties, and 1.5 million of whom continue to live in seriously overcrowded camp settings. An estimated 100,000 people are reported to have died as a result of the prolonged conflict". It described the LRA as "a violent criminal group with a severe disruptive capacity against the civilian population within its reach, humanitarian convoys in the area and personnel of the United Nations Mission in the Democratic Republic of the Congo (MONUC), UNMIS and other United Nations programmes, funds and agencies operating in the Great Lakes region." UN Secretary-General Kofi Annan, according to the report, shared "the view of the Security Council that, as such, LRA should be regarded as a threat to regional peace."

In March, Joseph Kony, head of the LRA, had left Southern Sudan and joined his deputy Otti in Garamba national park in northeastern DRC. On 4 July, the Uganda government offered an amnesty to LRA leaders, but only in the event of the conclusion of a peace agreement. The new Government of Southern Sudan (GoSS) was keen to rid its territory of this source of instability and also of the presence of Ugandan troops, and eventually GoSS Vice-President Dr. Riek Machar took up the role of chief mediator. In the capital, Juba, **peace talks** between the LRA and the Ugandan government opened on 14 July. The delegation from Kampala was headed by the internal affairs minister, Rugunda. The top LRA brass remained in hiding in Garamba: they feared they might be apprehended and handed over to the international criminal court in The Hague, which had issued arrest warrants for Kony, Otti and three others in 2005. The LRA leaders insisted on the cancellation of the warrants as a precondition for a comprehensive peace accord. However, these warrants are neither subject to political expediency nor can they be nullified by the Ugandan government. Consequently, they remained in force. In order to facilitate agreement with the LRA leadership, the idea was floated that traditional Acholi reconciliation procedures ('Mato Oput') could possibly be taken as meeting the requirement of doing justice through national legal action.

Though the Acholi people had suffered the most under the LRA's atrocities, several little-known Acholi from the diaspora accepted membership in the hurriedly assembled LRA delegation. For the LRA, a political programme had been conspicuously absent, but now it emerged with an agenda for the talks, starting with the demand to disband the government army (later dropped), and the ability to produce media statements. Yet steady and close rapport between the delegation in Juba, headed by Nairobi-based Martin Ojul, and LRA commanders still in the bush could not be taken for granted. Apparently, the LRA leadership was keen on personal safety and the rescinding of international arrest warrants, whereas the delegation in Juba – provided with accommodation and per diems – had an interest in power-sharing at the national level. Demands by the delegation in Juba included autonomous status for northern Uganda and participation in the national government.

On 4 August, Kony declared a unilateral ceasefire, but the government side refused to reciprocate. Despite occasional interruptions and mutual accusations, the talks led to the signing of an agreement on 26 August on the **cessation of hostilities** with effect from 29 August. Two places in Southern Sudan – Owiny Ki-Bul on the eastern side of the Nile and Ri-Kwangba on its western side – were designated as assembly points for the LRA and safe passage was assured. LRA fighters were also allowed to gather in any place of worship in Uganda. Should the peace talks fail, the LRA would be allowed to leave their assembly places. The Southern Sudanese army was given the task of monitoring and protecting the LRA at the assembly areas and the GoSS was to provide food for the LRA. Owiny Ki-Bul was deserted by the LRA by the end of September.

The ceasefire and the prescriptions for the assembly points were not strictly observed, both sides trading accusations and counter-accusations. Despite occasional interruptions, the negotiations went on. On 21 October, Museveni briefly met the LRA delegation in Juba. This was as unprecedented as the personal encounter between Kony and the UN under secretary-general for humanitarian affairs, Jan Egeland, at the Ri-Kwangba assembly point on 12 November. Egeland tried to have the children held by Kony released, but left empty-handed. The cessation of hostilities agreement expired in September, but continued to be regarded as valid. On 1 November, an addendum to the agreement was signed. The international community sustained its interest. In a statement on 16 November the president of the Security Council welcomed the efforts to solve the conflict and stressed "the importance . . . of both parties respecting that cessation of hostilities." He demanded that the LRA immediately release all women, children and other non-combatants and indicated the intention of the council to monitor developments closely. Outgoing UN Secretary-General Kofi Annan on 30 November appointed Joaquim Chissano, former president of Mozambique, as special envoy for the LRA-affected areas. The 1 November ceasefire extension was further extended on 16 December to the end of February 2007. By the end of the year, the final outcome of the peace process still appeared inconclusive.

Problems in the arid northeast, **Karamoja**, persisted, but were not associated with the situation further west. In order to deal with the challenge posed by cattle-rustling warriors, well-equipped with modern weaponry, government in May resumed exercises aimed at seizing guns. After allegations of human rights violations, a fact-finding mission was dispatched to Kotido district by the UN High Commissioner for Human Rights. Its report, released on 23 November, pointed to abuses in the course of operations, including summary executions, arbitrary arrests, torture and rape. The army agreed "to investigate reported mistakes". At the end of the year, government claimed its disarmament programme was a success, stating that about 3,500 guns, including many assault rifles, had been collected since May. Guns still in circulation are estimated to amount to several times that number.

Foreign Affairs

States of the **Great Lakes region** have endeavoured to ease the tensions characteristic of the region for a number of years. One of the tools is the tripartite commission that was set up in 2004 to advance peace and security in the region, comprising the DRC, Rwanda and Uganda. It was expanded through the admission of Burundi in 2005 and renamed the Tripartite Plus Joint Commission. In Kisangani in eastern DRC in early 2006, the tripartite fusion cell was established, a joint intelligence office of the four countries plus the US. In April, the commission met in Bujumbura, three weeks after the first secretary in the Rwanda embassy in Uganda had been arrested briefly in an Entebbe hotel over an allegedly adulterous incident. The Bujumbura meeting of the commission was chaired by Dr. Cindy L. Courville, senior director for African affairs at the national security council in Washington (the US being the facilitator of these meetings). Agreement was reached on action against the various rebel groups, including the LRA.

A further attempt to bring stability to the region was the second summit of the International Conference on the Great Lakes Region in Nairobi on 14 and 15 December 2006, attended by President Museveni. It concluded a pact on security, stability and development in the Great Lakes region and envisaged a $ 225 m security package and programmes on good governance and other issues.

Relations with the two neighbours that together with Uganda form the East African Community (**EAC**), Kenya and Tanzania, remained good. Close connections with the GoSS are crucial to resolution of the crisis in northern Uganda. Museveni's relationship with John Garang had been particularly cordial. A report released on 18 April blamed pilot error for the crash of a Ugandan helicopter that had led to Garang's death on 30 July 2005. Relations with the Sudanese central government turned sour after Museveni's October visit to Juba without prior notice to Khartoum, and those with the DRC remained edgy. Relations with Rwanda improved. This country, as well as Burundi was admitted to the EAC – effective mid-2007 – by the community's summit in Arusha on 30 November.

A reflection of Uganda's standing was the showing of fellow African leaders at Museveni's swearing-in for his new term of office in May. Prominent visitors were Presidents Mwai Kibaki (Kenya), Jakaya Kikwete (Tanzania), Robert Mugabe (Zimbabwe), Thabo Mbeki (South Africa), Meles Zenawi (Ethiopia), Paul Kagame (Rwanda), Armando Emilio Guebuza (Mozambique), Abdullahi Yusuf (Somalia), Ismail Omar Guelleh (Djibouti), Mohammed Abdelaziz (Saharawi Republic) and Pierre Nkurunziza (Burundi), as well as Sudanese First Vice-President Salva Kiir and DRC Prime Minister Mvouba Isidore.

Relations with donor countries were uneasy. The **UK** again cut its budgetary support over issues of governance. Relations with the **US** were close, including in the military field. In Gulu in March, the US navy's centre for civil-military relations conducted a seminar for army representatives, police and civil society organisations working in the north. A training exercise focusing on humanitarian assistance was held in August in Soroti district, being part of a joint disaster preparedness programme of the three East African armies and US military personnel.

Among the international meetings President Museveni attended was the forum on **China**-Africa cooperation in Beijing early in November and the European development days in Brussels in mid-November. There he took the opportunity to ridicule with one blow **European** emphasis on 'good governance' as well as what he regards as African backwardness in the economic field: "Export of raw materials is bad governance."

Socioeconomic Developments

In January, the **IMF** executive board completed its final review of Uganda's economic performance under the three-year PRGF arrangement and approved disbursement of about $ 2.9 m, bringing total PRGF payments to $ 19.5 m. It was placed on record that the country "achieved macroeconomic stability and a strong external position, and has implemented a range of key structural reforms." The achievement of higher growth and broad price stability was attributed to "prudent monetary and fiscal policies, complemented by large external inflows." The PRGF on 1 February was replaced by a 16-month Policy Support Instrument (PSI). This IMF instrument will monitor the Poverty Eradication Action Plan (PEAP), the Ugandan version of a PRSP. Successes in reducing poverty reported earlier might not have been as impressive as assumed by the Bretton Woods institutions, as noted in an IMF country report released in January.

As a token of closer East African cooperation, the finance ministers of EAC member states presented their budgets on the same day (15 June). Minister Suruma's **new budget** aimed at enhancing economic growth and household incomes through increased production and productivity. Suruma proclaimed as major budget objectives stimulating economic growth and development, providing resources for basic public goods and services and promoting and maintaining macroeconomic stability. The total budget amounted to roughly $ 2.3 bn.

The background to the budget was the estimate by the Uganda bureau of statistics of a **slowdown** in economic **growth** in the 2005–06 financial year (FY). Real GDP was estimated to have grown by 5.3%, compared to 6.6% in FY 2004–05. This slowdown was largely attributed to the prolonged drought, with its effects on agricultural production, and to the fall in hydroelectric generation capacity (due to the lower water level in Lake Victoria), which resulted in substantial power shortages that affected the manufacturing sector. The fastest growing sub-sector in the economy, according to the minister, was telecommunications: the number of mobile phone subscribers passed the 1.5 m mark in December 2005.

Growth of domestic savings, albeit slow, did finally favour the construction business, rather than productive investment. As Suruma pointed out, the share of private construction in GDP steadily increased from 8.8% (FY 2000–01) to 15% (FY 2005–06), thus accounting for almost the entire increase in private investment. Foreign direct investment was estimated at $ 261 m, i.e., 2.8% of GDP. The minister's estimate of export earnings was of growth by 10% in FY 2005–06, surpassing the $ 1.3 bn mark. This growth was largely attributed to an increase in world coffee prices, as well as in fish volumes and unit prices. Yet the export volume index declined slightly, owing to lower export volumes for coffee, cotton and tobacco. The average rate of underlying inflation (which excludes food crops) over the first 11 months of FY 2005–06 was 5.3%, slightly surpassing the government target of 5%. Uganda was affected by the constant rise in world oil prices, leading to increased transportation costs. Suruma praised the Bank of Uganda for having once again been successful in containing inflationary pressures. Underlying inflation in mid-2006 stood at 4.4%, compared to 6.4% in July 2005.

Proposed **taxation** changes in the budget for FY 2006–07 included good news for shareholders and bad news for beer drinkers. As an incentive to capital markets, the withholding tax on dividends distributed by companies listed on the country's stock exchange was to be reduced from 15% to 10%. Excise duty on non-malt beer would increase from 20% to 30%. On bottled water, a 10% duty was to be imposed, and a specific rate for each 50 kg bag of cement was proposed. To be exempted from value added tax were liquid petroleum gas, in order to increase its affordability as an alternative source for lighting and cooking, as well as contraceptive sheaths, in order "to promote the use of condoms in the fight against HIV/AIDS." With a view to minimising the importation of environmentally hazardous used goods, a 10% environmental levy on motor vehicles aged eight years and above, excluding goods vehicles, and a specific rate on household appliances was to be introduced. Parliament in September, however, scrapped the excise tax on cement and exempted beer brewed from locally grown sorghum from the increase.

Government remained "committed to broad based private sector led growth of the economy, through reform and privatisation of the parastatal sector." By the end of April 2006, 128 divestitures had been completed using various forms of privatisation and 24 public enterprises were in various stages of divestiture. Kinyara sugar works and the dairy corporation were in advanced stages of divesture while the IPOs for Stanbic Bank and the national insurance corporation were expected to be completed in FY 2006–07. The challenges posed by modern information and communications technology are to be dealt with in various ways. In the medium term, an E-government strategy and master plan is to be developed, not least to ensure efficient service delivery at both the centre and local government level. In this field, an important role is foreseen for the newly created ministry of communications and information and communication technology. According to the minister of finance, 59% of the budget in FY 2006–07 was projected to be financed from domestic revenues, "whilst the balance will be provided through the support of our donor partners."

Power shortages are expected to be overcome by the construction of new dams on the Nile. The controversial Bujagali dam is not expected to be operational before 2010 and the Karuma dam not before 2011. For the time being, spending on thermal electricity generators and hydroelectric projects will increase. This will lead to a widening deficit (which stood at 8.6% in FY 2005–06). Suruma did not fail to mention the recently discovered crude oil resources in western Uganda (close to Lake Albert), but was careful not to raise expectations too high. He pointed out that efforts were under way to determine the commercial viability of the sites.

In the **Corruption** Perceptions Index 2006 provided by Transparency International, Uganda was ranked 105th, an improvement from 117th in 2005.

While preparations for the Commonwealth heads of government meeting due at the end of November 2007 gained momentum, it emerged that considerable improvement in the **hotel** infrastructure is needed.

Debate on the best way to deal with the ongoing threat posed by the **AIDS** pandemic continued. According to an army spokesman, more soldiers were lost to AIDS than in combat with the LRA. UNAIDS figures showed a marginal increase in AIDS prevalence (6.7% in 2005 compared to 6.4% in 2000). There was concern that in order to please the US – Uganda is a major beneficiary of the US President's Emergency Plan for AIDS Relief (PEPFAR) – as well as local and foreign Christian fundamentalist organisations, the 'C' (use of condoms) element in the successful 'ABC strategy' might eventually be dropped in favour of the 'A' (abstinence) and 'B' (being faithful) elements only.

Volker Weyel

VII. Southern Africa

All states of the sub-region were members of SADC and met regularly in a variety of thematically focused sub-regional conferences. However, while SADC was considered the most advanced form of sub-regional cooperation on the continent, its further integration was at best modest. Globally negotiated relationships posed challenges to further unification on sub-regional levels. Zimbabwe remained the most obvious example of how a transition to independence was derailed once the liberation movement in power had lost its legitimacy, while the scandalous situation in Swaziland continued to be largely ignored within the sub-region and by the outside world.

Democracy, Politics and Elections

The generally positive trend towards enhanced minimum standards of at least formal democratic rule continued – at least relatively speaking – in most countries of the sub-region. Notable exceptions were Swaziland, which remained a no-party state in constitutional terms, and Zimbabwe, which continued to a large extent to base the rule of the party in power and its president, Mugabe, on coercion and repression. Behind the facade, however, manipulation and power struggles, which did not provide evidence of many (if any) internalised democratic values and norms, remained very much alive in other countries too.

Parliamentary and presidential elections in **Angola** had been repeatedly promised for this year but were once again postponed until 2008 and 2009 respectively. In contrast, the government in **Lesotho** reacted to a parliamentary majority that had dwindled to two seats because of floor crossings by announcing early elections for February 2007. Two national elections took place during the year. In **Zambia**, the electorate voted on 28 September for local governments, parliament and president. The election date was announced on short notice and caught the opposition by surprise. President Mwanawasa managed to stay in office as the clear winner with 43% of the votes, but Michael Sata emerged as a surprise runner-up with an impressive 29% (compared to 3.4% in 2001). In a parallel result, Mwanawasa's party, the Movement for Multiparty Democracy consolidated its parliamentary representation with 43% of the votes (73 seats), while Sata's Patriotic Front increased its seats from one in the 2001 elections to a remarkable 43 seats (28.7% of votes). Sata's supporters, misled by early announcements of a likely victory, protested violently in frustration at the final results, which they felt were manipulated. However, observers considered the elections generally free and fair. By contrast, the elections in **Madagascar**, which took place on 3 December, were rather unspectacular and uncontroversial. President Ravalomanana emerged as unchallenged winner with 54.8% of the votes (with the closest rival trailing behind with 11.7%) and his re-election was widely considered as a *fait accompli* even before the electorate had cast its votes.

While 2006 was a fairly peaceful election year, **political power struggles** raged – often within the dominant party with almost exclusive control of political power – in several other countries, most notably Malawi, Namibia and South Africa, as well as within the internally divided and split opposition party in Zimbabwe. In **Malawi**, the feud between President Mutharika and his predecessor Muluzi continued unabated. It dominated the political scene and resulted in legal proceedings as well as political dismissals. In **Namibia**, preparations for the next election of the dominant SWAPO party's president were reflected in deeply entrenched internal divisions. Potential aspirants for nomination by the party as the candidate for the next election of the state president tried to secure comparative advantages and started to close ranks. A crucial debate in this context was the question of whether the party president should be a person other than the head of state (which is the case in Namibia and the cause of much obstructionism and confusion as to who has the ultimate say). In **South**

Africa, similar competition dominated the political scene between the faction led by Mbeki as head of state and party president and the rival faction under the former state and party vice-president, Zuma. Here too, the next decisive stage in the power struggle is considered to be who will be elected as the party president, the result of which will have a large impact on the process and outcome of the African National Congress's nomination of its candidate in the election of the next head of state. In **Zimbabwe**, the opposition Movement for Democratic Change split over strategic policy issues and lost its counter-hegemonic weight by being much distracted by internal disputes. At the same time, factionalism in the ruling party remained a phenomenon, though more difficult to recognise, and subject to ongoing speculation about who had most control and was best positioned to succeed President Mugabe.

Human Rights and Stability

Organised violation of human rights and subsequent social instability has decreased in recent years and its decline corresponded with the strengthening of at least formally institutionalised democratic rule in most of the countries. The unfortunate exceptions remained Swaziland and Zimbabwe and, to a lesser degree, the far from consolidated crypto-democracy in Angola. Forms of politically motivated brutal violence on an organised scale continued to dominate the daily life of most Zimbabweans and, in combination with the unabated deterioration of living conditions, added to the millions of people who have left their home country for reasons of sheer survival and protection of their physical safety. Isolated acts of presumably politically motivated violence also made the public headlines in Lesotho, but generally the sub-region compared favourably with earlier years, when violence bordered on civil war.

The annual 'Freedom in the World' report issued by the Freedom House, which classifies countries according to **political rights and civil liberties**, showed little deviation from previous years but pointed out the continued gross violations committed by the government in Zimbabwe, which ranked lowest and was classified with Swaziland and Angola as not free. Mauritius, Botswana, South Africa, Namibia and Lesotho qualified as free, while Madagascar, Mozambique, Zambia and Malawi were partly free. The latest report indicated that South Africa was among the few countries whose overall rating was slightly less favourable than in the previous year.

Constitutionally enshrined principles were in several cases reaffirmed by courts and the rule of law (as opposed to the law of the rulers) was confirmed and consolidated through such independent verdicts. Most spectacularly, a high court in **Botswana** ruled on 13 December that a group of San (also known as Bushmen, the ethnic minority with the most ancient roots in the area) evicted by the government from a reserve that used to be their home were in lawful possession of the land and unconstitutionally deprived of their living right. While the government was initially reluctant to obey the verdict, it finally accepted the ruling but continued to restrict the San in whichever way possible from leading the life they felt entitled to. Another breakthrough in entrenching human rights was the enactment of a bill in the parliament in **South Africa** on 14 November that legalised same-sex marriages. In a sub-region in which policy makers and the larger public were still largely guided by homophobic tendencies in their moral judgments, this bordered on a cultural revolution. Unfortunately, the similarly strong xenophobic tendencies in most countries found no similar counter-expression by lawmakers. Refugees from Zimbabwe trying to find a means of survival in neighbouring countries were often the first victims of an exclusivist concept of entitlement in neighbouring states: they were denied residence and employment opportunities and were deported home as illegal immigrants.

Press freedom and freedom of expression continued to remain relevant criteria for gauging the degree of civil liberties and were a contested arena in most of the countries. Independent print media were increasingly harassed through lawsuits initiated by political office bearers and other prominent individuals or corporate agencies that sought through such interventions to inhibit the disclosure of unwanted information in the public sphere. The Media Institute of Southern Africa (MISA) on 18 September issued a media statement based on the deliberations of its annual general meeting in Johannesburg on 5 September and involving delegates from ten countries. It expressed grave concern about the ongoing **violations of media freedom** and freedom of expression in the SADC. MISA harshly criticised Botswana for its withdrawal of the draft broadcasting policy and asked "whether a conservative parliament is holding democracy to ransom" since legislation prevented – as in Lesotho and Zimbabwe as the only other SADC countries – the operation of community radio services. MISA called on governments to relinquish control and transform national broadcasters into public service broadcasters. Swaziland was criticised for having engendered a climate of fear for media practitioners, which resulted in self-censorship. The Interception of Communications Bill reviewed by Zimbabwe's parliamentary legal committee was condemned as highly intrusive, unreasonable and blatantly unconstitutional.

While most aggregated surveys trying to assess and rank societies according to so-called good governance criteria remained more or less dubious methodologically, they at the same time conveyed messages and shaped perceptions, not least with regard to the investment climate and stability. Hence, they needed to be registered. In contrast to the MISA criticism of Botswana and a series of interferences by the state infringing upon civil liberties and the rights of minorities, Botswana competed with Mauritius for top-ranking status within the sub-region in terms of democracy and human rights ratings. The **Bertelsmann Transformation Index** for 2006 placed Mauritius and Botswana 15th and 16th out of 119 reviewed countries in terms of its status index, followed by South Africa (18) and Namibia (26). The top scorers did even better in the management index, which was topped by Mauritius, while Botswana ranked third, followed by South Africa (11). Madagascar, ranked 25th, and was praised for achieving one of the greatest improvements, namely 35 ranks compared to 2003. Angola and Zimbabwe, with the latter classified as a 'defective democracy', scored worst among the SADC countries (the index did not include Swaziland).

Socioeconomic Developments

Like other states on the continent, the resource-rich countries of the sub-region benefited from the new competition for access to and control over their natural wealth (minerals, metals, precious stones, oil). China's continued commercial and business offensive left its traces on most SADC states and was reflected both in foreign policy as well as economic relations. Many of the export-oriented economies benefited from increased prices for their resources on the world market as a result of the higher demand from rapid industrialisation elsewhere. The average annual economic growth rate of the SADC countries was estimated at around 5% and higher than previous aggregated results. But few if any effects were visible in terms of value added manufacturing of raw materials. The sub-region remained largely – with the exception of South Africa – an exporter of unprocessed primary goods and reproduced the established patterns of unequal exchange.

The overall record of SADC states in terms of the **annual HDI** released by the UNDP remained disappointing. Mauritius ended up best, ranked as the last country among those with high human development at 63rd position among 177 countries. South Africa (121), Namibia (125), Botswana (131), Madagascar (143) and Swaziland (146) ended in the lower ranks of the medium human development category, while Lesotho (149), Zimbabwe (151), Angola (161), Zambia (165), Malawi (166) and Mozambique (168) trailed behind with a low human development classification. Botswana (-73), South Africa (-66), Swaziland (-50) and Namibia (-50) displayed the greatest discrepancies between the (higher) rank in per capita income and the (lower) rank in the HDI, which was testament to the extreme inequalities in income distribution. Ranked according to children under weight for age, Namibia ended third last among the sub-region's countries together with Mozambique (both 24% for the age group under 5 years), with only children from Angola (31%) and Madagascar (42%) worse off. Given the relative resource wealth of both the Namibian and Angolan economies, this was among the biggest scandals, along with the constant deterioration of Zimbabwe's economy with devastating effects for the majority of its people. Also as an effect of the AIDS pandemic, life expectancy rates decreased in nine of the countries, with only marginal increases in Angola, Madagascar and Mauritius.

As the special envoy for humanitarian needs in Southern Africa reported to the UN secretary-general after the mission to five of the countries between 7 to 15 December, the sub-region is "acutely vulnerable to the effects of flooding and drought because it relies largely on rain-fed agriculture." Notwithstanding the chronically depressing situation, **food security** for parts of the population improved considerably after the good rainfalls and the decent harvest expectations in many areas. The WFP had been able to reduce its sub-regional relief operations from a peak of 9 m people early in the year to a planned 4.3 m in the depths of the upcoming lean season. According to reports by the US-based Famine Early Warning Systems Network (FEWSNET), domestic maize output was expected to improve in all sub-regional countries except Angola and South Africa, with increases of from 11% in Mozambique to 385% in Botswana. The FEWSNET assessment in September/October predicted on the basis of official country reports that in the six countries previously most affected (Lesotho, Malawi, Mozambique, Swaziland, Zambia and Zimbabwe) the numbers of those identified as vulnerable to food insecurity had declined by 70% from about 10 m to 3 m people. Pockets of vulnerable groups were also identified in Angola, Madagascar, Namibia and Swaziland, but emergency food distribution was only anticipated for Angola and Zimbabwe. Figures released for the period April to October showed that maize exports from South Africa (as the region's major source of maize) to other SADC countries had significantly decreased, except to Zimbabwe. Imports into Zimbabwe made up 41%, while total exports to the structurally grain-deficient Botswana, Lesotho, Namibia and Swaziland (known as the BLNS countries) totalled 39%. While South Africa exported white maize from domestic production, Argentina remained an exporter of yellow maize to SADC countries, in particular Zimbabwe and South Africa. By the end of the year the food security status of many households across the sub-region remained stable. So did food prices, at a level below the average for previous years. Only Zimbabwe bucked the trend, with increased food insecurity across the country due to supply shortages, high market prices and loss of purchasing power as a result of extreme inflation.

Southern Africa remained the epicentre of the **HIV/AIDS epidemic**: 32% of all HIV positive cases and 34% of AIDS-related deaths were registered in the sub-region. Zimbabwe was the only country that showed a declining prevalence rate, although available data were unreliable, biased and inconsistent. With one of every five adults living with HIV, however, Zimbabwe remained among the most afflicted countries. Life expectancy among women was 34 years, among the lowest in the world (37 for men). Generally, young women were by far the highest risk group in the sub-region and in South Africa four times more likely to be infected with HIV (where between 5.5 m and 6 m people were estimated to be HIV positive) than men of their age. Swaziland, with an estimated one-third of its population infected, had the highest adult HIV prevalence in the world and approached an absolute decline in population numbers. National adult infection levels were also high in Botswana, Lesotho and Namibia, and ranged between 20% and 24%. The sub-region was home to above 3 m AIDS orphans and the socioeconomic consequences of the pandemic were disastrous. As the 3rd annual forum of the SADC national AIDS authorities (which took place on 12–14 December in Blantyre) stated in its press release, this sad state of affairs was also reflected in declining agricultural productivity, high drop-out rates especially in primary schools and a declining quality of education, since high numbers of teachers died of AIDS.

Sub-regional Organisations

All 12 countries of the sub-region were officially united in **SADC**, with Tanzania and the DR Congo as additional members. With the exception of Mozambique, all sub-regional member states of SADC were also members of one or more other configurations overlapping with SADC. **SACU**, the oldest customs union worldwide, included South Africa and all BLNS states. **COMESA** included seven of the 12 sub-regional SADC states. Mauritius and Madagascar were also members of the Indian Ocean Commission and Angola of ECCAS. Dual membership in SADC and COMESA was considered particularly problematic with respect to imbalances in trade, stiff competition faced by local industries in the SADC countries, rampant smuggling of cheaper goods produced in other COMESA countries and restricted mobility by SADC members in parts of the COMESA region.

SADC made only slow progress in achieving its ambitions of more integration. It had committed itself to achieving a free trade area by 2008 and a customs union by 2010. These commitments were renewed at the ordinary annual **SADC summit** in Lesotho's capital Maseru (17–18 August). Further goals included a common market by 2015, a monetary union by 2016 and a single currency by 2018. The Seychelles, earlier a SADC member, applied to rejoin SADC and attended the summit as an observer. President Mogae of Botswana observed in his address as the outgoing SADC chairperson that in contrast to the noble ambitions, the implementation of SADC programmes showed little evidence of full integration. He called for a scaling up of the integration process and appealed to member states to show a stronger commitment to regional programmes and projects. Mogae pointed to the fact that "as a regional organisation, we still have problems implementing any of our targeted development programmes with our own resources." He pointed out that the budget outlook for 2007–08 expected member states to contribute 39% and external partners 61%, and diagnosed "a need to instil a spirit of self-reliance in our community." At the time of the summit, the DR Congo, Madagascar, Swaziland, Zambia and Zimbabwe still owed their annual dues in full or in part.

Lesotho's Prime Minister Mosisili took over from Mogae as SADC chairperson, and Zambian President Mwanawasa was elected as his deputy to follow Mosisili. Namibia's President Pohamba handed over chairmanship of the organ on politics, defence and security cooperation to Tanzania's President Kikwete, while Angola was elected deputy chairperson of the organ. Earlier on, at an inter-state defence and security committee meeting, which ended on 21 July in Windhoek, the decision to inaugurate a SADC **standby force** for the sub-region at the SADC summit was postponed for a year for logistical and financial reasons. The brigade-sized force is supposed to be part of a larger African standby force under the AU to provide a peacekeeping contingent which is to be operational on the continent.

The summit reiterated that the Regional Indicative Strategic Development Plan (RISDP) and the Strategic Indicative Plan of the Organ on Politics (SIPO) were the main instruments in achieving the desired scaling up of the SADC **integration agenda**. It established a task force comprising ministers of finance, investment, economic development, trade and industry to work with the secretariat to define the road-map for eradicating poverty and to propose measures for fast-tracking implementation. The task force was requested to report to an **extraordinary summit**, which took place on 23 October in Midrand, to consider regional, economic and political integration. This extraordinary summit, which several heads of state did not attend, concluded that the free trade agreement programme was on course and would be launched as planned in 2008, but that trade patterns consisted mainly of commodities. It identified a need to diversify the SADC economies and to increase intra-regional trade and growth. It also reaffirmed its commitment to establishing a customs union by 2010. South Africa's President Mbeki expressed in his weekly column – circulated through the party newsletter 'ANC Today' (27 October-2 November) – strong support for a **consolidated SADC** as his preferred option, but also cautioned that this required "necessary analytical rigour to ensure that we do not make a false start." He noted that the negotiations would need to see ways for disengagement from all regional economic structures outside SADC, scrutinise all other extra-SADC trade and economic agreements and in particular ensure that the negotiated Economic Partnership Agreements (EPAs) with the EU did not turn into an obstacle for SADC.

Indeed, the multiple affiliations of SADC countries not only complicated internal efforts towards further harmonisation but also impacted the negotiations for **EPAs** with the EU. These required that each country be a member of one defined configuration. Four SADC countries, which were also members of COMESA, had decided to negotiate EPAs within the 16–member Eastern and Southern African (ESA) group. In marked contrast, Tanzania had entered the EPA negotiations together with Angola, Botswana, Lesotho, Mozambique, Namibia and Swaziland as part of the seven-country SADC group. South Africa had observer status, since it is not an ACP country, but had earlier entered a separate Trade, Development and Cooperation Agreement (TDCA) with the EU. This complicated matters further, given that the other SACU countries were directly affected by such an arrangement through the common tariff zone. On 7 March, during the 4th European Commission (EC)-SADC senior officials meeting, the SADC EPA group presented a paper that recommended the inclusion of South Africa as a party to the negotiations. The EU responded unofficially only on 1 December. It expressed doubt that an EPA would be completed in time and blamed configuration matters and South African involvement for the delayed negotiations. The EC accepted South Africa's inclusion into the configuration and implied that SACU would be the axis for regional integration as an "institutionally coherent and economically integrated core group." At the same time, the EC insisted on a separate trade regime for South Africa. The TDCA was considered a useful starting point for negotiations over imports from the EU, while tariff increases in the interests of the BLNS countries as SACU member states were opposed to prevent South Africa from benefiting. The SADC-EPA submission had proposed limiting the negotiations only to market access for goods, which the EC rejected as unacceptable. Instead, it emphasised that tariff concessions depended entirely on the sub-region's "efforts to integrate on the rules". WTO compatibility remained the exclusive point of reference. Initial responses by the South African chief trade negotiator indicated resistance to the introduction of a trade regime separating South Africa from the SADC-EPA. According to the South African newspaper 'Business Day' (13 December), he emphasised that South Africa did not differentiate under the TDCA between any of the EU member countries and that the call for uniform treatment was a principled position. Instead, the EU had established division.

Notwithstanding such efforts at further integration, **sub-regional coherence** remained a remote goal. With the NEPAD secretariat operating from Midrand, a new player was added to the challenge. Operating at times like a mega-NGO, the NEPAD secretariat also promoted and implemented sub-regional infrastructural investments and other related trans-national projects, which earlier on were supposed to be an integral part of SADC policy. Not surprisingly, the most visible expansion of SADC during the year beyond all the rhetoric was the construction work at its headquarters in Gaborone. An analysis published after the SADC summit by the South Africa-based Southern Africa Trust (an NGO in support of sub-regional local civil society actors) criticised SADC member states: they had "excelled in signing many progressive declarations, but failed dismally in translating these declarations and protocols into implementable policy initiatives." The integration agenda was too state-centric and elite-driven and lacked adequate participation by non-state actors. This was also lamented by the 2nd **SADC civil society forum**, which held its meeting from 14–16 August ahead of the annual summit in Lesotho. The forum recognised the transitions in most SADC countries from authoritarian rule to multiparty democratic systems but noted "that challenges for nurturing and consolidating democracy still confront many countries leading to periodic legitimacy crisis of governance which in turn results in political instability." It also expressed concern over the preference given by most SADC states to state security over human security. Notwithstanding all the positive tendencies, this was a more realistic perspective that showed there was still much to be done.

Henning Melber

Angola

There was little change in the year as the government consolidated its framework for the future, particularly its own continuation in power, and there was little sign of the promised decentralisation. Increasing elite confidence was shown in the cavalier stance on **elections**, now postponed until 2008 and 2009, six years after the end of the civil war.

There were initial improvements in transparency with the publication of oil revenues online (showing that signature bonuses for oil companies usually cost around $ 1,000 m, including some payments towards a social fund). Inflation was 13.2%. The government did not sign the Extractive Industries Transparency Initiative (EITI). The trade balance was in surplus for the second consecutive year, based almost entirely on oil exports. Despite this, the country was deemed the worst place to do business.

A report of the UK parliament's All-Party Parliamentary Group on Angola (APPG) following their visit during the year stated that "the link between war and lack of development is becoming increasingly tenuous given vast wealth and lack of urgency by government in social development programmes." Despite a new press law, media freedom seemed unchanged, with the state able to control or neuter most of the print and broadcast media.

Domestic Politics

In December, the 'Conselho da Republica' (a 23–member advisory body which includes the president, prime minister, chief legal officer and members of those political parties represented in the National Assembly and others) recommended unanimously that **elections for parliament and the presidency** will be in 2008 and 2009 respectively. This marks six years since the war and seventeen years since the last elections. By 2009, Dos Santos will have been in power for 30 years and it is assumed he will ignore his earlier statements about not standing in the presidential election. Although the elections were repeatedly promised for 2006, and UNITA ('União Nacional para a Indepêndencia Total de Angola') called for both to occur in 2008, the delay suited both government and opposition: the governing MPLA ('Movimento Popular de Libertação de Angola') with 129 of the 220 parliamentary seats hopes to have a sufficient peace and development dividend and the faction-ridden opposition needs time to reorganise itself.

The official launch of the **voter registration** and civic education campaign took place on 1 October and the actual registration started on 15 November. By the end of the year, 945,451 of the estimated 7.5 m strong electorate had registered. Civil society pointed out that a registration process between November 2006 and May 2007 falls in the rainy season and would create difficulties of access, that 4 m people are without identity documents owing to war and displacement and that **civic education**, especially in rural and remote areas, was needed, including mine awareness instruction in indigenous languages. Some civil society programmes started earlier in the year, given by locally based organisations like Development Workshop, Open Society, the Electoral Institute of Southern Africa (EISA) and Norwegian People's Aid, which concentrated its focus on women's participation in elections. The political parties have also begun training their cadres to be agents, etc. The government has no sustained programme of international assistance, rather asking for ad hoc help in areas it determines so as to control the process. Fr. Jacinto Pio Wakussanga (Padre Pio) called for the independent 'Radio Ecclesia' to be allowed countrywide programmes on voter education – a demand the government has consistently refused.

The **National Electoral Commission** (CNE) was appointed, despite legal challenges to its membership from civil society, with 11 members and offices in all provinces and most municipalities. The Inter-Ministerial Commission of Electoral Processes (CIPE) was set up to administer the elections, with doubts over the independence of both bodies.

There were two **assassination attempts** reported on the life of Gen. Fernando Miala, former head of SIE – external security services – who had been sacked in March amid numerous allegations about his relations with the French and the Congolese. The attempt on 24 December was described by the independent newspaper 'Folha 8' as having SINFO (internal security) involvement.

Demining is now largely carried out with Angolan government money using international NGOs or UNDP and did receive much international assistance throughout the year.

According to Sapapelo Nunda, technical director of the national demining institute, there were still 5–7 m mines – a figure that some outside experts have disputed. Despite expected delays, Angola destroyed its stockpile of 52,000 antipersonnel mines, complying with its obligations under the mine ban treaty. Further **reductions in the armed forces** were announced in July by General Francisco Antonio Andrade, Director of the Institute for Socio-Progressional Reintegration of Ex-Soldiers (IRSEM). The World Bank- and European Commission-funded programme has demobilised 15,000 soldiers, about half with disabilities.

Allegations abound about the ruling party creating **divisions inside the opposition** through completely open use of state coffers to buy off minor parties (including those not in parliament) at a cost of $ 100,000 per party. Cleverly, the money was paid in three tranches, with the second due in September dependent on an expenditure report for the first tranche of May. A planned demonstration by parties on 26 September was stopped by security forces, with the money being paid in October. There will be massive state expenditure to ensure MPLA wins the elections – in a situation where many fear elections, given the war that occurred after the 1992 election. The APPG reported that it was struck by the lack of political disagreement over policies between government and the main parties, asking the *faux naive* question – what was the war about then? The answer received was that UNITA and the opposition parties opposed the "personalities in government but not their policies."

The government's **divide and rule strategy** appeared successful. FNLA (Frente Nacional de Libertação de Angola) infighting saw the congress held in June by faction leader Lucas Ngonda denounced as illegitimate by the smaller faction led by historic leader Holden Roberto. The former rebel movement UNITA, with 67 seats, uneasily trying to unify its factions to transform itself into a fully functional political party, saw its efforts marred by interference from the MPLA (including allegations that 13 of its members had been killed). In March after a Luanda meeting of its political commission, UNITA expelled four leading members and suspended others. Expulsions included Jorge Valentim, a founding member but long-term critic of the leadership, and suspensions included Eugenio Manuvakola, who with Valentim had set up UNITA-Renovada in 1998. The row came to a head after UNITA leader Isaias Samakuva called in January on 16 UNITA deputies to step down in favour of deputies of his choosing – a demand that was refused. Another high-ranking dissident, Abel Chivukuvuku, then in June called for a party congress – a demand accepted by Samakuva in December. Subsequently there were (denied) allegations that Chivukuvuku was having discussions with MPLA about his running for presidential elections in opposition to UNITA leader Samakuva and seeking ruling party financial support and access to the state media. In December, Valentim accused Samakuva of bad management and embezzlement in respect of the $ 1.5 m that UNITA had received from the state. Similar faction fighting was reported inside the 'Partido Renovado Social' (PRS) and the civil opposition parties. On 31 May, for first time since November 2005 the bilateral mechanism for political consultation (agreed after end of war between government and UNITA) met and agreed to work together and overcome suspicions, such as the allegation that UNITA had begun to stockpile weapons.

Peace in the **Cabinda enclave** – from which 60% of oil wealth derives and where a low-intensity struggle for independence waged by the 'Forças de Libertação do Enclave de Cabinda' (FLEC) factions is distinct from but interwoven with the nearly 30-year civil war – remained partial despite the 1 August Namibe peace agreement. A series of meetings with the Cabindan Forum for Dialogue (CFD – a grouping of the resistance, human rights groups and the Catholic church, with the latter's delegation led by Catholic Vicar-General Raul Taty – led to a decrease in military activity and then acceptance at Namibe that Angola was a unitary and indivisible state, but with the specific characteristics of Cabinda province necessitating special status for it. However, the kind of special status is very unclear: there has been rejection of the deal by other parts of FLEC, notably the larger FLEC-FAC ('Forças de Libertação do Enclave de Cabinda-Forças Armadas de Cabinda') faction's president, N'Zita Henriques Tiago.

General Francisco Pereira Furtado, coordinator of the joint military commission set up to oversee the **peace process**, claimed in October that 86% of FLEC's forces had demobilised, with 615 officers from the former FLEC Renovada forces, including its leader Antonio Bento Bembe (wanted in the US for kidnapping a Chevron executive, president of CFD but now given retired general status), having joined training courses at the Luanda military school. General Furtado by then promoted to be the FAA chief of staff later admitted that the conflict was not yet over. Senior leaders of FLEC had by the end of the year not surrendered and there were reports (denied by government) that soldiers from the FLEC-FAC group were continuing the armed struggle, with reported tensions in northern Cabinda and attacks on army positions near Buco Zau and Belize. The National Assembly in December passed an amnesty law similar to that passed in 2002 covering crimes, including military ones.

The Cabindan human rights organisation, Mpalabanda Cabinda Civic Association (MACC), was banned on 20 July and its spokesperson Raul Danda arrested in September, moves described as Luanda's trade mark strategy of **dividing the separatists** and destroying their military capabilities, whilst rewarding others with ministerial posts and bringing in limited autonomy to ensure control of the process.

The legal system continued to lack resources and independence, with many seats on the supreme court remaining vacant and a constitutional court first called for in 1992 not established. **Independence of the judiciary** saw little improvement, with judges for the supreme court still being appointed by the president and subject to executive dictates. The space for civil society and in particular human rights activists, campaigners against forced removals and housing clearances and journalists appeared to have narrowed, also in Cabinda, where church initiatives brought a partial ceasefire. According to human rights NGO 'Maos Livres', redress for forced evictions, arbitrary rule and other **human rights violations** were impossible to obtain from the legal system. International human rights bodies welcomed the sentencing on 8 August of a police officer to 17 years' imprisonment for the deliberate and unlawful killing of a homeless boy: this was the first such sentence. This was followed by the court appearance in November of a former cabinet minister and general who was alleged to have terrorised local farmers as he sought to expand his land holdings at their expense.

Legislation covering **press freedom** was passed in February, with improvements including the elimination of the state monopoly over TV broadcasting, incorporating public interest principles into broadcasting and a defence of 'truthfulness' for journalists facing defamation charges. However, the climate for freedom of expression and overcoming journalistic self-censorship remained restrictive, particularly outside Luanda. A February Human Rights Watch response ('Still Not Protected') to the legislation pointed to deviations from international human rights standards, such as excessive limitations on press freedom, including defamation and licensing procedures for private broadcasters being subject to government discretion.

Women are under-represented at all levels of state administration, political life and at decision-making levels in churches and NGOs. Tensions and conflicts at a local level have manifested themselves in abuses of power relations in the home, including violence against women, with sexual abuse still not recognised as criminal. Norwegian Peoples Aid is working with Angolan NGOs on a project 'Women and Elections' and is looking to SADC guidelines of 30% women's participation in parliament.

Foreign Affairs

Angola has **hegemonic regional aspirations** rivalling those of South Africa to the south, but despite a cool relationship in the past it has lately signed a number of agreements with Pretoria (Tshwane), which may mark a change from competitiveness to a more cooperative relationship. Angola is a strong security state with no obvious internal or regional threats. Internationally, Angola appeared more concerned to counter images of its corruption, without giving up hegemonic notions in Central Africa, such as an increasingly warm relationship with fellow oil producer, **Equatorial Guinea**: it hosted a February meeting with President Obiang. Luanda remained aware that its fortunes were linked to international oil consumers, despite its military and economic assets giving it bargaining power.

The Angolan elite remained largely immune to what **international pressure** there was for good governance and transparency, and avoided a deal with international financial institutions through its loan from and cooperation with China. There appeared lessening outside capacity or will to induce an equitable distribution of the large oil profits or push issues of transparency. The West is aware of the need to engage with a booming economy and is keen to compete with China, which is getting the lion's share of contracts, etc. for infrastructural (re)construction. The continuing **geo-petroleum-strategic interest** of the US in the Gulf of Guinea – 'the American Lake' – and Angola in particular as alternative sources of supply to the Middle East was shown in continued good relations. Angola continued to have large shares of US and Chinese markets, but was keen in its foreign policy to diversify its economic relations.

Angola continued to forge **business with the Chinese**: Angola is now their third largest provider of crude oil. Prime Minister Fernando da Piedade Dias dos Santos paid a five-day visit before the Sino-Africa summit in 4–5 November. Chinese Prime Minister Wen Jiabao said during his earlier visit in June that Angola had become China's second biggest trading partner in Africa (shortly to become the biggest) and that Chinese medical specialists would train Angolan doctors in the future. It was also announced that another $ 2 bn loan would be forthcoming, some of which, according to later announcements, was to be spent on upgrading the fisheries industry.

Relations with Brazil, Israel and Russia continued warm as a counter-balance to both the West and to some extent China. There appeared to be some tensions in that relationship on the terms of the loans (70% goes to Chinese firms, who use Chinese labour). Dos Santos pointedly paid an official visit to Russia in late October rather than going to China and stressed the long ties of Russo-Angolan friendship – the first agreement on friendship and cooperation was signed in 1976 – and he claimed there that the entire $ 5 bn debt to Russia had been repaid. There were agreements signed between Angolan and Russian oil and diamond companies.

Reflecting moves towards a more united **SADC**, Angola continued to draw closer to South Africa, signing a number of agricultural, trade and energy agreements. Relations with the Congolese cooled after the expulsion and ill-treatment of illegal Congolese and Dos Santos's allegations of 'a silent invasion from Congo'. This was balanced by the need for security over the water supply from Inga dam in Congo and for the profitability of the Benguela railway being built and rehabilitated by the Chinese at a cost of $ 330 m as part of the $ 4 bn to be spent over 11 years on refurbishing the rail network. Relations with Namibia continued to be warm and there was a memorandum of understanding on establishing an Iona Park-Skeleton Coast cross-border conservation area in late 2006.

There were good relations between the first and second African oil giants, **Nigeria** and Angola, with Nigeria as chair of OPEC being instrumental in Angola's joining the organisation, despite opposition from the US, China and the oil companies. On 23 May, the Nigerian minister for oil, Admound Daukoru, visited to discuss stabilisation in the oil market. Angola hosted the Association of Petroleum Producers of Africa (APPA), which has 11% of world oil production.

Relations with **Switzerland** continued their improvement. The $ 21 m returned to Angola in October were earmarked for education and demining. The Swiss Agency for Development and Cooperation, SDC, denied that the money had been Dos Santos's personal money or that there were still unfrozen Angolan funds in Swiss banks. Relations with **France**, which had been cool due to the Falcone affair, may be warming slightly given that Total was granted operator rights in licences granted in May in blocks 17 and 18, with reports that it was in discussion with the Angolans on paying substantially higher signature bonuses than the Chinese had done. **British aid** is slowly being withdrawn, with (denied) reports of the withdrawal of the Luanda Urban Poverty Programme (LUPP) funding within two years owing to high levels of corruption, because Angola is not strategic to the UK, except for British Petroleum (BP). Despite earlier expressed scepticism on Angola with regard to EITI and transparency, the EU's development commissioner, Louis Michel, visited on 8 December and announced an **increase in EU funding** of € 170 m, which could increase to € 200 m with projects on good governance. Relations continued strong with Brazil and **Portugal**, although little transpired in the latter's offer of an alternative donors' conference. Angolan ambassador to **UN** Ismael Gaspar Martins was elected chair of the UN peacebuilding commission in June – a body ensuring the sustainability of peace agreements.

Socioeconomic Developments

How much Angola derived from oil revenues in 2006 is a matter of dispute depending on calculations, but between $ 29 and 30 bn has been suggested. Diamond wealth was estimated at $ 1 bn. Angola still has a **narrow economic and skills base**, which distorts its developmental priorities, since human capacity and industrial development are drawn into servicing the oil sector. Extractive industries employ only 1% of the population and are massive in personnel and human capacity. Taxation comes from customs duties or oil revenues (90%) so there is no citizen monitoring of their own money, meaning little popular pressure or, indeed, pressure through parliament, given state funding of parties and lack of direct constituency representation.

The World Bank described the government's oil-backed borrowing as the "core obstacle to the country's development." There was a Luanda conference in May on the use of oil revenues, although typically the government only allowed civil society into the latter part. In an October speech to EITI, the deputy finance minister, Job Graca, delayed committing the government to the initiative, claiming as usual observer status, which means little without **transparency conditionality**. Over the year, the World Bank, the World Economic Forum and the Economist Intelligence Unit ranked Angola very low, on occasion at the bottom, of lists of countries providing a welcoming business climate.

Growth was 14.6%, despite higher OECD and other predictions in June. There were few linkages to the rest of the economy. Angola underwent **negotiations with the IMF** for a Policy Support Instrument (PSI), which would give Luanda a closer degree of control over its spending than orthodox Bretton Woods programmes. The IMF visited in March for an Article IV consultation but did not conclude a full programme. It detailed its differences with Luanda over the latter's policy of negotiating huge bilateral loans, especially with the Chinese and Portuguese, rather than paying off its debts and thereby, according to the fund, increasing its ability to attract cheap concessional lending. A report later in the year called for greater concentration on structural and governance issues – a theme echoed by the

OECD, which saw structural reforms as leading to the long-awaited and postponed donors' conference. The World Bank granted Angola $ 102 m for the second phase of the Multi-Sector Emergency and Rehabilitation Project (PMER) in February. The trade balance according to a Deloitte study showed an expected surplus for the second consecutive year, based almost entirely on oil exports, although the government was also unable to spend more than 60% of its budget. In April, there were government negotiations with the Paris Club to reschedule its debts of an estimated $ 2.3 bn (out of an estimated total of $ 15 bn). Although some Paris Club countries favoured a rapid settlement, Angola needs some form of IMF-approved programme to get a comprehensive Paris Club debt write-off.

Attendance by the minister of petroleum, Desiderio Costa, at an OPEC meeting on 14 June in Venezuela resulted in December in an invitation to Angola to become an **OPEC member** from 1 March 2007. Such membership may mean future restrictions on output, although the limit is likely to be between 1.5 and 2 m b/d, whereas current production is 1.4 m and expected to rise to 2 m b/d by the end of 2007 (reserves are estimated at 12.5 bn).

On 4 November, Angola announced the setting up of the **African Association of Diamond Producing Nations** (ADPA), with its headquarters in Luanda, to coordinate policies of African producers for price protection and foreign investment and eventually gain greater profits from higher value activities such as cutting. However, unease over ADPA saw Botswana, the largest producer, not sending a delegation. Human rights activists expressed concern in December over the treatment of **illegal diamond miners** (*garimpeiros*) in the northeast, a month after a Botswana meeting of the Kimberley Process (KP, an organisation of states combating 'conflict diamonds') made Angola chair of a new KP group on artisanal alluvial diamond producers. Regime critic Rafael Marques Morais alleged that diggers were the victims of human rights abuses at the hands of security companies in the pay of the diamond corporations. The issue has raised the temperature between Kinshasa and Luanda, since many of the miners are Congolese.

Concern continued over the problem of the intensive use of **Chinese labour**, having high productivity but little engagement with the local population, which has no participation in the infrastructural planning. Local civil society and economists continued to express concerns that the deal would only contract 30% to local firms, with questions over elite-linked firms getting the 30% non-Chinese component without competition. A proposal was announced in November of a state-directed network of shops and markets to bring cheaper prices, create jobs and challenge the power of the big business groups, although previous initiatives were not successful. The concentration on **infrastructural improvements**, which can be justified in economic terms, is more aligned to the elite's accumulation strategy than to any anti-poverty programme. Chinese loans and labour are rebuilding railways and highways linking to the coast as well as upgrading Luanda port.

On 17 November, the National Assembly approved the 2007 **budget** in which the social sector received the highest proportion, with education and health spending estimated at 5.6% and 5.1% respectively. Most spending will go on administration, and most of even the expected spending of $ 75 per capita will be on prestige projects. The opposition parties abstained, rather than presenting alternatives. The 'education for all' programme, promising free compulsory and quality education by 2015 and full gender equality, was marked by the commencement of school-building.

There was **little improvement in social indicators**, with NGOs providing the bulk of health work, such as in the LUPP. There was one doctor per 13,000 people, maternal mortality was 1,800 deaths per 100,000 births and under-five mortality was 260 per 1,000 due to malaria, respiratory infections, diarrhoea, etc. Malnutrition affected almost half of the 7.4 m children. UNICEF stated, based on 2004 statistics, that Angola was the second worst place in the world to be a child. The outbreak of **cholera** that started in February killed at least 3,000 people, one-third in Luanda, although uncounted rural deaths may mean many more. Government promised a rubbish clean up and the provision of more standpipes, although NGO workers saw more value in rebuilding the waterworks. The literacy rate remained at less than 50%.

The government has made some commitment to addressing **HIV/AIDS** and associated vulnerabilities, with the president's wife, Ana Paula dos Santos, in February opening the first national meeting of civil society organisations working on the pandemic. While the rate is lower than the rest of Southern Africa (5% overall, according to Alberto Stella, the UNAIDS representative in Angola, at a meeting in February), there remains a great need for reliable statistics, given regional variations, increased movement of population and difficulties in accessing rural areas.

Of the Luanda population, 70% is in informal housing and therefore without title rights. In theory, after the 2005 land reform law, residents can obtain paper title, but only within a three-year period. However, obtaining title by rural and urban dwellers is dependent on their getting an identity card, entailing a two-year wait. Observers doubted the law would eliminate the possibility of **conflict over land**, given land grabs by the rich and powerful plus the complications of returning refugees and IDPs. The law contained no implementation clauses, meaning that although some foreign-funded local NGOs and the long-time international NGO Development Workshop have been attempting to register land for local communities, the process is difficult, given the lack of knowledge in local government. During the year, 500 land titles were registered.

There was increased conflict over **urban land** as the national reconstruction office, set up in 2006, produced plans for the biggest African urban project, 'Nova Cidade de Luanda', intended to house 4 m people as land pressure and the economy grew. Demonstrations against forcible evictions occurred during the year amid allegations that usual police procedure was to force out residents in areas like Cabamba in Luanda without inquiring into whether they had legal documentation. Government tended to allege that residents had illegally occupied in hopes of getting compensation, something the Catholic church hierarchy also alleged. No public inquiry was held, although the prime minister talked in May about the need for consultation and compensation. A March statement by the UN special rapporteur on housing rights, Miloon Kothari, on the evictions led to his proposed visit being postponed throughout the year.

Despite projections of harvests improving over the next five years and some good regional harvests, 2006 saw a downturn, with the **food deficit** being 54% (625,000 tonnes per year). Imported food was a huge burden on the cost of living, especially for poor people. The trend towards lack of international support meant that WFP could raise only $ 19 m of the $ 90 m it estimated it needed to feed 700,000 to 800,000 Angolans with no access to domestic food supplies. WFP warned on 26 May that it would have to provide half-rations and suspend food distribution, including to school children. It finished its programme at the end of the year.

There were still an estimated 80,000 **refugees in neighbouring countries** assessing whether to return. Of these, 52,000 refugees were expected to return home, according to UNHCR's repatriation programme.

Women and girls are particularly affected by lack of access to health, information, education and water. Angola has one of the highest maternal mortality rates in the world, low literacy among women and lower school matriculation, attendance and completion among girls than boys. Rural and urban women and girls take responsibility for water collection, which impacts negatively on health. Women as primary carers are responsible for sick family members. In urban areas, the lack of (male-dominated) formal employment possibilities has resulted in women becoming primary family breadwinners through informal commercial activity, in addition to remaining primary carers. Continuing government attempts to crack down on informal commercial activity will have the effect of further increasing poverty levels among poor urban women and their families.

Internal pressures on the ruling elite are few, since the latter do not rely on citizens for legitimacy or for tax revenue. Despite rhetoric on increased transparency, accountability and democratisation, little has yet been accomplished to overcome the gap between ruler and ruled or to overcome the needs of those in rural areas or *musseques* (slums). The challenges remained a **fragmented national economy**, an overvalued currency damaging to productive local non-oil sectors of the economy (although it keeps prices of food imports low), a history of financial embezzlement and misappropriation of funds, a lack of international confidence and donor coordination, poor administrative capacity, a large child population at risk from disease and largely weak (or at least fragmented) opposition and civil society unable to affect social and political developments.

Steve Kibble

Botswana

Celebrating its 40th anniversary of independence, Botswana continued to enjoy political stability. While the Botswana Democratic Party (BDP) – in power for all the 40 years – seemed to come to grips with factional strife, efforts to establish a formal agreement for opposition unity collapsed. The high court ruled the controversial relocation of the San from the Central Kalahari Game Reserve (CKGR) unconstitutional. Diamond production remained the engine of economic growth and the government signed a historic deal with the multinational De Beers allowing Botswana a greater share in the conglomerate. Notwithstanding numerous initiatives, HIV/AIDS continued to threaten socioeconomic development.

Domestic Politics

After some progress in opposition unity last year, the main opposition parties – the Botswana National Front (BNF, with 12 members in parliament), the Botswana Congress Party (BCP, with one MP) and two smaller parties – officially started negotiations on formal **opposition unity** on 18 February. Since a full merger was ruled out, discussions centred on three options. Under the 'pact' arrangement, the parties would compete under their own names and constituencies would be allocated to the party with the greatest relative strength in each district. This model had been tried with limited success in the 2004 elections but only the inclusion of the BCP in the pact in by-elections in 2005 had brought more encouraging results. The 'umbrella' model would mean that all parties would compete under the same name and symbol while in the 'alliance' model all parties would campaign under the colours of the BNF, the strongest opposition party.

It quickly emerged that **tensions among the parties**, particularly between the BNF and the BCP (an offshoot of the BNF), would complicate a settlement. BNF officials portrayed the smaller parties as 'splinter parties' that should join the BNF, while the BCP started negotiations to include the New Democratic Front (NDF) – another breakaway from the BNF that had not been invited to the talks – as a group member of the BCP. On 12 March on short notice, the BNF leadership refused to sign a 'people's unity charter'. After the negotiations made no real progress over the following months, the **opposition parties' congresses** in mid-July reaffirmed the principle of opposition unity. However, the BNF congress on 15 and 16 July overwhelmingly supported the 'alliance' model, prompting sharp criticism from the other parties, which feared BNF dominance. On 27 September, the four members of the opposition framework had to concede that BNF continued to favour the 'alliance' model despite its continued and bitter rejection by the other parties.

After the parties clashed over the fielding of candidates in council by-elections in the Naledi North ward in Gaborone city on 21 October, it became apparent that negotiations on **opposition unity had failed**. The BNF won the council seat in one of its traditional strongholds but lost another in Ngwaketse West to the BDP. The BNF also had to deal with a sudden six week 'sabbatical' by its leader Otsweletse Moupo, who had to sort out problems in his law firm, but apparently decided to stand alone in future. The other parties resolved to forge ahead without the BNF, which now entered a new period of infighting about the quality of its leadership. Moupo's reputation reached a further low when he, the official leader of opposition, failed to respond to President Mogae's state of the nation address on 13 November.

Unsurprisingly, the opposition's weakness strengthened the position of the ruling **BDP**, particularly because it had seemingly come to grips with its own **factionalism**. After a leadership retreat on 11 and 12 February, the leaders of the faction led by party veterans Ponatshego Kedikilwe and Daniel Kwelagobe – sidelined at a party congress in 2003 – declared themselves satisfied with the better representation of their faction in the party. President Festus Mogae openly regretted on 12 February and in April the one-sided support of the other faction, led by foreign secretary Mompati Merafhe and education minister Jacob Nkate, who had replaced former party vice-president Kedikilwe with Ian Khama in 2003 (Khama also being state vice-president since 1999). While the quarrels in and between the opposition parties continued, the BDP managed to hold an orderly **party congress** on 15–17 July. The congress held elections for the party's youth wing, which had been at the centre of party infighting in previous years. A 'unity team' that included supporters of both factions won easily and in August BDP's executive secretary declared his confidence that a united BDP would be 'certain of victory'.

Though party politics moved in favour of the BDP and a survey poll by Afrobarometer revealed 70% support for the president's performance (up from 59% in 1999), many problems remained obvious when Botswana celebrated its **40th anniversary of independence** on 30 September. Mogae's speech focused on 40 years of good governance but also conceded that Botswana was still a developing society. Given the country's dependence on diamonds, the international campaign of Survival International (SI) on the removal of the San from the CKGR was of particular concern. SI had accused the government of relocating the San in order to mine diamonds and thus portrayed Botswana's main source of wealth as 'conflict diamonds'. Already on 4 August, Mogae had invited the opposition leaders to discuss the issue. These leaders welcomed the consultation and condemned SI's campaign, but remained critical of the relocation policy.

In the trial before the high court in Lobatse in which a group of San challenged their **relocation from the CKGR**, the court finally delivered its long-awaited judgment on 13 December. The trial, the longest and most expensive in the country's history, had taken 130 days spread over more than two years and the typed record comprised some 18,900 pages, High Court Justice Maruping Dibotelo and his three fellow judges ruled that the applicants were in lawful possession of the land in the CKGR and that they were "deprived of such possession by the government forcibly or wrongly and without their consent." The court also ruled unconstitutional the government's refusal to issue special game licences for hunting to the San. While this was clearly a **victory for the San**, the high court also ruled – with one judge, Justice Unity Dow, dissenting – that the termination of basic services to the San was neither unlawful nor unconstitutional and the government was not obliged to restore them. Moreover, the court ruled, with Dow again dissenting, that each party should pay its own costs.

Though the San and their lawyers had never argued that **diamond mining** was behind the relocation, as claimed by SI, the government attorney succeeded in including this issue in the trial. The high court deemed this evidence irrelevant to the case but also found that there was no evidence that this was the reason for the government's policies. In only one of the six settlements from which the original 200 applicants had been relocated had prospecting for diamond mining taken place before 2002. After a visit to Gope, the settlement in question, the court found, however, that no prospecting was taking place anymore and the settlement had been established as a result of diamond prospecting – due to the availability of water – as opposed to having been closed down because of diamond mining.

The high court's decision was welcomed as a 'landmark ruling'. Particularly, opposition media and the human rights group Ditshwanelo, which had constantly supported the San case, cautioned the government to duly implement the ruling. After five days of internal consultation by government, a spokesman announced on 18 December that the **government**

accepted the ruling and had no intention of appealing it. Yet the government apparently chose to take a narrow interpretation of the ruling. On 14 December, Attorney-General Athalia Molokomme had already outlined the government's interpretation: only the remaining 189 applicants and their minor children would be entitled to return to the CKGR, and without any livestock or automatic right to special hunting licences. The government offered talks with the San and appealed to them not to return to the reserve before President Mogae had spoken to them at New Xade, the main new settlement created by the government outside the reserve.

Foreign Affairs

The removal of the San from their homelands in the CKGR and the court case continued to attract **negative international publicity**. Although the government in March was given support by a group of British parliamentarians, it was still under pressure from the international campaign coordinated by SI. SI's claim that diamond exploration in the CKGR was the prime reason for evicting the San and its strategy of – falsely – dubbing Botswana's diamonds 'conflict' or 'blood diamonds' proved to be effective in attracting worldwide attention. The movie 'Blood Diamond', starring Leonardo DiCaprio and dealing with diamond mining in Sierra Leone, made matters worse from the government's perspective. After the high court ruling on 13 December, international reactions were mainly positive, though SI warned the government to implement the ruling in an orderly way.

President Mogae sought support for the country's **'Diamonds for Development'** campaign abroad. On 1 January, Botswana assumed the chair of the Kimberley Process, an initiative that includes a certification scheme in order to precisely track the origins of rough diamonds being traded. On 12 October, Mogae spoke at the Center for Global Development in Washington, DC, trying to distinguish Botswana's diamonds from 'blood diamonds'. Furthermore, in early November, Botswana chaired the plenary meeting of the Kimberley Process. A representative pointed out that trade in conflict diamonds had been significantly reduced to 0.2% of all diamonds traded. On 4 December, President Mogae followed up the Kimberley meeting in Gaborone with an address to the UN general assembly on progress in implementing the certification scheme.

Botswana's **relations with Zimbabwe** remained the greatest regional diplomatic challenge for the country. Constant inflows of illegal immigrants from Zimbabwe caused domestic tensions and increasing criticism of Mogae's handling of this issue. Many Batswana and the media blamed the influx of Zimbabweans as the prime reason for the increased crime levels in the country. In particular, the president's visit to Zimbabwe on 28 August to open an agricultural show in Harare at the invitation of President Robert Mugabe, was widely criticised in view of Zimbabwe's poor human rights record and dismal economic situation. On 20 July, government confirmed in parliament that it had abandoned the controversial plans to electrify the fence along the Botswana-Zimbabwe border. According to government, the fence had been erected to contain the spread of foot and mouth disease from cattle herds in Zimbabwe.

Botswana played an active role at the ordinary **SADC summit** on 17–18 August in Maseru, Lesotho. At that meeting, President Mogae handed over the chairperson of the organisation, which he had held since August 2005. Botswana was also one of the prime proponents of deeper regional integration at the extraordinary SADC summit on 23 October. It discussed the scaling-up of regional economic integration, particularly the launching of the FTA by 2008. In contrast to its international reputation as one of Africa's political and economic success stories, Botswana's government again refused to participate in the **NEPAD APRM**, citing financial considerations and parallel reviews as the reasons.

Socioeconomic Developments

On 6 February, Minister of Finance and Development Planning Baledzi Gaolathe delivered the **state budget** for the fiscal year 2006–07 to the Botswana National Assembly. The theme of the budget was 'Building an Innovative Economy for the 21st Century'. The 2005–06 financial year (from 1 April to 31 March) showed a surplus of P (pula) 4.63 bn against an initially anticipated surplus of P 1.58 bn. Customs revenue from SACU grew strongest and contributed to a total state revenue of P 22.27 bn.

Inflation averaged 11.6%, compared to 8.6% in 2005, causing major public concern. The increased inflation was due to the combination of higher world prices for petroleum and the effect of a 12% devaluation of the local currency on 29 May 2005. Yet the rate declined to 8.5% for the twelve months to December, indicating that the Bank of Botswana aims to further reduce inflation. At the end of November, foreign exchange reserves stood at P 48.8 bn, a sum which translates to a remarkable $ 7.9 bn. Estimated real GDP growth in 2005–06 amounted to 4.2%, down from an estimated 6.2% in the previous financial year. The extraction of diamonds, Botswana's principal export commodity, rose to 33 m carats in the calendar year, from 31.9 m carats in 2005. However, the world price for rough diamonds went down by about 4% in the same period. Botswana remained the world's leading diamond producer in terms of value.

The government extended leases on the four diamond mines in the country by 25 years. On 23 May, President Festus Mogae and De Beers chairman Nicky Oppenheimer signed the deal **renewing the licence for Debswana**, a 50/50 joint venture between De Beers, the world's largest diamond mining conglomerate, and Botswana, to mine diamonds in the world's most valuable diamond mine at Jwaneng and the other three mines, Orapa, Letlhakane and Damtshaa. In concession, the state obtained a greater shareholding in De Beers and entered into agreements that will strengthen Botswana's diamond beneficiation industry. The **Diamond Trading Company of Botswana**, a joint venture between the government and De Beers, is to partly replace De Beers's marketing monopoly in diamonds and encourage local cutting. Construction of a new $ 83 m facility near Gaborone's airport was started and completion is expected by 2008.

After long delays, at the end of October the Public Enterprises Evaluation and Privatisation Agency (PEEPA) confirmed that the South African airline SA Airlink had been chosen as the preferred bidder for the national airline **Air Botswana**, which recorded a net loss of P 17 m for the year. The minister of finance and development planning announced that the opportunities for 'rationalisation' of other parastatals must be examined before any decision on privatisation could be made.

As in previous years, Botswana was awarded favourable international credit ratings and scored well on indices for good governance, such as the Corruption Perceptions Index (released on 6 November). Once again, Botswana was the **least corrupt country** in sub-Saharan Africa on the index. Yet in terms of providing a business environment for foreign investment, the picture looked less favourable. According to the World Economic Forum's 2006 global competitiveness report, out of 125 countries Botswana was ranked only 81st, as against 72nd in 2005. On 3 November, the local newspaper 'Mmegi' published extracts from the report of the **Business and Economic Advisory Council** (BEAC). The council had been established mid-year in order to develop proposals that would improve the business environment. It clearly criticised government programmes to support economic activity and noted that Botswana's economy remained relatively undiversified and relied heavily on diamond extraction.

According to the preliminary results of the official 2005–06 labour force survey, Botswana's **unemployment rate** dropped from 21.5% in 1995–96 to 17.6% in 2005–06. However, it was widely believed that these data underrated the problem of unemployment. At the beginning of the year, the government reintroduced **school fees** for secondary schools as part of its 'cost recovery' measures. For more than 20 years, the state has provided free secondary education. Opponents claimed that the fees would deter parents from sending their children to school. On the other hand, the government granted exemptions for poor families.

The high **HIV/AIDS prevalence rate** remained the most pressing social issue in Botswana. According to the 2004 Botswana AIDS impact survey, 17.1% of the population were infected with HIV. There were slight indications that the prevalence rate was decreasing: Sentinel Surveillance, which tests pregnant women (15 to 49 years) in government clinics, found that the HIV prevalence rate among them had dropped from 37.4% in 2003 to 32.4% (preliminary data). As of October, the total number of patients enrolled for anti-retroviral therapy was 75,785. This was an improvement of 39% compared to the previous year, but still short of the government target of 85,000 people by end of the year.

Matthias Basedau & Christian von Soest

Lesotho

The political calm that Lesotho had enjoyed since the general elections of 2002 was threatened by mounting discontent with government and the breakaway from the ruling **Lesotho Congress for Democracy** (LCD) of 18 of its own MPs to form the **All Basotho Convention Party** (ABC). This reduced the LCD's majority in parliament to just two, prompting Prime Minister Pakalitha Mosisili to call an early election, to be held on 17 February 2007. Although the government is faced by the daunting task of improving life for the majority of people within an impoverished labour-surplus economy, its immediate difficulties appear to have been caused by perceptions of its pursuing the interests of a privileged political elite at a time of a temporary fall back in employment in the textiles sector, service delivery failures and widespread hunger.

Domestic Politics

In June 2005, the government had announced **substantial salary increments** (some as high as 85%) for senior office-holders and MPs. It justified these on the grounds that, compared with regional salary levels, those in Lesotho were extremely low. For instance, the proposed increase would take the prime minister's salary to no more than maloti (M) 300,000. Nonetheless, within an impoverished economy where unemployment was standing at over

40% and the mass of public servants had recently received an increase of just 5%, the top-tier wage hikes drew severe criticism. Subsequently, the volume of complaints increased markedly after the government was rocked by a scandal resulting from revelations that, after a number of ministers had taken receipt of Mercedes Benz cars in 2005, its fleet contract with Imperial Fleet Services allowed senior government ministers and officials, judges and parliamentary officials to purchase their three-year-old government vehicles for just 1% of their original price. This precipitated a storm of public criticism, and even a go-slow by magistrates, who complained bitterly about their low salaries.

The public perception that the political elite was living high on the hog (however modest its emoluments in regional terms), contributed to a sense that the political peace the country had enjoyed since 2002 was fragile. This was confirmed by a couple of **violent incidents with sinister political overtones**. One was the attempted assassination of Foreign Minister Monyane Moleleki in the early hours of 29 January. He was shot only in the arm, but those responsible for the shootings were not apprehended. In contrast, Moleleki's two military bodyguards were subjected to a court martial, before which they claimed that they had been tortured by police who had tried to force them to make false statements against the minister. Moleleki proclaimed that the police seemed determined not to find his assailants. The second incident appears to have been the outcome of an internal rift within the one-time ruling Basotho National Party (BNP). Bereng Sekhonyana, a former deputy leader of the party who had fallen out with its leader, former military strongman Major-General Justin Lekhanya, had been nominated by the speaker of parliament to attend a conference in Botswana. Lekhanya had objected and organised protests by the BNP's women and youth leagues outside parliament. The upshot was passage of a motion in parliament, which was supported by Sekhonyana, reprimanding Lekhanya and other senior BNP MPs for seeking to intimidate the speaker and suspending them from parliament. Two days after the passage of this motion, on 2 June, Sekhonyana was gunned down outside his house.

It was against this unsettled background that on 13 October, Tom Thabane, minister of communications, science and technology, resigned from the government and crossed the floor of the house with 16 other LCD MPs where, along with an independent MP for Mokhotlong who had been expelled from the LCD in 2004, he formed the ABC. Of the **17 ex-LCD MPs crossing the floor**, five were from Maseru districts and the rest were from all districts except Quthing and Qacha's Nek, thereby ensuring that the new party could lay claim to a significant national presence and could pose a significant electoral threat to the LCD.

Thabane, who had served in every post-independence government whether as a senior civil servant or a minister, complained in an interview that the LCD had betrayed the heritage of the radical Congress tradition. The government was failing in the provision of basic services to the people and was more interested in its own well-being. When the ABC held its first major public rally in Maseru on 29 October, he spoke of the decline of health and other services, but referred also to the rising tide of crime, none of which the government was capable of tackling because of a "lack of political will". When challenged about his acceptance of a relatively new car for just 1% of the original price, under the Imperial scheme, Thabane agreed to return it, although the government refused to receive it back.

It was in this context that Mosisili, with his parliamentary majority reduced to just two seats, decided to call an **early election** on 17 February 2007. On the same night that the king dissolved parliament, a Dutch medical volunteer was shot dead late at night outside a guest-house owned by Trade and Industry Minister Mpho Malie. The latter claimed that the taxi in which the volunteer had returned home had been mistaken for his official Mercedes Benz and that the bullets had been meant for him, hinting that responsibility lay with the ABC. Moleleki now made public his suspicions that the attack made on him previously had come from within his own party, from those elements who had later created the new political party. Thabane dismissed the allegations as nonsense, but it was distressingly clear that the country was set for a potentially turbulent, if not violent election.

Foreign Affairs

Following the upgrading of the status of the Irish consul-general to that of full ambassador in 18 May, Lesotho received a **state visit by the Irish president**, Mary McAleese, who took the opportunity to visit a number of Irish aid projects. A further important aid project was completed with the prime minister's inauguration, in February, of 17 new schools funded at a total cost of M 60 m by Japan. The schools formed part of a government school-building programme that had so far reportedly led to the opening of 180 new schools.

The **SADC summit** met in Maseru on 26–27 August. At the meeting, President Festus Mogae of Botswana handed over the chairmanship of the organisation to Prime Minister Mosisili.

Socioeconomic Developments

Migrant labour remains very important to Lesotho's economy. Despite the rapid expansion of the textile industry, which employs some 40–50,000 Basotho, it remains the major source of employment. Yet the consequences of the shift in employment patterns are dramatic, not least because miners' average earnings of between M 40–50,000 per annum are up to four times better than those of Lesotho's factory workers. In addition, whereas the overwhelming majority of migrant workers are men, the overwhelming majority of workers in the clothing and textile industry are women.

Lesotho is today less a labour reserve than a labour-surplus economy. **Unemployment** remains endemic, in excess of 40%. Furthermore, while Lesotho's growth rate averaged over 5% during the 1990s, this has fallen to around 1.5% since 1998, despite high praise from the World Bank and other financial observers for the government's fiscal management. Meanwhile, long-term economic prospects are bleak due to factors such as continuing external suspicion about the country's political stability; the continuing decline in migrant earnings; the decline in investment associated with the completion of the first phase of the Lesotho Highlands Water Project (LHWP); an expected drop in revenue accruing from the SACU with the establishment of a free trade area between the EU and South Africa; and, finally, the uncertainty about the future of the textile and garment industry attendant upon the limited life expectancy of the AGOA of 2000 (and subsequent amendments) and the 2005 lapse of the WTO's Multi-Fibre Agreement (MFA), which constrained the global impact of Asian, notably Chinese, competition.

The sum of all this is that **poverty continues to deepen**. The government's own estimate (which is more conservative than other studies) is that 58% of the population is living in poverty, and that the proportion of those living in 'ultra-poverty' has risen above 38%. The poor are necessarily dependent upon the informal and subsistence agricultural sectors, but their capacity to survive is undermined by the alarmingly high level of HIV/AIDS infection (reckoned to be in excess of 31%). The WFP continued to complain in 2006 that funding shortages were hampering the distribution of food aid and that Lesotho needed food aid for more than half a million people but was in a position to assist only between 250,000 and 300,000. As a consequence, there had been a dramatic reduction in the 100,000 orphans previously receiving assistance. Early this year, the heaviest rainfall in nearly two decades destroyed more than one-third of the crops in the ground ahead of the April harvest, leading WFP to predict further food shortages.

The government announced its intention to tackle these challenges through its **Poverty Reduction Strategy** (PRS), which, after wide consultation with civil society, it published in June. This had eight priorities: the creation of employment; the improvement of agricultural production and food security; the development of infrastructure; the deepening of democracy, governance, safety and security; the improvement of access to healthcare and social welfare; the improvement of quality of and access to education; the management and conservation of the environment; and the improvement of public service delivery. Cross-cutting priorities were listed as the combating of HIV/AIDS and problems related to gender, youth and children.

When delivering his **2006–07 budget** on 8 February, Finance Minister Tim Thahane foreshadowed the official publication of the PRS by stating that the greatest threat to the attainment of its goals was a lack of resources. He therefore recorded the government's acute disappointment at the exclusion of Lesotho from the debt cancellation afforded 18 HIPCs by the G8 countries in 2005. He had earlier indicated that debt cancellation would have saved Lesotho M 312 m per year. The PRS and MDGs were achievable, he said, but only with greater support from Lesotho's "development partners".

Estimated **government spending** would be M 4,907.5 m, of which M 3,655.4 would be recurrent and M 1,252 would be capital expenditure. Revenue was expected to be M 5,352.4 m, providing an envisaged surplus of M 277.8 m (some 2.2% of GDP). Notable among the expenditures would be an allocation of M 30 m for the building of a new parliament, a venture for which China would contribute technical expertise.

Thahane proclaimed that the country's economic fundamentals remained sound, but noted that the **textiles sector** was going through a rough patch as a result of the end of the MFA, increased competition from Asian producers and the appreciation of the rand/loti against the dollar. Between 1999 and 2004, textile exports had increased from about $ 100 m to $ 450 m, and employment had reached 50,000 at the peak of the country's exports. However, employment had fallen back to 37,500 in 2005. Growth was expected to increase to 1.7%. Many textile companies were struggling. As a result, government was taking bold steps to support and diversify the sector. Rather than calling for the restriction of Chinese exports, it was seeking Chinese help to solve problems and generate jobs; in forming joint ventures; in training workers in quality assurance; and in financing and constructing Knotted Fabric Mills to anchor these textiles. Government was also reviewing tax policy in order to make life easier for existing companies.

By mid-year, it was reported that the textile industry was recovering, with factories reopening and the number of jobs back to 47,000. The turnaround was ascribed to increased demand from the US and European markets and Lesotho's hard work in making the country a destination of ethical choice, Lesotho having made considerable efforts to engage employers in the fight against HIV/AIDS.

Further good news was provided by steady growth in the **diamond industry**. Not only was there the prospect of opening two further mines, but the mine at Letseng-la-Terai, which had reopened in 2004, was gaining a reputation for producing large high-quality stones. However, mine managers warned against unrealistic expectations. The mine employed only some 400 Basotho and was producing only 3,000 carats a month – in contrast to Botswana's production of about 2.5 m carats a month. Nonetheless, it was the mine's growing reputation that facilitated its sale in June by its majority shareholders, JCI and Matodzi, to another South African company, Gem Diamonds, for R 879 m, with the Lesotho government increasing its stake in the enterprise to 30%.

Lesotho continued to earn international goodwill for its **prosecution of corruption** arising from the LHWP. Early in the year, Lesotho's former top official on the highlands water commission, Reatile Mochebele, had been charged along with his former deputy, Letlafuoa Molapo, with receiving bribes amounting to over R 1 m from various companies. In November, a leading NGO, the Transformation Resource Centre (TRC), called for the widening of the corruption investigations into tenders allocated for the LHWP. The call followed public hearings during which residents affected by the construction of the Katse dam had alleged that they had had to bribe officials involved in relocating them. TRC further stated that while 30,000 people had been affected by the LHWP relocations, agreed compensation had yet to be paid to many of them. Prior to this, a crack in the wall of the Katse dam had sparked safety concerns. The TRC argued that the compromising of construction standards was a concomitant of the alarming degree of corruption surrounding the LHWP and posed dangers to those who had been displaced.

Roger Southall

Madagascar

The elections of 3 December went off smoothly and President Ravalomanana was re-elected. He embarked on implementing his bold Madagascar Action Plan (MAP), introduced in March. Though Marc Ravalomanana no longer had the lustre at home he once enjoyed, the donor community continues to embrace him. High profile state visits by UN Secretary-General Kofi Annan and German President Horst Köhler, as well as President Ravalomanana's own official travels indicated his continued international appeal. Nonetheless, Ravalomanana closed the year facing shifting domestic political terrain, stubborn poverty levels and somewhat unstable market conditions marked by economic inequalities and rapid but difficult-to-manage growth in the mining and oil sectors.

Domestic Politics

The **elections** of 3 December were peaceful, transparent and, with only modest challenges from disgruntled opposition members, anticlimactic. No serious challenger arose to compete against President Marc Ravalomanana and his victory was clear months before the balloting took place. As ratified by the 'Haute Cour Constitutionnelle de Madagascar', President Ravalomanana won an easy victory with 54.8% of the vote nationwide. The closest challengers were Jean Lahiniriko with 11.7% of the vote and Roland Ratsiraka with

10.1%. On 17 November, General Andranafidisoa had announced that he had formed an interim military government. The **coup effort** never materialised and Andranafidisoa was ultimately arrested, but not before eight opposition members announced their support for him.

While the elections met the benchmarks necessary for positive feedback from domestic and international observers, they were marred by problems in the **election laws**. President Ravalomanana rejected advice to change to a single ballot. Instead, he maintained the system of a different ballot for each candidate while introducing a new requirement that candidates must provide their own ballots to the population. A multiple ballot system is more easily subverted and gave rise to challenges of propriety at the local level. Candidates complained that the new requirement introduced an economic and logistical hurdle to competing. The short campaigning window allowed under the electoral code made it difficult for challengers to gain name recognition outside their home territory. The electoral code limits funding opportunities for candidates, essentially opening the process only to those who can afford it. Two days before the election, the national election committee, the government body responsible for the elections, announced that there were problems with the electoral lists leading opposition members to claim fraud even before the balloting.

President Ravalomanana's margin of victory was great but should not be confused with the energy and enthusiasm that he elicited five years ago. He gained support as much from the **lack of a viable opposition** as by his own popularity: his support base was both more fractured and narrow. A poll in the capital (his base of power) shortly before the elections appeared to reflect a willingness to give him one more opportunity to prove he can right the economic woes of the country while uniting its identity and forging its path towards global market engagement. This is a far cry from a similar poll before the 2001 elections in which people saw him as an infallible saviour.

One of the most notable changes in Madagascar's domestic politics was the **composition of the opposition**. In 2005, there were three distinct opposition groups in Madagascar with more radical tendencies: the 'Comité de Réconciliation National' (CRN) led by former President Zafy Albert, the 'Solidarité Parlementaire pour la Défense de la Démocratie et l'Unité Nationale' (SPDUN) led by Pastor Richard Andriamanajato, and the 'Rassemblement des Forces Nationales' (RFN) led by Pastor Edmond Razafimahefa. Other, more moderate opposition parties included former President Norbert Ratsirahonana's 'Asa Vita no Ifapitsarana' (AVI) party, Roland Ratsiraka's 'Toamasina Tonga Saina' (TTS) party, Alain Ramarson's 'Mouvement des Citoyens pour la Saufgarde de la Republique' (MCRS), Manandafy Rakotonirina's 'Mpitolona ho amin'ny Fanjakan'ny Madinika' (MFM) party and Moxe Ramandimbilahatra's TEZA party. Of these, only Norbert Ratsirahonana, Manandafy Rakotonirina and Roland Ratsiraka were positioned to run in the elections and even they could muster only 4.2%, 0.3% and 10.4% respectively. Such an opposition would not pose much of a challenge to most incumbents.

The real challenge to President Ravalomanana was from his own party **TIM** ('Tiako i Madagasikara'). The TIM is still a young, inchoate party. It is at a crossroads of several political trends. Madagascar is an emergent democracy with growing institutional needs for a viable party system led by a stable governing party. Yet, like former ruling parties, the TIM was built around a single man. There has been a real opportunity for the TIM to grow in new directions, garnering support from beyond its ethnic base and institutionalising itself to the benefit of the broad ruling elite to serve primary party functions such as recruiting new leaders and building a platform. Yet, Marc Ravalomanana, once bordering on shy about his presidential powers, has grown more centralised, secretive and, according to his critics, autocratic. As challenges rose in the National Assembly, even one-time supportive legislators began complaining of the use of the party by the executive to infringe upon legislative activities. By mid-year, it became clear that the reason a leader would join TIM could be closely associated with his or her position on President Ravalomanana's leadership position. Broadly speaking, TIM members can be categorised into four groups: those who joined TIM because they seek reform, those who joined TIM for opportunistic reasons, those who joined TIM because they were conforming to the ruling party and those disenfranchised, disaffected leaders formerly close to Ravalomanana that have nowhere else, politically speaking, to go. For the first group, allegiance to the party is likely tied to gains made by the president's policies. Those who are opportunistic will stay loyal as long as there is no viable opposition to offer other opportunities. Those in the third and fourth groups are the most fickle as they hold little allegiance and could move, or create, an alternative block to the ruling party. At present, the TIM is factionalised and dominated by a narrow group closely aligned with the president. The rest of the party, even those who are disaffected, are still supporting the TIM platform. Yet one can imagine a scenario in which these inter-party personalised networks become more important than the parties themselves. For the first time since the party was formed five years ago, there is reason to watch cautiously to see if the fissures widen to a point where the party splits.

The elections also made clear that President Ravalomanana has not been successful at overcoming a **geographic divide** in his base of support. Voter turnout for the elections was 61.9%, down from 67.9% in 2001. There was a significant voter turnout bias towards Antananarivo and Fianarantsoa where President Ravalomanana is the strongest. Voter turnout in Antananarivo province was 66.8% and in Fianarantsoa 60.3%. Where Ravalomanana is weakest, Tulear province, the turnout rate was the lowest in the country, 57.7%. The population of Antananarivo and Fianarantsoa provinces exceeds half of the national population ensuring that a candidate need only win these provinces to secure victory. The voter turnout difference adds an additional advantage to these provinces of more than five points. A candidate like Jean Laniriko, from Tulear province, thus cannot compete even though he won 46% in his home province to Ravalomanana's 35.4%, unless he can win over voters in Antananarivo and Fianarantsoa. This is an unlikely proposition given

Madagascar's historic political divides and made impossible by the small window for campaigning allowed under electoral law. In the end, President Ravalomanana won with 54.8% of the vote, compared to 51.5% in the recounted 2001 vote. Yet his performance in the farther provinces was comparatively lower. The election results thus point to a **centralisation of support** for the president as opposed to a broadening of his populist base. This is a sign of increasing disenchantment and of growing political space for an oppositional challenger, if one should emerge.

The civil service and corruption were critical concerns for the president. There was a growing perception that the **civil service** itself was dividing between upper (secretaries-general, directors) and lower staff. The lower showed a greater propensity for adaptation to new bureaucratic models being introduced but were more outspoken on wage and benefit challenges. On 31 December, President Ravalomanana addressed growing disquiet by announcing a 10% wage increase across the board for civil servants, though it is far from certain that this is sufficient.

One of President Ravalomanana's hallmark policy agendas is **anti-corruption**. He has placed tremendous resources in the 'Bureau Indépendant Anti-Corruption' (BIANCO) and the 'Conseil Supérieur de l'Intégrité' (CSI), garnering support from leading donors. Yet even his foreign advisors have criticised these efforts as not significant enough or expeditious enough. In addition, in an evaluation released on 13 December, the Independent Evaluation Group (IEG) of the World Bank was critical of CSI and BIANCO even as the World Bank country mission continued to support them. It argued that there have been important strides but these are mostly institutional or related to petty crimes. More importantly, these independent organisations are attached to the presidency, thus placing the executive beyond their oversight. The IEG rates the progress in good governance – anti-corruption and public management – as 'moderately unsatisfactory'.

Foreign Affairs

President Marc Ravalomanana came to power with a tremendous reserve of goodwill from the international community. His capitalist worldview made him a **natural ally of the US** but he also embraced US President George Bush's 'war on terror'. On 16 September, the US joined the UN, EU and others by offering $ 1 m in extra-budgetary spending for the election. In July, the US demonstrated its continued dedication to Malagasy environmental initiatives by helping sponsor a biodiversity summit. Americans were active advisors to the president, from offering governance advice for new oil resources (June) to providing election campaign advice to the president.

On 6 April, **German President** Horst Köhler visited Madagascar. This was a first as German president but Köhler had visited earlier as head of the IMF. He commented that the country was heading unequivocally in the right direction and pledged to continue to grow trade ties. The visit by **French President** Jacques Chirac on 21 July 2005 had ramifications in 2006 as it mended fences between France and this ex-French colony. At the meeting, the two heads of state discussed trade cooperation, population growth, development and other common concerns. Chirac also apologised for the French suppression of the 1947 uprising that left as many as 100,000 Malagasy dead. Both trade and aid have blossomed in response and, on 16 May, Chirac encouraged Russian President Vladimir Putin to invite NEPAD members (including Madagascar) to the **G8 meeting** in St. Petersburg (15–17 July). While this did not happen, other state visits to diverse countries in Europe and Asia, and his attendance at the non-aligned summit in Cuba on 13 September, showed that President Ravalomanana took seriously his voiced commitment to opening trade partnerships outside ideological positions or strategic alignments.

On 16 March, Kofi Annan made a visit to Madagascar, a first for a **UN secretary-general**. Annan pledged to forge closer ties between the UN and Madagascar. Other international organisations have shown similar support for Ravalomanana. Despite its slow acceptance of Ravalomanana as president in 2002, the AU ultimately embraced him, sending election observers at his request. Given his market-oriented proclivities, the **SADC** is a more obvious partner for Ravalomanana. It also sent an observer mission for the elections. In a speech on 6 January, Ravalomanana declared that "[w]e will continue to improve the business sector or the three Ps [partnership between private and public sectors]", offering a particular pledge to SADC markets to which he had opened the country in 2004.

Socioeconomic Developments

Poverty in Madagascar is both broad and deep. According to a 2005 household demographic study released by the Madagascar statistical office in April, 78.3% of subsistence farmers live in poverty, with an intensity rating of 31.4%. In all, some 68.7% of Malagasy live in poverty, 52% of the urban population and 73.5% of the rural population.

The year 2006 marked an important shift in Madagascar's socioeconomic policy process. President Ravalomanana came to politics from the business sector, where he had founded Tiko, the country's leading milk products company. Over the years, he built an empire with a multitude of sub-corporations and affiliates touching on a vast number of economic sectors. In March, President Ravalomanana rolled out his **MAP**. This far-reaching initiative came during significant programmatic redressment by donors, in particular the writing of the country assistance strategy by the World Bank. In the aggregate, these efforts have been complementary, but there has nonetheless been friction between domestic and international efforts to address development concerns. These, combined with the sharp turn towards the mineral and oil economy, are the hallmarks of the socioeconomic changes.

MAP was designed to address the MDGs while taking into account the priorities seen by the Ravalomanana government, particularly in areas of governance and market reform. There are **eight areas of commitment**: responsible governance; connected infrastructure; educational transformation; rural development and green revolution; health, family planning and the fight against HIV/AIDS; high growth economy; cherish the environment; and national solidarity. The intent is, according to the speech given by the president at MAP's release, to "create strategies and actions that will ignite rapid growth, lead to the reduction of poverty, and ensure that the country develops in response to the challenges of globalization and in accordance with the national vision." It set specific commitments for the 2007–12 period that follow the MDG. Each of the commitments addressed specific challenges. Each challenge addressed a goal and each goal is measured by an indicator. So, for instance, the challenge of reducing corruption is met by the goal that "corruption will be substantially reduced through a change in values, mindsets and the enforcement of the Code of Conduct. We will increase the confidence of people and companies to be rightly and fairly treated by courts, public administration (customs, tax, land tenure) and by security forces." The indicators will be those employed by the international NGO Transparency International.

The creation of indicators for the goal of each challenge of every commitment made for an ambitious undertaking. More ambitious still is the fact that these commitments are linked. For instance, the challenges articulated in connecting infrastructure require a ministry of public works, transport and meteorology that is responsibly governed. Because of its complexity, President Ravalomanana has set out his **Big Goals** to guide the process and the Immediate Priorities already under way. The Big Goals include raising Madagascar's UN HDI ranking from 146 out of 177 to 100; decrease the poverty rate from 85.1% to 50%; reduce the fertility rate from 5.4% to 3%– 4%; increase life expectancy from 55.5 to 58 to 61; increase literacy from 63% to 80%, increase the number of students completing primary school to 56% from 19% and secondary school to 40% from 7%; increase the GDP growth rate from 4.6% to 8%–9%; increase the GDP from $ 5 bn to $ 12 bn; increase the GDP per capita from $ 309 to $ 476; increase private investment from $ 600 m to $ 1.7 bn; improve the World Bank Business Climate Ranking from 131 to 80 and the Corruption Perceptions Index of Transparency International from 2.8 to 5.2; and, increase the households having land title from 10% to 75%. The Immediate Priorities, already under way, are public finance reform; increasing international private investment through the new economic development board; provide the seeds, fertilisers and other inputs for a green revolution; crack down on rural security problems; introduce contraception and other health programmes; and transform the judiciary.

Financing for the enormous MAP effort is dependent on two funding streams: private sector investment and **donor assistance**. The former is another co-dependent part of the plan. Donors have flocked to fund Marc Ravalomanana. The combined donor portfolio grew to over $ 2.2 bn with the World Bank leading the way with a new $ 947 m commitment. The first part of the new commitment came on 13 July with $ 10 m to stabilise the ailing parastatal JIRAMA (Electricity and Water of Madagascar). The largest commitment by the World Bank, EU and ADF, separately and together, is in the transportation sector. Yet the World Bank has also continued to renew its $ 40 m environment programme, its $ 30 m governance project and a number of others. It also introduced on 14 November a $ 30 m irrigation and watershed management project and on 3 August a new $ 18 m community development fund (its fourth). This year also saw the coming together of the $ 129 m integrated growth poles project, introduced on 12 July 2005, which seeks to "help provide the adequate business environment to stimulate and lead economic growth in three selected regional poles." Other aspects of the World Bank's new country assistance strategy, to be released in 2007, will be growing rural sector funding, governance and other areas. Despite the complementary visions of MAP and the World Bank's country assistance strategy, the introduction of MAP elicited strong criticism on 13 March from then country director James Bond, but this was short- lived and MAP was ultimately released by the IMF as a PRSP.

Much of the rallying to find a new path came amid new optimism for the **mining and oil sectors**. Component D of the World Bank's integrated growth poles project is for mining- and tourism-led growth in Toalognaro. By far the greatest part of the $ 166 m project will go to infrastructure that services the growing mining sector (particularly ilmenite and gemstones) in the region. The Bank's portion is less than one-third of the total cost, as mining interests, particularly a subsidiary of Rio Tinto, are shouldering the rest as part of a $ 650 m commitment. In 2006, the project began billing itself as a model for dynamic mineral resource management that can serve international, national and local interests by strengthening sector governance and enabling economic growth through holistic land-use planning. Mining accounted for 4% of GDP but estimates are that by 2011 it will reach 12%. The potential is high but regular community meetings brought out local concerns that, outside low-wage labour, foreign workers and contracting with foreign companies has to date undermined local gains.

This year may be come known as the year Madagascar's **oil boom** began in earnest as the country made ExxonMobil's hot list and a Wood Mackenzie report heralded in September that 35% of 75 test wells drilled yielded oil or natural gas. Norsk Hydro, Chevron-Texaco, ExxonMobil, Total, Royal Dutch Shell and (British) Madagascar Oil have been among those companies that won rights. Projections are that by 2009 Madagascar will be producing 60,000 barrels of oil per day (adding approximately 9% to the GDP). Yet despite the opportunity, there were warnings from such organisations as Global Watch that resources can produce the curse of political instability and that there is no automatic mechanism for oil revenues to alleviate poverty. The World Bank began working on a set of rules to ensure the good fortunes are well distributed, but this has not quieted critics.

The mining and oil opportunities came at a propitious time. There is a persistent current account deficit, which the IMF estimated leapt from -1.3% of GDP in 2001 to -10.5% in 2006. **Inflation** remained a stubborn 11.2%. This disproportionately reflects sector-specific prices, in particular, ironically, oil. The marginal shift in these figures from 2005 implies that Madagascar has not learned to live within its means.

It is still unclear if **Madagascar's liberalisation** is creating sustainable economic growth, if MAP will bring real development across and between sectors and if the mining and oil sectors will benefit the population as a whole. At 4.7%, the real GDP growth rate in Madagascar fell far short of the IMF's 7% projection. Madagascar moved from 146th to 143rd (of 177) on the UNDP's HDI. The UNDP gave Madagascar a 26 on its GDP-HDI score, as opposed to a 24 in 2005, indicating an improvement in human development in comparison to overall GDP. Yet, the GINI index was persistently 47.5, indicating a worse problem in income distribution than oft-cited cases such as China or Nigeria. All of this is a sign of mixed results, requiring patience before determining an outcome.

Richard R. Marcus

Malawi

The power struggle between President Bingu wa Mutharika and his predecessor, Bakili Muluzi, continued to dominate the political scene. The political feuding was exacerbated by the government's anti-corruption campaign, which was directed mainly against Muluzi, the vice-president and other opposition supporters. The opposition was seeking to undermine Mutharika, initially through impeachment procedures and, latterly, by trying to enforce a constitutional clause that bars floor crossing, which would reduce the president's support in parliament. The political impasse affected government business throughout the year. Political turmoil took up a considerable amount of Mutharika's attention and distracted him from dealing with governmental matters.

Domestic Politics

The feud between President Mutharika and Muluzi was responsible for much of the domestic political turmoil throughout the year. Muluzi and his United Democratic Front (UDF) attempted to remove the president from power, initially by trying to impeach him. However, in mid-January, Maxwell Milanzi, the MP whose motion had commenced **impeachment proceedings** in parliament the previous October, withdrew the indictment on the grounds that "it has become very unpopular amongst the majority of Malawians and the donor community." He was quickly condemned by his party for the withdrawal and subsequently resigned from the UDF to become an independent MP. It was alleged that Milanzi had acted to avoid corruption allegations being made against him by the government. The UDF made it clear that the impeachment motion could be re-introduced, but it was apparent that for the immediate future the threat of impeachment had ended.

Malawi's opposition accused Mutharika of initiating **selective corruption investigations** to 'persecute' his opponents. It claimed that corruption probes targeted especially senior UDF politicians, particularly ex-President Muluzi, the current Vice-President Cassim Chilumpha and certain MPs, such as Maxwell Milanzi, who had supported the impeachment motion. Dr. Chilumpha was Mutharika's running mate in the 2004 presidential election. He was, however, a close ally of Muluzi and his relations with Mutharika became increasingly strained, particularly as he refused to quit the UDF and join the president's Democratic Progressive Party (DPP). Chilumpha was the only cabinet minister who remained a member of the UDF. On 8 February, the president announced the **dismissal of the vice-president** for alleged insubordination, running a 'parallel' government and failure to perform his duties. Chilumpha claimed that for over a year the president had "humiliated me and victimised me" to force him out. On 1 March, the constitutional court ruled that Chilumpha be reinstated, since the president did not possess the powers to dismiss Chilumpha: only parliament could do this, and only following impeachment. However, on 28 April Chilumpha and two businessmen were arrested and charged with treason and conspiracy to commit murder. They were accused of plotting to have the president assassinated and for Chilumpha to assume power as the next in line. Ten opposition leaders and businessmen were detained in May in connection with the **alleged plot**. They were subsequently released for lack of evidence. Chilumpha was put under house arrest pending the outcome of his request to the constitutional court to declare that the charges be dropped on the grounds that he was constitutionally immune from prosecution while holding the office of vice-president. However, on 7 November, the constitutional court ruled that Chilumpha had no immunity from prosecution and that the alleged subversion case against him should proceed. On 20 November, the courts ordered that Chilumpha be released from house arrest, as he could not be detained indefinitely. By year's end, Chilumpha was still awaiting trial for treason and conspiracy to murder.

On 3 February, a former education minister, Yusuf Mwawa, was convicted on **charges of fraud**, abusing public funds and corruption. On 14 February, he was sentenced to five years in jail, although on 21 September the high court granted him bail on medical grounds. Mwawa was a minister in Mutharika's cabinet when he used public funds to cover part of his wedding expenses, but he had also been a government minister in a previous Muluzi administration. It was alleged that he was targeted, as with others, because of his continuing close connections to the former president. Certainly the sum involved – he was convicted for corruptly and fraudulently using Malawi K (kwacha) 170,000 (about $ 1,500) from the ministry of education – was small.

The Anti-Corruption Bureau (ACB) had begun to investigate former President Muluzi for corruption in 2005. On 27 July, Muluzi was arrested on **corruption charges**. He was called in to answer 42 counts of theft, corruption and breach of trust after millions of dollars of donor funds were allegedly diverted to his personal account during his term of office. He was released the same day on unconditional bail. The following day all the charges were dropped. Just hours after arresting Muluzi, the director of the ACB, Gustav Kaliwo, was suspended from office on the orders of President Mutharika, "for not following the right procedures". Two weeks later, Kaliwo formally resigned his position. Kaliwo's suspension prompted the director of public prosecutions, Ishmael Wadi, to drop unconditionally all the counts of corruption against Muluzi. Wadi reasoned that as a result of the suspension of Kaliwo, the ACB had no one to investigate the case. In early August, the President fired Wadi for withdrawing the corruption charges. Mutharika said Wadi's decision to drop the charges against Muluzi "has done the country more harm than he realises." It "has destroyed my credibility as president against corruption," he said.

President Mutharika has dismissed a number of government ministers and senior officials in his time in office. More than 35 top public servants have been fired. These have included an inspector-general of police, the National Intelligence Bureau director, two directors of public prosecutions, a reserve bank governor and a director of ACB. On 17 May, Mutharika dismissed Ralph Kasambara as attorney-general. Media reports claimed that Kasambara had been implicated in a number of scandals. On 26 October, the president dismissed Minister of Economic Planning and Development David Faiti, allegedly for working with a former Mutharika ally and cabinet minister, Gwanda Chakuamba, who had fallen out with Mutharika and become an opposition leader.

President Mutharika's DPP did not have majority support in parliament. It actually had only the six seats it had won in the December 2005 by-elections. However, a number of Malawi Congress Party (MCP) and UDF MPs crossed over to the DPP, which claimed mid-year that it had 70 MPs in the 193-aseat National Assembly. The **collapse of the impeachment bid** against Mutharika set off a flurry of resignations by opposition parliamentarians to distance themselves from the parties that had sponsored the motion to remove the president. Other MPs who were disgruntled with their parties also joined the DPP.

Top opposition party officials also **defected to the DPP**. The MCP had suffered a severe blow the previous year when its secretary-general, Kate Kainja Kaluluma, moved to the DPP and was appointed education minister by the president. On 1 June, Mutharika appointed three opposition MPs to his new cabinet. One was Bob Khamisa, the treasurer-general of the UDF, who became minister of home affairs and internal security. Two MCP MPs, Bintony Kutsaira and Ted Kalebe, accepted posts as deputy ministers. The president declared he had included members from the other parties in his desire to form a government of national unity.

Yet despite the desertions to the DPP, almost one-third of MPs remained loyal to the MCP, which made it the party holding the largest number of seats in parliament. The MCP's

John Tembo was the official leader of the opposition. Mutharika sought in vain to woo the MCP to strengthen his parliamentary standing. Tembo accused the president of bribery and corruptly enticing MPs to support government business in the National Assembly. The DPP did have working relations with a few small parties and a number of independents. However, in July a few MPs announced their **resignation from the DPP** partly because of Mutharika's alleged authoritarian tendencies, but more likely because they had been overlooked for ministerial positions. Political bickering stalled several government bills, and approval of the national budget was delayed by the political crisis surrounding the arrest of the vice-president.

The opposition set moves afoot to bring section 65 of the constitution to bear on the speaker of the National Assembly to declare vacant the seats of all MPs who had moved to the DPP. Section 65 bars sitting legislators from crossing the floor to another political party. At a **constitutional review conference** in April, President Mutharika proposed that the section be removed from the constitution. He argued that it ran counter to the constitutional provisions of freedom of association.

The constitutional amendment process also centred on limiting the age of a presidential candidate to a maximum of 70 years. This would effectively bar political leaders such as Mutharika and Tembo. On 7 December, a **constitutional court ruling** confirmed the validity of the clause in the constitution that disallows MPs from crossing the floor in parliament. The speaker of the National Assembly, Louis Chimango, could therefore invoke section 65 and declare vacant the seats of MPs who had defected to the DPP. The ruling sent shock waves among pro-DPP parliamentarians and the government. Commentators linked the long delay in convening parliament to the fear in government ranks that the speaker might enforce the constitutional ruling when the National Assembly resumed. The DPP stood to have over 60 of its around 70 seats in parliament declared vacant as they were gained through floor-crossing.

The president's attempts to remove Dr. Chilumpha led to some **tension in the DPP** between senior members who harboured ambitions to take the vice-president's place and become Mutharika's running mate in the 2009 presidential elections. As well, there were government ministers who aspired to stand as presidential candidates for the DPP in 2009, especially if Mutharika was ruled out through the age limits. On 26 October, the president fired Uladi Mussa, the minister of agriculture, partly for professional incompetence but primarily for campaigning to be DPP's presidential nominee in 2009.

Lobbying to be the **UDF's presidential candidate** in 2009 also began in earnest. Within the UDF there was pressure on Muluzi to desist from running for the presidency. Privately, he was said to have indicated his willingness to retire from active politics. A group of former Southern African presidents also urged Muluzi to play a more international role in African conflict mediation rather than remain immersed in Malawian partisan politics. Although there were a few presidential aspirants for the UDF, it was evident that a suitable candidate other than Muluzi had yet to emerge. The MCP also saw calls from some of its members for the ageing John Tembo to step down well before 2009 so that his successor had time enough to strengthen the party in the next general election.

On 14 May, Mutharika honoured Dr H.K. Banda, Malawi's first president, with a $ 620,000 mausoleum. He described **Banda as a national hero**, despite his record of political repression and human rights abuses. Banda's MCP appreciated Mutharika's gesture, and observers noted that some MPs could move to the DPP as a result. On the other hand, some concerns were raised that Mutharika might be emulating the authoritarian tendencies in Banda's leadership style. His detractors accused him of leadership by dictates. His decision-making was less than transparent, and he was alleged to be flouting rules and procedures in appointing and dismissing ministers and senior officials.

The Malawi constitution specifies that local government elections be held one year after national elections. **Local elections** should therefore have taken place in May 2005. However, the polls were postponed because the government decided that scarce resources were needed for emergency food aid. Donors accepted this with the caveat that local elections would be held as soon as practicable. As the food crisis passed, donor pressure increased on government to hold the elections. In June, the government announced its intention, allegedly for budgetary reasons, to amend the constitution to delay local elections to 2009 to coincide with the next presidential and parliamentary elections. The opposition condemned this postponement as another move by Mutharika to centralise power in the office of the presidency. The DPP may also have been unsure of its local-level support. As a newly established party it lacked the grassroots network of the main opposition parties. In September, however, the electoral commission gave notice that local government elections would be held in June 2007.

Foreign Affairs

Malawi is extremely dependent on external financial assistance. In the 2006–07 budget, **donor resources** were estimated to cover 55% of government expenditure. This gave donors considerable say as well as some influence in Malawi's affairs. The donors were firmly behind President Mutharika, whom they saw as committed to donor-sponsored economic reforms. The IMF lauded the government for maintaining budgetary discipline, especially observing expenditure targets at a time of severe food shortages. It commended the government's performance in implementing the PRGF. The government met the various targets and thereby became eligible for substantial debt relief from its external creditors. On 1 September, the IMF and the World Bank cancelled the bulk of Malawi's $ 2.9 bn worth of external debt, which at year's end was reduced to $ 590 m, and possibly even lower to $ 400 m. Malawi qualified for debt cancellation under the multilateral debt relief initiative, which had been introduced in 2005 by the G8 industrialised countries.

The donors also exerted much **pressure on the opposition parties** to abandon impeachment proceedings against President Mutharika. In January, the IMF even described the grounds for impeachment of the president as "weak". As well, donors urged the opposition to support the government in parliament, especially when key legislation or the national budget needed to be passed. Donors called on the country's political leaders to end their differences for the good of the nation and urged them to initiate political dialogue. A panel of six former presidents of SADC member countries also urged opposition leaders to drop impeachment proceedings.

In May, the country witnessed a four-day **state visit by Zimbabwe's President** Robert Mugabe. On 4 May, he opened a newly refurbished highway named after him. Local opposition and human rights groups protested the visit as well as the naming of the road because of his poor human rights record at home. Mutharika said the road honoured "a distinguished son of Africa". Western diplomats were also displeased with Mugabe's visit although they did attend the road opening ceremony. During a state banquet organised in honour of the Zimbabwean leader, Mutharika stressed the need for SADC countries to support one another closely.

President Mutharika also spoke ardently about the Shire-Zambezi waterway as an object of possible cooperation between **Mozambique and Malawi** to help address Malawi's serious problem of limited and expensive transportation links to external markets. However, neither donors nor the private sector nor the Mozambican government have shown much interest in this project. As well, the waterway would face competition from a project currently under way to rehabilitate the Sena railway line in Mozambique, which runs from near Malawi's southern border to the Indian Ocean port of Beira.

An incident that attracted much international media coverage occurred in October when American musical star **Madonna** arrived in Malawi to help raise the profile of children orphaned by HIV/AIDS. However, when she adopted a Malawian boy after being given permission to do so by the government, much controversy was sparked both within Malawi and the Western world on the pros and cons of adoption by white people of black children in a developing African country.

Socioeconomic Developments

Malawi's economic performance is heavily dependent on its **agricultural sector**. In 2005, a severe drought had hit agriculture very hard. Maize production declined, as did production of burley tobacco. Both of these are crops grown by smallholder farmers. In the estate sector, which produces mainly flue-cured tobacco, output also declined slightly. In 2006, the rains returned and there was a major recovery in the agricultural sector. **Maize** is the staple food of most people and the annual harvest exceeded the level of domestic consumption. Malawi recorded its biggest maize crop ever, some 2.6 m tonnes, which was half a million tonnes more than its annual requirement. The bumper harvest was only partly due to better rainfall, since heavy rains in February damaged crops in the southern region. The policy of subsidised seed and fertiliser may also have contributed to the buoyant maize crop, even though there were problems in its effective implementation. Better weather conditions and the improved availability of fertiliser also increased output of tobacco. Malawi's two other main crops, tea and sugar, saw increased production as well.

GDP growth recovered from 2.1% the previous year to an estimated 6.9%. Improved food supplies led to a drop in inflation from 15.4% to around 11%. Lower maize prices were the principal reason behind lower food price inflation while non-food inflation rose because of higher fuel prices. A recovery in tea and to some extent tobacco exports plus a reduction in maize imports led to a **surplus in the balance of trade**. Tobacco is Malawi's main export, earning just over half of export receipts. Export earnings were affected by the slump in the auction prices of tobacco early in the year, but they picked up from mid-June. Tea production increased significantly, as did tea auction prices. However, imports of food in the first three months of the year as well as high international oil prices meant that the fall in the **current account deficit** was only from 11.2% to 8.7% of GDP.

External financial assistance and a rise in domestic revenue led to an increase in total revenue. However, strong government spending pressures, for instance, to pay for maize imports and social expenditures, meant a continued albeit slightly lower **budget deficit** in the 2006–07 fiscal year, which was forecast at about 3.5% of GDP.

About 40% of the population – some 5 m people – were in need of **emergency food assistance** ahead of the maize harvest in March. Of these, 2.2 m were children. UNICEF reported in January that nearly half of all children under five years of age were stunted and one-fifth were underweight or malnourished. Malawi's children were also affected by the country's high prevalence of HIV/AIDS. Around 14% of the population aged between 15 and 49 were infected and the disease has orphaned some 550,000 children under 15.

The **AIDS pandemic** has cut life expectancy to 37 years. UNAIDS estimated that some 87,000 people lost their lives to AIDS-related illnesses during the year while about 187,000 people living with HIV/AIDS were in need of antiretrovirals (ARVs). However, only 46,000 were receiving free ARV drugs. The government intended increasing ARV therapy by about 40,000 patients a year for the next three years. However, concern was expressed that the scaling-up of ARVs would be constrained by the unavailability of adequately trained nurses, clinical officers and doctors. Many medical personnel leave Malawi each year. It was estimated that nearly two-thirds of nursing posts were unfilled, and the number of doctors practising was only one-sixth of those needed.

This **lack of medical professionals** was attributed to low salaries and poor working conditions, which have sent many nurses and doctors to the UK, Australia and South Africa. It was not surprising that these same factors were behind the proliferation of industrial strikes at various public and private sector organisations. Striking academics at the University of Malawi demanded a salary increase of over 500%, and similar demands were voiced elsewhere, such as at the Malawi national examination board.

A **human development report** released by the UNDP at the end of the year indicated that over 4 m Malawians, one-third of the population, did not have access to clean water.

In this situation, illnesses such as cholera and diarrhoea were rife. In fact, between July and October over 4,500 cases of cholera were confirmed. The majority of rural people rely for their washing and drinking water on natural water sources, such as streams contaminated by human and animal waste. This was of major concern for both the government and civil society organisations, particularly as safe drinking water is a key indicator for the achievement of the MDGs by 2011.

Roger Tangri & Lewis B. Dzimbiri

Mauritius

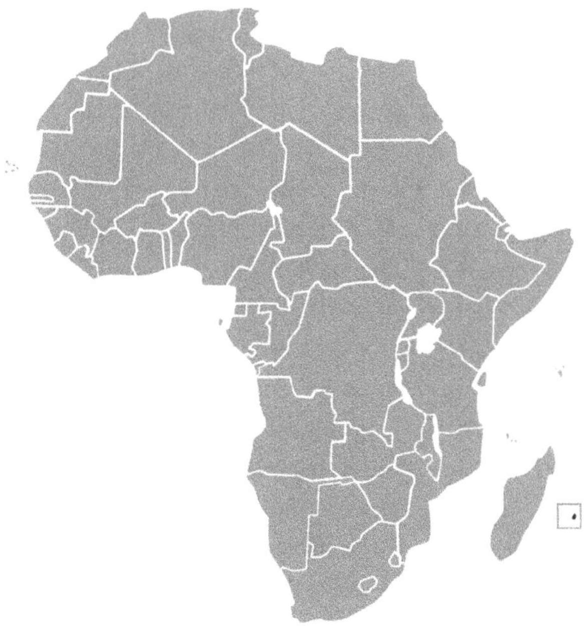

Mauritius enjoyed political stability as the new Labour/Alliance government stayed securely in office but had to address serious economic problems by adapting to a globalised world without preferential trade terms. A high fiscal deficit, a potentially unsustainable public debt and a permanent deterioration in the terms of trade were the challenges. A loss of trade preferences in textiles and sugar, which together make up 12% of GDP, 20% of employment and over 50% of exported goods (excluding free port), were the main issues. These challenges came on top of a secular economic slowdown, exacerbated by higher world oil prices: average real GDP growth has sunk to below 3.5% during the past five years. Instead of addressing the social concerns of the ordinary people, as Labour had proclaimed in the election campaign, government had to redress public deficits and growing threats from globalisation.

Domestic Politics

After the clear victory in the general elections last year, in which Paul Bérenger and Pravind Jugnauth were ousted as prime minister and deputy prime minister and minister of finance respectively, Mauritian society experienced a short **political 'honeymoon'**. Free bus transport for students and senior citizens, the most notable promises of Ramgoolam's election campaign, was introduced, a measure that, however, widened the deficit effect in the government budget. Yet, this honeymoon was rapidly over. The socio-political atmosphere deteriorated as a result of rising prices and drastic reforms in social services. Since the alliance headed by the Labour Party leader Dr. Navinchandra (Navin) Ramgoolam had campaigned in opposition for continuation of the established **social welfare model** during the parliamentary election campaign, but now in office was urging massive sacrifices, the people were disappointed. Accustomed to economic success and relative prosperity over about 15 years, they were not yet prepared to face the need for adjustment.

On the other side, there was a **split in the alliance** between the Mauritius Socialist Movement (MSM) and the Mauritius Militant Movement (MMM): Bérenger and MMM put the blame for the lost elections on Pravind Jugnauth, the president of MSM. Jugnauth, it was argued, had stayed in the political shadow of his father, the president of the republic, Sir Anerood Jugnauth, and seemed too detached from the majority of the Hindu electorate. Since Pravind Jugnauth had lost his parliamentary seat, there was a real problem within the leadership of the MSM. Consequently, the MMM openly asked Pravind Jugnauth to step down in favour of his uncle, Ashock Jugnauth who had served as health minister in previous governments. As a barrister and self-made man, he would be more attractive to the ordinary Hindu electorate. The MSM found these declarations provocative and in turn questioned the leadership of Bérenger, who as a figure of the white 'cultivated, intellectual minority' would have brought about the alienation from the Hindu majority. On 3 March, Ashock Jugnauth had a meeting with the president of the republic. After weeks of escalation in February and March in the discussions of domestic issues, **Bérenger retired** as the official leader of opposition, since the MMM was in a minority inside the opposition coalition (10 as against 12 seats). In April, the previous minister of labour and social affairs, Showkutally Soodhun (MSM) was being discussed as a replacement for Bérenger, but finally Bérenger was replaced on 4 July by Nandoo Botha, secretary general of MSM. Ashock Jugnauth himself left MSM and founded his own party (National Union), consisting of himself as MP and some members of the previous government, the most notable among them being the previous foreign and tourism minister, Anil Gayan.

Paul Bérenger continued to be an important actor in domestic politics, even after resigning as leader of the opposition. He was everywhere present, organised press conferences and his MMM party tried to attract a young next-generation leadership. Many observers felt that Bérenger had not yet retired from active political life and still harboured personal ambitions to become prime minister again, probably through a redesigned alliance with Ramgoolam. Due to the disappointment in the population, the political parties are seduced into thinking in terms of alternative alliances, and MMM was already talking about the need for convergence in programmes and action in order to win the 2010 elections.

The domestic conflicts abated for some days after the **death of Sir Satcall Boolell** at the age of 85 on 23 March. The funeral on 25 March of this historic political figure (heir of

Seewoosagur Ramgoolam as chairman of the Mauritius Labour Party) was a demonstration of national unity, since all the current leaders of the country from government and opposition hailed Satcall's work as prime minister from 1984 to 1991, when Navin Ramgoolam took office.

Again, **corruption** was on the national agenda. A previous minister of lands and housing Dulull (MMM), was questioned about having received Mauritius Rupees (MRs) 50 m as a bribe during the construction of the integrated resort scheme of the Bel Air Sugar Estate (BASE). This case again raised the question of the efficiency of the Independent Commission Against Corruption (ICAC), which celebrated its fourth anniversary in April. It had identified 600 cases of bribery, but the society was nevertheless left with the impression that it was a virtual institution without real impact. On 6 June, the director of investigations at ICAC, Roshi Baddhain, resigned. Officially this was the result of an offer of employment as a forensic expert with the International Criminal Court in The Hague, but the real cause (it was said) was frustration with anti-corruption work in Mauritius in general and particularly within the ICAC.

On 3 July, the question of **electoral reform** was raised in parliament again. In 2002, the Sachs commission had proposed a proportional vote component of 30 MPs, but this had never been adopted into parliamentary procedure. The deputy prime minister and minister of finance, once again urged the need to modernise the electoral system. He proposed a smaller number of parliamentarians to be elected under proportional representation (20 instead of 30), but even so the reform got stalled. The different political parties put forward various scenarios under which they would be penalised by the proposed reform and consequently rejected all changes.

During the preparation period for the budget in April and May, the Mauritian government and particularly Finance Minister Sithanen tried to prepare the society for harsh cuts in the **national budget** for 2006–07 to be presented in June. Thus, the Mauritian society was put on notice that there would be no repetition of the economic miracle of the 1980s and that the change of government did not change the need for economic and social reforms. Large sections of the society were accustomed to a certain level of welfare and well-being and previous governments had not really launched fundamental reforms.

Foreign Affairs

Foreign policy was marked by continuity. The Labour government retained the integration of foreign affairs, trade and cooperation into one **super ministry for global integration**, which was headed by Madan Murlidhar Dulloo. With respect to its global orientation, a certain diversification was discernable: even if Mauritius is still very dependent on exchanges with the EU – let alone its historical, linguistic and cultural affinity with Europe – it has discovered 'emerging economies' such as India and mainland China. With respect to globalisation, Mauritius increased its cooperation with the category of 'small and vulnerable island states'. This group wishes to retain special status and preferences in the international multilateral system.

A second move towards a more **polycentric orientation** in Mauritius's foreign policy was Ramgoolam's visit to the non-aligned conference in Havana, Cuba, where the prime minister negotiated a cooperation agreement with Venezuela's President Chávez and Cuba. Mauritius was elected as one of the **vice-presidents of the non-aligned movement**. This trip continued to the UN general assembly in New York and to the conference of the Francophonie in Bucharest.

Particularly intense relations developed with **India**. The government had intensified its exposure through a weeklong visit by Prime Minister Ramgoolam to India in October 2005. At the end of that year, Mauritius signed a preferential treaty and a double tax avoidance treaty with India. Now, in October 2006, the Economic Cooperation and Partnership Agreement (ECPA) focused on trade, exchange of services, an investment treaty and economic cooperation. India is particularly interesting for Mauritius as a market for rum and textiles. On the other hand, Mauritius is as an offshore banking centre for Indian companies and of interest not only for making financial arrangements for the domestic Indian market but particularly too for **emerging African investment markets**, in which Indian firms want a share. The ECPA is considered as a test case for bilateral treaties with other countries in the region or on the Indian Ocean rim.

Prime Minister Ramgoolam went on an official visit to **France** from 29–31 March. The main topic was French aid, which should compensate the loss of preferential sugar prices of the order of 36% on the EU market from 2009 onwards. Although Mauritius's relations with **Madagascar** are considered to be those of a good neighbour, the reality was more complex, since both countries live in a state of mutual ambivalence. In terms of area and population, Madagascar is a giant compared to Mauritius, and hence the Malagasy elite considers itself as dominant. Yet in economic terms, Madagascar is extremely poor and Mauritius a middle income country, providing the Mauritian elite with the advantage of self-esteem and superiority. Astonishingly, it took 18 months to nominate a new Mauritian ambassador to Madagascar. Finally, Ernest Gérard Lemaire, belonging to the 'minor' Republican Movement in the Labour-Alliance, was named to the post. The accreditation process in Madagascar itself took some months, too. Politically, relations between Madagascar and Mauritius were marked by **mischief in certain economic activities** (potato-growing and marketing project and the blockade of an oil tanker bound for Mauritius in the port of Tamatave). These events show the complex nature of relations despite the fine wording of the declarations. The Malagasy agriculture minister visited Mauritius with a large delegation to sort out misunderstandings between the different economic partners and entrepreneurs on both sides. The most critical issue was the intent of Malagasy opposition leader Pierrot Rajaonarivelo (in exile in Paris) in November to use Air Mauritius and Mauritius territory for his assault on Madagascar in preparation for his standing as a candidate in the presidential election on 3 December. After an abortive attempt to reach Madagascar from Réunion, Rajaonarivelo tried to get to Madagascar as a passenger on an Air Mauritius plane, which was prevented from landing by the Malagasy authorities. Rajaonarivelo subsequently filed a suit against Air Mauritius in Port Louis.

Socioeconomic Developments

Mauritius went through a difficult year of adaptation. According to the IMF assessment letter of 8 September in the context of the aid for trade initiative, Mauritius must overcome **two major economic challenges**: a high fiscal deficit and potentially unsustainable public debt; and a permanent deterioration in the terms of trade resulting from the loss of trade preferences in textiles and sugar. As noted above, these goods account for 12% of GDP, 20% of employment and over 50% of goods exports (excluding free port). These challenges came on top of a secular economic slowdown, exacerbated by higher world oil prices: average real GDP growth has slowed from over 7.5% in the second half of the 1980s to below 3.5%. The IMF noted further that the loss of trade preferences had seriously hurt the economy. Declines in export prices in combination with higher oil prices contributed to a 17% reduction in the terms of trade, equivalent to an estimated cumulative loss of income of over 4% of GDP.

Against these alarming signs and tendencies, the finance minister and deputy prime minister, Rama Sithanen, proposed a radical neo-liberal **national budget** for 2006–07, focusing on growth and liberalisation; investment facilitation; opening up the economy; labour market reform; radical reforms in social policies; controlling wastage and securing efficiency gains in the public sector; fiscal consolidation and discipline; tax reform; and broadening the circle of opportunities. The concrete proposals consisted of a sequence of measures to abolish the classic achievements of the Mauritian model: making hiring and firing procedures more flexible; linking salaries to productivity gains; unifying the corporate tax; reducing custom duties; exclusively restricting government borrowing to investments; simplifying procedures to start an economic activity; abolishing licences and the economic processing zones (except for integrated resorts and free port); and closing down of the public Development Works Corporation (DWC) and police garage.

This was a totally neo-liberal approach under a Labour prime minister. Consequently, **commentaries and reactions** by the public were as controversial as the proposals. The trade unions had particular difficulty in accommodating the reforms proposed by the government. Given their shared historical background, they had anticipated that the Labour government would be closer to trade union demands and had expected now to reap the benefits of the change in government in social terms: the essence of Labour's election campaign had been putting people and their social concerns first. Indeed, the Labour-led alliance had called itself the 'Social Alliance'. Yet it was exactly these expectations that were not fulfilled. The **dismantling of subsidies** on the most basic consumer products such as flour, bread, milk, cooking gas, construction material, etc. (as announced in the budget) induced inflationary pressures on these items. In his budget speech, too, Finance Minister Rama Sithanen had proposed **linking salaries to productivity** and abandoning previous wage-setting councils, such as the Pay Research Bureau and the National Remuneration Board, which negotiated public sector compensation. A new national wages council was tasked with aligning salaries with productivity gains and not exclusively with the price index and budgetary room for salary increases.

All this provoked strong **criticism by the trade unions**, but the social unrest did not feature on the daily political agenda, partly because of the highly fragmented structure of the trade unions. Of a total population of about 1.2 m, roughly 525,000 are part of the gainfully employed labour force, of which 105,000 workers are effectively organised in trade unions. Some 350 individual trade unions, more than half of which have fewer than 50 members, have merged into 12 federations. Moreover, given the membership structure and the economic changes, trade unionism is losing affiliates, and the new booming sectors such as the free port, offshore banking and information technology are barely unionised, if at all. Only after the closure of the state-owned DWC did massive unrest surface in November, when the workers staged a hunger strike against the decision to close, which had been announced in the budget speech.

In previous years, the outgoing MSM/MMM government had failed to table the **labour market** reforms in the shape of an Industrial Relations Act in parliament because of electoral considerations. This had been interpreted as a victory, but might, however, turn out to be a Pyrrhic victory due to the fact that the labour-intensive sectors such as sugar cane and textiles will shrink even more drastically and rapidly in the future, further reducing the room to manoeuvre. Since the existing labour laws are incompatible with ILO convention 87 ('Freedom of Association and Protection of the Right to Organise', signed in 1948), reform will be inevitable. The Labour government established a new tripartite commission in order to find consensus on the labour law reforms, but the proposed reform elements found only critics in the society.

Klaus-Peter Treydte

Mozambique

Mozambique remains the donor darling, with aid rising. The economy continues to grow at more than 7% a year, but concern increases about the lack of rural development and Mozambique's inability to reach the MDGs. It was a politically quiet year with few changes.

Domestic Politics

Frelimo's 9th congress in Quelimane (11–15 November) produced few dramatic changes. Frelimo is no longer the party of workers and peasants: more than half the congress delegates worked for the party or the state. Of 1,326 delegates, only 90 were subsistence peasants and just 9 were industrial workers. Only 20 said they were members of the trade union federation OTM ('Organização dos Trabalhadores de Moçambique'), while 48 were business people. In contrast, 470 delegates worked in the state apparatus (183 teachers and 27 nurses) and 276 were in the Frelimo party apparatus. President Armando Guebuza consolidated his leadership but ex-President Joaquim Chissano remained a major force in the party and was elected honorary president. Some old-timers have been pensioned off and replaced by younger, better educated people, but the liberation movement generation remained a powerful force. The total openness and smooth running of the congress suggested that the sharp tensions between the various groups inside the party were successfully managed. Prime Minister Luísa Diogo proved to be the brightest rising star. In elections for the central committee, she came second with 1,105 votes, 33 votes behind Alberto Chipande (1138 votes), who fired the first shots of the liberation war in 1964, and ahead of Graça Machel (1,084 votes). Diogo must now be seen as a serious presidential candidate in 2014 (when Guebuza cannot stand again): at the time of the central committee elections she was 48 years old, compared to 61 for Graça Machel.

The **Political Commission** met almost weekly and set government policy. Next to Guebuza, Chissano and Chipande it includes five ministers – Diogo, Aiuba Cuereneia (development and planning), Aires Aly (education), Alcinda Abreu (foreign) and José Pacheco (interior) – as well as Maputo Mayor Eneas Comiche and the speaker of parliament, Eduardo Mulémbwè. Former Nampula provincial Governor Filipe Paunde was elected unopposed as secretary-general and is also a member of the Political Commission.

In April, the eldest son of former President Joaquim Chissano was formally charged with ordering the **murder of Carlos Cardoso**, Mozambique's best investigative journalist, in 2000. Nyimpine Chissano has also been charged with various economic offences. Initially, Albano Silva, the lawyer husband of Prime Minister Luísa Diogo, was the surprise choice as defence lawyer, but he had to step down as he had been a witness in a related case.

Three **elections** are due in the coming three years: 2007 for new provincial parliaments, 2008 for municipal assemblies and 2009 national elections for president and parliament. An ad hoc parliamentary commission began work on new election laws in March 2005 but ad hoc commissions require unanimity, so it was hamstrung by demands from the opposition party Renamo that it must be able to veto any decision by an election commission, and that the ad hoc commission could not consider any other issue unless this was granted. On 15 June, parliament remitted the laws to a standing commission, with normal voting. The new laws were approved in parliament on 20 December. Despite substantial concessions to Renamo, the opposition staged a noisy protest and stormed the speaker's table in an attempt to prevent a vote.

The **new election laws** largely maintained the present electoral system, with some important changes. The national elections commission, CNE ('Comissão Nacional de Eleições'), was reduced from 19 to 13 members – three Frelimo, two Renamo and eight nominated by civil society and chosen by parliament, so Frelimo is guaranteed a majority. Elections will be on one day rather than two. Mozambique has proven unable to update its electoral roll, so there will be a new registration every five years, for each electoral cycle. Presidential candidates will be required to submit a nomination petition of 10,000 names (as at present) and a $ 4,000 deposit. The 5% threshold for parliamentary elections is removed, which may permit small parties to gain seats. In national elections, only registered parties can stand, but in parliamentary and local elections independent citizens' lists will be allowed. The new election law did not, however, end the secrecy of the national count, which had been heavily criticised by international and national observers as well as Mozambique's own constitutional council. In past elections, the CNE made significant changes to the results without any public explanation.

In a radical shift, the administration of the **civil service** was split. A national public service authority, ANFP ('Autoridade Nacional da Função Pública'), sworn in on 11 July was made responsible for both national and provincial civil servants. The ministry of state administration, which previously had been responsible for all government employees, will only be responsible for districts and lower levels. The ANFP is headed by Victória Dias Diogo, former permanent secretary of tourism and sister of the prime minister, Luísa Diogo.

President Armando Guebuza continued to tour the country regularly, giving speeches in which he stated that it was possible to overcome poverty and underdevelopment. He put great stress on decentralisation. Each district was given a special budget of $ 280,000 per year to be spent on locally determined economic development projects. Consultative councils are being established at district and community level, while the national government is attempting to increase the number of skilled people in district governments. In his speeches, he emphasised the need for a change in attitude – for local people to believe that it is possible to overcome poverty and to take the initiative and not wait for central government.

Foreign Affairs

Mozambique remains a **donor darling**: aid continued to rise, from $ 1,246 m in 2004 to $ 1,285 m in 2005 (announced by DAC in January 2007). Aid is one-fifth of GDP and half of the government budget. Mozambique receives 50% more aid per capita than its neighbours Tanzania and Malawi. "Mozambique is a success story in Sub-Saharan Africa" wrote the IMF in a report on 1 December.

With an estimated 60 bilateral and multilateral donors and 150 international non-government organiations, the **bureaucracy** became increasingly complex. In a report for the British department for international development, the Mozambican academic Elisio Macamo wrote in June that the "regular review exercises, working groups, and high and middle level meetings between Government . . . officials and donors . . . may be necessary to reassure donors [but] consultation mechanisms appear to have become an end in itself." Government lacks people and time to fully participate, while "donors themselves have not always been able to prepare themselves adequately for these various meetings."

More than one-quarter of aid goes directly into the government budget, but this has increased rather than decreased the administrative burden. The 18 **budget support donors** have created an extremely cumbersome procedure for working with the government. To agree on goals for the coming year and assess performance in the past year, 24 working groups involved hundreds of donor and government staff during two months. Some very senior government officials did little other work in that period. At a press conference on 13 April, the minister for planning and development complained about the number of sleepless nights for his staff in the weeks before the meeting, while the Swedish ambassador, whose embassy led the donor side, admitted she was shocked by the amount of work involved. There was a time-consuming mid-term evaluation in October, which occupied people for a month.

The Confederation of Mozambican Business Associations (CTA) is totally dependent on USAID, which pays 93% of its expenses, the CTA revealed on 21 July.

Ireland is one of the budget support donors and President Mary McAleese visited on 14 June. **British** Chancellor of the Exchequer Gordon Brown visited on 10 April and promised extra aid for education. Guebuza visited London on 4–5 December. Economist and US special advisor Jeffrey Sachs visited in June: Mozambique is to have 11 of Sachs's special **millennium villages**. These are to be model villages on which $ 110 per person per year is spent.

Mozambique is taking control of the **Cahora Bassa dam**, following an agreement signed by President Armando Guebuza and Portuguese Prime Minister Jose Socrates in Maputo on 31 October, just a year after the deal was agreed in principle. Mozambique will buy two-thirds of the dam for $ 950 m, raising its share of 'Hidroeléctrica de Cahora Bassa' (HCB) from 18% to 85%. Mozambique is paying $ 700 m and refuses to say how it has raised the money. The other $ 250 m comes from profits of HCB itself. The delay in signing the Cahora Bassa deal occurred because Eurostat, the EU's independent statistical agency, initially refused to accept it. Portugal was under heavy EU pressure because of its large budget deficit, and it hoped the $ 950 m would partly plug the hole. But Portugal had claimed that HCB owed the Portuguese treasury over $ 2 bn, so Eurostat wanted Portugal to treat the deal as a $ 1 bn loss, which would worsen rather than help the Portuguese budget deficit.

Mozambique refused to take the dam at independence in 1975 because Portugal had agreed to sell electricity to apartheid South Africa at a loss in exchange for support for its colonial wars, which meant the dam would have been a drain on the Mozambican economy. Cahora Bassa is the highest dam in Africa and second largest in Africa by volume of water held (after Lower Usuma in Nigeria) and by hydroelectricity production (after Aswan in Egypt). Cahora Bassa can generate 2,075 megawatts and is running at 95% of capacity, selling 1,100 megawatts to South Africa, 450 megawatts to Zimbabwe and the rest to Mozambique. Ownership is particularly important because Mozambique wants to build **a second dam** at Mpanda Ncua, 70 km downstream: it would use the same water and thus the two dams would need to be managed together. Mpanda Nuca would generate 1,200 megawatts and cost $ 2.3 bn: funding was offered by China's Export Import Bank on 20 April. This is further linked to a proposal for an 1,800 megawatt coal-fired power station associated with the nearby Moatize coal mine, which has been privatised to a Brazilian firm 'Companhia do Vale do Rio Doce'.

President Guebuza has strongly defended African links with **China**, for example in a speech at Davos on 26 January. China is heavily involved in central Mozambique, where it is negotiating agriculture projects in the Zambesi valley. It will also build a new national stadium in Maputo, it announced on 18 November. A Chinese company is carrying out the project to expand the Maputo city water system. Guebuza went to China and met Chinese President Hu Jintao on 4 November. But there was controversy in December when a study revealed extensive illegal exports of timber to China.

Privatisation of the northern railway system and Maputo port has proved problematic, and on 23 March the chairman of the national ports and railways company said the new operators were not living up to their contracts. In particular, they were failing to make the promised investment. The northern railway was privatised to a US company because of continued US military interest in the deepwater port of Nacala. Rebuilding of the central railway system by an Indian leaseholder, with World Bank money, progressed rapidly, but the crisis in Zimbabwe cut traffic along one branch of the railway and through the port of Beira.

In July, Mozambique set up its national commission to participate in the **APRM**. Prime Minister Luísa Diogo was co-chair of the UN secretary-general's high-level panel on **UN system-wide coherence** in areas of development, humanitarian assistance and environment, which reported on 9 November. President Guebuza addressed the UN General Assembly on 21 September. The first meeting of the former heads of state club, the **Africa Forum**, was held in Maputo on 11 January. Former President Joaquim Chissano organised the meeting of 16 former heads of state.

Socioeconomic Developments

Inflation for 2006 was just under 10%, above the target of 7.5%, and economic growth was 7.8%. **Aid** and loans account for half the state budget. Military spending is only 2% of the government budget while education is 22% and health 12%: 526 new schools were built in 2006.

HIV/AIDS is a serious problem and by the end of the year 38,000 patients were receiving antiretroviral (ARV) drugs, out of 250,000 who needed them. In early 2006, donors criticised the government for not doing enough about AIDS, and the number of centres providing ARVs increased from 46 in June to 150 by the end of the year. The target for 2007 is 96,000 people on ARVs. It is estimated that more than 16% of Mozambicans between 15 and 49 years of age are infected and that 97,000 have already died. Life expectancy has fallen to 38 years, compared to an expected 46 without AIDS. About 1.5 m are infected – 800,000 women, 570,000 men and 80,000 children. In a speech on 15 March, Health Minister Dr. Ivo Garrido said that 15% of health workers and 9,000 teachers would die of AIDS by 2010. At least 380,000 children have lost one or both parents to AIDS. Linked to this is a growing tuberculosis epidemic. **Malaria** remains the second main cause of death, and is on the increase: 4,985 died of malaria compared to 4,209 the previous year.

Mozambique's new **poverty reduction strategy paper** (PARPA II, 'Plano de Acção para a Redução da Pobreza Absoluta, 2006–09', Action Plan to Reduce Absolute Poverty, 2006–09) was approved by the council of ministers on 2 May. It was negotiated with donors but was not presented to parliament. It puts more stress on the economy than the previous one and directs attention away from the social sectors, but it still largely follows the neo-liberal Washington Consensus line that it is for the private sector to develop the country and end poverty. It says "the function of the private sector is to grow the economy" and create jobs. "The success of the private sector depends on the functioning of the market economy, which, in large measure, depends on the force and quality of the private sector itself." The role of government is largely seen as creating a good business environment, improving 'human capital' through health and education, and building infrastructure such as roads and electricity.

UNDP released its Mozambique national human development report for 2005 on 6 September, which showed that of 12 measurable **MDGs**, Mozambique was unlikely to reach four: share of the poorest fifth in national consumption, child malnutrition, under-five mortality and children in upper primary education (6th and 7th grade). The report showed that despite continuing official GDP growth of more than 7% a year for nearly a decade, there has been a dramatic fall in real GDP per capita from $ 210 in 1998 to $ 131 in 2002, and that this had risen to only $ 149 in 2004 – the last year for which data were available. The report found that although the human development index was rising steadily, the percentage of underweight children and low birth-weight babies was improving only very slowly.

Donors are increasingly concerned about **corruption**. The April evaluation found that government had met 23 of 26 economic and development targets, but only 5 of 13 governance targets. In another British department for international development report, Tony Vaux in April warned that despite Mozambique's positive progress and willingness to engage with the agenda of donors, the trend was towards centralization and consolidation of power within a narrow elite, which will be obliged to offer patronage to a wide and 'greedy' circle of clients. The tendency towards corruption will undermine development and democratic processes, potentially creating a vicious spiral.

USAID issued a report in May that claimed "political considerations dominate the highest level of the **court system**", while justice officials "sell verdicts and lose evidence and case files in exchange for bribes." There is "active involvement of individuals within government or the ruling party in criminal activity, including drug trafficking, money laundering and theft of public funds." The report personally attacked supreme court President Mario Mangaze, who is given "a significant portion of the blame for slow reform" of the justice system. "He is a Frelimo stalwart who is widely considered to be a key interlocutor for political leaders when important interests are at stake in court cases."

Attorney-General Joaquim Madeira on 11 April told parliament that "chronic situations of manifest corruption" in the criminal investigation police, PIC ('Polícia de Investigação Criminal'), even involving high-ranking officers, "leave us in despair and suffocate the work of the honest." He said that some officers had blocked the investigation of the assassination of journalist Carlos Cardoso in 2000 and had been taken off the case, but were subsequently promoted. In his speech, he called for PIC to be transferred from the notoriously corrupt interior ministry to become part of a public prosecutors' office, but later in the year this was blocked politically.

Donors had forced the government to carry out a forensic audit of the plundered and collapsed **Austral** bank, and the audit was delivered early in the year. Although it was believed to highlight high-level corruption and might point to the killer in 2000 of the acting head of the bank, António Siba-Siba Macuacaua, no action had been taken on the report. After ten years during which it was managed by the British company, the Crown Agents, Mozambique took back control of its customs service on 5 July.

The **administrative tribunal**, TA ('Tribunal Administrativo', a kind of auditor-general), reported at the end of the year on the government's 2005 accounts. The report exposed some corruption and a lot of incompetence. It also highlighted loans to the elite, which are not being repaid. A highly controversial issue has been more than $ 40 m in loans made to companies by the state treasury in 1999 to 2002: many of these had been **political loans**, or at least reflected a conflict of interest. For example, a company partly owned by Albano Silva received a loan when his wife, Luisa Diogo, was finance minister. The TA reported that of 42 companies that received loans from the treasury, only 13 had made any repayments by the end of 2005. Silva's company is repaying its loan. A company partly owned by President Armando Guebuza has repaid only 1% of its loan, but companies linked to other members of the Frelimo elite are not repaying. Meanwhile, when Banco Austral collapsed and was renationalised and then re-privatised in 2002 (to ABSA in South Africa, itself taken over by Barclays), 70 loans for $ 17 m were left for the state to collect. These are believed to be the politically sensitive loans. By the end of 2005, only 15% had been collected. Of the 70 bad loans, attempts were being made to collect 44, while 26 "are still being analysed". The TA report also analysed income and expenditure and made some interesting points, for example, that twice as much is spent on each school pupil in Maputo city as in Zambezia. In health, the spending in Maputo city per person is three times the spending in Nampula province.

Labour Minister Helena Taipo took a hard line on employers not meeting proper **labour standards**, including those in cashew factories in the north of the country. But the most public conflict was with the British firm Group 4 Securicor and its subsidiary Wackenhut. An arbitration panel ruled in 2005 that Wackenhut had improperly failed to pay overtime since 1994 to 600 workers, and that it owed present and former workers $ 1.36 m. Wackenhut refused to pay, and on 28 August Taipo issued a formal order insisting on payment. Then the company lost the contract to guard the US embassy and in November dismissed 250 staff without compensation. The labour ministry ruled that the company owed the staff a total of $ 300,000 in redundancy pay. Local managing director Jon Mortimer held a press conference at which he stated his refusal to pay. In December, Taipo withdrew his work permit.

Mozambique's press is now freer than that in the US, according to Reporters Without Borders in their annual **press freedom** index. In the ranking, Mozambique came 45th and the US 53rd. In 2002, the US was number 17 and Mozambique ranked 70th.

An **earthquake** on 23 February measuring 7.5 on the Richter scale was the strongest in recorded history in the country. It was centred in remote Machaze district and caused little damage. The earthquake was felt 530 km away in Maputo, where tall buildings swayed. The total lack of damage there is due to strict building codes, which took into account that Mozambique is in an earthquake zone. **Landmines** and unexploded ordinance from three wars continued to be a problem, with 23 people killed in 2005 compared to only three in 2004, Deputy Foreign Minister Henrique Banze said on 13 July.

On 1 July, the country switched over to a **new metical** (MTn), which simply drops three 0s off the old currency. Old coins and banknotes were slowly replaced: they were no longer legal tender in shops but could be exchanged in banks for several more years. On 2 May, the **minimum wage** was increased from the equivalent of $ 53 per month to $ 56.60: for agricultural workers the rise was from $ 38.10 to $ 40.15 per month.

Electrification expanded rapidly. The final provincial capital, Lichinga, was linked to the national grid on 17 April, and the grid should reach all 128 district capitals by 2010. The government has stepped up development of bio-fuels based on agricultural products: work started on two factories. Wherever he went, President Guebuza urged peasants to grow jatropha. Previously treated as a weed, its seeds can be pressed locally for an oil that can be used in lamps, and when pressed commercially can be mixed with diesel.

The grain harvest was 2.1 m tonnes, up 10% on 2005. Pulse and cassava production were also up. On 16 January, Industry and Trade Minister Antonio Fernando launched a **Made in Mozambique** campaign to encourage people to buy locally made goods.

Joseph Hanlon

Namibia

This year, there were no spectacular political events to report. President Pohamba pursued a low-profile policy aimed at reconciling the different factions in the SWAPO party, which continued to dominate the political scene unchallenged. Since Pohamba took office in March 2005, there have been no cabinet reshuffles. However, the internal power struggles continued unabated and showed that the different factions remained in fierce competition for control of political power. In foreign policy, closer links to China emerged as the most remarkable feature. Concerning socioeconomic performance, little improved for the majority of people despite the first projected annual budget surplus since independence, while the self-enrichment schemes for the new elite flourished.

Domestic Politics

The main theme in domestic affairs remained the question of which of the **two presidents** really exercised power and governed the country: the former head of state Sam Nujoma, who remained president of the dominant (though much divided) SWAPO party or his own candidate for succession, the elected head of state Hifikepunye Pohamba. In public, the new head of state maintained a loyal attitude towards Nujoma as the party president and tolerated his predecessor's interference in substantive matters. The two did not engage in public power struggles, but it was evident that Pohamba sought to heal the wounds inflicted in the bitter inner-party power struggles over Nujoma's successor as head of state. Pohamba reappointed some of the ousted party members into higher positions and did not pursue a confrontational policy. The inner-party conflicts, however, simmered on. All eyes were on Nujoma, who prepared to secure his party presidency for at least another term at the next party congress (end of 2007). His cohorts started visible mobilisation while other factions did likewise in an effort to prevent this eventuality, all at the expense of a secure and stable policy environment. Speculation and strategic moves dominated the scene, while President Pohamba at least publicly stayed out the fray and tried to limit the damage. In a symbolic encounter, which received much media coverage, the motorcades of the two presidents travelling in opposite directions met unexpectedly on the tar road in northern Namibia on 5 December. Reportedly, the motorcade of Namibia's head of state had to make way for that of his party president.

The **internal power struggles** were reproduced on a number of fronts. The politics of firm control by the dominant party faction acting on behalf of Nujoma resulted in continued interference in local government matters, where elected office bearers on district or town levels and party members elected to regional or local party offices were replaced if they did not have the confidence of the Nujoma faction. The SWAPO-affiliated National Union of Namibian Workers (NUNW) dismissed its secretary-general for the critical stance he had taken earlier towards Nujoma. The 4th national NUNW congress, which preceded May Day, was marred by dissent and tumult, and delegates from the teachers' and the mineworkers' unions walked out in protest over the procedures adopted, which prevented dissenting views from being voiced. Leading independent-minded trade unionists were replaced by Nujoma loyalists. The leadership of member unions – notably the Namibian national teachers' union – was subsequently also replaced by Nujoma followers. At the congress of the SWAPO women's council on 8–10 December, a similar revamp occurred when one of Nujoma's confidantes, the deputy minister of health, was appointed new secretary of the influential body. She replaced a long-time activist alleged to be an 'imperialist' who had insulted the 'old man' (Nujoma). All these manipulative interventions pointed at the forthcoming SWAPO congress in 2007, which decides the next party president and indirectly also the presidential candidate for the elections in late 2009.

Nujoma remained publicly active at the party level. On 1 July, he blamed the white community for committing a crime against humanity and warned the British they would face consequences for interfering in Zimbabwe: "You touch Zimbabwe, you touch SWAPO", he said. Speaking on 15 July, he threatened that Namibia could use its uranium resources to "make its own atomic bombs" if external forces "create[d] nonsense". Upset by the demands of a group of former SWAPO combatants (see below), he allegedly made veiled death threats to members of this committee at a party meeting on 30 July. This prompted the UN special rapporteur on human rights to inquire of the foreign ministry in a letter of 10 August as to the substance of these allegations. On 3 August, Nujoma provoked students of the University of Namibia and the polytechnic to walk out in protest – a hitherto unknown form of open defiance, which illustrated the growing frustration over the offensive behaviour displayed by the 'founding father of the nation'. Nevertheless, at the annual SWAPO central committee meeting on 16–17 December, Nujoma declared that leaders must ensure that they promoted party and national unity, patriotism and solidarity and must embrace democratic norms and principles in their intentions, deeds and actions. He also dismissed claims by "some treacherous elements" and some local media that the party was divided.

Anti-corruption initiatives were a priority in President Pohamba's policies. On 27 March, he launched a zero-tolerance campaign, which laid the basis for cooperation between the newly established anti-corruption commission, the office of the ombudsman and various civil society organisations. However, self-enrichment schemes in the private sector and in the public services reached unprecedented heights. Black Economic Empowerment (BEE) and affirmative action schemes served as smokescreens for dubious, if not fraudulent practices. Financial scandals were under investigation in a number of parastatals and state institutions such as the Offshore Development Cooperation, which reported that Namibian dollars (N$) 100 m had gone missing. Misappropriation of funds in the social security commission resulted in over 50 employees being arrested during the year. Forensic investigation into the government institutions pension fund's development capital portfolio took place following the discovery that more than N$ 600 m were earlier allocated to BEE business operations, with many of these not repaying the preferential loans.

While the ousted CEO of the agricultural bank declared in mid-October in a labour lawsuit that his monthly salary of N$ 83,000 was "mid-range" and "moderate", hundreds of disappointed **war veterans** had been publicly mobilised since mid-year in pursuit of adequate compensation. President Pohamba dismissed their material claims as excessive in a televised address to the nation on 4 August and argued that meeting their demands would amount to an estimated annual expenditure of N$ 6 bn or 40% of the budget. However, government showed its concern by appointing the SWAPO party's secretary-general to a newly created portfolio for war veterans. In contrast, the party's president, Nujoma, categorically dismissed claims by the war veterans that in the course of negotiating independence they had been promised material compensation for their sacrifices during the struggle.

Foreign Affairs

Namibia remained committed to friendly relations with **other African countries** but sceptical about the APRM. The foreign minister reiterated on 10 March that while NEPAD would be considered part of the continental policy Namibia rejected the APRM. At the end of April, Botswana's President Mogae opened the town council's civic centre in the northern Namibian main town Oshakati and pointed out that both governments shared a commitment to decentralisation as a form of regional development. Tanzania's President

Kikwete used his visit in mid-April to hold talks between the two governments as chair and deputy chair respectively of the SADC organ on politics, defence and security and to call for strong support for the forthcoming elections in DR Congo. On 26 April, President Pohamba opened a SADC consultative conference in Windhoek with all member states in attendance to discuss sub-regional development as well as politics, defence and security. He visited the Republic of Congo for three days at the end of October and signed four agreements with his counterpart Sassou Nguesso. The Namibia-Angola joint commission on defence and security held its 13th session in early July in northern Namibia. On 21 September, the minister of information held a press conference in the presence of diplomats from Angola, South Africa and Botswana to clarify that a document circulating and claiming that there was an Angolan-Namibian 'defence protocol' was a fabrication. The document suggested that there was a military pact on bilateral assistance in the event of military conflict with other SADC states. Another row erupted over a visit by the deputy minister of lands to Zimbabwe in June. According to local media reports, he had expressed admiration for Zimbabwe's land policy. The government issued a press release at the end of June that this did not imply a shift in land policies in Namibia and that the minister was quoted out of context.

In May, relations with **South Africa** improved with the drafting of an agreement on the contested issue of water use from the Orange River, the common border. On 21 November, the 6th presidential meeting on economics between Namibia and South Africa took place in Windhoek. Presidents Pohamba and Mbeki updated the bilateral economic agreement, which included a total of 48 trans-border projects. The further exploration and utilisation of the offshore Kudu gas field along the southern coastline of Namibia was identified as a priority to contribute to the sub-regional energy supply. The talks also included discussions on special arrangements to allow Mozambique, Malawi and Zambia limited benefits from SACU.

Namibia's role in the **UN** featured prominently. On 27 January, President Pohamba demanded a bigger role for Africa on the Security Council by supporting the call for five non-permanent seats. He emphasised that Namibia's contribution to peace missions in Liberia, Sudan and Sierra Leone demonstrated the country's multilateralism at all levels. A fifth peacekeeping contingent of 610 soldiers left for Liberia at the end of September. Addressing the UN General Assembly on 20 September, Pohamba urged all parties in the Sudan to respect the transition from the AU to the UN peacekeeping force. But Namibia's role in the UN was not free of controversy. At the end of March, a government decision to object to the participation of local NGOs in the General Assembly's special session on AIDS caused uproar among advocacy groups. Namibia's ambassador to the UN provoked adverse international headlines when he proposed on 28 November on behalf of several African countries the deferment of adoption of the declaration on the rights of **indigenous peoples** until the end of the General Assembly session to allow for further consultations. Observers considered this a strategic move to prevent the adoption of the original declaration. Namibia was backed by Botswana, several other African countries, Canada, Australia, New Zealand and Russia. However, the 14 African member countries of the UN Human Rights Council that had approved the declaration on 29 June were among those recommending adoption. Finland, on behalf of the EU, urged a vote against delaying the declaration. Several human rights groups and similar agencies advocating indigenous minority rights harshly criticised Namibia, which like Botswana is accused of neglecting the local Bushmen (San) communities.

Friendly relations with **China** were consolidated. The ministry of foreign affairs issued a statement in early March confirming the government's support for the one-China policy. More than 20 business people were included, along with the president and his entourage, in the Namibian delegation that toured Singapore from 30 October and then attended the Sino-African summit in Beijing. The trip was described as an 'eye opener' and Chinese industry was viewed as eager to do business with its Namibian counterparts, notably in the mining sector. A total of seven twinning arrangements between Chinese and Namibian towns underscored the exceptionally close ties. **Russian interests** were evident in the inaugural session on 27–28 July in Windhoek of the Namibia-Russian intergovernmental commission on trade and economic cooperation. **Cuban** assistance continued in the health sector, in which 170 Cuban health professionals worked during the year. Military cooperation with the **US** took place in September, when Namibian defence force officers received training as international peacekeepers. Namibia was among the 21 countries that were in mid-October again declared eligible for US military training programmes. Their participation was earlier denied because of their refusal to sign an agreement with the US administration that would exempt Americans from prosecution by the International Criminal Court.

The special relations with **Germany** were underscored in Windhoek in mid-May in the bilateral talks on development cooperation: these resulted in a further increase in development aid by the single largest donor country. On 26 October, Namibia's parliament adopted without any objections a motion recalling the genocide under German colonial rule a century ago and demanding dialogue with Germany on reparations. In December, the implementation of a special reconciliation initiative by the German government was advertised. Not considered to be reparations, the tender invited consultancy services to define the framework for a € 20 m development programme over a ten year period. This initiative had earlier been blocked by the Namibian government, which had wanted further clarification. As the tender specified, "the special initiative is meant for development projects in areas and for communities that had 'historic ties' with the German colonial government and which the present German government considers as a special moral and political responsibility towards Namibia to aid the said communities." The Namibian government reportedly requested that the San communities be included as beneficiaries of this initiative.

Socioeconomic Developments

Minister of Finance Saara Kuugongelwa-Amadhila tabled the **annual budget** for 2006–07 on 16 March. It was the first since independence that presented a balanced account and predicted a surplus for the year and was described by her as "pro-poor, pro-growth". The only feature that possibly deserved such praise was the announced increase in the monthly pension for the elderly from N$ 300 to N$ 370. It became effective half a year later and was the first increase since 2004. Total expenditure for the financial year (April to March) was expected to increase by 18.6% to N$ 15.2 bn, with income expected to increase by 23.6% to N$ 15.25 bn through favourable revenue flows from, in particular, the SACU pool: these were expected to increase by 65% to some N$ 6.1 bn. However, dependence on these revenues at the same time showed the continued vulnerability of the Namibian state budget, especially as SACU revenue is likely to decline considerably with new free trade arrangements. Against the background of this **unsustainable revenue base**, the continued expansion of the budget was called into question, while local economists criticised the budget for bringing about neither long-term poverty reduction nor incentives to stimulate local economic growth and investment. The **additional budget** announced on 8 November adjusted the expected total government spending for the financial year to N$ 15.28 bn, with a much higher budget surplus of N$ 799 m.

In contrast to this positive balance, the **debt burden** remained a challenge. Government's debt-to-revenue ratio had soared from 7% in 1992 to more than 100%. Repayment of interest on debt equalled around 10% of budget allocations to the ministries of defence and of health and social services, which both received about the same allocations. For the purchase of farms under the land reform and resettlement policy, N$ 50 m was allocated. In contrast, slightly more was earmarked for security services, while double the amount was put aside to finance the soaring costs of the new state house complex (built by Chinese and North Korean contractors) and slightly more for the protection of VIPs. In its analysis, the Institute for Public Policy Research (IPPR) characterised the budget as "piecemeal and opportunistic reform rather than change according to a well thought-out, long-term plan." Expenditure was expected to rise to 35.6% of GDP. While the finance minister described the civil service as bloated and as unsustainable on the basis of current expenditure (with capital expenditure always on the low side), the public service wage bill for the year was estimated to rise again from N$ 5.5 bn to N$ 6.1 bn. The finance minister repeated her warnings in earlier budget speeches that a continued increase of the country's debt load placed a heavy burden on future generations – but increased expenditure and borrowing. As the IPPR concluded, the government continued to spend every cent it could lay its hands on. The state-owned Namibia Post and Telecom Holdings (NPTH) obtained additional income on 25 July when it finalised the country's biggest commercial deal of the year with the sale of 34% of the share capital in Mobile Telecommunications (MTC) to Portugal Telecom for N$ 1.02 bn.

Article IV discussions were held by an **IMF mission** from 6–14 November in Windhoek. The statement issued on 14 November commended authorities for the fiscal consolidation over the last two years that had reduced the fiscal deficit from over 7% of GDP to close to balance. It critically noted that one-off receipts from the partial privatisation of the state-owned MTC could have been used to reduce public debt and recommended continued reduction of the public debt ratio. This was required because of the projected substantial decline in SACU revenue and the country's significant public investment needs in health, education, poverty reduction and infrastructure. The statement warned that "more determined efforts [were] needed to reduce poverty so as to maintain social cohesion."

The outgoing local **EU representative** voiced his **criticism** of the government's poor planning, misjudgements and haphazard decision-making and noted that these harmed investor confidence. In an interview published by the state-owned 'New Era' (30 June), he stated his impression that the government executed "development plans without proper planning and the necessary research needed for the implementation of its socio-economic projects." He further maintained that implementation of aid projects was hampered by red tape and that investors had complained of the risks of doing business in Namibia.

Such criticism, combined with the increase in graft scandals and corruption, was also reflected in Namibia's **international ranking**. The World Economic Forum released its global competitiveness report at the end of November and the local business community noted with concern that Namibia's ranking had dropped from 79 to 84. According to TI's corruption perceptions index presented on 6 November, Namibia dropped from 47th to 55th. In the UNDP HDI, released in mid-November, Namibia remained in 125th position.

The **energy supply** remained high on the agenda, as Namibia imported about half its electricity, mainly from South Africa. One of the biggest single investments in infrastructure development in the annual budget was the N$ 250 m allocated for the development of the offshore Kudu gas power project to avert the imminent power crisis, which was evident in the increasingly irregular power supply from South Africa. Delivery failures caused black-outs in parts of Namibia and forced local electricity distributors to implement contingency plans. On 14 December, the CEO of Namibia's parastatal energy provider Nampower announced in Windhoek, at the opening of a working meeting with energy utilities from Botswana, Mozambique, South Africa, Zimbabwe and Zambia, that the **Kudu gas field** would be developed further in collaboration with South Africa's Eskom and the South Africa-based continental energy company Tullow Oil. He added that a Caprivi link would connect Namibia at an estimated cost of N$ 3 bn with Zambia, Botswana and Zimbabwe. Furthermore, Namibia and Angola planned to undertake a study for a hydro-electric power project on the Kunene river (their joint border) and Nampower explored a western corridor project providing a link to the Inga project on the Congo River in the DR Congo. The permanent secretary of the ministry of mines and energy disclosed to a local newspaper at year's end that government had decided to use its own uranium resources to produce nuclear power. Already on 30 January he had unsettled participants at a renewable energy workshop exploring the possibilities of solar and wind power when he announced that nuclear energy would be an option.

While the ailing fisheries sector was unable to recover from the setbacks in 2005 and the quota for the total allowable catch remained low, the **mining sector** thrived. Diamond production remained the most important single source of income to the economy, but there was notable diversification as a result of the favourable world market for the country's other minerals and metals. Scorpion Zinc and Rössing Uranium alone contributed 36% of the mining sector's total income (and 49% of non-diamond mining income), which peaked at N$ 11.4 bn for the year, an increase of 52% as against 2005. The lower exchange rate of the N$ against the US$ as well as increased demand by Asian economies contributed to the favourable conditions. Namibia produced some 7.5% of the world's **uranium** output, with a new mine at Langer Heinrich soon to be operational. At that point, Namibia was expected to account for 10% of the world's uranium, a figure that was likely to increase further to 15% given all the concessions issued, much to the disquiet of environmental groups, which vainly tried to limit the damage. **Zinc** was produced in the Anglo American-owned Scorpion mine and the Exxaro subsidiary Rosh Pinah mine, with huge profit margins due to world market price increases of more than 100% over 2005.

Notwithstanding such favourable conditions, the marginalisation of large parts of Namibia's population continued unabated. In early December, the local UNICEF office presented a study that showed a continued marked increase in **violence** against women, children and elderly people. Even young children and seniors were not spared rape, physical abuse and other forms of violence. The report suggested that women and girls were under constant siege wherever they went, and held attitudes of male superiority responsible. The imbalance in gender relations was a local focus of the acting secretary-general of the Namibian Red Cross when the organisation presented its global report on catastrophes on 14 December. Another area of concern was the situation of an estimated 120,000 orphans, most of whom had lost their parents to AIDS.

Another worrying feature was the continued destitution of the **San population**. The roughly 32,000 members of the various San communities had by far the lowest average income and 60% were dependent on food aid. Most of these communities formed part of the local populations in the Omaheke and Caprivi regions, on which the national planning commission presented regional poverty profiles in mid-year. According to these reports, a quarter of the Omaheke population lived in extreme poverty, while 40% of the Caprivi region's households were considered poor (with the national average 29.1%). The desperate situation of some San communities was brought into the limelight by the local newspaper, 'The Namibian' (14 March). It disclosed that San communities in western Caprivi had out of sheer hunger eaten mouldy rice distributed to them as food aid, even though officials told them it was unfit for human consumption. Samples tested afterwards in the state veterinary laboratory proved the rice to be unfit for both human and animal consumption.

In marked contrast to bread and butter issues, there was exceptional hype over **Hollywood celebrities** when Angelina Jolie stayed with Brad Pitt for several weeks in a coastal resort to give birth to their daughter on 28 May. They received VIP treatment, including the screening of all journalists trying to enter the country during the period and police action against any person suspected of trying to intrude on the couple's privacy. According to the deputy minister for tourism, the government offered the newborn child Namibian citizenship. The frenzy culminated in proposals to declare the birthday a public holiday. Less spectacular were visits later in the year by the British Prince Harry and Sir Richard Branson.

Meanwhile, the initiative by a church-based coalition demanding a **Basic Income Grant** (BIG) received less favourable response. The BIG coalition asked for an unconditional grant of N$ 100 to every Namibian under retirement age. This would amount to 2% of GDP, but was rejected by the cabinet in May.

Henning Melber

South Africa

Politics in South Africa continued to be dominated by the controversy surrounding former Deputy-President Jacob Zuma. The African National Congress (ANC) appeared split into similarly strong factions between the 'Mbeki camp' and the 'Zuma camp'. The macro-economic picture remained favourable, although the treasury estimated economic growth at 4.4%, somewhat lower than the anticipated 4.9%. The government initiated more comprehensive policies on job creation and social security benefits to address poverty.

Domestic Politics

The controversial **Jacob Zuma** resumed his duties as deputy-president of the ANC. He was acquitted on 14 May of raping a 31-year-old HIV-positive AIDS activist and family friend. Zuma admitted to having sex, but said it had been on a consensual basis. The trial harmed Zuma's reputation as he demonstrated his ignorance of HIV transmission as well as questionable assumptions about women and their sexual needs. Asked by the judge whether he had considered the health implications of having sex with HIV positive partners, he replied that he had taken the precaution of having a shower after the sexual intercourse. He also invoked 'Zulu traditions' that compelled him to fulfil women's sexual needs. In August, Archbishop emeritus Desmond Tutu advised Zuma against pursuing the race for the presidency. Tutu said that he could not condone Zuma's behaviour and also blamed him for doing nothing to prevent demonstrations by his supporters outside the Johannesburg high court, where they vilified the woman who had laid the complaint and threatened her life.

Zuma still faced unrelated charges of fraud and corruption connected with the 1999 strategic arms deal. The former deputy-president was once regarded as the man most likely to succeed President Thabo Mbeki. Since Mbeki dismissed him as deputy-president, Zuma has maintained that he is the victim of a conspiracy by unidentified people within the ANC who want to torpedo his political career. ANC regions and even local branches found themselves paralysed by the **internal divisions** between the 'Zuma camp' and the 'Mbeki camp'. The ANC Youth League (AYL), Zuma's staunchest supporter, purged prominent members for being 'anti-Zuma', as did the Young Communist League. The South African Communist Party (SACP) and the Congress of South African Trade Unions (COSATU), the ANC's allies in the Tripartite Alliance, were also strongly affected by divisions between perceived Mbeki and Zuma loyalists. The Tripartite Alliance is widely expected to unravel in the near future, but SACP and COSATU have thus far resisted growing pressure to leave the alliance.

On 20 September, the Pietermaritzburg high court dropped the **corruption case against Zuma** and two subsidiaries of the French arms manufacturer Thales. Judge Herbert Msimang said that the prosecutors "had limped from one disaster to the other". They should have investigated further before charging Zuma. He refused the request from the prosecution for a further delay. Prosecutors said they might bring new charges, but Zuma supporters welcomed the court decision as vindication of their claims that he is the victim of a conspiracy. On 6 November, the supreme court of appeal rejected a bid by Schabir Shaik, Zuma's associate in the arms scandal, to have his conviction for corruption overturned. The court upheld Shaik's sentence of 15 years of imprisonment. This means that Zuma's close links to his formal financial advisor will continue to haunt him if he insists on making his bid for the presidency.

Zuma cultivates the image of a pro-poor politician, although as deputy-president he had never questioned Mbeki's business-friendly policies. After the court dropped the charges, Zuma received a roaring welcome at the **COSATU congress** (18–21 September). COSATU called for all legal moves against Zuma to be laid to rest once and for all, and for his reinstatement as deputy-president of South Africa. Although a pro-Zuma mood prevailed among the delegates, COSATU President Willie Madisha, who is reputed to be pro-Mbeki, was re-elected by a small margin. The roundly pro-Zuma secretary-general, Zwelinzima Vavi, was re-elected unopposed. COSATU's congress was characterised by a militant mood, with resolutions adopted against key elements of the liberal economic policies pursued by the government. The congress blamed Mbeki for following 'the agenda of capital'. Criticism of privatisation policies was vocal, but further privatisations had already been put on hold. According to the reserve bank, the number of strikes in South Africa has reached a ten-year high, with 1.6 m working days lost during the first half of the year.

In May, Vavi had criticised the dictatorial tendencies within the ANC, complaining that the National Executive Committee (NEC) had become the preserve of cabinet ministers and businessmen, while labour and civil society were being marginalised. On 6 September, the chairman of the 'Friends of Jacob Zuma Trust' in Gauteng, Zobaphi Sithole, was shot dead in Soweto. Amid speculation that he had been assassinated, police treated it as a straightforward criminal case. Sithole's predecessor as chair of the trust, George Nene, was killed in a car accident earlier in the year.

In his **state of the nation address** on 3 February, President Thabo Mbeki proclaimed an 'Age of Hope'. South Africa had experienced more than five consecutive years of sustained growth – an upswing longer than any in the post-Second World War period. The president announced policies to spread the benefits of economic growth to South Africa's poor, including free primary schools for the poorest students and the elimination of shack settlements. More land will be allocated for housing developments near to economic centres, reversing apartheid practice of locating poor blacks far from the city centres. The notorious 'bucket system' by which human waste is collected from people's homes every morning should be eradicated by the end of 2007. He announced considerable increases in spending on public sector investment in the supply of electricity and water and the expansion of telecommunications. An expanded public works programme in underdeveloped urban and rural regions is designed to provide jobs while also opening up new opportunities for skills acquisition. Mbeki devoted only a brief paragraph to HIV/AIDS. The health budget has increased by 10%, with the HIV/AIDS sub-programme taking up a larger share of expenditures. It now stands at 18% of the health budget. The HIV/AIDS allocations for the provinces also grew substantially, by 32%.

Shortly before the local elections on 1 March, Mbeki reminded voters that spending on social development and public service delivery is being increased substantially. He cited the booming economy as evidence that the neoliberal economic model GEAR (Growth, Employment and Redistribution) adopted in 1996 had been correct. Towards the end of the year, the government indicated that it would work towards a more comprehensive social security safety net. This may include an extension of the child allowance to the age of 16, but the government remains reluctant to concede the Basic Income Grant (BIG) advocated by the left in the Alliance. The left, the main churches and civil society organisations have been campaigning for a social grant of Rands (R) 100 per month for all South Africans.

The theme of service delivery dominated the **local elections** on 1 March. The ANC used the elections for a massive clean-up among its councillors: 60% of incumbent councillors were not renominated. This was partly caused by the ANC's commitment to gender parity at local level: incumbent men had to make place for female newcomers. The ANC received 66.5% of the vote and kept control of 194 councils. The only setback was Cape Town, where the Democratic Alliance (DA) became the biggest party with 41%, while the ANC won 39% of the vote and Patricia de Lille's Independent Democrats 11%. Overall, the DA won 14.9% of the votes, giving it control of 10 councils. With 7.5% of the votes, the Inkatha Freedom Party (IFP) maintained control of 18 councils, all in the KwaZulu-Natal heartland.

In spite of Thabo Mbeki's call to celebrate the election victory, party insiders were increasingly concerned about **voter apathy**, particularly among young South Africans. The turnout for the local elections was 48% of registered voters. Registered voters numbered 22 m, the same number as for the 1994 elections. In view of the demographics, registered voters should number some 28 m. Millions of South Africans apparently did not bother to register.

Cape Town became the only major city controlled by the opposition DA, as well as the only major city with a white mayor. The ANC staged numerous attempts to unseat Mayor Helen Zille and her DA-led coalition. On 19 September, the ANC-controlled Western Cape government delivered a letter to Zille stating that it intended to replace the office of the mayor with rule by a committee of major parties. This unusual intervention was motivated by the need for 'stable government' in the lead-up to the 2010 football World Cup. Zille labelled the manoeuvre unconstitutional and said the city would take legal action if necessary. The ANC wanted to change the mayoral system only in Cape Town, not anywhere else in the Western Cape province.

After a meeting behind closed doors in May, the ANC NEC came out with a public show of unity, but infighting continued. With the **presidential succession race** focused on the December 2007 ANC conference, names of probable candidates – apart from Jacob Zuma – included Cyril Ramaphosa, Tokyo Sexwale, Deputy-President Phumzile Mlambo-Ngcuka, Minister of Foreign Affairs Nkosazana Zuma and ANC Secretary-General Kgalema Motlanthe. The person elected president of the ANC in December 2007 is likely to become president of South Africa in 2009, although in the Eastern Cape a lobby emerged to have Mbeki stay on as head of the ANC for a third term. Ramaphosa has a long history in the trade union movement, having led the National Union of Mineworkers. A former secretary-general of the ANC, he was popular with grassroots membership. In the 1997 elections for the NEC, Ramaphosa won most votes. He led the ANC team in the constitutional negotiations with the National Party government, but was subsequently sidelined by Thabo Mbeki. Ramaphosa then opted for a business career and amassed a considerable fortune in black empowerment deals. As a businessman, he is no longer the likely candidate of the left, although he could be a compromise candidate. Sexwale also has impeccable struggle credentials. Like Ramaphosa, he has built an extensive business empire, largely in diamond mining. However, he left a mixed record after his brief stint as premier of Gauteng, leading local analysts to believe that as president Sexwale would depend heavily on civil servants.

Much criticism centres on **Mbeki's authoritarian style** of government and his centralisation of powers in the Office of the President. Mbeki's view is that a 'developmental state' needs central strategic planning and management. The Office of the President now consists of the president, the deputy-president, the minister in the office of the president (Essop Pahad), the cabinet office and the Policy Co-ordination and Advisory Service (PCAS), headed by Mbeki loyalist Joel Netshitenzhe, who left the government information service in order to join the presidential staff. Within the Office of the President an intelligence unit also operates, separate from the state intelligence services. Concentration of powers in the executive office has been at the expense of parliament and the influence of the ANC. Yet many analysts also agree that coordination between government departments has improved considerably and that the Office of the President has brought more cohesion to government policy. SACP Deputy Secretary-General Jeremy Cronin, who joined the attack on the centralisation of powers, conceded simultaneously that a 'developmental state' has a need for a strong presidency.

There were a number of noteworthy **party political events**. On 31 August, Roelf Meyer announced that he had joined the ANC. Meyer was the chief negotiator on behalf of the National Party government in the constitutional talks in the early 1990s. In December, the ANC sacked its chief whip, Mbulelo Goniwe, for sexually harassing a parliamentary intern. Following an investigation by an ANC disciplinary committee, Goniwe was expelled from the party and removed as an MP. DA leader Tony Leon declared on 21 November that he would not seek re-election when his party meets to choose a new leader at its congress in May 2007. Leon will remain an MP till the next parliamentary elections in 2009.

In the wake of the **unresolved murder of Brett Kebble**, the scandal stories about the mining magnate's web of patronage assumed massive proportions, tainting the commissioner of police, Jackie Selebi. Kebble was one of the biggest funders of the ANC, as well as the ANC Youth League. In November, Scorpion detectives arrested a local tycoon, Glenn Agliotti, as part of their investigations into the Kebble murder. Agliotti, a friend of Selebi, was described in court as "one of those syndicate bosses who tend not to get their hands dirty but manage their enterprises from a distance." According to the arrest warrant, Agliotti is one of 12 suspects wanted for crimes ranging from money laundering to corruption, drug trafficking and defeating the ends of justice. Mbeki dismissed calls for a commission of inquiry into allegations against Selebi and expressed his confidence in the commissioner. Selebi is now under investigation by the Scorpions, the specialised unit that deals with organised crime. The Scorpions investigation is potentially damaging for the ruling party, as it could reveal money flows to the ANC and individual party bosses. The investigation into Selebi's links with organised crime is likely to fuel the tensions between the Scorpions and the South African Police Service.

As public protests against the **high crime rate** began to mount towards the end of the year, crime became a more urgent issue on the political agenda. With an average of 50 murders a day, or 18,528 a year, South Africa still has the world's second-highest murder rate. Violent robberies stood at 119,726 over the financial year 2005–06, and the number of reported rape cases at 54,926. The government stated that serious crime has declined by 10% over the past years.

The South African Broadcasting Corporation (SABC), the **public broadcaster, banned high-profile critics** of the government from its programmes. After an investigation, it was reported that the head of news, Snuki Zikalala, had drawn up a blacklist, which included the names of Moeletsi Mbeki (brother of the president), Eleanor Sisulu, William Gumede, Aubrey Matshiqi, Xolela Mangcu and other political analysts.

Brain drain statistics are hard to come by, but indications are that a serious loss of skills is taking place. According to the Southern African Migration Project (SAMP) it is not only disenchanted whites who are searching for opportunities abroad, but a substantial number of skilled blacks as well. However, black people were typically thinking of going to work abroad for a relatively short period of about two years.

New **anti-mercenary legislation** passed on 29 August set strict limits on South Africans seeking to work in security or military jobs abroad. They have to register with an arms control committee, and even when permission for foreign service is granted, they will be barred from serving in conflict zones. The new law will also affect the nearly 800 South African citizens serving in the British army. The legislation originated after the fiasco of a failed mercenary coup in 2005 in Equatorial Guinea, but is increasingly targeted at ex-security personnel working in Iraq. The number of ex-security staff working for British, American or South African companies in Iraq is estimated to be several thousand.

With a nominal rise of 1.3%, the **defence budget** was set at R 23.83 bn. However, if the declining expenditures on the arms deal (Strategic Defence Package) are taken into account, the military has 9% more to spend. Annual payments for the strategic arms package of jets, helicopters, submarines and frigates began dropping for the first time since South Africa started payments in 2000–01. This will free up more than R 1.8 bn, which will largely be used on equipment for the long-neglected army and for a rejuvenation of troops through the intake of new recruits. A group of 4,000 recruits joined the South African National Defence Force (SANDF) in January. The navy took in 612 recruits while 196 recruits joined the air force.

Critics contend that the **SANDF's capacity** for peacekeeping missions in Africa is seriously hampered by the obligations incurred by this massive arms package. The army bears the brunt of the new direction towards peacekeeping in Africa, but the Strategic Defence Package of 1999 was largely aimed at purchasing planes and helicopters for the air force and submarines and frigates for the navy. Ahead of the delivery of new jet fighters, the air force barred whites from training as fighter pilots in an effort to give the air force a more balanced racial profile. Since 2004, 70 pilots have resigned. Some missions had to be outsourced to chartered commercial flights because of a lack of aircrew. In addition to the pilots, a few hundred technicians also left the SAAF. The SANDF remains two-thirds white officered at middle management level. Lower ranks are predominantly black. More racial balance is being achieved by pensioning off the old guard while creating more top positions. Wage and pension costs weigh heavily on the defence budget. Despite efforts to recruit young, well-educated soldiers, the average age of the troops is about 31 years. The army is reluctant to let go the many ageing former guerrilla fighters who have no qualifications for civilian employment. Defence Minister Mosiuoa Lekota admitted in parliament that only 13,000 jobs had been created for the R 29 bn that had been paid for the arms deal. According to DA leader Tony Leon, that is a shortfall of 52,000 jobs, in view of the original agreement.

A new, largely black-owned **arms company** was launched on 20 September at the Africa Aerospace and Defence exhibition by Minister of Transport Jeff Radebe. According to Radebe, the Ngwane Defence Group combines the expertise of Umkhonto we Sizwe (MK, the ANC's armed wing in exile) and the SANDF. The CEO is Siphiwe Nyanda, who was head of the SANDF and is known as a vocal supporter of Jacob Zuma. Also involved were Fana Hlongwane, an ex-official from the defence department, George Nene, deputy director-general of the department of foreign affairs, and Brig.Gen. Damian de Lange (ex MK, now SANDF).

The **arms procurement deal** continued to haunt prominent politicians, given the suspicions of bribery and influence peddling. A **corruption probe in Germany** into the sale of the frigates disclosed that some $ 18 m might have been paid in bribes and 'commissions'. Up to 1999, bribes by German exporters to foreign officials could be accounted for legally as tax-deductible expenses. After a change in the law in February 1999, this practice became illegal. Although the name of then Deputy-President Thabo Mbeki has been mentioned in connection with talks about the German component of the arms deal in 1995, Mbeki welcomed the German investigations.

An APRM report warned that crime, corruption and xenophobia threaten to undermine post-apartheid democracy. **Corruption** was seen as particularly worrisome: South Africans feel a sense of betrayal, "regarding corruption as a negation of democratic gains after a long period of struggle." South Africa ranks seventh in the 'world bribe payers index' compiled by Transparency International. The index measures perceptions of corruption rather than actual records. South Africa scores behind India, China and Russia, which were perceived as the top bribers. Questions arose early in the year over a holiday trip by Deputy-President Phumzile Mlambo-Ngcuka to the United Arab Emirates in December 2005, using an air force jet at the cost of an estimated R 700,000. She was accompanied by family and friends. The presidency defended the trips, saying that protocol allowed the use of official planes for private trips. Sixteen current and former ANC MPs have been found guilty of theft and fraud after an investigation into the abuse of parliamentary travel privileges. The 16 admitted the charges and where fined and given suspended jail sentences of between three and five years.

South Africa felt part of the global backlash against the **Danish cartoons** featuring Islam and the prophet Mohamed. Mass demonstrations were staged in cities with a substantial

Muslim population, such as Cape Town and Durban. Threats were made to newspaper vendors, editors and staff. In a pre-emptive action, the Council of Muslim Theologians (Jamiat-ul Ulama) of Transvaal sought an interdict against Johncom Media and Independent Media. Johannesburg high court Judge Mohamed Jajbhay ruled that the right to dignity outweighs the right to freedom of expression and that the Sunday papers should refrain from publication. The human rights commission stated that the challenge was to balance the two important rights at stake – the right of the media to freedom of expression and the right to dignity on the part of the Muslim community. 'Sunday Times' editor Mondli Makhanya commented that the court ruling amounted to "a serious blow to the freedom of the press". When protests mounted and at times turned violent, several papers printed an apology for publishing some of the cartoons or featuring critical articles on the issue.

HIV/AIDS remained a controversial political issue. More than 60 leading AIDS scientists wrote a letter to President Mbeki demanding the dismissal of Minister of Health Manto Tshabalala-Msimang after she told an AIDS conference in Toronto that garlic, beetroot and African potatoes are effective in managing the disease. The scientists described the minister as an "embarrassment" whose "immoral" and "pseudo-scientific" views had disastrous consequences. Stephen Lewis, the outgoing UN AIDS envoy to Africa, lambasted South Africa at the conference in Toronto as "the only country in Africa whose government is still obtuse, dilatory and negligent about rolling out treatment." In early September, the cabinet stripped Tshabala-Msimang of responsibility for commenting on HIV/AIDS policies. Deputy Health Minister Nozizwe Madlala-Routledge, who took over the AIDS portfolio, succeeded in establishing a cooperative relationship with the Treatment Action Campaign (TAC), the main umbrella organisation of HIV/AIDS activists. After her appointment as head of an inter-ministerial committee in October, Deputy-President Mlambo-Ngcuka also engaged with civil society organisations active in the field of AIDS awareness and treatment. By the end of the year, 235,378 patients were receiving treatment through state-funded programmes, against an estimated need of 800,000.

The government launched the **treatment plan** in 2003, but the percentage of infected patients taking up antiretroviral (ARV) treatment remained far below target. The slow pace has been blamed on government reluctance to prioritise treatment because of the high costs involved, as well as on Mbeki's 'denialism'. However, a study by the Bureau for Economic Research at the University of Stellenbosch concluded that the economic benefits of treatment far outweigh costs. If 50% of patients are on ARV treatment, the impact of HIV and AIDS on economic growth will be reduced by 17% over the period 2000–20. The government has proclaimed that it aims to halve the number of infections by 2011. There are plans to extend treatment to 80% of HIV-positive patients.

Figures on **AIDS mortality** remain uncertain, as many doctors are still hesitant to list AIDS as the cause of death. It had been expected that this would change after insurance companies dropped the rule that death from AIDS-related illness would disqualify surviving relatives from insurance payouts. According to Stats SA, female death due to HIV/AIDS had quadrupled from 1997 to 2004. Projections of the **economic impact** of AIDS vary enormously. A study by the Joint Economic AIDS and Poverty Programme concluded that the effect would be negligible, but analysts at ABSA bank forecast that GDP would be almost 10% smaller in 2015 than it would have been without the pandemic. Most studies agree that AIDS will disrupt the educational system, with potentially serious economic repercussions. South African enterprises are developing different strategies to ward off at least some of the effects of the epidemic. Common strategies include the introduction of labour-saving technologies and work methods, outsourcing of work and casualisation of labour. Many companies are cutting back on death and disability benefits, while the workers' contributions to the premiums are increased.

In order to speed up the process of **land restitution and redistribution**, more pressure will be used on white farmers unwilling to sell. Chief Land Claims Commissioner Tozi Gwanya stated on 21 April that the government has identified 335 white-owned farms that could be earmarked for expropriation if negotiations with the farmers fail. Farmers will then be compelled to accept the price offered by the government. Under the land restitution laws, government can expropriate land without a court order. Thus far the government has been very reluctant to use these powers, fearing Zimbabwean-style chaos, with all its consequences. Lulu Xingwana, the new minister of agriculture, added at an agricultural briefing in mid-August that white farmers risk being expropriated if they fail to agree to sell for acceptable prices within the next six months. She accused white farmers of not being committed to the empowerment of black people. Lourie Bosman, the president of AgriSa, the largest farmers' union, rejected the ultimatum as 'unacceptable'. He warned of serious consequences for the economy and the risk of stirring up racial tensions.

The date for the completion of the restitution process has been extended to 2008. Over 90% of the claims have been settled, but in many cases with financial compensation rather than through actual restitution of land. Restitution of land rights applies to people who have been dispossessed under segregationist land legislation. **Land reform** refers to a broader process that includes the transfer of land to emerging black farmers and granting land rights to tenant labourers. The government has set a target for the transfer of 30% of agricultural land by 2014. Thus far the process has moved at a slow pace, with only 4% of white-owned agricultural land transferred to black farmers, while the establishment of emerging black farmers has also seen a number of failures. Moreover, many farm workers have lost access to land since the ANC took power in 1994. Ben Cousins, director of a land research project at the University of the Western Cape, noted that white farmers have forced nearly 1 m black workers and their families off the farms in an attempt to forestall claims to parts of their property.

On 14 November, parliament passed the controversial Civil Union Act by 230 votes to 41, legalising **same-sex marriages**. In view of the strong and diverse criticism from various quarters, including the churches and traditional leaders, the ANC had instructed its MPs to be present and vote in favour. In 2005, the constitutional court had ruled that existing laws discriminate against homosexuals. South Africa now is the only African country where same-sex marriages can be legally concluded.

On 31 October, former President **P.W. Botha died** at the age of 90 in his house in Wilderness near George. Botha's adult life was entirely devoted to the National Party, first as party organiser and later as minister of defence, prime minister and president. Under Botha's leadership, South Africa embarked on a policy of limited reforms to apartheid and began tentative contacts with the imprisoned Nelson Mandela, but at the same time he gave unprecedented powers to the military and the police. In the second half of the 1980s, his government became more repressive and ruthless, fuelling ethnic rivalries and destabilising neighbouring countries that offered sanctuary to liberation movements. Botha consistently refused to cooperate with the Truth and Reconciliation Commission. President Thabo Mbeki offered the family a state funeral, but they declined the offer.

Foreign Affairs

South Africa has firmly established itself as the economic powerhouse and the main political and diplomatic broker on the African continent, and even beyond, as in the crises evolving from Iran's and North Korea's nuclear policies. Thabo Mbeki has become a habitual guest at the G8 summit. At the same time, however, resentment in Africa against South Africa's role as self-appointed spokesperson on behalf of Africa is building. On 16 October, South Africa was elected to a non-permanent seat on the **UN Security Council**, by 186 of 192 votes. South Africa's term runs from January 2007 to January 2009. Foreign Minister Nkosazana Dlamini-Zuma pledged that her country would work to prevent violence in Africa and to pursue peace, particularly in the Middle East.

South Africa undertook to contribute 15% of the budget of the AU over 2006, almost doubling of its previous contribution. The increase follows an AU decision that countries' contributions should be proportional to the strength of their economies. South Africa also hosts the Pan-African Parliament in Midrand. South African troops continued to serve in **peacekeeping forces** in Burundi, the DR Congo and Sudan, in the context of AU or UN operations. In November, Deputy Foreign Minister Aziz Pahad announced that the 1,500 SANDF troops serving in Burundi with the UN will be redeployed to a task force under the aegis of the AU. This has been set up to oversee the incorporation of the 'Forces Nationale de la Libération' (FNL), the last remaining Hutu rebel group, into the national Burundian army. Pahad urged the UN Security Council to take over the AU peacekeeping force in Darfur. South Africa has made a modest contribution of a few hundred troops and police to this AU mission, but prefers continued involvement under a UN mandate.

Minister of Defence Mosiuoa Lekota stated in parliament on 8 September that about 50,000 rounds of ammunition, 97 mortar bombs, 46 R-1 assault rifles, three light machine guns, two pistols and two grenades had been lost or stolen in the course of various peacekeeping missions. In the DR Congo, South Africa contributed not only troops to MONUC, the UN peacekeeping force, but also assisted in the preparation of elections in October-November. The South African air force flew presidential and provincial ballot papers to 14 electoral coordination centres. South Africa contributed a few hundred troops to an AU force sent to the notoriously coup-prone Comoro Islands to help ensure a peaceful change of power.

Mbeki's **mediation efforts in Côte d'Ivoire** ran into vocal criticism from some West African leaders, who alleged that he lacks sensitivity towards local dynamics. Speaking during the Francophone summit in Bucharest, President Abdoulaye Wade of Senegal invited the South African president to step back and let ECOWAS deal with the issue. Many West African leaders believe that Mbeki is too soft on Ivorian President Laurent Gbagbo, whose politics of 'Ivoirité' have resulted in ethnic purges, driving hundreds of thousands immigrants from Burkina and Mali back home. On 17 October, the peace and security council of the AU relieved Thabo Mbeki of his mandate as a peace broker in Côte d'Ivoire. The council instituted a new 12-month transition period with increased executive powers for Prime Minister Charles Konan Banny and paid tribute to Mbeki for his "untiring efforts".

On 21 June, Chinese Premier Wen Jiabao arrived in South Africa for two days of talks on nuclear power, textile imports and regional alliances, as part of his eight-day Africa tour. Trade between **China** and the African continent has nearly quadrupled since 2000, and South Africa figures high on the list of trading partners. According to government statistics, over 2004 South Africa's exports to China were valued at R 5.5 bn, while it imported Chinese manufactured goods to a value of R 18 bn. Cheap Chinese textiles and shoes have caused much concern in the textile and footwear sector: an estimated 65,000 jobs have been lost because of the cheap imports. South Africa pressed for an agreement that would limit Chinese imports until the end of 2008: this period of voluntary restraint should provide a breathing space for the industry to restructure. It was reported that a memorandum of understanding had been worked out that could cut Chinese imports by a third.

On 4–5 November, President Thabo Mbeki was among the 41 African presidents and prime ministers at the Sino-African summit in Beijing, where a broad range of new trade, investment and aid deals was announced. Mbeki emphasised the importance of NEPAD and the need for transparency and 'corporate good governance'. Earlier in the year, Mbeki had suggested the possibility of joint ventures between South African and Chinese firms. South African companies, including Sasol and beer producer SABMiller have invested over $ 400 m in China, while Chinese investments in South Africa are in the range of $ 130 m.

South Africa remains outspoken in its **support of NEPAD's principles** of good governance and transparency, but Chinese officials at the Beijing summit repeated that China would not impose conditionality on trade, investment and aid. China's relentless drive for minerals in Africa is likely to undermine NEPAD's commitment to good governance. In 2005, South Africa cancelled contracts with Uganda because of reports that gold, diamonds and other minerals from that country were in fact obtained by plundering the eastern regions of the DR Congo. Subsequently, China stepped into the gap and increased the import of gold and diamonds from Uganda. South Africa is also worried about China as arms supplier to Africa, as South Africa's state arms manufacturer Denel aspires to capture a bigger share of this market.

A state visit on 5–6 September by Russian President Vladimir Putin, accompanied by around 100 business leaders, raised expectations for cooperation in aerospace, energy and military-industrial sectors. Trade between **Russia** and South Africa has been insignificant, but both sides see room for improvement. Among the deals concluded between the two countries are agreements in the banking sector, a financing agreement with regard to mining, energy and infrastructure and investments in metal processing plants. De Beers signed an agreement with the Russian diamond company Alrosa that opens the way for joint exploration in African countries.

South Africa fostered good relations with **Iran**, which continues to be one of its main suppliers of crude oil. South Africa also has substantial investments in Iran, with Sasol as one of the main investors. Pretoria has asserted Iran's right to develop nuclear energy for peaceful purposes and was involved as mediator between Iran and the UN Security Council.

To secure its **access to oil resources** in the face of increasing competition from China, the US and European countries, South Africa announced in June that it was opening an office of the state oil company PetroSa in Equatorial Guinea, its first African office outside South Africa. PetroSa has a 45% partnership in an oil exploration concession with the National Oil Company of Equatorial Guinea. Oil production in this small West African state has risen sharply over the past few years, with the bulk of oil exports directed to the US, China and Spain. Like other customers, South Africa did not mention the bleak human rights record of Equatorial Guinea. The oil company Ophir, set up in 2004 and controlled by Tokyo Sexwale's Mvelaphanda Holdings, opened negotiations with the Polisario Front for an offshore oil exploration licence in the Western Sahara.

The state-owned manufacturer Denel continued its **arms exports**, also exploring new markets outside the African continent. South Africa and Brazil were working on a R 300 m project to develop a short-range air-to-air missile system. Attempts to sell Rooivalk helicopters to Turkey met with competition from American and Italian arms manufacturers. A missile test site in the southern Cape is to become the basis for a South African Space Agency. Science and Technology Minister Mosibudi Mangena told MPs on 26 May that space science and astronomy would generate billions of rands in foreign investment. South Africa has signed agreements with NASA in the US, the European Space Agency and the Russian Space Agency.

South Africa signed a cooperation agreement with the **Central African Republic**, in spite of the AU's rule that regimes that came to power through unconstitutional means should be isolated. President Francois Bozizé, who overthrew the government of Ange-Felix Patassé in 2003, paid a visit to South Africa and discussed future cooperation in the field of defence and security, energy and mines and capacity building in the public service.

The influx from **Zimbabwe** has caused the South African government to double its expenditures on immigration control. Official figures released in Harare suggest that about 3.4 m people – a quarter of the population – are now living abroad. Some 1.2 m are believed to be in South Africa, more than in any other country. On average, 10,000 illegal Zimbabweans are deported from South Africa every month. The statistics were recorded at the Beitbridge reception and support centre established to assist deportees. Former Zimbabwean MP Roy Bennett, who is also treasurer of the Movement for Democratic Change, was denied asylum in South Africa. Zimbabwean police said he is wanted in connection with an alleged plot to kill Mugabe. The Zimbabwe exiles' forum stated its concern about South Africa's refusal to grant political asylum to Zimbabweans. Zimbabwean President Robert Mugabe pardoned three apartheid-era spies (Kevin Woods, Michael Smith and Philip Conjwayo) who were sentenced to life imprisonment in 1988 for a failed attempt to blow up a car carrying exiled ANC activists.

Socioeconomic Developments

The macroeconomic picture remained favourable, although the treasury estimated **economic growth** at 4.4%, somewhat lower than the anticipated 4.9%. Over the next three years, economic growth is still expected to average around 5% per year, largely owing to strong investment, massive spending on infrastructure and high commodity prices. Spurred on by the promise of sustained growth and mounting discontent on the left, the government initiated more comprehensive policies to address widespread poverty through job creation and an expanded system of social security.

Finance Minister Trevor Manuel emphasised that **redistribution**, as envisaged in the original Reconstruction and Development Programme (RDP), remains part and parcel of government policy. He explained the latest policy model, ASGI (Accelerated and Shared Growth Initiative), as a plan to broaden the benefits of growth by improving social provisions and job creation among the marginalised sectors of the population. Manuel again tabled a mildly expansionary budget seeking to consolidate growth by encouraging investment, while also paying attention to poverty alleviation. This task was made easier by a R 41 bn revenue overrun, thanks to more efficient tax collection and high commodity prices. The fiscal deficit for 2005–06 fell to 0.5% of GDP, the second lowest deficit in South African history. The extra income will be used to pay off debt, raise expenditure and provide moderate tax relief mainly to low and middle income earners. In his medium-term budget policy statement on 25 October, Manuel pointed out that South Africa can expect revenue growth to outpace spending growth in 2007, allowing the treasury to budget for a 0.5% surplus in 2007–08, the first budget surplus in 30 years.

Total **public expenditure on infrastructure** is scheduled to grow 14.2% over the next three years, with R 372 bn to be invested in housing and community infrastructure, water, sewage, power generation and better roads, rail and ports. In view of the football World Cup in 2010, improvement of sports stadiums, public transport, justice and crime prevention will be prioritised. Hospitals and schools also ranked high on the priority list. Education remains the single largest category of spending, with an annual budgetary increase of 9.7%. There is new emphasis on 'employment in community services', with a budget allocation of R 4 bn to provide payment for people providing community services.

Major **bottlenecks** continue to be the skills shortage and underspending by government departments and by the provinces, which are responsible for infrastructure, housing, education and health. The provinces spent only 55% of their 2005–06 capital budgets. Manuel announced initiatives to tackle the lack of capacity in public service delivery by providing support to provincial and local government.

In May, construction work began on an ambitious new public transport system, the **Gautrain**, linking Johannesburg and Pretoria and O.R. Tambo international airport. Costs of this high-speed train are estimated at R 20 bn. The first section of the project, linking Johannesburg's northern suburb of Sandton to Pretoria, is due to open in June 2010, just in time for the World Cup.

Minister of Public Enterprises Alec Erwin indicated in July that service delivery will be prioritised over **Black Economic Empowerment** (BEE) in the transport and power-generating sector. Erwin stressed that BEE or women's advancement could not be allowed to slow down urgently needed modernisation of infrastructure. This change in policy will not affect the momentum of BEE in the rest of the economy, where sectoral charters have been introduced to ensure that blacks gain control of an increasing share of companies. BEE has been fiercely criticised by the left in the Tripartite Alliance for promoting a very rich black elite without obvious benefits for workers or the poor. Erwin's statement came amid other indications that the government is seeking a more balanced policy that not only caters to the interest of the black middle class but increasingly to the poorest segments of the population.

Industrial growth and electrification schemes have stretched the **power supply** to its limits, resulting in frequent electricity cuts. Projects envisaged include coal, gas and hydropower in the SADC region, as well as a pre-feasibility study for the construction of a third nuclear plant. According to the Petroleum Agency SA, foreign and local companies are showing growing interest in exploring the oil and gas potential of South Africa's west coast. Over the past few years, over $ 1 bn has been spent on oil and gas exploration in South Africa. To meet the rising demand for electricity, the coal sector is expanding rapidly. South Africa ranks as the fifth-largest producer of coal in the world. The bulk of coal production is consumed locally, but exports are rising. The coal sector has also witnessed substantial growth in black-owned companies, which now run about 20% of the coal sector. Coal mines require less capital and are easier to operate than gold or platinum mines and are therefore more within the reach of BEE entrepreneurs. Platinum has over the past few years overtaken gold as South Africa's largest commodity export earner. South Africa produces about 75%

of the world's platinum. Coal comes second and gold now stands at third. The gold price recovered but gold mines are not considering opening new shafts.

Sustained economic growth did not translate into a corresponding growth in jobs. According to official statistics, 26.5% of South Africans are jobless, but analysts agree that the real **unemployment** figure still hovers around 40%. The majority of jobless people are considered unemployable because of their lack of skills. The best performing sector in terms of job growth was the construction industry, followed by trade, hotels and restaurants. Tourism remains a growth industry. The mining sector and the textile industry topped the list of industries with declining employment. On 18 May, COSATU called a day of protest action against the loss of more than 100,000 jobs over the past three years and the increasing casualisation of labour. However, according to Pieter Laubscher of the Bureau for Economic Research at the University of Stellenbosch, the formal sector of the economy is creating jobs at the rate of 2.5% per year. Between September 2004 and September 2005, 300,000 new jobs were created in the formal sector. In terms of job creation, the government has put its hopes in small- and medium-sized business. Integrating **the 'second economy'** into the mainstream economy is part of the governments' ASGI, whose main objectives are to halve unemployment and eradicate poverty by 2014. Speaking at a May Day rally for a crowd of farm workers in Swellendam in the Western Cape, Mbeki emphasised that an expansion of the skills base is a vital condition if more people are to profit from the growth in the 'first economy'. In view of continued high unemployment, the government remains reluctant to relax the stringent restrictions on recruiting skilled workers outside SA.

During a visit in November, the IMF's deputy managing director, John Lipsky, praised the "sound macro-economic management" that had resulted in unprecedented sustained economic expansion. He expressed support for ASGI but suggested that job creation could be encouraged by liberalisation and deregulation of the labour market and the trade regime. Government policy has been especially successful in its avowed aim of creating a **black middle class**. According to a survey by the Advertising and Research Foundation, blacks now make up about one-third of the country's middle class. The middle-income bracket is defined as people earning between R 6,500 and R 11,800 a month. The proportion of blacks in the top income bracket is now around 20%. However, the black middle class still constitutes only 10% of the black population. These 10% make up 43% of total black buying power. Greater black spending power has fuelled the consumer boom of the past years, although concern is growing that this boom may not be sustainable, as many households have made purchases on credit. Between 1994 and 2005, the black share of car ownership increased from 29% to 42%.

According to a study by the Institute of Justice and Reconciliation (IJR), **South Africa's elite** is very closed: political and economic interests are closely intertwined and a small group of prominent individuals figures in many BEE deals. The report, entitled 'Money and

Morality' lists 118 names of politicians, their spouses, ambassadors, senior civil servants and business people. IJR director Charles Villa-Vicencio emphasised that those on the list were not being identified as corrupt. There has been a sharp rise in the number of **black graduates** with tertiary degrees: the black graduation rate has increased by 334% over the past 14 years. In 2005, blacks constituted 30% of students registered for MA or PhD degrees.

A long and violent **strike by security guards** in the first half of the year revealed the extent to which South Africa has become dependent on private security. Their union, the Transport and Allied Workers Union, demanded higher wages, but negotiations became very complicated because a total of 14 unions were involved, resulting in deadlocks caused by intra-union disputes. Hundreds of strikers went on the rampage during May Day celebrations in Cape Town. COSATU had to abandon its rally and called in the police to deal with strikers who looted vendors and damaged property. The strike was the most violent since 1994, with nine people murdered and substantial damage to public and private property. According to the SA Institute of Race Relations, there are almost three private security guards for every policeman.

With regard to the **trade balance**, imports increased at a much faster pace than exports. Notable was the rapid growth of imports from Africa. South African exports to the US increased by 30%. The main beneficiary of the preferential tariffs under the AGOA scheme, renewed by the US Congress in December 2006, is the car manufacturing industry. Motor vehicles, parts and accessories reported excellent export figures. The EU remains South Africa's biggest trade partner, accounting for some 40% of its imports and exports. EU countries also account for about 70% of donor funding for South Africa.

The downward slide of the Rand continued throughout the year. The **weak performance of the currency** was blamed on the rapid increase in the external current account deficit. The manufacturing sector expressed cautious optimism that the weak Rand will help to reclaim export orders that had been lost over the two previous years when the currency was strong. Growing consumer demand on the domestic market has, however, mitigated the impact of declining exports.

The **wine industry** experienced its worst season in many years due to a global oversupply of red wine in the lower-priced market segment. By September, average bulk prices of the most widely produced red wines had fallen by almost 40% compared to 2001.

Ineke van Kessel

Swaziland

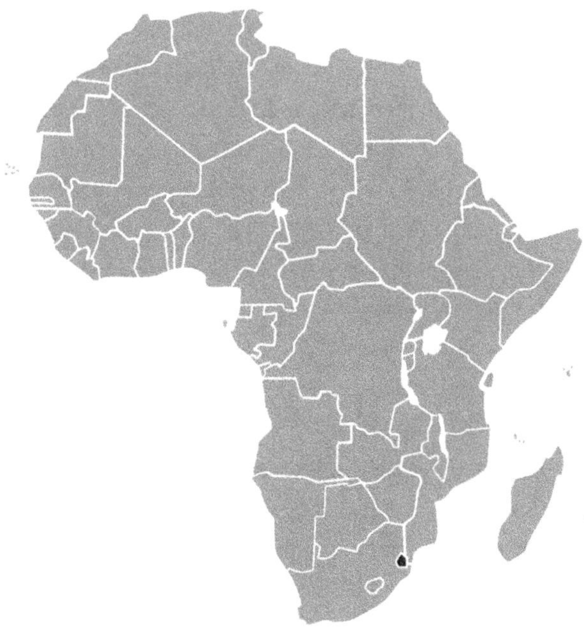

The diet of authoritarianism, repression, corruption and socioeconomic decay continued to characterise political life. The extent of the last of these characteristics was dramatically illustrated by new IMF data which revealed that life expectancy had declined from 60 years of age in 1980 to 31.3, making it the worst country in the world in terms of the duration of life for its citizens. According to the Economist Intelligence Unit's (EIU) Country Report, the chances of a 25 year-old Swazi reaching the age of 50 were only 28% for males and 22% for females. These figures would have been 94% and 97% respectively if it had not been for AIDS.

Domestic Politics

A nine-year-long **constitutional review process** costing millions of dollars came to an end on 26 July when King Mswati III signed into law a new constitution. Basically, nothing changed politically and the monarch was left with the same unfettered powers appropriated by his father, Sobhuza II, in his emergency decree of 1973. Mswati had appointed a constitutional review commission in 1996. At the time, it had seemed the monarchy was under threat from a combination of rising domestic opposition and a perception that a newly democratic South Africa, having pledged to place human rights considerations at the core of its foreign policy, might use its dominance of the region to press for democratic reform in Swaziland.

The king signed the constitution into law on 26 July 2005 but announced it would come into force six months hence. It took effect on 7 February. It was widely anticipated at the time that Mswati would then promulgate the repeal of the emergency proclamation of 12 April 1973. He did not. Constitutionally, Swaziland remains **a no-party state**. A number of political groupings hostile to the monarchy do function and enjoy a degree of tolerance. The most prominent of these are the Peoples United Democratic Movement (PUDEMO) and the Swazi Youth Congress (SWAYOCO). Two weeks after promulgating the new constitution, the king told the international press that the country was "not ready for political parties", a view affirmed by the attorney-general, who on 11 May, suggested that the constitution did not "disallow political parties because it did not address the issue, but that the Swazi people were not yet ready for them."

The constitution also proposed no changes to the **electoral system**, which means that the King retains the power to fill by nomination 42% of the seats in the legislature as well as the power to appoint the prime minister, all cabinet members, all judges and all chiefs. While losing the power to rule by decree, he retained the power to veto legislation and to dissolve parliament at any time. His immunity from the courts of law was also retained.

A series of **bomb attacks** targeting the offices of two important traditional institutions as well as the homes of three police officers and two politicians close to the royal family had occurred in 2005. Of the 19 surviving alleged PUDEMO and SWAYOCO members and sympathisers then arrested (one died in custody after being tortured), 15 (including the deceased's husband) were charged with the destruction of government property, attempted murder and treason. On 10 March, they were released on bail after the acting chief justice of the high court, Jacobus Allandale, stated that the prosecution had failed to make a convincing case of a link between the accused and the bombings. He also ordered an investigation into allegations that the accused had been tortured. No such inquiry ensued. A rally convened to welcome the release of the accused was forcibly dispersed by the police. In September, four of the accused were re-arrested on further charges of damage to property. By the end of 2006, no trial date had been set amid indications that the state was having difficulty building a credible case.

Suspicion and hostility has for years characterised the state's attitude to the media. **Freedom of speech** and of the press in Swaziland is not legally protected and the government has frequently acted against the media, especially to discourage critical coverage of the royal family. This has included closing down newspapers and magazines as well as detaining and generally harassing journalists and broadcasters. There are two daily newspapers in Swaziland, one of which is government-owned. The state has a monopoly over television and radio ownership.

A **censorship policy** for the state-owned Swaziland Broadcasting and Information Services has since 2003 prohibited the dissemination of negative information about the government. The courts have also been used to intimidate journalists. In 2004, Deputy Prime Minister Albert Shabangu sued the 'Times of Swaziland' for defamation for an article in which Shabangu's past links to opposition groupings were cited. In July 2005, the high court awarded him Elangeni (E) 750,000 (approx. $ 116,000) in damages, but this was overturned by the court of appeal on 18 May. Shabangu was also ordered to pay the newspaper's legal costs. This was indicative of the relative autonomy of this court of last resort, which nearly four decades after independence is not only headed by a foreigner but is entirely composed of largely retired judges drawn from English-speaking SADC states. This, it should be noted, must be consonant with the king's wishes for it is he who makes all judicial appointees on the basis of recommendations from a judicial services commission, which he also nominates.

On 29 August, the minister of public service and information extended a **warning to the media** against criticising the king. This came after the state broadcaster had aired critical comments made by a local human rights lawyer following the visit to the kingdom by an AU human rights group. Management of the radio station was told to 'toe the line'. A senior journalist at the radio station was quoted by the Media Institute of Southern Africa as saying that "censorship is an everyday occurrence here. As a government medium, there is very little we can do."

Foreign Affairs

In a departure from established diplomatic practice, a number of foreign governments articulated **public criticism** of the political situation in Swaziland. Both the British high commissioner and the Netherlands ambassador strongly criticised the political system when presenting their diplomatic credentials to the king early in the year. Britain's Paul Boateng stated that, "corruption, violence, intimidation and torture have no place in the new Africa of the 21st century. It is on issues such as these that the reputation of Swaziland rests."

On 18 May, the EU ambassador announced the **suspension of direct funding** to the government. The EU has been one of the major donors in Swaziland in recent years, having provided aid to the value of € 4.1 m in 2005. Announcing the decision, Ambassador Peter Beck said the action was being taken "due to the absence of adequate fiscal controls" and would be reviewed only when "government implements a solid accounting and auditing mechanism to monitor its coffers." As he noted further, "Swaziland is behind other African countries."

International criticism of the situation also emanated from the British Trade Union Congress and the International Confederation of Free Trade Unions. In a joint letter sent to the Commonwealth secretariat in March, the two bodies described the new constitution as "consolidating the absolute monarchy with a few cosmetic changes." A month earlier, the central executive of Congress of South African Trade Unions (COSATU) adopted a resolution strongly critical of the situation and resolved to join a blockade of border crossings into Swaziland. At several of these border points, protesters clashed with the South African police and at least 25 were arrested, including some senior COSATU office bearers.

Relations with South Africa remained low key and the long-planned visit to South Africa by King Mswati – postponed at the last minute in 2005 – did not materialise. Nor were there any meetings of the Joint Bilateral Commission for Cooperation (JBCC) set up to, among other things, find a solution to the border dispute between the two countries. Swaziland has a longstanding claim on parts of Mpumalanga province and the Ingwavuma region of northern KwaZulu-Natal. On 20 November, the Swazi government announced its intention to take its land claims to the International Court of Justice as years of representations had, according to government officials, "fallen on deaf ears".

Socioeconomic Developments

As a consequence of a variety of factors (mismanagement, corruption, uncontrolled expenditure on the part of the monarchy and a persistent drought), the performance of the economy has weakened steadily over the past decade. The overall **growth rate** was estimated by the IMF at 1.8% in 2005 and the predictions for 2006 put the figure at about the same level. Of the population, 69% were said to be living below the poverty line of E 128 per month, with an estimated 300,000 Swazis dependent on food aid for survival. In October, the government blamed **budgetary constraints** for stopping payments of its monthly grants of E 80 to orphans and vulnerable children as well as to widows and the elderly. A rare protest by MPs resulted in the reinstatement of the payments. The national unemployment rate was put at around 40% for all workers, while the rate for women alone was estimated at 70%. In May, the inflation rate was 5.54%.

Compounding Swaziland's economic woes was a reduction in the price paid by the EU for **sugar**, which is the major source of export revenue, accounting for 24% of GDP and some 91,000 jobs. For the past 30 years, Swaziland has been one of 18 ACP countries to benefit from a preferential pricing arrangement to supply the EU with a fixed quota of sugar at prices that matched those paid to European producers and which was approximately three-and-a-half times higher than the world market price. A WTO ruling that deemed the arrangement unfair resulted in the EU deciding to reduce the price paid to the ACP beneficiaries by 36% over three years, starting with an immediate cut of 5%. According to the Swaziland sugar association, the effect was a loss of $ 30 m in revenue. This situation will deteriorate even further.

An EIU report described **corruption** as endemic. It suggested that this was not a product of excessive bureaucratic regulations or registration requirements but stemmed from the undemocratic nature of the political order and from a view within the political establishment that state resources are, as the EIU put it, "an entitlement". Corruption, it estimated, cost up to E 40 m ($ 6.5 m) monthly. These figures exceed the annual budget of the ministry of health in a country with the world's highest HIV/AIDS infection rate. In response to this criticism, and that by various national and international groupings, parliament passed the Prevention of Corruption Act. In terms of the act, an anti-corruption commission and an anti-corruption unit were established as dedicated entities for the investigation of corrupt activities involving public officials, companies and public enterprises. These units replaced an earlier one established in 1998, but which had never produced any indictments as it lacked all the necessary legal powers fully to investigate suspects. The two bodies started functioning in July, but by year's end had not moved against any individuals or groups.

In October, police in South Africa's Mpumalanga province – which borders on both Swaziland and Mozambique – announced that they were investigating a **child-trafficking** racket involving trade in girls aged between 10 and 16 from Swaziland and Mozambique. After being lured into South Africa, the girls were then forced into prostitution. Police stated that they believed the racket had been operating for some six years.

Swaziland is confronted by a human disaster of epic proportions in the form of the highest **HIV/AIDS infection** rate in the world. According to a 2005 survey by the Swazi ministry of health, the proportion of sexually active adults between the ages of 19 and 49 infected with HIV/AIDS was 42.6% in 2004 with the rate as high as 56% in the 25–29 age category. World Vision, an NGO involved in food distribution in Swaziland, reported that 42.6% of pregnant Swazi women attending antenatal clinics were HIV positive. In June, the number of orphaned children stood at 69,000, with projections suggesting that the figure would rise to 120,000 by 2010. The impact of the epidemic in Swaziland is such that the US census bureau has predicted that the population of Swaziland will actually begin to decline from its current level of just under 1 m.

John Daniel & Marisha Ramdeen

Zambia

Domestic and even foreign politics were under the sway of disease, death and xenophobia, which had a major impact on the outcome of the presidential and parliamentary elections. While President Levy Mwanawasa was safely re-elected, the opposition was totally shaken up by the above tripartite menace and by the surprising re-emergence of an old challenger, Michael Sata, the new populist leader of the opposition.

Domestic Politics

The election year started with a portent for the opposition parties. On 19 January, in **three by-elections** the ruling Movement for Multiparty Democracy (MMD) won constituencies previously held by opposition parties, one each from the Forum for Development and Democracy (FDD) (Chama South) and the United National Independence Party (UNIP) (Milanzi) in Eastern province, and one from UNIP (Roan) in Copperbelt province. The opposition had failed to form electoral alliances and had split the vote over a number of parties to the benefit of the ruling MMD.

Partly in reaction to the defeat, and having learned some lessons from previous elections, the various opposition parties started more seriously than before to form election alliances. On 28 February, the leaders of the United Party for National Development (UPND)

Anderson Mazoka, Tilyenji Kaunda of UNIP and Edith Nawakwi of FDD formed the **United Democratic Alliance** (UDA), comprising the strongest opposition parties in parliament, which held 63 out of 150 seats at that time. The intention was to field one common presidential candidate and joint candidates in parliamentary elections.

Hardly two weeks later, on 11 March, another group of parties announced the formation of the **National Democratic Front** (NDF), the so-called 'Northern Alliance', as it was supposed to include parties with a base mainly in Northern and Luapula provinces among the Bemba speakers. This group comprised Ben Mwila's Zambia Republican Party (ZRP), Nevers Mumba's Republican Party (RP), Daniel Pule's Zambia Development Congress (ZADECO), Chitalu Sampa's Party of Unity, Development and Democracy (PUDD) and Michael Sata's Patriotic Front (PF). However, before the final agreement was signed, Sata with his PF dropped out, while Ken Ngondo's All People's Congress (APC) joined the NDF, which consequently was re-named to **National Democratic Focus**. The NDF national congress (14–16 June) elected Ben Mwila as the alliance's presidential candidate.

Late in March, the prospects of the ruling party for the upcoming elections were overshadowed by the president's falling ill. He suffered what was, after some secrecy, officially called a 'minor' stroke, and was flown to London for treatment. About two months later, Anderson Mazoka, the most prominent and respected opposition politician and leader of UPND, died in a South African hospital after a prolonged illness. While Mwanawasa recovered and was able to take up his duties again, despite some doubts as to whether he would be sufficiently fit for campaigning, **Mazoka's death** caused major turmoil in UPND and the UDA electoral alliance, from which both never recovered.

UPND became caught up in a leadership wrangle that finally split the party. Some of Mazoka's friends first wanted his wife to succeed. Later, playing the ethnic card, they demanded that only a Tonga such as Mazoka himself could be his successor. The Tonga used to be one of the UPND stalwarts in Southern province, and the MMD had long tried to discredit UPND as a 'tribalist' Tonga-party. After a nasty power struggle, Hakainde Hichilema, a rich Lusaka businessman and newcomer to politics, but a Tonga, was elected as UPND's president by a 69% majority at the party's convention (14 July). Independent observers saw nothing wrong with the elections. The defeated competitor, the party's former vice- and acting president, Sakwiba Sikota, a Lozi from Western province, left the party and formed the **United Liberal Party** (ULP).

When Sikota wanted to join the UDA with his new party, the UPND leadership blocked the move. Consequently, ULP finally agreed with Sata's PF on an electoral pact aimed at avoiding competition between the two parties in the same parliamentary constituencies. While PF was supposed to be strong in the Northern, Luapula and Copperbelt provinces, ULP's strength was expected to be in the Western province. Finally, the UDA leadership agreed on Hichilema (UPND), the leader of the party with most opposition seats in parliament, as their presidential candidate and Edith Nawakwi (FDD) as running mate for the vice-presidency.

The elections had to take place within the framework of the **old constitution and its electoral law**, which favoured the incumbent. Civil society organisations as well as opposition parties had been mobilising against this constitution for many years. After a new wave of demonstrations at the end of 2005, President Mwanawasa seemed to have given in to the opposition's major demands in February by agreeing to the idea of a constituent assembly and a national referendum. Ostensibly all the arguments that Mwanawasa had deployed against this idea did not count any more. Yet what appeared to be a victory for the opposition, turned out to be a trick to buy time and goodwill for the government. It soon became clear that it was impossible to come to grips with a new constitution before the elections. Although the government introduced a new election law in May, it did not include a change to the 50% plus one vote for the presidential election as demanded by the opposition and civil society organisations.

On 26 July, the president announced 28 September as the date for the **trilateral elections** of local governments, parliament and president. The early date took the opposition by surprise because elections used to be held in December. As a result, the opposition parties had problems getting ready for the campaigns in time, while the ruling MMD, with the support of the state machinery, was in a better position.

In the preparations for the parliamentary elections, only MMD held **primary elections**, which they did as early as mid-April, although these were marred by widespread malpractices and corruption. The final adoption of candidates for each constituency, however, was decided by the party's national executive committee. In all the other major parties, candidates were nominated by the leadership alone. Only MMD was able to field candidates in all constituencies, while UDA (9 August) tried but failed in a number of constituencies (Luapula), and PF managed only 122 nominations, disregarding a number of provinces where they had hardly any party structures. MMD had already nominated its presidential candidate at a national congress in 2005, and nomination was not an issue in PF, since Sata was the only possible candidate. In the UDA, the three party leaders agreed among themselves (3 August) on the leader of the strongest party, the UPND-newcomer Hichilema.

The **electoral campaigns** were conducted with the usual bickering and personal attacks among the candidates, without any focus on particular issues. The government emphasised economic achievements, economic growth over several years and debt reduction, while the opposition pointed to the lack of trickle-down effects and the persistence of poverty. The atmosphere finally heated up when PF-leader Michael Sata, also called 'King Cobra', notorious for his aggressive style, focused his campaign on socioeconomic grievances by turning on foreign investors. He promised the deportation of Chinese, Lebanese and Indian investors if he were elected president. This resonated well with the urban electorate's complaints about foreign investors, namely their poor working conditions and the substandard wages for Zambians and their competition with small traders and entrepreneurs on the local market. Sata's repeated statements on the issue not only caused an uproar among politicians and in the media, but also a diplomatic row with China. Sata had singled out the Chinese whose "investment has not added any value to the people of Zambia." On top of that, he tried to have his campaign funded by Taiwanese businessmen in exchange for the promise of acknowledging Taiwan diplomatically. Sata was reprimanded by the head of the Electoral Commission of Zambia (ECZ) for stirring-up racial sentiments. Sata also promised to introduce legislation that would allow foreigners to hold only 51% of a Zambian company. In a final attempt to get votes, Sata declared that he would stop all corruption charges against former President Chiluba and his friends. In exchange for this promise, Chiluba called on his supporters to vote for Sata: in 2001 the latter had already supported Chiluba's failed attempt to change the constitution to allow for a third presidential term.

Partly due to the electoral alliances, only five candidates – down from 11 in 2001 – competed for the **presidency**, of which only three were expected to muster a substantial number of votes. President Mwanawasa clearly won the elections with 43% (1,177,846) of the vote, trailed by Michael Sata (PF) in second place with 29.4% (804,748) and Hakainde Hichilema (UDA) in third with 25.3% (693,772). The result was surprising inasmuch as at the beginning of the year nobody would have expected Sata to be in the position of a challenger, since he had won only 3.4% of the vote in 2001. In 2001, Mwanawasa had been elected with only 28.7% of the vote and by a narrow margin of only 34,000 votes, with (credible) widespread accusations of vote-rigging.

In the **parliamentary elections**, MMD won 73 seats with 43% of the vote, while PF repeated its dramatic gain with 21% and 43 seats (up from 2.76% and one seat in 2001) and UDA secured only 26 seats with 21.7% of the vote. The remaining seats were taken by NDF (one), ULP (two) and by independents (three seats). In two constituencies, the parliamentary elections had to be postponed because one of the candidates died shortly before the elections. Clearly the parties forming the UDA, which together had won 75 constituencies in 2001, lost out in the elections. With the president's prerogative to nominate eight additional MPs, who enjoy the same privileges as the 150 elected members, the MMD secured a safe majority in parliament.

The early announcement of some of the election results in urban constituencies put Sata in the lead, but this changed later when the rural results came in. In response, Sata supporters started rioting in Lusaka and Copperbelt towns for two days. The **violent crowds** felt betrayed and were reminded of the 2001 electoral shambles. An additional reason for the frustration on Sata's side was an awkward opinion poll by University of Zambia lecturers (based on urban areas only) that had put Sata in front with an unbelievable 52% in early September. A more reliable survey weeks before had forecast Sata as being fairly firmly in second place. Only Sata was able to stop the violence after some days, which he did by calling on his supporters to be calm and accept the result.

There were a number of remarkable points about the elections. By the end of the year no total results were available for the local government elections. The **voter turnout** was 70.8% of the registered voters (3,941,229), the highest percentage and absolute number since the return to multiparty elections. Local and international observers rated the election as generally **free and fair**, and, above all, a significant improvement on the 2001 elections, although they pointed out a number of necessary improvements for the future. The EU observers also mentioned the very low number of women candidates in all parties. It was evident that the ECZ under a new chairperson, Justice Irene C. Mambilima, had made a major effort to render the elections more credible, for example, by using 30,000 **transparent ballot boxes** for the first time. During previous elections, there had been many complaints about ballot boxes being stuffed with pre-marked ballot papers in favour of the ruling MMD. Another problem in former elections, allegations of double registration, was solved by using a centralised computer system: ECZ was able to detect about 2,000 double registrations. However, a number of problems remained, such as delays in opening several polling stations, while the collation, counting and transmission of results was not only delayed but full of inaccuracies, resulting in more than 50 electoral petitions.

A closer **analysis of the results** revealed several changes in the electorate. First, MMD experienced substantial losses in the northern part of the country, in the heartland of Bemba-speaking people (Northern and Luapula provinces), but gained substantially in North-western, Western and Eastern provinces. Second, PF won substantially in Northern and Luapula provinces at the cost of MMD, so the Bemba vote was split. Third, PF also won in the urban areas of the Copperbelt and all constituencies of Lusaka. These are areas with a substantial number of formally employed workers where MMD used to find its support, but also among petty traders, etc. This means Sata was successful with his xenophobic social 'agenda' mainly in the multiethnic setting of towns. Fourth, UDA was reduced to an alliance of Southern and partly Eastern provinces. Fifth, most significantly UNIP, the former state party, experienced dramatic losses in Eastern province where the party used to have its regional stronghold after democratisation. In 2001, UNIP had gained 35% of the vote, winning 12 of 19 constituencies in that province. Now UNIP, in alliance with UPND and FDD – the latter also had its stronghold in Eastern province (26% and 5 constituencies in 2001) – gained only four of the 19 constituencies, the remaining 15 going to MMD. The four UDA seats were evenly shared between UNIP and FDD in Eastern province. This very likely signified not only the end of UNIP as a regional party but also perhaps the end of an era. Sixth, UPND was confined to its traditional stronghold in Southern province and proved in the end to be a Tonga party.

Mwanawasa's **new cabinet**, which was not reduced in size, did not represent a major surprise, apart from the new vice-president, Rupiah Banda (69), a veteran politician and a member of Mwanawasa's campaign team in Eastern province, whence he also originated. A number of ministers were completely new because some previous ministers did not make it back into parliament. At least five ministers retained their posts, the most prominent being Minister of Finance Ng'andu Magande, while another six were shifted to different ministries.

Mwanawasa's **anti-corruption drive** lost further credibility. The efforts lasting more than four years to investigate and try members of Chiluba's administration have resulted in hardly any major convictions, with three exceptions. After two failed trials, a final court case against former President Chiluba commenced without him, because a court ruled in November that he was unfit to stand trial. After some haggling, the government allowed him to travel to South Africa for treatment. Local civil society organisations such as Transparency International Zambia as well as newspapers denounced the government policy as 'fighting corruption with rhetoric' and demanded a proper anti-corruption strategy that would include the present government and administration, and not only the past. The fate of the Task Force Against Corruption, whose mandate expired at the end of the year, remained unclear.

Foreign Affairs

The president's severe illness as well as the election campaign slowed down foreign policy activities. The president launched the first **national defence policy** (13 June), which emphasised the country's commitment to promoting peace and security, advancing military cooperation, non-aggression, non-interference in the internal affairs of other states and advocating peaceful settlement of disputes. The plan did not specify any external threat but identified internal risks in the form of "politically inspired strikes, demonstrations, growth of organised crime, armed robbery . . . ultra nationalist and secessionist tendencies . . . designed to destabilise the country."

Zambia's **dual membership in SADC and COMESA** has come under pressure. In January, the government announced it had started studying which of the unions would be best for Zambia. In the end, the country would belong to only one. However, on the 12th anniversary of COMESA (8 December) the Zambian vice-president reaffirmed the country's commitment to the customs union, which has its headquarters in Lusaka. Critically, he pointed out that other countries have benefited more from COMESA than Zambia has, for it has become the recipient of goods from other countries with negative effects on local industries.

On 23 January, Mwanawasa signed the **APRM** under NEPAD at the 4th summit of the APR forum held in Khartoum. The implication is that Zambia will participate in the process and that its democratisation will be voluntarily scrutinised through a series of studies. Zambia was the 26th member of the AU to join the initiative.

In May, an old **border problem with Malawi** re-emerged when Zambian authorities discovered that the beacons in the Chama-Lundazi border area (Eastern province) marking the border line had been wilfully removed by Malawians. At the same time, a Malawian was accused of 'grabbing' 71.5 hectares of land that was being cultivated by 265 Malawian workers. The incident signified an unresolved border dispute about the demarcation line between the two countries. When Malawi's President Bingu wa Mutharika visited Lusaka for the celebration of Zambia's Independence Day (24 October) he committed himself to demarcating the international boundary between the two countries. He commended the close cooperation between the two countries, to be institutionalised through regular meetings of the joint permanent commission of cooperation. He was also satisfied with the Zambian government's commitment to complete the Mchinji-Chiapata railway line that crosses the border of the two countries. The line is part of the Nacala development corridor, which will link Zambia and Malawi with the Indian Ocean port of Nacala (Mozambique).

In a major move to improve infrastructural and trading links with its neigbours, the president together with his counterparts from Zimbabwe and Botswana signed an 'historic agreement' during a **visit in Harare** (28 August). This took the form of a memorandum of understanding on the construction of a bridge across the Zambezi river at Kazungula (Southern province), where currently there is only a ferry.

A couple of weeks later, Mwanawasa commissioned the construction of Chembe bridge across Luapula river (Luapula province), which will ease contacts with the DR Congo. The bridge will be constructed by a Chinese company with support from the Chinese government. The Chinese government and corporations are also involved in the planned privatisation and rehabilitation of the major infrastructural link with Tanzania, the Tanzania-Zambia Railway (TAZARA), linking Kapiri Mposhi and Dar es Salaam, the Indian Ocean harbour. The 1,860 km long railway, Zambia's most important connection to the sea and once financed by an interest-free loan and built by China (1970–75), is dilapidated and has been in deficit for many years. A private Chinese company, selected by the Chinese government, is supposed to run TAZARA. The railway line is crucial for the transporting of Zambian copper to the coast for shipment to China. The good relationship between Zambia and Tanzania was underlined when Mwanawasa attended mainland Tanzania's 45th independence anniversary on 9 December.

Early in September, however, cordial **Chinese-Zambian relations** were strained when Beijing's ambassador 'intervened' in an 'unacceptable' way in the Zambian elections, according to local commentators and trade union leaders. The ambassador had threatened to cut ties with Zambia and stop Chinese investments if Michael Sata, the leader of the opposition PF, won the elections. The stark reaction by the Chinese ambassador was triggered by Sata's announcement that, once he had been elected president, he would expel Chinese, Lebanese and Indian entrepreneurs from Zambia. Although these were not the remarks of a government official but of an opposition politician, the president was swift to apologise to the Chinese government during talks with the ambassador. To counter-balance the poor image of Chinese investors, the two countries signed a memorandum of understanding on harmonising labour relations. The Zambian government's understanding was that this will enhance working conditions in businesses run by Chinese in Zambia.

The president, together with more than 40 other African leaders, attended the **Forum on the China-Africa Cooperation** (FOCAC) in Beijing, 4–5 November, to celebrate the 50th anniversary of Sino-African relations. During the visit, Zambia was granted a debt cancellation of $ 211 m. In addition, Zambian representatives concluded an agreement with the

China Non-Ferrous Metal Mining Company (CNFC) on the construction of a new smelter at the CNFC-owned Chambishi mine (worth $ 200 m, and allegedly good for 1,000 jobs). The mine, privatised to CNFC in 1998, had become notorious for the strained Chinese-Zambian relations on the ground and for poor working conditions, after 46 workers had been killed in an unexplained explosion (2005), and again in July when six workers were shot and wounded during **riots over wages**. Zambia also got Chinese support to construct a modern stadium for the 2010 soccer World Cup.

The new Vice-President Rupiah Banda participated in the newly established **Africa-South America summit** held in Abuja, Nigeria, on 30 November. In August, the president attended the SADC heads of state and government meeting in Lesotho.

At the end of November, Zambia, Angola and the UNHCR signed an agreement to assist the voluntary **repatriation** of about 60,000 Angolan refugees still in Zambia. Earlier in the year, many of them had experienced a food crisis. These refugees are the remainder of the more than 400,000 people who had fled the civil war in Angola.

Socioeconomic Developments

Despite the elections and worries about unrestrained expenditure resulting in an increasing deficit, macro indicators of economic and financial development proved to be another success story. The **annual budget**, under the promising title "From Sacrifice to Equitable Wealth Creation", delivered on 3 February by Finance Minister Ng'andu Magande, clearly indicated strict austerity policies to comply with conditions laid down by the IMF and international donors. Major austerity measures were a freeze on public sector pay (public sector wages to be not more than 8% of GDP) – which caused national labour protests – and a rise in domestic revenue through increased income taxes on higher incomes.

Civil society organisations viewed the budget as a 'mixture of pain and relief', as it increased the allocations for health and education but failed to lay out a clear policy for job creation. Trade union leaders called it a 'betrayal of workers'. According to government information, in the education sector 7,100 new teachers were recruited and pupil enrolment in elementary schools increased by 13.1%, among other improvements. In the **health sector**, more than 700 additional personnel were employed and a number of new health posts and health centres were either constructed or commenced. However, the increased investment in the health sector contributed little to solving the 'crisis of health staff', as there were only 600 doctors available for a population of almost 11 m, only one doctor for 18,000 Zambians. In addition, the shortfall of 8,000 nurses remained unresolved. To ease the burden of the rural poor, the government scrapped user fees for health care in rural areas. The reintroduction of free health care for these people was made possible by the debt cancellation under the HIPC initiative.

Most of the **economic and financial targets** outlined in the budget were achieved. Real GDP growth increased again, from 5.2% in the previous year to 5.8%, but missed the 6%

target. The fight against inflation took a major step forward when the annual rate was brought down to 8.2%, below the 10% target, as compared to 15.9% in 2005. This was the lowest level of inflation in the last 30 years. On the income side, the government failed to achieve its aim. Domestic revenues remained at Zambian kwacha (ZK) 6,600.7 bn, while the target was ZK 6,959.8 bn. According to the government, this shortfall was mainly due to under-collection of value added tax and excise duty.

The **economic performance** was driven by the mining sector, with an 11.8% growth rate (2005: 7.9%), construction at 9% (2005: 21.2%) and the transport sector at 13.4% (2005: 11%). The fuel supply was stable after problems at the Indeni oil refinery were solved. These had caused a fuel shortage for three weeks in 2005. After the partial drought in the previous season, agricultural growth recovered by 3.9%. A bumper harvest of 1.4 m metric tonnes of maize was recorded as compared to 0.87 m during the 2004–05 season. The government attributed this success not only to favourable weather conditions but also to improved provisions of credit, fertiliser and food security packs for the 800,000 small-scale farmers.

External economic relations remained problematic, although the trade balance continued with a surplus of $ 1,176 m compared to only $ 10 m in 2005. The surplus was mainly due to record world market prices for copper, which led to an increase in export earnings by 77.3% to $ 3.9 bn, up from $ 2.2 bn in 2005 (imports were $ 2.7 bn). Income from non-traditional exports (tobacco, cotton, sugar, maize seeds, electrical cables) increased by 29.3%. Overall, the current account deficit remained at about $ 780 m and was financed by foreign direct investments, project grants and portfolio inflows.

The kwacha experienced strong appreciation against the US dollar. While the **currency** had been at about ZK 4,300 and ZK 4,700 to $ 1 in previous years, it climbed to about ZK 3,500 over 2006. The strong kwacha was caused by the weak dollar, strong copper exports, donor support and the substantial debt relief.

As a result of the **HIPC debt relief** granted in 2005, the government was able to proclaim that the country was 'no more a Heavily Indebted Poor Country'. It recorded a reduction by 86.7% of the country's external debt stock, down from $ 4.5 bn (2005) to $ 635 m. The foreign debt service was lessened to $ 33.9 m, down from $ 373.2 m (2004).

One of the last **privatisation** projects, the 'private sector participation' (as it is officially called) in the crucial TAZARA railway, made substantial progress. In October, based on a World Bank-sponsored study and one commissioned by the Chinese government, the two governments involved, Zambia and Tanzania, decided to grant a concession to run the railway line to a Chinese company that had been identified by the Chinese government. The conditions of the contract were still to be negotiated.

On 24 July, the government made public the **Fifth National Development Plan** (FNDP) for 2006–10. The plan aimed at broad-based wealth and job creation "through citizenry participation and technological advancement." The strategic focus is development of the economic infrastructure and human resources. FNDP is part of 'Vision 2030', a first long-term plan in which government declared its very ambitious target to build "a prosperous Middle Income Country by the Year 2030", to reduce hunger and poverty plus foster a competitive and outward-oriented economy. The government indicated that the long-term goals would require growth rates beyond the average 4.7% that had been achieved over the past five years.

Gero Erdmann

Zimbabwe

Zimbabwe began the year with a split opposition. Intra-opposition animosity, coupled with the traditional tension between the major political parties, meant that the political scene did not rise above bickering, scapegoating and mudslinging among the major players. The economy continued its downward trend. This was matched by the state's zeal to arrest the decline. The social scene saw no improvement from the sharp decline of the previous year. Zimbabwe's alienation from the West was hugely compensated for by the continuing drive to look to the East and the public support of most of Africa. The relationship with major multilateral agencies remained mixed.

Domestic Politics

The split in the major opposition party, the Movement for Democratic Change (MDC), was confirmed with the holding of separate congresses by the two factions. On 1 February, the 'pro-senate' faction elected Arthur Mutambara, a former student leader, as its president. On 16 March, the much bigger 'anti-senate' faction re-elected Morgan Tsvangirai as its leader. By the end of the year, despite much speculation on talks about reconciliation between the two factions, unity had not materialised.

On 27 May, Lovemore Madhuku and other leaders of the **National Constitutional Assembly** (NCA) changed the constitution of the country's largest pro-democracy group, resulting in their retaining control. Government and sections of civil society condemned the move, pointing out that the NCA had lost the moral authority to condemn President Mugabe's putative desire to remain in power forever.

In a **by-election** in the Harare constituency of Budiriro on 21 May, the Tsvangirai faction of the MDC won, brushing aside challenges from both the Mutambara faction and ZANU-PF. On 7 October, ZANU-PF won a by-election in Chikomba constituency, beating the MDC (Tsvangirai). ZANU-PF won another by-election in Rushinga, defeating the same MDC faction. In **rural district council elections** on 21 September, ZANU-PF won 403 of the 1,277 wards unopposed after opposition parties failed to field candidates for the elections slated for 28 October. Opposition parties claimed that their candidates had been unfairly disqualified or had been prevented from presenting their nomination papers by violent ZANU-PF supporters.

The perennial **factionalism in the ruling ZANU-PF** was significantly muted during the year. It only became apparent at the party's annual congress (8–10 December). The resolution to postpone the 2008 presidential elections to 2010 could not be adopted, reportedly because not all provincial branches were in favour of the motion. Reports linked the positions for and against the resolution to the two main factions within the party. The resolution was subsequently referred to the party's central committee. Those who favoured the postponement justified the proposal in the name of harmonising parliamentary and presidential elections, to ease the administrative burdens and save money. Opponents of the proposal, including civil society and the opposition, saw this as a ploy to extend President Mugabe's term by two years by dodging the 2008 elections. ZANU-PF's succession politics was complicated by speculation surrounding the poor health of Vice-President Joseph Msika: persistent rumours of his impending retirement clouded the issue further.

In a sign of **increasing uneasiness within ZANU-PF**, it was reported on 14 July that the party was planning a major cleansing exercise to remove elements seen to be tarnishing the party's image with bad behaviour. President Mugabe told the central committee that the elements who were "wanting to enrich themselves are increasing in number" and that "some people are just being crookish *[sic]*." Speaking at the 23rd ZANU-PF national consultative assembly on 15 July, President Mugabe said there were stories circulating regarding the succession issue, with reports that some people had resorted to consulting witchdoctors for guidance. He said succession would be decided by the people of Zimbabwe.

On 9 May, the **power struggle within ZANU-PF** over succession was brought to the high court in a case in which the former state information minister, Jonathan Moyo, was suing two senior party members, ZANU-PF Chairperson John Nkomo and senior politburo member Dumiso Dabengwa, for defaming him when they allegedly told Mugabe that Professor Moyo had funded and led the hatching of a 'coup plot' against Mugabe in 2004.

Corruption was a topical issue during 2006. On 20 September, the industry and international trade minister, Mpofu, sensationally told a parliamentary committee that there was a report that implicated senior politicians in the looting of Ziscosteel, the steelmaking parastatal. He later denied ever making the statement and the existence of the report. In November, Matonga, the deputy information minister, was arraigned on corruption charges in a scandal that sucked in Chombo, the local government minister.

On 16 May, President Mugabe swore in seven commissioners of the reconstituted **Zimbabwe Electoral Commission** (ZEC) in a move that would see the Electoral Supervisory Commission (ESC) merging with ZEC in accordance with the 2005 constitutional amendments, creating a single body to run all elections and referendums in the country.

In **local government**, on 16 June, the government for the fourth consecutive time reappointed Sekesai Makwavarara and four members of the commission running the city of Harare for a further six months. The opposition and civil society, particularly the combined Harare residents' association, condemned the decision, accusing government of imposing an unelected body on Harare residents because it was afraid of democratic elections.

Public protests increased in the major cities, with government responding with force in each case. This spawned accusations of repression and the **violation of basic constitutional freedoms**. Government defended itself by stressing that it was enforcing the rule of law. On 3 May, police in Bulawayo arrested more than 170 women and school children for demonstrating against an increase in tuition fees in schools and tertiary institutions. The demonstrators belonged to the Women of Zimbabwe Arise (WOZA) protest group, known for tenaciously staging similar demonstrations in cities and towns over the worsening economic situation in Zimbabwe. In March, the MDC (Tsvangirai) announced that it would mount a **campaign of resistance** during the winter. Tsvangirai threatened to lead mass demonstrations in late June and July in a bid to dislodge President Mugabe from power.

On 1 June, MDC (Tsvangirai) claimed that over the previous week at least 13 families had been forced to flee their rural homes in a fresh wave of **political violence** by militant ZANU-PF supporters. On 5 July, police arrested an opposition legislator, Willas Madzimure, accusing him of inciting Harare residents to revolt against the government. About 200 vendors were arrested in Bulawayo after demonstrating against harassment by city authorities. They were released without charge on 7 July. On 13 September, the secretary-general of the Zimbabwe Congress of Trade Unions (ZCTU), Wellington Chibebe, and 15 others were arrested in Harare for holding a demonstration that the government had earlier banned. Defence lawyers said the people were assaulted "excessively and brutally" during arrest. Security forces put up roadblocks sealing off the capital and were out in force in other major towns, forcing the ZCTU to announce an end to the demonstrations that had been organised to protest against the deteriorating economy as well as demanding higher wages, lower taxes and more medicine to combat HIV/AIDS. President Mugabe rejected widespread international condemnation of the assaults on the trade unionists, saying his government had no apologies to make.

While government continued its tight grip on the **print and electronic media**, save for verbal threats, attacks and litigation or threats of litigation, there was a considerable let-up on the state's assault on the private press. But in what was seen as continuing disregard for freedom of expression, the state continued its clampdown on private broadcasting. On 26 June, it was reported that government, using technology acquired from China, had been able to partially jam the signal from the Washington-based Voice of America's Studio 7 radio station. On the same day, SW Radio Africa, a UK-based Zimbabwean radio station, claimed its signal was also being jammed in Harare. Government considered the private radio stations hostile and illegal.

On 26 May, government gazetted the **Interception of Communications Bill**. It sought to establish a communications centre to monitor and intercept certain communications in the course of their transmission through a telecommunication, postal or any other related service. The transport and communications minister would be empowered to issue an interception warrant to authorised persons where there were reasonable grounds to believe that a serious offence had been or was being or would probably be committed or that there was a threat to safety or national security. The warrant issued by the minister would be valid for three months. The Media Institute of Southern Africa urged the African Commission on Human and People's Rights (ACHPR) to pressure government not to pass the controversial law.

State-church relations were in the limelight throughout the year. On 23 March, the Zimbabwe Council of Churches (ZCC) produced a **pastoral letter** that was distributed amongst member churches and other stakeholders. Among other issues, the controversial letter addressed the socioeconomic and political climate in the country, rising corruption, land reform and constitutional issues. On 25 May, President Mugabe met church leaders from ZCC, the Zimbabwe Catholic Bishops Conference (ZCBC) and the Evangelical Fellowship of Zimbabwe (EFZ) at state house. After the meeting, the clergymen expressed support for government saying that their five-hour meeting with Mugabe had resulted in agreement that the church and government must play complementary roles and should not be regarded as competitors or rivals. Apparently at the president's suggestion, the church leaders deferred the national prayer day to 25 June.

In a move that indicated the **diverging viewpoints in the church** on how to deal with the state, the meeting was publicly condemned by the more radical Zimbabwe Christian Alliance (ZCA). It was claimed that insiders had said the decision to cancel the prayer day was spurred by the fear that the pro-opposition ZCA would take over the proceedings. On 25 June, the organisations that had earlier met the president held the national day of prayer with President Mugabe as guest of honour. Critics saw this as a political ploy to divide the church. President Mugabe urged churches to help state efforts to revive the country's economy: he warned that priests who dabbled in politics could face a "vicious" backlash. On 18 September, the churches produced a document entitled "The Zimbabwe We Want: Towards a National Vision for Zimbabwe." Significantly, the document recommended the drafting of a new constitution and the institution of widespread reforms. Mugabe personally received a copy of the document, but dismissed the need for a new constitution.

On 6 March, police claimed to have unearthed an **arms cache** in the eastern city of Mutare. They arrested a white ex-Rhodesian soldier Peter Hitschmann and two ex-policemen. Top MDC (Tsvangirai) officials – including Mutare North MP Giles Mutsekwa and former Chimanimani MP Roy Bennett – were arrested over the cache of what the state described as arms of war. Bennett later escaped to South Africa, while charges against Mutsekwa were dropped. By the end of the year, Hitschmann was still in custody. While government stressed that the discovery revealed the MDC's terroristic agenda to unseat government violently, critics dismissed the alleged arms cache as a political gimmick by the state.

Police executed controversial operations around the country. In a move reminiscent of 'Operation Murambatsvina', on 12 May, as part of a fresh clean-up operation code-named '**Operation Round Up**', police in Harare rounded up 10,224 people, many of them street children, squatters, vagrants, touts and what the authorities called 'disorderly elements' whom they planned to send to rural areas. On 21 November, in conjunction with the Reserve Bank of Zimbabwe, police launched '**Operation Chikorokoza Chapera/Isitsheketsha Sesiphelile**' to deal with illegal mining. It was prompted by rampant smuggling of precious stones and environmental degradation in mining areas. By the end of the year, police had arrested more than 16,000 people.

On 30 June the Domestic Violence Bill was gazetted. The legislation aimed to afford victims of domestic violence the maximum protection the law could provide and to introduce measures to ensure that the relevant organs of state gave full effect to the provisions of the law.

Foreign Affairs

Relations with **African countries** and organisations remained largely good, with most leaders supporting Zimbabwe in its squabbles with the West: the quarrel was reduced to the West's opposition to Zimbabwe's land reform programme. On 2 May, President Mugabe arrived in **Malawi** on a state visit. He was granted the freedom of Blantyre and had a road named after him, a move that angered some civil society groups in Malawi. Mugabe visited **Uganda** to attend the inauguration of President Museveni on 12 May.

President Mugabe attended and addressed the 14th summit of the **Non-Aligned Movement** (NAM) in Havana, Cuba (11–16 September). In his address he highlighted "the evils of a uni-polar world; a world that is characterised by unilateralism at the expense of multilateralism." On 20 September, he addressed the 61st session of the **UN General Assembly** in New York. He condemned the 'illegal sanctions' by some Western countries against Zimbabwe. On 5 December, President Mugabe arrived in Khartoum, Sudan to attend the 5th **ACP** summit. In his address on 7 December, he said ACP states should stand together in denouncing practices by powerful nations that are in defiance of international law.

At the end of March, President Teodoro Obiang Nguema of **Equatorial Guinea** paid a state visit to Zimbabwe. The visit did not result in a widely expected oil deal that could ease Zimbabwe's energy crisis. Instead, Obiang invited Zimbabwean businessmen to visit Equatorial Guinea to explore possible business opportunities. President Jakaya Kikwete of **Tanzania** paid a state visit, during which he officially opened the 47th Zimbabwe international trade fair in Bulawayo on 29 April. He urged Zimbabwe and Tanzania to concentrate on their efforts to fight against poverty and disease.

Relations with **South Africa** continued to be mixed. On 24 May, responding to reports from London quoting South African President Thabo Mbeki as saying the UN held the key to solving "an economic and political crisis" in Zimbabwe, the secretary for information and publicity said the Zimbabwe Government was unaware of any UN intervention on Harare. On 19 May, the South African government denied the treasurer-general of the MDC (Tsvangirai) Roy Bennett **asylum** on the grounds that his application lacked merit and he did not face any danger in Zimbabwe.

On 14 July, it was reported that President Mugabe would seek the support of regional heads of state to fund **mediation efforts**, led by former Tanzanian President Benjamin Mkapa, between Zimbabwe and Britain. Diplomatic sources said Zimbabwe was lobbying the region to endorse the initiative when it was tabled at the **SADC summit** in August in Maseru, Lesotho. Contrary to expectations, the SADC did not publicly confront Mugabe over Zimbabwe's political and economic problems. Mugabe reportedly left Maseru without signing the finance and investment protocol, reportedly after Zimbabwe had been pencilled-in for deliberation in a closed-door session. Zimbabwe denied that it had ever been on the agenda. According to an EU communiqué, at the **EU-SADC ministerial troika** in Maseru on 17 November, the EU raised concerns about the deteriorating situation in Zimbabwe and its spill-over effects in the region. SADC indicated its "continuing support to Zimbabwe in finding solutions to improve the situation and underlined the need for continuous, constructive engagement with . . . Zimbabwe."

Relations with multilateral organisations never improved. On 24 May, it was announced that **UN** Secretary-General Kofi Annan was no longer expected to visit Zimbabwe to assess the impact of 'Operation Murambatsvina' because the purpose of the invitation had fallen away. On 31 May, Annan said he still planned to visit Zimbabwe. Annan held talks with Mugabe in the course of the 25 June-2 July biennial AU summit in Gambia. He announced afterwards that he would no longer be travelling to Zimbabwe. Annan said Mugabe had informed him that former Tanzanian President Mkapa was already mediating, albeit between Zimbabwe and former colonial ruler Britain, rather than between government and the opposition.

On 26 May, in London, during a visit that was part of a diplomatic offensive, Tsvangirai called for **UN intervention** in the southern African country's political and economic crises. He rejected claims by government earlier that week that there was no need for UN involvement in Zimbabwe. On 13 June, the government rejected a recommendation by the UN Committee for Development Policy (CDP) that the country be downgraded to **LDC status**. In a letter to the CDP, government said it would not consent to being downgraded. On 15 February, Zimbabwe revealed that it had paid off its debt to the IMF ahead of the March deadline. Zimbabwe had made a final payment of $ 9 m to clear its debt with the IMF general resource account. On 8 March, the IMF executive board, however, upheld sanctions against Zimbabwe since the country still had overdue obligations to the Fund's PRGF amounting to $ 119 m.

The country remained **ostracised by the West**, towards which it also maintained its hostile attitude. On 29 June, President Mugabe scoffed at reports of initiatives by some Western countries to come up with a rescue plan for Zimbabwe. He said Zimbabwe was suffering but did not need rescuing, although it would welcome financial assistance. He insisted Zimbabwe was not about to die and would "not die ever". He said what Zimbabwe needed was "just and lawful treatment by the Western world, a recognition that it is a full, sovereign country which has the right to own and control its own resources, the right to chart its own destiny unhindered." On 14 July, while marking the French national holiday, **France's ambassador** to Zimbabwe urged government to mend relations with its own population before launching international initiatives. On 30 January, the European Commission announced that the **EU** had extended targeted sanctions against Zimbabwe for another year. The sanctions included an arms embargo, travel bans on top officials and a freeze on their financial assets. The target list included President Mugabe and more than 100 ministers and senior ZANU-PF officials. On 28 February, **US** President George Bush extended by one year a series of sanctions against Zimbabwean officials, including President Mugabe, for undermining democracy.

On 26 May, it was reported that President Mugabe was pushing for talks with **British Prime Minister** Tony Blair to resolve the current crisis and had roped in former Tanzanian President Mkapa to act as mediator. On 5 July, the British foreign office said that mediation between Britain and Zimbabwe was not required, as Harare's problems did not arise from a bilateral dispute. On 8 October, **Swedish Ambassador** to Zimbabwe Sten Rylander admitted he now had little enthusiasm to 'build bridges' between Zimbabwe and the EU. When he had arrived earlier in the year, the envoy was optimistic that he could influence normalisation of strained relations between the two parties. The basis of his optimism was a long conversation with President Mugabe on 16 February when he presented his credentials. On 17 May, Britain denied asylum to fugitive former high court judge **Benjamin Paradza**. He found refuge in New Zealand. He had been jailed *in absentia* for three years for corruption after skipping bail, alleging political persecution.

The country's '**Look East**' policy suffered a snag. On 12 May, it was reported that **Chinese companies** assigned to a number of projects in the country were abandoning the sites because of non-payment. RBZ Governor Gideon Gono left for **Russia** on 31 May, hardly a month after visiting Moscow and just over a week after returning from **South Korea**, in search of an economic rescue package. On 9 October, Zimbabwe signed five memorandums of understanding with Russia on trade, investment and economic cooperation worth $ 300 m. The agreements followed talks with a 48-member Russian delegation, which included the businesspeople and journalists that had arrived in the country the previous week to explore investment opportunities in Zimbabwe's various economic sectors. It turned out that the agreements might have been hoaxes. It later emerged that the 'business delegation' and the businesses it represented were virtually unknown in Russia. On 9 October, the ministry of health and child welfare received drugs worth $ 50,000 from **South Korea**, which were expected to augment supplies at state health institutions. On 19 November, President Mugabe made a four-day state visit to Iran. He said that Zimbabwe and Iran "think alike [and] should fight against Western superpowers and their evil systems." He secured fuel deals.

Vice-President Joice Mujuru left for **China** on 8 June to garner support for Zimbabwe's economic revival. Mrs. Mujuru, who was accompanied by a high-powered delegation of government officials and the country's business sector, was said to be seeking support for the National Economic Development Priority Programme (NEDPP). Reports on 14 June revealed that government ministries and companies had signed **deals with Chinese firms** for the supply of broadcast transmission, irrigation, tillage and construction equipment. On 19 June, the China Development Bank (CDB) reportedly expressed willingness to help Zimbabwe with its economic recovery programme. President Mugabe was one of 35 African heads of state at the 4–5 November Beijing Summit of the Forum on China-Africa Cooperation (FOCAC). During one-to-one talks with Mugabe, Chinese President Jintao described China's expanding relationship with Zimbabwe as an "unshakeable policy".

Socioeconomic Developments

Economic indicators did not improve. **Inflation**, which had been about 400% in November 2005, edged over 600% in January. It began to soar after government revealed that it had paid the IMF $ 221 m to cover arrears that threatened Zimbabwe's membership. On 16 February, government admitted that it had printed at least Z $ 21 trillion in currency to buy the US dollars to pay off the debt. By March, inflation had risen 914% a year. In April, inflation crossed the 1,000% threshold. By the end of the year, the consumer price index was 1,033.5%. According to Economist Intelligence Unit estimates, the GDP closed the year at $ 4.19 bn, down from $ 4.28 bn the previous year. The decline in the real GDP slowed down to -4.4%, from -7.7% in 2005. The current accounts balance improved from -$ 569.5 m to -$ 297.8 m, while foreign exchange reserves excluding gold fell from $ 155 m in 2005 to $ 135 m.

The total **external debt** rose from $ 4.9 bn to $ 5.3 bn. Figures from the RBZ revealed that government domestic debt, which had marginally declined since the beginning of the year, increased by more than Z$ 2 trillion to settle at Z$ 15.7 trillion in March. On 13 July, President Mugabe told a group of journalists from the state media and Reuters that Zimbabwe was besieged by its enemies, but that his government would survive an escalating crisis he blamed on sabotage by former colonial ruler Britain. Mugabe admitted to being "very worried" about Zimbabwe's economic crisis.

On 7 May, government surprisingly announced that the **unemployment rate** in the country was less than 9%, this being in contrast to other estimates that put the rate at over 80%. Government insisted that the figure reflected the real definition of unemployment as comprising people who were actively looking for employment. Experts and critics dismissed the figure as unrealistic, with sceptics pointing out the fact that people were not actively looking for employment was an indication of loss of confidence and hope in the economy. On 28 April, government announced **massive pay hikes** of over 300% for civil servants. This was seen as an attempt to pre-empt the mass protest planned by the MDC (Tsvangirai) scheduled for winter. Inflation was then at 913.6%. The salary increases were set to push up the government's wage bill to well over 50% of GDP.

There was much of activity in **economic and fiscal policy**. In mid-April, government launched another economic revival programme, the NEDPP, the 7th economic recovery plan since 1991. NEDPP was formulated by the government through the Zimbabwe national security council chaired by President Mugabe. The $ 2.5 bn programme sought, among other things, to arrest inflation, stabilise the exchange rate and raise agricultural production. On 31 July, RBZ Governor Gideon Gono announced a 60% **devaluation** of the Zimbabwean dollar from 101,000 to 250,000 to the US dollar. Presenting his mid-term monetary policy review statement, Gono also announced a currency reform by dropping three zeros from the country's bearer cheques.

He announced the introduction of a new family of bearer cheques that would be in circulation following the move to drop the three zeros. The change was also aimed at compelling individuals and companies to bring in billions of dollars stashed away in safes and at combating the burgeoning black market in currency. The deadline for switching to the **new currency** was 21 August. On 9 October, the RBZ banned 16 money transfer agencies for 'deviant behaviour'. The RBZ also announced tough measures to force commercial banks to lend money to agriculture and other key sectors of the economy. It decreed that banks should, with immediate effect, lend 30% to the farming sector, 15% to mining and 10% each to manufacturing, tourism and small- and medium-scale enterprises.

The Z$ 4.6-trillion 2007 **budget** was presented on 30 November. The budget would have a projected deficit of Z$ 1.6 trillion. Government increased the tax-free threshold to Z$ 100,000 – up from Z$ 20,000 – with effect from January 2007. This would release an extra Z$ 430 m into taxpayers' hands. The new figure fell short of the Z$ 175,000 suggested by stakeholders during the pre-budget consultative process. In what commentators regarded as an unrealistic projection, government set an annual **inflation target** of between 350% and 400%, with a possible drop to below 10% by the end of 2008. The minister set the target real GDP growth at between 0.5% and 1%.

On 30 May, the RBZ secured and signed a one-year deal with a European bank, BNP Paribas, and a South African financial institution, Loita Capital Partners, for a $ 50 m **revolving fund to import fuel**. According to the RBZ chief, the loan deal had been "secured and leveraged" with mineral exports from Zimbabwe's largest nickel producer, Bindura Nickel Corporation, and had been underwritten by two private Zimbabwean commercial banks.

The country's **educational and heath** delivery system continued to experience problems of staffing, equipment and funding. On 4 July, medical aid societies and clinics hiked fees by between 85% and 100%, putting the cost of health care beyond the reach of many Zimbabweans. The increases came barely three months after private hospitals and clinics had effected a 240% hike in consultation fees. The fee hike would see individuals on medical aid forking out an average of Z$ 4 m every month, up from about Z$ 2.5 m. On 13 July, junior doctors went on strike demanding better salaries and working conditions. The strike action brought operations to a standstill at the two largest public hospitals, which reportedly turned away hundreds of patients seeking treatment. Zimbabwe continued to experience one of the harshest **HIV/AIDS** epidemics in the world. About one-fifth of its adult population was living with HIV and an estimated 565 adults and children were infected every day. However, there was evidence that Zimbabwe's HIV prevalence had genuinely fallen. Some 50,000 of an estimated 500,000 Zimbabweans in need of anti-retroviral drugs received them from state institutions.

On July 7, Bulawayo city council reported that 33 people, 28 of them children below the age of four, had died of **malnutrition-related illnesses** in March alone. The deaths brought to 110 the total number of people who had reportedly died in the city because of malnutrition-related diseases in just the first three months of the year. Critics interpreted this as a shocking illustration of the humanitarian crisis unfolding in Zimbabwe after six years of acute food shortages and economic and political turmoil. In the first two months, 77 malnutrition-related deaths had been recorded in Bulawayo. On 7 June, statistics released by the consumer council of Zimbabwe reported that the **cost of living** for a family of six for the month of May had surged to Z$ 49.1 m, up by 19.5% from the April figure of Z$ 41 m. The figure closed the year at Z$ 245,500 (revalued) (Z$ 245.5 m old currency). In an effort to enforce **price controls**, in late November, police arrested two managers of Lobels, a private company, for flouting price control regulations by raising the price of bread without government approval. On 30 November, the two were jailed for an effective four months each for unilaterally increasing the price of bread.

In a new twist to **land reform**, on 1 June, government announced that it would evict about 4,000 black farmers who had illegally occupied commercial farms and conservancies in Masvingo province. On 26 June, there were reports that government was reneging on a pledge to invite white farmers back to work the land and was moving to evict the few who were still on the farms. Scores of eviction notices were delivered to white farmers. Didymus Mutasa, the lands and security minister, told Western diplomats that he did not care if Zimbabwe's land remained unproductive "as long we [blacks] own it." On 4 May, the high court issued judgments ordering newly resettled farmers to return the farms to their owners. On 9 November, government issued the first batch of 99-year leases to beneficiaries of the controversial land reforms. On 10 June, Mutasa said government had begun paying out compensation to some of the country's displaced white farmers. He announced that the state was paying those who needed money, particularly those whose land fell under the Bilateral Investment and Protection Act.

There was unease in the **mining sector** after the 18 April confirmation by President Mugabe that government was moving to restructure mining ownership to increase the participation of blacks in the sector. On 1 June, President Mugabe allayed fears of mining companies about government threats to take over all mining companies in its indigenisation drive. He said the miners had nothing to fear, as government's aim was to economically empower black Zimbabweans. On 27 October, the Zimbabwe tourism authority reported that **tourist arrivals** had increased by 45% in the first nine months compared to the same period in 2005. The increase came from Africa and Asia. Arrivals from the West were down by 20%.

The **food situation** remained critical. On 8 May, it was reported that relief agencies had run out of food but could not appeal for more aid until government gave them the clearance. At risk were hundreds of thousands of widows, orphans, school children and AIDS patients. It was estimated that at least 3 m Zimbabweans (a quarter of the population) required food aid in the period leading up to the year's harvests. On 16 May, the agriculture minister said Zimbabwe was projected to harvest about 1.8 m metric tonnes of maize, of which 900,000 would be delivered to the Grain Marketing Board (GMB). On 14 June, it was reported that the government had stationed soldiers and police on roads leading into cities to prevent farmers from moving maize to the black market for the grain in urban areas and forcing them to sell to the state-owned GMB.

On 10 June, government reported that it had spent over Z$ 1.563 trillion on '**Operation Garikai/Hlalani Kuhle**' whose aim was the building of 3,325 houses for victims of the 2005 'Operation Murambatsvina'. Some 2,043 families reportedly benefited. An additional 30,000 residential stands were made available countrywide, with local authorities expected to expedite the allocation of the stands and the servicing of land. A revolving fund drawing money from payments by buyers reportedly stood at Z$ 9 bn. Some 170 factory shells built under the programme had been completed, while 344 vendor marts had become operational.

On **new legislation**, government gazetted the Petroleum Bill on 26 June. The legislation sought to establish a petroleum regulatory authority that would regulate and license persons in respect of retailing, producing and procuring petroleum products.

Amin Y. Kamete

List of Authors

Jon Abbink, Researcher, African Studies Centre, Leiden, Professor of Anthropology at the Free University of Amsterdam, The Netherlands

An Ansoms, Researcher, Institute of Development Policy and Management, University of Antwerp, Belgium

Matthias Basedau, Senior Researcher, Institute of African Affairs, German Institute of Global and Area Studies, Hamburg, Germany

Rémy Bazenguissa-Ganga, Lecturer, University of Lille, France

Linnea Bergholm, Research Candidate, University of Wales, Aberystwyth, Department of International Politics, United Kingdom

Heinrich Bergstresser, Media Consultant, Freelance Research Associate of the Institute of African Affairs in Hamburg, of the Friedrich Naumann Foundation and of InWent, Germany

Anders Bjørkelo, Research Director, Centre for Middle Eastern and Islamic Studies, University of Bergen, Bergen, Norway

John Daniel, Academic Coordinator of the School for International Training's programme in Reconciliation and Development in Durban, South Africa

Mirjam de Bruijn, Researcher, African Studies Centre, Leiden, The Netherlands

Qinisile Delwa, South African Participant of "Managing Global Governance" Programme by DIE and InWent and Research Intern at Institute for African Affairs, German Institute of Global and Area Studies, Hamburg, Germany

Lewis Dzimbiri, Senior Lecturer in Public Administration, University of Botswana, Gaborone, Botswana

Stephen Ellis, Researcher, African Studies Centre, Leiden, The Netherlands

Gero Erdmann, Senior Researcher, Institute of African Affairs, German Institute of Global and Area Studies, Hamburg, Germany

Jonas Ewald, Assistant Researcher, Centre for Africa Studies, Gothenburg University, Sweden

Sven Grimm, Research Fellow, German Development Institute, Bonn, Germany

Joseph Hanlon, Senior Lecturer, Development Policy and Practice, Open University, Milton Keynes, United Kingdom

Gerti Hesseling, Researcher, African Studies Centre, Leiden, Professor at the Study and Information Centre for Human Rights (SIM), University of Utrecht, The Netherlands

Kurt Hirschler, Freelance Political Scientist, Hamburg, Germany

Nicole Hirt, Freelance Research Associate, Institute of African Affairs, German Institute of Global and Area Studies and Senior Consultant at HACOS – "Horn of Africa Consultancy Service", Hamburg, Germany

Rolf Hofmeier, Former Director, Institute of African Affairs, German Institute of Global and Area Studies, Hamburg, Germany

Cord Jakobeit, Professor of International Relations, University of Hamburg, Germany

Amin Kamete, Senior Researcher, Nordic Africa Institute, Uppsala, Sweden

Steve Kibble, Regional Advocacy Coordinator, Africa Middle East Asia, Progressio, United Kingdom

Dirk Kohnert, Deputy Director, Institute of African Affairs, German Institute of Global and Area Studies, Hamburg, Germany

Piet Konings, Researcher, African Studies Centre, Leiden, The Netherlands

Bruno Losch, Senior Economist, Centre de Coopération Internationale en Recherche Agronomique pour le Développement, Montpellier, France

Sabine Luning, Lecturer Cultural Anthropology and Development Sociology, Leiden University, Leiden, The Netherlands

Roland Marchal, Senior Researcher, Centre National de Recherche Scientifique/Centre d'Etudes et de Recherches Internationales, Paris, France

Richard Marcus, Assistant Professor and Internship Director, International Studies Program California State University, Long Beach, USA

Cédric Mayrargue, Researcher, Centre d'Etudes d'Afrique Noire, Bordeaux, France

Mike McGovern, Assistant Professor of Anthropology, Yale University, USA

Andreas Mehler, Director, Institute of African Affairs, German Institute of Global and Area Studies, Hamburg, Germany

Henning Melber, Executive Director, The Dag Hammarskjöld Foundation, Uppsala, Sweden

Paul Nugent, Professor of Comparative African History and Director of the Centre of African Studies, University of Edinburgh, United Kingdom

Claes Olsson, Political Scientist and Editor at Global Publications Foundation, Uppsala, Sweden

Helena Olsson, MSc in political sciences and staff member at the Nordic Africa Institute, Uppsala, Sweden

Krijn Peters, Lecturer, Centre for Development Studies, Margam Building, University of Wales, Swansea, United Kingdom

Marina Rafti, Research Assistant, Institute of Development Policy and Management, University of Antwerp, Belgium

Marisha Ramdeen, Research Intern at the Human Sciences Research Council and MA student in political science at the University of KwaZulu Natal, South Africa

Marcel Rutten, Researcher, African Studies Centre, Leiden, The Netherlands

Abdoulaye Saine, Associate Professor in Political Science, Miami University of Ohio, Oxford, USA

Gerhard Seibert, Post-doctorate Fellow at the Instituto de Investigação Científica Tropical (IICT), Lisbon, Portugal

Roger Southall, Honorary Research Professor, Sociology of Work Unit, University of the Witwatersrand, Johannesburg, South Africa

Roger Tangri, Associate Professor in Political and Administrative Studies, University of Botswana, Gaborone, Botswana

Klaus-Peter Treydte, Economist, Freelance writer and Consultant, Former (2000–2004) country representative Friedrich-Ebert-Foundation Madagascar and Mauritius

Denis Tull, Senior Research Fellow, German Institute for International Affairs, Berlin, Germany

Walter E.A. van Beek, Researcher, African Studies Centre, Leiden and Lecturer in anthropology at the University of Utrecht, The Netherlands

Han van Dijk, Researcher, African Studies Centre, Leiden and Professor of Law and Governance in Africa, chair group Law and Governance, Dept of Social Sciences, Wageningen University and Research Centre, The Netherlands

Ineke van Kessel, Researcher, African Studies Centre, Leiden, The Netherlands

Klaas van Walraven, Researcher, African Studies Centre, Leiden, The Netherlands

Martin van Vliet, Institute of Multiparty Democracy at The Hague, The Netherlands

Nuno Vaz, Researcher, Head of the Humanitarian Aid Division at IPAD – Instituto Português de Apoio ao Desenvolvimento (Portuguese Institute for Development Support), Lisbon, Portugal

Christian von Soest, Research Fellow, Institute of African Affairs, German Institute of Global and Area Studies, Hamburg, Germany

Volker Weyel, Former Editor-in-chief 'Vereinte Nationen' (1977–2004), specialised journalist and consultant, Bonn, Germany

Douglas Yates, Assistant Professor of Political Science in the Department of International Affairs, The American University of Paris, France

www.ingramcontent.com/pod-product-compliance
Lightning Source LLC
LaVergne TN
LVHW080115011026
849160LV00013B/1109
* 9 7 8 9 0 0 4 1 6 2 6 3 1 *